Principles of Money, Banking, and Financial Markets

The Addison-Wesley Series in Economics

Principles of Money, Banking, and Financial Markets

Ninth edition

Lawrence S. Ritter
New York University

William L. Silber
New York University

Gregory F. Udell
New York University

 **ADDISON-WESLEY**

An imprint of Addison Wesley Longman, Inc.

Reading, Massachusetts • Menlo Park, California • New York • Harlow, England
Dan Mills, Ontario • Sydney • Mexico City • Madrid • Amsterdam

Executive Editor: **John Greenman**
Developmental Editor: **Barbara A. Conover**
Project Editor: **Elizabeth LaManna**
Design Manager: **John Callahan**
Electronic Production Manager: **Su Levine**
Desktop Administrator: **Laura Leever**
Art Studio: **Electra Graphics, Inc.**
Cover Designer: **Kay Petronio**
Compositor: **York Graphic Services, Inc.**
Printer and Binder: **R.R. Donnelley & Sons Company**
Cover Printer: **The Lehigh Press, Inc.**

Library of Congress Cataloging-in-Publication-Data
Ritter, Lawrence S.
  Principles of money, banking, and financial markets / Lawrence S. Ritter, William L. Silber, Gregory F. Udell.—9th ed.
      p.   cm.
  Includes bibliographical references and index.
  ISBN 0-673-98053-7
  1. Money. 2. Banks and banking. 3. Finance. I. Silber, William L. II. Udell, Gregory F., 1946-
. III. Title.
HG221.R536   1996
332—dc20   96-14985
                                            CIP

ISBN 0-673-98053-7
2 3 4 5 6 7 8 9 10-DOC-00 99 98 97

For Jonathan, who likes to win
Danny, who likes his way
Tammy, who likes people

For Steve and Peter

And for Betty, Clare, Ashley, Ryan and Jill

With love

"... be careful in teaching, for error in teaching amounts to deliberate sin."

The *Mishnah, Pirkei Avot,* 4

BRIEF TABLE OF CONTENTS

PART III

Banks and Other Intermediaries 177

PART IV

Financial System Architecture 241

PART VII

Grand Finale 545

CONTENTS

PART I

The Basics 1

CHAPTER 1

Introducing Money, Banking, and Financial Markets   3

CHAPTER 2

The Role of Money in the Macroeconomy   6

PART

Financial System Architeture 241

PART V

The Art of Central Banking   313

PART VI

Monetary Theory   397

NOTES TO THE INSTRUCTOR

The completely revised ninth edition of *Principles of Money Banking and Financial Markets* focuses on modern analytical perspectives while maintaining the casual conversational style you have come to expect. More specifically, the treatment of financial markets and institutions now appears center stage in Parts I through IV, and the discussion has been recast in the asymmetric information framework; extensive examples have been interspersed throughout so that students can understand exactly what is going on. Since just about everything is new in these sections, let's take a look at how they are organized.

Part I briefly introduces the role of money, markets, and institutions within the framework of the overall economy. Part II then launches an intensive examination of financial instruments and markets, including an analysis of the level and structure of interest rates (Chapters 4 and 5), the pricing of risky assets (Chapter 7), and an overview of derivatives (Chapter 9) and foreign exchange (Chapter 10). We then turn in Part III to a discussion of financial institutions, including how asymmetric information explains the fundamental nature of financial intermediation (Chapter 11). In fact, the focus in Part II on markets and in Part III on intermediaries sets the stage for our unique analysis of financial system architecture in Part IV. This is sufficiently innovative to warrant some further detail.

We begin our discussion of financial system architecture with Chapter 14's analysis of how financial contracts address the information problems presented by small and large businesses. After explaining why some borrowers are drawn to intermediaries while others have access to publicly traded markets, Chapter 15 provides a parallel treatment of the regulatory structure of financial markets and financial intermediaries. Chapter 16 tops it off with a foray into an international comparison of financial system design. Japan and Germany illustrate how intermediary-dominated systems work while the

United States and United Kingdom represent markets-oriented systems. The chapter ends with speculation on how the formerly centrally planned economies of Eastern Europe will end up (it's a surprise so we won't say how it turns out).

The final two parts of the book return to the traditional macroeconomic framework to deal with the art of central banking (Part V) and monetary theory (Part VI). All the chapters have been updated and some have been consolidated so that the discussions are more focused. The last chapter of the book ties everything together by showing how to combine observations on institutions, markets, and the overall economy to understand current financial sector developments.

Exactly how you organize this course depends on what you want to accomplish. With this in mind we have written the chapters so that for the most part they are self-contained, thereby permitting maximum flexibility. Nevertheless, the ordering of chapters reflects the fact that most instructors now teach a financial-markets and institutions-oriented course, with central banking as the backdrop. Thus, there are good reasons for following the book chapter by chapter, with omissions reflecting your own particular emphasis. For example, it is possible to omit Chapters 6 through 8 to avoid capital market theory and performance and to drop the discussion of derivatives in Chapter 9 without sacrificing continuity. On the other hand, Chapter 10 on foreign exchange should appear early in the course because international discussions are interspersed throughout the text. Similarly, for a course focused on monetary theory and policy it is possible to jump to Part V (the art of central banking) and Part VI (monetary theory and policy) right after completing Part I and Chapters 4, 5, and 10 from Part II.

Whatever route you choose, we have tried to make this the most readable, analytically correct book you will ever adopt. We hope that neither you nor your students will be disappointed. Please let us know how it turns out. Good luck.

Lawrence S. Ritter
William L. Silber
Gregory F. Udell

ACKNOWLEDGMENTS

We would like to thank Mary Jaffier for her considerable help in preparing this manuscript, and Elizabeth LaManna, project editor, for managing the book through the production process. We would also like to thank the following students and teachers for taking the time and effort to comment on the text and help in the various editions (affiliations are those at the time the comments were received):

G. Abraham, *Grambling State University*
Burton Abrams, *University of Delaware*
Paul L. Altieri, *Central Connecticut State College*
Ernie Ankrim, *Pacific Lutheran University*
Eddie Ary, *Ouachita Baptist University*
William T. Baldwin, *Eastern Kentucky University*
John Bay, *University of Southern Maine*
Allen N. Berger, *Federal Reserve Board*
Herbert Bernstein, *Drexel University*
W. Carl Biven, *Georgia Institute of Technology*
Deborah Black, *Hunter College of City University of New York*
Dwight M. Blood, *Brigham Young University*
Scott Bloom, *North Dakota State University*
Elbert V. Bowden, *Appalachian State University*
Maureen Burton, *California Polytechnic State University-Pomona*
Robert C. Burton, *Frostburg State College*
Ralph T. Byrns, *Metropolitan State College*
John A. Carlson, *Purdue University*
Stephen Cecchetti, *Ohio State University*
Arthur D. Chesler, *Kentucky Wesleyan College*

Thomas C. Chiang, *Drexel University*
Dale Cloninger, *University of Houston at Clear Lake*
Eleanor Craig, *University of Delaware*
Wilfrid Csaplar, *Hampden-Sydney College*
Bob Curl, *Northwest Nazarene College*
J. Kenneth Davies, *Brigham Young University*
Robert M. Domine, *University of Michigan*
James S. Earley, *University of California, Riverside*
Fisehe Eshete, *Bowie State University*
William P. Field, Jr., *Nicholls State University*
Stanley Fischer, *Massachusetts Institute of Technology*
Kaya Ford, *Northern Virginia Community College*
Mark Foster, *University of Northern Alabama*
Ramzi Frangul, *Sacred Heart University*
Ian Giddy, *Columbia University*
Micha Gisser, *University of New Mexico*
Harry Greenbaum, *South Dakota State University*
John B. Guerard, Jr., *University of Texas*
Satya P. Gupta, *Augsburg College*
Jerry W. Gustafson, *Beloit College*
Philip J. Hahn, *Youngstown State University*
David Hait, *York University*
David R. Hakes, *University of Northern Iowa*
Gabriel Hawawini, *INSEAD (The European Institute of Business), Fontainebleau, France*
Naphtali Hoffman, *Elmira College*
Robert S. Holbrook, *University of Michigan*
Mary Jaffier, *New York University*
Karen Johnson, *Baylor University*
Edward J. Kane, *Ohio State University*
Maryann Keating, *Valpariso University*
Peter M. Kerr, *Southeast State College*
Jimmie King, Jr., *Tuskegee Institute*
Richard W. Kjetsaa, *Fairleigh Dickinson University*
Leora Klapper, *New York University*
Kajal Lahiri, *State University of New York at Albany*
Gregor Lazarcik, *State University of New York at Geneseo*
Tom Lee, *California State University at Northridge*
Marie Lobue, *University of New Orleans*
Darryl W. Lowry, *Roanoke College*
Morgan J. Lynge, *University of Illinois at Urbana*
John McArthur, *Claremont Graduate School*
Neela Manage, *Florida Atlantic University*
Louis Manzell, *Monmouth College*
W. Douglas McMillin, *Louisiana State University*
John J. Merrick, *New York University*

Loretta J. Mester, *Federal Reserve Bank of Philadelphia*
Stephen Miller, *University of Connecticut at Storrs*
H. Brian Moehring, *University of the Redlands*
Robert L. Moore, *Harvard University*
Douglas W. Morrill, *Centenary College of Louisiana*
Alan Norton, *St. John Fisher College*
John A. Orr, *California State University at Chico*
Peter Parker, *Randolph-Macon College*
Braxton I. Patterson, *University of Wisconsin at Oshkosh*
Thomas J. Pierce, *California State University at San Bernardino*
Dean Popp, *San Diego State University*
Thomas P. Potiowsky, *Portland State University*
Alan Rabin, *University of Tennessee at Chattanooga*
Charu Raheja, *New York University*
John D. Rea, *Investment Company Institute*
Henry Rennie, *University of Toledo*
Deborah E. Robbins, *Wellesley College*
M. Richard Roseman, *California State University at Los Angeles*
David Sandberg, *Brigham Young University*
John M. Sapinsley, *Rhode Island College*
Donald J. Schilling, *University of Missouri*
Carole Scott, *West Georgia College*
Larry J. Sechrest, *University of Texas at Arlington*
Edward Shapiro, *University of Toledo*
Milton M. Shapiro, *California Polytechnic State University*
Thomas J. Shea, *Springfield College*
Cathy Sherman, *University of Texas*
William O. Shropshire, *Oglethorpe University*
Harinder Singh, *San Diego State University*
Theodore R. Snyder, Jr., *University of New England*
Milton H. Spencer, *Wayne State University*
Charles E. Staley, *State University of New York at Stony Brook*
H. Joe Story, *Pacific University*
Harry C. Symons, *Ursinus College*
Ronald L. Teigen, *University of Michigan*
John Thorkelson, *University of Connecticut*
Kenneth N. Townsend, *Hampden-Sydney College*
Dang Tran, *University of Baltimore*
Irwin T. Vanderhoof, *New York University*
Pearl S. Vogel, *Sacred Heart University*
Joan Walters, *Fairfield University*
Jonathan B. Wight, *University of Richmond*
Douglas A. Wion, *Lock Haven State College*
Stuart Wood, *Tulane University*

ABOUT THE AUTHORS

Lawrence S. Ritter is Professor of Finance and Economics at the Stern School of Business of New York University. A former Chief of the Domestic Research Division of the Federal Reserve Bank of New York, he has served as a consultant to the U.S. Treasury, the Federal Deposit Insurance Corporation, the Board of Governors of the Federal Reserve System, the American Bankers Association, the Association of Reserve City Bankers, and the Garvin Guy Butler Corporation. He has been the Editor of the *Journal of Finance* and is a past President of the American Finance Association. Professor Ritter is also the author of numerous articles in professional journals and of *The Glory of Their Times*, a best-selling book about the early days of baseball.

William L. Silber is the Dean Abraham Gitlow Professor of Finance and Economics and Director, Glucksman Institute for Research in Securities Markets at the Stern School of Business of New York University. A former Senior Staff Economist with the President's Council of Economic Advisers and a former Senior Vice President at Lehman Brothers Kuhn Loeb, he has served as a consultant to the Board of Governors of the Federal Reserve System, the President's Commission on Financial Structure and Regulation, the U.S. Senate Committee on the Budget, the House Committee on Banking, Currency and Housing, the Justice Department, the Federal Home Loan Bank Board, the National Commission on Electronic Funds Transfers, and the Department of Housing and Urban Development. He is on the Economic Advisory Panel of the Federal Reserve Bank of New York and is the author of five books and numerous articles in professional journals.

Gregory F. Udell is Associate Professor of Finance at the Stern School of Business of New York University. He was formerly a banker and commercial loan officer in Chicago specializing in lending to small and midsized midwestern companies. Currently his academic research focuses on banking and financial contracting. He has published numerous articles in academic journals including the *Journal of Political Economy*, the *Journal of Monetary Economics* and the *Journal of Business*. He is an Associate Editor of the *Journal of Money, Credit and Banking* and the *Journal of Banking and Finance*. Professor Udell has been a visiting economist and consultant to the Board of Governors of the Federal Reserve System.

Principles of Money, Banking, and Financial Markets

PART I

The Basics

CHAPTER 1

Introducing Money, Banking, and Financial Markets

Oscar Wilde wrote that a cynic knows the price of everything and the value of nothing. Although that's certainly worthy of further reflection, for our purposes, price and value refer to the same thing: how much a security or financial asset is worth. **Financial markets** generate prices whenever securities are bought or sold. **Financial institutions** value financial assets whenever making loans to businesses or consumers. Thus pricing and valuation of financial assets are at the heart of the financial marketplace. One of our objectives is to link the behavior of securities prices, such as for stocks and bonds, to the performance of the economy as a whole, as well as with the behavior of financial institutions and markets.

But first things first. What exactly do we mean by money, banking, and financial markets? The **money** in *money, banking, and financial markets* refers not only to the greenbacks we spend, but more broadly to the monetary economy. As you will learn, money plays a key role in the performance of the economy. It not only facilitates transactions among the millions of economic players in the economy, but it represents the principal mechanism through which central banks attempt to influence aggregate economic activity, including economic growth, employment, and inflation. The **banking** in *money, banking, and financial markets* refers to banks and other financial intermediaries. A financial intermediary is an institution that takes funds from one group of investors and redeploys those funds by investing in financial assets. Banks serve as the principal caretaker of the economy's money supply and, along with other financial intermediaries, provide an important source of funds for consumers and businesses. The financial markets in *money, banking, and financial markets* refer to the markets in which financial assets can be traded. Financial markets provide a mechanism for those with excess funds to purchase securities, such as stocks and bonds, issued by those who need funds. Moreover, financial markets provide prices for those stocks and bonds, so that we know whether to conceal or brag about our most recent purchases.

AN OVERVIEW

Money in the modern economy is sometimes viewed as a lubricant that greases the wheels of economic activity. Without money, the transactions that make up our daily economic routine would be unimaginably difficult, and saving and investing would be almost full-time jobs. Money, however, is more than just a lubricant which enables the economy to operate smoothly. Money also plays a key role in influencing the behavior of the economy as a whole and the performance of financial institutions and markets. More specifically, changes in the supply of money and credit can affect how rapidly the economy grows, the level of employment, and the rate of inflation—and these, in turn, can affect the value of financial assets held by individuals and institutions.

Banks play a particularly critical role in the economy. Banks provide a place where individuals and businesses can invest their funds to earn interest with a minimum of risk. Banks, in turn, redeploy these funds by making loans. In this regard, banks are remarkably similar to other financial intermediaries like finance companies and insurance companies, which also acquire funds from individuals and businesses and pass on these funds to other individuals and businesses. Like finance companies and life insurance companies, banks are particularly well-equipped to invest in the most challenging types of financial investments—loans to individuals and small businesses.

Why are banks singled out for special treatment? As it turns out, most of what we call money in the United States is represented by the deposits issued by banks. Consequently, banks serve as the principal caretakers of the payments system because we write checks on our bank accounts to pay for things we buy. Moreover, because money has linkages to the overall performance of the economy, banks are intimately involved in how the central bank of the United States, called the **Federal Reserve,** influences overall economic activity. In particular, the Federal Reserve directly influences the lending and deposit creation activities of banks. This, in turn, helps determine how much people are willing to save and how much businesses are willing to invest and whether the prices of stocks and bonds go up, down, or sideways in the financial markets.

How does this all work? For the complete answer, you have to read the rest of this book! But here's a preview of what you will find. The remaining chapters in Part I set the stage. We define money and look at its relationship with economic performance. Then we'll provide an overview of financial institutions, instruments, and markets and how they serve as a mechanism for the flow of saving and investment. In Part II we examine the performance and behavior of financial markets where funds move directly from those who have funds to those who need funds. We pay special attention to how all types of securities are valued, how interest rates are determined, and how complicated markets, such as derivatives and foreign exchange, actually work. In Part III we look at intermediated markets where funds move between borrowers and lenders via financial intermediaries, such as banks, insurance companies, pension funds, and some institutions you may not have heard of. In Part IV we examine the overall financial system. This will involve looking at the relationship between financial markets and intermediated markets, the regulation of these markets, and an international comparison across different financial systems.

Having examined the financial landscape in Parts II, III, and IV we will then be ready to tackle the issue of overall economic performance. Part V begins this process by discussing the art of central banking. We can then address questions about the linkages among money, inflation, growth, and employment in Part VI. Along the way we'll learn that not everyone agrees on just what these linkages are, so you'll have to make up your own mind about what seems right. Part VI brings us 'round full circle linking monetary policy, prices in the stock and bond markets, and the performance of the economy.

CHAPTER 2

The Role of Money in the Macroeconomy

"The lack of money is the root of all evil," said George Bernard Shaw. Although that may be something of an exaggeration, there have been numerous periods in history when it appeared to be more true than false. There have also been rather lengthy episodes when the opposite seemed true: when economic disruption apparently stemmed not from too little money, but from too *much* of it.

From this line of thought, the question naturally arises, what is the "right" amount of money? Not too little, not too much, but just right? And how can we go about getting it?

Actually those are fairly sophisticated questions requiring careful consideration to produce answers that stand the test of time. Although we will devote a fair amount of attention to the relationship between money and economic activity, a number of somewhat more fundamental issues spring to mind as well. For example, exactly what is this thing called money that has obsessed princes and paupers throughout the centuries? In the good old days money was gold, kept under lock and key until it was sent by ship or stagecoach to meet the payroll. Nowadays money is paper that we carry around until it is worn and frayed. Can these really be the same thing?

In truth our discussion will have to extend far beyond the traditional confines of money if we want to understand the workings of our financial system. Financial institutions and markets have become so complex during the second half of the twentieth century that commercial banks are no longer the only financial institutions that matter, and stocks and bonds no longer tell the entire story of how financial markets operate.

INTRODUCING MONEY

What *is* money, anyway? And how much of it do we actually have?

Money is just what you think it is—what you spend when you want to buy something. The Indians used beads, Eskimos used fishhooks, and we use **currency** (coins and bills) and, most of all, **checking accounts.**

Money is used as (1) a means of payment, but it has other functions as well. It is also used as (2) a store of value, when people hold on to it, and (3) a standard of value (a unit of account), when people compare prices and thereby assess relative values. But most prominently money is what you can spend, a generally acceptable means of payment or medium of exchange that you can use to buy things or settle debts.

How large a money supply do we have? It amounted to $1,125 billion at the end of December 1995, roughly $373 billion in the form of currency and about $752 billion in checkable deposits at banks and other financial institutions. This definition of money—currency outside banks plus checking accounts—is frequently called M1 (to distinguish it from two other definitions of money, M2 and M3, which we will get to in a moment). If you want to know what the

---

GOING OUT ON A LIMB

It's Time to Change Our Small Change

The coinage system in the United States consists of five coins—the penny, nickel, dime, quarter, and half-dollar. With the dramatic rise in consumer prices since World War II, these five coins are no longer adequate to serve the small-change needs of the American public. Prices are now about ten times higher than they were in 1940, so nowadays a dollar bill buys only what a dime bought back then, while it takes a dime to buy what a penny used to purchase. Yet we have the same coins we had in the dim distant past.

What we should do is promptly abolish the penny and the half-dollar and in their place mint a brand-new dollar coin. With prices as high as they are, pennies are a waste of time and effort. Unwanted, pennies lie undisturbed on sidewalks; for most people, apparently they aren't even worth the effort of bending down to pick them up. Half-dollars should also be abolished, in this case because no one uses them. The half-dollar is a cumbersome coin that is rarely received in change because experience has demonstrated that neither shoppers nor cashiers in retail establishments like them.

A new dollar coin should be introduced, and possibly the dollar bill should be phased out at the same time. Memories of failed efforts to introduce dollar coins make people apprehensive about trying it again. "Eisenhower dollars" were coined from 1971 to 1978, but people felt they were too heavy and, like the half-dollar, they were not kept in circulation. Similarly, the "Susan B. Anthony dollar" was introduced in 1979, but because of its size people confused it with quarters and after a short while it also disappeared from circulation.

The Treasury is now considering still another version of the dollar coin. Perhaps with the year 2000 on the horizon the public will find it both practical and useful.

money supply is today check the *New York Times* or the *Wall Street Journal;* both newspapers list it every Friday.

Since currency and checking accounts are spendable at face value virtually anywhere, at any time, they are the most **"liquid" assets** a person can have. A liquid asset is something you can turn into the generally acceptable medium of exchange quickly without taking a loss, as compared with illiquid assets, which usually can be sold or liquidated on short notice only at a substantially lower price. Currency and checking accounts are the most liquid assets you can have (because they *are* the medium of exchange), but they are not the only liquid assets around. Savings deposits and government bonds are rather liquid, although you can't spend them directly. To spend them, you first have to exchange them for money. At the other extreme, real estate and vintage automobiles typically rank fairly low on the liquidity scale; if you have to sell quickly, you might suffer a loss.

Thus liquidity is a continuum, ranging from currency and checkable deposits at the top of the scale to a variety of frozen assets at the bottom. As a result, what we call **money** is not a fixed and immutable thing, like what we call water (H_2O), but to a great extent a matter of judgment; there are several different definitions of money, each of which drops one notch lower on the liquidity scale in drawing the line between "money" and "all other assets." Table 2.1 summarizes the three different definitions of the money supply.

M1 refers to the most liquid of all assets, currency plus all types of checking accounts at financial institutions. In addition to commercial banks, the so-called thrift institutions—savings banks, savings and loan associations, and credit unions—can also issue checking accounts. However, most **demand deposits** (noninterest-bearing checking accounts) are still in commercial banks. As indicated in Table 2.1, other checkable deposits, such as negotiable order of withdrawal (NOW) accounts, are also considered part of M1. These interest-

TABLE 2.1   Three Definitions of the Money Supply (December 31, 1995)

M1	Currency outside banks ($373 billion), plus demand deposits at banks ($390 billion), plus other checkable deposits at banks and at all thrift institutions ($353 billion), plus travelers' checks ($9 billion)	$1,125 billion
M2	Add small-denomination time deposits ($936 billion), plus money market deposit accounts and savings deposits at all depository institutions ($1,135 billion), plus retail money market mutual funds shares ($465 billion)	$3,661 billion
M3	Add large-denomination ($100,000 and over) time deposits at all depository institutions ($417 billion), plus institutional money market mutual funds shares ($227 billion), plus bank repurchase agreements and Eurodollars ($269 billion)	$4,574 billion

Source: Federal Reserve Bulletin.

Note: Money market mutual funds, money market deposit accounts, repurchase agreements, and Eurodollars are all explained and discussed in subsequent chapters.

bearing checking accounts were made available to individuals and households during the 1970s as banks and thrifts circumvented a prohibition which existed at the time against paying interest on demand deposits. Since M1 is confined to these highly liquid assets, ones that can be used in an unrestricted way as a means of payment, it is the narrowest definition of money (as well as the most traditional one, by the way).

M2 drops a shade lower on the liquidity scale by adding assets that are most easily and most frequently transferred into checking accounts when a payment is about to be made. This category includes household **savings accounts** and small-denomination (under $100,000) **certificates of deposit** (CDs). Unlike savings accounts, CDs have a scheduled maturity date. If you want to withdraw your funds earlier, you suffer a substantial penalty by having to forfeit part of your accrued interest.

M2 also includes **money market deposit accounts** at banks and thrift institutions as well as shares in consumer (retail) **money market mutual funds.** Actually, most money market deposit accounts and money market mutual fund shares carry limited check-writing privileges, so many people believe they should really be listed in M1. However, the data as presently compiled include them in M2.

M3 adds a number of other items, the largest of which is large-denomination ($100,000 and over) CDs, most of which are held as short-term investments by business firms. We will discuss them further in Chapter 12.

So what is the money supply in the United States? Is it $1,125 billion (M1) or $4,574 billion (M3), or something in between? Each definition of money has its adherents, but we use the narrow definition of the money supply, M1, because that and only that is generally acceptable as a means of payment. Once you go beyond currency and checking accounts, it is hard to find a logical place to stop. Throughout this book, therefore, we will for the most part stick to the narrow definition of money: currency plus checkable deposits.[1] As we will see in Chapter 22, however, the Federal Reserve has shown a preference for M2 in recent years.

Who Determines Our Money Supply?

Why do we have $1,125 billion of money in the United States? Who, or what, determines how much there will be?

Regardless of what you may have heard, gold does *not* determine the money supply. Indeed, it has very little influence on it. In 1968 the last remaining link between the money supply and gold was severed when a law requiring 25 percent gold backing behind most of our currency was repealed. If that is

---

[1] Which is not to say that M1 is a perfect measure of how much of the means of payment is in existence. As just one example of its shortcomings, notice that M1 does not include any estimate of existing bank "overdraft" facilities (which are arrangements that allow people to write checks—legally—even when they don't have enough in their checking accounts to cover them). These as well as other funds available for immediate payment are not included in M1 mainly because of the absence of reliable data on them.

all news to you, it is a good indication of just how unimportant the connection between gold and money has always been, at least in the past half century.

Both currency and checking accounts can be increased (or decreased) without any relation to gold. Does that disturb you? Does it lead you to distrust the value of your money? Then send it to us. We'll be delighted to pay you 90 cents on the dollar, which should be a bargain if you believe all you read in the papers or hear on television about a dollar being worth only 60 cents, or 50 cents, or whatever the latest figure may be.[2]

If gold is not the watchdog, then who (or what) does determine how much money we will have?

The monetary authority in most countries is called the **central bank.** A central bank does not deal directly with the public; it is rather a bank for banks, and it is responsible for the execution of national monetary policy. In the United States the central banking function is carried out by the Federal Reserve System, created by Congress in 1913. It consists of 12 district Federal Reserve banks, scattered throughout the country, and a **Board of Governors** in Washington, D.C. This hydra-headed monster, which some view as benign but others consider an ever-lurking peril, possesses ultimate authority over the money supply.

As noted earlier, the money supply (M1) consists of currency and checking accounts. **Currency** is manufactured by money factories—the Bureau of Engraving and Printing and the Mint—and then shipped under heavy guard to the U.S. Treasury and the Federal Reserve for further distribution. For the most part it enters circulation when people and business firms cash checks at their local banks. Thus it is the public that ultimately decides what proportion of the money supply will be in the form of currency, with the Federal Reserve banks wholesaling the necessary coins and paper to local banks. The Federal Reserve is not particularly concerned with the fraction of the money supply that is in one form or another, but rather with the *total* of checkable deposits plus currency.[3]

As Table 2.1 shows, about 66 percent of the money supply is in the form of checking accounts. These deposits come into being, as we will see later in the

---

[2]Actually, when you read that the dollar is worth only 50 cents you have a clue to why gold has little to do with the *value* of money, in addition to having little to do with determining the amount outstanding. Money is valuable only because you can buy things with it, like clothes and books and stereos. The value of a dollar is therefore determined by the prices of the things we buy. When people say a dollar is worth only 50 cents they mean that nowadays it takes a dollar to buy what 50 cents could have bought a few years ago (because prices have doubled).

[3]Just in case you're curious, here are some miscellaneous facts about coins and bills. Coins are manufactured by the U.S. Mint, which has production facilities in Philadelphia, Denver, and San Francisco. All bills are manufactured by the U.S. Bureau of Engraving and Printing, which has facilities in Fort Worth, Texas, and in Washington, D.C. The largest denomination of currency now issued is the $100 bill; there used to be $500, $1,000, $5,000, and $10,000 bills in circulation, but their printing was discontinued in 1945. The average life of a $1 bill is about a year and a half, before it is torn or worn out, which is why the government tried to popularize the Susan B. Anthony dollar coins in 1979. Coins last much longer than bills. Banks send worn-out bills back to the Federal Reserve, which destroys them and distributes newly printed bills in their place.

chapter, when banks extend credit, that is, when they make loans or buy securities. Checking deposits vanish, as silently as they came, when banks contract credit—when loans are repaid or banks sell securities. It is precisely here, through its ability to control bank behavior, that the Federal Reserve wields its primary authority over the money supply and thereby implements monetary policy.

This process of money creation by banks, and the execution of monetary policy by the Federal Reserve, will be introduced shortly and discussed at length in Chapters 18 through 22. But before we get into the details, we should back off for a moment and ask, why all the fuss? Why is money so important to begin with?

The Importance of Money I: Money Versus Barter

What good is money in the first place? To appreciate the importance of money in an economic system, it is instructive to speculate on what the economy might be like without it. In other words, why was money invented (by Sir John Money in 3016 b.c.)?

For one thing, without money individuals in the economy would have to devote more time to buying what they want and selling what they don't. In other words, people would have less time to work and play. A barter economy is one without a medium of exchange or a unit of account (the measuring-rod function of money). Let's see what it might be like to live in a barter economy.

Say you are a carpenter and agree to build a bookcase for your neighbor. This neighbor happens to raise chickens and pays you with four dozen eggs. You decide to keep a dozen for yourself, so you now have three dozen to exchange for the rest of the week's groceries. All you must do is find a grocer who is short on eggs.

What's more, you have to remember that a loaf of bread exchanges for six eggs (it also exchanges for 11 books of matches or three boxes of crayons or one Yankee Yearbook, but never mind because you don't have any of these things to spare). And of course all the other items on the grocer's shelf have similar price tags, listing the various possible exchanges. The tags are bigger than the items.

Along comes something called money and simplifies matters. Workers are paid in money, which they can then use to pay their bills and make their purchases. Money becomes the medium of exchange. We no longer need price tags giving rates of exchange between an item and everything else that might conceivably be exchanged for it. Instead, prices of goods and services are expressed in terms of money, a common denominator.

The most important thing about the medium of exchange is that everyone must be confident that it can be passed on, that it is generally acceptable in trade. Paradoxically, people will accept the medium of exchange only when they are certain that it can be passed on to someone else. One key characteristic is that the *uncertainty* over its value in trade must be very *low*. People will be more willing to accept the medium of exchange if they are certain of what it is worth in terms of things they really want. The uncertainty of barter transactions makes people wary of exchange. If I want to sell my house and buy a car and you want to do just the reverse, we might be able to strike a deal, except for the fact that I'm afraid you might sell me a lemon. Hence I don't make a deal; I'm uncertain about the value of the thing I'm being asked to accept in exchange. A medium of exchange, which is handled often in many transactions, becomes familiar to us all and can be checked carefully for fraud. Uncertainty in trading is thereby reduced to a minimum.

Closely related to the low-uncertainty–high-exchangeability requirement is the likelihood that the medium of exchange will not deteriorate in value. It must be a good store of value, otherwise as soon as I accept the medium of exchange I'll try to get rid of it; it thereby might be worth fewer and fewer goods and services tomorrow or the day after. Thus if price inflation gets out of hand and I have little confidence that the medium of exchange will hold its value, I'll be reluctant to accept it in exchange; in other words, it won't be the medium of exchange for very long. If that happens, we'll begin to slip back into a barter economy.

The medium of exchange also usually serves as a unit of account. In other words, the prices of all other goods are expressed in terms of, say, dollars. Without such a unit of account, you'd have to remember the exchange ratios of soap for bread, knives for shirts, and bookcases for haircuts (and haircuts for soap). The unit of account reduces the information you have to carry around in your brain, freeing that limited space for creative speculation.

So money is a good thing. It frees people from spending too much time running around bartering goods and services and allows them to undertake other endeavors—production, relaxation, contemplation, and temptation.

It is important to emphasize, once again, that people use the medium of exchange—money—not because it has any intrinsic value but because it can be exchanged for things to eat, drink, wear, and play with. The *value* of a unit of money is determined, therefore, by the prices of each and every thing—more accurately, the average level of all prices. If prices go up, a unit of money—a dollar—is worth less because it will buy less; if prices go down (use your imagination) a dollar is worth more because it will buy more. Thus the value of money varies inversely with the price level.

The Importance of Money II: Financial Institutions and Markets

Money also contributes to economic development and growth. It does this by stimulating both saving and investment and facilitating transfers of funds out of the hoards of savers and into the hands of borrowers, who want to undertake investment projects but do not have enough of their own money to do so. Financial markets give savers a variety of ways to lend to borrowers, thereby increasing the volume of both saving and investment and encouraging economic growth.

People who save are often not the same people who can see and exploit profitable investment opportunities. In an economy without money, the only way people can invest (for example, to buy productive equipment) is by consuming less than their income (saving). Similarly, in an economy without money the only way people can save—that is, consume less than their income—is by acquiring real goods directly.

The introduction of money, however, permits the separation of the act of investment from the act of saving: Money makes it possible for a person to invest without first refraining from consumption (saving) and likewise makes it possible for a person to save without also investing. People can now invest who are not fortunate enough to have their own savings.

In a monetary economy, a person simply accumulates savings in cash because money is a store of value. Through financial markets, this surplus cash can be lent to a business firm borrowing the funds to invest in new equipment, equipment it might not have been able to buy if it did not have access to borrowed funds. Both the saver and the business firm are better off: The saver receives interest payments, and the business firm expects to earn a return over and above the interest cost. And the economy is also better off: The only way an economy can grow is by allocating part of its resources to the creation of new and more productive facilities.

In an advanced economy such as ours, this channeling of funds from savers to borrowers through financial markets reaches highly complex dimensions. A wide variety of financial instruments, such as stocks, bonds, and mortgages, are utilized as devices through which borrowers can gain access to the surplus funds of savers. Various markets specialize in trading one or another of these financial instruments.

And financial institutions have sprung up—such as commercial banks, savings banks, savings and loan associations, credit unions, insurance companies, mutual funds, and pension funds—that act as intermediaries in transferring funds from ultimate lenders to ultimate borrowers. Such financial intermediaries themselves borrow from saver-lenders and then turn around and lend the funds to borrower-spenders. They mobilize the savings of many small savers and package them for sale to the highest bidders. In the process, again both saver-lenders and borrower-spenders gain: Savers have the added option of acquiring savings deposits or pension rights, which are less risky than individual stocks or bonds, and business-firm borrowers can tap large sums of money from a single source. None of this would be possible were it not for the existence of money, the one financial asset that lies at the foundation of the whole superstructure.[4]

Uncontrolled, money may cause hyperinflation or disastrous depression and thereby cancel its blessings. If price inflation gets out of hand, for example, money ceases to be a reliable store of value and therefore becomes a less

---

[4]Strictly speaking it is theoretically possible for transfers between savers and borrowers to occur within a barter framework. Thus credit arrangements could exist without money. But only the existence of money permits the complex and efficient channeling of funds between savers and borrowers.

efficient medium of exchange. People become reluctant to accept cash in payment for goods and services, and when they do accept it, they try to get rid of it as soon as possible. As we noted above, the value of money is determined by the price level of the goods money is used to purchase. The higher the prices, the more dollars one has to give up to get real goods or buy services. **Inflation** (rising prices) reduces the value of money. **Hyperinflation** (prices rising at a fast and furious pace) reduces the value of money by a lot within a short time span. Hence people don't want to hold very much cash; they want to exchange it for goods or services as quickly as possible. Thus if money breaks down as a store of value, it starts to deteriorate as a medium of exchange as well, and we start to slip back into barter. People spend more time exchanging goods and less time producing, consuming, and enjoying them. A severe depression causes different but no less serious consequences.

So once we have money, the question constantly challenges us: How much of it should there be?

MONEY, THE ECONOMY, AND INFLATION

Many people persist in thinking that money must somehow be based on gold, or maybe silver, or at least on *something* that has tangible physical substance. As we saw above, however, money is mostly an accounting phenomenon, reinforced by social convention and the legal power of government. There simply isn't any backing behind our currency, and checking accounts, which constitute most of our money, are nothing more than liabilities on the books of financial institutions.

How do such checking accounts come into existence? How does the central bank—the Federal Reserve ("the Fed")—regulate their amount? How does the Federal Reserve know how large the money supply should be in the first place? Finally, just what is the relationship between the money supply, economic activity, and inflation?

The remainder of this chapter is devoted to a preliminary exploration of such questions. Later in the book, especially in Parts V and VI, we will dig deeper into many of these same matters; meanwhile, we will provide some background information intended to make the material in the intervening chapters more meaningful.

Bank Reserves and the Money Supply

Checking accounts come into being when banks extend credit, that is, when they make loans or buy securities. Checking accounts disappear when banks contract credit, when bank loans are repaid or banks sell securities. Here is how it works.

When a bank makes a loan to a consumer or business firm, it typically creates a checking account for the borrower's use. For example, when you borrow $1,000 from your friendly neighborhood bank, the bank will take your promissory note and give you a checking account in return. From the bank's point of view, it has an additional $1,000 of assets (namely, your promissory note); this is matched by an additional $1,000 of liabilities (namely, your checking account). The creation of this $1,000 in checking deposits means the money supply has increased by $1,000.

Similarly, when a bank buys a corporate or government bond, it pays for it by opening a checking account for the seller. Assume you are holding a $1,000 corporate or government bond in your investment portfolio, and you need cash. You might sell the bond to your local bank, which would then add $1,000 to your checking account. Once again, from the point of view of the bank, its assets (bonds) and liabilities (checking accounts) have gone up by $1,000. Again, money has been created; the supply of money in the economy has increased by $1,000.

Conversely, when you repay a bank loan by giving the bank a check, the bank gives you back your promissory note and at the same time lowers your deposit balance. If a bank sells a bond to an individual, the same reduction in deposits occurs. The supply of money declines. Conclusion: Banks create money (checking accounts) when they lend or buy securities and destroy money when their loans are repaid or they sell securities.

A bank cannot always expand its checking account liabilities by making loans or buying securities. Banks are required by the Federal Reserve to hold reserves against their checking account liabilities—the current reserve requirement is about 10 percent reserves against checking deposits. These reserves must be held in the form of vault cash or a deposit in their regional Federal Reserve bank. Therefore, only if a bank has "excess" reserves, reserves over and above its requirements, can it create new checking deposits by making loans and buying securities.

Once a bank is "loaned up," with no more excess reserves, its ability to create money ceases. And if it has deficient reserves, not enough to support its existing deposits, the bank must somehow get additional reserves. Otherwise it has no choice but to call in loans or sell securities in order to bring its deposits back in line with its reserves.

It is through the fulcrum of these reserves that the Federal Reserve influences bank lending and investing and thereby the money supply. How the Federal Reserve manipulates the reserves of the banking system will be explored in detail in Chapter 20. For now, let's just take it for granted that the Federal Reserve controls bank reserves, hence the money supply, and move on to the next question.

How Large Should the Money Supply Be?

In theory, the answer is simple enough. Presumably the supply of money affects the rate of spending, and therefore we should have enough money so that we buy, at current prices, all the goods and services the economy is able to produce. If we spend less, we will have idle capacity and idle people; if we spend more, we will wind up with higher prices but no more real output. In other words, we need a money supply large enough to generate a level of spending on new domestically produced goods and services—the economy's gross domestic product (GDP)—that produces high employment at stable prices. More money than that would mean too much spending and inflation, and less money would mean too little spending and recession or depression.

In practice, unfortunately, the answer is not nearly that simple. In the first place, decisions about the appropriate amount of money are often linked with the notion of countercyclical monetary policy, that is, a monetary policy that deliberately varies the amount of money in the economy—increasing it (or, more realistically, increasing the rate at which it is growing) during a recession, to stimulate spending, and decreasing it (or increasing it at a less than normal rate) during a boom, to inhibit spending. As we will see in later chapters, such attempts at economic stabilization are quite controversial.

The more fundamental issue for us is to understand how changes in the money supply can influence people's *spending* in a consistent way. What a change in the money supply can do is to alter people's **liquidity.** Money, after all, is the most liquid of all assets. A liquid asset, as mentioned previously, is something that can be turned into cash, that is, sold or liquidated, quickly, with no loss in dollar value. Money already *is* cash. You can't get more liquid than that!

Since monetary policy alters the liquidity of the public's portfolio of total assets—including, in that balance sheet, holdings of real as well as financial assets—it should thereby lead to portfolio readjustments that involve spending decisions. An increase in the money supply implies that the public is more liquid than formerly; a decrease in the money supply implies that the public is less liquid than before. If the public had formerly been satisfied with its holdings of money relative to the rest of its assets, a change in that money supply will presumably lead to readjustments throughout the rest of its portfolio.[5]

In other words, these changes in liquidity should lead to more (or less) spending on either real assets (cars and television sets) or financial assets (stocks and bonds). If spending on real assets expands, demand for goods and services increases, production goes up, and GDP is directly affected. If spending on financial assets goes up, the increased demand for stocks and bonds drives up securities prices. Higher securities prices mean lower interest rates. The fall in interest rates may induce more spending on housing and plant and equipment, thereby influencing GDP through that route.[6]

---

[5]Of course, if monetary policy could increase the money supply while all other assets of the public remained unchanged, people would be not only more liquid but also wealthier. As we will see in Chapter 20, however, monetary policy can alter only the composition of the public's assets; it cannot change total wealth *directly*.

[6]Since this point will come up again and again, it is worth devoting a moment to the *inverse* relationship between the *price* of an income-earning asset and its effective *rate of interest* (or yield). For example, a long-term bond that carries a fixed interest payment of $10 a year and costs $100 yields an annual interest rate of 10 percent. However, if the price of the bond were to rise to $200, the current yield would drop to 10/200, or 5 percent. And if the price of the security were to fall to $50, the current yield would rise to 10/50, or 20 percent. Conclusion: A rise (or fall) in the price of a bond is reflected, in terms of sheer arithmetic, in an automatic change in the opposite direction in the effective rate of interest. To say the price of bonds rose or the rate of interest fell is saying the same thing in two different ways. We will return to these matters in a somewhat more formal way in Chapter 4.

Underlying the effectiveness of monetary policy, therefore, is its impact on the liquidity of the public. But whether a change in the supply of liquidity actually does influence spending depends on what is happening to the demand for liquidity. If the supply of money is increased but demand expands even more, the additional money will be held and not spent. "Easy" or "tight" money is not really a matter of increases or decreases in the money supply in an absolute sense, but rather increases or decreases relative to the demand for money. In the past half century we have had hardly any periods in which the money supply actually decreased for any sustained length of time, yet we have had many episodes of tight money because the *rate* of growth was so small that the demand for money rose faster than the supply.

If people always respond in a consistent manner to an increase in their liquidity (the proportion of money in their portfolio), the Federal Reserve will be able to gauge the impact on GDP of a change in the money supply. But if people's spending reactions vary unpredictably when there is a change in the money supply, the central bank will never know whether it should alter the money supply a little or a lot (or even at all!) to bring about a specified change in spending.

The relationship between changes in the money supply and induced changes in spending brings us to the speed with which money is spent, its *velocity* or rate of turnover. When the Federal Reserve increases the money supply by $1 billion, how much of an effect will this have on people's spending, and thereby on GDP? Say we are in a recession, with GDP $100 billion below prosperity levels. Can the Fed induce a $100-billion expansion in spending by increasing the money supply by $10 billion? Or will it take a $20-billion—or a $50-billion—increase in the money supply to do the job?

Velocity: The Missing Link

Clearly, this is the key puzzle that monetary policymakers must solve if the policy is to operate effectively. Money is only a means to an end, and the end is the total volume of spending, which should be sufficient to give us high employment but not so great as to produce excessively rising prices.

When the Federal Reserve increases the money supply, the recipients of this additional liquidity *probably* spend some of it on domestically produced goods and services, increasing GDP. The funds thereby move from the original recipients to the sellers of the goods and services. Now the sellers have more money than before, and if they behave the same way as the others, they, too, are *likely* to spend some of it. GDP thus rises further, and the money moves on to yet another set of owners, who, in turn, *may* also spend part of it, thereby increasing GDP again. Over a period of time, say a year, a multiple increase in spending and GDP could thus flow from an initial increase in the stock of money.

This relationship between the increase in GDP over a period of time and the initial change in the money supply is important enough to have a name: the **velocity** of money. Technically speaking, velocity is found after the process has ended, by dividing the cumulative increase in GDP by the initial increase in the money supply.

Similarly, we can compute the velocity of the *total* amount of money in the country by dividing total GDP (not just the increase in it) by the *total* money supply. This gives us the average number of times each dollar turns over to buy goods and services during the year. In 1995, for example, with a GDP of $7,246 billion and an average money supply of $1,123 billion during the year, the velocity of money was 7,246 divided by 1,123, or 6.5 per annum. Each dollar, on the average, was spent 6.5 times in purchasing goods and services during 1995.

With this missing link—velocity—now in place, we can reformulate the problem of monetary policy more succinctly. The Federal Reserve controls the supply of money. Its main job is to regulate the flow of spending. The flow of spending, however, depends not only on the supply of money but also on that supply's rate of turnover, or velocity, and control of this the Federal Reserve does *not* have under its thumb.

A central problem of monetary theory is the exploration of exactly what determines the velocity of money—or, looked at another way, what determines the volume of spending that flows from a change in the supply of money. As we shall see, disagreements over the determinants and behavior of velocity underlie part of the debate over economic stabilization policy.

But there's more. The Federal Reserve has to worry not only about the relationship between money and spending but also about whether prices or production responds to increased spending. More GDP is good if it corresponds to more production but not so good if it means higher prices. Either outcome is possible. And that brings us to the subject of inflation. While the next few pages provide an overview, the nitty-gritty is reserved for Chapters 27 and 28 on monetary theory.

Money and Inflation

Consumer prices are now more than ten times higher than in 1940 and nearly triple what they were in 1975. Since 1975 prices have risen at an average annual rate of almost 6 percent a year; at that rate, prices double every 12 years.[7]

Who is responsible for inflation? Is money the culprit? Can we bring an inflationary spiral to a halt if we clamp down on the money supply? The classic explanation of inflation is that "too much money is chasing too few goods." The diagnosis implies the remedy: Stop creating so much money and inflation will disappear.

Such a diagnosis has been painfully accurate during those hard-to-believe episodes in history when runaway hyperinflation skyrocketed prices out of sight and plunged the value of money to practically zero. Example: Prices

---

[7]As a special bonus, we give you "the rule of 72" for growth rates. If something (anything) is growing at a compound annual rate of x percent, to find out how many years it will take to *double*, divide 72 (the magic number) by x. For example, if prices are rising at 6 percent a year, they will double in $72 \div 6 = 12$ years. It isn't precise to the dot, but it's a useful rule of thumb.

quadrupled in Revolutionary America between 1775 and 1780, when the Continental Congress opened the printing presses and flooded the country with currency. The phrase "not worth a continental" remains to this day. The situation in Germany after World War I was even more extreme; prices in 1923 were 34 billion times what they had been in 1921. In Hungary after World War II, it took 1.4 nonillion pengo in 1946 to buy what one pengo could purchase a few years earlier (one nonillion equals 1,000,000,000,000,000,000,000,000,000,000).

Severe breakdowns of this sort are impossible unless they are fueled by continuous injections of new money in ever-increasing volume. In such cases money is undoubtedly the inflation culprit, and the only way to stop inflation from running away is to slam a quick brake on the money creation machine.

However, hyperinflation is not what we have experienced in this country in recent years. From 1950 through 1995, the cost of living increased in every year but one (1955). The annual rate of inflation over the entire period averages out at more than 4 percent per year. Moreover, even during periods of recession, such as 1974, 1981, and 1991, inflation was still with us, with prices rising 12, 9, and 4 percent respectively in those years.

Unlike its role in hyperinflation, money is not so obviously the only culprit when it comes to this everyday variety of creeping inflation we have experienced in recent years. Let's take a look at some evidence before jumping to conclusions. The following list shows annual money supply growth and the inflation rate from 1930 to 1995, using M1 as the definition of money. It shows that the two tend to move together, although not as closely in recent years. If we use M2 as our definition of money, the relationship remains relatively close even more recently.[8] We can also look at each individual decade. Again using the 1930–1995 period and M1 as our definition of money:

1. During the 1930s the money supply (M1) increased by 35 percent, but consumer prices *fell* 20 percent.

2. In the 1940s the money supply increased by 200 percent, but prices rose by "only" 70 percent.

3. The 1950s provide the best fit: The money supply and prices both rose by about 25 percent.

4. In the 1960s the relationship deteriorated slightly: The money supply increased by 45 percent, and consumer prices rose by slightly less than 30 percent.

---

[8]There is a reason why in recent years inflation has tracked M2 more closely than M1. M2 includes money market deposit accounts and money market mutual funds, both of which pay short-term market rates of interest. When interest rates go up lots of "money" flows from noninterest-paying demand deposit and low-interest-paying NOW accounts into the more profitable money market accounts. This dramatically decreases M1 but has no effect on M2. Why? Because M2 *already* includes these money market accounts. When rates go down, the opposite happens. The net effect: M1 bounces all over the place with interest rates while M2 does not. Hence, most economists now place more weight on M2 than M1 because it isn't so unstable.

GOING OUT ON A LIMB

Can It Happen Here?

Many Americans were frantic when consumer prices in the United States rose at a double-digit rate (13 percent) back in 1979 and 1980. What would life be like if inflation hit not double but *quintuple* digits, as it actually did—at 11,700 percent—in Bolivia in 1985?

Life in the world of hyperinflation was both tragic and absurd. People had to carry around suitcases full of money in order to buy ordinary goods and services, since all payments had to be made in paper money. Paper money was necessary because the rapid rate of inflation made the use of checks and credit cards impractical; the time they took to clear made the figures on them obsolete. A startling example: The number of pesos a new luxury Toyota automobile cost in 1982 would buy just three boxes of aspirin in 1985.

According to the *Wall Street Journal,* the 1,000-peso bill, the most commonly used, cost more to print than it purchased. It bought one tea bag. To buy an average-size television set with 1,000 peso bills, customers had to haul money weighing more than 68 pounds to the store. A new 100,000-peso note was printed to ease the burden. At the official exchange rate, however, it was only worth $2 (U.S.). On the black market, where it was more realistically valued, it was worth only 80 U.S. cents.

The financial system practically ceased to exist, the economy could not function on a day-to-day basis, and barter replaced money in many parts of the country. The hyperinflation ended when the government stopped creating so much money.

Can hyperinflation take hold in the United States? We doubt it as long as the Federal Reserve remains independent of the U.S. Treasury (see Chapter 18).

5. During the 1970s the money supply rose by 90 percent, and prices rose by 105 percent.
6. In the 1980s the money supply doubled, and prices rose by 60 percent.
7. In the first half of the 1990s the money supply rose by 45 percent, and prices rose by only 20 percent.

You can be your own judge, but the data seem to imply that money has a lot to do with all types of inflation. People cannot continue buying the same amount of goods and services at higher and higher prices unless the money supply increases. If the money supply today were no larger than it was in 1950 ($115 billion), prices would have stopped rising long ago—and so would real economic activity.

A qualification is in order: An increase in the money supply is a *necessary* condition for the continuation of inflation, but it is probably not a *sufficient* condition. Increases in the money supply will not raise prices if velocity falls (as in the 1930s). Even if velocity remains constant, an increase in the money supply will not raise prices if production expands. When we are in a depression, for example, the spending stimulated by an increase in the money supply is likely to raise output and employment rather than prices. Furthermore, in the short run at least—and sometimes the short run is a matter of several years—increased spending and inflation can be brought about by increases in velocity without any increase in the money supply.

Let us end this section with a summary statement of the role of money in the inflation process. Does more money *always* lead to inflation? No, but it can under certain circumstances, and if the increase is large enough it probably will. Case 1: If the central bank expands the money supply while we are in a recession, the increased spending it induces is likely to lead to more employment and a larger output of goods and services rather than to higher prices. Case 2: As we approach full employment and capacity output, increases in the money supply become more and more likely to generate rising prices. However, if this increase is only large enough to provide funds for the enlarged volume of transactions accompanying real economic growth, inflation still need not result. Case 3: Only when the money supply increases under conditions of high employment *and* exceeds the requirements of economic growth can it be held primarily responsible for kindling an inflationary spiral.

The time factor and the extent of inflation are also relevant. In the short run, an increase in monetary velocity alone (generated by increasing government or private spending), with a constant or even declining money supply, can finance a modest rate of inflation. The longer the time span, however, and the higher the rise in prices, the less likely that velocity can do the job by itself. Over the longer run, the money supply must expand for inflation to persist.

SUMMARY

1. Money serves a number of functions in the economy. Perhaps the most important is its use as a medium of exchange. It also serves as a store of value and as a unit of account. In general money is considered the most liquid asset, because it can be spent at face value virtually anywhere at any time.

2. The precise definition of the asset called money varies with the economic system. In the United States we have three definitions: M1, M2, and M3. Each represents a slightly different definition of liquidity and spendability. M1 is the narrowest and most popular definition: the sum of currency and all checkable deposits at banks and thrift institutions. This is the definition we use throughout the book unless we say otherwise.

3. Without money the economy would have to rely on the more cumbersome barter system to exchange goods and services. Only a primitive mechanism would exist for channeling savings into productive investments. The level of economic welfare would be lower on both counts.

4. Control over the money supply rests with the central bank. In the United States the central banking function is carried out by the Federal Reserve,

which tries to regulate the supply of money so that we have enough spending to generate high employment without inflation. The Federal Reserve regulates bank lending and the money supply through its control over bank reserves. By changing bank reserves and thereby the money supply, the Fed alters people's liquidity and, it is hoped, their spending on goods and services, which, in turn, helps determine GDP, the level of unemployment, and the rate of inflation.

5. The relationship between money and spending depends on how rapidly people turn over their cash balances. This rate of turnover of money is called the velocity of money. Since any given supply of money might be spent faster or more slowly—that is, velocity might rise or fall—a rather wide range of potential spending could conceivably flow from any given stock of money.

6. Inflation has historically been one of our most troublesome economic problems. Increases in the money supply are a necessary but not a sufficient condition for the creeping type of inflation we have been experiencing. In cases of hyperinflation, the money supply is clearly the main culprit. More money does not always lead to inflation, because velocity can fall and output can expand. In the long run, however, inflation cannot continue unless it is fueled by an expanding money supply.

QUESTIONS

2.1 Which definition of money supply, M1, M2, or M3, is most appropriate if the most important function of money is its role as medium of exchange? Why?

2.2 What are the most important characteristics of a good medium of exchange?

2.3 Explain why the value of money is inversely related to the price level.

2.4 "Without deposit-type money the financial sector would be less developed and the level of economic activity would be lower." Explain.

2.5 Assuming the Federal Reserve can successfully control the money supply, does this mean that the Fed can also control aggregate spending and GDP?

2.6 Is inflation clearly due to "too much money"?

2.7 Prices have roughly tripled in the last 20 years. If they do the same over the next 20, how much will it cost annually to go to your college 20 years from now?

2.8 *Discussion question:* Communist leader Vladimir Lenin is supposed to have said that inflation will undermine a country's financial system and eventually ruin the nation. But we have had inflation for many years, and the country is still standing. Does this mean that the statement is wrong?

CHAPTER 3

Financial Instruments, Markets, and Institutions

Financial markets are basically the same as other kinds of markets. People buy and sell, bargain and haggle, win and lose, just as in the flea markets of Casablanca and Amsterdam or the gold markets of London and Zurich. In financial markets they buy and sell securities, like stocks and bonds, which are less tangible than hot bracelets or cold gold bars but are no less valuable. In this chapter we introduce the instruments and institutions of the financial sector. But before getting into the details, let's provide an overall perspective.

FLOW OF FUNDS

All financial systems must provide a mechanism by which funds flow from those who have money, called saver-lenders, to those who want money, called borrower-spenders. While financial systems vary from country to country, there are basically two fundamental transmission mechanisms through which the process can take place. Funds can flow directly through **financial markets** or indirectly through what we call **intermediated markets** via financial intermediaries. The process is called the flow of funds and is described schematically in Figure 3.1. Funds flow from left to right and financial claims flow from right to left. When funds flow through financial markets, borrower-spenders sell financial claims called securities, such as stocks and bonds, to saver-lenders. In this case, the link between lenders and borrowers is "direct"

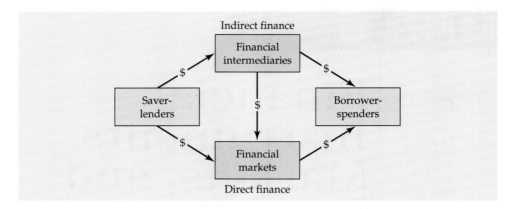

FIGURE 3.1   Flow of funds from lenders to borrowers.

because funds flow from lenders to borrowers and securities flow from bor-rowers to lenders.

When funds flow through intermediaries, the process is "indirect". This is because lenders purchase the financial claims of financial intermediaries who, in turn, purchase the financial claims of borrowers. For example, lenders might purchase a bank certificate of deposit while the bank, in turn, makes a business loan, which is like purchasing the IOU of a business firm. Here lenders do not purchase business loans directly, but rather provide the funds indirectly by investing in bank deposits. In addition, however, financial intermediaries buy securities from the financial markets—such as a life insur-ance company buying a corporate bond. Hence, you will note in Figure 3.1 that there is an arrow between financial intermediaries and financial markets.

Through a wide variety of techniques, instruments, and institutions, the financial system channels the savings of millions into the hands of borrowers who need more funds than they have on hand. Financial and intermediated markets are conduits through which those who do not spend all their income can make their excess funds available to those who want to spend more than their income.

Saver-lenders stand to benefit because they earn interest or dividends on their funds. Borrower-spenders stand to gain because they get access to money to carry out investment plans they otherwise could not finance (and that presumably earn more than the interest they pay). Without financial and intermediated markets, savers would have no choice but to hoard their excess money, and borrowers would be unable to realize any investment plans except those they could finance by themselves.

Saver-lenders are typically households, although from time to time busi-ness firms and governmental bodies—federal, state, and local—also lend sub-stantial amounts. Borrower-spenders are mostly business firms and govern-ments, although households are also important as consumer credit and mortgage borrowers.

The existence of highly developed, widely accessible, and smoothly functioning financial and intermediated markets is of crucial importance in transmitting savings into the hands of those desiring to make investment expenditures. Those who can visualize and exploit potentially profitable investment opportunities are frequently not the same people who generate current saving. If the financial transmission mechanisms are underdeveloped, inaccessible, or imperfect, the flow of funds from household saving to business investment will be impeded, and the level of economic activity will fall below its potential.

In order for this flow of funds process to function smoothly, there must be adequate information about these markets and how they operate, and adequate information about the financial claims issued by borrower-spenders. For example, if borrowers are unaware of the financial and intermediated markets in which they can issue their financial claims—or if knowledge about sources of funds is not widely disseminated—then some investments that could have been undertaken won't be, even though there are savers who would have willingly lent the funds at rates of interest equal to, or less than, what borrowers would have been willing to pay. A similar situation could arise as far as savers are concerned. Some may not be aware of lending opportunities. Instead of being put to work, funds are put under the mattress and less investment takes place (which, in turn, lowers saving as income declines). Furthermore, if savers are ill-informed about the quality of borrowers, then they may be unwilling to purchase their claims at a fair price—or at any price at all. Thus an efficient financial system must disseminate information to lenders about the quality of the financial claims issued.

Lots of interesting questions arise concerning the flow of funds. How are financial claims issued and how are securities traded in the financial markets? What determines the mix between direct finance and indirect finance? Does access to information play a role in determining this mix? What are the differences in the mix across countries? We will begin to address some of these questions in this chapter by first providing an overview of financial instruments and markets and by then profiling the major financial intermediaries. This is a prelude to a more extensive discussion of financial system architecture in Part IV.

FINANCIAL INSTRUMENTS AND MARKETS

Since we will be discussing bonds, stocks, and mortgages throughout this book, we will devote this section to explaining the similarities and differences among such financial instruments. In addition we provide a bird's-eye view of the money and capital markets, where billions of dollars worth of these and other instruments are bought and sold every day.

When borrower-spenders raise funds in the financial markets they do so by issuing securities in what is referred to as the **primary market.** Issuing securities in the primary market involves choosing the appropriate security and then distributing it to saver-lenders. One particular kind of financial institution, an investment bank, specializes in helping borrowers in the primary market. For example, investment banks, such as Smith Barney, Goldman Sachs, and Morgan Stanley, gather information about the demand for particular securities by potential buyers and for a fee, help borrowers structure and price those securities and then sell them at the most favorable price. In essence, investment bankers are information and marketing specialists for newly issued securities.

Once securities are issued, another related set of institutions helps to provide a **secondary market,** where existing securities can be bought and sold. Perhaps the most prominent secondary market is the New York Stock Exchange, but there are also so-called over-the-counter markets in many securities as well.

We will return to these topics in Chapter 6, where we discuss the structure and performance of securities markets and in Chapter 8 where we examine the money and capital markets. At this point let's review the instruments themselves, so that we can better appreciate why stocks, bonds, and mortgages are so valuable, even if they are only pieces of paper.

Bonds Represent Borrowing

Bonds exist in a wide variety of forms. For example, there are corporate bonds, U.S. government bonds, and state and local government (often called **municipal**) bonds. But in each and every case they represent the same thing, namely, the borrowing of money by the corporation or governmental body that originally sold the bond.

When Microsoft, let's say, or Uncle Sam, or the state of Wyoming want to raise a few million dollars, what they frequently do is print up fancy pieces of paper—called **bonds**—and try to sell them. Many individuals and financial institutions are interested in buying these securities because the paper states that the issuer, such as Microsoft, promises to pay whoever owns the bond (the lender) certain interest payments at specified dates in the future.

The paper also states when the bond will mature, that is, the date when the loan will be paid off to whoever owns the bond at that time. Some bonds have an original maturity of only a few years, while others may not come due for 20 or 30 years. At times in the past some governments have even sold bonds without a maturity date at all, called **perpetuities** or **consols,** and therefore keep paying interest forever.

Most bonds promise to pay a certain number of dollars of **interest** each year for a stated number of years and then to repay the principal at maturity. In the United States, bonds traditionally have been issued with coupons that bondholders redeem every six months to collect the interest that is due. For that reason, bonds are often referred to as **coupon securities.**

More recently, however, some bonds have been issued *without* coupons. Naturally enough, they are referred to as **zero-coupon bonds.** These securities are sold at a price well below their stated face value, with the difference representing the interest that will be earned by the bondholder over the life of the instrument. U.S. savings bonds are the most familiar securities of this sort. In Chapter 4 we will go into the details of how interest is calculated on coupon-bearing and zero-coupon securities.

There are many other differences among bonds. One of the most important has to do with the way their interest is taxed. State and local bonds, or municipals, are often called **tax-exempts,** because their interest is exempt by law from federal income taxation. Their interest is also usually exempt from state income taxes in the state where they are issued. Interest on corporate bonds and on federal government securities are subject to federal income taxes. On the other hand, interest on federal government bonds is not subject to state and local income taxation.

Stocks Represent Ownership

While bonds denote borrowing, **stocks** represent ownership.[1] Holding a stock certificate means that the holder owns part of the corporation. Thus there are only *corporate* stocks, no U.S. government or state and local government stocks, since individuals cannot "own" governments (at least not legally). Corporations raise money in several ways: by borrowing from banks, for instance, or by selling bonds, or by selling shares in ownership—that is, selling stocks. While bondholders receive interest, the income that stockholders receive is called **dividends.**

The two main types of stocks (often they are called equities or shares) are **preferred stock** and **common stock.** Preferred stockholders get a *fixed* dividend, and they are entitled to it before the common stockholders get anything. Common stockholders, which is what most of us are who buy stocks, get what is left over after preferred stockholders have received their fixed payments; in other words, common stockholders get a *residual* or *variable* dividend that fluctuates with the company's profits. That's nice if the company has been doing well, but not so pleasant otherwise. There is also **convertible preferred stock,** which can be converted into common stock at a predetermined price.

Once stocks are issued, they can be bought or sold, that is they can be traded, on a number of markets in this country and abroad, with common stock prices fluctuating with the fortunes of particular companies and with economic conditions in general. Actually, many buyers of common stocks seem to be more interested in capital gains (the difference between the purchase price and the selling price) than in dividends, possibly because they think they can get rich more quickly with capital gains than with dividends.

There are several measures of trends in overall common stock prices. Two of the broader measures are Standard & Poor's 500 Stock Index (called the

---

[1]Stocks are purchased by saver-lenders. Technically a stockholder is not a "lender" because a stockholder purchases equity, not debt. Nevertheless, we prefer to use the term saver-lender because it is simpler than saver-lender-owner. Sometimes, as you may have noticed, we drop all the hyphens and collapse everyone into the word *lenders* or *savers*.

S&P 500 for short), which is based on the prices of 500 stocks, and the New York Stock Exchange Composite Index, which is based on all the stocks (more than 1,500) listed on the New York Stock Exchange. However, the most popular and widely followed measure of all, even though it is the least representative, is the Dow Jones Industrial Average, which is based on the prices of only 30 stocks.

A market in which stock prices are rising, by the way, is called a **bull market,** while one in which stock prices are falling is a **bear market.** Similarly, bulls are traders who expect stock prices to rise, while bears expect them to fall. (It is often said on Wall Street that bulls make money and bears make money but pigs never do, so don't be a hog!)

With bonds and preferred stocks having fixed income payments, and common stocks variable income payments, we have come upon one of the main similarities as well as one of the main differences among securities. *All securities share a common characteristic in that they represent a claim to a stream of payments, often called cash flows, in the future.* In particular, the purchaser or owner of a security has a claim against the issuer or original seller of the security. It is the precise nature of that claim that distinguishes different types of securities. Bonds and preferred stocks generate fixed dollar payments in the future, while common stocks produce variable dollar payments. The key message, however, is that *all* securities represent claims to cash flows, and the nature of those cash flows is what helps to determine the value of the securities.

Mortgages Involve Real Estate

Mortgages are debts incurred by someone who is borrowing in order to buy land or buildings, with the land or buildings serving as "security", or **collateral,** for the lender. Like bonds, mortgages are debt instruments that promise to pay interest for a stated number of years and then repay the face value or principal at maturity. They are frequently amortized, which means that the principal is gradually repaid, along with the interest, during the life of the mortgage.

Mortgages are classified into three types: one- to four-family home mortgages, multifamily residential mortgages (apartment houses), and commercial (including farm) mortgages. They often run 25 to 30 years until maturity, although some are considerably shorter. Mortgages are also classified by whether or not they are insured by a government agency, either the Federal Housing Authority (FHA) or the Veterans Administration (VA). These so-called **FHA-VA mortgages** are contrasted with conventional mortgages, which do not carry any government insurance.

Traditionally mortgages were normal **fixed-rate** securities, with the interest rate fixed over the life of the loan. But they now come in many varieties, including **variable-rate** (or **floating-rate**) debt, with the interest rate adjusted periodically—say, every six months—to reflect changes in the overall level of interest rates.

An unusual characteristic of mortgages is the uncertainty that exists for the lender with respect to inflows of cash. Even if the interest rate is fixed, homeowners have the right to repay their mortgages early, which they may very well do if they move to a new location or if interest rates fall and they can refinance their indebtedness (borrow again) on better terms. This prepayment uncertainty makes mortgages less desirable than other forms of debt from the lender's viewpoint.

Some of the uncertainty is reduced when individual mortgages are packaged together into a "pool" and sold as a unit. Mortgage pools have become a popular form of financial investment, with buyers (lenders) relying on the large number of mortgages in the pool to help smooth out cash flows. One of the most popular type of mortgage pool is insured by the **Government National Mortgage Association** (Ginnie Mae), a division of the Department of Housing and Urban Development.

Some mortgage pools are referred to as **pass-through securities** (such as Ginnie Mae Pass-Throughs), because the interest and principal on the underlying mortgages are passed through to the saver-lenders in the pool by the originators of the mortgages. For example, after a savings and loan association (which we meet in the next section) makes a series of mortgage loans to individuals, it applies for insurance from Ginnie Mae and is then allowed to form a pool of mortgages that can be sold to the investing public. All interest payments and principal prepayments on the mortgages are passed through to the saver-lenders who have purchased the pool. Obviously there's a lot of bookkeeping involved, so the originator of the pool (the savings and loan association) receives a servicing fee for its time and trouble.

Mortgage pools come in still more complicated varieties, such as the collateralized mortgage obligation (CMO), which we discuss in Chapter 8. At this point it is useful to note that these pools represent a form of **securitization.** Securitization occurs when funds that used to flow through intermediated markets now flow through financial markets. Until residential mortgages were securitized they were exclusively owned by depository institutions such as banks, savings and loan associations, and mutual savings banks. Now, however, individual saver-lenders can own residential mortgages by buying a passthrough or CMO, which can be later resold in the secondary market. Other types of financial claims have also been securitized over the past decade including automobile loans and student loans. When securitization occurs it changes the mix between direct finance and indirect finance. We explain why this occurs in Chapter 16.

Derivatives: Options and Futures

Options and futures contracts are not used by corporations or individuals to raise funds. Nevertheless, they have become such important financial instruments in managing risk exposure that it is helpful to have at least a nodding acquaintance with them. Options and futures are often lumped together, because they both represent contractual agreements between two parties concerning some third asset. For example, there are options contracts on gold and on Treasury bonds, and there are also futures contracts on gold and Treasury bonds. Thus both options and futures are often called **derivative financial instruments,** because they derive their value from a so-called underlying asset. Options and futures are also similar in that they are both traded on organized exchanges. For example, the Chicago Board Options Exchange conducts trading in options on common stock and the Chicago Board of Trade sponsors trading in Treasury bond futures.

But the differences between these two instruments far outweigh their similarities. First let's look at **futures contracts,** because they are less complicated. A futures contract deals in both rights and obligations regarding the underlying asset. In particular, the buyer of a futures contract, also called the **long,** has the right and obligation to receive the underlying asset, say Treasury bonds, at some future date. The seller of the contract, also called the **short,** has the right and obligation to deliver the Treasury bonds on a specific date in the future. The price at which the Treasury bonds will be transferred is negotiated when the contract is sold by the short to the long on the floor of a futures exchange.

Thus both parties know exactly how much Treasury bonds (or gold) will cost them in six months or a year. If prices go up in the meantime, the long (who is entitled to pay the lower agreed-upon price) makes money and the short (who has agreed to deliver at the lower price) loses money. One reason people buy and sell futures contracts, therefore, is that they disagree on the future course of prices for an underlying asset and hope to profit as prices move in their anticipated direction. Another reason is that selling or buying the asset at a known price at a specific date in the future eliminates the risk of price fluctuations for someone who must buy or sell the asset in the future.

Options contracts also deal in rights and obligations with respect to an underlying asset, but these rights and obligations are separated. In particular, a **call option** gives the owner the right to buy the underlying asset, such as IBM stock or gold or Treasury bonds, at a fixed price (called the **strike price**) for a specific time interval, such as six months. A **put option** gives the owner the right to sell the underlying asset at a fixed price. The sellers of these options, called **option writers,** have the obligation to sell or buy the underlying assets as the case may be, and in return receive a payment, called the **option premium.**

Obviously, options are a complicated business, one that we cannot get into in detail right now. But it should be clear that options are potentially important instruments for dealing with the risks of price movements in the underlying assets. We will return to these topics in Chapter 9.

The Money and Capital Markets: A Summary

Before leaving the subject, let's take another look at how the financial markets as a whole are organized. Generally, an arbitrary distinction is drawn between the market for long-term securities and the market for shorter-term issues. The **capital market** refers to that segment of the marketplace where financial instruments have original maturities of more than a year (including equities, which have no maturity at all), and the **money market,** which is where financial instruments have original maturities less than one year.

TABLE 3.1   The Capital Market: Securities Outstanding (1995)

Type of instrument	Amount outstanding*
Corporate stocks (at market value)	$7,984
Residential mortgages	3,635
U.S. government securities (marketable, long-term)	2,531
Corporate bonds	1,326
State and local government bonds	1,062
Commercial and farm mortgages	1,081

*In billions of dollars, December 31, 1995.

Source: Federal Reserve Flow of Funds Accounts and *Federal Reserve Bulletin.*

By far the largest part of the capital market, in terms of dollar volume of securities outstanding, is the stock market, as Table 3.1 indicates. About half of all the outstanding stocks are owned by individuals; the rest are held by institutions such as pension funds, mutual funds, and insurance companies (in that order), all of which we will meet in greater detail in the next section.

As homeowners, individuals are most familiar with residential mortgages. As far as investment goes, however, some residential mortgages are held to maturity by savings and loan associations and by commercial banks, while other residential mortgages are securitized. Commercial mortgages (shown at the bottom of Table 3.1) arise in connection with financing business properties. Most commercial mortgages (and farm mortgages as well) are held by commercial banks and life insurance companies.

In the corporate bond market, life insurance companies are the main lenders (they own a third of the corporate bonds), followed by pension and retirement funds. State and local government bonds are bought primarily by wealthy individuals for their tax-exempt feature: Their interest is exempt from federal income taxes.

U.S. government securities are generally bought by a wide variety of purchasers, including the Federal Reserve, commercial banks, individual Americans, and foreigners. The same is true of the securities of various government agencies, such as the **Federal Home Loan Banks,** the **Federal National Mortgage Association,** and the **Federal Land Banks.** Most of these are guaranteed, formally or informally, by the full faith and credit of the federal government.

In many of these sectors of the capital market, active trading takes place daily for outstanding issues—especially for stocks and U.S. government securities, and to a lesser extent for corporate and municipal (state and local) bonds. Trading is facilitated by a variety of institutions, including securities dealers and brokers, with extensive communications facilities, under the watchful eye of government regulators such as the Securities and Exchange Commission. We will explore the functioning of all these markets in greater depth in Chapters 6 and 8.

In contrast to the capital market, with its long-term securities, the money market deals with short-term instruments that almost by definition are highly liquid—that is, readily marketable. If you need to raise cash quickly and are forced to dispose of long-term securities, you can take a beating, but if you have short-term securities, chances are you can sell them without taking much of a loss. The short-term securities will mature pretty soon anyway, so if you can hold off a little while you can redeem them at face value when they mature. In addition, it is simply a fact of life, embedded in the mathematics of bond yields and prices, which we discuss in Chapter 4, that for long-term securities a small change in interest rates involves a large change in price, whereas for short-term securities even a large change in yield involves only a small change in price.

For this reason, business firms and others with temporary surplus funds buy money market instruments rather than long-term securities. Commercial banks are particularly important participants in the money market, both as lenders and as borrowers, as they adjust their legal reserve positions, invest temporarily idle balances, or sell some of their securities to raise funds in anticipation of forthcoming business demands for loans.

U.S. **Treasury bills** are the most liquid money market instrument and currently, as Table 3.2 indicates, the most popular one, with about $761 billion outstanding. Treasury bills are short-term debts of the U.S. government. Typically, they are issued for three months or six months or a year. They are highly marketable and are actively traded by both financial institutions and nonfinancial corporations.

Commercial paper is mostly held by money market mutual funds. It represents short-term liabilities of the most creditworthy business firms and finance companies and has grown rapidly in recent years.

Negotiable CDs are bank deposits with a fixed maturity date, and thus are liabilities of the issuing banks. But they are interest-earning assets to whomever buys them. They are attractive because they are negotiable, which is a legal term meaning they can be transferred to a third party. Negotiable CDs are also readily marketable through securities dealers who specialize in buying and selling them. Thus a corporate treasurer who needs cash quickly

TABLE 3.2 The Money Market: Securities Outstanding (1995)

Type of instrument	Amount outstanding*
U.S. Treasury bills	$761
Commercial paper	675
Negotiable bank CDs (large denomination)	420
Bankers' acceptances	20

*In billions of dollars, December 31, 1995.

Source: Federal Reserve Flow of Funds Accounts and Federal Reserve Bulletin.

can sell off these CDs before they mature. The negotiable CD offers an alternative to Treasury bills or other money market instruments. By raising the rate they pay on CDs, banks can entice funds that might otherwise go into Treasury bills. **Bankers' acceptances,** the least important of the main money market instruments, arise in the course of international trade transactions.

This overview of the money and capital markets has included a number of references to the financial institutions that invest in these markets. Let's turn now to a somewhat more formal introduction to these financial intermediaries in order to complete our overview of the financial system as a whole.

FINANCIAL INTERMEDIARIES: PURPOSES AND PROFILE

Financial institutions such as banks, insurance companies, and pension funds, are called by a special name: **financial intermediaries.** They dominate the financial scene at home and abroad. It is virtually impossible to invest money nowadays without getting involved with some kind of financial intermediary in one way or another. In this section we formally introduce the various kinds of financial intermediaries that are prominent in this country and show how they go about their business. In order to set the stage, let's try to understand why the transmission of funds between lenders and borrowers, as described earlier in this chapter, frequently is accomplished through the good offices of financial intermediaries.

The Role of Financial Intermediaries

Financial intermediaries are nothing more than financial institutions—commercial banks, savings banks, savings and loan associations, credit unions, pension funds, insurance companies, and so on—that transfer funds from saver-lenders to borrower-spenders. They borrow from Peter in order to lend to Paula. What all financial intermediaries have in common is that they acquire funds by issuing their own claims to the public (savings deposits, savings and loan shares) and then turn around and use this money to buy traded securities, such as stocks and bonds, or nontraded financial instruments, such as consumer loans and commercial loans.

The role of financial intermediaries as "go-betweens" is reflected in their balance sheets. Unlike most companies, financial intermediaries have financial instruments on *both* sides of their balance sheet. Thus, like any other company, financial intermediaries have financial claims (liabilities and/or equity) on the liabilities side of the balance sheet. However, unlike most companies, financial intermediaries also have financial claims as assets—financial claims they invest in. A manufacturing company, for example, has mostly **real assets** (heavy things that you can kick and touch). In contrast, a commercial bank has mostly loans and government bonds as assets. This balance sheet characteristic of financial intermediaries creates a special management challenge that we will focus on in Part III.

Two questions spring to mind at this point: Why do financial intermediaries exist, and why do they have such big buildings, like the Citicorp Center in New York and the John Hancock Center in Chicago? Unfortunately, we don't have a very good explanation for the financial intermediary edifice complex, so let's focus on the first question, why do financial intermediaries exist? This question is more puzzling after we take another look at Figure 3.1, where we see that saver-lenders could accomplish their investment objectives by putting their savings directly in the financial markets and avoiding financial intermediaries altogether. So why bother with these institutions?

We can identify three reasons that explain why financial intermediaries play a major role in one financial sector: transactions costs, diversification, and information. Each is discussed in turn.

Let's take transactions costs first. Suppose you decide to buy a nice car this summer, say a Jaguar XJ6, primarily because Jaguar is now owned by the Ford Motor Company. You bargain hard and get the dealer down to $73,000. To pay the dealer, you could just give her securities from your portfolio worth $73,000. This approach, however, raises several problems. First, it turns out that all of your bonds are in $5,000 and $10,000 denominations. Second, the dealer doesn't want bonds because she's afraid they'll get stolen and she owes Ford cash. Third, once she gets the bonds, she has to sell them and pay a brokerage commission. As a result, the dealer says she has to add $500 to the price of your XJ6 for all the trouble your bonds cause her. The solution? Write a check drawn on a bank and save the $500 in transactions costs. We can think of other examples. Suppose you have $10,000 to invest and you want to buy a little bit of 100 different stocks. The brokerage commissions associated with buying one or two shares of each of these stocks would be prohibitively expensive. The solution? Buy $10,000 shares in a **mutual fund,** which invests in the 100 stocks you want and pay a commission on only one purchase.

Diversification is the second big reason saver-lenders often choose to invest in financial intermediaries. We will see in Chapter 7 that investing in a portfolio of many securities (as opposed to putting all of your eggs in one basket) diversifies away a substantial amount of risk without necessarily sacrificing expected return. Investing in a bank certificate of deposit, for instance, effectively gives the depositor a claim against a large portfolio of assets (the assets owned by the bank, which consist of bonds and loans). Mutual funds are another example. A widely diversified mutual fund can spread investor risk over hundreds of securities (as well as reducing the transactions costs associated with buying all of those securities individually).

The third reason for the existence of financial intermediaries is the production of information. Many borrower-spenders have financing needs that are difficult to evaluate. Consumers and small businesses are good examples. Unlike large corporations, little is publicly known about their financial condition. Evaluating their creditworthiness requires time and expertise, which individual saver-lenders generally do not have. Consequently, it makes sense for individual lenders to delegate to the financial intermediary the responsibility of producing information about the borrowers whose financial claims they will purchase.

Some financial intermediaries exist strictly to reduce transactions costs and provide diversification, while others add information production to their menu of services. An example of the former is an **index fund.** An index fund is a mutual fund that simply buys the stocks (or bonds) that compose a well-known index, such as the S&P 500 mentioned previously. No information is produced by an index fund on the securities it invests in; it simply buys the securities in the index, so that investors can mimic the performance of the index with minimum transactions cost.

At the other extreme, some financial intermediaries specialize in producing information needed to purchase the IOUs of individuals and small businesses. For example, consumer finance companies focus on consumer loans that might very well not exist without finance company expertise.

The existence of financial intermediaries has a very beneficial effect on economic growth. Their ability to lower transactions costs, provide diversification, and produce information lowers the cost of funds that are channeled from saver-lenders to borrower-spenders. As we will explore later in Part IV, without financial intermediaries some enterprises might not get any funds at all—including new start-up companies that provide the seeds for the economy's growth.

Financial Intermediaries in Profile

Let's now turn to the different types of intermediaries. Our purpose here is to introduce these institutions. We will pay special attention to the composition of their liabilities and their assets. Recall that the liabilities reflect how they acquire funds from ultimate lenders and the assets reflect how they deploy those funds. Because both their assets and their liabilities are financial claims, financial intermediaries profit by earning a higher rate of interest on their assets than they pay on their liabilities. In fact, from this perspective, financial intermediaries are just like any other firm—they are motivated by profits. In the process of turning a profit they just happen to accomplish an important economic objective, channeling funds from lenders to borrowers.

Although all financial intermediaries have a lot in common, there are also substantial differences among them. Ranked in terms of asset size, for example, as in Table 3.3, commercial banks are easily the largest. However, in addition to size, financial intermediaries differ significantly in terms of the composition of their assets and liabilities.

1. **Commercial banks** are the most prominent of all financial institutions. There are about 10,000 of them, ranging from Citibank, with hundreds of *billions of dollars* in assets, to thousands of small banks scattered throughout the country, many of which have less than a hundred *million dollars* in assets. Commercial banks are also the most widely diversified in terms of both liabilities and assets. Their major source of funds used to be demand deposits

TABLE 3.3   Financial Institutions, Ranked by Asset Size (1995)

Institution	Asset size*
Commercial banks	$4,501
Private noninsured pension funds	2,627
Life insurance companies	2,086
Mutual funds (stock and bond)	1,853
State and local government retirement funds	1,387
Savings and loan associations and mutual savings banks	1,016
Commercial and consumer finance companies	827
Property and casualty insurance companies	746
Money market mutual funds	745
Credit unions	310

*Total financial assets, in billions of dollars, December 31, 1995.

Source: Federal Reserve Flow of Funds Accounts.

(checking accounts), but in the past few decades savings and time deposits—including certificates of deposit—and other liabilities have become even more important than demand deposits. As we saw in Chapter 2, the main difference between savings deposits and time deposits is that time deposits have a scheduled maturity date. With these funds commercial banks buy a wide variety of assets, ranging from short-term government securities to long-term business loans and home mortgages. Because of their importance we will devote much of Chapter 12 to commercial banks.

2. **Life insurance companies** insure people against the financial consequences of death. They receive their funds in the form of periodic payments (called *premiums*) that are based on mortality statistics. Insurance companies can predict with a high degree of actuarial accuracy how much money they will have to pay out in benefits this year, next year, even ten or twenty years from now. They invest accordingly, aiming for the highest yield consistent with safety over the long run. Thus a high percentage of their assets is in the form of long-term corporate bonds and long-term mortgages, although the mortgages are typically on commercial rather than residential properties. We will look more closely at life insurance companies and other nondeposit financial institutions in Chapter 13.

3. **Pension and retirement funds** are similar to life insurance companies in that they are mainly concerned with the long run rather than the short run. Their inflow of money comes from working people building a nest egg for their retirement years. Since they face few short-term uncertainties, they invest mainly in long-term corporate bonds and high-grade stocks.

4. **Mutual funds** are frequently stock market–related institutions, but there are also mutual funds specializing in bonds of all kinds and in mortgages as well. A mutual fund pools the savings of many people of moderate

means and invests the money in a wide variety of securities, thereby obtaining diversification that individuals acting alone might not be able to achieve. Shareholders can always redeem or sell back their shares if they wish, but the price they'll receive from the fund depends on what has happened to the securities it holds. Buying shares in a mutual fund is thus more risky than buying a savings deposit or a money market instrument like a Treasury bill, but because of diversification, it is less risky than buying individual stocks or bonds on one's own.

5. **Money market mutual funds** are something else again. They were introduced in the early 1970s and grew to a startling $200 billion in about ten years. They are like the old-fashioned kind of mutual fund just described, in that people buy shares in a fund. However, the fund's management does not invest the money in the stock market or in corporate or municipal bonds. Instead, it purchases highly liquid short-term money market instruments that we discussed previously, such as large-size bank negotiable CDs, Treasury bills, and high-grade commercial paper.

6. **Savings and loan associations** (S&Ls) have traditionally acquired almost all their funds through savings deposits, usually called shares, and used them to make home mortgage loans. This was their original purpose—to encourage family thrift and home ownership. They now issue checking accounts and also make a limited amount of consumer loans and business loans. They encountered serious problems in the 1980s, which we discuss in Chapter 11.

7. **Commercial and consumer finance companies** specialize in lending money to people to buy cars and take vacations and to business firms to finance their working capital and equipment. Many of them, like the General Motors Acceptance Corporation, are owned by a manufacturing firm and lend money mainly to help retailers and customers buy that firm's products. Others, like Household Finance and Beneficial Finance, mainly make small consumer loans. They get their funds primarily by selling their own short-term promissory notes (commercial paper) to business firms that have funds to invest for a short while.

8. **Property and casualty insurance companies** insure homeowners against burglary and fire, car owners against theft and collision, doctors against malpractice suits, and business firms against negligence lawsuits. With the premiums they receive—big ones from car owners under 25 years old—they buy high-grade municipal and corporate bonds, high-grade stocks, and short-term money market instruments, such as Treasury bills.

9. **Credit unions** are generally included, along with S&Ls and mutual savings banks, in the category of "thrift institutions." There are about 13,000 of them, some in every state in the union, most quite small but a few with assets exceeding $1 billion. They are organized as cooperatives for people with some sort of common interest, such as employees of a particular company or members of a particular labor union, fraternal order, or church. Credit union members buy shares, which are the same as deposits, and thereby become eligible to borrow from the credit union. Until the early 1980s credit unions offered only savings deposits and made only consumer loans. They now offer

checking accounts (called *credit union share drafts*) and also make long-term mortgage loans.

10. **Mutual savings banks** are practically identical with savings and loan associations except that they are concentrated mostly on the East Coast. As their name implies, mutual savings banks are legally structured as "mutuals" or "cooperatives," with the depositors or shareholders "owning" the institution. As a result of the Garn-St. Germain Act of 1982, named after Congressman Ferdinand St. Germain and Senator Jake Garn, they can now easily switch from a mutual to a stock form of ownership, and many of them have done just that. Like S&Ls, savings banks traditionally have obtained most of their funds in the form of savings deposits and used the money mainly to make home mortgages, but they now can issue checking accounts and make consumer loans and some business loans. There are now only about 2,050 S&Ls and savings banks.

SUMMARY

1. Financial markets are the transmission mechanism between saver-lenders and borrower-spenders. Saver-lenders supply funds to borrower-spenders either directly, by buying securities, or indirectly, by buying the liabilities of specialized financial intermediaries. These intermediaries, in turn, either buy securities from, or make loans to, borrower-spenders. Well-functioning financial markets facilitate the growth of GDP by giving both saver-lenders and borrower-spenders options they would not otherwise have.

2. Government, corporate, and municipal bonds all indicate the same thing—that the issuer has borrowed funds at a specified interest rate for a stated period of time. When saver-lenders buy these debt claims they become lenders. Traditionally, bonds have been coupon-bearing securities. Recently, however, zero-coupon bonds have become popular.

3. Stocks represent ownership rather than indebtedness. Owners of preferred stock receive fixed dividends, similar to bond interest, but owners of common stock get variable dividends that depend on the company's profitability. When saver-lenders buy stock they become owners.

4. Mortgages are debts incurred by borrowers who are buying land or buildings. The property serves as collateral for the lender in case of borrower bankruptcy. Mortgage pools are groups of mortgages put together and purchased by an investor as a unit.

5. Options and futures contracts, called derivatives, are contractual agreements between two parties concerning a third underlying asset. Although they are not used for borrowing by corporations or individuals, they are important tools in managing risk.

6. The capital market refers to the market for long-term securities, such as corporate stocks and bonds. The money market refers to the market for short-term securities (one year or less in original maturity), such as Treasury bills and negotiable bank CDs. Money market instruments are more liquid than capital market securities.

7. Financial intermediation involves financial institutions acquiring funds from the public by issuing their own financial claims and then using the funds to buy the claims of borrower-spenders. Financial intermediation leads to lower interest rates because: i) intermediaries reduce transactions costs associated with buying financial claims; ii) intermediaries facilitate diversification; and iii) intermediaries efficiently produce information about borrower-spenders, whose claims would otherwise be difficult or impossible to sell.

8. Financial intermediaries come in all shapes and sizes, including commercial banks, insurance companies, mutual funds, and finance companies. Some specialize in diversification (mutual funds) while some specialize in information production (finance companies).

QUESTIONS

3.1 Define *direct finance, indirect finance, saver-lenders,* and *borrower-spenders.*

3.2 What is the function of financial markets?

3.3 People buy bonds to get interest. Why, then, would anyone buy a bond that has no interest coupons attached (that is, a zero-coupon bond)?

3.4 Why do saver-lenders sometimes choose to invest indirectly through financial intermediaries?

3.5 *Discussion question:* Explain how financial intermediaries might promote overall economic growth. Should the government subsidize intermediaries in order to promote growth?

PART II

Financial Instruments and Markets

CHAPTER 4

Interest Rate Measurement and Behavior

Interest rates are the most pervasive element in the financial world. They affect everything that financial institutions do, and their implications extend into just about every nook and cranny of financial markets. Bank managers wouldn't dream of making investment decisions without first considering the outlook for interest rates. Consumers decide where to put their savings depending in large part on where they can get the best interest rate on their funds. Business managers take interest rates into account in deciding when to borrow, how much, from whom, and for how long. Most importantly, interest rates serve as a yardstick for comparing different types of securities.

Given the importance of interest rates, it is worthwhile exploring how they are calculated and their relationship to the prices of securities. We can then turn to see what determines whether rates are high or low and how they have behaved historically.

CALCULATING INTEREST RATES

Suppose you lend someone $100 for a year at 8 percent annual interest. How much would you get back at the end of the year? The answer depends on how the interest is paid. The most elementary case is called, not surprisingly, **simple interest.**

Simple Interest

There is a formula, which you probably remember from high school, for calculating the dollar amount of interest earned based on simple interest:

$$Principal \times Rate \times Time\ (in\ years) = Interest$$
$$\$100 \quad \times .08 \times \qquad 1 \qquad = \quad \$8$$

The amount you'd get back at the end of the year would be the principal ($100) plus the interest ($8) or a total future amount of $108:

$$
\begin{aligned}
Total\ Future\ Amount &= Principal + Interest \\
&= Principal + (Principal \times Rate) \\
&= Principal\ (1 + Rate) \\
&= \$100\ (1 + .08) \\
&= \$108
\end{aligned}
$$

This example illustrates that if you are offered a choice between a dollar today and a dollar a year from now, you should take the dollar today, because you could lend it out and turn it into more than a dollar a year from now. Time, in other words, is worth money. A dollar in hand is worth *more* than a dollar due a year from now. Another way of expressing the same thought is to say that a dollar due a year from now is worth *less* than a dollar today (because interest can make today's dollar grow over the course of a year).

What if you lent money for more than a year, say, for three years? With *simple* interest at an 8 percent annual rate, $100 loaned out today will yield $8 interest at the end of a year, another $8 interest at the end of the second year, and $8 interest at the end of the third year.

$$
\begin{array}{ccccccc}
Principal & \times & Rate & \times & Time\ (in\ years) & = & Interest \\
\$100 & \times & .08 & \times & 3 & = & \$24
\end{array}
$$

Thus, the total amount you'd have at the end of three years would be the principal ($100) plus the interest ($24) or $124.

It's hard enough to get rich to begin with, but even harder if you lend your money out at simple interest. At least insist on **compound interest,** which is just as easily available—usually more so—and over time generates much more rapid growth.

Compound Interest

Compound interest produces more rapid growth because it involves interest on interest. With annual compounding, the interest that accumulates during a year is added to the principal at year's end, so that the following year your money earns interest on interest.

Banks, for example, usually pay compound interest to depositors who put their money into bank savings accounts. The interest depositors earn is periodically added to their principal, so that it in turn starts to earn interest. Some banks convert the interest to principal annually, while others do so semiannually, quarterly, monthly, or even daily. They advertise that interest is compounded annually, semiannually, or whatever it may be. We'll stick to annual compounding to illustrate how compound interest works.

With annual compounding at an 8 percent interest rate, $100 loaned out today will yield $8 interest at the end of a year, an additional $8.64 interest at the end of a second year, a further $9.33 at the end of a third year, and so on. Compare this $25.97 of total interest after three years to the $24 that accumulates with simple interest. The difference appears small, but over long periods of time it becomes stupendous. For instance, $100 lent at 8 percent simple interest would grow to $900 in a hundred years; at 8 percent compound interest over the same time period, $100 would grow to $219,976!

Let's examine compound interest a bit more closely to understand why it's so powerful. If you deposit $100 in a bank at 8 percent annual interest, what is your deposit worth after a year? The answer, of course, is $108. More formally: $100 (1 + .08) = $108. What is it worth after two years? Because of compounding (receiving interest on interest), it becomes $108 (1 + .08) = $116.64. What the second year really amounts to is $100 (1 + .08) (1 + .08), or $100 (1 + .08)^2 = $116.64. On the same basis, after three years the deposit would be worth $100 (1 + .08)^3, after four years $100 (1 + .08)^4, and so on. After 100 years, the deposit would be worth $100 (1 + .08)^{100}, which is equal to $219,976—all because of interest on interest.

If $100 today at 8 percent interest is worth $108 a year from now, and $116.64 two years from now, we can work *backward* and say that $108 a year from now must be worth only $100 today, and that $116.64 two years from now must also be worth only $100 today. In the previous paragraph, we applied an interest rate to increase a present sum into the future; we can also work backward to reduce or discount a future sum back to its **present value** (time is money). Putting it a bit more formally, we have simply transposed the previous paragraph's

$$\$100 \ (1 + .08) \ = \ \$108 \qquad \text{into} \qquad \frac{\$108}{(1 + .08)} = \$100$$

and

$$\$100 \ (1 + .08)^2 \ = \ \$116.64 \qquad \text{into} \qquad \frac{\$116.64}{(1 + .08)^2} = \$100$$

We will return to the concept of present value shortly. First, though, let's become better acquainted with some interest rates on marketable **coupon-bearing securities,** like corporate, municipal, and government bonds. The interest rate that is most frequently referred to in bond markets is called **yield to maturity,** but a couple of other bond interest rates are often mentioned by securities buyers and sellers and are quoted in the financial sections of many newspapers—namely, the coupon rate and the current yield. Let's look first at the coupon rate and the current yield and then return to yield to maturity.

Coupon Rate on Bonds

Suppose you pay $900 for a $1,000-face-value 8 percent–coupon bond that will mature in ten years and that you expect to hold until maturity. *What annual interest rate will you be getting on that security?* In particular, what return will you be earning if you invest in the security?

You have to be careful to keep clear exactly which interest rate you are talking about. In this instance the **coupon rate,** which is equal to the annual coupon divided by the face value, is 8 percent ($80/$1,000 = 8 percent). This also means that printed on the face of the bond is a statement that each year the holder of the bond will get an interest payment from the bond's issuer, amounting to 8 percent of the $1,000 face value, or $80. (Most bonds pay interest semiannually, which in this case would mean payments of $40 twice a year, but for simplicity we'll assume only one payment a year of $80.)

If you had paid the full $1,000 face value for the bond, you would indeed be getting 8 percent interest. But bond prices may rise and fall for many reasons, as we'll see later in the chapter. In our case, you are paying only $900, so although the coupon rate printed on the bond specifies 8 percent, you will actually be earning more than 8 percent because you paid less than $1,000. But *how much more* than 8 percent?

Current Yield

We take a step in the right direction by examining the **current yield.** The current yield is calculated as the annual dollar interest payment divided by the price you paid for the bond, or $80/$900 = 8.89 percent. At first glance this looks like a reasonable way to figure the interest rate, until you realize that it neglects the fact that when the bond matures in ten years you'll have a $100 **capital gain** (because you paid only $900, but when the bond matures it will be redeemed at its $1,000 face value).

Yield to Maturity

Yield to maturity is the most accurate and widely used measure of interest rates in financial markets. It takes into account the factors that current yield neglects. In our discussion of compound interest we noted that, at 8 percent annual interest, $100 today will be worth $108 a year from now, $116.64 two years from now, $125.97 three years from now, and so on. Putting this formally: $100 (1 + .08) = $108; $100 (1 + .08)^2 = $116.64; and $100 (1 + .08)^3 = $125.97.

We also noted that we could work backward and *discount a future sum back to its present value:* At 8 percent interest, $108 due a year from now would be worth $100 today (its present value), $116.64 due two years from now would be worth $100 today, and $125.97 due three years from now would also be worth $100 today. That is:

$$\frac{\$108}{(1 + .08)} = \$100; \quad \frac{\$116.64}{(1 + .08)^2} = \$100; \quad \frac{\$125.97}{(1 + .08)^3} = \$100$$

This concept of present value enables us to compare securities with different time dimensions. The illustration above, for example, shows that when the annual interest rate is 8 percent, three pieces of paper—one promising $108 in a year, one promising $116.64 in two years, and one promising $125.97 in three years—are all equally valuable. Each of them is worth exactly the same ($100).

With this background in mind, let's now turn to the concept of yield to maturity. *The yield to maturity of a security is that particular interest rate (or rate of discount, as it is sometimes called) that will make the sum of the present values of all the future payments of the security equal to its purchase price.*

The easiest way to understand the above italicized sentence is with a concrete example. We have been discussing paying $900 for a $1,000-face-value 8 percent–coupon bond that will mature in ten years. What annual interest rate will it provide? Unless we can answer that question, we have no way of comparing it with other bonds that are available in the market, so we won't be able to tell if it's a good buy or a poor one.

Assuming that the interest is paid annually rather than semiannually, this piece of paper promises ten future payments—interest payments of $80 each and one final payment consisting of $80 in interest and $1,000 face value (or principal). The price of the bond is $900, which means that anyone who wants to receive those future payments has to give up $900 today. The yield to maturity of this bond is defined as *that particular rate of discount* (let's call it *r*) *that will make the sum of the present values of all ten expected future payments equal $900.*

If we can find *r* in the following equation, we will have calculated the annual yield to maturity of this security:

$$\$900 = \frac{\$80}{(1+r)} + \frac{\$80}{(1+r)^2} + \frac{\$80}{(1+r)^3} + \cdots + \frac{\$1,080}{(1+r)^{10}}$$

We could figure out *r* by trial and error, trying one rate of discount (say 9 percent) and then another (10 percent) until we isolate one that makes all the terms on the right-hand side of the equation add up to $900. But that would be a time-consuming process. It would be a lot quicker and easier just to look it up in a book of bond yield tables, where it's all worked out for us. Such tables show the yield to maturity in this particular case to be 9.58 percent per annum. (Notice that this is well above the current yield of 8.89 percent, because it implicitly takes account of the capital gain—the difference between the $1,000 face value and the $900 paid for the bond.)

What if you don't have a book of bond yield tables handy? Well, most business-oriented hand calculators are programmed to do the job. If you have such a hand calculator, with keys labeled in the usual way, enter $80 for the yearly coupon payments (use the *PMT* key); $1,080 for the final payment (with the *FV* key); 10 for the number of periods to maturity (the *N* key); and $900 for the bond's purchase price or present value (the *PV* key). Press the appropriate key (usually *r* or %) and in a flash the display will show the annual yield to maturity: 9.60 percent.

The hand calculator's 9.60 percent yield to maturity differs slightly from the bond table's 9.58 percent. The reason is that we assumed only one interest payment a year when entering data into the calculator, whereas bond tables are constructed on the assumption of semiannual interest payments. Since we've been simplifying all along in this example by assuming interest is paid annually, we might as well stick with that assumption and, to be consistent, use 9.60 percent as the appropriate yield to maturity.

In terms of yield to maturity, therefore, if you invested $900 in this particular security you'd get an annual yield of 9.60 percent on your money from now until the bond matures ten years from now. The yield to maturity is an accurate measure of the return on your investment in the security, because it compares all future dollar payments (including any capital gain) with the amount of money needed to get those future payments (namely, the price of the security).

So far we've been discussing yield to maturity in very specific terms, using the example of a particular security. The concept is too important, however, to leave it at that. We should generalize the concept so it can be applied to a variety of cases. Here is the general formula we can use to calculate the yield to maturity *(r)* of a fixed-income security that pays a dollar coupon *(C)* in each of *n* years, has a face value *(F)* that will be paid off at maturity *n* years from now, and has a current price *(P)*:

$$P = \frac{C_1}{(1 + r)} + \frac{C_2}{(1 + r)^2} + \frac{C_3}{(1 + r)^3} + \cdots + \frac{(C_n + F_n)}{(1 + r)^n}$$

What the general formula tells us is that if we know the price of a security, its coupon payments, its face value, and its maturity, we can find its annual yield to maturity *(r)*. The yield to maturity is whatever rate of discount will make the sum of the present values of all future payments equal the purchase price.

OFF THE RECORD

The Million Dollar Lottery: A Case of Misleading Advertising?

One illustration of the time value of money arises in connection with state lotteries in which the lucky winner gets paid over a period of time rather than getting the entire sum all at once. "Buy a ticket and win a million dollars!" reads the advertisement. But often it turns out that what the winner really gets is $50,000 now followed by $50,000 a year for the next 19 years.

However, $50,000 now followed by $50,000 a year for 19 years is worth considerably less than a million dollars. Following the present value formula in the text and assuming an 8 percent interest rate:

Present Value = $50,000 + $50,000/(1 + .08) + $50,000/(1 + .08)^2 + $\cdots$
+ $50,000/(1 + .08)^{19}

Converting each of the payments to present value and adding produces a sum total of $530,180. Not bad, but it's a long way from a million!

We could also use the same general formula to determine a security's *price*, provided we know the yield to maturity to begin with. In other words, if we know *r*, the coupon payments *(C)*, the face value *(F)*, and the years to maturity *(n)*, we can solve for the present value of the bond or the price *(P)* we should be willing to pay for it. We'll come back to this way of looking at the equation later in the chapter.[1]

Zero-Coupon Bonds

Most bonds are like the $1,000-face-value 8 percent–coupon bond that we have been using for illustrative purposes; most corporate, government, and municipal bonds do indeed have coupons attached to them that entitle the holder to periodic interest payments. In the case of our bond, the coupon rate of 8 percent means that each year the holder of the bond will get an interest payment, from the bond's issuer, amounting to 8 percent of the bond's $1,000 face value, or $80.

However, recent years have witnessed the growing popularity of a new kind of bond—**zero-coupon bonds,** which do not entitle the holder to get any coupon interest payments whatsoever. The only thing the owner of such a bond gets is the face value, when the bond eventually matures.

Why would anyone ever think of buying a bond that doesn't make any interest payments? As with many things, whether or not it is worth buying depends on how much it costs. We've already seen that if you pay $900 for an 8 percent–coupon bond with a $1,000 face value, you'll get an annual yield to maturity of 9.60 percent on your money over the next ten years. What if someone offers you the same bond but without any coupons—that is, a piece of paper promising $1,000 in ten years and nothing else? In fact, if you can get that piece of paper at a price of only $400, you will *also* get 9.60 percent on your money over the next ten years!

Yields to maturity on zero-coupon bonds follow the same principles as on coupon securities, but they are easier to calculate because there is only one payment—the face value, which is due on maturity. Thus the basic formula simplifies to:

$$Price = \frac{Face\ Value}{(1 + r)^n}$$

In the case of zero-coupon bonds, yield to maturity is that rate of discount *(r)* which makes the present value of a single payment (the face value), due in *n* years, equal to the current price. If we already know what *r* is, we can use the same formula to solve for the present value or price of the bond.

---

[1]Actually the "present value" formula in the text can be used quite generally to value anything with future cash flows, not just securities. An investor might project future cash flows for an investment in a firm or building as C_1 through C_n. If the purchase price of the firm or building were given, then the formula would generate what is known as the internal rate of return on the investment. In fact, the yield to maturity on a bond is nothing more than the internal rate of return on the cash flows of the bond.

In our example, with a face value of $1,000 due in ten years, if we know the annual interest rate—say it is 9.60 percent—then we can solve for the price. With a hand calculator, the price turns out to be $399.85.

READING THE FINANCIAL NEWS

Government Bond Market Quotations

(1)			(2)	(3)	(4)	(5)
Rate	Mat.	Date	Bid	Asked	Bid chg.	Yld.
8¼s,	2000–05	May	105.25	106.1	+ .4	7.53
12s,	2005	May	141.12	141.20	+ .4	7.72
10¾s,	2005	Aug.	129.8	129.16	+ .2	7.73
9⅜s,	2006	Feb.	117.10	117.18	—	7.61
7⅝s,	2002–07	Feb.	100.25	101.1	+.5	7.51
7⅞s,	2002–07	Nov.	103.4	103.12	+.2	7.51
8⅜s,	2003–08	Aug.	106.26	107.2	+ .8	7.62
8¾s,	2003–08	Nov.	110.4	110.12	+ .3	7.64
9⅛s,	2004–09	May	113.18	113.26	+ .7	7.67
10⅜s,	2004–09	Nov.	125.6	125.14	+ .8	7.77
11¾s,	2005–10	Feb.	137.18	137.26	+ .6	7.81
10s,	2005–10	May	122.12	122.20	+ .11	7.68
12¾s,	2005–14	Nov.	147.24	148	+ .7	7.83
13⅞s,	2006–11	May	158.30	159.6	+ .5	7.76
14s,	2006–11	Nov.	160.24	161	+ .4	7.87
10⅜s,	2007–12	Nov.	126.16	126.24	+ .5	7.76
12s,	2008–13	Aug.	143	143.4	+ .7	7.83
13¼s,	2009–14	May	156	156.8	+ .9	7.86
12½s,	2009–14	Aug.	148.23	148.27	+ .6	7.85
11¾s,	2009–14	Nov.	142.8	142.16	+ .8	7.75
11¼s	2015	Feb.	140.10	140.14	+ .6	7.71
10⅝s,	2015	Aug.	133.19	133.27	+ .9	7.68
9 7.8s,	2015	Nov.	125.4	125.12	—	7.68
9¼s,	2016	Feb.	119.10	119.18	+ .9	7.58
7¼s,	2016	May	97.8	97.12	+ .8	7.47
7½s,	2016	Nov.	101.11	101.15	+ .9	7.38

Column (1) identifies each government bond in terms of its coupon rate and maturity date. For example, the *second* bond in Column (1) carries a 12 percent coupon and will mature in May of the year 2005. (Conversationally, it is referred to as "the twelves of oh five," which explains the s following each coupon rate.) The next bond has a 10¾ percent coupon and will mature in August of 2005 (the ten and three-quarters of oh five).

Many bonds—like the first one, the eight and a quarters of May 2000–05—have *two* maturity dates. Such bonds mature on the second date but are **callable** by the Treasury starting with the first date. The 8¼s of May 2000–05, for example, will mature in May of 2005, however, if it wishes, the Treasury can call them for redemption, that is, buy them back from you at a predetermined price, in May of 2000 or at six-month intervals thereafter until it *has* to redeem them, at face value by May of 2005.

(continued)

Columns (2) and (3) indicate what government securities dealers were "bidding" and "asking" for each bond at the close of trading the previous day—that is, their "buying price" (bid) and "selling price" (asked). Not surprisingly, their bid price is slightly below their asked price, allowing dealers to expect a profit when transacting with the public. Government bonds normally have a face value of $1,000 and their price is conventionally expressed as a percentage of face value. Note that the numbers after the period are not decimals but 32nds. Thus, with respect to the last bond on the list, the $7\frac{1}{2}$s of 2016, government securities dealers were willing to buy at $101^{11}/_{32}$ (= $1,013.4375) and willing to sell at a slightly higher price of $101^{15}/_{32}$ (= $1,014.6875).

Column (4) is the change in the dealers' bid price at the close of trading compared with the previous day's close. It is also in 32nds. For example, the $7\frac{1}{2}$s of 2016 closed at $101^{11}/_{32}$ bid, up $^{9}/_{32}$ from the previous day's close of $101^{2}/_{32}$.

Column (5) is the bond's yield to maturity. For callable bonds, the yield to maturity is calculated in one of two ways: (a) to first call date when the asked price is above par (100), and (b) to maturity date when the asked price is equal to or below par. The asked price is used in the yield to maturity calculation since that is the price you would have to pay when buying the bond. In Column (5) the period is a true decimal point, so there is an implied percent sign (%) after each yield.

The Inverse Relationship Between Yields and Bond Prices

We mentioned earlier that higher interest rates mean lower bond prices and lower interest rates mean higher bond prices. We can use the general present value formula just developed to demonstrate why this is so: If a bond's coupon payment *(C)* and face value *(F)* are fixed, a higher yield to maturity *(r)* must imply a lower bond price *(P)*. Similarly, a lower yield must imply a higher bond price. If either *r* or *P* changes, the other will automatically change in the opposite direction.

For instance, what if you paid not $900 but $925 for our illustrative ten-year 8 percent–coupon bond with a face value of $1,000? What annual yield to maturity would you be getting then? Plug $925 instead of $900 into your trusty calculator and the yield to maturity would fall from 9.60 to 9.18 percent. What if you paid only $875? Then yield to maturity would rise to 10.04 percent.

We have been assuming that we know *P* and want to find the resulting interest rate. We could do it the other way around: We could ask what price is implied by a particular yield. For instance, we could assume an interest rate of 12 percent and calculate the price that would produce that annual yield to maturity (assuming, of course, that *C* and *F* are fixed). The answer must be a price *below* $875, since $875 gives us only a 10.04 percent yield. We find that a price of $774 would produce a 12 percent yield to maturity.

The special case of a consol, or perpetual bond, best illustrates the inverse relationship between yields and bond prices. A consol is a bond with no maturity date at all. It promises that the holder will receive a fixed annual dollar payment forever, with no redemption date. In that case, with n approaching infinity, the general present value formula collapses (you'll have to take our word for it) into simply:

$$Price = \frac{C}{r}$$

Here it becomes obvious that, with C given, the rate of interest (r) and the price have to move inversely. For example, if $C = \$1$ and $r = 0.05$, then $P = \$20$; but if r rises to 0.10, then P falls to $10. The inverse relationship between P and r follows directly from the mathematical formula for bond pricing.

Why Long-Term Bonds Are Riskier than Shorts

We can also use the general formula for the present value or price of a bond to explain why a change in interest rates affects long-term bond prices so much more than it affects prices of short-term securities. For long-term securities, a small change in interest rates involves a large change in price, whereas for short-term securities even a big change in yield involves only a small change in price.

Here's an illustration. Take two bonds, each of which has a face value of $1,000 and an 8 percent coupon; one has 20 years until maturity and the other has only two years. Both are currently priced at par (that is, at $1,000), so that yield to maturity in each case is 8 percent, the same as the coupon rate.

Assume that suddenly, for reasons no one fully understands just yet, all interest rates rise by two percentage points. Yield to maturity in each case goes up to 10 percent. This rise in yield involves a fall in price from $1,000 to $830 for the 20-year bond, but a fall in price from $1,000 to only $965 for the two-year security.

In brief, the longer a bond's maturity, the more its price will be affected by a change in the general level of interest rates. This has enormous implications for capital gains and losses. When all interest rates fall, long-term securities rise dramatically in price, but not short-term ones. Similarly, when all interest rates rise across the board, long-term bonds—but not the shorter ones—drop drastically in price.[2]

The general present value formula explains why this is so. The formula shows that the price or present value of a bond consists of the sum of the dis-

---

[2]Length of time to maturity is the most important factor affecting bond prices when interest rates change, but it is not the only one. Coupon size is also relevant: The smaller the coupon, the more a bond's price will be affected by a change in interest rates. An 8 percent–coupon bond will be more volatile in price than a bond with a 10 percent coupon. (Most volatile of all would be a long-term zero-coupon bond.) Portfolio managers often mathematically combine maturity and coupon size in order to estimate a bond's riskiness more precisely than is possible with maturity alone. The combination of the two is called a bond's **duration.** For more on the subject, see the Appendix to Chapter 5.

counted present values of all its future payments. The longer the maturity of a security, the greater will be the effect of a change in r on the price, because there are more future payments and they will be discounted over a longer period of time. The longer period of time is crucial: Remember that discounting a payment due in 20 years isn't just dividing by $(1 + r)$ but by $(1 + r)^{20}$.

In other words, you can get rich quickly with long bonds, but you can also go down the drain. Long-term bonds are riskier than short-term bonds because the threat of potential loss is greater. Then why do people buy them? Because they often yield more than short-term bonds, and also because hope springs eternal: Maybe interest rates will fall and long-term bond prices will skyrocket!

Nominal Versus Real Interest Rates

So far we have discussed only nominal interest rates. "Nominal" means measured in money as distinct from purchasing power. Nominal interest rates— that is, market interest rates as quoted in the newspapers—provide an accurate measure with respect to purchasing power when prices are stable, because then the purchasing power of money remains constant over time. But when prices are rising, as during periods of inflation, nominal interest rates become misleading with respect to purchasing power.

Inflation means that lenders will get back dollars that have less purchasing power than the dollars they loaned out. Assume a 10 percent nominal interest rate and a 6 percent annual rate of inflation. If you lend someone $100 for a year, at 10 percent interest, you'll receive back $110 a year later. But with prices 6 percent higher, it will take you all of $106 to buy what you could have gotten for $100 last year. In terms of purchasing power, the $110 you now have buys only $4 more of goods and services than the $100 you loaned out a year ago. Although the nominal interest rate is 10 percent, 6 percent inflation has shrunk the inflation-adjusted or real interest rate to only $4/$100, or 4 percent.

The **nominal interest rate** measures the increment in dollars as a percent of dollars loaned out ($10/$100). The **real interest rate** measures the increment in purchasing power as a percent of purchasing power loaned out ($4/$100). *In a nutshell, the real interest rate is the nominal interest rate minus the inflation rate.*[3]

Actually, there are two concepts of the real interest rate: the ex ante or expected real rate and the ex post or realized real rate. The ex ante or expected

---

[3]The 4 percent real interest rate in this example is an approximation. It takes $106 to buy what $100 could have bought a year ago, leaving an apparent $4 increment in purchasing power. But that $4 can no longer buy what $4 could have bought a year ago. Because of the 6 percent inflation, $4 now can only buy what $3.77 could have bought last year ($4/1.06 = $3.77). Thus the precise real rate of interest in this example is not 4 percent but only 3.77 percent. Nevertheless, it has become customary to ignore this refinement, so that the real rate of interest is generally calculated simply as the nominal interest rate minus the inflation rate.

real interest rate is the nominal interest rate minus the expected rate of inflation. The ex post real rate is the nominal interest rate minus the actual or
realized rate of inflation. More on this later in the chapter.

Return Versus Yield to Maturity

Just as inflation creates a divergence between nominal and real yields, the fact
that people often sell bonds before the final maturity date creates a divergence
between the concept of yield to maturity developed above and the concept of
return, or what the bond returns to the investor over the time period the bond
is actually held. To illustrate this point, we first define **return** and then present a series of numerical examples.

The concept of return or rate of return measures the cash flows received
during a period relative to the amount invested at the beginning. For our
purposes, it makes sense to measure returns per annum so that we have a
uniform standard for comparison. Thus, the annual rate of return on a
bond that is held for one year is measured as the selling price minus the
purchase price plus the coupon payment, all divided by the initial price. Or,
more formally:

$$Return = \frac{Selling\ Price - Purchase\ Price + Coupon}{Purchase\ Price}$$

For example, a bond that is purchased for $1,000 at the beginning of the year,
pays a coupon of $80 at the end of the year, and is sold for $1,000 at the end of
the year has an annual return of 8 percent:[4]

$$Return = \frac{1,000 - 1,000 + 80}{1,000} = 0.08$$

If the bond were sold for $1,100, the return would be 18 percent:

$$Return = \frac{1,100 - 1,000 + 80}{1,000} = 0.18$$

Now let's go back to our favorite 8 percent–coupon ten-year bond that we
purchased for $900. Recall that the yield to maturity on that bond was 9.60
percent. Suppose that after buying the bond for $900 the investor decides to
sell it after one year. What will be the annual return earned on the investment? The answer depends crucially on the selling price. More specifically,
suppose the investor sells the bond at a lower price, say $880, because the

---

[4]Note that our example specifies that the coupon is paid at the end of the year because if it were
paid earlier in the year the return measure would have to include interest earned on the coupon
from the time it is paid until the end of the year. All return measures assume that cash distributions are made at the end of the period.

level of interest rates has gone up at the end of one year (remember that bond prices move inversely with interest rates). The annual return is then 6.6 percent:

$$Return = \frac{880 - 900 + 80}{900} = 0.066$$

On the other hand, if yields had gone down at year's end and bond prices had increased, the annual return would be much higher. For example, if the investor had sold the bond for $950 the annual return would be 14.4 percent:

$$Return + \frac{950 - 900 + 80}{900} = 0.144$$

Yield to maturity is, in general, a poor guideline to the annual returns earned on a bond when selling before maturity. Whether the investor is pleasurably surprised or utterly disappointed depends on what happens to bond prices between one year and the next; and whether bond prices go up or down depends on whether interest rates rise or fall. And that brings us to our next major topic: What determines movements in the overall level of interest rates?

WHAT DETERMINES THE LEVEL OF INTEREST RATES?

Now that we are experts in how to calculate interest rates, let's see what determines whether they are high or low and how they have behaved historically. There are interest rates on many different types of loans—rates on car loans, home mortgages, government securities, corporate bonds, and so on. However, most interest rates move up and down together, so that we can simplify matters by discussing "the" interest rate, with "the" rate conveniently standing for all rates taken as a group. In the next chapter we will look separately at interest rates on alternative securities and explore differences among them. In all cases, however, whenever we use the term *interest rate* we mean yield to maturity.

Supply and Demand Determine the Interest Rate

The interest rate is a price, like the price of Lamborghinis or Maseratis or copies of your favorite video game. With the interest rate, however, the price we are talking about is the price of credit or borrowing money—the price that lenders receive and borrowers have to pay. Because the interest rate is a price, like all prices, it is determined by supply and demand. Supply of and demand for what? Of credit or **loanable funds**—funds that lenders are willing to make available for borrowers to borrow.

In any competitive market, whether for automobiles or personal computers, interaction between supply and demand determines price and quantity

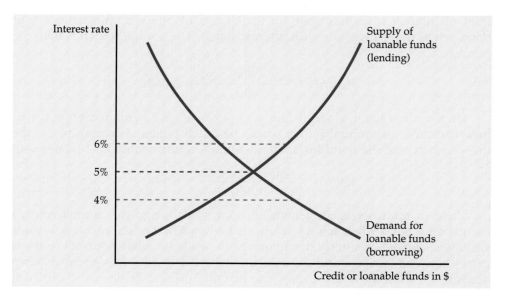

Interest rate

Supply of
loanable funds
(lending)

6%

5%

4%

Demand for
loanable funds
(borrowing)

Credit or loanable funds in $

FIGURE 4.1   Supply and demand determine the interest rate.

exchanged. Financial markets are no exception. In fact, we can best illustrate the story by drawing familiar supply and demand curves. In Figure 4.1 the interest rate is shown on the vertical axis and the quantity of credit or loanable funds on the horizontal axis. The upward-sloping supply-of-funds curve represents the commonsense notion that lenders will be willing to extend more credit the higher the interest rate they receive (holding everything else constant, including things like borrower creditworthiness). The downward-sloping demand-for-funds curve represents borrower behavior: The lower the interest rate, the more funds borrowers are willing to borrow (once again holding everything else constant, like the prospects for business activity).

It should not be terribly surprising that the **equilibrium interest rate** is at the intersection point of the supply and demand curves—producing a yield of 5 percent in Figure 4.1. Equilibrium, you may recall from basic economics (or high school physics, if that's a better memory), means no tendency for change. Thus, in Figure 4.1 the interest rate will stay at 5 percent because that's where the quantity of funds lenders want to lend just equals the quantity of funds borrowers want to borrow. At any other interest rate, there is an excess of either borrowers or lenders, and competitive pressure will force the rate toward its equilibrium level. For example, at 6 percent lenders want to lend more than borrowers want to borrow; competition among lenders forces the interest rate down. Similarly, at 4 percent borrowers want to borrow more than lenders want to lend; competition among borrowers forces the interest rate up. Once the interest rate gets to 5 percent, there is no tendency for it to change as long as the supply and demand curves stay where they are.[5]

Analyzing interest rates by supply and demand assumes that financial markets are competitive, so that supply and demand pressures will be reflected in price (interest rate) changes. It rules out the conspiracy theory of interest rates—the view that rates are rigged by a few insiders with substantial market power.

It is hard to believe that any one person, institution, or group of institutions has anywhere near enough power to rig interest rates in this country. There are simply too many lenders engaged in the business of lending, and therefore too many alternatives open to most would-be borrowers, to permit any tightly knit clique of lenders to control the price of credit. Lenders charging more than prevailing rates would price themselves out of the market and lose business to their competitors. Similarly, borrowers trying to borrow at

---

[5]Instead of talking about how the supply of and demand for credit or loanable funds determine the rate of interest, we could talk about the same thing in terms of how the demand for securities and the supply of securities determine the price of securities (see the diagram below). To supply credit (lend) is equivalent to *demanding* debt securities—financial institutions lend, for example, by purchasing debt instruments. To demand credit (borrow) is the same as *supplying* securities— business firms borrow by selling their bonds or other IOUs. Look at the diagram and compare it with Figure 4.1 in the text. At a price of $833 (which corresponds, let us say, to the 6 percent *yield* in Figure 4.1) relative eagerness to buy securities—or lend—would drive up the price of securities, just as Figure 4.1 shows that it would drive *down* the rate of interest. And at a price of $1,250, corresponding to a 4 percent yield, relative eagerness to sell securities—to borrow—would drive down the price of securities, just as Figure 4.1 shows that such circumstances would drive *up* the rate of interest.

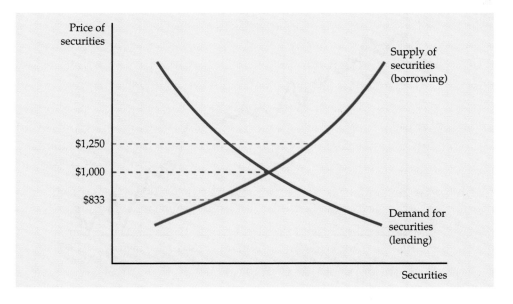

cheaper than prevailing rates would find themselves outbid for funds by others who are willing to pay the market price.

Why Does the Interest Rate Fluctuate?

Once the interest rate reaches equilibrium—like 5 percent in Figure 4.1—does it stay put? Hardly. Figure 4.2, which records the daily yield movements on ten-year Treasury bonds during the first half of 1995, shows that yields can fluctuate considerably from day to day. Why do rates change so often?

The interest rate fluctuates, like other competitive prices, because of shifts in the demand and/or supply curves. Before going into detail, let's focus on the mechanics. Perhaps you remember from your introductory economics course that we should distinguish between movements *along* a demand or supply curve and a *shift* in the curve. When the amount demanded or supplied changes in response to a change in the interest rate, then we have a movement *along* a demand or supply curve. On the other hand, a *shift* in a curve occurs when the amount demanded or supplied changes, at each interest rate, in response to something else—such as, for example, a change in expectations regarding inflation.

Figure 4.3 illustrates (a) a movement along a demand curve and (b) a shift in the curve. Moving down demand curve (a) from *x* to *y* to *z* is a movement along the demand curve. As the interest rate falls, the amount of credit demanded increases. A shift in demand takes place when the amount demanded increases at each interest rate, as from demand curve (a) to demand curve (b).

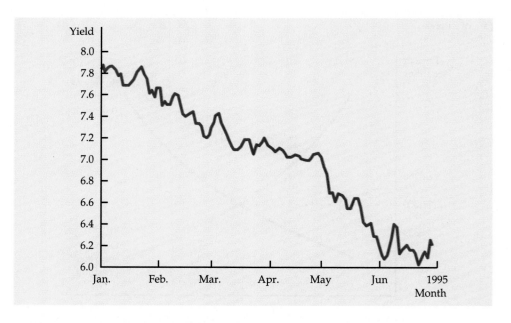

FIGURE 4.2   U.S. Treasury bond yields fluctuate from day to day (1995).

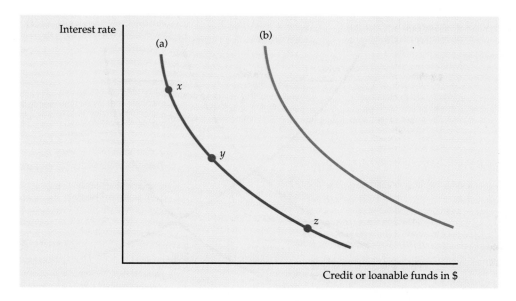

FIGURE 4.3 Movement along a demand curve versus a shift in demand.

Of course, the amount demanded could also *decrease* at each interest rate, in which case the curve would shift to the left.

When talking about a movement along a single demand or supply curve, we'll always refer to a change in "amount demanded" or "amount supplied." On the other hand, when we say demand or supply has increased (or decreased), we'll mean the whole curve has shifted to the right (or the left).

Making this distinction helps to avoid confusion. When mortgage interest rates fall, for example, many potential home buyers decide to borrow funds and buy a home because now they can afford the monthly mortgage interest payments. That's an increase in the amount of loanable funds demanded in response to a change in the interest rate—a movement down *along* a single demand curve. In this case, a fall in the interest rate causes an increase in the amount demanded. On the other hand, say many tenants suddenly find themselves with more money and decide they can afford to buy their own homes, even at higher mortgage rates. This is a rightward *shift* in the demand curve.

It should be fairly obvious that anything that causes the demand or supply curves to shift position will cause the equilibrium interest to change. For example, in Figure 4.4, starting out with supply curve *S* and demand curve *D* produces a 5 percent equilibrium interest rate. If the demand curve shifts from *D* to *D'* and the supply curve stays put, the equilibrium interest rate will rise to 6 percent. If, on the other hand, the supply curve shifts from *S* to *S'* and the demand curve stays where it was (at *D*), then the new equilibrium interest rate will be 4 percent.

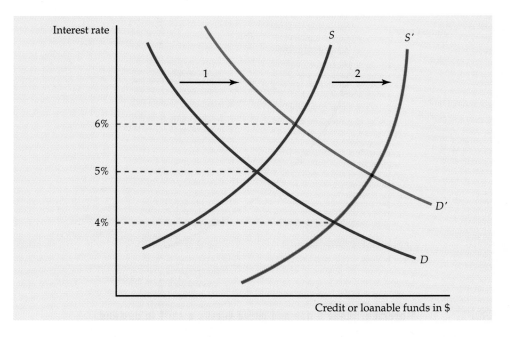

FIGURE 4.4 **Shifts in demand (1) or supply (2) curves can change the equilibrium interest rate.**

Behind Supply and Demand

Now that we know that shifting supply and demand curves for loanable funds underlie gyrations in interest rates, let's see if we can go one step further. The level of interest rates will go up when the demand for loanable funds increases or when the supply of loanable funds decreases. What might lie behind such shifts in the demand and supply curves? First, let's look at demand.

Most borrowing comes from:

1. Business firms, borrowing to acquire inventories or buy capital equipment;
2. Households, borrowing to buy cars, consumer goods, or homes;
3. State and local governments, borrowing to build sewer systems, roads, schools, and so on; and
4. The federal government, borrowing to finance federal budget deficits.

Anything that increases the eagerness to borrow in any of these sectors would shift the demand for loanable funds to the right and drive interest rates higher. Some such factors might be anticipated improved profits on the part of business firms; expectations of higher incomes on the part of consumers;

large population increases resulting in the need for more state and local services; or a big buildup in military outlays producing larger federal budget deficits.

Now let's turn to supply. Why might the supply of loanable funds—lending—decrease? Most lending comes from financial institutions or directly from individuals. Banks and other financial institutions sometimes have to curtail their lending because government authorities, like the Federal Reserve, make it difficult for them to lend. The ability of individuals to lend depends in part on how much they save; if they save less, they will generally lend less, exerting upward pressure on interest rates.

We will not go behind supply and demand in similar detail with respect to declines in interest rates. We trust your own ingenuity. In general, of course, what makes interest rates fall are decreases in the demand for loanable funds (for example, because of slower economic activity) and/or increases in the supply (for example, because individuals save more). You can take it from there.

In The News

Slower Economic Activity Raises Bond Prices and Lowers Interest Rates

Treasuries Jump On Subdued Retail Sales

U.S. Treasury prices surged yesterday after figures from the Commerce Department showed that the widely expected rebound in retail sales failed to take place in May.

Late in the session, the benchmark 30-year Treasury was up $13^1/_{32}$ at $113^3/_4$ to yield 6.561 percent. At the short end of the maturity spectrum, the two-year note was yielding 5.612 percent, and yields on all but the 10- and 30-year notes had fallen below 6 percent.

Retail sales increased by 0.2 percent in May, or by just 0.1 percent without the motor vehicle component. Economists had expected the rise to be closer to 0.6 percent, reversing April's 0.3 percent decline.

The figures were closely watched because economists were counting on a rebound from consumers to put some life back into the economy. Weakness in the figures renewed speculation that the Federal Reserve would lower interest rates this summer.

Since late last month, traders have gone through swift changes in sentiment as they have tried to determine the course of monetary policy. Bonds soared earlier this month after a string of weak economic data only to sink last week after Mr. Alan Greenspan, Fed chairman, made comments the market took to mean that rates would be left unchanged.

Adding fuel to the speculation that the Fed might ease was weakness in consumer price figures, also released yesterday. The Consumer Price Index rose 0.3 percent in May as most economists had expected, but the core index—which excludes the food and energy components—was up 0.2 percent, not the 0.3 percent most had forecast.

The Importance of Inflationary Expectations

One element underlying *both* supply and demand deserves special mention because it is so important. That element is expectations.

In our earlier discussion of nominal versus real interest rates, we showed how to calculate the real rate of interest given a particular nominal interest rate and a specific rate of inflation. Now we have a somewhat different concern: Will a change in *expectations* of inflation alter the equilibrium nominal interest rate itself?

Changes in inflationary expectations affect equilibrium interest rates by shifting the curves for both the demand for and the supply of loanable funds. Borrowers expecting inflation to accelerate *will increase their demand* for loanable funds, shifting the demand curve to the right, because they look forward to repaying their borrowings in depreciated dollars. On the other hand, lenders expecting a speedup in inflation will *decrease their supply* of loanable funds, shifting the supply curve to the left, because they anticipate getting repaid with money of diminished purchasing power. On both counts, the end result of increased inflationary expectations will be higher *nominal* interest rates. Similarly, expectations of a slowdown in inflation will decrease demand, increase supply, and produce lower rates.

Usually, however, matters are not so neat and tidy. Our example assumed that everyone agrees in their expectations about inflation. In the real world, such unanimity about the future, or about anything else for that matter, hardly ever exists. Under such circumstances, the consequences for interest rates are more complicated.

Cyclical and Long-Term Trends in Interest Rates

Now let's see if our supply-demand framework can shed some light on how interest rates have behaved over the past four decades. Figure 4.5 plots the yields on ten-year government bonds since 1950 to represent the overall movement in interest rates. The chart also shows the annual rate of inflation represented by the rate of increase in the consumer price index. The shaded areas on the chart indicate periods of business cycle recession—that is, periods when the economy is growing relatively slowly and unemployment is increasing. Each shaded area begins at the peak of a business cycle expansion and ends at the bottom (or trough) of the ensuing recession.

Three generalizations can be drawn from Figure 4.5:

1. *The level of interest rates tends to rise during periods of business cycle expansion and fall during periods of cyclical recession.* Yields go up when business conditions are good, because that's when business firms and households generally increase their demand for loanable funds. Businesses borrow more to accumulate inventories in anticipation of increased sales, and households buy more goods and services on credit because the future looks bright for them, too. The opposite takes place in recessions, when both businesses and

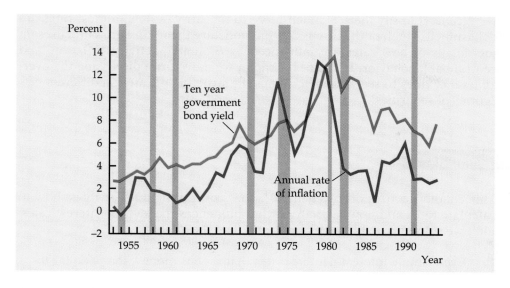

FIGURE 4.5   Trends in interest rates since 1950.

consumers rein in their use of credit so that the demand for loanable funds shifts to the left and interest rates fall.

Supply-curve shifts reinforce these effects on interest rates. The Federal Reserve usually tightens credit in business cycle expansions, shifting the supply of loanable funds to the left, raising interest rates. And the Federal Reserve typically eases credit during recessions, which increases the supply of credit, lowering interest rates.

2. *The level of interest rates was on an upward long-term trend from 1950 to 1980.* For the most part each cyclical trough in interest rates was higher than the previous trough, and each cyclical peak similarly higher than the one before. This upward trend was probably due to a number of factors, the two most important of which were large federal budget deficits, which forced the U.S. Treasury to borrow huge amounts every year, and investor concern with future inflation. Inflationary expectations, as we have seen, can generate forces that raise interest rates. Figure 4.5 shows that inflation accelerated between the 1950s and the early 1980s, so it is not surprising that nominal interest rates followed suit as investor's expectations of inflation caught up with the trend in actual inflation.

3. *Since the early 1980s rates have trended downward.* This decline cannot be due to smaller federal budget deficits because deficits got larger than ever during this period, so it must be due to expectations of inflation. As can be seen in Figure 4.5, actual inflation dropped from double digits in the early 1980s to under 3 percent by the early 1990s, so it is not surprising that nominal interest rates have followed a similar trend. The big question as we approach the turn of the millennium is whether interest rates will continue their decline or whether the uptrend that ended in the early 1980s will resume.

Needless to say there is much more to the story of how interest rates are determined. Much of the discussion on monetary theory in Part VI focuses on the details of how rates are influenced by economic activity, inflation, and central bank behavior. In the next chapter we move from discussing the overall level of rates to see what determines the structure of rates on different categories of securities.

SUMMARY

This chapter focuses on two general issues concerning interest rates: how to calculate rates and how to analyze what influences the level of interest rates. First we summarize the calculations and then the analysis.

1. Even simple interest demonstrates that time is money, that a dollar today is worth more than a dollar due a year from now (because today's dollar can grow to more than a dollar by earning interest during the year). Compound interest produces more money than simple interest because compounding involves the payment of interest on interest.

2. The yield to maturity of a security is that rate of discount that will make the sum of the present values of all future payments flowing from the security equal to its purchase price. Conversely, the present value or price of a security consists of the sum of the discounted present values of all its expected future payments. The yield to maturity is a useful yardstick for comparing returns on different securities.

3. Because many buyers do not hold securities to maturity, annual return is often used as an alternative yardstick. Return on a bond is defined as price change plus coupon expressed as a fraction of price.

4. The present value formula shows why there is an inverse relationship between yields and bond prices. It also shows why a change in interest rates affects the prices of long-term securities by more than the prices of short-term ones, making long-term securities riskier than short-term securities.

5. It is important to distinguish between "real" and "nominal" interest rates. The real interest rate is the nominal rate minus the rate of inflation.

6. The interest rate is the price of credit and as such is determined by the supply of and demand for credit or loanable funds. It fluctuates because of shifts in demand and/or supply.

7. Interest rates rise when the demand curve for loanable funds shifts to the right and/or when the supply curve shifts to the left. Rates fall when the demand curve shifts to the left and/or the supply curve shifts to the right. Behind demand and supply are the borrowing require-

ments of businesses, households, and governments, and the monetary policies of the Federal Reserve. Expectations also underlie the demand for and supply of loanable funds, especially expectations regarding inflation.

8. Interest rates tend to rise during periods of business cycle expansion and fall during recessions. This reflects increased demand for loanable funds during expansions and decreased demand during recessions.

9. The long-term trend of all interest rates was upward from 1950 to 1980. Much of this uptrend was a reflection of the increase in inflation between 1950 and the early 1980s. Interest rates have fallen since the early 1980s, primarily because inflation declined.

QUESTIONS

4.1 Explain why yield to maturity is higher than current yield when you buy a coupon-bearing bond for less than its $1,000 face.

4.2 Explain why zero-coupon bonds sell for less than identical maturity coupon-bearing bonds.

4.3 Is it correct to say that bond prices vary inversely with the interest rate because of simple mathematics? Why?

4.4 Why do you subtract the rate of inflation from the nominal rate of interest to derive the real rate?

4.5 If interest rates suddenly fall, would you rather be holding a portfolio consisting mostly of short-term securities or of long-term securities?

4.6 Show how the supply of and demand for securities is the mirror image of the supply and demand curve for loanable funds as a framework for determining the equilibrium level of interest rates.

4.7 What are the main forces underlying demand for funds that cause the level of interest rates to go up? What are the forces underlying supply that cause rates to rise?

4.8 Explain how an increase in inflationary expectations can cause nominal interest rates to rise because of the effect on supply and demand for funds.

4.9 What would you expect the historical record to show about the behavior of the level of interest rates during cyclical expansions? Did rates in fact behave as you would expect?

4.10 *Discussion question:* Common stocks are often said to be "risky" investments while bonds are considered "safe." Do you agree with this assessment? Why or why not?

CHAPTER 5

The Risk and Term Structure of Interest Rates

Whether interest rates go up or down often depends on which ones you focus on. Short-term interest rates can go up while long-term rates may stay put. Or vice versa. It's time to examine the details. After all, that's where the money is. The structure of yields on different maturities of the *same* class of securities is explored first. We then turn to the relationship among yields on different categories of securities (such as government bonds versus corporate bonds).

THE TERM STRUCTURE OF RATES AND THE YIELD CURVE

The relationship among yields on different maturities of the same type of security is called the **term structure** of interest rates (from "term to maturity"). For government bonds we might compare the yields on three-month Treasury bills, two-year notes, and 20-year bonds.

The relationship between yield and maturity is sometimes depicted graphically by a **yield curve,** as in Figure 5.1, where yield is measured on the vertical axis and term to maturity is on the horizontal axis. Often the yield curve is upward sloping—that is, short-term securities yield less than long-term securities (curve *A*). Sometimes it is rather flat—short-term yields equal long-term yields (curve *B*). And sometimes the yield curve is even downward sloping— short-term interest rates are *above* long-term rates (curve *C*).

What determines the shape of the yield curve? A number of analytical explanations have been proposed, ranging from the application of basic supply and demand to more complicated theories based on expectations and preferred maturity ranges of different investors. Each approach is aimed at explaining real-world observations, such as why yields on all maturities tend to

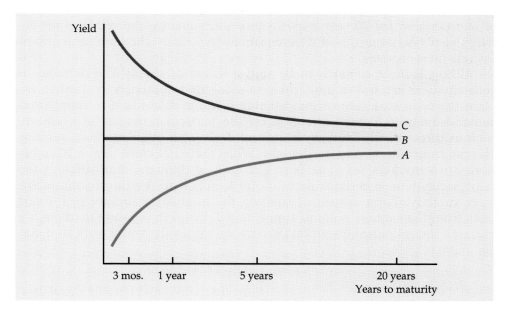

Yield

3 mos.   1 year   5 years   20 years

Years to maturity

C
B
A

FIGURE 5.1   Three alternative yield curves.

move together while at the same time there are distinct, divergent, patterns between movements in short-term and long-term yields. First we will develop the alternative theories of the term structure, and then we will describe how they best explain actual events.

Supply and Demand.   Just about everything in economics is determined by supply and demand, and the term structure of interest rates should be no exception. In the previous chapter we showed how the overall level of interest rates was determined by the supply of and demand for loanable funds or, alternatively, by the supply of and demand for securities as a whole. A simple extension of that approach suggests that the interest rates on different maturity categories of securities are determined by the relative supply of and demand for each maturity class. For example, the interest rate on three-month Treasury bills is determined by the supply of and demand for three-month Treasury bills, while the interest rate on 20-year bonds is determined by the supply of and demand for 20-year bonds. Thus when the supply of three-month bills goes up, the yield on bills rises to induce investors to buy the additional supply; when the supply of bills falls, the yield on bills falls to ration the smaller supply among eager investors.[1] If nothing happens to the supply

---

[1]Do not be confused by the fact that a decrease in supply causes yields to fall; yields decline because the decrease in supply raises security *prices* and prices and yields are inversely related.

of and demand for 20-year bonds, these shifts change the relationship between yields on securities of different maturity; that is, the term structure of interest rates changes.

Although there is much to be said in favor of supply and demand in general, there are severe limitations to using that approach by itself to explain the term structure of interest rates. The problem is that supply and demand analysis focuses attention on the particular market in question, such as three-month Treasury bills, and deals with other markets, such as 20-year securities, as an afterthought. When there is a close relationship between two markets, as there is in the case of different maturities of the same security, it is perhaps more useful to focus on the interrelationships more directly. Thus instead of treating the maturity structure of interest rates from the vantage point of supply and demand in separate markets, we examine the relationships among securities within the framework of a single market.

The Pure Expectations Approach.   There are many—and here financial analysts and economists often find much common ground—who argue that short-term securities and long-term securities are very good substitutes for each other in investor portfolios, not for every investor but for enough so that their decisions *collectively* make a significant impact on the market. For such investors the important feature of the security they buy is not the maturity date of the final payment, but rather what it *returns* over the period for which they want to invest (see the previous chapter for a definition of returns). This concern with returns implies that expectations of future short-term rates determine how long-term rates are related to short-term rates. Let's illustrate that with a particular example.

Say you are the portfolio manager of a bank and you want to invest funds for two years. Suppose you could buy a one-year Treasury security today yielding 8 percent, and you expect that next year the rate on one-year securities will be 10 percent. If you buy the one-year security today and reinvest in a one-year security next year, you expect an average return over the two years of about 9 percent. If you had the option of buying a *two-year* Treasury security today that yielded $9\frac{1}{2}$ percent, you'd jump at it (so would everyone else). On the other hand, if two-year Treasury securities were yielding only $8\frac{1}{2}$ percent, you wouldn't touch them (neither would anyone else). This means that unless the two-year security yielded exactly 9 percent (the average of the current and expected short-term rate), portfolio managers would try to buy it (if it yielded more) or sell it (if it yielded less). This buying and selling pressure by portfolio managers maintains the long-term (two year) rate as an average of the current short-term (one year) rate and the expected future short-term (one year) rate.

A somewhat more general statement is as follows: The relationship between the yield on a two-year (long-term) security and a one-year (short-term) security depends on the expected future short-term rate. If next year's *expected* short-term rate is above the current short-term rate, then the current long-term rate will be above the current short-term rate, and the yield curve will be upward sloping. On the other hand, if next year's expected short-term rate is below the current short-term rate, the yield curve will be downward sloping.[2]

The key to this **expectations theory** of the term structure is that short-term securities and long-term securities are very good substitutes for each other in investor portfolios. In fact, they are perfect substitutes: If expected returns are the same, the portfolio manager is indifferent between "shorts" and "longs." Instead of separate markets for short-term and long-term securities, there is a single market. Note in this case that if the supply of long-term securities goes up and the supply of short-term securities goes down, it makes absolutely no difference as far as yields are concerned. Because investors are indifferent among maturity categories of the same security, they will happily exchange long-term securities for short-term securities, with no change in yields, as long as expected future short-term rates are unchanged.

The Liquidity Premium Modification.   It is difficult to argue that investors are unconcerned about differences between short-term securities and long-term securities. It is simply a fact of life—embedded in the mathematics of bond prices—that the *prices* of long-term securities are more volatile than those of short-term securities (see Chapter 4 or, for a more rigorous discussion, the appendix to this chapter). If you have to sell a security before it reaches maturity and interest rates have increased, a long-term security will have fallen in price much more than a short-term one. If you might have to sell to raise cash, you'll prefer short-term securities. They are safer. Commercial banks, for example, prefer short-term securities precisely because their needs for cash are often unpredictable.

Recognition of the greater capital uncertainty of long-term securities leads to the "liquidity premium" modification in the expectations theory of the term structure. If most investors are like commercial banks and prefer the capital certainty of short-term securities, while most bond issuers prefer to issue long-term securities, then investors on balance will demand a premium for holding long-term securities. This is often called a **liquidity premium,** but it is really a **risk premium**—a reward for exposure to the capital uncertainty of long-term securities. Thus in our previous numerical example a two-year security would have to yield more than the average of the current one-year rate and next year's expected one-year rate. Otherwise investors wouldn't want to hold the riskier two-year security.

---

[2]The story of the downward-sloping yield curve is as follows. If the current one-year rate is 8 percent and investors expect next year's one-year rate to be 6 percent, portfolio managers could earn an average return of 7 percent by investing in two successive one-year securities. If the current rate on a two-year security were above 7 percent, all investors would buy it, forcing up the price and reducing the yield. If the current two-year rate were below 7 percent, no one would buy it, forcing down the price and raising the yield. Thus the two-year security must yield 7 percent when the current one-year security yields 8 percent and the expected one-year rate is 6 percent. Since the short-term (one-year) rate is 8 percent and the long-term (two-year) rate is 7 percent, we have exactly what we call a downward-sloping yield curve.

The Preferred Habitat Approach.   It seems reasonable to suggest that many investors prefer short-term securities. But to leave it at that would be misleading, because some investors actually have a *preference* for long-term securities. Life insurance companies and pension funds, for example, don't worry that much about surprising needs for cash. Their liabilities are actuarially predictable. In fact, they want to make sure they earn at least 8 (or 10 or 12) percent on their assets over the next ten (or 20 or 30) years. That way they are sure of a profit because they promise to pay pension holders something less than that. These institutions therefore prefer long-term securities.

Because some institutions prefer long-term securities while others prefer short-term issues (like members of the animal kingdom, they have **preferred habitats**), it would seem that the supply-demand emphasis in explaining the term structure could make a healthy comeback. For example, when the supply of five-year securities increases relative to other maturities, the yield on such issues will have to increase above the "expectations theory average" in order to induce investors to leave their preferred maturity ranges and to invest in the unfamiliar "five-year" territory. The same would be true for any increased supply of a particular maturity category. Thus the yields on various maturities would seem to have relatively little to do with expectations, and much more to do with relative supply and demand.

Not so fast, say the proponents of the expectations theory. While many institutions have preferred maturity ranges for their investments, they can also be induced rather easily to switch between short-term securities and long-term securities when yields get out of line with expectations. Commercial banks, for example, require only a "liquidity premium" to invest in longer-term securities. A large increase in the supply of five-year bonds may therefore initially push up their yield to a higher level than is warranted by the expectations theory alone. But commercial banks will then be lured away from their preferred one-year securities by the attractive yields on five-year bonds. And pension funds will be enticed as well. Both these actions mitigate the upward pressure on five-year bond yields caused by the increased supply of securities in that maturity category. In the process, the role of expectations is restored.

Real-World Observations.   Each of the theories outlined above is aimed at explaining the real world. We started with the pure expectations approach and then modified it to make the theory conform more closely to reality. A further step is to recognize that investors do not usually have precise numerical predictions of short-term rates for next year or the year after. More likely, investors form expectations of when the "level" of rates is in general relatively high and when the "level" of rates is in general relatively low. While this is a rather casual version of the expectations theory, it provides a powerful explanation of when the yield curve is likely to be upward sloping (curve *A* in Figure 5.1) or downward sloping (curve *B*).

When interest rates are high relative to what they have been, investors generally expect them to decline in the future. Falling interest rates mean rising bond prices, and those investors who are holding long-term bonds in their portfolio will reap their just reward—big capital gains. Therefore, when all rates are relatively high, investors will prefer to hold long-term securities rather than short-term securities (because the potential capital gains on short-term securities are relatively low). This additional demand for long-term securities drives their prices up and their yields down, relative to short-term securities. Thus long-term yields are below short-term yields (that is, the yield curve is downward sloping) when the overall level of rates is high.

Similarly, when the general level of rates is low and yields are expected to rise in the future, investors prefer not to hold long-term securities because they are likely to incur large capital losses. This drives the price of long-term securities down (and the yield up), thereby producing long-term rates above short-term rates (an upward-sloping yield curve).

Figure 5.2 demonstrates the accuracy of these conjectures with yield curves during the mid-1970s, a particularly illustrative period. The actual yield curve on August 30, 1974, was downward sloping, and that's when the overall "level" of rates was quite high by then-current historical standards. On the other hand, the most sharply upward-sloping curve is for January 23, 1976, when the "level" of rates was relatively low.

Figure 5.2 also emphasizes another empirical regularity: Short-term rates fluctuate more than long-term rates over the course of the business cycle. Indeed, over the 16-month period covered by the yield curves, short-term rates fluctuated by about 5 percentage points, while 20-year bond yields hardly

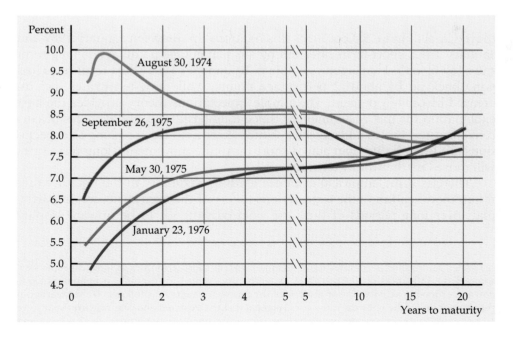

FIGURE 5.2   Yields on U.S. government securities.

When the "level" of rates is high, the yield curve is likely to be downward sloping.

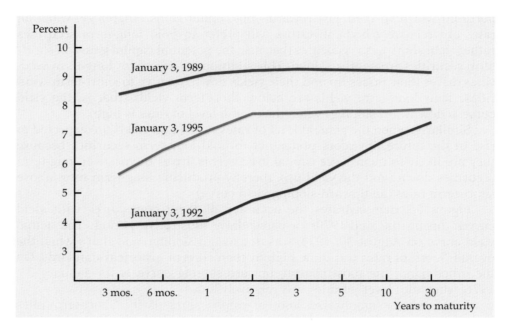

FIGURE 5.3   Short-term rates fluctuate by more than long-term rates over the business cycle.

moved at all. Figure 5.3 confirms this relationship. Between January 1989 and January 1992, short-term rates fell by $4\frac{1}{2}$ percentage points while long-term rates fell by only $1\frac{1}{2}$ percentage points. By January 1995 short-term rates had gone back up by about 2 percentage points, while long-term rates had increased by only $\frac{1}{2}$ percent. The simple expectations theory provides the best explanation for this phenomenon: Since long-term rates are averages of current short-term rates and expected future short-term rates, as long as expectations are less volatile than actual short-term rate movements, long-term rates will move less than short-term rates.[3]

There is some empirical evidence lending credibility to the liquidity premium modification to the expectations theory of the term structure. In particular, over long periods of time the yield curve tends to be upward sloping

---

[3]Expected future short-term rates move less than current short-term rates as long as people view some of the influences on interest rates as temporary events—for example, a temporary slowdown in economic activity. The arithmetic of the rate movements is as follows: We saw earlier in the chapter that if the one-year rate were 8 percent and the expected one-year rate next year were 10 percent, then two-year rates would be 9 percent. If the one-year rate jumped to 12 percent and the expected one-year rate rose to 11 percent, then the equilibrium long-term rate would be $11\frac{1}{2}$ percent (the average of 12 and 11). Thus when the short-term rate jumped by 4 percentage points, the long-term rate rose by only $2\frac{1}{2}$ percentage points. And that is what we said in the text: Short-term rates fluctuate more than long-term rates.

more often than it is downward sloping. Under the pure expectations theory this should not happen. After all, there is no reason to think that expected future short-term rates are usually above current short-term rates—and that's the only thing that would explain this phenomenon according to the pure expectations approach. But once a liquidity premium is added to the story, long-term rates exceed the average of the current short-term rate and expected future short-term rates. This implies an upward-sloping yield curve more of the time.

A final observation comes from market participants. Most practitioners would stress that over the very short run, large supplies in a specific maturity range would raise the interest rate on that particular category of security. Such anecdotal evidence supports the supply/demand or preferred habitat approach to the term structure of interest rates. In point of fact, in the very short run (such as over a week or two), there is little doubt that relative supplies of securities must be brought into the picture. After all, it takes time for the expectations-based substitution between short-term and long-term securities to occur. But after all is said and done, and all portfolio adjustments have been completed, the impact of relative supplies is swamped by expectations of future short-term rates.

To summarize, the best approach to the term structure is ecumenical. The expectations theory forms the foundation; liquidity premiums then enter as a permanent modification to the yield curve; and finally, over short periods of time, even relative supplies of securities have an impact.

GOING OUT ON A LIMB

Is the Shape of the Yield Curve a Crystal Ball?

Predicting the course of economic activity is serious business. Many corporations pay large sums for the forecasts generated by high-priced consultants. Perhaps they would be better off, and would save money, if they simply looked at the shape of the yield curve.

Figure 5.2 shows that short-term rates fluctuate more than long-term rates over the course of the business cycle. It also shows that at just about the peak of the business cycle in August 1974, the yield curve was negatively sloped, partly in response to the antiinflationary policy pursued by the Federal Reserve. The result was a steep recession that did not hit bottom until March 1975. About that time the yield curve became positively sloped and remained that way until the end of the decade, when the economic expansion came to an abrupt halt.

Coincidence? The Federal Reserve Bank of Cleveland reports that negatively sloped segments of the yield curve preceded all but four of the 17 business-cycle downturns since 1910 (the exceptions were 1926, 1945, 1948, and 1953). Indeed, stock market forecasters (who make economic forecasters look like geniuses) have jettisoned many of their arcane charts in favor of the yield curve as the key predictor of stock price movements.

The message is clear: A negatively sloped yield curve is a danger sign for the economy and the stock market. If you see one, proceed with caution (sell first).

An Aside on Marketability

We could continue with more details on the term structure relationship. But we've gone about as far as we should without recognizing that nicely shaped curves such as those drawn in Figures 5.2 and 5.3 hardly ever occur in nature. Not that the yield curve for any of the dates shown in the figures is wrong. It's just that the yield curve depicts the relationship between yield and maturity, and there are other factors that influence yields—even on a relatively homogeneous group of securities such as government bonds.

One of the most important explanations for differences in yield to maturity on government bonds with the same maturity are differences in the marketability of specific issues. The most recently issued government bonds in each maturity range, often referred to as the **current coupon,** or **on the run,** issue, are usually the most actively traded securities in the secondary market. Although we discuss the details of marketability and the related concept of liquidity in the next chapter, it is sufficient to recognize that government securities dealers are most willing to buy and sell the most recently issued securities, so that investors can count on finding a ready market for these issues in case they want to alter their existing portfolios. Because these "current coupon" issues are highly marketable, they carry somewhat lower yields to maturity than the older, so-called "off the run" issues.

RISK AND TAX STRUCTURE OF RATES

Once we step away from the safety of governments, default risk plays an important role in explaining yield relationships. Indeed, for lack of a better name, this is often called the risk structure of interest rates, even though other factors, such as differential tax treatment, come into play in addition to the relative risk of default. We'll take a look at the relationship among yields on governments, corporates, and municipals, staying away from term structure influences by looking at long-term bonds only.

As with term structure theory, a straightforward supply-demand analysis can be tried in explaining yield relationships. For example, as the supply of corporate bonds rises relative to, say, governments, the yield on corporates should increase. But as with the term structure, a simplistic supply-demand approach ignores important relationships between these markets that dominate the yield structure. In particular, because all bonds are substitutes for each other in investor portfolios, as soon as one yield begins to rise relative to others, investors switch into that security. This substitution process holds down the widening yield differentials among securities.

In fact, when you think about it, every security entitles the holder to receive exactly the same thing—a stream of dollar payments in the future. One reason investors pay a different price for each of these contracts is that sometimes people break their promises. They don't wind up doing what they said

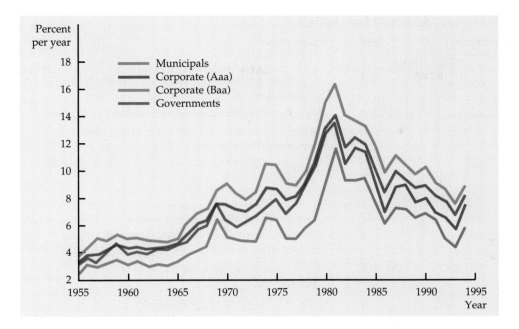

FIGURE 5.4   Riskier securities carry higher yields.

they'd do. In some religions you do penance for such transgressions; in the financial world you go bankrupt. So, bonds are risky—they may not pay either the interest or the principal. Since the federal government has substantial taxing power there is little risk of **default** on government securities.[4] But for corporations, individuals, and even municipal governments, the risk of default is prominent. Since people usually have to be paid to bear more risk (see Chapter 7), yields on corporate bonds exceed those on governments, as is evident in Figure 5.4.

In a similar vein, within the corporate sector firms have differing degrees of **default risk.** As is summarized in Table 5.1, private credit-rating agencies, such as Standard & Poor's and Moody's Investors Service put the bonds of these firms into different risk categories, depending on the strength of the company's balance sheet, cash flows, and management. The highest rating, Aaa in Moody's rating system, goes to companies such as AT&T. The credit rating used by some investors (such as pension funds) as a cutoff for so-called "investment grade issues" is Baa. At the other end of the scale, those bonds that are in default get a C rating. Figure 5.4 illustrates what we would expect: Lower-rated corporate bonds (Baa) have higher yields than bonds in the higher-rated category (Aaa).

---

[4]Although the government always has the ability to repay its debt, it can simply refuse to do so. This is called sovereign risk (as in sovereign monarch). Because repudiating debt has severe consequences for future borrowing, however, this option is rarly considered a viable strategy.

TABLE 5.1   A Guide to Bond Ratings

Moody's	S&P	Description
Investment Grades		
Aaa	AAA	Best quality with least risk; strong ability to pay interest and principal
Aa	AA	High quality, slightly more long-term risk than the top rating
A	A	Strong capacity to pay interest and principal, but a bit vulnerable to changes in economic conditions
Baa	BBB	Adequate current financial strength, but could be threatened by changes in the economy
Speculative Grades		
Ba	BB	Currently paying interest but with an uncertain future
B	B	Little assurance that interest and principal will continue to be paid
Caa to C	CCC to C	Highly speculative bonds that may be in or near default
	D	Used only by S&P for bonds in default

Municipal bonds—the debt issued by state and local governments—have a number of interesting features. The default risk of such bonds used to be considered quite low, with the only significant bankruptcies occurring during the Great Depression. The taxing power of state and local governments is the ultimate backing for municipal bonds. But the taxing power of states and cities is limited by people's willingness to stay put and subject themselves to the burden of ever-increasing local taxes. As a result of this and the de facto defaults of New York City in 1975, Cleveland in 1978, and Orange County, California, in 1995, default risk considerations exert considerable influence on the yield relationships among municipals and between municipals and other bonds.

The tax-exempt status of interest payments on municipal bonds is, however, the most important influence on municipal yields versus governments and corporates. Assume it's the bad old days and you pay 50 percent of your income in federal income taxes. If the yield on a government bond is 8 percent, you get $80 per $1,000 invested, but after taxes you'll wind up with only $40—or an after-tax yield of 4 percent. But if you own a municipal bond that pays $80 per $1,000 invested, you keep it all, because interest on municipal bonds is immune from the Internal Revenue Service. If the municipal bond had no chance of default and if everyone were in the 50 percent bracket, then investors would refuse to buy government bonds and would buy all the municipals they could lay their hands on if both yielded 8 percent before taxes. This would drive down the price of governments and push up the price of municipals. When would investors be indifferent between these two securities? Clearly when the municipal bond yielded 4 percent and the government bond yielded 8 percent; they would both pay their owners $40 after taxes, and the market would be in equilibrium.

At a lower income tax rate, the yield on municipals would have to be higher—say $5\frac{1}{2}$ percent versus 8 percent on governments.[5] Furthermore, municipal bonds ain't what they used to be in terms of their default-free reputation. This tends to push such rates even closer to the yield on fully taxable U.S. government bonds. As can be seen in Figure 5.4, the yields on municipal bonds have usually stayed well below comparable maturity governments, as dictated by tax considerations. But back in the Great Depression and in more recent times when default risk jitters surfaced and income tax rates were reduced, the yields on municipal bonds were forced toward yields on fully taxable governments.

SUMMARY

1. The relationship between yields on short-term and long-term securities is frequently illustrated graphically by a yield curve. The yield curve can be upward sloping (short-term rates are below long-term rates), downward sloping (short-term rates are above long-term rates), or flat (the yields on shorts and longs are the same).

2. The basic expectations theory maintains that the shape of the yield curve is determined by investors' expectations of future short-term interest rates. In particular, if short-term rates are expected to rise, the yield curve will be upward sloping, while if short-term rates are expected to fall, the yield curve will be downward sloping. A specific result is that long-term rates are averages of current and expected future short-term rates.

3. There are a number of modifications to the pure expectations theory that reflect other influences on rate structure. For example, since investors are usually considered risk averse, and since long-term securities have greater capital uncertainty than short-term securities, a liquidity premium is likely to be attached to long-term yields. In addition, some investors, such as life insurance companies, prefer long-term securities because they can "lock in" a guaranteed return on funds. This suggests that there are preferred maturity ranges for investors, and changes in supplies of securities will alter yields on different maturities.

4. The fundamental role of expectations in shaping the yield curve is emphasized by the following empirical regularity: When the overall level of

---

[5]If your tax rate is t, the yields on governments is G, and the yield on municipals is M, then after-tax yields are equal when $G(1 - t) = M$. Hence the ratio of M to G equals $(1 - T)$. With a marginal tax rate of 30 percent, the equilibrium yield on governments would be 8 percent compared with 5.6 percent on municipals.

rates is high compared with the recent past, the yield curve slopes downward; when the level of rates is low compared with recent experience,
the yield curve slopes upward.

5. Default risk helps to explain the excess of corporate bond yields over the
yield on government bonds of comparable maturity. The probability of
default also influences the structure of yields within the corporate bond
market.

6. Municipal bonds yield less than government bonds because the interest
payments on municipals are exempt from federal income taxes. Nevertheless, when default probabilities on municipal debt increase, their tax-
free yields can approach taxable yields on governments.

QUESTIONS

5.1 Describe the market pressures that, according to the pure expectations
approach to the term structure of interest rates, force the equilibrium
long-term rate to equal an average of the current short-term rate and the
expected future short-term rate.

5.2 Why does the liquidity premium approach to the term structure maintain that the equilibrium long-term rate is above the average of the current and expected future short-term rate?

5.3 Why do long-term rates tend to fluctuate less than short-term rates over
the course of the business cycle?

5.4 If the marginal income tax rate were 30 percent, what would be the equilibrium yield relationship between municipals (ignoring default risk)
and governments?

5.5 *Discussion question:* If your parents called and asked for advice on what
types of bonds they should buy for their retirement fund, what would
you tell them?

Bond Price Volatility: Duration Versus Maturity

We have mentioned on a number of occasions that long-term bonds are riskier than short-term bonds—not because we don't like long-term bonds, but because numerical examples show that a one-percentage-point change in the yield to maturity on a long-term bond produces a larger change in the price of the bond than the impact of a one-percentage-point change in yield on the price of a short-term bond. Now, this statement is correct—usually. Which is okay most of the time, but not good enough for mathematicians and bond market professionals, who like things somewhat more precise.

The problem with the relationship between bond price volatility and maturity stems from the rather casual way people define maturity. In particular, we identify the maturity of a bond with the date of final repayment of principal. Thus, a bond with ten years to maturity and an 8 percent coupon makes a series of coupon payments equal to $80 per year and then pays the principal borrowed ($1,000) plus the final $80 coupon at the end of the tenth year. Our definition of maturity ignores the fact that the bond makes coupon payments in each of ten years before it repays the principal. This is not necessarily bad; we can define maturity as we wish. In fact, this definition of maturity reminds holders of corporate bonds that they have ten years to worry about potential defaults on promised payments. But by ignoring the coupon payments, we have in a sense overstated the maturity of the bond; lenders get some of their money back before the ten-year maturity date.

A more comprehensive measure of a bond's maturity, called **duration,** takes into account the timing of both coupon and principal payments. We will define duration very precisely below. But first let us focus on a key relationship: A bond with longer duration has greater price volatility than a bond with shorter duration when yields on both bonds change by the same amount in percentage points. We can even write down a simple formula relating the percentage change in the price of a bond to the bond's duration. Let P stand for price, D for duration, i for yield to maturity, and Δ for "change in." Then, we have:

$$\Delta P/P = \frac{-\Delta i}{(1 + i)} \times D$$

This says that the percentage change in the price of a bond is opposite in sign (yields go up and bond prices fall) and equal to the percentage change in yield to maturity times the duration of the bond.[1] Thus, if the duration of a bond is five years, for example, and the yield to maturity falls from 8 percent (0.0800) to 7.99 percent (0.0799), we can readily calculate the percentage change in the price of the bond as follows:

$$\begin{aligned}\Delta P/P &= -[\Delta i/(1 + i)] \times D \\ &= -[-.0001/(1.08)] \times 5 \\ &= -[-.000092] \times 5 \\ &= +.00046\end{aligned}$$

In particular, if the price of the bond were 100 and the yield to maturity decreased by one basis point (equal to 0.01 percent or 0.0001), from 8 percent to 7.99 percent, then the price of the bond would increase to 100.046 (with $\Delta P/P = .00046$ and $P = 100$, $\Delta P = .046$ and the new price is 100.046). If the duration of the bond were ten years, the price would have increased to 100.09, and so on.

This is obviously a handy formula to have. It lets you calculate how a bond's price varies with changes in the yield to maturity. Note that this relationship has nothing at all to do with economics. It all follows from the definition of the price of a bond (displayed in Chapter 4) and the definition of duration. Although we cannot show you why combining the definitions produces this magic result (we trust the mathematicians), we can move one step in that direction by presenting the formula for duration.

Duration is defined as a weighted average of the time periods when a bond's payments are made. That's the easy part. The more difficult part is the weight applied to each time period. In particular, the weight attached to each time period is the present value of the payment at that time divided by the price of the bond. This is most easily understood by way of specific example. Suppose we have our five-year bond with $80 annual coupon payments and a $1,080 principal-plus-coupon payment at the end. Thus, there are five time periods: years 1, 2, 3, 4, and 5. The formula for duration is:

$$D = \frac{\left[\frac{\$80}{(1+i)}\right](1) + \left[\frac{\$80}{(1+i)^2}\right](2) + \left[\frac{\$80}{(1+i)^3}\right](3) + \left[\frac{\$80}{(1+i)^4}\right](4) + \left[\frac{\$1,080}{(1+i)^5}\right](5)}{\frac{\$80}{(1+i)} + \frac{\$80}{(1+i)^2} + \frac{\$80}{(1+i)^3} + \frac{\$80}{(1+i)^4} + \frac{\$1,080}{(1+i)^5}}$$

[1]This formula is precisely correct only for infinitesimally small yield changes. Otherwise, it is an approximation.

This looks messy, but it's really not that bad. First, the numerator: Each of the time periods—1, 2, 3, 4, and 5—is in parentheses and preceded by a term in brackets. The bracketed terms are either the present value of $80 (for the first four years) or the present value of $1,080 (for the fifth year). These weights are each divided by the price of the bond, which appears in the denominator of the formula (see Chapter 4 to convince yourself that the formula in the denominator is equal to the price of the bond).

The duration of a bond clearly depends on more than just the date of the final principal payment (five years). For example, if the yield to maturity (i) were 8 percent, so that the bond were selling at par, the duration of our bond would measure 4.2 years. Duration is less than five years because the earlier time periods in the formula receive some weight in the computation. For example, year 2 receives the weight $[\$80/(1.08)^2]$ divided by the denominator. If the yield to maturity increased to 12 percent, the duration of the bond would decrease to 4.1 years, because the especially large weight attached to the last time period (5) would become smaller in present value terms. *Thus, it is generally the case that the higher the yield to maturity, the lower the duration of a bond* (holding everything else constant, of course).

The coupon payment clearly plays an important role in the duration calculation. Returning to our initial case of an 8 percent yield, if the coupon of the bond were $40 rather than $80, the duration would be 4.5 years. It is generally the case that *lower coupons mean longer duration* (everything else the same), because the weights attached to the earlier years in the formula would be smaller.

One special case is worth emphasizing. When the coupon payments are zero, the duration of our bond is equal to five years. In fact, *duration always equals maturity for a zero-coupon bond (and is less than maturity for bonds with coupons).* To convince yourself of this, simply write out our duration formula without the first four terms in both the numerator and denominator (they are equal to zero for a zero-coupon bond). We then have the same term in the numerator and denominator, except that it is multiplied by 5 in the numerator. Thus, everything cancels except the 5 in the numerator, which is the date of the final payment. This makes considerable sense, of course, since we started our discussion by noting that the date of the final principal payment is an imprecise measure of "true" maturity because it ignores coupon payments. If there are no coupon payments, however, the date of the final principal payment is all that matters.

Finally, to show how duration varies with the conventional definition of maturity, Table 5A.1 lists five bonds with 8 percent coupons, all priced at **par** and thus yielding 8 percent, but with maturity dates varying between five and 30 years. Obviously, longer maturity means longer duration as long as the bonds have the same yield and same coupon. But duration hardly increases at the same pace as maturity. For example, doubling the maturity of a 15-year bond to 30 years increases its duration by less than a third (from 9.0 to 11.8). Moreover, if our 30-year bond had a 17 percent coupon and yielded the same 8 percent, its duration would be 10.1 years, less than the duration of the 20-year bond shown in the table.

TABLE 5A.1   Duration of Bonds with Different Maturities

Coupon	Yield	Maturity	Duration
8%	8%	5 years	4.2 years
8%	8%	10 years	7.1 years
8%	8%	15 years	9.0 years
8%	8%	20 years	10.3 years
8%	8%	30 years	11.8 years

The moral of the story is keep your eye on duration, not maturity. First, you have a handy little formula that describes how price risk varies with duration. Second, to focus attention on maturity can sometimes be quite misleading.

CHAPTER 6

The Structure and Performance of Securities Markets

Kathleen Turner needs a script, Richard Avedon a camera, and Pete Sampras a tennis racket. Each performer uses the props appropriate for the medium in question. Performances can be stimulating, comical, pleasurable, disappointing. That's how it is in the world of entertainment.

Well, it's not so different in securities markets. Brokers, dealers, specialists, and traders are the actors. Telephones and computer terminals are the props. Stocks, bonds, and mortgages are the media. Performances are described as resilient, deep, broad, thin, liquid. Our task is to describe who goes with what and why. You can then decide whether to applaud or hiss after your next financial transaction.

NATURE AND FUNCTION OF SECURITIES MARKETS

In the previous two chapters we examined the forces that influence the equilibrium prices of different types of securities. For the most part we ignored the structure of these markets, taking for granted that somehow the interested buyers and sellers of the securities would find their way to the marketplace. And that is precisely the main assumption underlying the equilibrium price that emerges from the intersection of supply and demand curves: The price balances the supplies of and demands for the security by *all* potential market participants.

In practice, bringing all buyers and sellers together is not quite so simple. Trading interests are not uncovered costlessly, because buyers and sellers may be in different locations and therefore not aware of each other. Similarly, time may elapse between a buyer's arrival at the marketplace and the appearance of a compatible seller. Such geographical and temporal fragmentation makes the prices at which transactions actually take place differ from the equilibrium price. Real-world trading at prices that straddle the true equilibrium is the best we can hope for. In fact, we might think of the ideal situation as actual transactions prices doing a little dance around the theoretical equilibrium price.

Securities markets are organized to help bring buyers and sellers together, so that both parties to the transaction will be satisfied that a fair transactions price, close to the true equilibrium price, has been arranged. There are three main types of market organization that facilitate the actual purchase and sale of securities: an **auction market,** a **brokered market,** and a **dealer market.** In each case, the aim is to match up buyers and sellers.

Auction Market. The main feature of an auction market is that buyers and sellers confront each other directly to bargain over price. There is nothing that stands between buyers and sellers, just an auctioneer who records bids and offers tendered by potential buyers and sellers. The particular rules of the auction determine exactly how buyers and sellers are matched up. For example, there can be a single trade between all buyers and sellers at a single price or a series of trades at different prices. Under all circumstances, the key characteristic of the auction is that orders are centralized, so that the highest bidders and lowest offerers are exposed to each other. The most popular example of an auction market is the New York Stock Exchange, where auctions for individual securities take place at specific locations, called *posts,* on the floor of the exchange. The auctioneer in this case is the **specialist** who is designated by the exchange to represent (as an agent) orders tendered by public customers. A second example of an auction market is the twice daily London gold fixing. Representatives of five London bullion dealers gather together to expose public orders to competitive bidding. One of the dealers is designated by the group as the auctioneer.

Brokered Market. When there are insufficient participants in an auction market, so that potential traders do not always find "reasonable" bids and offers, it may pay traders to employ the services of a broker to search for the other side of a trade. Thus a seller of securities may ask a broker to show the securities to potential buyers or a buyer may ask a broker to uncover potential sellers. Unlike the auctioneer, whose role is completely passive, the broker provides information about potential buyers and sellers and earns a commission in return. Many of us are familiar with real estate brokers who provide information for potential buyers and sellers of homes. Municipal bonds are the best example of securities that trade primarily in a brokered market.

Dealer Market. During the time it takes a broker to uncover a compatible trading partner, the equilibrium price of the security may change. It can be profitable, therefore, for a person to remain in the marketplace to provide the service of continuously bidding for securities that investors want to sell and offering securities that investors want to buy. This person acts as a **dealer** (also called **market-maker**), buying securities for his or her own account when the public is selling and selling from her or his own account when the public is buying. Unlike brokers, dealers commit capital to the process of bringing buyers and sellers together and take on the risk of price changes in the securities they hold in inventory. Dealers expect to earn a profit, because they always quote a bid price (at which they buy) that is below their offer price (at which they sell).

Many securities trade in dealer markets, including government bonds, corporate bonds, and equities traded in the so-called **over-the-counter** (OTC) market. There are usually many dealers in each security. They are linked together either by telephone or by computer hookup. In fact, many over-the-counter stocks trade in a semiautomated system called **NASDAQ** (National Association of Securities Dealers Automated Quotation System). On the New York Stock Exchange the specialists who are the designated auctioneers also quote bids and offers in their capacity as dealers. Thus trading on the New York Stock Exchange is a cross between a dealer market and an auction market.

The organizational structure of a market, the existence of brokers, dealers, exchanges, as well as the technological paraphernalia, such as quotation screens, computer terminals, and telecommunications are all mobilized to keep transactions prices as close to true (but unknown) equilibrium prices as is economically feasible. Easy access to a trading forum, with many potential buyers and sellers, means that a security can be bought or sold quickly with little deviation from its equilibrium value. That is what is meant by marketability, a catch-all term indicating small deviations of actual transactions prices about the true equilibrium.

Good marketability implies that a security can be sold, liquidated, and turned into cash very quickly without triggering a collapse in price. Because a highly marketable security is more desirable to investors, its equilibrium price will be higher, and its return lower, relative to less marketable securities.

The rest of our discussion is devoted to examining the efficiency of securities markets. First we look at how effective markets are in bringing buyers and sellers together, the so-called **operating efficiency** of securities markets. We then turn to pricing efficiency and related regulatory concerns.

Primary Versus Secondary Markets

Before detailing the nature of trading in securities markets, it is important to emphasize the distinction between **primary markets** and **secondary markets.** Most of the popular markets, such as the New York Stock Exchange and the Tokyo Stock Exchange, are secondary markets where existing securities are exchanged between individuals and institutions. The primary markets—markets for newly issued securities—are much less well known.[1]

In the United States, for example, new issues of stocks or bonds to raise funds for General Motors, General Electric, or General Mills are not sold to saver-lenders on the floor of the New York Stock Exchange, the American Stock Exchange, or even the Midwest Stock Exchange in Chicago. Rather, the matchmaking takes place behind closed doors, aided by Wall Street's **investment banks.** Names such as Morgan Stanley, Goldman Sachs, Smith Barney, and Merrill Lynch dominate the list. They often act as brokers and dealers in secondary markets as well. But in their role as investment banks they help distribute newly issued stocks and bonds to ultimate investors, insurance companies, pension funds, mutual funds, and individuals throughout the country.

These distributions are called **underwritings:** The investment bank guarantees an issuer of securities a price on the new issue. Often a number of investment banks band together in a syndicate to market a new issue; by sticking together they share the risk of adverse movements in stock prices or interest rates between the time an issue is bought from the corporation and the time it goes out of the investment banks' inventory, safely tucked away in the portfolio of an individual investor or a financial intermediary. The idea is to get rid of the issue as quickly as possible, within a day or two. That minimizes the risk exposure of the investment banking firm's capital. Announcements of successful underwritings, called *tombstones,* appear frequently in the financial press.

A number of features of this new-issue market are noteworthy. First, as with many, or most, markets, it is not located in any particular spot. Underwritings of new issues do not take place on the floor of an organized exchange. Rather, the marketplace is a series of conference rooms of investment banking firms, linked by telephone with each other, with corporations, and with ultimate investors. Second, the most important commodity sold by these investment banking firms is information about the price required to sell an issue and who the likely buyers are. That's one of the most important functions of markets, dissemination of price and trading information. To market the new issue, investment bankers in effect sell the services of their capital by purchasing the issue outright from the corporation and thereby ensuring that the firm pays only the agreed-upon price. Subsequent adverse or favorable price movements do not affect the issuing firm, just the vacation prospects of the investment bankers. As compensation for their time and trouble, investment bankers earn a fee, called an **underwriting spread,** on each newly issued security.

---

[1]As we will see in Part III in our discussion of financial intermediaries, there are many kinds of newly issued (primary) financial assets, such as commercial loans made by banks to small and medium-size businesses, that rarely, if ever, trade in secondary markets. These nontraded assets are purchased by financial intermediaries and held until maturity. In addition to commercial loans, this group includes privately placed debt of midsize companies that is purchased by life insurance companies and commercial mortgages, also purchased by life insurance companies.

This announcement is not an offer to sell or a solicitation of an offer to buy any of these securities. The offering is made only by the Prospectus, copies of which my be obtained in any State in which this announcement is circulated only from such of the several underwriters as may lawfully offer these securities in such State.

June 8, 1995

4,844,605 Shares

NGC Corporation

Common Stock

Price $8 1/2 Per Share

Lehman Brothers		Donaldson, Lufkin & Jenrette
		Securities Corporation
Bear, Stearns & Co. Inc.	CS First Boston	Dean Witter Reynolds Inc.
Dillon, Read & Co. Inc.	Goldman, Sachs & Co.	Kemper Securities, Inc.
Morgan Stanley & Co.	Oppenheimer & Co., Inc.	PaineWebber Incorporated
Incorporated		
Salomon Brothers Inc	Smith Barney Inc.	The Chicago Dearborn Company
Howard, Weil, Labouisse, Friedrichs		Petrie Parkman & Co.
Incorporated		
Hanifen, Imhoff Inc.		McDonald & Company
		Securities, Inc.
Principal Financial Securities, Inc.		Rauscher Pierce Refsnes, Inc.

Newspaper advertisement.

An underwriting syndicate floats a new issue.

The near-invisibility of primary markets, compared with the immense popular recognition of secondary markets for equities, does not change the fact that both serve essential functions. Moreover, there is a close interrelationship between prices and yields on securities in secondary markets and those in primary markets. One important clue to the required new-issue yield on a corporation's bonds, for example, is the recent yield on the firm's obligations in the secondary market. How useful these yields are depends, in part, upon the "quality" of secondary market prices. Are they close to equilibrium prices, or do they reflect one or two transactions that might not be representative? Only by recognizing the nature of the secondary market can the prices and yields recorded there be evaluated.

EFFICIENCY OF SECONDARY MARKET TRADING

As we indicated at the beginning of the chapter, secondary markets work well if they bring together buyers and sellers of securities so that they transact at prices close to the true equilibrium price. Markets that accomplish this objective have low transactions costs and are considered liquid. One measure of the liquidity costs of a market is the spread between the bid price and the offer (or asked) price quoted by a dealer who "makes a market" in the particular security. In order to understand how the dealer's **bid-asked spread** measures liquidity costs, let's begin with a market that operates as an auction and then introduce dealers as participants.

The equilibrium price that we identify with the intersection of supply and demand curves emerges from the following type of auction. At a prearranged point in time, buyers and sellers interested in a particular security gather before an auctioneer. The auctioneer announces a price for the security (perhaps the price from the previous auction) and asks buyers and sellers to submit quantities they want to buy or sell at that price. If the quantity supplied exceeds what is demanded, the auctioneer announces a lower trial price and asks market participants to resubmit orders to buy or sell. If at the new lower price there are more buyers than sellers the auctioneer tries a slightly higher price and asks for still a new set of orders. This iterative "recontracting" process continues until a price emerges at which buying and selling interest are equal. At that point, the auctioneer instructs buyers to tender cash and sellers to tender the securities, and the exchange takes place at what has been established as the equilibrium price. This auction is known as a *Walrasian auction,* after Leon Walras, a nineteenth-century French economist who conceptualized the auction underlying the determination of equilibrium prices in this way. There is, in fact, one very real marketplace that operates as a Walrasian auction, namely the twice-daily London gold fixing, where the price of gold bullion is determined.

Most markets operate quite differently from the Walrasian auction. Transactions usually occur continuously throughout the day rather than at a single point in time. In most cases, buyers and sellers of securities do not want to wait until a scheduled auction takes place. They prefer to transact immediately in order to eliminate the uncertainty over where the new equilibrium price might be. To provide this service of immediate execution, dealers (market makers) enter the marketplace to quote a bid price at which they will

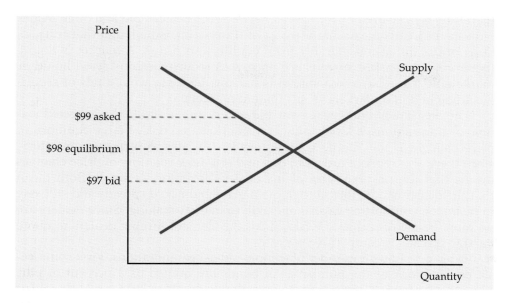

FIGURE 6.1   Bid-asked spreads cause actual transactions prices to hover about the true equilibrium price.

buy from potential sellers and an offer price at which they will sell to potential buyers.

Figure 6.1 shows the **bid** price ($97) at which a dealer will buy from the sellers (on the supply curve) and the **asked** or **offer** price ($99) at which the dealer will sell to the buyers (on the demand curve). Unlike the buyers and sellers on the demand and supply curves, the dealer is not interested in the security itself. Rather the dealer's sole objective is to sell whatever inventory has been purchased before the equilibrium price has a chance to change. The dealer's reward is the spread between the bid and offer, in the case of Figure 6.1, the $2 difference between the $99 asked price and the $97 bid.

Note that if trading in this security were conducted in a Walrasian auction, all transactions would have occurred at the equilibrium price of $98 (that's the price where the quantity people want to sell just matches what others want to buy). But since buyers and sellers were concerned that the equilibrium price might change before the auction took place, they chose to transact at the dealer's bid and offer prices.[2] The cost of transacting immediately,

---

[2]One puzzling question is how does a dealer know where the equilibrium price is? An important source of information about the equilibrium price comes from the dealer's inventory of securities. For example, if a dealer quotes a very high bid and offer relative to where the equilibrium price is, the dealer will buy a lot more at the bid than he or she sells at the offer, producing an increase in the inventory of securities held. This provides a signal to the dealer to lower the bid and offer. If the bid and offer are too low, the dealer's inventory falls, and that signals the dealer to raise the bid and offer. So the answer is that by trial and error the dealer's bid and offer prices hover around the equilibrium price.

therefore, is measured by the spread between the dealer's bid and offer. Wider bid-asked spreads mean that the cost of transacting is high and that transactions prices differ considerably from equilibrium prices. A market is liquid, therefore, if bid-asked spreads are narrow. A security is considered liquid or marketable if the bid-asked spread is narrow. Let's see what kinds of securities trade in liquid markets versus illiquid markets.

The dealer will quote a narrow bid-asked spread if: (1) the expected volume of transactions is large; and (2) the anticipated risk of large equilibrium price changes is low. Large volume means it is easy to turn over inventory, since there are frequent orders to buy and sell. Low volatility of price changes means that the risk exposure of the dealer's inventory is small. Both mean that the dealer can be forced to quote narrow bid-asked spreads and still stay in business, committing capital and skill to market-making. Since dealers are no more benevolent than the rest of us, the element forcing dealers to quote narrow spreads is competitive pressure.

Table 6.1 shows a number of sample bid-asked quotations. First some basic explanations of the numbers. All bonds are quoted as a percent of **par.** Thus the Treasury 7.25 percent–coupon bonds due May 2016 could be sold at $82^{10}/_{32}$ (the bid price) per $100 face value and could be bought at $82^{14}/_{32}$ (the asked price) per $100 face value. Since minimum denominations of most bonds are $1,000, that means it costs $824.38 to buy such a bond, while I get $823.13 if I sell it. The spread (asked minus bid) recorded in the last column is $1/_8$ or 12.5 cents per $100, or 1.25 per $1,000 transaction. In other words, if I buy a $1,000 Treasury bond and decide to sell immediately because I get a hot stock tip, my schizophrenia will cost me $1.25. A $2,000 round trip, as they call it, costs $2.50, a $3,000 trade, $3.75, and so on. This is a measure of the liquidity costs of the security: the transactions costs of buying and selling.

The bond of the Federal National Mortgage Association in the second line of Table 6.1 trades on a $3/_{16}$-point spread, or $1.88 per $1,000, compared with the $1.25 per $1,000 round-trip transaction in the Treasury bond. This suggests that these securities have somewhat less liquidity than Treasury obligations, which is true.

The explanation for the variation in the spreads lies primarily in the volume of trading in the particular issues. Since Treasuries trade more than just about any other kind of security, it is not surprising that they have smaller bid-asked spreads.

The last section of Table 6.1 records the bids and offers for two over-the-counter equities. Barton Inc. trades on a $1/_8$-point spread, and so does Belmac Inc. Like point spreads in football, these quotations must be scrutinized before you jump to costly conclusions. It would seem, for example, that both securities have liquidity costs that are similar to Treasury bonds. In fact, this is not the case. Quotations in the equity market are *per share.* Thus to buy 100 shares of Barton costs $650 ($6^1/_2$ times 100), with an immediate sale netting $637.50. A 200-share purchase would cost $1,300, and a sale would net $1,275. Thus it costs $25 for a $1,300 round trip in Barton, while a $1,000 round trip in Treasuries costs only $1.25. The lesson is clear: Bid-asked spreads must be related to the price of the security and the implied cost of

TABLE 6.1   Sample Bid and Asked Quotations on Securities

Name of market	Particular issue		Bid	Ask	Spread
	Coupon	Maturity			
1. Governments and Agencies					
Treasury Bond	7.25	May 2016	$82^{10}/_{32}$	$82^{14}/_{32}$	$^1/_8$
Federal National Mortgage Association	4.95	Sept. 1998	$96^8/_{32}$	$96^{14}/_{32}$	$^3/_{16}$
2. OTC Stocks					
Barton Inc.		—	$6^3/_8$	$6^1/_2$	$^1/_8$
Belmac Inc.		—	$5^7/_8$	6	$^1/_8$

Sources: *Wall Street Journal, New York Times.*

trading or liquidating a specific dollar amount. In general, there are higher transaction costs for equities compared with bonds. In part this reflects the greater risk of price fluctuation a dealer is exposed to with equities.[3]

But there's more to the story than bid-asked spreads. For one thing, we haven't mentioned bid-asked spreads on the organized exchanges. The reason is that they aren't published in the newspapers, even though a specialist on the trading floor will quote a spread. IBM, a very active New York Stock Exchange security, was quoted on a spread of $^1/_8$ when it was selling for about $100 per share. That's $12.50 per $10,000 round trip, just about what it would cost to trade $10,000 in Treasury bonds. For trades of that size, equities can be just about as liquid as Treasury securities, if not more so.

The real difference between liquidity in Treasuries and liquidity in *any* equity lies in the size of transaction that can be handled without causing either a widening of the bid-asked spread or a shift up (in the case of a buy) or down (for a sale) in the implicit equilibrium price. Quotes in equities must be good for at least a round lot—100 shares. Quotes in the Treasury market must also be good for a round lot, usually $1 million in face value. A $10 million order in Treasuries can also be filled without much trouble. But for equities, there's simply no way to liquidate a $5 million block of stock, or even a $1 million position, without causing dealers to back away after the purchase of 100 or 200 shares. Thus the bid-asked spread measures the liquidity cost of normal-size transactions, and what's normal in the Treasury market would be abnormal in any common stock. In fact, blocks of stock are not brought to the auction market on the floor of the New York Stock Exchange unless a trade has been arranged beforehand by dealers. While the public auction of organized exchanges looks good and has distinct advantages, it simply cannot handle the large trades of institutional investors.

---

[3] In addition to these bid-asked spreads, your broker charges a fee, called a *commission,* for executing your trades. This expense depends more on whether you deal with a discount broker or a full service broker than whether you are buying a stock or bond.

In The News

Dealers Make Money Buying at Their Bid and Selling at Their Offer

Market Makers: A Dying Breed?

For most of the last 20 years, being a NASDAQ market maker has been a very profitable occupation. If you didn't get caught committing too much capital to one or two stocks, and if you managed to arrange for a steady flow of orders, you had a right to profit by buying low and selling high.

You accomplished that because every stock had two prices, the lower bid price (at which you bought stock) and the higher ask price (at which you sold stock). The rules of the game were that the public had no right to get inside that spread.

In that atmosphere, the number of market makers has soared to around 400, with some stocks having 40 market makers and the average stock having 11. The market makers have competed vigorously, but not by narrowing the spread. The competition has been on getting access to order flow, which has led to some offering low commissions to the public while others paid (perfectly legal) kickbacks to other brokers for directing order flow to them.

But the rules are changing, and the probable result is a shrinkage in the ranks of market makers. On Friday, the Securities and Exchange Commission approved a new NASDAQ rule that will make it relatively easy for all investors to get inside the spread. If a stock is trading, say, at $15 bid and $15.25 asked, you can put in an order to buy it at $15. Whichever market maker gets that order, called a limit order, will have to fill it before he can buy a single share of stock for his own account at $15.

The implications of that are clear. It is in the interest of investors trading in reasonably liquid NASDAQ stocks to put in limit orders, rather than market orders that will be executed at the wrong end of the spread. And those orders ought to go to the market maker with the most volume in a stock, simply because that one is most likely to have to execute your order. Such a rule has already been in effect for some market makers, but starting next month, it will expand to all of them, even those who do not deal directly with the public. To be sure, no broker has to accept limit orders. But if yours won't, find another broker.

Source: Copyright © 1995 by The New York Times Co. Reprinted by permission.

This discussion suggests a somewhat more sophisticated measure of market performance, one that focuses on the ability of a market to absorb large trading volume without causing wild gyrations in transactions prices. The qualitative description of such markets is relatively easy: They have *depth*, *breadth*, and *resiliency*. A market is deep if it is easy to uncover buy and sell orders above and below current transactions prices; if these orders exist in large volume, then the market has breadth; if new orders quickly pour in when prices move up or down, the market is called resilient.

All of these characteristics imply low transactions price volatility. For example, even if a dealer's bid and asked quotes are good for 100 shares only, if a larger purchase order causes institutions that continuously monitor dealer quotes to call in sell orders, then prices won't gyrate much. Markets that are *not* deep, broad, and resilient are called **thin markets;** only a small volume of trading can be absorbed without producing wide price swings.

Having said all that, there's not much else to do. There just aren't any good measures of this aspect of liquidity. Simply looking at price volatility is not enough, equilibrium price changes are part of everyday price movements and do not reflect poorly on a market's liquidity.

One important observation can be made, however, concerning the impact of communications technology on the ability of any market to absorb large orders without becoming "disorderly." Traders who can continuously monitor quotation screens can participate more quickly in buying and selling if prices deviate from their view of equilibrium. When prices fall, they buy; when prices rise, they sell. This very process contributes to price stability and liquidity. Moreover, the reduction in price volatility also leads to narrow bid-asked spreads, since dealer inventories are subject to less risk.

We have extended our discussion of secondary market trading, efficiency, marketability, and liquidity to the point of no return. Price changes should be small when trading is motivated by liquidity needs; that's the characteristic of highly marketable securities. But new information affecting the underlying

---

GOING OUT ON A LIMB

The Computer Will Prevail

The New York Stock Exchange celebrated its 200th anniversary in 1992, but not much has changed since the exchange abandoned the buttonwood tree for its home at Eleven Wall Street. Buyers and sellers still bargain face-to-face on the stock exchange floor, with orders recorded on pads of paper in barely legible script. A similar situation prevails in the nation's commodities exchanges, where open outcry among buyers and sellers determines the price of everything from pork bellies to Treasury bond futures.

Not all modern trading markets mimic the procedures of the eighteenth century. London stocks now trade via computers and telecommunications, as do futures markets in Japan and Germany. In fact, the accompanying newspaper clipping describes plans to create a fully automated trading system for German stocks and bonds. There is little doubt that electronics will eventually prevail, even where the New York Stock Exchange is concerned.

The real question is why haven't computers already replaced all trading floors, the way word processors have replaced electric typewriters in the offices of the 1990s? The answer is liquidity. The New York Stock Exchange and the U.S. commodities exchanges are extremely liquid, with narrow bid-asked spreads that attract orders from public investors. Competing computer-based exchanges have difficulty breaking into the vicious cycle: Liquidity attracts trading volume that generates more liquidity. At some point, however, technology will prevail with a quantum improvement in the technique for matching buyers and sellers. At that point the exchange floor will go on the chopping block, the same one the buttonwood tree ended on.

value of the security should be reflected quickly in equilibrium price changes. Indeed, if prices of financial assets did not reflect news about bankruptcies, earnings trends, lawsuits, and whatever else affects the payments promised by the issuer of the financial instrument, then the market would be inefficient. Some call this aspect of a market **allocational efficiency.** Up to now we have analyzed the operating efficiency of financial markets. Actually, the popular discussion of "efficient capital markets" focuses on allocational efficiency, without calling it by that name. In the next section we provide an overview of efficient capital markets within the framework of regulation of securities markets.

EFFICIENT CAPITAL MARKETS AND REGULATION

A vast literature has developed during the past twenty years based on a relatively straightforward proposition: The current price of a security fully reflects all publicly available information. Put somewhat differently: There is no unexploited publicly available information that would lead to superior investment performance. If securities prices fully reflect all available information, the capital market is called efficient.

It's hard to argue with the statement that markets will be efficient. If securities prices didn't reflect all publicly available information, market pressures would quickly force them to do so. Suppose that dealers ignored a news flash that an OTC-traded company had discovered how to make oil out of used textbooks. Everyone else would find the price of the security relatively cheap in view of the fantastic profits the company will reap. Buy orders would pour into brokerage offices and sell orders would disappear. Dealers would meet their commitment to sell 100 shares at the old asked price and then would more than double the quoted asking price to avoid selling what they didn't have at ridiculously low prices. As soon as the dealer quoted a price sufficiently high to reflect the rosy profit outlook, buy orders would drop to normal (the security would no longer be such a bargain), sell orders would reappear (let's take some profits), and the new equilibrium price would fully reflect all publicly available information.

There's nothing wrong with that story. It happens all the time, and that's precisely what we mean when we say that capital markets are efficient. The problem arises in the implications for buying and selling securities. The implication is quite simple: don't trade. If prices quickly incorporate all information affecting the fortunes of a company, then you can't earn above-average returns by selling so-called overvalued securities or buying undervalued ones. There aren't any bargains. Moreover, the fancy charts sold by investment advisers, suggesting that you buy when the price of a stock rises by 5 or 10 percent, aren't worth the paper they are printed on.

Needless to say, securities analysts have little use for such academic ranting and raving. How quickly do you think markets absorb new information? Within a day is the best estimate of academic researchers. If that's the case, there is little to gain from buying or selling after reading the investment bulletins of your favorite brokerage house. By the time you've finished reading, there's nothing to do but watch which way the price of your security went.

Our discussion of market efficiency made specific reference to publicly available information. It's quite possible, indeed, quite probable, that nonpublicly available information can be used to make extra profits or avoid undesirable losses. The Securities and Exchange Act of 1934 provided for the establishment of the Securities and Exchange Commission (SEC) to prevent fraud and promote equitable and fair operations in securities markets. The focal point of SEC regulations is the disclosure of information that might be relevant for the pricing of securities. The SEC insists that investors should not be at a disadvantage when purchasing or selling securities. Not only must there be full disclosure of all pertinent information, but misinformation and dissemination of false or misleading reports are specifically prohibited.

The SEC's job is not an easy one. As we will see in Chapter 15, the SEC has enlisted the aid of the various organized exchanges and the National Association of Securities Dealers (NASD) in supervising brokers and dealers, and in monitoring transactions in secondary markets. The exchanges and the

NASD take these disciplinary and supervising responsibilities seriously. And with good reason. The specter of more detailed SEC involvement in day-to-day operations is more than enough to encourage vigorous self-regulation.

It would be a mistake, however, to assume that manipulation, fraud, misinformation, and deception have disappeared from financial transactions simply because the SEC plays watchdog. Markets are efficient because investors and traders scrutinize and search and screen all information for themselves. **Caveat emptor et venditor** are still the watchwords that ensure market efficiency.

SUMMARY

1. The equilibrium price that emerges from the familiar supply-demand picture assumes that all buyers and sellers have been brought together in the marketplace. Actual transactions prices in real-world markets may differ from the theoretical equilibrium price, because it is costly to bring together all potential traders.

2. Markets that trade existing securities are organized as either auction, broker, or dealer markets. In all cases, resources are devoted to uncovering compatible trading interests. The New York Stock Exchange is the best example of an auction market, while government and corporate bonds are traded primarily in dealer markets. Brokers are frequently used in the municipal bond market.

3. It is important to distinguish these secondary markets for securities from the primary market, where newly issued securities are initially placed with investors. Virtually all corporations use investment bankers to help market new issues of stocks and bonds.

4. The operating efficiency of secondary markets is measured by how closely actual transactions prices conform to theoretical equilibrium prices. A narrow bid-asked spread in a dealer market produces transactions prices that are close to the true equilibrium price. Other dimensions to operating efficiency include the size of order that can be accommodated at a given quotation. In terms of these criteria, the market for Treasury securities is the most liquid secondary market.

5. Because investors place a positive value on liquidity, securities that are more liquid sell for higher prices than less liquid securities, all other things being equal, of course.

6. Securities markets are highly efficient processors of new information. Most evidence suggests that current prices fully reflect all publicly available information. Regulatory supervision by the Securities and Exchange Commission is aimed at preventing fraud and promoting fair and equitable trading.

QUESTIONS

6.1 Describe the characteristics that distinguish auction, broker, and dealer markets. What is the main common objective of these different forms of market organization?

6.2 What determines whether a dealer will quote a narrow or a wide bid-asked spread?

6.3 Ignoring for a moment the size of the bid-asked spread, explain why Treasury bonds are more liquid than equities.

6.4 What are the implications for investor decision making of the proposition that markets are efficient?

6.5 How do investment bankers help companies issue new securities?

CHAPTER 7

The Pricing of Risky Financial Assets*

Risk is a double-edged sword: It complicates decision making but makes things interesting. That's true of life in general and financial markets in particular. In the last three chapters we have described how the price of a financial asset, like the price of just about everything else, depends upon supply and demand. We have also seen that shifts in supply and demand produce price changes and that this price variability means that financial assets are risky. Our main objective in this chapter is to explain how investors are compensated for holding **risky securities** and how investor portfolio decisions influence the outcome.

At the most general level, a financial asset is a contractual agreement that entitles the investor to a series of future cash payments from the issuer. The value of the asset depends upon the nature of the future cash payments and on the credibility of the issuer in making those payments. Bonds versus equities illustrate different future payment profiles, with bonds promising fixed dollar payments at prespecified dates, while equities offer variable payments depending upon the fortunes of a particular company. Similarly, government bonds versus corporate bonds illustrate that similar cash flows can differ because issuers have different degrees of credibility in meeting their scheduled obligations. Nevertheless, because all securities involve future cash flows, they share certain common valuation principles.

Every risky security must compensate investors for two things: (1) delayed payment of future cash flows and (2) uncertainty over those future cash flows. The form of the compensation is expected return, that is, what the investor expects to earn when holding those securities. To anticipate our results, we will

---

*The material in this chapter is conceptually more difficult than what has been covered thus far in the book. The remaining chapters in Part II are written so that it is possible to omit this chapter.

show that an investor's expected return on a security consists of a riskless rate of return to compensate for saving rather than spending plus a return for bearing risk.

We distinguish riskless and risky securities in the following way. Recall the definition of annual return on a bond in Chapter 4:

$$Return = \frac{Selling\ Price - Purchase\ Price + Coupon}{Purchase\ Price}$$

For a one-year security with a guaranteed cash flow, such as a government bond, the annual return is riskless because the return is known with certainty. For example, if the current price is $1,000 for a government bond that repays $1,000 in principal plus $50 in interest at the end of one year, substitute the $1,000 principal payment for the selling price, add the $50 coupon, and our formula generates a return of 5 percent. This return is riskless because the repayment of principal and the coupon payment are guaranteed. On the other hand, suppose that a company would like to issue stock costing $1,000 that has a selling price of either $1,080 or $1,020 at the end of the year, depending upon how much money the company makes. The return on this security is uncertain: It is either 8 percent or 2 percent.[1]

The key question is whether investors will pay $1,000 for this uncertain return of 8 percent or 2 percent, given that 5 percent is available with certainty. The answer depends, in part, on the probabilities that the risky security will earn 8 percent versus 2 percent as well as on whether investors like or dislike the uncertainty. If investors end up paying less than $1,000 they will expect to earn more than 8 percent and 2 percent and if they pay more than $1,000 they will expect to earn less. Our ultimate objective is to determine, therefore, the equilibrium price, hence the equilibrium expected return, on this risky security.

We proceed from here in two steps. The first step is to specify the factors influencing the return on a *riskless* investment. This is equivalent to seeing what determines the yield or interest rate on a one-period riskless loan, and reviews the discussion in Chapter 4. The second step is to see how risk enters the picture. This formal analysis of decision making in a risky environment will generate some powerful insights into how investors are compensated for risk.

A WORLD OF CERTAINTY

Without risk there are no disappointments. All plans proceed as conceived; all expectations are fulfilled; no promises are broken. Life is perfectly predictable, and so is the financial sector. One person's promise to repay a loan is as good as anyone else's. No one is a welcher—not even your in-laws. Under such ideal conditions the same interest rate is applicable to each and every

---

[1]In the formula for return, substitute $1,080 for the selling price, $1,000 for the purchase price, and set the coupon equal to zero and that produces a return of 8 percent. Substituting $1,020 for the selling price rather than $1,080 produces a return of 2 percent.

loan. Anyone trying to charge more will not succeed in making a loan; anyone charging less will be deluged with requests for funds. All securities are perfect substitutes for each other; hence they must sell for the same price, which means they offer the same return. Thus the interest rate is the same for all—it is the yield earned by lenders on a riskless loan, one that will be repaid in full by all borrowers, without a shadow of a doubt.

Since this is a rather peculiar world, to say the least, it's worth asking whether there will be any borrowing or lending at all under such mythical conditions? The answer is yes, as long as people and businesses differ regarding the desired time patterns of their consumption. Those preferring instant gratification (IG) may want to consume more today than their current income, while prudent providers (PP) may want to consume less than their current income. The PPs lend to the IGs at the rate of interest. That rate is determined, in fact, by the balancing of the total demand for funds by the IGs with the total supply of funds from the PPs.

The rate of interest doesn't have anything to do with risk, because there isn't any. Rather, the interest rate influences people's consumption decisions. If more people want to borrow—either to buy a new hat (consumption) or to build a new factory (real investment)—than want to lend, the rate of interest will be pushed up by the unsatisfied (and still-eager) borrowers. The rise in the rate of interest causes some to rethink their borrowing and spending plans, while others may decide to save and lend more; with a higher interest rate it pays to be a prudent provider. Thus the key decisions influenced by the riskless rate of interest are consumption versus saving.

CONSEQUENCES OF UNCERTAINTY AND RISK AVERSION

At the very least, the world as we know it is rife with unanticipated disappointment. Borrowers, however well intentioned, may be simply unable to fulfill their promises to repay borrowed funds. Factories built to produce polyester fabrics may become obsolete because of renewed enchantment with natural fibers. Thus the manufacturer who raised capital with every intention of paying dividends out of expected polyester sales may not make the expected payments. In general investors will be disappointed whenever their returns turn out lower than expected. Of course, they will be happy if their returns wind up higher than expected, but the uncertainty itself makes investors unhappy. This characteristic is referred to as **risk aversion.** It doesn't mean investors will never take on risk, it means that they must be compensated for the risk. We will see later that there is good evidence suggesting that investors are, in fact, risk averse.

The principle of risk aversion is so important that it is worth examining in some detail. It will lead us directly to the strategy employed by most investors to reduce risk, namely, **portfolio diversification.** After seeing how diversification helps investors reduce risk exposure we can return to our basic question of how investors are compensated for the risk that they cannot diversify away.

To illustrate risk aversion, let's return to our earlier example and show that investors who are risk averse prefer a security that is certain to return 5 percent compared with one having an *equal chance* of returning either 8 percent or 2 percent. The second security has an average return of 5 percent: About half the time its return is 8 percent, and about half the time its return is 2 percent. Its *expected* return is 5 percent, where the formal definition of expectation is the sum of the possible outcomes multiplied by their respective probabilities: 8% × $\frac{1}{2}$ plus 2% × $\frac{1}{2}$ = 5 percent. Note that the *expected* return is nothing more than the average return.

Why does a risk averter prefer the certain return of 5 percent to an equal chance of 8 percent or 2 percent, even though the expected values of the two securities are identical? Simply put, with the risky security, the extra pleasure when the return is 8 percent is less than the additional pain when the return is 2 percent. Sound familiar? It should, because it's nothing more than the principle of diminishing marginal utility of income that we all remember from basic economics: Each additional dollar is worth less (although you always want more!).

Would the risk averter ever be indifferent between a security paying a fixed return with certainty, such as a 5 percent savings deposit in a commercial bank, and a security whose return is uncertain? Yes, but only if the risky security had a higher expected return to compensate for the undesirable uncertainty. For example, if the risky security's equally probable outcomes were either 10 percent or 2 percent, so that the expected return would be 6 percent (10 percent × $\frac{1}{2}$ plus 2 percent × $\frac{1}{2}$ = 6 percent), then our risk-averting investor might be indifferent. If the possible outcomes are 12 percent and 2 percent, so that the expected return is 7 percent, the investor might even prefer the risky venture, since the compensation in terms of higher expected return might be enough to induce risk-taking. The required trade-off of higher return per unit of risk—the degree of risk aversion—is a subjective measure, quite different for every individual.

Does all this mean that someone who is not a risk averter must have deep-seated emotional problems? Not at all—he or she is simply a risk lover (also known as a compulsive-degenerate gambler). We conclude that most people in the real world are risk averters, not because they tell us so in any direct way, but because most people hold diversified portfolios—many different securities rather than just one with the highest possible return. Diversification, the simple idea of not putting all your eggs in one basket, is what helps risk-averting investors cope with risky investments.

An Aside on Measuring Risk

Before proceeding to the principles of diversification, it is useful to note that we have just used what is formally called a *probability distribution* to represent the outcomes of our risky security. Each of the possible "events" (8 percent and 2 percent) has a probability of occurring ($\frac{1}{2}$ in our case), and the sum of the probabilities is unity (at least one of the possible outcomes must occur). Moreover, we have used a statistic called the *arithmetic mean* (the common average) to summarize the most likely outcome—the expected value. In this vein, we can try to specify more carefully the meaning of risk.

Uncertain outcomes make for risky investments. While the expected value of our equally probable 8 percent and 2 percent investment is 5 percent, sometimes the return will be 3 percent more than the mean (8 minus 5 is 3) and sometimes the return will be 3 percent less (2 minus 5 is -3). The deviation of actual returns from expected returns is a useful measure of risk. But the deviations of actual outcomes from the mean can be either positive or negative, and if one were to add them up, the pluses and minuses would cancel! We could apply either of two arithmetic operations to sum up the deviations and avoid the canceling problem: (1) take absolute values; (2) square the deviations (recalling that a negative number squared is a positive number). The second is used in calculating what is called the *standard deviation,* which we now describe in somewhat greater detail.

We begin our calculation of the standard deviation by taking the deviation of each outcome from the mean and squaring it. Each of these squared deviations is weighted by the probability of occurring; that is, each is multiplied by its respective probability. This makes the standard deviation a still more intuitive measure of risk. We then add up all of the weighted squared deviations and restore the numbers to their original scale by taking the square root of the entire mess. In our example, we have the following: $(8 - 5)^2 \times \frac{1}{2} + (2 - 5)^2 \times \frac{1}{2} = 9 \times \frac{1}{2} + 9 \times \frac{1}{2} = 9$, the square root of which is 3. In particular, for this investment the standard deviation of the probability distribution of returns is 3 percent. With a more complicated probability distribution, the numerical results are not quite so simple.

A potential drawback of the standard deviation is the use of both positive and negative deviations around the expected value. Shouldn't risk measure only the disappointments—that is, when actual outcomes are below expectations? That's a reasonable suggestion. But when the probability distribution is symmetrical above and below the mean, it makes no difference (below the mean is just half the total). Since there is evidence suggesting that security returns have this symmetry (they are normally distributed), and since the standard deviation has nice statistical properties (whatever that means), much of the analysis used to see how to put securities together into a portfolio—called *portfolio analysis*—works with the standard deviation to measure risk.

We are now prepared for one of the most useful bits of investment advice you will ever encounter. It also turns out to be the most fundamental proposition of **modern portfolio theory:** An asset may seem very risky when viewed in isolation, but when combined with other assets, the risk of the portfolio may be substantially less—even zero! Holding many securities in a portfolio is what is meant by portfolio diversification. Since portfolio diversification is crucial to risk reduction, let's examine the principle in some detail.

PRINCIPLES OF DIVERSIFICATION

The idea behind diversification can be illustrated by considering a portfolio of just two assets. The first we'll call asset A for Adventure Inc. We're not quite sure what business they're in, but it's a good one. In good times (probability = 0.5) it pays 16 percent and in bad times (probability = 0.5) it pays 2 percent—clearly a cyclical industry. The expected return is 9 percent, but with fairly large uncertainty over the actual outcome, which varies directly with the pulse of economic activity. Now consider asset B for Badlands Inc. In good times they lose money, producing a return of −2 percent. But in bad times they rake it in, earning 12 percent for the misanthropic investors. The expected return is 5 percent, with substantial variance in the actual results. Note, however, that asset B's outcomes are countercyclical—they are better when the economy is worse.

Could it make sense to buy both of these highly risky investments—apparently exposing oneself to all sorts of disappointment? The answer is definitely yes. In fact, dividing your funds equally between assets A and B yields a return of 7 percent, in both good times and bad; there is no uncertainty at all.[2]

Does that mean the investor would definitely prefer the half-and-half portfolio to either A or B by itself? The investor clearly prefers the portfolio to B alone, because B's expected return is only 5 percent and it is uncertain at that, while the half-and-half portfolio returns 7 percent without risk. In this case, the risk averter clearly chooses the combination portfolio. Less clear is whether the investor would choose the fifty-fifty strategy or put everything in A. While A has uncertainty, it also has a higher expected return (9 percent versus 7 percent). The choice of A versus the combination depends upon the precise nature of the risk averter's preferences—whether the extra 2 percent expected return compensates for the increase in risk.

The principal lesson derived from the example is twofold. First, the uncertainty of return of an individual asset (its standard deviation) is *not* by itself a measure of its riskiness. Rather it is the contribution of the asset's uncertain return to total portfolio risk that matters. Second, a key determinant of the

---

[2]Here's the arithmetic: Start with $200. Put $100 in A and $100 in B. In "good times" A pays $16 (= 16 percent of $100) and B loses $2. The investor earns $14 ($16 minus $2) on $200 invested, or 7 percent (14/200). In "bad times" the $100 in A earns $2 while the $100 in B earns $12, for a total of $14, which is once again 7 percent. *Note:* The standard deviation of the returns on the half-and-half portfolio is zero, even though each security's return has a positive standard deviation.

latter is how asset returns are interrelated with each other. This is so important it has a name of its own—*covariance*.[3]

In the example just given, assets A and B are perfectly negatively correlated: When asset A's return is low, that of B is high, and vice versa, and the magnitudes are such that there is perfect offset. That's why combining the two reduces risk (in this case to zero). Indeed, this *is* the principle of portfolio diversification: Hold a number of assets (rather than one), so that the exposure to risk is reduced. An asset such as B, whose returns are countercyclical (high when everything else is low), is an ideal addition to a risk averter's portfolio.

But assets such as B are relatively hard to come by. If portfolio diversification to reduce risk depended on finding assets with "negative covariance of returns," we'd be in for tough times (and lots of risk). But the magic of portfolio diversification extends to other cases as well. In particular, as long as assets do not have *precisely* the same *pattern* of returns, then holding a group of assets can reduce risk.

Take the case where each asset returns either 6 percent or 2 percent, but the outcomes are independent of good times or bad times, *and of each other*, like the flip of a coin. Does dividing the portfolio between two such assets, X and Y, reduce risk? Well, if the investor holds both X and Y in equal amounts and *both* happen to return 6 percent or both happen to return 2 percent, the investor is in the same situation as with holding just one asset. But it's also possible, in fact *just* as possible, that when X returns 6 percent, Y returns 2 percent, or when X returns 2 percent, Y returns 6 percent. In these cases, uncertainty is zero, because half of the portfolio is in X and half is in Y, hence the return is the average—4 percent. In fact, holding many, many such assets, perhaps one thousand assets, all with an equal chance of 6 percent or 2 percent, and the outcome of each one is *independent* of every other asset, makes the portfolio virtually certain of always earning 4 percent. About half of the outcomes will be 6 percent and half will be 2 percent. This is the law of large numbers at work, driving the risk of the portfolio to zero.

You should recognize that the key assumption in this last example is the word *independent*. When asset returns are relatively independent (zero covariance), putting many together tends to produce the average return just about all of the time. Risk is thereby reduced to zero. Does that mean that most people who hold diversified portfolios have zero risk? No, it doesn't, because

---

[3]Covariance has a simple intuitive definition: comovement. It also has a precise mathematical measurement. In our case, the deviation of each security's return from its mean is derived; the product of the paired observations is then weighted (as in the standard deviation) by the probability of each of the paired observations actually occurring. Positive covariance indicates that when one security's return is above its mean, so is the other. Negative covariance indicates that when one security's return is above its mean, the other is below.

The term *correlation*, which is used in the following sentence of the text, also has a specific mathematical connotation. It is the covariance divided by the product of the standard deviations. It rescales covariance so that *perfect* comovement is +1.0 and perfectly offsetting movement is −1.0, with intermediate relationships between these two extremes. A zero correlation means that the returns of the two securities are independent.

In The News

Sometimes More Is Less as Far as Risk Is Concerned

For a Calmer Portfolio: Just Add a Little Risk

NEW YORK—If you want to make your mutual fund portfolio more tranquil, try buying some risky funds.

Sound absurd? It's not at all, says Gerald Perritt, editor of the *Mutual Fund Letter,* a Chicago newsletter: "People look at a fund and say, 'how risky is it?' But it's not the risk of the individual fund that counts, but what the addition of that fund does to your overall portfolio."

Venturing into high-risk funds—such as those specializing in small-company, foreign or natural-resource stocks—is a way to spread your market bets. And that, in turn, lowers the risk that all your investments will sink at once. In the long run, such diversification tends not only to smooth returns, but also to boost them.

Unfortunately, edgy stock-fund investors often shortchange themselves by sticking solely with safe-looking stock funds that don't bounce around in price very much. These funds, which invest heavily in larger U.S. companies and are typically less volatile than other stock funds, account for almost 60 percent of the $699 billion in stock-fund assets, according to fund researchers at Lipper Analytical Services.

Such lower-risk investments might be a good bet if you're only buying one fund, financial advisers say. But for those who are putting together a portfolio of stock funds, investing exclusively in sedate offerings can be a big mistake. A better strategy, say financial advisers, is to select the types of stock funds that tend to blaze a different path than the large-stock bellwethers.

Funds that hold shares of small companies, foreign firms, or natural-resource producers fit that bill. But these funds also are prone to wild swings in price.

Paradoxically, when you combine these risky funds with large-company stock funds, they can have a marvelously soothing effect. How come? Such funds often provide offsetting gains when large-company stocks are tumbling, so including them in your mix will tend to damp the gyrations of your overall portfolio.

Source: Jonathan Clements, "For a Calmer Portfolio: Just Add a Little Risk," *Wall Street Journal,* June 24, 1994. Reprinted by permission of *The Wall Street Journal.* Copyright © Dow Jones & Company, Inc. All Rights Reserved Worldwide.

most assets are affected in a systematic way by economic conditions—hence most asset returns are not completely independent of each other. But as long as returns are not perfectly correlated, portfolio diversification reduces risk.

THE RISK PREMIUM ON RISKY SECURITIES

The examples of portfolio diversification just given permit some refinement in the first principles discussed earlier. The standard deviation of returns is a good measure of risk for analyzing a security by itself. It is also a good measure of risk for an entire portfolio. But it is a relatively poor measure of the risk contribution of a single security to an entire portfolio. That depends much more on the covariance of returns with other securities; more precisely, the *average covariance* of a security's returns with all others. The reason lies in the magic of diversification: The risk contribution to a portfolio of a security's returns that are substantially independent of all other returns is nearly zero. This *nonsystematic* risk is diversified away as the number of securities held increases (as in our coin flipping example). Only the *systematic* movement of the return on a security with all others adds to portfolio risk. This suggests that the best portfolio may in fact be the mostly widely diversified portfolio imaginable—one that includes literally every security in the marketplace. Not surprisingly this is called the **market portfolio.**

If most asset holders are risk averse, then it also follows that they will demand extra compensation—higher expected returns—in proportion to the **systematic risk** of a security. They will not, however, demand compensation for **nonsystematic risk** because they can diversify nonsystematic risk away by sticking the security in a portfolio. In other words, *the* **risk premium** *that investors demand will be in proportion to the systematic risk of the security.*

This leads us back to the question that we started with: How are investors compensated for holding risky securities? The simplest answer is that riskier securities must offer investors higher expected returns compared with less risky securities. Put somewhat differently, it is a sad fact of financial life that investors who want to earn higher returns will have to take on more risk. But

---

GOING OUT ON A LIMB

Buy an Index Fund

Although many people recognize the validity of diversification, relatively few small investors take full advantage of the principle. In particular, many investors hold "blue chip" stocks such as IBM and General Electric, but few hold the smaller, less well-known, stocks. This is a mistake. The IBMs of the world are all subject to similar economic risks, hence diversifying among them reduces portfolio risk relatively insignificantly.

Two reasons often explain why investors do not fully diversify. First, they don't know about the less popular stocks. Second, brokerage commissions make it expensive to hold so many different issues.

Investors can circumvent these problems by holding a well-diversified mutual fund, especially one that delivers no-frills diversification. In particular, so-called index funds are designed to mimic the performance of some benchmark index of the stock market, such as the S&P 500. These funds hold all 500 securities that make up Standard & Poor's index of the U.S. equity market. Thus, investors are well diversified across all segments of the stock market and do not have to pay exorbitant fees to the management of the mutual fund. The reason: Managers of index funds have the relatively easy job of diversifying to match overall market performance rather than trying to beat the stock market as a whole. For those who want diversification, buy an index fund—it's the most efficient way to diversify.

there is more to the story than this seemingly obvious conclusion. We can specify a more precise relationship between risk and return based on the portfolio behavior of risk-averse investors just discussed. In particular, the extra expected return on a risky security above the risk-free rate will be proportional to the risk contribution of a security to a well-diversified portfolio. And the risk contribution depends primarily on how closely a security's returns move with all other securities.

This specific relationship between expected return and risk produces some very surprising results. Suppose an investor considers lending money to the typical mad scientist in your university's biology department, perhaps to find a vaccine against watching too much TV. Obviously, the chances of success are very low and the risk is very high. The investor might, in fact, choose not to lend at all. On the other hand, if the scientist went to a venture capital firm that specializes in mad scientists whose schemes are unrelated to one another, the risk of a portfolio of mad scientists would be quite low. In fact, the law of large numbers suggests that investing in 1,000 of these crazy professors will almost certainly produce at least ten discoveries that will hit the jackpot. So the professors get their money on reasonable terms.

Similar reasoning also explains why companies that have poor credit ratings who issue so-called junk bonds are able, as we see in Chapter 8, to raise funds in the capital markets. Viewed in isolation each company is quite risky, but some of these risks cancel each other within a portfolio.

The final example applies to an investor who holds all of the securities available in the marketplace, that is, the investor who holds the market portfolio. Our principles of portfolio diversification suggest that the investor earns a return above the risk-free rate that compensates for the comovement of returns among all securities, rather than the risks inherent in each and every security. The risk of the market portfolio (the standard deviation of its returns) is less than the sum of each security's risk (each security's standard deviation) because some of the individual variability tends to cancel out. All of this comes from the magic of diversification.

Thus it should not be terribly surprising to discover that when risk-free securities pay investors about 5 percent, those investors might expect to earn about 12 percent on a well-diversified portfolio of stocks. The portfolio is simply not risky enough to offer 20, 30, or 40 percent that would make us really ecstatic. We have to be content to earn about 7 percent as compensation for holding the extra risk of the market portfolio.

SUMMARY

1. Securities represent claims to future cash flows. All securities, therefore, must compensate investors for delaying consumption as well as for bearing risk.

2. In a world without risk, one asset is as good as any other. In fact, each and every asset offers the same return. Risk stems from uncertainty over the payments that will actually be received from investing in an asset.

3. Investors must, in general, be compensated for bearing risk. An investor will prefer an asset that always returns 5 percent to one that returns 5 percent *on average* but at any particular time may return less or more. This preference is called risk aversion.

4. Risk-averse investors will try to combine securities in a portfolio in order to reduce risk. Such risk reduction through portfolio diversification occurs because the uncertain outcomes on each security can offset each other somewhat. Therefore, do not judge the riskiness of a security by its own variability of possible outcomes. More important to a risk averter is whether the security's uncertain outcomes offset some of the risks on other securities in the portfolio.

5. A risky security must offer investors an expected return above the risk-free rate in proportion to the risk contribution of the risky security to a well-diversified portfolio.

QUESTIONS

7.1 What is the definition of risk aversion? Why are people risk averse?

7.2 How is it possible that if you combine two risky securities (each with a high standard deviation of returns) into a portfolio, the risk of the portfolio can be zero (the standard deviation of returns on the portfolio is zero)?

7.3 What is the main characteristic of investor behavior that forces riskier securities to pay higher returns?

7.4 *Discussion question:* If portfolio diversification makes so much sense, how come many people invest in only one or two stocks?

CHAPTER 8

Money and Capital Markets

The market for U.S. government securities is at the center of the money and capital markets. The U.S. Treasury has to sell many hundred billion dollars worth of securities each year to pay off maturing issues and to finance current government operations. The sheer magnitude of these activities has made the government securities market the reference point for both the money market, where securities under one year to maturity are traded, and the capital market, which includes both longer-term debt instruments and equities.

Our first step in this chapter, therefore, is to discuss in some detail the workings of the government securities market. We then turn to a brief discussion of bank-related securities because bank debt, which is mostly short term, is closely linked to short-term government bonds. With this background we then examine the markets for corporate securities, municipals, mortgages, and finally—as a reward for reading to the very end—we explain how the stock market really works and why you might want to look at what's happening to interest rates before you decide to buy or sell.

THE GOVERNMENT BOND MARKET

When the U.S. government runs a deficit, which it has in just about every year since 1930, it has to get the funds somehow. It usually gets the money not by printing brand new dollar bills but by *borrowing*—which means selling government securities to individuals, to banks, to insurance companies, to foreigners, indeed to anyone willing to lend to the Treasury by buying government bonds. To attract buyers, the Treasury issues a wide variety of maturities and types of government securities.

Types of Securities and Investors

At the end of 1994, there were $4.8 trillion or $4,800 billion worth of government securities outstanding. Of this amount, about 65 percent or $3,125 billion was in *marketable* form, consisting of securities that can be bought and sold on financial markets. The remaining $1,675 billion was in *nonmarketable* securities, such as the familiar U.S. savings bonds, in which no secondary market trading is permitted. If you want to sell some savings bonds, you have to sell them directly back to the Treasury at a fixed price.

Naturally enough, it is only marketable securities that are interesting from the point of view of how financial markets function. The $3,125 billion of marketable government securities consists of Treasury bills ($734 billion), Treasury notes ($1,867 billion), and Treasury bonds ($524 billion).

Treasury bills are the shortest-term government securities. As a rule, they are issued with original maturities of three months, six months, or a year. Bills are a kind of zero-coupon security (see Chapter 4), in that they are sold originally at a price below their face value, with face value payable at maturity. The difference between the price and face value (called the discount) constitutes the interest payment.

Treasury notes are issued with an original maturity of between one and ten years. Generally, the Treasury issues two-year and five-year notes on a regular schedule, such as at the end of each month. Unlike bills, which are issued on a discount basis, both notes and bonds are coupon instruments. That is, they have a statement printed on them specifying the rate of interest (as a percent of face value) that they carry. A coupon rate of 8 percent, for example, means that each year the holder of the note or bond will get an interest payment, from the Treasury, amounting to 8 percent of the security's face value. Interest is usually paid semiannually, so that with a $1,000 face value note or bond each semiannual coupon would entitle the holder to receive $40 from the Treasury.

Treasury bonds may be issued with any maturity longer than ten years. The longest bonds that are currently issued have an original maturity of 30 years.

Although Treasury notes and bonds begin life as coupon securities, government securities dealers often take newly issued notes and bonds and convert them to zero-coupon form by "stripping" the coupons from the body of the security. Dealers then market the coupons and the body of the security separately, as zero-coupon securities.

For example, a newly issued 15-year Treasury bond can be "stripped" into 31 separate zero-coupon securities. Why 31? Because there are two coupons per year (remember that interest is payable semiannually), and $15 \times 2 = 30$ plus the corpus or body of the bond = 31 (of course, there are only 30 different maturities, since the corpus and last coupon have the same maturity).

The $3,125 billion of marketable U.S. government securities are widely held not only in this country but throughout the world. In the first place, the Federal Reserve owns $375 billion as a result of current and past **open market operations.** Virtually all Federal Reserve open-market purchases and sales are conducted with government securities, mostly bills. The Fed's portfolio of governments provides the central bank with most of its income; after all, even a modest 4 percent yield on a $375 billion portfolio amounts to more than $15 billion a year. This leaves about $2,750 billion of marketable government debt held by the private sector—by commercial banks, individuals, insurance companies, nonfinancial corporations, pension funds, money market mutual funds, and foreign investors.

Since the late seventies, *foreigners* have been particularly large buyers of Treasury issues. They now own approximately $690 billion, about 22 percent of the marketable national debt (in 1969 they owned less than 5 percent).

Foreigners have acquired hundreds of billions of U.S. dollars by successfully selling automobiles, television sets, computers, and just about everything else to Americans. They have invested many of these dollars in U.S. stocks and bonds, especially government bonds. Money from abroad has been attracted here because of this country's political stability, financial freedom, and relatively high real interest rates.

In recognition of these substantial foreign investments in Treasury securities, it is often said, quite accurately, that recent U.S. budget deficits have been financed largely by foreigners. If it weren't for foreign purchases of Treasury securities, U.S. interest rates would be much higher than they have been.

How the Market Works

Most of the trading in governments takes place in the over-the-counter dealer market. At the heart of the market are forty or so government securities dealers. Some of the dealers are departments of major banks, like Citibank and Chase, while others are departments of large brokerage firms, like Merrill Lynch and Goldman Sachs. Most have their principal offices in New York, but some are headquartered in Chicago, San Francisco, and Los Angeles.

Trading in governments averages more than twenty times a typical day's trading on the New York Stock Exchange. Normal trading hours are from 9 A.M. to 4 P.M. New York time, but trading often extends beyond those hours when there is a lot of market activity. In fact, U.S. government securities are increasingly traded around the clock on virtually a nonstop basis, with trading following the sun around the globe.

Dealers get much of their inventory of bonds by bidding at competitive auctions. All marketable government securities are initially issued at auctions held by the Treasury. These auctions take place regularly, not just to raise new funds for the government, but to replace the funds of maturing securities. Three- and six-month Treasury bills, for example, are auctioned weekly (on Mondays), one-year bills monthly, and notes and bonds also on a regularly scheduled basis. Potential buyers at the auctions range from government securities dealers and large banks, with hundreds of millions to invest, to individuals with no more than a few thousand dollars to spare. The large investors wait until the very last minute before submitting their bids, trying to get the best price, while individuals usually submit theirs several days before the auction begins. If you would like a schedule of the forthcoming auctions simply write to the Federal Reserve Bank of New York (33 Liberty Street, New York, New York 10045) and they will be happy to accommodate your request.

The best way to understand what happens at an auction is to be there, so we'll do the next best thing and report on the details of a typical Treasury bill auction. First, though, let's refresh our memories about the basics of calculating yields on zero-coupon securities in general and on Treasury bills in particular.

Treasury Bills: Auctions and Yields

We saw back in Chapter 4 that the *general* formula for the yield to maturity *(r)* on a zero-coupon bond with *n* years until maturity is:

$$Price = \frac{Face\ Value}{(1 + r)^n}$$

It is fairly easy to specify the formula for calculating the annual yield on a Treasury bill with *one year* to maturity since in this case the value of $n = 1$. Thus, we have:

$$Price = \frac{Face\ Value}{(1 + r)}$$

We can also solve this formula for an explicit value for r:[1]

$$r = \frac{Face\ Value - Price}{Price}$$

When this expression is multiplied by 100, it generates r in percentage terms. For example, if a $100 face value Treasury bill is purchased for $95, the formula produces a yield of 5.263 percent. In effect, this formula measures the rate at which an initial sum of money (the purchase price) grows to the final sum (the face value).

But the expression must be modified when the growth takes less than a year, because all yields are commonly understood as per annum. For example, if a six-month Treasury bill costs $95 and grows into $100 in just half a year, the annual yield should be $5.263 \times 2 = 10.53$ percent.

The general formula for the annual yield on Treasury bills of three, six, or 12 months' maturity is:

$$r = \frac{Face\ Value - Price}{Price} \times t$$

---

[1] Take $P = F/(1 + r)$, multiply both sides by $(1 + r)$, producing $P(1 + r) = F$. Now divide both sides by P, giving $(1 + r) = F/P$. Subtract 1 from both sides, so $r = F/P - 1$. Getting the common denominator for the right-hand side gives $F/P - P/P$, which yields the formula in the text.

TABLE 8.1   Results of a Typical Treasury Bill Auction

	Three-month bills	Six-month bills
Amount applied for at auction	$22.9 billion	$21.3 billion
Amount scheduled to be sold	$7.6 billion	$7.6 billion
Noncompetitive tenders	$1.8 billion	$1.3 billion
Sales by competitive bidding	$5.8 billion	$6.3 billion
High price paid at auction	$98.074	$96.143
Yield on a discount basis	7.62%	7.63%
Coupon equivalent yield	7.88%	8.05%
Average price paid at auction	$98.066	$96.133
Yield on a discount basis	7.65%	7.65%
Coupon equivalent yield	7.91%	8.07%
Low price paid (stop-out price)	$98.064	$96.127
Yield on a discount basis	7.66%	7.66%
Coupon equivalent yield	7.92%	8.08%

Source: United States Treasury.

where t is the *inverse* of the fraction of a year the bill takes to mature. This entire expression is often called the coupon equivalent yield of a Treasury bill, as we shall see in a moment.

With this background in mind, let's turn to an illustrative Treasury bill auction. Table 8.1 shows the results of a typical weekly auction of three- and six-month bills. Before the auction, the Treasury announced that it would sell $7.6 billion of three-month bills and an equal amount of six-month bills (see the second line of the table).

Some potential buyers, fearful of not getting their bills by competitive bidding, submitted noncompetitive tenders (line 3), which guaranteed they would receive bills at the *average* price resulting from the auction. Because $1.8 billion of noncompetitive tenders were submitted for the three-month bill, the Treasury had to use competitive bidding for only the remaining $5.8 billion; and because $1.3 billion of such orders were submitted for the six-month bill, the Treasury had to sell only the remaining $6.3 billion competitively (line 4).

Competitive bids can be submitted at any Federal Reserve Bank or Branch until 1:00 P.M. on the day of the auction. At that time the Treasury closes the books and begins ranking the bids from the highest price on down. Table 8.1 shows that $22.9 billion of bids (both competitive and noncompetitive) were received for the three-month bill and $21.3 billion for the six-month issue—in both cases close to three times what the Treasury wanted to sell.

The highest bid for the three-month bill was $98.074 for a $100 face value bill. (Actually, $10,000 is the minimum denomination for Treasury bills, so

$98.074 really means $9,807.40. However, it is easier to do the calculations on the basis of $100 rather than $10,000.) Everyone bidding at that price was a successful bidder. The Treasury continued to accept bids at lower and lower prices until they aggregated $5.8 billion for three-month bills and $6.3 billion for six-month bills. At that point—the stop-out price—the auction was over, and those who submitted lower bids got nothing.

Because the successful bidders bought their bills at different prices, they will be receiving different yields. Two kinds of yield computations are used in the Treasury bill market: (1) **yield on a discount basis,** and (2) **coupon equivalent yield** (also called **bond equivalent yield**).

1. *Yield on a discount basis* is calculated as the face value minus the purchase price (let's call this *D*, for discount) divided by the face value. For example, Table 8.1 shows that high bidders for the new three-month bill received a $100 face value Treasury bill for $98.074. They paid $98.074, but in three months they'll get back $100. The difference *(D)* is $1.926:

$$\frac{1.926}{100} = 1.926 \text{ percent}$$

However, all yields are commonly understood to be on an *annual* basis. Three-month bills are really 13-week bills; they mature 91 days from issue date. Assuming as a rough approximation that a year has 360 days, a yield of 1.926 percent for 91 days can be annualized by multiplying it by 360/91 or 3.956. Thus the annual yield on a discount basis for the three-month Treasury bill high bidders is 1.926 percent × 3.956 = 7.62 percent (see Table 8.1).

The general formula for calculating yield on a discount basis is:

$$\frac{D}{\text{Face Value}} \times \frac{360}{\text{Number Days to Maturity}}$$

Yields have been quoted on a discount basis in the money market for generations. They keep being used because custom and tradition are hard to overcome. Nevertheless, the yield on a discount basis is a poor indicator of the *true* yield for two reasons. First of all, an investor doesn't pay the full face value of a bill when buying it, so 100 shouldn't be the denominator in the first term of the expression. Second, there aren't 360 days in a year, so 360 shouldn't be the numerator in the second term of the equation.

2. The *coupon equivalent yield* of a Treasury bill, which we mentioned above, corrects for these two flaws in yield on a discount basis. The formula for calculating the annual coupon equivalent yield is:

$$\frac{D}{\text{Purchase Price}} \times \frac{365}{\text{Number Days to Maturity}}$$

For example, low bidders for the six-month bill who paid $96.127 for a $100 face value security received a coupon equivalent yield of:

$$\frac{3.873}{96.127} \times \frac{365}{182} = 8.08 \text{ percent (see Table 8.1)}$$

As Table 8.1 shows, coupon equivalent yield is always *larger* than yield on a discount basis, because the denominator of the first term is necessarily smaller (it is the purchase price instead of the face value) and the numerator of the second term is larger (365 or 366 rather than 360).

The details of auctions for other types of Treasury securities differ somewhat from bill auctions, but the basics are still the same. Highest bidders buy first until the supply to be auctioned is exhausted. The yield calculations for the coupon-bearing Treasury issues follow the calculations described in Chapter 4, but without the discount yield complication.

At this point, let's spend some time on a market that is intimately connected with Treasury securities—the market for repurchase agreements.

Repurchase Agreements

With the Treasury auctioning billions of dollars in securities to government securities dealers, it should not be surprising that the dealers have developed **repurchase agreements (repos** or **RPs)** as an efficient mechanism for financing such activities. It also should not be surprising that once in place, this financing mechanism has taken on a life of its own. In particular, the market for repurchase agreements is, along with the federal funds market, the focal point of overnight borrowing and lending.

In a typical repurchase agreement, a government securities dealer, such as a major commercial bank, sells government securities (perhaps those just purchased at an auction) and agrees to repurchase them at a higher price the next day. The price the dealer agrees to pay for the securities the next day has nothing to do with what those securities sell for in the marketplace the next day. Rather the price is set to reflect the overnight cost of funds. And that's because the repurchase agreement is really a vehicle for borrowing money. In particular, when the owners of securities sell them they take in dollars; when they repurchase the securities the next day at a fixed price they are simply repaying those dollars plus interest. Notice that the other side of the repo transaction is called a *reverse RP,* and involves lending funds overnight.

The repo market is closely related to the market for borrowing and lending reserves owned by banks, called the **federal funds** market. To really understand that market requires a discussion of bank reserves, and that takes place in Chapters 21 and 22. At this point, it is useful to recognize that the RP and federal funds markets share a number of common characteristics. First, both markets are sources of overnight funds. Second, both markets settle payments the same day the transaction is completed. For example, in the case of the repo, the same day the dealer sells the securities with an agreement to repurchase them at a fixed priced, the funds are transferred into the dealer's accounts by whoever did the other side of the transaction (the reverse RP). The main difference between a repo and a federal funds transaction is that the latter is an unsecured overnight loan between financial institutions, while the former is essentially a collateralized loan, with the securities that are subject to repurchase acting as the collateral. Thus the overnight federal funds rate and the rate on repurchase agreements tend to move closely together. Whenever one rate moves up significantly relative to the other, borrowers borrow in the cheaper market, lenders lend in the more expensive market, and the rates are driven together—except that the federal funds rate is always slightly above the repo rate (about $\frac{1}{4}$ of one percent) to reflect the fact that repos are collateralized.

Although the repo market began as a mechanism for financing government securities on an overnight basis, the transaction has evolved into much broader use. First, repos are now done over a wide variety of maturities, ranging from the traditional one day to three months. Second, it is somewhat misleading to view the underlying collateral as what the repo is financing. In a sense, the repurchase agreement is used to raise funds for anything the borrower chooses. The underlying securities are simply acting as collateral for the lender. With this in mind it is useful to extend our discussion to other bank-related securities that are especially related to short-term Treasuries.

BANK-RELATED SECURITIES: CDS AND EURODOLLARS

When commercial banks consider how to finance their activities, they examine an array of opportunities in the money market rather than just looking at Federal funds and repurchase agreements. In fact, the most important segment of the money market is for Eurodollar time deposits, or Eurodollars for short. In recent years Eurodollars have mounted a legitimate challenge to Treasury bills as the centerpiece of the money market. Although the details of bank borrowing and lending activities is best left to a more complete discussion in Chapter 12, we focus here on how bank-related securities interact with other money market securities.

Most of us are personally familiar with at least some form of short-term bank liability—perhaps the popular savings account that we opened back in grade school. Banks also raise funds by issuing certificate of deposits, called CDs, which are essentially savings deposits with a specific time to maturity, hence they are formally called time certificates of deposit. Large-sized CDs, referred to as Jumbo CDs if they are more than $100,000 in value, are negotiable instruments (that is, they can be transferred to a third party) and are traded through a network of dealers just like Treasury bills.

Negotiable certificates of deposit have been an important part of the short-term money market since the early 1960s. They have been eclipsed, however, by their offshore counterparts known as Eurodollar time deposits. **Eurodollars** are dollar-denominated time deposits held abroad in foreign banks or in foreign branches of U.S. banks. Thus, these offshore deposits can be used by U.S. banks to raise funds in the same way that domestic CDs are used. But the market for Eurodollar time deposits has exploded in recent years as trading among banks in the London money market has taken on a life of its own. In

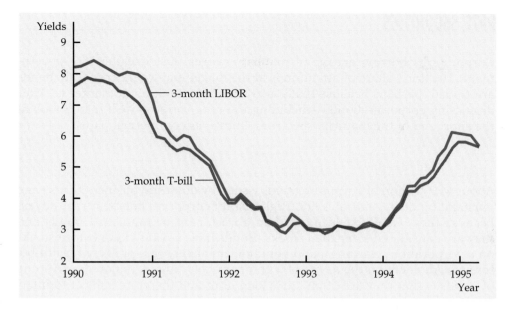

FIGURE 8.1   Yields on three-month Treasury bills and LIBOR move closely together.

particular, there is an active *interbank* market in Eurodollars that operates around the clock and around the world. Eurodollars are bought and sold as banks borrow and lend among themselves in response to short-term inflows and outflows of funds.

A number of large banks in London act as dealers in Eurodollars, quoting rates at which they are willing to borrow and lend. The rate they will lend at is called the *London interbank offered rate*, more commonly referred to as **LIBOR,** and the rate they will borrow at is the *London interbank bid rate* (known as LIBID, although hardly anyone ever mentions LIBID). Thus overnight LIBOR represents the cost of overnight funds to banks just like federal funds or overnight repurchase agreements. Three-month LIBOR represents the cost of three-month funds to banks—an alternative to selling three-month Treasury bills to generate cash. Because banks try to raise cash in the cheapest way, if any one of these rates were very much different from any of the others, borrowers would rush to the cheapest source and lenders would flock to the most expensive one. Borrowers would drive up rates where they were cheap and lenders would drive them down where they were high. Not surprisingly, therefore, Figure 8.1 shows rates on three-month LIBOR and three-month Treasury bills moving closely together.

The Eurodollar market has become so active in recent years that LIBOR is now the reference rate in many financial contracts. As we will see in the next chapter, derivatives contracts known as swaps often use LIBOR as the reference rate.

CORPORATE SECURITIES

Corporations borrow across all maturity ranges, just like the U.S. government. The lion's share of attention is at the longer end where corporate bonds are traded, perhaps because that's also where the junk bond market is. After discussing corporate bonds—including the junk variety—we'll take a look at the short end of the maturity spectrum, known as commercial paper.

Corporate Bonds

About $1.3 trillion of corporate bonds issued by domestic business firms were outstanding at the end of 1995. High-quality corporate bonds attract buyers because they usually yield more than government or municipal bonds and they are considered safer than stocks. Bonds have a prior claim before stocks on a corporation's earnings, and bondholders also have a preferred claim before stockholders on the assets of a company that fails. A major shortcoming of bonds is that they are often fairly long term and therefore subject to interest-rate risk—if interest rates rise, their prices plummet.

All corporate bonds are not identical. Differences among them include **call provisions** and **conversion features.** Many corporate bonds are **callable** after a certain specified date; that is, the issuer (the borrower) has the right to pay off part or all of the bond before the scheduled maturity date. Call provisions are exercised by the borrower when it is in the borrower's interest to do so—for instance, when the level of interest rates has fallen, so that the borrower can reborrow more cheaply. In partial compensation to the lender, the borrower has to pay a higher interest rate on a callable bond compared with one that is not callable.

Some corporate bonds are **convertible,** that is, they offer holders the right to convert their bonds into shares of the company's common stock at a predetermined price. This feature, which is attractive to many lenders, enables a corporation to sell such bonds at a lower interest rate than it would otherwise have to pay.

Corporate bonds also differ from one another in *quality.* Some borrowers are more likely and some are less likely to make their scheduled interest payments on time and to pay back the principal (face value) when the bond comes due (that is, when it matures). There is no question about the ability of the U.S. government to service its debts, but the same cannot always be said about corporate borrowers. As we saw in Chapter 5, Standard & Poor's and Moody's rate bonds according to their ability to repay interest and principle.

Bonds in the top four rating categories (Aaa, Aa, A, and Baa according to Moody's, for example) are often called **investment grade.** Bonds rated below Baa are called either **high-yield** or **junk bonds.** Before the late 1970s, almost all junk bonds were obligations of corporations that had fallen on hard times and consequently were having trouble meeting their interest payments; these bonds, often referred to as *fallen angels,* had started out as Baa or better and

GOING OUT ON A LIMB

Junk Is Good

Junk bonds have a bad name. In polite circles they are referred to as high-yield securities. And that's why people buy them, because they promise to pay more in interest to compensate for their lower credit rating.

In point of fact, junk bonds have been excellent investments over the years. For example, between 1977 and 1995 there are only two years (1980 and 1990) when investors would have lost money buying a diversified portfolio of junk bonds at the beginning of the year and selling at the end. Investors holding a portfolio of junk bonds over any two years would have lost money only in 1989–1990. Investors holding the portfolio over any three consecutive years would never have lost money.

More importantly, an investor who combines high-yield bonds with stocks and other securities will have a portfolio that has higher expected returns for any level of risk than the same portfolio without the junk bonds. This is a concrete (if somewhat surprising) example of the gains from diversification discussed in Chapter 7. So after all the smoke has cleared, junk is really something to consider as part of an overall portfolio.

were downgraded when the issuing firms encountered financial difficulties. Starting in 1977, however, companies began issuing original junk—that is, bonds rated below Baa to begin with—especially in connection with corporate takeovers and mergers. Investors buy such bonds because of their high yield, which presumably compensates for their extra risk.

Investment banker Michael Milken and the firm he worked for, Drexel Burnham Lambert, pioneered the issuance of such securities. The market for junk bonds held up well for a decade, but when the economy slowed down and many issuers could not make the required high interest payments, the securities plunged in price, forcing Drexel Burnham Lambert into bankruptcy in 1990. At about the same time, Milken pleaded guilty in federal court to six felony charges of securities fraud and conspiracy and agreed to pay $600 million in fines and restitution.

With respect to corporate bonds in general, life insurance companies and pension and retirement funds hold most of the outstanding bonds. Such institutions have a minimum need for liquidity because a large fraction of their expenditures can be scheduled many years in advance on the basis of average life expectancies and similar mortality statistics. Thus they can afford to buy long-term bonds and not worry about interest rates so much, since they won't have to sell prior to maturity in order to meet a sudden need for cash. Foreigners have also become large buyers of American corporate bonds, just as they have become big buyers of U.S. government securities.

While the bonds of some large corporations are listed and traded on the New York Stock Exchange, most corporate bond trading takes place in the over-the-counter market, through market-making dealers. The telephone is still the dominant mechanism for uncovering the best bids and offers of the numerous bond-dealing firms. A life insurance company portfolio manager,

READING THE FINANCIAL NEWS

Corporate Bond Market Quotations

(1) Bonds	(2) Cur yld.	(3) Vol.	(4) High	(5) Low	(6) Close	(7) Net chg.
AGS 7½11	cv	20	130	130	130	−1
AMR 10¼06	10.1	1	101½	101½	101½	−½
ANR 10⅝95	10.4	102	102	102	+1	+1½
ANR 13¼97	12.4	20	107¼	107¼	107¼	+¼
ARX 9⅜05	cv	85	109	108¾	108¾	−1¼
AVX 13½00	12.9	5	105	105	105	—
Advst 9s08	cv	6	109	109	109	—
AlaP 9s2000	8.9	10	101⅜	101⅜	101⅜	+¼

Column (1) shows the name of the company that issued the bond and the particular bond involved as identified by its coupon rate and maturity date. For example, the first bond in the column was issued by AGS Computers, a computer engineering and software company; it carries a 7½ percent coupon and will mature in the year 2011. (Conversationally, it is referred to as "AGSs seven and a halves of eleven.") The next one was issued by the AMR Corporation, which provides services for airlines; it carries a 10¼ percent coupon and will mature in the year 2006 (AMR's ten and a quarters of oh six). The last one is an Alabama Power Company bond with a 9 percent coupon that matures in the year 2000 (the nines of two thousand).

Column (2) is the bond's current yield—the coupon interest payment divided by yesterday's closing price (see column 6). Where cv appears, the bond is convertible into a specified number of shares of the company's common stock. Although the current yield is just as easy to calculate for convertibles as for ordinary bonds, it is usually omitted for convertibles because the market value of a convertible bond is often more closely related to the price of the stock for which it is exchangeable.

Column (3) (volume of trading) indicates the number of $1,000 bonds that changed hands yesterday on the New York Stock Exchange. Twenty AGS bonds were traded, only one AMR bond, 85 ARX bonds, and so on.

Columns (4), (5), and (6) show the highest, lowest, and closing (last) price at which each bond traded yesterday. Corporate bonds normally have a face value of $1,000 and their price is conventionally expressed as a percentage of face value. AGS's seven and a halves closed yesterday at 130 or $1,300 per bond. AMR's ten and a quarters closed at 101½ or $1,015 per bond. Advest's nines of oh eight closed at 109 or $1,090 per bond. Alabama Power's nines of two thousand closed at 101⅜ or $1,013.75 per bond. Notice that corporate bonds are quoted in one-eighths of a point (= $1.25 per $1,000 bond).

Column (7) is the change in the closing price from the previous day's close. For example, AGS's seven and a halves closed at 130 ($1,300) down 1 ($10) from the previous day's close of 131 ($1,310).

for example, may telephone a number of bond dealers to locate the best bid for a bond the company has decided to sell. There are so many individual corporate debt issues that trades in a particular bond are sometimes days or weeks apart. It does not really pay to invest in highly automated trading facilities when the volume of transactions doesn't warrant the huge outlay.

On the other hand, most dealers do maintain extensive computer-based information systems to record the bond preferences and holdings of ultimate investors (insurance companies, pension funds, and other institutions). This helps the dealer unearth buyers and sellers when needed. More importantly, it helps dealers place the corporate bonds they buy in their capacity as underwriters. Almost all corporate bonds are sold through underwriting syndicates of securities dealers. More on this in Chapter 14.

Commercial Paper

Commercial paper is to corporate bonds as Treasury bills are to Treasury bonds. That is, the government can borrow short term (bills) or long term (bonds), and corporations can similarly borrow short term (commercial paper) or long term (bonds). Commercial paper is a form of unsecured corporate borrowing that typically has an original maturity of between five and 270 days, with 30 days the most common.

By convention, issuers of commercial paper are divided into two categories: financial companies (such as finance companies and bank holding companies) and nonfinancial companies. The first group—financial companies—issues three-quarters of the dollar volume outstanding. Many finance companies are associated with well-known manufacturing firms, such as General Motors Acceptance Corporation (GMAC), the financing arm of General Motors.

Most commercial paper is bought by institutional investors, especially money market mutual funds, but nonfinancial firms and state and local governments also buy significant amounts. Since institutional investors dominate the market, the most popular denomination is $1 million. Historically, yields on commercial paper are somewhat above yields on Treasury bills of comparable maturity, because there is a greater risk of default with commercial paper than with Treasury bills, even for the highest-quality commercial paper. As can be seen in Figure 8.2, the commercial paper rate moves closely over time with the three-month Treasury bill rate.

In the primary market, new issues of commercial paper are often sold directly from the issuer to the buyer without any intermediary (called *directly placed paper*) or are sold through commercial paper dealers (dealer-placed paper). Most finance companies, for example, issue their paper directly to investors, but many other corporations go through commercial paper dealers who underwrite the issues.

Unlike Treasury bills, commercial paper does not have much of a secondary market. Investors who want to sell their paper before it comes due generally turn to the issuers, who will usually redeem their own obligations before maturity as a gesture of goodwill. Corporations that use dealers to sell their paper needn't be concerned about this nuisance, because the dealers often make a limited secondary market, agreeing to buy back paper from customers only.

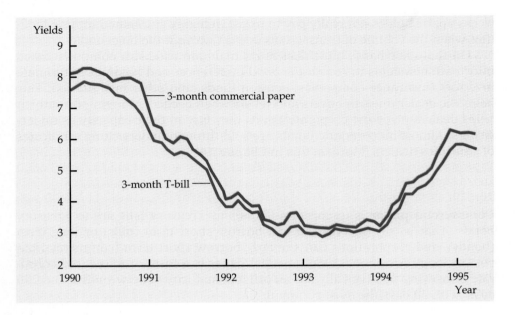

FIGURE 8.2   Yields on three-month Treasury bills and commercial paper.

Since investors can buy either Treasury bills or commercial paper, the two rates are competitive and move closely together.

Source: Federal Reserve.

MUNICIPAL SECURITIES

State and local government bonds, usually called **municipals,** carry the lowest yields of all securities of similar maturity and risk, as we know from Chapter 5. This low yield reflects the fact that their interest is legally exempt from federal income taxation. (Interest on municipal bonds is also usually exempt from state and local income taxes in the state where they are issued.) The federal tax exemption of interest on municipal securities was established by the Supreme Court in the 1895 *Pollock v. Farmers' Loan and Trust Company* case and was reaffirmed in 1913 in the first federal income tax law. In *South Carolina v. Baker* (1988) the Supreme Court reversed the *Pollock* decision and ruled that Congress does indeed have the power to tax the interest on municipal bonds if it wishes to do so. But so far, Congress has decided not to tap this source of revenue.

Municipals are usually issued in "serial" maturity form, as contrasted with the single maturity of government and corporate bonds. Serial maturity means that a portion of the total issue matures each year until the entire issue is eventually retired. Each portion carries its own interest rate and is separate from the rest of the issue. Thus when a state issues a ten-year serial bond, it is really issuing a series of one-year, two-year, and so on up to ten-year maturities.

Denominations of single bonds are usually $5,000, as compared with $1,000 denominations for corporate bonds. Municipal bonds are sold initially through underwriting syndicates, just like corporate bonds. The underwriting syndicates buy new issues in large blocks from the borrowing governmental authorities and market the securities to ultimate investors at a slightly higher price, making their profit on the differential, the so-called underwriting spread.

It is important to distinguish between the two kinds of municipal bonds: **general obligation bonds,** which are the majority of municipal bonds, and **revenue bonds.** General obligation municipals are issued for a wide variety of reasons, such as borrowing to build schools or to provide social services. They are backed by the general taxing power of the state or local government. Revenue bonds, on the other hand, are issued to finance a specific project—a toll highway, for example—and the interest and principal are paid exclusively out of the receipts that the project generates.

As might be expected, general obligation bonds are usually considered the safer of the two. Revenue bonds are riskier, because the particular project they are tied to might falter financially. A case in point is the 1983 default of the state of Washington on $2.25 billion of Washington Public Power Supply System (WPPSS) bonds, the largest municipal bond failure in U.S. history. The WPPSS (often called Whoops for obvious reasons) bonds were originally sold to finance several nuclear power plants in the state of Washington, and the payment of interest and principal depended on the financial success of those specific projects. Two of the plants were plagued by troubles for years; their financial difficulties eventually resulted in defaults. Revenue bonds usually carry a higher interest rate than general obligation bonds to compensate for the higher risk, but as the accompanying news item indicates, this relationship is sometimes reversed.

Secondary trading in municipals is conducted entirely in the over-the-counter dealer market. There are so many small issues of tiny and virtually unknown municipalities that the secondary market is not particularly active. Although the securities of some large states and cities have above-average liquidity (for a municipal bond, that is), many municipals are traded infrequently or not at all. As a result, the bid-asked spreads on municipal bonds are much wider than they are on either government or corporate bonds. To minimize this problem, when institutional investors want to sell some of their municipal bonds they frequently employ the services of a specialized municipal bond broker. Perhaps the best-known broker is J. J. Kenny and Company. The broker disseminates information on the bonds—coupon, maturity, and issuer—to potential investors, namely other institutions. Bids for the bonds are reported back to the seller, who can then decide whether to sell or not.

Most municipal bond prices and yields are not printed in the daily newspapers, but trade papers contain such information. The *Daily Bond Buyer* publishes data on new issues, and the *Blue List of Current Municipal Offerings* specializes in secondary market activity.

The two most popular short-term securities issued by state and local governments are **tax-anticipation notes** (TANs) and **bond-anticipation notes**

In The News

General Obligation Bonds Might Yield More than Revenue Bonds

Orange County Gets a Message

What would you do if someone owed you a lot of money and showed no intention of paying it back? Would you lend more money?

That's what municipal bond investors did last week, as they lent $295 million to bankrupt Orange County, California, which shows every intention of stiffing its previous lenders.

Orange County, as you no doubt recall, went broke by speculating on interest rates and is in bankruptcy court trying to weasel out of its obligations.

Looked at in isolation, the buyers last week got a pretty good deal. Orange County's latest bond issue was insured by MBIA, the nation's largest municipal bond insurer, and locks up some revenue streams that might otherwise have gone to pay the creditors that the county wants to avoid paying. The county paid a premium of about one-quarter percentage point over normal rates.

But the lending also sent a message to the county, that money will be available to it in the future no matter what it does about its past debts. Next week the county's voters are expected to turn down a proposal to raise sales taxes by one-half of a percent. Without that, default looms.

That message should surprise no one. To be sure, the bond industry has been talking tough, threatening not to lend any more money to Orange County, and maybe not to anyone in California, unless the state and the county live up to their responsibilities. But this market's history is one of a total inability to act tough when confronted with the most outrageous conduct. Never forget the Washington Public Power Supply System, a group of local utilities that was able to borrow again only shortly after walking away from its obligations and getting the State Supreme Court to approve the repudiation.

Still, it is breathtaking to see MBIA, a company that has the most to lose from a widespread repudiation of obligations by municipalities, stepping up to guarantee the bonds of a deadbeat that is certainly wealthy enough to pay but whose elected leaders see no reason why it should do so.

Joe Mysak, the editor of *Grant's Municipal Bond Observer*, thinks this could lead to a historic reversal in which revenue bonds, those backed by a project like a toll bridge, yield less than comparably rated general obligation bonds. After all, those bonds have something that may be seized by angry creditors.

Source: New York Times, June 18, 1995.

(BANs). Tax receipts flow in intermittently, rather than regularly, so TANs are used to borrow funds in the intervals between tax payment dates. The notes have maturities ranging from a few days to a few months and are paid off when tax receipts come in. BANs similarly provide stopgap financing for large projects, such as sewers or roads, and are paid off when long-term bonds are floated.

Money market funds that specialize in the purchase of short-term **tax exempts** have grown rapidly in recent years. Their popularity stems from the fact that they allow people of moderate wealth to diversify their portfolios of such securities. Many require a minimum investment of only $1,000, whereas the smallest denomination in which one can buy municipals directly is $5,000 for each security.

MORTGAGE SECURITIES

Mortgages are the most complicated of all debt instruments. Not because real estate acts as collateral and not because individuals, rather than governments or corporations, are the primary borrowers. Although these characteristics do make mortgages different, as we saw in Chapter 3, most mortgages are insured by some type of government agency, such as the **Government National Mortgage Association** (Ginnie Mae) or the **Federal Home Loan Mortgage Corporation** (Freddie Mac). Thus potential defaults by borrowers are usually not a primary concern for investors.

The biggest problem for investors is that mortgages can be repaid at the option of the borrower prior to the scheduled maturity date. Thus investors are never really certain of the maturity of their investment. This characteristic, known as prepayment risk, makes mortgages especially undesirable from the standpoint of institutional investors, such as pension funds who require fixed long-term cash flows to match the profile of their liabilities.

Numerous innovations in the basic mortgage instrument have taken place to make these securities more attractive to investors. The basic mortgage, as described in Chapter 3, is a 20- or 30-year amortizing loan, that is, the mortgage borrower repays interest and returns principle over a 20- or 30-year period. Unlike most conventional bonds, therefore, the loan is gradually repaid according to a predetermined schedule over time. Of course, just to complicate matters there are so-called balloon payment mortgages which resemble conventional bonds in that they do not amortize principal but require a lump sum payment at the end. In either case, however, the problem for investors is that the borrower has the option to repay (prepay) the entire loan earlier than scheduled.

To reduce prepayment uncertainty and, therefore, to broaden the appeal of mortgages among potential investors, securities dealers invented the **collateralized mortgage obligation** (CMO). In this case a number of mortgages are placed in a trust. The interest and principal repayments are then divided by the trustee (often a bank) into four (or more) segments according to a predetermined formula. The formula allocates prepayments to the first segment until it is paid off, then to the second segment until it is paid off, and so on. Investors then choose whether to receive their payments from the first, second, third, and so on, segments. These segments, by the way, are called tranches (*tranche* is slice in French). In this way the cash flow becomes more (but not perfectly) predictable for each investor.

Trading in CMOs takes place in the over-the-counter market between dealers just like corporate bonds. Because they are complicated securities, however, it is best to leave them and turn to something we may not know very much more about, but is certainly a lot more fun—the stock market.

THE STOCK MARKET

People have been known to make money in the stock market and also to lose some. It is a fact of life that the total number of stocks in existence changes rather slowly. What does change from year to year is not so much the number of shares but rather the price of each.

Why do stock prices go up and down? Not so much particular stocks, like IBM and Xerox, but why does the entire market, more or less, rise or fall? How important is monetary policy in driving stock prices up or down? We will examine these pricing issues in a moment, but first let's take a look at the marketplace itself.

Structure of the Stock Market

According to the New York Stock Exchange, there are now about 35 million individual shareholders in the United States. Nevertheless, in the past decade institutional investors—especially pension funds, mutual funds, and insurance companies—have edged individuals to the side and begun to dominate the stock market.

The "stock market" refers principally to the secondary market for common stocks. The primary market—that is, the original distribution of new stock issues—operates through investment banks, as we saw in Chapter 6. It is mostly the subsequent trading of securities that constitutes what is generally called the stock market.

The New York Stock Exchange (NYSE)—the Big Board—is the most visible part of the stock market, in part because shares of the largest and best-known corporations are traded there. High visibility also comes from the fact that you can actually see the marketplace. Trading in the shares of about 1,800 corporations takes place on the floor of the exchange at 11 Wall Street. Business is conducted by members of the exchange, and transactions are recorded on an electronic ticker tape flashed on the floor itself as well as in brokerage offices throughout the country. This is a real marketplace, the same as at the county fair, except that it's a lot more hectic.

Individual stocks are traded at particular locations, called *posts,* on the football-field floor. Traders receiving orders via telephone from brokerage offices throughout the country scurry about placing orders with particular specialists. The job of specialists is to maintain orderly trading for the securities in their charge.

READING THE FINANCIAL NEWS

Stock Market Quotations

(1) 52 Weeks High	Low	Stock	(2) Div.	(3) Yld. %	(4) P/E ratio	(5) Sales 100s	(6) High	(7) Low	(8) Close	(9) Net chg.
$15\frac{7}{8}$	$10\frac{3}{4}$	Huffy	.40	2.9	17	215	14	$13\frac{1}{2}$	$13\frac{5}{8}$	$-\frac{1}{4}$
$12\frac{3}{4}$	$6\frac{3}{4}$	HughTl.	.08	0.7	—	4366	$11\frac{1}{4}$	$10\frac{7}{8}$	$11\frac{1}{8}$	$+\frac{1}{8}$
$30\frac{3}{8}$	$20\frac{5}{8}$	HughSp.	.40	1.7	12	94	24	$23\frac{1}{2}$	$23\frac{7}{8}$	$+\frac{1}{8}$
$33\frac{7}{8}$	$19\frac{1}{8}$	Human	.76	3.7	51	1634	$20\frac{1}{2}$	20	$20\frac{3}{8}$	—
$36\frac{3}{8}$	$20\frac{1}{2}$	HuntMf.	.44	1.7	26	107	26	$25\frac{5}{8}$	26	—

Stock market quotations appear on a daily basis in many newspapers. Column (1) lists the high and low price per share for each stock over the past 52 weeks. For example, the common stock of the Huffy Corporation, which makes bicycles and outdoor power equipment, fluctuated between a high of $15.875 a share and a low of $10.75 in the past 52 weeks. Hughes Tool Company fluctuated between $12.75 and $6.75 a share, and Hughes Supply Corporation between $30.375 and $20.625 a share.

Column (2) is the current annual cash dividend being paid by the company, Humana Corporation, a hospital-operating company, is paying its stockholders 76 cents a share annually and Hunt Manufacturing is paying 44 cents a share.

Column (3) is the stock's dividend yield, which is the current annual dividend payment divided by yesterday's closing price (Column 8). Hunt, for example, is paying 44 cents and closed at $26: thus 0.44 ÷ 26 = 1.7 percent.

Column (4) is the company's price-earnings ratio—yesterday's closing stock price divided by the company's after-tax earnings per share over the last twelve months. Humana's high P/E multiple of 51 indicates that its stockholders apparently anticipate substantial future earnings growth (or else they wouldn't pay such a high price for the stock relative to the company's current earnings).

Column (5) records the number of shares traded yesterday in terms of hundreds of shares exchanged. Trading in the stock of Hughes Tool Company was quite active—436,600 shares changed hands—while Hughes Supply, which retails electrical and plumbing items, was relatively inactive, with only 9,400 shares traded.

Columns (6), (7), and (8) show the highest, lowest, and closing (last) price at which each stock traded yesterday. For example, Humana Corporation traded as low as $20 a share but closed at $20.375.

Column (9) is the change in the closing price from the previous day's close. Huffy Corporation closed down 25 cents a share while Humana was unchanged.

Specialists may simply match publicly tendered buy and sell orders submitted at the same price. Floor traders stand at the post and compete for orders that are not matched on the specialist's order book. When neither of these occur, specialists step in and buy for their own account (at the bid price) or sell from their inventory (at the asked price) in order to prevent excessive gyrations in transactions prices.

Smaller companies are not listed for trading on the New York Stock Exchange. Some trade on the American Stock Exchange, which is also located in New York City, but an increasing number of companies, even some large ones such as Microsoft, have their shares trade in the over-the-counter market (OTC). As compared with the organized exchanges, the OTC market has no single place of business where trading activity takes place. Rather, it is a linkage of many dealers and brokers who communicate with each other via telephone and computer terminals. The National Association of Securities Dealers Automated Quotation System (NASDAQ) shows bid and asked prices for thousands of OTC-traded securities on video screens hooked up to a central computer system. For some of the larger OTC stocks, like Intel, more than twenty firms make a market—that is, they quoted bid and asked prices that account executives at brokerage firms could rely on when selling or buying for their customers. For smaller OTC securities, perhaps only a couple of firms would make a market.

What Determines Whether Stock Prices Rise or Fall?

Now that we know something about the marketplace, let's see whether we can explain what makes the stock market go up or down. This won't necessarily help us make a lot of money, but at least we'll understand why it's so tough. Although we are most interested in the stock market as a whole we must start at the beginning with individual stocks and work our way up.

Stocks, more formally called **equities,** represent ownership in a company. If the company is profitable it generates earnings which can be passed on to the stockholders in the form of dividends. Thus equities entitle investors to future cash flows in the form of dividends. In Chapter 4 we showed that in order to value the future cash flows on a bond, it was necessary to discount those cash flows to take account of the time value of money. This principle can be applied to equities as well. To get to the bottom line (when to buy or sell) we make some simplifying assumptions.

Suppose we expect a company to earn $10 per share forever and that its management decides to keep stockholders happy by paying out all earnings as dividends. Based on Chapter 4 we can calculate the price of these future cash flows with the following equation:

$$P = \frac{\$10}{1 + r} + \frac{\$10}{(1 + r)^2} + \frac{\$10}{(1 + r)^3} + \cdots$$

where r represents the average annual rate used to discount the $10 dividend payments. The three dots at the end of the formula indicate that this series of numbers continues indefinitely (because earnings go on forever), with $(1 + r)$ continuing to be raised to higher and higher powers.

Although this looks like a complicated formula, it isn't. In fact, we mentioned in Chapter 5 that a bond known as a perpetuity or consol has precisely the same formula. Moreover, the formula simplifies to

$$P = \frac{\$10}{r}$$

OFF THE RECORD

The Dow Jones Versus the S&P 500

The **Dow Jones Industrial Average** (DJIA) is the most widely watched measure of what is happening in the stock market. Although it is very popular, the Dow is not nearly as comprehensive as other stock market indicators.

Some other—and in many ways better—market indicators are **Standard & Poor's 500 Stock Index** and the New York Stock Exchange Composite Index. Others are the NASDAQ, Over-the-Counter Composite Index and the American Exchange's AMEX Market Value Index.

The DJIA is an average of the prices of only 30 stocks. Included in the 30 are such blue-chip (that is, high-quality) corporations as General Electric, IBM, and Sears Roebuck. However, 30 stocks is an extremely small sample to use as a measure of what is happening in the whole stock market.

One reason for the Dow's popularity is that it has been around so long. Charles H. Dow, the first editor of the *Wall Street Journal,* and Edward D. Jones began to calculate it as far back as the 1880s. From 1905 to 1925 the Dow fluctuated mostly between 80 and 100. In the stock market boom of the late twenties, it rose to a peak of 381 on September 3, 1929, and then nose-dived to a low of 41 on July 8, 1932. It took more than two decades for the market to recover from the crash. It was November 1954 before the Dow again reached 381. The average hit 500 in March 1956, 1,000 in November 1972, and reached 2,722 on August 25, 1987. A few weeks later, on Black Monday (October 19, 1987), it fell more than 500 points! In November 1995 the Dow more than made up for its 500-point loss in 1987 by pushing through the 5,000 level.

The DJIA is expressed in terms of "points," not dollars. It is computed in such a way that all stocks have the same influence on the average. This is not the case with the S&P 500 or the NYSE Composite Index, which are calculated so that corporations with a greater total value of shares outstanding have more influence on the index than corporations with less total value.

The S&P 500 consists, not surprisingly of the prices of 500 stocks. The NYSE Composite includes all stocks listed on the New York Stock Exchange. Broader than both is the Wilshire 5000 Equity Index which includes 5,800 stocks—all those listed on the NYSE and the AMEX as well as many actively traded over-the-counter issues. Most financial experts prefer the S&P 500 as their favorite indicator of overall market behavior; it is usually the measure that index funds use as they try to match the market's performance, and mutual fund and trust fund managers are "graded" on whether or not they have done as well as or better than the S&P 500.

For example, if the rate required to discount those cash flows is 10 percent, then the stock price will be $100, while if the rate were 5 percent, the price would be $200.[2]

---

[2]This simple formula makes considerable sense if looked at from the following perspective. How much should you pay for a believable promise to pay $10 forever? The price, P, should be no more and no less than what it would take to generate $10 forever by investing the money at the going rate of interest. Thus, the price P should be such that $P \times r = \$10$, where r is the annual rate of interest. Or, $P = \$10/r$, which is the formula in the text.

Although we made a number of simplifying assumptions to get a relatively simple formula for pricing stocks, there is enough truth in this approach to warrant using it to explain what causes gyrations in stock prices.[3] Here are some general principles. The numerator of our formula is quite straightforward. Higher expected future earnings mean higher stock prices. This makes considerable sense for a single stock, like IBM, or for all stocks taken together, such as the 30 stocks in the famous Dow Jones Industrial Average or the less famous but more representative 500 stocks in Standard & Poor's 500 stock index. Not surprisingly, stock prices respond positively to higher projected earnings and negatively to lower projected earnings.

The denominator of the formula is somewhat more complicated. If stocks were just like government bonds, then the denominator would be simply the government bond rate. But common sense suggests (and the formal analysis of Chapter 7 makes clear) that risky securities such as equities require higher expected returns than government bonds to compensate for investor's risk aversion. So, for example, if government securities yield 5 percent, the required return on equities that appears in the denominator of our formula might be 12 percent—a 5 percent riskless government bond rate plus a 7 percent risk premium.

This perspective provides a second explanation for movements in stock prices: Higher government bond rates will increase the denominator of our formula and reduce stock prices while lower government bond rates will decrease the denominator and raise stock prices. This makes considerable common sense as well. If equities are expected to earn $10 per annum in dividends, that stream of payments is worth a lot more if government bonds pay 5 percent per annum than if government bonds pay 10 percent per annum.

Now that we know precisely why stock prices move in the same direction as company earnings and move *inversely* with interest rates, do we have the keys to instant riches? Unfortunately, the answer is a resounding no. Current stock prices respond to *expected* future earnings and to interest rates that discount those future earnings. To predict stock prices, therefore, requires knowing where the economy as a whole is headed, because that's what will determine the future course of earnings and interest rates. And economic forecasters are the only people that make weather forecasters look good. Nevertheless, let's turn to a discussion of how knowledge about money and mone-

---

[3]One complication that we omitted is that earnings tend to grow over time, so that stocks should be priced as a growing perpetuity. Our formula is easily modified to account for growth by replacing r in the denominator with $r - g$, where g is the growth in earnings. So if earnings (and dividends) are expected to grow by 3 percent and if r were 10 percent, then the stock price would be

$$P = \frac{\$10}{.10 - .03} = \$142.86$$

rather than $100 when growth is zero. Not surprisingly, if dividends and earnings are expected to grow, the stock price will be higher. Overwise, not much else changes and our discussion in the text is just fine as it is.

tary policy might help (or hurt) so that you can be prepared to apply what you learn in the rest of this course.

Money and Stock Prices

There are some economists who believe that fluctuations in the money supply provide the key to movements in stock prices. The reasoning follows the discussion in Chapter 2 and goes like this: When the Federal Reserve increases the money supply at a faster than normal rate, the public, finding itself with more cash than it needs for current transactions, spends some of its excess money buying financial assets, including stocks. Since the supply of equities is more or less fixed, especially in the short run, this incremental demand raises their price. Some stocks will go up more than others and some may go down, depending on the prospects for particular companies, but overall the *average* of stock prices will rise.

Conversely, decreases in the money supply—or increases at a slower rate than necessary to provide for the transactions needs of a growing economy—leave the public with shortages of funds. The result is, among other things, a cutback in stock purchases. This reduced demand for stocks lowers their prices.

Conclusion: A rapidly expanding money supply leads to higher stock values; inadequate monetary growth leads to a falling market.

Persuasive as the underlying reasoning seems, all too often the facts simply do not bear it out. Evidently too many other cross-currents simultaneously impinge on the stock market, such as business expectations and political developments. Like so many other single-cause explanations in economics, this simplified view of stock price determination contains too much truth to ignore but not enough to make it very reliable in the clutch.

For example, there are a number of instances that seem to support the notion that money supply matters a lot for stock prices. In particular, it is quite true that declines in stock prices *were* preceded or accompanied by declines in the rate of growth of the money supply in 1957, 1960, 1969, and 1981. And often increases in stock prices were indeed associated with increases in the growth of the money supply, as in 1967, 1968, 1975, and the early and mid-1980s.

In at least some of these instances, however, both stock prices and the money supply might conceivably have been reacting to a third causal force, perhaps an upturn in business conditions stimulated by the outbreak of war ( ) peace ( )—check one—a spurt in consumer spending, or something else. An improvement in business conditions, regardless of cause, typically leads to an expansion in bank business loans, a larger money supply, brighter profit prospects, and thereby higher stock prices. As the history of business cycles indicates, such upswings (or downturns) are capable of generating a cumulative push that can work up considerable momentum, carrying *both* the money supply and stock prices along with it.

GOING OUT ON A LIMB

The Crash of 1987 and Market Efficiency

On October 19, 1987, stock prices declined by more than 20 percent for no apparent reason. This led many people to doubt the proposition that the stock market is efficient. As we explained in Chapter 6, most academics believe that stock prices are efficient in the sense that prices reflect all publicly available information. Practitioners in the stock market view this dictum with considerable suspicion, especially since they make their living trying to take advantage of market pricing inefficiencies. The Crash of '87 bolsters their claim that stocks are buffeted by whimsical investor fantasies rather than hard facts.

We believe that the Crash of '87 not only doesn't prove that markets are inefficient, but might actually suggest market efficiency. The simple formula for pricing stocks developed in the text, and modified for growth in footnote 3, explains what might have happened. Suppose that the best estimate of future dividends is $10 per share and that the market expects this to grow by 9 percent per annum. If the risk-adjusted rate required to invest in stocks is 12 percent, then the stock price formula from footnote 3 produces a predicted stock price of 10/(.12 − .09) or 333. This number is quite close to the price level of Standard & Poor's 500 stock average on the day before the crash.

Now suppose that on the morning of October 19, 1987, investors demanded a modest increase of 1 percent in the risk premium for holding stocks because they became nervous that Congress would carry out its threat (announced the week of October 12, 1987) to put a prohibitive tax on the frenzy of mergers and acquisitions that sparked the stock market rally during the first seven months of 1987. Our formula now predicts a stock price average of $10/(.13 − .09) or 250—a drop of 33 percent from the previous level.

What does this numerical exercise suggest? Even relatively small changes in the underlying determinants of stock prices—a 1 percent increase in the risk premium demanded by investors—can cause enormous price swings in the market.

Unfortunately, this brings on an embarrassment of riches. Now we have to explain why the stock market doesn't move by 20 percent or more every day, rather than just once every fifty years. The facts are that such consensus revaluations of underlying market parameters do not usually occur for no apparent reason. But if you wait long enough, just about everything is possible, even low probability events like resurrecting dinosaurs, putting a man on the moon, or 20 percent stock market declines in one day.

The fact that stocks don't gyrate wildly for no apparent reason every other day suggests that a good rule of thumb is that the stock market might very well be an efficient processor of information.

Figure 8.3 provides a classic example of the pitfalls involved in reading a cause-and-effect relationship into two sets of statistics simply because they move together. The line labeled *S* indicates the movement of stock prices, annually, from the end of 1960 through the end of 1966, using stock prices at the end of 1960 as the base (= 100).

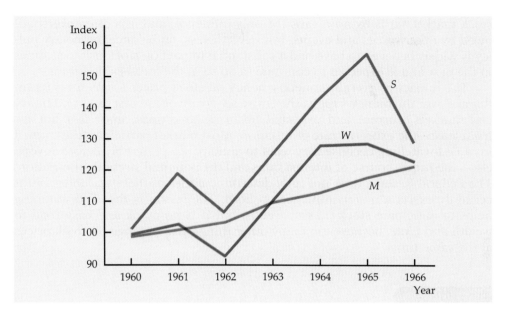

FIGURE 8.3   Stock prices and other variables, 1960–1966.

Sources: For stock prices: Dow Jones Industrials, monthly closing averages for December of each year (December 1960 = 100). For money supply: Demand deposits plus currency, monthly averages for December of each year (December 1960 = 100).

The line labeled *M,* on a similar index basis, is the movement of the money supply annually, also from the end of 1960 through the end of 1966. Over this particular six-year period, changes in the money supply clearly bore little relationship to turning points in stock prices.

Finally, the chart includes a third line, *W.* Its movements are obviously closely related to changes in stock prices. Almost without exception, the line labeled *W* and the line tracing stock prices move up and down together.

Cause and effect? The line labeled *W,* make of it what you will, is an annual index (1960 = 100) of the number of times members of the old Washington Senators baseball team struck out each year, over the period 1960 through 1966. (*Source: The Sporting News's Official Baseball Guide and Record Book,* Annual, 1960–1966.) For at least those years, evidently, an investor trying to forecast turning points in the stock market would have been better off reading *Sports Illustrated* instead of the *Wall Street Journal.*

Once we expand our horizon to encompass more than the money supply alone, however, there is widespread agreement that the Federal Reserve's execution of monetary policy *in general* does have considerable influence on the stock market.[4] It is by no means the only influence, and it is often overshadowed by other forces and events, but nevertheless, on balance, monetary policy is widely believed to have had a substantial impact on stock prices at times in the past and is expected to continue to do so in the foreseeable future.

The impact of overall monetary policy on stock prices stems from its influence over the money supply, the entire spectrum of interest rates and financial markets, current and expected business conditions, and—last but far from least—the expected rate of inflation. Most market participants are tuned in to Fed-watching because they want to anticipate—preferably before anyone else—the future course of interest rates and the potential strength of inflation. The Federal Reserve does not fully determine either of these variables, but it certainly exerts a major influence on both. The lesson is that Fed-watching helps to anticipate stock market trends, but it is no quick and easy road to wealth and fame, because too many other things also impinge on stock prices at the same time.

SUMMARY

1. The federal budget has generally been in deficit since 1930, so that the U.S. Treasury has had to borrow large sums by selling government securities. Commercial banks hold large amounts of governments, as do foreigners. It is often said that recent U.S. budget deficits have been financed largely by foreigners. Money from abroad has been attracted here because of this country's political stability, financial freedom, low inflation, and relatively high real interest rates.

2. Most trading in governments takes place in the over-the-counter dealer market. Government securities dealers are at the heart of the market. Dealers stand ready to buy and sell all the various maturities at quoted

---

[4]This is quite aside from the power of the Federal Reserve to set **margin** requirements on stock purchases. In an attempt to prevent a repetition of the speculative wave, financed heavily with borrowed funds, that carried the market to dizzy heights until the Fall of 1929, Congress in the 1930s authorized the Federal Reserve to impose margin (or minimum down payment) requirements on the purchase of stocks. If the margin requirement is 100 percent, then 100 percent cash must be put up and no borrowing at all is permitted. If the margin requirement is 80 percent, that much of one's own cash must be put up when one buys a security, and only the remaining 20 percent can be financed by borrowing from a bank or a broker. Of course, you could always finance the entire amount by borrowing from your sister-in-law and no one would be the wiser (except perhaps, in the long run, your sister-in-law). High margin requirements have probably helped restrain speculation in stocks, especially by those who could least afford it. Nevertheless, if the Federal Reserve had only this device to influence the market, it would be relying on a weak reed indeed. Margin requirements are 100 percent at Santa Anita and Hialeah racetracks, but at last report speculative activity by those who could not afford it as well as by those who could appeared unimpaired.

"bid" and "asked" prices. Dealers get much of their inventory by bidding at competitive auctions, which is how the Treasury initially issues all marketable government securities. Dealers often use repurchase agreements to finance their holdings of governments.

3. Treasury bill yields are calculated in two different ways: yield on a discount basis and, more accurately, coupon equivalent yield (also called bond equivalent yield).

4. The markets for Eurodollars and bank CDs are closely related to the Treasury bill market. In fact, the Eurodollar market together with the London interbank money market has mounted a legitimate challenge to Treasury bills as the centerpiece of the money market. LIBOR, the London interbank offered rate, is the most frequently used reference rate in financial contracts.

5. Corporate bonds differ from each other in many respects, including default probabilities, call provisions, and conversion features. Private companies rate corporate bonds with respect to quality, that is, with respect to the ability of the borrower to pay interest when scheduled and repay principal when due. Although some corporate bond trading takes place on the New York Stock Exchange, most trading is over the counter through market-making dealers. These are the same dealers who act as underwriters when a corporate bond is first issued.

6. Municipal bonds appeal mainly to high-income individuals and to institutions subject to high tax rates, because of their federal income tax exemption. Underwriting syndicates dominate the primary market, and subsequent trading takes place in the over-the-counter market. General obligation municipal bonds are backed by the general taxing power of the state or local government. Revenue bonds are related to a specific project, with interest and principal payments generated by that project's revenues.

7. Mortgages are more complicated than other debt instruments primarily because borrowers have the option to repay the loan prior to its scheduled maturity. Collateralized Mortgage Obligations (CMOs) were invented to minimize the effect of this uncertainty on mortgage investors.

8. Stocks are traded primarily on the New York Stock Exchange and in the over-the-counter market. These are secondary markets because only existing securities trade there.

9. Stock prices rise and fall with interest rates and company earnings. Monetary policy plays an important role in influencing stock price movements because of its effect on overall economic activity, inflation, and, of course, interest rates.

QUESTIONS

8.1 Which is the more accurate way to calculate yield on a Treasury bill: discount yield or coupon equivalent yield? Why?

8.2 How are repurchase agreements used by dealers to finance their inventory of government bonds?

8.3 Why does the yield on three-month Treasury bills move together with the yield on three-month Eurodollar deposits?

8.4 Why are junk bonds not really junk (or are they)?

8.5 Why do municipal general obligations bonds have lower yields than municipal revenue bonds? Might this relationship be reversed?

8.6 How do collateralized mortgage obligations (CMOs) make some investors more willing to hold mortgages?

8.7 *Discussion question:* Explain why higher interest rates cause stock prices to go down. Do you think you can use this analysis to make money in the stock market (think before you do anything)?

CHAPTER 9

Demystifying Derivatives

Life was a lot simpler when bonds were bonds, stocks were stocks, and futures were pork bellies. But those days are gone forever. Futures contracts on Treasury securities have grown to the point where the Federal Reserve was asked by Congress to study the effects of Treasury bond futures on the cost of the federal debt. A similar explosion in options trading on stock indices forced the Securities and Exchange Commission to consider the implications for the liquidity of the capital markets. And swaps have forced regulators to rethink traditional measures of bank risk exposure.

Although futures, options, and swaps are complicated instruments, they have found their way into the risk management toolbox of just about every major financial institution. They are called **derivatives** because each of these instruments is a financial contract that derives its value from some other underlying asset. Considering the importance of derivatives in the daily operation of our financial markets, it seems like a good idea to understand what they are, how they work, and most importantly, how to avoid losing money in the process. First we look at futures, then at options, and finally at swaps.

AN OVERVIEW OF FINANCIAL FUTURES

A futures contract is a contractual agreement that calls for the delivery of a specific underlying commodity or security at some future date at a currently agreed-upon price. There are contracts on interest-bearing securities (such as Treasury bonds, Treasury notes, and Eurodollar Time Deposits), on stock indices (such as Standard & Poor's 500 and Japan's Nikkei index), and on foreign currencies (such as the German mark and the Japanese yen). Trading in these contracts is conducted on the various commodity exchanges alongside the conventional agricultural commodities. For example, Treasury bonds

In The News

Regulators Worldwide Worry About Derivatives

German Banker Seeks Tighter Rein on Derivatives

FRANKFURT—A German central banker stepped up the pressure to improve controls over financial derivatives, saying it is time for banks and regulators to act.

The remarks by Hans Georg Fabritius, vice president of the Hesse regional central bank, suggest that the Bundesbank is becoming impatient with the slow progress in regulating the highly volatile instruments. While Mr. Fabritius isn't a member of the policy-making Central Bank Council, he is responsible for daily market supervision in Frankfurt's financial center.

"Although there's no reason for crisis hysteria, it also would be wrong to play down the derivatives problem," he said. "There's much more of a need for action, primarily by those banks and securities houses in the center of the business."

German banks haven't disclosed any large-scale losses linked to derivatives trading, but Metallgesellschaft, a blue-chip engineering and metals company, was driven to the brink of bankruptcy by making wrong bets on oil prices on the New York Mercantile Exchange. Several insurance companies also have announced that they lost money through derivatives transactions. Overall, however, German firms release almost no information on their financial investments.

One reason for the collapse of United Kingdom merchant bank Barings PLC in late February was massive loss-making positions taken in Japanese equity derivatives by Nicholas W. Leeson, a former trader in its Singapore subsidiary.

In his speech, Mr. Fabritius praised the Basel group for allowing banks to submit their own risk-management systems for approval under certain conditions. However, "the responsibility for the selection and continued development of proper methods for risk management must remain with the management of the individual banks," he said.

Source: Silvia Ascarelli, "German Banker Seeks Tighter Rein on Derivatives," *Wall Street Journal,* June 16, 1995. Reprinted by permission of *The Wall Street Journal.* Copyright © 1995 Dow Jones & Company, Inc. All Rights Reserved Worldwide.

trade on the Chicago Board of Trade (CBT) along with futures contracts on wheat, corn, and soybeans. Eurodollar Time Deposits are traded on the Chicago Mercantile Exchange alongside the venerable pork belly and live cattle futures contracts.

Although futures contracts on agricultural commodities have been in existence since the middle of the nineteenth century and financial futures were introduced about 25 years ago, the volume of trading in financial futures now exceeds the more traditional agricultural commodities. **Financial futures** have obviously become quite popular in a very short time period. They share a number of common characteristics with all futures contracts that help determine how they are used. The best way to understand these characteristics is by way of specific example.

All futures contracts are standardized agreements to buy or sell a particular asset or commodity at a future date at a currently agreed-upon price.[1] The terms of the contract specify the amount and type of asset to be delivered, as well as the location and delivery period. In the case of financial futures, the underlying asset is either a specific security or the cash value of a group of securities. For example, the Treasury bond contract calls for the delivery of $100,000 in Treasury bonds, and the Treasury bill contract calls for the delivery of $1 million in Treasury bills. In the case of stock index futures, the contract calls for the delivery of the cash value of a particular stock index. For example, the popular S&P 500 contract calls for the delivery of $500 times the value of the S&P 500 Stock Index.

The precise terms of each contract are established by the exchange that sponsors trading in the contract. Let's take a closer look at the Treasury bond futures contract. If you buy one December 1998 Treasury bond futures contract, you have the right and obligation to receive $100,000 of 15-year maturity government bonds during December 1998. The seller of the contract has the right and obligation to deliver those bonds at that time. In futures market terminology the buyer of the contract is called **long** and the seller is called **short.** All of the terms of the contract—$100,000 of 15-year government bonds, December delivery, and so on—are established by the Chicago Board of Trade, which sponsors Treasury bond futures trading. The only matter left for negotiation between the buyer and seller of the contract is the price at which the bonds will be delivered. And that is determined by the often frenetic bidding and offering that occurs at the location (called a *pit*) on the floor of the Chicago Board of Trade where the auction in Treasury bond futures is conducted.

Note that the standardization of contract terms is designed to promote liquidity, the ability to buy and sell quickly with low transactions costs. Large trading volume promotes narrow bid-asked spreads, as we saw in Chapter 6. Futures exchanges promote large trading volume by standardizing the terms of futures contracts, allowing many individuals to trade the identical commodity.

Of equal importance in promoting the liquidity of futures contracts is the nature of the auction process itself. All orders for a particular contract are directed to a single pit on the exchange floor. The trading pit is circular in shape, with tiered steps where traders stand facing each other. Buying and selling interests must be represented quite literally by open outcry. The scene most closely resembles controlled chaos. But the result is that all orders are exposed to the highest bid and lowest offer, thereby guaranteeing execution at the best possible price.

---

[1]A nonstandardized agreement to buy or sell an asset at a future date at a currently agreed-upon price is called a **forward contract.** Market participants use forward contracts in much the same way as futures, except that forwards are customized and traded over the counter rather than on organized exchanges.

For example, if you are interested in buying the December 1998 Treasury bond futures contract, you might be told by your account executive that the prevailing bid in the Treasury bond pit is $97\,^2/_{32}$ per $100 face value of bonds, with the best offer at $97\,^3/_{32}$. You may then instruct your account executive to buy one contract from someone in the trading pit who is offering at $97\,^3/_{32}$. You will then be long one December bond future at a price $97\,^3/_{32}$, and the trader in the crowd will be short one December bond future at $97\,^3/_{32}$.

At this point a number of institutional arrangements in futures markets take over. Although both you—the long—and the short have a contractual agreement to receive and deliver the underlying bonds, respectively, you no longer look to each other to exercise those rights and obligations. Rather the **clearing corporation** associated with the futures exchange, consisting of well-capitalized members of the exchange, interposes itself between you and the short. In particular, the long looks to the clearing corporation to satisfy the delivery obligation, and the short looks to the clearing corporation to pay the amount due on the delivery date. In this way the clearing corporation reduces the credit risk exposure associated with future deliveries of the underlying securities. Shorts and longs do not have to worry that the other party will not perform their contractual obligations.

The clearing corporation, in turn, has a number of special institutional practices to reduce its own credit risk exposure. First, both the short and long must place a deposit, called **margin,** with the clearing corporation. Margin is a performance bond that *both* buyers and sellers must deposit. If it were a down payment on the ultimate purchase price, it would be required of the buyer only. Second, the clearing corporation requires that gains and losses be settled each day in what is called **mark-to-market settlement.** Thus, if the price of the December Treasury bond future rises from $97\,^3/_{32}$ to $98\,^3/_{32}$, the value of your (long) position has increased by $1 per $100 face value of bonds. On the $100,000 contract you have a profit of $1,000, and the short has a loss of $1,000. The clearing corporation collects this sum from the short and transfers it to you at the end of the trading day as part of its mark-to-market settlement. In order to facilitate the collection process, the futures exchange imposes *price limits* on the amount that the futures contract can change each day. For example, in the Treasury bond contract, prices cannot change by more than $3 per $100 face value. Thus, a maximum of $2,000 can be transferred out of or into your account each day.[2]

The rights and obligations represented by having a long or short position in Treasury bond futures can be intimidating to say the least. The short must

---

[2]Do not let this give you a false sense of security. In particular, this does not mean that your losses are limited by the futures exchange's price limits. Prices can continue to rise or fall the next day, before you have had a chance to reverse your position. For example, if you are short and the price of the Treasury bond contract rises the limit because there are many buyers and literally no sellers, you must remain short until trading is resumed the following day. If the preponderance of buying interest continues, your losses are extended the following day.

READING THE FINANCIAL NEWS

Financial Futures Quotations

(1)	(2)	(3)	(4)	(5)	(6)	(7)	(8)	(9)
(L1)			Treasury Bonds (CBT)—$100,000; pts. 32nds of 100%					
June	100–13	100–25	100–13	100–23	+ 14	7.928	−0.44	192,839
Sept	99–13	99–26	99–13	99–24	+ 15	8.025	−.048	13,051
Dec	98–16	98–26	98–15	98–24	+ 13	8.328	−.041	3,779
Mr	97–25	97–28	97–23	97–27	+ 13	8.221	−.043	3,680
June	96–26	97–00	96–22	97–00	+ 14	8.310	−.047	3,293
Sept	95–29	96–05	95–29	96–04	+ 13	8.403	−.044	1.744
(L2)			Est vol 135,000, vol Wed 125,793, open int 233,373, + 1,972.					
			Treasury Notes (CBT)—$100,000; pts. 32nds of 100%					
June	103–24	103–30	103–24	103–29	+ 6	7.439	−.027	44,841
Sept	103–02	103–97	103–02	103–06	+ 6	7.540	−.027	5,092
Dec	—	—	—	102–18	+ 7	7.629	−.031	260
			Est vol 11,000; vol Wed 7,239; open int 54,213, + 976.					
			Treasury Bills (IMM)—$1 mil.; pts of 100%					
June	94.44	94.45	94.30	94.43	+.02	5.57	−.02	29.938
Sept	94.49	94.30	94.47	94.49	+.02	5.51	−.02	5,757
Dec	94.53	94.53	94.46	94.49	+.01	5.51	−.01	1,698
Mr	94.46	94.46	94.40	94.45	+.01	5.55	−.01	739
June	94.34	94.37	94.30	94.35	—	5.65	—	293
			Est vol 5,745; vol Wed 5,814; open int 38,574, + 91.					
			Indices					
(L3)			S&P 500 Index (CME) 500 times Index					
June	305.30	305.70	302.65	303.40	−.20	305.70	228.90	95,994
Sept	307.20	307.50	304.70	305.35	−.10	307.50	229.90	1,532
Dec	308.00	309.20	306.80	307.30	−.05	309.20	243.20	922
			Est vol 70,300; vol Wed 69,149; open int 98,453, + 1.129					
			Index (prelim.) High 302.72; Low 300.38; Close 300.93 + 55					

Futures market quotations appear in a variety of formats in daily newspapers, so you have to read the headings of the columns and rows in each case. In the accompanying example, line (L1) indicates that Treasury bond contracts follow immediately below, that the exchange on which the bond contract is traded is the CBT (Chicago Board of Trade), that the size of the contract is $100,000, and that quotations are in percentage points plus thirty-seconds per $100 face value. Each of the lines listed beneath the Treasury bond heading refers to a specific contract month. At the bottom of the Treasury bond listings, line (L2) records a number of items: The particular day's trading volume in contracts for all months is estimated at 135,000 contracts; the exact volume traded on the previous day (Wednesday) is listed as 125,793 contracts. The last item on line (L2) is open interest. That refers to the total number of long positions outstanding (equal to the total number of short positions outstanding) and is reported at 233,373 contracts, which is an increase of 1,972 contracts over the previous day.

(continued)

Now let's look at the nine columns of information. Column (1) lists the specific contract month. The first entry is June and the last entry is for September of the following year. In other words, the CBT sponsors trading in six different contract months for Treasury bond futures. Columns (2), (3), (4), and (5) refer to the opening, high, low, and closing (or settlement) price of the contract. Thus for the first June contract, the closing price is recorded at $100^{23}/_{32}$. Column (6) indicates that the settlement price is up $^{14}/_{32}$ compared with yesterday's settlement. Since each full percentage point in the Treasury bond contract is worth $1,000, column (6) suggests that the futures contract is worth $437.50 more than the previous day ($^{14}/_{32} \times \$1,000$). Column (7) translates the settlement price into a yield based on an 8 percent-coupon 15-year Treasury bond. Because the settlement price is above par ($^{23}/_{32}$ above par), it is not surprising that the yield is listed as 7.928 percent (less than the 8 percent coupon assumed for the underlying bond). Column (8) shows that the change in yield from the previous close is −.044 (which means that yesterday the yield was 7.972 percent). Column (9) lists the open interest of the particular contract month. The June contract has 192,839 contracts outstanding, which is considerably larger than any other contract month.

Columns (7) and (8) are used to report historical high and low prices for the contracts that do not have interest rate components. For example, in the S&P 500 Stock Index contracts listed under line (L3), the June contract has a historical high price of 305.70 in column (7) and a historical low price of 228.90 in column (8).

actually deliver $100,000 in Treasury bonds during the delivery month, while the long must come up with the cash when delivery takes place. This can be embarrassing if the long doesn't have the money or the short doesn't have the bonds. Most traders in futures markets, therefore, choose **settlement by offset** rather than delivery. In particular, longs may settle their rights and obligations at any time by making an offsetting sale of the identical December 1998 Treasury bond contract, while shorts may cancel their rights and obligations at any time by making an offsetting purchase. The clearing corporation keeps track of all buyers and sellers and closes out a trader's position when there is both a purchase and a sale of the identical contract on its books for the same account. Don't ask what happens when the clearing corporation's computer goes haywire.

Settlement by offset permits hedgers, speculators, and arbitrageurs to make legitimate use of the futures market without getting into the technical details of making or taking delivery of the underlying asset. Now let's see exactly what these legitimate activities by hedgers, speculators, and arbitrageurs actually are.

Using Financial Futures Contracts

The most important activity provided by futures markets is the opportunity to hedge legitimate commercial activities. **Hedgers** buy or sell futures contracts to reduce their exposure to the risk of future price movements in the underlying asset. For example, a government securities dealer who has just purchased newly issued government bonds at the Treasury's auction must hold those bonds in inventory until ultimate investors (pension funds, insurance companies, and individuals) place orders to buy the securities. In the meantime, the dealer is exposed to the risk that interest rates will rise and the bonds will fall in price.

Nothing makes dealers more unhappy than losses on their inventory. The dealer can avoid that outcome by taking a short position in Treasury bond futures. Since the price of bond futures moves almost in lockstep with the price of the underlying bonds (thanks to the activities of arbitrageurs, as we will see in the next section), a decrease in the value of the dealer's inventory because bond prices decline will be offset by the dealer's short position in Treasury bond futures. For example, if the bonds in the dealer's inventory fall in price from $99 to $98, the dealer loses $1 for each $100 in inventory. If the dealer sold Treasury bond futures short, however, the associated $1 decline in the futures contract will provide an offsetting profit.

Notice that as soon as the dealer's inventory of government bonds has been sold to ultimate investors, the dealer should offset the short position in the futures market by buying back the identical Treasury bond futures. Reversing the position is proper, because once the bonds have been sold there is no need to maintain the short position in bond futures as a hedge against price decreases. The moral of the story is that legitimate hedging use of the futures market occurs with a sale of a futures contract and a subsequent offsetting purchase. Despite contrary propaganda by assorted members of Congress, a hedger does not have to make delivery, or even intend to make delivery, when using futures contracts to offset risk.

Another type of hedge involves taking a long position in a futures contract rather than a short position. For example, a pension fund may anticipate a need to buy bonds one month in the future, after it has accumulated sufficient cash from pension-holder contributions. If the pension fund manager waits until the month is out to buy the bonds and bond prices rise in the interim, then the funds will be invested at lower yields. To hedge the risk that bond prices will rise before the funds are actually invested, the pension fund manager buys Treasury bond futures. If bond prices go up under these circumstances, the long position in Treasury bond futures generates a profit to offset the higher price the pension fund pays for the bonds.

We have just seen that legitimate hedgers in financial futures can be either buyers or sellers of futures contracts. "Short hedgers" offset inventory risk by selling futures, while "long hedgers" offset anticipated purchases of securities by buying futures. Sometimes short hedgers sell contracts to long hedgers. But that would be an accidental occurrence. There is nothing to guarantee that legitimate hedging activities by shorts and longs will coincide in the marketplace. That is where speculators enter the picture.

Unlike hedgers, **speculators** purposely take on risk when buying or selling futures contracts. For example, if short hedgers depress the price of the Treasury bond contract by their sales, speculators will be induced to buy those contracts in anticipation of a price increase once the hedging pressure has subsided. Similarly, speculators will be induced to sell contracts if the buying activity of long hedgers temporarily drives up the price of the Treasury bond contract. Speculators take on the risk of price movements from hedgers. They expect to earn a profit in the process. If they're good at their craft they earn a return for their time, skill, and invested capital; if they're not so good they go into some other line of business very quickly—with a lot less capital than before.

Pricing Financial Futures Contracts

The buying and selling activities of hedgers and speculators together determine the price of a futures contract. More selling drives the price lower; more buying drives the price higher. Although this sounds trite, it's the best way to describe price determination in the futures market (or any market, for that matter). We can be somewhat more sophisticated, however, when describing the *relationship* between the price of the futures contract and the price of the assets that underlie the futures contract. The relationship between the price in the so-called "cash market" and the price in the futures market is determined by **arbitrageurs.** Their activities are crucial for hedgers, because, as we saw in our example in the previous section, the price of the futures contract and the price of the underlying securities must move together if hedgers are to be able to reduce their risk by taking offsetting positions in the futures market.

The main reason the price of the futures contract moves closely with the price of the underlying security is that during the delivery period (say, December 1998) there are rights and obligations to deliver the *actual* securities specified in the contract. During the delivery period, in fact, these rights and obligations force the price of the futures contract and the price of the underlying security to be one and the same. Here's why. If the price of the futures contract were higher than the price of the actual securities during the delivery period, then it would pay arbitrageurs to sell the futures at the higher price, simultaneously buy the securities at the lower price, pocket the price difference, and deliver the securities in satisfaction of their obligations as shorts. This activity drives down the futures price and drives up the price of the underlying securities until they are equal.

On the other hand, if the price of the futures contract were below the price of the underlying security, it would pay the arbitrageur to buy the futures contract and sell the actual security. This time, as the buyer of the futures contract, the arbitrageur would take delivery of the securities and then turn around and deliver them to whoever bought them in the cash market, pocketing the price differential in the process. In this case the arbitrageurs drive up the futures price and drive down the price of the underlying commodity until they are equal.

It doesn't take a genius to make money as an arbitrageur. Just about anyone who can participate in the cash and futures markets simultaneously will recognize the wisdom of instant profits and will undertake these arbitrage activities. Thus, the activities of arbitrageurs will be massive and cause the price of the futures contract and the price of the underlying securities to converge on the delivery date.

A similar arbitrage prior to the final delivery date reinforces the comovement between futures prices and the price of the underlying securities, as long as the securities can be stored by arbitrageurs. The main difference is that prior to the delivery period, the arbitrageur would compare the futures price with the price of the underlying securities plus the cost of carrying those securities to the final delivery date. Price discrepancies will lead to buying and selling in the cash and futures markets until prices are brought into proper alignment. In particular, at any point the price of the futures contract would be equal to the price of the underlying security plus carrying costs.[3] More importantly for hedgers, whenever the price of the underlying security changes, arbitrageurs will push the price of the futures in the same direction.

The activities of hedgers, speculators, and arbitrageurs combine to make futures markets important risk management arenas for financial institutions. It pays for banks, insurance companies, pension funds, and others to participate in futures markets, because the standardization of the contracts creates a facility for managing risk exposure at low transactions costs. The fact that the futures contract mirrors the cash market, but with lower transactions costs, is the main contribution of futures markets to the financial marketplace. A very different dimension to risk management is offered by options contracts, as we will see in the next few sections.

AN OVERVIEW OF OPTIONS CONTRACTS

Options contracts have both a shorter and a longer history in financial markets than futures contracts. Options on individual stocks have been traded in the over-the-counter market since the nineteenth century. The public visibility of options increased dramatically, however, in 1972 when the Chicago Board Options Exchange (CBOE) standardized the terms of the contracts and introduced futures-type pit trading. As shown in Table 9.1, in addition to the CBOE, options contracts are now listed on the American Stock Exchange, the Philadelphia Stock Exchange, the Pacific Stock Exchange, and the New York Stock Exchange. In addition, most of the nation's futures exchanges sponsor options on futures contracts. At this point, the options listings in the newspaper rival the stocks themselves for investors' attention.

---

[3]The main cost of carrying securities is the interest rate on the funds tied up in the purchase. Thus, in September 1998, the price of the December 1998 Treasury bond futures would equal the price of the underlying Treasury bonds plus the net interest cost of carrying those bonds from September 1998 until they can be delivered in December.

TABLE 9.1   Examples of Options Contracts

Specific contracts	Exchange
Options on Individual Equities	
IBM, GM, GE	Chicago Board Options Exchange
Disney, GTE, DuPont	American Stock Exchange
Honda, Dell	Philadelphia Stock Exchange
Genentech, Gannett	Pacific Stock Exchange
NYNEX, Campbells Soup	New York Stock Exchange
Options on Indices	
S&P 100, S&P 500	Chicago Board Options Exchange
Major Market Index	American Stock Exchange
New York Stock Exchange Index	New York Stock Exchange
Options on Interest Rate Futures	
Treasury bonds, Treasury notes	Chicago Board of Trade
Eurodollar, Treasury bills	Chicago Mercantile Exchange
Options on Foreign Currency Futures	
German mark, Japanese yen	Chicago Mercantile Exchange

To appreciate what this options activity is all about, we must examine the contractual obligations of buyers and sellers of options. These contractual obligations are more complicated than futures contracts.

Like futures contracts, options are derivative financial instruments; that is, they derive their value from some underlying asset. In traditional stock options, the underlying asset refers to 100 shares of a particular stock, such as General Motors or IBM. In other cases, the underlying asset is a basket of equities represented by some overall stock index, such as the S&P 500 Index or the S&P 100 Index. These are called stock index options, and the contractual obligations are defined by some dollar value of the index, either $500 times the index or $100 times the index. Finally, in options on futures contracts, the contractual obligations call for the delivery of one futures contract. Although the precise value of an option depends upon exactly what the underlying asset is, there are a number of elements common to all options contracts that we can explore.

All types of options come in two varieties: **puts** and **calls.** Let's begin our story with calls, because they are somewhat more popular. The buyer of a call option has the right (but not the obligation) to buy a given quantity of the underlying asset at a predetermined price, called the **exercise** or **strike price,** at any time prior to the expiration date of the option. For example, you may instruct your account executive at a brokerage firm to place an order at the CBOE to buy a call on IBM with an exercise price of $150 and an expiration date of September 1998. Once your order is executed, you are "long" the IBM

$150 call. This option gives you the right to purchase 100 shares of IBM at a price of $150 at any time prior to September 1998. The seller of that option, called the short (or the option writer), has the *obligation* (not the right) to deliver those shares to you at a price of $150.[4]

Note that, unlike futures contracts, the rights and obligations of option buyers and option sellers are not symmetrical. The buyer of the option acquires rights and the seller of the option takes on obligations. The buyer of the call option pays a price to the seller for the rights acquired. This makes considerable sense, because the option seller would be foolish to take on obligations without any compensation. The price paid for the option is often called the *value of the option* or the **option premium.** The premium is paid by the long to the short as soon as the option is purchased.[5]

Before examining the determination of option premiums, let's see what rights and obligations are conveyed by put options. The buyer of a put option on IBM with a strike price of $150 and an expiration date of September 1998 has the right (but not the obligation) to *sell* 100 shares of IBM at a price of $150 on or before September 1998. The seller of the put option, called the short or the option writer, has the *obligation* (but not the right) to receive or buy those shares at a price of $150. In consideration of those rights, the buyer of the put option pays a premium to the seller of the put option.

This has been pretty complicated, so let's summarize: Option buyers have rights; option sellers have obligations. Call buyers have the right to buy the underlying asset; put buyers have the right to sell the underlying asset. In both puts and calls the option buyer pays a premium to the option seller.

Note that in our example of the IBM call and put we used the same strike price and the same expiration date. Although there are a number of different strike prices and expiration dates for each exchange-traded option, the exchange sponsoring the trading establishes rules for determining which strike prices and expiration dates will be traded for each option (see the Reading The Financial News box for an example with options on Treasury bond futures). This standardization is designed to elicit interest by many potential traders, thereby promoting contract liquidity.

As with futures contracts, there is also a clearing corporation that guarantees the performance of contractual obligations, so that buyers and sellers of exchange traded options do not have to be concerned with the creditworthiness of their trading partners.[6] The only matter up for negotiation on the floor of the exchange is the option premium—the price the option buyer pays to the

---

[4]The option described here is called an American option, because it gives the right to buy IBM at any time until September 1998. European options (which are also traded in the United States) give the right to buy the underlying asset on (but not before) the expiration date.

[5]Note that in futures contracts both the long and short have rights and obligations, so that there is no premium paid at the time the contractual obligation is struck. In a futures contract only the price at which the future delivery will take place is agreed upon.

[6]Unlike futures contracts, options do not have mark-to-market settlement, nor are there any price limits associated with options.

seller for the rights conferred. Let's turn to the determinants of the option premium and see how options are used by individuals and institutions.

Using and Valuing Options

Perhaps the best way to understand why individual investors and financial institutions use options is to look at what an option is worth on the expiration date of the contract. In doing so it is important to remember that investors who buy options, either calls or puts, have rights but no obligations. Therefore option buyers will do whatever is in their best interest on the expiration date. Let's take a look at the value of our IBM call with a $150 exercise price.

Although options are complicated, there are only two possibilities on the expiration date that must be evaluated: The price of IBM can be above $150 or the price can be below $150. If the price of IBM stock is below $150, say $145, the call option to buy IBM at $150 on the expiration date is worthless. The call buyer obviously chooses not to exercise the right to buy IBM at $150. Thus the value of the call is zero. On the other hand, if the price of IBM on the New York Stock Exchange is above $150, say $155, then the option to call (buy) the stock at $150 has value. In fact, if IBM is trading at $155, the call is worth exactly $5 per share of stock on expiration. The call is worth $5 per share because the investor can exercise the option—that is, demand that the option writer deliver IBM at $150—and then immediately sell the shares for $155.

This discussion implies that the payoff on expiration to a long call position is either equal to zero (if the stock is below the exercise price) or equal to the stock price minus the exercise price (if the stock price is above the exercise price); this is called the **intrinsic value** of the option. A similar argument shows that on expiration, a long put position has a value of zero if the stock price is *above* the exercise price and a value equal to the exercise price minus the stock price (this is just the opposite of the call) if the stock price is below the exercise price. For example, the owner of a $150 put on IBM will not want to exercise the right to sell IBM at $150 if IBM is selling at $155 on the stock exchange; but if IBM is selling for $140, then the put owner's right to sell IBM at $150 is worth exactly $10 on expiration.

One of the main advantages of buying options is the asymmetrical payoff just outlined. Buying a call provides unlimited upside potential, if the underlying asset rises in price, but a maximum downside risk of the premium paid initially if the underlying asset falls in price. Similarly, buying a put provides everincreasing profit as the underlying asset falls in price but a maximum loss of the initial premium if the asset rises in price. This asymmetrical payoff has the characteristic of insurance, which may be the reason the price paid for an option is called the option premium. As with all insurance policies, if nothing happens (your car does not get hit by a tree), the premium paid is gone and you receive no benefits. For option buyers, the premium paid is a cost and there are no offsetting benefits if the price of the underlying asset does not move up significantly (in the case of a call) or down significantly (in the case of a put).

Options Quotations

(1)	(2)	(3)	(4)	(5)	(6)	(7)

(L1) T-Bonds (CBT) $100,000; points and 64ths of 100%

Strike	Calls—Last			Puts—Last		
Price	Jun-c	Sep-c	Dec-c	Jun-p	Sep-p	Dec-p
96	4–50	4–33	—	0–07	0–56	1–35
98	2–62	3–04	—	0–19	1–27	2–12
100	1–32	1–58	2–00	0–49	2–10	3–10
102	0–36	1–09	1–21	1–52	3–22	—
104	0–12	0–41	—	3–27	—	—
106	0–03	0–22	0–32	—	—	—

(L2) Est. vol. 35,000, Wed vol. 19,189 calls, 17,065 puts
Open interest Wed; 250,647 calls, 186,050 puts

T-Notes (CBT) $100,000; points and 64ths of 100%

Strike	Calls—Last			Puts—Last		
Price	Jun-c	Sep-c	Dec-c	Jun-p	Sep-p	Dec-p
100	3–60	—	—	0–02	0–18	0–37
102	2–03	1–52	1–41	0–08	0–41	1–07
104	0–36	0–46	0–51	0–42	1–33	—
106	0–05	0–15	0–21	2–08	2–60	—
108	0–01	0–05	—	4–04	—	—
110	0–01	0–02	—	—	—	—

Est. vol. 9,200, Wed vol. 1,508 calls. 1,803 puts
Open interest Wed; 42,402 calls, 25,466 puts

Although options quotations in the daily newspaper differ slightly depending upon whether the underlying asset is a particular stock or a futures contract, they all share a number of common characteristics. In the accompanying example, for options on futures, line (L1) indicates that what follows immediately below are options on Treasury bond futures, that these options are traded on the Chicago Board of Trade (CBT), that the size of the underlying futures contract is $100,000, and that the quotations are percentage points plus sixty-fourths (per $100 face value). Immediately beneath the Treasury bond listing, line (L2) records the day's estimated trading volume for both puts and calls as 35,000 contracts and the previous day's volume as 19,189 call contracts and 17,065 put contracts. Beneath that line the open interest as of the previous day is recorded. Open interest is the number of open long (equal to short) positions. The open interest for calls is recorded as 250,647 contracts and the open interest for puts as 186,050 contracts. Since puts and calls are completely separate contracts, there is no need for the open interest on the two types of options to be related.

Now let's look at the columns of information. Column (1) shows the strike (exercise) price for each of the options available for the Treasury bond contract. The first line refers to options with a strike price of 96 and the last line refers to options with a strike

(continued)

price of 106. As you can see, the rules of the CBT call for strike prices that are 2 points apart. Columns (2), (3), and (4) list the closing (settlement) prices for call options with three different expiration dates—June, September, and December. For example, the 100 calls with a September expiration have a closing price of $1^{58}\!/_{64}$. Since each full percentage point on the Treasury bond contract is worth $1,000, the September 100 call costs $1,906.25. Notice that for some specific options—the 104 calls with a December expiration, for example—no price is listed because there was no trading in that particular contract. Columns (5), (6), and (7) record the closing prices for the June, September, and December put options.

The main difference in the quotation conventions for options on individual stocks is that the closing price of the stock itself is listed (usually in the extreme left-hand column). In addition, open interest and option trading volume are not usually recorded for individual equities.

This analogy with insurance, in fact, provides the best insight into how options are used by hedgers. Let's return to our earlier example of hedging with Treasury bond futures. We showed that securities dealers who have just bought Treasury securities in the auction could protect their inventory by selling Treasury bond futures. As an alternative strategy, a dealer could buy puts on Treasury bond futures. In this case, if bond prices fall, the value of the inventory falls, causing a loss. But as our discussion of puts has just showed, the value of the put increases as the price of the underlying asset falls. This offsets the loss in the dealer's inventory.

The main difference in the two hedging strategies occurs if bond prices rise rather than fall. The dealer who bought puts is clearly better off: Rising bond prices increase the value of the inventory, while the worst the puts can do is go out worthless on expiration day. The asymmetrical payoff on the put means that the dealer has protected his or her downside risk by buying the put while retaining upside potential through inventory. The dealer who sold bond futures as a hedge has an offsetting gain on the future if bond prices fall but also has an identical offsetting loss on the future if bond prices rise. Thus, selling futures as a hedge gives downside protection but also eliminates upside potential.

Why, then, doesn't everyone hedge with put options rather than futures? The answer, of course, is the premium. The option buyer pays something for the asymmetrical payoff. If bond prices don't fall, the put option expires worthless and the premium is lost. Hedging with futures, on the other hand, does not involve any premium payments. If option premiums are low it may very well pay to hedge with options, while if premiums are high futures may turn out to be more attractive hedging vehicles.

Note that hedging is not the only reason people buy options. Speculating that the price of Treasury bonds will go up is a lot less nerve-racking if an investor buys calls rather than the underlying securities (or the futures contract). In particular, buying a call limits your loss to the premium if prices go in the wrong direction (which is usually the case for most of us). Thus, even from the speculator's vantage point, option premiums represent the cost of insurance.

What Determines Option Premiums?

Since option premiums are important to both hedgers and speculators, let's take a look at what determines whether they are large or small. The obvious answer is that option premiums are determined just like any other price—by supply and demand. What we would like, however, is to provide an idea of what underlies the desire to pay a high price for an option (demand) compared with the willingness to sell options (supply). Since this is an extremely complicated subject, our discussion will be brief and intuitive rather than rigorous and mathematical. We'll examine calls first and then extend the discussion to puts.

Let's take our favorite option, the IBM calls with a strike price of $150. The price of such equity options is usually quoted per share, which means that multiplying by 100 (the number of shares the call owner is entitled to buy) gives the dollar price of the option. For example, if this IBM option were quoted at $5, it would cost $500 to buy; if the option were quoted at $15, it would cost $1,500, and so on. What determines whether the price of the IBM 150 calls is $5, $15, or $35? The three main factors are the current price of IBM stock, the volatility of IBM's stock price, and the time to expiration of the option. We will look at each factor in turn.

It should be fairly intuitive that a call option with a given exercise price will be worth more the higher the price of the underlying asset. If IBM stock is selling for $160, the $150 call gives you the right to buy 100 shares at a price which is $10 below the price at which you could sell the shares. Thus everyone would pay at least $10 for the IBM $150 calls if IBM stock sells for $160, since they could lock in an immediate profit if the call were selling for less. If IBM stock were selling for $180, for example, the $150 call would be worth at least $30. Somewhat more generally, options will sell for at least their intrinsic value at any time, even prior to expiration. And that means that a higher stock price implies a higher call value at all times.

But that can hardly be the entire story. If IBM stock were selling at $150 per share, the intrinsic value of the $150 calls would be zero, but the options could still be quite valuable. And that is especially true if the calls have a significant amount of time left before expiration. In particular, if the price of IBM is very volatile, and there is a lot of time before the option expires, then there is always a chance that the price could move up significantly between now and expiration. The greater the volatility of IBM stock, the higher its price can go, hence the more the call could be worth on expiration. Therefore, given the current price of the stock, call buyers will pay more for a call option

GOING OUT ON A LIMB

Don't Blame Derivatives

Derivatives were the scapegoat in the bankruptcy of California's Orange County municipal investment fund and were also blamed for the demise of Barings, the 300-year-old British investment bank. The facts are that in both cases derivatives were the side show rather than the main event. The root cause of Orange County's problems was an investment manager who overstepped his bounds speculating on the future course of U.S. interest rates. And Barings was brought down because a young trader went unsupervised by senior management even as he compounded speculative bets on Japan's Nikkei stock index.

In both of these cases, derivatives were used to implement the grand scale of the speculation. But that is not the usual case against these instruments. Allegations that derivatives are dangerous stem from their supposedly complicated payoffs, so that even sophisticated investors can be unpleasantly surprised by the outcome of a particular derivatives strategy. Clearly, that was not the problem with Orange County and Barings. In these two cases, derivatives were knowingly misused by sophisticated investors.

It is highly doubtful that derivatives are too complicated for sophisticated investors to use properly in designing a risk reduction strategy. Options, futures, and swaps are employed routinely on a daily basis by thousands of risk managers, often applying the basic strategies outlined in this chapter. Just because a few participants misuse these instruments should not lead to wholesale condemnation. That would be similar to banning scalpels just because Jack the Ripper probably used that particular surgical tool to murder his victims.

if the underlying stock is more volatile than otherwise. A similar argument makes option sellers less willing to write options on stock with large price volatility. Thus for any given price of the underlying asset, call option premiums will be larger for stocks with high price volatility.[7]

The impact of time to expiration on the value of a call is easily seen as an extension of what we have just said. A call option that expires six months from now has more time for the price of the underlying asset to rise above the exercise price than an option with only three months to expiration. Thus call option premiums will be higher the longer the maturity of the option.

To summarize, call options will be worth more the higher the price of the underlying asset, the greater the volatility of the underlying asset, and the longer the time to expiration of the option.

A similar discussion would show that premiums on put options will be higher the *lower* the price of the underlying asset, since the put gives the owner the right to sell at the exercise price. In particular, an IBM put with an

---

[7]Note that even though high volatility can mean large declines in price as well as large gains, the greater downside risk is less important to the call buyer than the enhanced upside potential because of the asymmetrical payoff to the call. The worst that can occur to the call buyer is that the call goes out worthless, while the upside potential is unlimited.

exercise price of $150 will be worth more if IBM is selling at $140 rather than $150. Higher price volatility of the underlying asset and longer time to expiration make put options more valuable for the same reason they make call options more valuable: There is more chance that the option will have higher intrinsic value on the expiration date.[8]

Option pricing comes in much more complicated varieties than we have described here. Mathematical arbitrage arguments produce a more rigorous set of results. But for our purposes we have gone far enough to recognize that options will be an expensive way to hedge portfolio risks if those risks are substantial. There is, after all is said and done, no such thing as a free lunch. In particular, if stock and bond prices are highly volatile, then option premiums will be large. Financial institutions will then have a difficult choice: Hedge with options to keep the upside potential while paying a substantial premium, or hedge with futures and forget about premiums and extra profitability. At last glance both options and futures markets had active participants from major financial institutions. Conclusion: Risk reduction takes many forms, depending upon its price (or put somewhat differently, you pay your money and take your chances).

AN OVERVIEW OF SWAPS

Swaps are relatively new on the derivatives landscape, having been invented in 1981 to help firms reduce interest rate risk. Since then swaps have grown to the point where they now involve transactions worth several trillion dollars per year. Swaps come in two broad varieties: **interest rate swaps** and **currency swaps.** Although both are important, to keep matters under control we will stick to the interest rate variety to illustrate how swaps work.

Like futures and options, a swap is a contractual agreement. In the case of a swap the two parties (referred to as **counterparties**) agree to exchange interest payments over a specific time period. One party to the transaction is called the **fixed-rate payer** and the other is called the **floating-rate payer.** Their obligations to each other might look like the following: The fixed-rate payer agrees to pay 10 percent per annum in each of the next five years; the floating-rate payer agrees to make payments based on some reference rate, such as the Treasury bill rate or LIBOR (the London interbank offered rate). The dollar amount of the payments made between the counterparties is determined by multiplying the interest rates by an agreed-upon principal, known as the **notional principal amount.** Before trying to understand why individuals or companies might enter into such a contract, let's see exactly what the counterparties have agreed to.

---

[8]As in footnote 7, only the favorable outcome of volatility gets priced in the option; the unfavorable price movements at worst only make the option value go to zero.

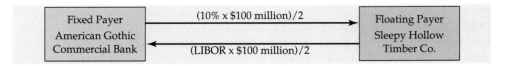

FIGURE 9.1   Obligations of payments every six months for the duration of the swap.

Unlike exchange traded futures and options contracts, swaps are customized agreements designed to the requirements of the counterparties. Nevertheless, there are some conventions adhered to. For example, suppose the American Gothic (AG) Commercial Bank agrees to pay 10 percent per annum over the next five years to Sleepy Hollow (SH) Timber Company, while SH agrees to pay to AG whatever six-month LIBOR is. Thus AG is the fixed-rate payer and SH is the floating-rate payer. The counterparties agree that the notional principal amount is $100 million. By convention the interest payments are made every six months. Thus, AG will pay SH $5 million (10 percent times $100 million divided by 2) every six months for the next five years. The payments by SH to AG depend upon six-month LIBOR. So if six-month LIBOR is currently 8 percent, then SH pays AG $4 million (8 percent times $100 million divided by 2) six months from now. The second payment by SH to AG will depend on what six-month LIBOR turns out to be. Thus if six-month LIBOR is 7 percent in six months, the payment will be $3.5 million (7 percent times $100 million divided by 2) at the end of one year. Note that the fixed-rate payer (AG) always pays the same amount, while payments by the floating-rate payer (SH) vary according to the reference rate. The notional principal amount is never exchanged, just the interest payments. Figure 9.1 illustrates the specific obligations between the two counterparties.

Swaps can be structured just about any way to accommodate the counterparties. Although LIBOR has emerged as the most popular reference rate for establishing payments by the floating-rate payer, Treasury bill rates and commercial paper rates are some obvious alternatives.

What determines whether the fixed-rate payer pays 10 percent or 11 percent when receiving LIBOR? Two important factors are the shape of the yield curve and default risk (both of which are discussed in Chapter 5). In the case of our five-year swap, if five-year Treasury securities were yielding 9.0 percent and American Gothic were an Aaa-rated company, AG might pay 1 percent over five-year Treasuries for a total of 10 percent. On the other hand, if AG were a less creditworthy bank it might have to pay 1.5 percent above five-year Treasuries for a total fixed payment of 10.5 percent. Notice that default risk plays a role even though the notional principal amount is not exchanged because the counterparties might default on the scheduled interest payments.

Financial institutions, such as banks and securities dealers, help bring the counterparties to a swap together, often interposing their own credit between counterparties who may not know each other. Thus, American Gothic and Sleepy Hollow may prefer to exchange payments with the Safe and Sound

National Bank, rather than each other. Safe and Sound will be more than happy to accommodate them and will charge a fee accordingly. This makes AG and SH more comfortable, but may leave Safe and Sound with the obligation to make either fixed or floating payments in case one of the counterparties defaults. Needless to say, Safe and Sound checks out AG and SH and varies their fee according to the respective credit ratings.

Why Swap?

As conservative businesses, American Gothic and Sleepy Hollow enter into a swap to reduce risk exposure. For example, suppose AG makes a five-year $100-million commercial loan and raises funds the old-fashioned way, by issuing six-month certificates of deposits to its favorite depositors. The five-year commercial loan yields 12 percent and the six-month CDs cost 7 percent. Although this is profitable, closer examination by AG's chief financial officer shows that the package is risky because six months from now CD rates might rise, causing AG's profit to decline or disappear. AG could reduce this risk by finding a counterparty who would be willing to pay AG the six-month interest rate (so AG could cover its CD costs) and in exchange AG would pay a fixed rate for five years. If that fixed payment were 10 percent per annum (as in our example above) AG would still make a profit on its loan (which yields 12 percent).

Now let's turn to the Sleepy Hollow Timber Company. Suppose Sleepy Hollow has just completed a successful debt offering, issuing ten-year notes at a fixed rate of $9\frac{3}{4}$ percent. Having been in business for over one hundred years, SH has a long-term outlook and does not anticipate needing any of its newly raised cash for five years. So it takes the proceeds and invests in six-month Eurodollar deposits because the London branch of its long-standing banker promises a very attractive rate, especially since SH promises to renew the Eurodollar deposits every six months for the next five years. The main problem with this strategy is that Eurodollar rates may decline over the next five years, leaving SH to pay the fixed $9\frac{3}{4}$ percent on its debt but earning less on its short-term investments. Clearly SH could reduce its risk exposure by finding a counterparty who would pay SH a fixed rate (say 10 percent over the next five years) and in exchange SH would pay a floating rate based on six-month LIBOR (which is the rate earned by SH on its six-month Eurodollar deposits).

Along comes the Safe and Sound National Bank and brings AG and SH together in a swap agreement: AG pays fixed and receives floating; SH pays floating and receives the fixed; and Safe and Sound earns a commission for realizing that a 10 percent fixed payment works for both. More generally, Safe and Sound earns a commission for arranging a transaction that allows both AG and SH to reduce their risk exposure while maintaining a profit.

What we have just described is a generic swap, sometimes referred to as a "plain vanilla" swap. The objective of both participants in this example was to undo maturity mismatches in their respective balance sheets. The controversy over derivatives, in general, and swaps, in particular, does not revolve around cases such as these. Rather, swaps become unpleasant when they generate losses and when one of the counterparties is a closet speculator rather than a hedger. To understand the danger involved let's see what causes the value of a swap contract to go up or down.

Valuing a Swap

Swap contracts are traded in the over-the-counter market just like corporate bonds. Thus American Gothic could sell its swap obligation (to receive floating and pay fixed) to someone else. The question is whether AG would have to pay someone to take over its contractual obligations or might it receive something in exchange? Let's see what determines how much the swap contract is worth, using the numerical example developed above.

American Gothic has the following contractual agreement: It has agreed to pay $5 million every six months for the next five years and, in exchange, will receive every six months a dollar payment equal to six-month LIBOR times $100 million divided by 2. If AG asked Citibank to take on this contract one day after the contract was entered into, what would Citibank do? The first step would be to see what today's swaps are paying for the right to receive six-month LIBOR. If five-year interest rates have increased, say, to 12 percent, then a payment of $6 million would be needed (12 percent times $100 million divided by 2) to receive six-month LIBOR, while if five-year interest rates declined to 8 percent, then a payment of $4 million would be needed. Thus if interest rates rise, the fixed-rate payer (AG) has a valuable swap on its hands because it pays $5 million rather than $6 million every six months to receive six-month LIBOR. In this case, AG will be able to sell its swap contract to Citibank at a profit. On the other hand, if interest rates decline, AG has an unprofitable swap contract because it pays $5 million rather than $4 million every six months to receive six-month LIBOR. Thus AG would have to pay Citibank to take on its swap contract.

A similar exercise would show the reverse for the floating-rate payer, although in the interest of mercy we'll spare the details. The point of the exercise is that swaps produce gains and losses just like options and futures contracts.[9]

Now we understand why swaps can be dangerous. Both American Gothic and Sleepy Hollow entered into a swap agreement with the objective of reducing risk. And that not only wasn't dangerous, it was eminently sensible. However, there is nothing to prevent some swashbuckling speculator from entering into a swap agreement hoping to profit on future movements of interest rates. In this case, swaps can easily inflict losses. And if that speculator happens to work for a bank, insurance company, or pension fund manager, the

---

[9]In fact, swaps are identical to a series of custom-designed futures contracts—called forward contracts—on interest rate securities. For example, if interest rates go down and bond prices go up, the fixed-rate payer loses money, just like someone who has sold Treasury bond futures, while if interest goes up and bond prices go down the fixed-rate payer makes money, just like someone who has sold Treasury bond futures. This is not surprising since the fixed-rate payer has contracted to pay a fixed amount to receive a payment that will be higher if interest rates are higher and smaller if interest rates are lower.

headline that reads "Swaps Cause Bankruptcies" should read "Speculators Cause Bankruptcies." Now that might not make the losses any smaller, but it certainly puts swaps in a very different light.

SUMMARY

1. Financial futures contracts include the following: interest rate futures, such as Treasury bonds and Eurodollars; stock index futures, such as the S&P 500; and foreign currency futures, such as the German mark. They are used by financial institutions to reduce risk of price changes in the underlying securities. Long hedgers reduce risk by buying futures contracts, short hedgers reduce risk by selling contracts.

2. Futures contracts are priced by the balance of supply of and demand for contracts by hedgers, speculators, and arbitrageurs. The activities of arbitrageurs produces a close relationship between the price of futures contracts and the underlying financial asset.

3. Options are divided into puts and calls. Buyers of puts have the right to sell at a fixed exercise price, while buyers of calls have the right to buy at a fixed exercise price. The option sellers (or writers) have the obligation to do what the buyers want. In consideration of the rights received, option buyers pay a premium to option sellers.

4. Financial institutions can use options to hedge their risks. The asymmetric payoffs to both puts and calls—unlimited gains with limited losses—can make options especially attractive.

5. The prices of all options—their premiums—are larger the greater the price volatility of the underlying asset and the longer the time to expiration of the option. In addition, puts are worth more when the price of the underlying asset is low, and calls are worth more when the price of the underlying asset is high.

6. Interest rate swaps are contractual agreements between two parties who agree to exchange interest payments over a specific time period. Financial institutions can use swaps to reduce the risk exposure associated with a mismatch of maturities on their balance sheets.

7. The value of a swap changes when interest rates move up and down. Hedgers don't mind so much when this happens, but speculators do.

QUESTIONS

9.1 Do legitimate hedgers in the futures market normally expect to deliver (or take delivery of) the underlying asset? Why or why not?

9.2 Explain the process forcing the price of the futures contract into equality with the price of the underlying asset during the delivery period.

9.3 Explain the rights and obligations of the buyer and seller of a call option. Compare these with the rights and obligations of the buyer and seller of a futures contract.

9.4 What is the difference in terms of potential profit and loss of hedging an inventory of Treasury bonds by selling futures contracts versus buying put options?

9.5 Why is an option worth more the greater the volatility of the underlying stock?

9.6 Explain why the fixed-rate payer in an interest rate swap is happy when interest rates go up?

9.7 *Discussion question:* Since swaps, options, and futures are complicated instruments, should we have laws that restrict participation in these markets to "suitable" investors?

CHAPTER 10

Understanding Foreign Exchange

Big banks and corporations used to do only a small part of their business overseas, but now many of them have branches worldwide. Before World War II, only the wealthy could afford to vacation in Europe, but now tens of thousands of college students fly there every summer. Any time a transaction takes place between the residents of two different countries, one kind of money has to be exchanged for another. What matters to most of us is whether we will have to pay a little or a lot for a French franc or a German mark.

Exchanges of one kind of money for another are made on the foreign exchange market, which consists of a network of foreign exchange dealers, such as banks, that buy and sell foreign monies in the form of foreign currencies and deposits in foreign banks throughout the business day. More familiar to most people are currency exchanges, which deal mainly with tourists; they are found downtown, at airports, and at railroad stations in all the major tourist centers.

The price of foreign money, the **foreign exchange rate,** like the price of anything that is bought and sold, is determined by demand and supply. The main problem is to identify the underlying determinants of the demand for and the supply of foreign money.

WHAT DETERMINES FOREIGN EXCHANGE RATES?

Whenever we import foreign goods, buy foreign stocks or bonds, or travel abroad, we have to make payments to people in other countries. Naturally enough, these people want to get paid in their own money. So we have to get

Foreign Exchange Quotations

A Sample Table of Foreign Exchange Rates

Country	# of Dollars for a Unit of Foreign Money	# of Units of Foreign Money for a Dollar
Argentina (Peso)	1.01	0.99
Australia (Dollar)	0.69	1.449
Austria (Schilling)	0.088	11.36
Belgium (Franc)	0.0303	33.00
Brazil (Cruzeiro)	0.00009	11,111.00
Britain (Pound)	1.5100	0.6623
30-day forward	1.5053	0.6643
60-day forward	1.5013	0.6661
90-day forward	1.4966	0.6682
Canada (Dollar)	0.7878	1.2694
30-day forward	0.7857	1.2728
60-day forward	0.7835	1.2763
90-day forward	0.7813	1.2799
Chile (Peso)	0.002707	369.41
China (Yuan)	0.1753	5.7045
Finland (Mark)	0.1919	5.2110
France (Franc)	0.1815	5.5096
Germany (Mark)	0.6180	1.6181
30-day forward	0.6151	1.6258
60-day forward	0.6126	1.6324
90-day forward	0.6100	1.6393
Greece (Drachma)	0.004678	213.77
India (Rupee)	0.0346	28.902
Ireland (Punt)	1.6350	0.6116
Israel (Shekel)	0.3729	2.6817
Italy (Lira)	0.000682	1,466.00
Japan (Yen)	0.008019	124.70
30-day forward	0.008016	124.75
60-day forward	0.008015	124.77
90-day forward	0.008013	124.80
Mexico (New Peso)	0.3205	3.12
Netherlands (Guilder)	0.5581	1.7918
Norway (Krone)	0.1466	6.82
Portugal (Escudo)	0.006875	145.45
Russia (Ruble)	0.002413	414.42
S. Korea (Won)	0.001269	788.02
Spain (Peseta)	0.008803	113.60
Sweden (Krona)	0.1411	7.0872
Switzerland (Franc)	0.6837	1.4626
Thailand (Baht)	0.03923	25.49
Uruguay (Peso)	0.000278	3,597.00

The left-hand column of numbers shows how much U.S. money exchanges for one British pound, one French franc, one German mark—in other words, it shows how much U.S. money it takes to buy *one unit of foreign money*. The entries in this column

(continued)

indicate that on this particular day it took $1.51 to buy one British pound (look under Britain and ignore the "forward" quotations for a moment), a bit over 18 cents to get a French franc, and 61.8 cents to buy one German mark.

The right-hand column shows how much foreign money exchanges for *one U.S. dollar:* $1 would get you about 66 British pence (66.23 to be precise), or 5.5096 French francs, or 1.6181 German marks. Notice that the two columns are reciprocals—that is, 1 divided by 1.01 equals .99 (Argentina) and so on.

Major currencies have four different price quotations: the "spot" price, 30-day forward, 60-day forward, and 90-day forward. The spot price is what you pay to buy the money today. Forward prices are what you pay if you sign a contract today to acquire the money on a specific future date (30, 60, or 90 days from now). Many business firms deal in this so-called forward market for foreign exchange because they anticipate the need for foreign currencies to conduct their normal business. By contracting now to buy or sell foreign exchange at some date in the future, business firms avoid the risk that the foreign exchange rate might change.

hold of foreign exchange, which we can do by going to a bank or currency exchange and buying some. Our imports thus give rise to a *demand for foreign exchange.* Notice, by the way, that when we buy foreign money we do so by offering dollars, so that a demand for foreign money also amounts to a supply of dollars on foreign exchange markets.

On the other hand, whenever we export our goods, sell our securities to others, or are host to foreigners traveling here, payments have to be made to us. Naturally, we also want to get paid in our own money. So foreigners have to buy American dollars, which they can do by going to a bank or currency exchange and offering their own money to get dollars. Our exports thus give rise to a *supply of foreign exchange.* Notice that when they offer foreign money they are trying to buy dollars, so that the supply of foreign money also amounts to a demand for dollars on foreign exchange markets.

Payments to and from foreigners are conveniently summarized in a national **balance of payments.** Each country's balance of payments shows the payments made to foreigners and the receipt of funds from them, in the same way that a family might keep a record of all its expenditures and receipts. A deficit in the U.S. balance of payments is similar to a deficit in a household's budget. It means that collectively we are paying out more money abroad than we are taking in. A surplus in the U.S. balance of payments is just the opposite. It means we are taking in more money than we are paying out.

At the heart of movements in foreign exchange rates is the deficit or surplus in balance of payments:

1. A *deficit* in our balance of payments means that we are paying out more money abroad than we are taking in. This produces a demand for foreign exchange greater than the supply. As a result, the price of foreign money will rise—foreign exchange will **appreciate** in value relative to the dollar. We can also think of this as a supply of dollars greater than the demand for them

on the foreign exchange market, so the dollar will **depreciate** in value relative to other kinds of money.

2. On the other hand, a *surplus* in our balance of payments means that we are taking in more money from abroad than we are paying out. This produces a supply of foreign money (trying to buy dollars) that is greater than the demand for foreign money, so the price of foreign money will fall. Foreign exchange will depreciate, and the dollar will appreciate.

When exchange rates freely react to demand and supply, as just described, they often generate self-correcting changes in imports and exports and in other types of international transactions, which eliminate balance-of-payments deficits and surpluses. For example, assume we are importing more goods than we are exporting, so that we are running a payments deficit. The price of foreign exchange will rise. The dollar will depreciate. As a result, foreign goods and services will become more expensive for us, so we are likely to import less. At the same time, we will probably export more because foreigners will find our products less expensive (they can now get more dollars for the same amount of their money). With fewer imports and more exports, our balance-of-payments deficit should shrink.

The same reasoning applies if we have a payments surplus because we are exporting more goods than we are importing. The price of foreign money will fall, increasing our imports (because foreign goods are now cheaper for us to buy) and decreasing our exports (our products are now more expensive for foreigners), thereby reducing our surplus.

Figure 10.1 illustrates these principles in the case of Djibouti francs. The dollar price for one franc is on the vertical axis (for example, 25 cents for one franc), and the number of francs is on the horizontal axis. The demand and supply curves for francs have the conventional shapes: The amount of francs demanded increases as their dollar price falls, because when francs become less expensive, Djibouti products become cheaper for us, we import more from Djibouti, hence we demand more francs. The amount of francs supplied decreases as their dollar price falls, because when francs become cheaper our goods become more expensive for the Djiboutians, so we export less to them, hence they supply fewer francs on the foreign exchange market.

As drawn, the demand and supply curves for francs imply an equilibrium price of 25 cents for one franc. At that exchange rate, the demand for francs equals supply and our balance of payments shows neither a deficit nor a surplus (at least with respect to Djibouti).

Why Do Exchange Rates Fluctuate?

It is obvious from Figure 10.2, which shows historical movements in the exchange rate between the dollar and other major currencies, that exchange rates vary considerably over time. Although equilibrium occurs at the intersection of supply and demand curves as depicted in Figure 10.1, whenever those curves shift to the right or left the equilibrium exchange rate will

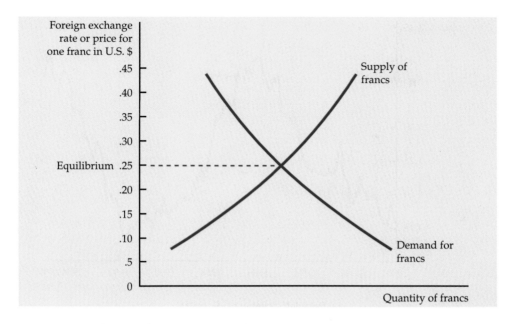

FIGURE 10.1   Supply of and demand for foreign exchange and foreign exchange rates.

change. For example, Figure 10.3 shows that a rightward shift in the demand curve for francs causes the price of francs in terms of dollars to increase, say from 25 cents to 35 cents. This occurs because at the old equilibrium of 25 cents, the quantity of francs demanded on the new demand curve is greater than the supply (there is an excess demand for francs), forcing up the price of francs. Figure 10.4 shows that a rightward shift in the supply curve for francs causes the dollar price of francs to decline, say from 25 cents to 15 cents, because at the old equilibrium of 25 cents there is a larger quantity of francs supplied than is demanded (there is an excess supply of francs).

The key to understanding movements in exchange rates, therefore, is to identify the factors causing shifts in the supply and demand curves for foreign currency. At the most general level, whatever causes U.S. residents to buy more or less foreign goods (at every exchange rate) shifts the demand curve for foreign currency, while whatever causes foreigners to buy more or less U.S. goods shifts the supply curve of foreign currency. More specifically, we can identify three factors that influence long-run supply and demand conditions:

1. *Relative Prices of U.S. Versus Foreign Goods.* Suppose prices of American motorcycles rise relative to Japanese bikes, so that a 1200-cc Harley now costs more than a similar-size Yamaha. U.S. bikers will switch to buying Yamahas (even though they make less noise), creating an excess demand for yen, driving up its price in terms of dollars. Thus the yen tends to *ap*preciate and the dollar *de*preciates whenever U.S. price levels rise relative to foreign

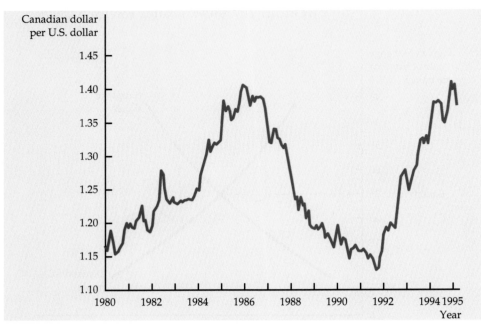

(a) Canadian dollar per U.S. dollar.

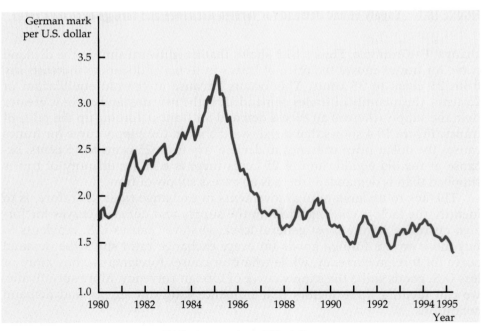

(b) German mark per U.S. dollar.

FIGURE 10.2   Fifteen years of exchange rate history between the U.S. dollar and other major currencies.

Note: Each of these charts shows the amount of foreign currency per U.S. dollar. Therefore, higher numbers mean a stronger dollar and lower numbers a weaker dollar.

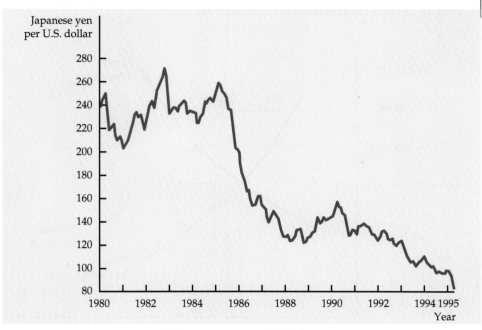

(c) Japanese yen per U.S. dollar.

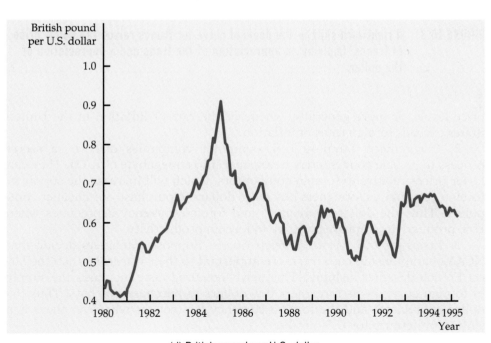

(d) British pound per U.S. dollar.

FIGURE 10.2   (Continued)

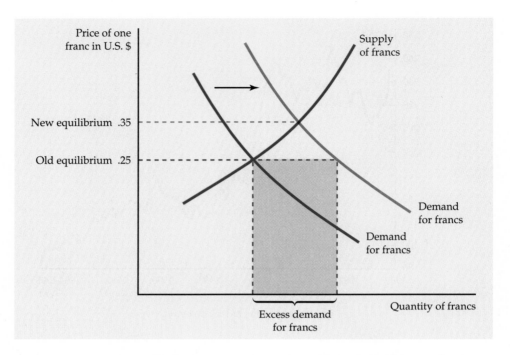

FIGURE 10.3   A rightward shift in the demand curve for francs raises the dollar price of francs, implying an appreciation of the franc and a depreciation of the dollar.

price levels, or more generally, whenever the rate of inflation in the United States exceeds foreign rates of inflation.

2. *Productivity.* Suppose U.S. computer companies discover a secret process to recycle your Sunday newspaper into a megabyte of RAM. They can lower prices relative to foreign competitors, which will increase the supply of foreign currency as foreigners buy more dollars to purchase our cheaper computers. Thus the dollar appreciates and foreign currency depreciates when U.S. productivity improves relative to foreign productivity.

3. *Tastes for U.S. Versus Foreign Goods.* Suppose foreigners decide that NCAA championship caps are more important to their wardrobe than the latest French designer fashions. This newly acquired taste increases the supply of foreign currency as foreigners buy dollars to purchase our hats. Thus the dollar appreciates and the foreign currency depreciates whenever there is a shift in preference for U.S. products.

Inflation, productivity, and tastes are clearly at the root of the long-run movements in exchange rates such as depicted in Figure 10.2. By their nature, however, these factors change rather slowly over time, so that they cannot explain the often violent daily and weekly movements in exchange rates. For example, Figure 10.5 shows the considerable day-to-day volatility in major

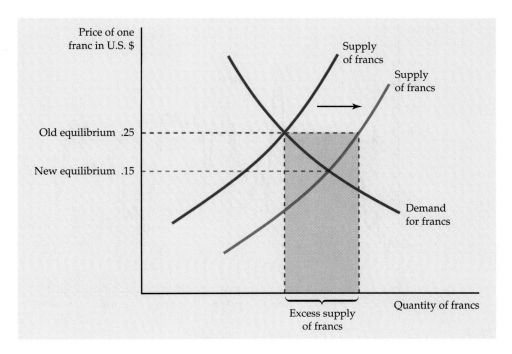

FIGURE 10.4   A rightward shift in the supply curve of francs lowers the dollar price of francs, implying a depreciation of the franc and an appreciation of the dollar.

foreign exchange rates during the first half of 1995. At the root of the short-term volatility in foreign exchange markets is the behavior of global investors seeking the highest return commensurate with risk.

How Global Investors Cause Exchange Rate Volatility

Investment funds flow across national borders because U.S. citizens are free to purchase foreign securities and overseas investors can easily purchase U.S. securities. In this environment of capital mobility, investors compare the expected return on domestic securities versus foreign securities to determine which are most attractive. And whenever U.S. investors prefer foreign securities they must first go into the foreign exchange market to buy foreign currency. Similarly, when foreign investors prefer our securities they must first go to the foreign exchange market to buy dollars. Thus changes in preferences for foreign securities give rise to excess demand for or supply of foreign currency in the same way as varying preferences for hats and motorcycles. Only in this case *expectations* of future exchange rates play a central role in the decision making, so the entire process becomes somewhat more volatile. This is best illustrated by way of example.

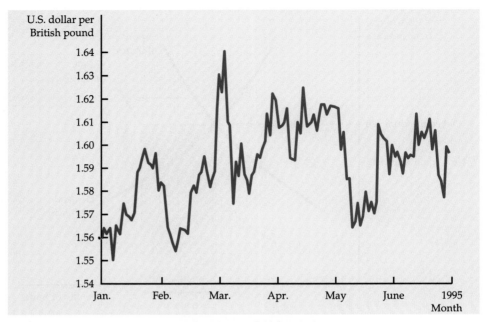

(a) U.S. dollar per British pound.

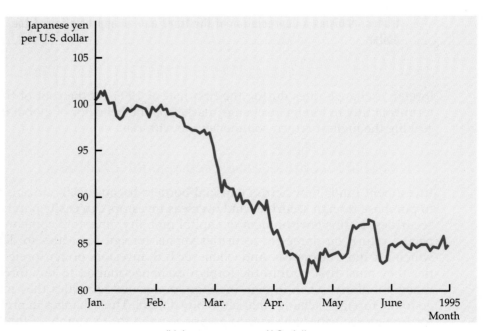

(b) Japanese yen per U.S. dollar.

FIGURE 10.5   Daily fluctuations in foreign exchange rates can be quite volatile (1995).

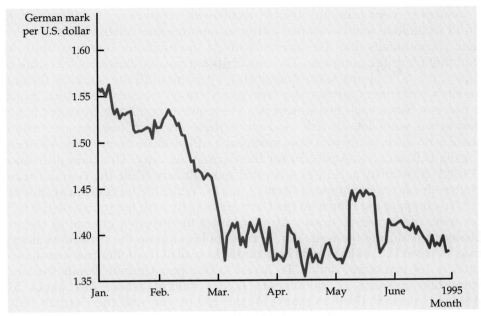

(c) German mark per U.S. dollar.

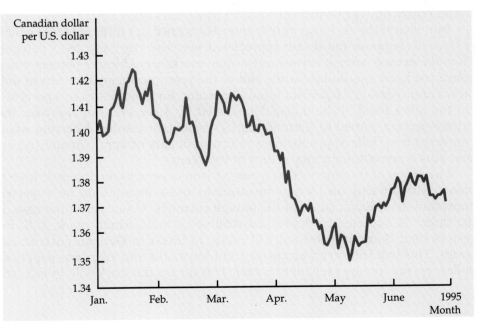

(d) Canadian dollar per U.S. dollar.

FIGURE 10.5   (Continued)

Suppose your school's athletic department receives a $1 million gift to build an indoor tennis complex. After an appropriate celebration the president recommends that the university invest the funds for one year until the building plans are complete. The university's treasurer considers investing in one-year U.S. Treasury securities earning 4 percent until she is told by the university's investment adviser that one-year German treasury securities return 6 percent. Since each investment is a government bond, the treasurer is not concerned with default risk. And since these are both one-year securities, there is no uncertainty over how much each will produce in one year: 4 percent for the U.S. security; 6 percent for the German security. The main difference is the U.S. security generates 4 percent more dollars while the German security produces 6 percent more German marks. Which is the better investment?

To compare the return on the German security with the return on the U.S. security, the treasurer must add or subtract the *expected* change in the exchange rate during the next year. For example, suppose the current exchange rate between U.S. dollars and German marks (called the dollar/mark exchange rate) is 1.4 marks per dollar. To invest in one-year German bonds the treasurer first converts $1 million into DM1.4 million (where DM stands for deutsche mark or German mark). At the end of one year the German bond produces DM1.484 million (DM1.4 multiplied by 1.06 = DM1.484). If the treasurer can convert this back into dollars at the same 1.4 exchange rate, then the investment will generate $1.06 million (DM1.484 divided by 1.4 DM per $ equals $1.06). This is clearly better than buying U.S. Treasury securities that would return only $1.04 million.

But what if the exchange rate in one year turned out different from where it started? Suppose the dollar appreciated over the year, say, by 3 percent. Then the extra 6 percent earned in German marks would lose 3 percent when converted back into dollars at the end of the year, producing a return in dollars of approximately 6 percent minus 3 percent, for a net return of 3 percent.[1] On the other hand, if the dollar depreciated by 3 percent over the year, the extra 6 percent earned in German marks would gain another 3 percent when converted into dollars, producing a return in dollars of approximately 6 percent plus 3 percent, for a total return of 9 percent.

The moral of the story is that a comparison of returns on domestic investments with returns on foreign investments must incorporate an expected appreciation or depreciation of the foreign currency. In our particular case, if the dollar is expected to depreciate relative to the German mark, U.S. investors (and German investors) will prefer to invest in German government bonds. This will lead to an excess demand for marks and an excess supply of dollars on the foreign exchange market. This means the mark will, in fact, ap-

---

[1]The precise calculation is as follows: The German government securities generate DM1.484 million. But if the U.S. dollar appreciates by 3 percent, then the exchange rate at the end of the year is 1.442 marks per dollar (1.40 multiplied by 1.03). Dividing DM1.48 million by 1.442 produces $1.029 million—or a return of 2.9 percent on the $1 million investment.

In The News

Global Investors Chase High Yields

High Yields in Mexico Spell Huge Risk

Stephen Hechtman recently traveled down to Puerto Vallarta to take in the sun, the beautiful bay, the delicious seafood—and he figures he didn't spend a dime of his hard-earned paycheck.

To pay for his trip, the Connecticut furniture retailer is just scooping the interest off a $10,000 investment he made in Mexican money market securities this year. The investment generates an annualized return of about 50 percent in pesos, which was more than enough to finance the vacation and which he plans to use to finance similar trips to the resort every six months. "I am new at this game, but I find this very exciting," Mr. Hechtman says.

With annualized yields of 50 percent to 60 percent available in Mexico these days on short-term government and corporate IOUs, lots of investors outside Mexico are asking how they, too, can get in on the game.

After all, the peso has stabilized at around 5.9 to the dollar, reducing the likelihood that it will crash fast enough to wipe out the principal of an investment in money market securities with maturities of either 28 or 91 days. Meanwhile, interest rates are likely to stay high through the summer because the government is committed to squeezing the economy, to prevent hyperinflation following the Dec. 20 devaluation of the peso.

Money managers say the first thing someone should consider before investing in Mexican money market instruments is that the strategy is among the riskiest on the planet these days. After all, high yields imply high risks.

Investors don't need long memories to remember what can happen in Mexico. As recently as six months ago, the Mexican economy had seemed to be in strong shape, and the government was promising it would never devalue the currency. Yet the government did devalue Dec. 20, and the near-total loss of confidence that resulted drove the Mexican currency down 53.5 percent against the dollar at its low point. The plunge shattered returns on Mexican money market investments held at the time. There isn't any promise today that the currency will remain at 5.9 pesos to the dollar, so currency risk is the biggest peril facing any short-term investor in Mexican money market securities.

Jorge Suarez-Velez, president of Afin Securities International Ltd., the U.S. subsidiary of a large Mexican broker, cautions that "we do not think that the peso has much upside potential." In a shock, the currency could fall sharply, he adds, so "for dollar-based clients it remains a high-risk investment."

Source: Wall Street Journal, May 24, 1995. Reprinted by permission of The Wall Street Journal. Copyright © 1995 Dow Jones & Company, Inc. All Rights Reserved Worldwide.

preciate and the dollar will depreciate. On the other hand, if the dollar is expected to appreciate a lot (by more than the 2 percent interest rate differential in our example), U.S. investors (and German investors) will prefer U.S. Treasuries. This will lead to an excess demand for dollars and an excess supply of marks on the foreign exchange market, implying that the mark will, in fact, depreciate and the dollar will appreciate.

This example suggests that the equilibrium foreign exchange rate is sensitive to investor expectations of future movements in exchange rates. Since these expectations might be quite unstable and susceptible to change, it is not surprising to observe considerable volatility in actual exchange rates.

FIXED VERSUS FLOATING EXCHANGE RATES

Volatility in foreign exchange rates represents a cost of doing business internationally. For many years governments tried to avoid that cost by fixing exchange rates at some predetermined level. A system of **fixed exchange rates** was maintained globally from 1944 until the early 1970s under the supervision of the **International Monetary Fund** (IMF). When that system collapsed it was resurrected with a more limited scope in 1979 for the major European countries. The **European Monetary System** (EMS) operated quite smoothly until 1992, when a number of countries, such as the United Kingdom and Italy, were forced to abandon the system and allow their currencies to float freely. At various times, certain governments have tried to fix their exchange rate to specific countries, such as Mexico linking the peso to the U.S. dollar—until that exploded in December 1994. Since fixing exchange rates at a predetermined level seems to be a fixation of government authorities that always seems to fall apart, let's see how it's done and what the problems are.

How Fixed Rates Are Supposed to Work

Under **floating exchange rates,** if a country runs a balance-of-payments deficit, the supply of its money offered on world financial markets exceeds the demand, and its money depreciates in value relative to other monies. But with *fixed* exchange rates, as they existed from the end of World War II until 1973, fluctuations in exchange rates were stopped before they could get started. By international agreement, under the supervision of the International Monetary Fund, a deficit country that saw its money start to depreciate had to step in promptly and prevent the decline. How? By buying up its own money in order to absorb the excess of supply over demand at the pegged exchange rate.

As an illustration, say France is initially in a situation where the supply of and demand for francs is equal, so that the foreign exchange rate is in equilibrium. Suddenly the French people decide they no longer like French wine and pastry but prefer American soda pop and Twinkies, which they begin to import in huge quantities.

As Figure 10.6(a) shows, this change in tastes would shift the entire supply curve of francs to the right, as the French offer more francs (at every exchange rate) to buy the increased number of dollars they need to pay American soda

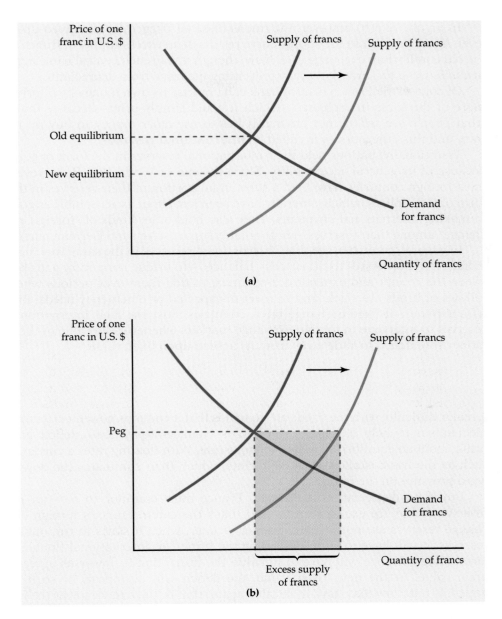

FIGURE 10.6   **In (a), with floating rates, the franc depreciates; in (b), with pegged rates, the French central bank prevents the decline by buying up the excess supply of francs.**

pop and Twinkies exporters. At the old equilibrium exchange rate, France now has a deficit in its balance of payments, which translates into a supply of francs greater than the demand. With exchange rates free to fluctuate, the franc will depreciate and move down toward a new lower equilibrium level.

In Figure 10.6(b) however, the rate is fixed, or pegged, at an agreed-upon level. Again the shift in the supply curve results in an excess supply of francs at the old equilibrium exchange rate. Now, though, the French central bank steps in *and buys up this excess,* thereby preventing the franc from depreciating.

Of course, the French central bank can't buy up its own money by offering more of the same in exchange—which it could simply print—because that's what people are *selling,* not buying. It has to use *other* money to buy up its own, and this other money is called its **international reserves.**

Traditionally, nations held their international reserves in the form of gold, because of its general acceptability. Since the end of World War II, however, most foreign countries have held a substantial portion of their reserves in the form of U.S. dollars, which generally have been just about as acceptable as gold in making international payments. They also hold other kinds of "foreign exchange" among their reserves—most notably Japanese yen and German marks.

In general, countries use their international reserves in the same way individuals and businesses use their cash balances—to bridge temporary gaps between the receipt and expenditure of funds, to tide them over periods when inflows of funds are slack, and to meet unexpected or emergency needs. But with a system of fixed exchange rates, countries must use their international reserves to intervene in foreign exchange markets whenever the value of their money threatened to slide away from its agreed-upon fixed value.

International Financial Crises

A major difficulty with the fixed rate system is that it contains no self-correcting mechanism to help eliminate a country's balance-of-payments deficit and bring about an equilibrium in its exchange rate. With floating rates a currency such as the franc is allowed to depreciate, which then eliminates the downward pressure on the franc.

But if no depreciation is allowed, France must continue to pay out its reserves to buy up excess francs—and that's the catch. France's foreign exchange reserves are not infinite. Sooner or later, when it starts to run out of reserves, it will have to stop "defending the franc." In international financial terminology, France will have to **devalue** the franc, that is, lower its agreed-upon value. At the new lower value, the deficit will disappear, or so it is hoped. If not, they may have to devalue again, that is, once more lower the international value or price of the franc.

Once the international financial community senses that **devaluation** is a possibility, no matter how remote, it is likely to take actions that increase the probability of its occurrence. People who own francs, or liquid assets payable in francs, and suspect that the franc may be devalued would be inclined to get out of francs and into some other kind of money—say, German marks—until the devaluation has been completed. Then, with the marks, they could buy back more francs than they originally had. Such "speculative" sales of francs by private holders must of course be purchased by the French monetary authorities, as they try to prevent the franc from depreciating. This puts an added strain on their reserves, thereby increasing the likelihood of devaluation which, in turn, stimulates renewed "speculative" activity.

Since devaluations are an ever-present fact of life under a fixed exchange rate system, countries with balance-of-payments deficits were viewed with some suspicion by those who manage large pools of mobile funds—treasurers of multinational corporations, bankers, oil sheiks, financial consultants to private investors, and others with similar responsibilities. Indeed, fund managers often got nervous about holding a country's money as soon as that country's rate of inflation exceeded that of other countries, since, as we saw above, a faster rate of inflation leads to a depreciating currency.

Despite the difficulties inherent in a fixed exchange rate system, governments have found it nearly impossible to follow a hands-off policy with respect to exchange rates. Although the industrialized countries have permitted most major exchange rates to float since the early 1970s, there are frequent interventions by central banks trying to nudge exchange rates one way or another.

This system has been dubbed **managed floating,** but that hardly describes what's really going on. The foreign currency markets are simply too big for anyone to manage, including the world's central banks. And if it looks as though the central banks are having their way, it's probably because the marketplace was going in that direction anyway.

SUMMARY

1. Our payments abroad create a demand for foreign exchange (which can also be viewed as a supply of dollars). Payments from foreigners to us create a supply of foreign exchange (or a demand for dollars).

2. An international balance of payments is an accounting record of all payments made across national borders. A deficit in our balance of payments creates a demand for foreign exchange greater than the supply, leading to appreciation in the value of foreign exchange. Alternatively, we could say that it leads to depreciation of the dollar. A surplus in our balance of payments creates a supply of foreign exchange greater than the demand, leading to depreciation in the value of foreign exchange. Alternatively, we could say that it leads to appreciation of the dollar.

3. Differential movements in the rate of inflation, changes in tastes, and differences in productivity account for the long-run movements in exchange rates. The short-run volatility of exchange rates is caused by global investors seeking the best international investments.

4. If foreign exchange rates are free to respond to market forces, movements in exchange rates should eliminate both deficits and surpluses. With fixed exchange rates, a deficit country must intervene and buy up its own money to prevent its depreciation on the foreign exchange market. It uses its international reserves for this purpose, but the process

ends when a country runs out of reserves. International financial crises tend to develop under fixed rates when fears of devaluation lead to speculative dumping of a country's money.

QUESTIONS

10.1 Assume that you are back in a system of fixed exchange rates and that you own a lot of Mexican pesos. A rumor starts circulating that Mexico will soon devalue the peso. What will you do? Why?

10.2 What will happen to the dollar/mark exchange rate if the Germans decide to dump a lot of the U.S. securities they have purchased over the years?

10.3 Under a system of fixed exchange rates, how did countries keep the rates fixed? Why is that so difficult?

10.4 Why do expected movements in foreign exchange rates influence the investment decisions of global investors?

10.5 *Discussion question:* Explain why the dollar has declined relative to the Japanese yen and German mark during the past ten years.

PART III

Banks and Other Intermediaries

CHAPTER 11

The Nature of Financial Intermediation

It is virtually impossible to spend or save or lend nowadays without getting involved with some kind of **financial intermediary.** Back in Chapter 3 we explained briefly why intermediaries are such pervasive phenomena. Now it's time to dig a little deeper into the nature of these institutions. We begin by examining the economics underlying **financial intermediation.** Our objective is to understand why these institutions exist in the first place and where they fit in the overall financial landscape. Using this framework we then take a look at how intermediaries have evolved in the United States over the past 50 years and explore the dynamic forces driving their development. We conclude by analyzing how the economic role performed by these institutions translates into a specific set of managerial challenges.

THE ECONOMICS OF FINANCIAL INTERMEDIATION

From the vantage point of Adam Smith, it is difficult to explain the existence of financial intermediaries. More specifically, applying the principles of perfect markets to the financial sector means that buyers and sellers of securities can transact with each other without cost, that securities are infinitely divisible (bonds, stocks, and so on, can be bought in any denomination), and that buyers and sellers of financial instruments know the true quality of what they are buying and selling. Thus in a world where markets are perfect, there seems little reason for financial intermediaries to exist—who needs a middleman?

From this perspective, it seems logical to attribute the existence of financial intermediaries to so-called market imperfections, especially *transactions costs*. In the fanciful world of perfect markets, funds would flow effortlessly from lenders to borrowers through the financial markets in exchange for traded securities. However, when small savers and small borrowers are involved, the transactions costs associated with selling securities in small amounts are often prohibitively expensive. It would take a lot of time, for example, for small savers to look through the Yellow Pages to find small borrowers to lend money to. Instead, small savers give their money to banks, then banks give that money to small borrowers, and all the small savers and borrowers involved are better off because they avoid a major transaction cost—the cost of searching. Thus banks and other financial intermediaries reduce transactions costs—a boring job, but somebody has to do it!

Portfolio diversification is another important function of financial intermediaries. The principle of not putting all your eggs in one basket implies that investors should hold many different securities to spread out their risk exposure. More formally, modern portfolio theory emphasizes that investors are only compensated for the risk that remains after diversifiable risk has been eliminated in a large portfolio (see Chapter 7 for more details). The direct implication is that prudent investors should hold widely diversified portfolios. This can be difficult if an investor has only a few thousand dollars to invest. Along come financial intermediaries that make it easy and simple to hold financial claims backed by many different securities. More specifically, a stock index mutual fund is an intermediary that offers small investors a way to participate in the performance of the stock market as a whole, thereby benefiting from diversification with all available securities.

But there are even more fundamental forces underlying the role of financial intermediaries than just greasing the wheels of finance and providing an easy way to diversify (although these surely are important). Financial intermediaries are major contributors to *information production*. Specifically, many intermediaries are in the business of producing information about borrower creditworthiness. The need for this information arises because of public enemy number one: **asymmetric information.**

Asymmetric information occurs when buyers and sellers are *not* equally informed about the true quality of what they are buying and selling. The asymmetry always runs in the same direction—the seller knows more than the buyer. With respect to financial instruments, asymmetric information refers to the security issuer (borrower) having more information than an investor (lender) about the issuer's (borrower's) future performance.

A survey of commercial bankers conducted by your favorite textbook authors during spring vacation showed not a single reported instance of a borrower warning a loan officer, "I am really much riskier than you think. Please charge me a higher interest rate, make me pledge more collateral, and do not lend me as much money as I am requesting." Instead, borrowers tend to understate their risk and make promises they may not keep. This would not pose much of a problem if a borrower's true quality was always obvious. Unfortunately, it often is not. This is particularly true in the case of loans to consumers and small businesses where lenders are typically at a huge informational disadvantage. Asymmetric information is much less of a problem for large businesses because there is so much publicly available information about their quality and behavior.

Asymmetric information occurs in two forms, adverse selection and moral hazard. **Adverse selection** arises before a financial transaction is consummated. For example, adverse selection is related to information about a business *before* the bank makes the loan. All small businesses tend to represent themselves as high quality (that is, low risk) despite the fact that bankers know that some are good and some are bad. However, in the absence of information about exactly who is good and who is bad, bankers face a problem. On the one hand, if they charge too high an interest rate, the good borrowers may withdraw from the loan market, leaving only the bad borrowers. On the other hand, if bankers charge too low a rate they will lose more money on their bad borrowers than they will make on their good borrowers. In the worst case scenario, bankers may decide not to lend to any small business who seeks credit. This is known as *market failure*.

Moral hazard arises *after* a financial transaction is consummated. It arises because borrowers covertly engage in activities that increase the probability of poor performance. For example, a small business borrower may deliberately choose riskier projects after receiving a bank loan. At first blush this may seem surprising. Why would a small business take on more risk when that would necessarily increase its chances of defaulting on the loan and going bankrupt in the process? Simply put, the reason is that owners share disproportionately in the upside potential while lenders share disproportionately in the downside. To see this, note that a lender is no better off when a business is a modest success than when it is a big success because the lender receives only principal and interest. The owner, however, is much better off when the company is a big success than when it is a modest success because the owner gets to pocket all of the big profits. On the other hand, the owner loses the same amount whether the company is a moderate disaster or a major disaster. And that is because with limited liability the owner can lose only the equity that was put in, and no more. Thus as a result of the way owners and lenders participate in success and failure, taking on more risk works to the owner's advantage. Naturally enough, this asymmetry is likely to keep lenders awake at night figuring out how to protect themselves.

In the absence of solutions to the adverse selection and moral hazard problems, lenders will simply make considerably fewer loans to individuals and small businesses. More information, however, solves the problem. And in most cases, it is *financial intermediaries* that become specialists in the production of this additional information—both at the loan origination stage to address the adverse selection problem, and after lending the money by monitoring borrowers to address the moral hazard problem. Financial intermediaries use information in conjunction with tailor-made financial contracts designed to help them sort out the good from the bad (and the ugly) before any money is lent—and to provide appropriate incentives for responsible borrower behavior afterward. Sometimes these contracts can be quite restrictive. For example, a bank might restrict a corporate borrower from making a substantial investment in new equipment without the bank's permission. However, as the bank develops a relationship with the borrower by monitoring the borrower's performance over time, it may grant permission if the borrower has done well and can justify the investment. In Chapter 14 we examine in greater detail how intermediaries design appropriate financial contracts.

But why is it that information production is delegated to financial intermediaries? Why don't individual investors produce their own information about borrowers instead of intermediaries? The principal reason is that financial intermediaries enjoy economies of scale in information production. Suppose a small business wants to borrow $1 million. It could go to 100 small saver-lenders and borrow $10,000 from each. However, each of these savers would have to evaluate the borrower and each one would incur the cost of information production. Suppose this cost is $4,000 per evaluation. Then the total cost of information production, $100 \times \$4,000 = \$400,000$, would most likely be prohibitive. On the other hand, if these 100 small savers each deposited $10,000 in a bank and delegated to the bank the responsibility for evaluating the borrower, then information would have to be produced only once, by the bank. Thus total information production costs are reduced from $400,000 to $4,000, and the bank becomes the sole lender.

Because the financial intermediary has the exclusive use of the information it has produced, it also makes sense to delegate the responsibility of **monitoring** borrower behavior over the life of the loan to the intermediary. Thus it is not surprising that bank loans, for example, are **nontraded financial contracts** that are held by the bank until maturity so that the bank can keep a close watch on its money until the end of the loan.

The role of financial intermediaries can be summarized in the flow of funds diagram in Figure 11.1. This is similar to Figure 3.1 except that we now highlight the alternative routes by which funds flow from saver-lenders to borrower-spenders. When saver-lenders invest directly in the financial markets by purchasing securities issued by borrower-spenders that can be resold on secondary markets (which we call **traded securities**), Case III applies. Borrowers (issuers) in this market are well-known entities, such as large companies or federal and municipal governments, with an abundance of publicly available information. However, other borrowers, such as individuals and smaller businesses are *information problematic*. They can obtain funding only from financial intermediaries that specialize in information production. Case I applies for them, where savers delegate to financial intermediaries the responsibility for information production and for the design of nontraded financial contracts.

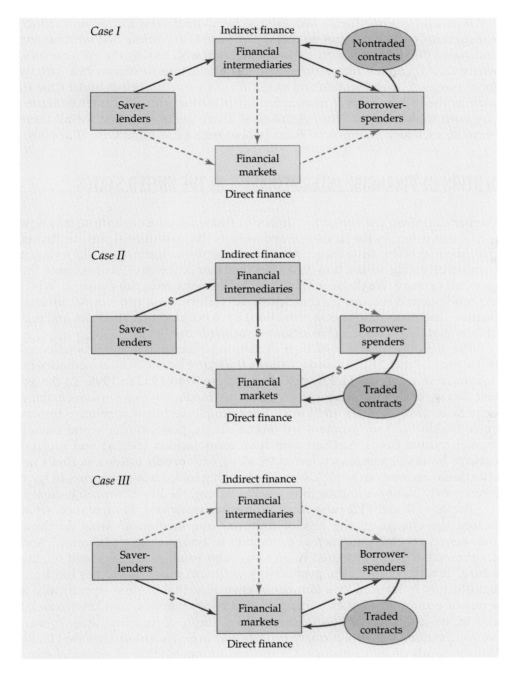

FIGURE 11.1   Flow of funds from savers to borrowers.

Financial intermediaries also exist to facilitate diversification and reduce transactions costs. They can do this under Case I, in conjunction with buying nontraded financial contracts, or in conjunction with buying traded securities, where Case II applies. Interestingly, some financial intermediaries exist strictly for purposes of diversification and reduction of transactions costs under Case II, such as the money market mutual fund, while other financial intermediaries buy both traded and nontraded financial instruments and exist for all three reasons, such as a commercial bank (where both Case I and Case II applies).

THE EVOLUTION OF FINANCIAL INTERMEDIARIES IN THE UNITED STATES

Having examined the economic theory of financial intermediation, it is now time for us to survey the landscape and identify the institutional players. Rather than starting off by describing what financial intermediaries look like today, it is more revealing to see how financial intermediaries have evolved over the past half century. We discover that these institutions are quite dynamic. While the fundamental reasons for their existence (information production, diversification, and transactions cost reduction) have not changed, the form and mix of financial intermediaries has changed rather dramatically.

The evolution of financial intermediation in the United States is reflected in Tables 11.1 and 11.2. Table 11.1 shows the major financial intermediaries by dollar assets and Table 11.2 by percentage share from 1952 to 1995. To the extent that we can view the pace of financial intermediation as a horse race, there seem to be clear winners and losers. For example, in terms of relative importance (Table 11.2) the winners are mutual funds, pension funds, and money market mutual funds. **Savings and loan associations (S&Ls)** and **mutual savings banks** (sometimes referred to, along with **credit unions** as **thrift institutions**) are obviously big losers. The banking industry also appears to have fared poorly along with, though to a lesser extent, the life insurance industry.

Tables 11.1 and 11.2 raise some interesting questions. For instance, what caused the change in the mix of financial intermediaries? How do these changes reflect the fundamental economics of financial intermediation? And are these changes interrelated in any way, and what do they portend for the future? It turns out that the profitability of financial intermediaries has been significantly influenced by a number of environmental factors—specifically, a series of economic "shocks," changing regulatory barriers, and key financial and technological innovations. Rather than simply chronicling these events, we will examine this evolutionary process via three overriding themes: (1) the shifting sands of interest rates, (2) the institutionalization of financial markets, and (3) the decline of banking.

The Shifting Sands of Interest Rates

The period encompassing the 1950s and early 1960s is often thought of as the age of innocence. Smoking was cool. Cars had big engines. Motorcycle riders

TABLE 11.1   **Financial Intermediary Assets in the United States, 1952–1995 (in billions of dollars)**

	1952	1960	1970	1980	1990	1995
Depository institutions						
Commercial banks	169	229	517	1,482	3,338	4,501
Savings and loans and mutual savings	48	112	253	792	1,358	1,016
Credit unions	2	6	18	68	217	310
Insurance companies						
Life insurance	71	116	201	464	1,367	2,086
Property and casualty	14	26	51	182	533	746
Pension funds						
Private	11	41	123	495	1,566	2,627
Public (state and local government)	7	20	60	197	820	1,387
Finance companies						
	12	28	64	205	611	827
Mutual funds						
Stock and bond	6	23	53	70	654	1,853
Money market	0	0	0	76	498	745
Total	340	601	1,340	4,030	10,964	16,098

Source: Federal Reserve Flow of Funds Accounts.

Note: Columns may not add due to rounding.

didn't wear helmets. Rock and roll spawned songs about Peggy Sue and dances like the Peppermint Twist. Life was simple. And so was the world of finance. Interest rates were stable. Federal Reserve regulations imposed ceilings on deposit rates so that banks and thrifts had little competition for the short-term funds provided by small savers. Managers of these institutions also had things easy. Go to work at 9:00 A.M. Make a mortgage or business loan by 12:00 noon. Play 18 holes of golf in the afternoon. The only challenge in banking was finding a way to put all those cheap deposits to work.

By the mid-1960s, however, this comfortable world began to change. As the economy grew, loan demand grew with it—demand for mortgages, demand for consumer loans, and demand for business loans. As a result, the amount of total loans as a percentage of bank assets jumped from approximately 45 percent in 1960 to nearly 60 percent by 1980. Thus the challenge in banking shifted from finding enough loans to finding enough deposits to satisfy an increasing loan demand. Meeting this challenge initially was the typical good news–bad news phenomenon. The bad news was that the interest rate environment for intermediary deposits became increasingly unstable. The good news was that depository institutions still enjoyed the protection of

TABLE 11.2   Share of Financial Intermediary Assets in the United States, 1952–1995 (percent)

	1952	1960	1970	1980	1990	1995
Depository institutions						
Commercial banks	49.7	38.1	38.6	36.8	30.5	28.0
Savings and loans and mutual savings	14.1	18.7	18.9	20.0	12.4	6.3
Credit unions	0.1	1.0	1.3	1.7	2.0	1.9
Insurance companies						
Life insurance	21.0	19.3	15.0	11.5	12.5	13.0
Property and casualty	4.2	4.4	3.8	4.5	4.9	4.6
Pension funds						
Private	3.1	6.8	9.2	12.3	14.3	16.3
Public (state and local government)	2.0	3.3	4.5	4.9	7.5	8.6
Finance companies						
	3.5	4.6	4.8	5.1	5.6	5.1
Mutual funds						
Stock and bond	1.9	3.9	4.0	1.7	6.0	11.5
Money market	0.0	0.0	0.0	1.9	4.6	4.6
Total	100.0	100.0	100.0	100.0	100.0	100.0

Source: Federal Reserve Flow of Funds Accounts.

Note: Columns may not add due to rounding.

deposit rate ceilings under the Federal Reserve's **Regulation Q,** which was designed to insulate intermediaries from interest rate competition.

The Regulation Q Security Blanket.   Regulation Q gave the Federal Reserve the responsibility of imposing ceilings on deposit rates. The intent of the regulation was to promote stability in the banking industry by preventing "destructive competition" among depository institutions trying to outbid each other by offering increasingly higher deposit rates. The fear was that the resulting higher cost of funds would lead to more bank and thrift failures and increase the chances of a systemwide banking panic, such as had occurred during the Great Depression.

The consequences of Regulation Q were somewhat different. When short-term market interest rates exceeded Regulation Q ceilings, money market instruments, such as Treasury bills and commercial paper, became more attractive investments than deposits. Small savers, however, were out of luck because these money market instruments were not sold in small denominations. Wealthy individuals and corporate depositors, on the other hand, who could afford to buy money market instruments led the exodus from deposits, in a process known as **financial disintermediation.**

The Birth of the Money Market Mutual Fund.   Figure 11.2 traces the history of short-term interest rates (represented by the three-month Treasury bill rate) and the Regulation Q ceiling on bank passbook savings accounts from 1950 to 1995. While market rates occasionally exceeded Regulation Q ceilings in the 1950s, these periods tended to be brief, and the differences between market rates and the Regulation Q ceilings were not that large. Thus hardly anyone noticed when the first crack in Regulation Q appeared in 1961 as banks offered negotiable certificates of deposit (CDs) that escaped Regulation Q because they were issued in denominations of $100,000 or more. However, when interest rate volatility escalated in the mid-1960s, wealthy investors switched from savings accounts to large CDs; and when interest rates soared in 1969, banks found still other loopholes to Regulation Q, such as issuing commercial paper through their holding companies and obtaining funding with Eurodollar deposits (dollar denominated deposits held abroad).

But it was the invention of the **money market mutual fund** in 1971 that put the nail in Regulation Q's coffin. In a money market fund, small investors pool their funds to buy a diversified portfolio of money market instruments, such as Treasury bills, commercial paper, and negotiable CDs, that would otherwise be inaccessible because they are sold only in large denominations. The fund pays its investors the interest earned on its investments less a small management fee. Investors can withdraw their funds at any time: Most funds even offer limited withdrawal by check. Thus for the first time, small savers had easy access to money market interest rates as an alternative to Regulation Q-constrained bank deposits. This new investment vehicle for the small saver permanently altered the financial landscape.

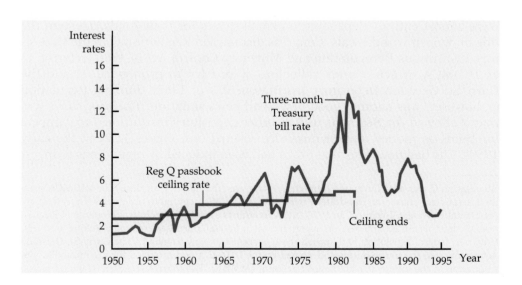

FIGURE 11.2   Interest rates and Regulation Q.

Source: Federal Reserve Bulletin.

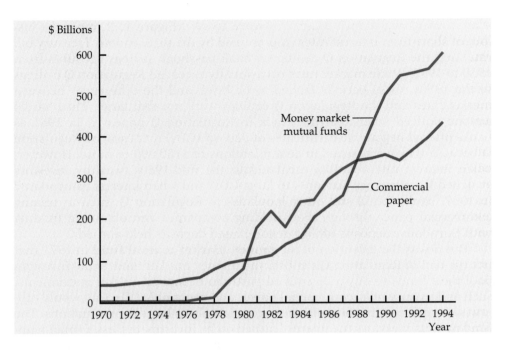

FIGURE 11.3 **Commercial paper and money market mutual funds.**

The Savings and Loan Crisis. Figure 11.3 shows that in the late 1970s the growth in money market mutual funds accelerated as small savers shifted funds out of banks and thrifts in response to rising market interest rates. For S&Ls, this marked the beginning of a disaster because, unlike banks, they were almost entirely dependent on small savers for their funds. To stem the tide of deposit withdrawals, Congress dismantled Regulation Q in the Depository Institutions Deregulation and Monetary Control Act of 1980 (referred to as DIDMCA, which sounds ridiculous if you try to pronounce it) and the Garn–St. Germain Depository Institutions Act of 1982.[1] Junking Regulation Q, however, was another good news–bad news situation. The good news was that it allowed the S&Ls (as well as other depository institutions) to compete for funds as money market rates skyrocketed (see Figure 11.2) in the early 1980s. The bad news was that S&Ls had been induced by regulations to invest

---

[1]Regulation Q was not eliminated immediately but was phased out over time. The DIDMCA specified a six-year phaseout. In addition it authorized NOW (negotiable order of withdrawal) accounts nationwide. ("Invented" in 1970, **NOW accounts** exploited a technical loophole in Regulation Q that permitted interest on what, for all practical purposes, was a checking account. However, federal legislation had limited these accounts to New England.) The Garn–St. Germain Act accelerated the phase-out period started by the DIDMCA and provided for the immediate introduction of the money market deposit account (MMDA). The MMDA is a deposit which pays a money market–linked interest rate and offers limited checkability. Its introduction had an immediate and dramatic impact. Bank MMDAs grew from zero in December 1982 when they were first permitted to $340 billion by April 1983.

primarily in long-term (usually 30-year) fixed-rate residential mortgages. Thus, S&Ls were stuck with mortgages made in the 1970s or earlier, most of which were earning less than 8 percent, while they were renewing their short-term deposits at rates that were nearly double that. By 1980 the *rate spread* between the average yield on assets and the average cost of funds for the S&L industry had turned from a positive number, where it represented profits, to a negative number, where it generated losses.

More importantly, as a result of rising rates and the structure of S&L balance sheets, the value of S&L assets fell below the value of liabilities, making the industry economically insolvent. To see this, recall from Chapter 4 that bond values decline when interest rates rise, with longer maturities suffering larger declines for any given increase in rates. The mortgages held by S&Ls behaved like long term bonds, so that market values plummeted as mortgage rates rose from 8 percent to more than 16 percent. There was little benefit on the liability side of S&L balance sheets because S&Ls had issued very few long-term deposits, so they failed to lock in the old low rates.

How badly were the S&Ls underwater? Estimates by academics at that time indicate that the industry had a negative net worth of as much as $150 *billion* by the end of 1981.[2] However, these academic estimates were largely ignored by the regulatory and financial communities. Instead, the general perception in the early 1980s was that the S&Ls were just suffering from a short-run hiccup in profitability. After all, only 11 S&Ls were closed in 1980. Depositors were not concerned, moreover, because they were insured by an agency of the federal government, the **Federal Savings and Loan Insurance Corporation (FSLIC).**

How could just about everyone have been so much in the dark about the industry's insolvency? In great part the answer has to do with the rules governing S&L financial statements (no doubt your favorite subject). Instead of showing a huge *negative* net worth, the industry's collective financial statement showed a *positive* net worth of more than $30 billion because S&L financial statements were constructed on an *historical cost basis*, meaning that any loss in the market value of a mortgage was not recorded unless the mortgage was actually sold by the S&L. Not surprisingly, very few mortgages were sold under such conditions, hence losses went unreported and undetected.

Essentially the S&L industry crisis was managed as a big gamble. If interest rates fell soon enough the whole problem would disappear, except for a year or two of losses from the negative interest-rate spread. To allow the S&Ls to buy some time, Congress passed the Garn–St. Germain Act, which freed

---

[2]See Table 2 in Edward J. Kane, "The Role of Government in the Thrift Industry's Net-worth Crisis" in *Financial Services: The Changing Institutions and Government Policy,* edited by George J. Benston (New York: Prentice Hall, 1983). Kane notes that this estimate was subject to several upward biases, most notably that it did not incorporate a maturity distribution for mortgage portfolios. He cites one other study made at the time, however, that attempted to correct for these biases and still estimated losses at approximately $100 billion.

S&Ls to invest in higher yielding consumer loans, business loans, construction loans, real estate equity, junk bonds, and more. Thus the S&Ls were permitted to invest in areas they had little expertise in. And, like gamblers deep in debt, they had every incentive to bet on a long shot by investing in these risky assets in hopes that a big payoff would offset the monumental, but unreported, economic losses they had suffered in their mortgage portfolios.

How did the gamble turn out? Interest rates eventually came down, but not until the mid-1980s, and by then it is not surprising that S&Ls racked up huge losses on their risky new investments. After all, what did S&Ls know about junk bonds? The general public became aware of the problem in 1986, as the Reagan administration sought $15 billion in Congressional funding—only a fraction of what was ultimately needed—to shore up the S&L insurance fund. Most estimates put the ultimate losses on the order of $150 billion. In Chapter 15 we return to the S&L crisis to examine the lessons for deposit insurance.

The Rise of Commercial Paper. The competitive impact of money market mutual funds was by no means confined to the S&L industry. There was also a dramatic effect on the banking business. The flow of money into money market funds created an enormous reservoir of funds looking for short-term money market investments. This increasing appetite for money market instruments was satisfied in part by an equally dramatic increase in the issuance of commercial paper. Before money market funds, some very large corporations issued commercial paper, but these were relatively few and in small amounts compared to today. As shown in Figure 11.3, growth in the commercial paper market parallels growth in money market funds. At whose expense did this growth occur? Mostly commercial banks. Essentially, banks lost their largest and highest quality borrowers to the commercial paper market via money market mutual funds.

Banks responded to the loss of their loans to high-quality borrowers, in part, by replacing them with loans to less creditworthy businesses, commercial real estate loans, and loans to **lesser developed countries (LDCs).** As a result, by the end of the 1980s bank loan portfolios, on average, consisted of riskier borrowers than they did in the 1970s.[3]

The migration of corporate financing from the short-term bank loan market to the commercial paper market represented a shift from nontraded loans (Case I in Figure 11.1) to traded commercial paper (Cases II and III in Figure 11.1). While the creation of the money market mutual fund was the trigger that prompted this shift, technological innovations were also important in a number of dimensions. First, advances in computers and communications technology permitted money market funds to offer transactions services cou-

---

[3]See Allen N. Berger and Gregory F. Udell, "Collateral, Loan Quality, and Bank Risk," *Journal of Monetary Economics* 25 (January 1990), pp. 21–42, for an analysis of the changes in bank loan portfolios between the 1970s and 1980s.

pled with a diversified money market investment vehicle at very low costs. Second, new and sophisticated analytical techniques were introduced during this period, including mathematical models of asset valuation and default prediction, which, when combined with high-powered computers, meant that the specialized monitoring services of a commercial bank were no longer necessary to evaluate many borrowers. Just about anyone could tell which firms warranted access to the commercial paper market. This opened the floodgates for new commercial paper issuers.

Innovations in information technology also had an impact on how banks compensated for the loss of their large corporate clients. Borrowers who had previously been too difficult even for banks, became "bankable" for the first time. For example, as we will see in more detail in Chapter 14, **collateral** is an important mechanism that banks use to solve the asymmetric information problem, especially for small business. But the cost of monitoring collateral in the form of accounts receivables and inventory had been very labor intensive. However, as computer and information technology improved during the 1970s, these costs plummeted, making it profitable for banks to provide collateralized financing to an increasing number of companies. Today, more than half of all short-term bank loans to small business are collateralized by accounts receivable and/or inventory.

The Institutionalization of Financial Markets

When individual savers buy securities themselves, funds flow *directly* from savers to borrowers, as in Case III of Figure 11.1. When savers put their money into a financial intermediary that buys traded securities, the process is *indirect*, as in Case II of Figure 11.1. **Institutionalization** refers to the fact that more and more funds in the United States have been flowing indirectly into the financial markets through financial intermediaries, particularly pension funds, mutual funds, and insurance companies (Case II) rather than directly from savers (Case III). As a result, these "institutional investors" have become much more important in the financial markets relative to individual investors. For example, individual investors owned 86 percent of all equities outstanding in 1960, but they owned only 51 percent in 1995. Institutionalization has made it easier for companies to distribute newly issued securities via their investment bankers, as we will see in Chapter 14.

What caused institutionalization? Quite simply, it was driven by the growth of these financial intermediaries, particularly pension funds and mutual funds. And this growth stemmed, in part, from the financial and technological innovations just discussed. But there's more to the story than that. Pension fund growth was also encouraged by government policy. Tax laws, for instance, encourage employers to help their employees by substituting pension benefits for wages. This is good for employees because they do not pay taxes on their pension benefits until they are received after retirement. By deferring taxes until retirement employees earn compound interest on more money. Employers are happy to help out because both pension benefits and wages are *nontaxable* to the employer.

Legislation in the 1970s and 1980s also created a number of new and attractive alternatives to the traditional employer-sponsored **defined benefit plan,** the most significant of these being the **defined contribution plan.** In the traditional defined benefit plan, the sponsoring company contributed to a pension fund that promised specified benefits to its employees upon their retirement. In contrast to these plans, employees covered under a defined contribution plan may choose (within limits) the assets they want to invest in. This flexibility is extremely attractive to employees, even though the benefits they receive upon retirement depend on how well the assets perform (as well as on how much has been contributed to the plan). The two major defined contribution plans are the 403(b) plan for nonprofit organizations and the 401(k) plan for everyone else.

Mutual funds gained considerably from these changes in pension plan laws. Defined contribution plans were allowed to include mutual funds on the menu of assets from which plan members could choose. As a result, approximately 28 percent of all 401(k) assets are in mutual funds and about 70 percent of all new money currently flowing into mutual funds (that is, new subscriptions) is from 401(k) plans. In addition, aggressive marketing by **mutual fund families** (different funds managed under the same umbrella, such as Fidelity Investments or the Vanguard Group) and the increasing attractiveness of specialized funds, such as bond funds and index funds, have also fueled mutual fund growth.

The Decline of Banking

"Banking Buried by Bad Loans," could have been the epitaph of the banking industry. As we noted previously, as high-quality borrowers moved to the commercial paper market during the 1970s and 1980s, banks extended loans to borrowers with riskier prospects. Thus banks were especially vulnerable to the international debt crises that emerged during the 1980s and to the economic shocks that plagued the oil, farming, and real estate industries. As a result, by the late 1980s bank failures had reached unprecedented levels, as is shown in Figure 11.4. Although bank profitability rebounded after 1992 and bank failures dwindled to a trickle, dire predictions for the industry persist based primarily on increased competition from other financial intermediaries. Perhaps the most telling statistic for the doomsayers is shown in Table 11.2 above, which shows the decline of banking's fraction of total intermediated assets from 50 percent in 1952 to 28 percent in 1995.

To paraphrase Mark Twain, the reports of banking's demise are greatly exaggerated. First, the so-called decline of commercial banking is limited to a decline in the *relative* importance of commercial banking. While Table 11.2 shows that the fraction of intermediated assets in banking has declined, Table 11.1 shows that banking industry assets actually increased between 1970 and 1995 (even after adjusting for inflation). In other words, bank assets have actually increased—just not as fast as the assets of other financial intermedi-

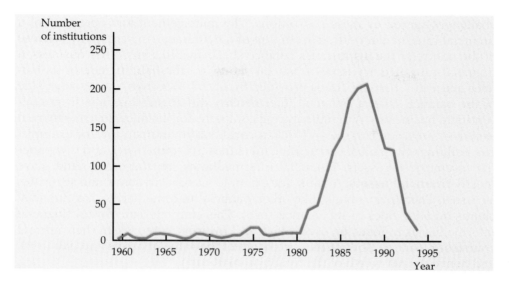

FIGURE 11.4   Bank failures.

Source: Federal Deposit Insurance Corporation, *1993 Annual Report and Quarterly Banking Profile.*

aries. Second, as we will see in the next chapter, many new banking activities are not reflected on bank balance sheets as assets (and, therefore, are not included in Tables 11.1 and 11.2), even though they add significantly to bank revenue. These include, for example, trading in interest rate and currency swaps, merger and acquisition advisory services, securities underwriting, and other nontraditional activities.

Finally, banks still have a strong comparative advantage in lending to individuals and small businesses. Our discussion above shows that as specialists in the production of information, banks are ideally suited for making non-traded loans to these types of information-problematic borrowers. And unlike finance companies (as we will see in Chapter 13), banks sell a whole menu of products to their customers, including personal and commercial loans, checking accounts, retirement products, trust activities, payroll processing, and so on. Thus banks are uniquely equipped to develop comprehensive relationships that make it easier for them to monitor their borrowers and mitigate some of the problems arising from asymmetric information. For these reasons, it is hard to imagine that banks will become as irrelevant as some of their more ardent critics contend.

FINANCIAL INTERMEDIARIES: ASSETS, LIABILITIES, AND MANAGEMENT

We have analyzed the economic role of financial intermediaries and how intermediaries have evolved to fill that role. Now we turn to the managerial challenges shared by these institutions. The management and operation of a financial intermediary differs from that of a manufacturing company because of the nature of the institution's balance sheet. Just like any other business, a financial intermediary issues financial claims on the liability side of its balance sheet in return for funds provided by savers. However, on the asset side of the balance sheet a financial intermediary differs substantially from conventional businesses. A manufacturing company, for instance, has mostly **real assets**—things you can see and kick. A cardboard manufacturer, for example, has buildings (its *plant*), corrugating machines (its *equipment*), and raw paper (its *inventory*) as assets. Financial intermediaries, on the other hand, have mostly **financial assets.** A bank, for example, has mostly loans and securities as assets. Therefore, a bank, like other financial intermediaries, has financial claims on *both* sides of its balance sheet. This characteristic forces financial intermediaries to focus on **credit risk** and **interest rate risk** in their normal course of business. Both of these risks affect the value of assets and liabilities, and hence the net worth of the financial institution.

When a financial intermediary purchases the nontraded claims of either a business or an individual, its main concern is with *credit risk* because it tends to hold these assets to maturity and expects to earn the cash flows promised by the borrower. A default means no cash flow (such as a failure by the borrower to make an interest payment), which is bad news for the intermediary. All of this suggests that a financial intermediary has an incentive to monitor its borrowers continuously. This relationship enables the financial intermediary to acquire information over time about the true quality of its customers so that it can then charge its high-quality customers a low rate and its low-quality customers a high rate.

Managers of financial intermediaries must also worry about *interest rate risk.* If a bank, for example, invests in *five-year* fixed-rate loans and acquires funds by issuing *six-month* deposits, it will be extremely vulnerable to swings in interest rates. In particular, let's start out on a happy note by assuming the loans earn 9 percent and the deposits cost 6 percent. This strategy currently earns the bank an *interest rate spread* of plus 3 percent (9 percent minus 6 percent). If short-term interest rates increase to 10 percent six months from now, however, the bank will be forced to renew its deposits at 10 percent but will still be stuck with its 9 percent loans for another four and a half years. The bank's spread will thus decrease from plus 3 percent to minus 1 percent, making shareholders very unhappy because instead of making big profits, the bank will lose money. On the other hand, if short-term interest rates decrease to 4 percent, shareholders will be ecstatic about the increase in the bank's interest rate spread to 5 percent and the improvement in the bank's profitability. In reality, shareholders should have been concerned at the outset because of the mismatch between the maturities of assets and liabilities. A maturity mismatch is simply a form of interest rate speculation. To avoid this most financial intermediaries tend to have assets whose maturities on average mirror the maturities of their liabilities. A notable exception, as we discussed in the previous section, was the S&L industry which got into trouble during the early 1980s.

Financial intermediaries must implement risk management procedures so that they can monitor these risks and set appropriate limits for each. How credit and interest rate risks differ across financial intermediaries is reflected in their balance sheets. Figure 11.5 shows condensed balance sheets (T-accounts) for some of the major financial intermediaries in the United States. Assets are shown on the left-hand side of the T-accounts, and liabilities and equity are on the right-hand side.

Depository institutions are shown at the top of the figure. As their name implies, these institutions all have deposits on the right-hand side of their balance sheets. Because these deposits tend to be short term in maturity, it is not surprising that depository institutions usually invest in relatively short-term assets. Depository institutions also face credit risk because they invest heavily in nontraded private loans. Specifically, banks make commercial (business) loans, commercial real estate loans, and consumer loans. Mutual savings banks, savings and loan associations, and credit unions make consumer and mortgage loans.

The **nondepository financial intermediaries** are shown at the bottom of Figure 11.5. Like depository institutions, some of these institutions face credit risk associated with nontraded financial claims. Life insurance companies, for instance, invest in nontraded bonds (called **private placements**) to midsized companies; commercial finance companies make business loans; consumer finance companies make consumer loans; and venture capital firms invest in the nontraded equity of small start-up firms.

As with the depository financial intermediaries, the asset maturities of nondeposit financial intermediaries reflect the maturity of their liabilities. Because the liabilities of life insurance companies consist mostly of insurance policies and long-term annuities, life insurance companies prefer long-term bonds, mortgages, and real estate equity. Similarly, pension funds invest in stocks, long-term bonds, mortgages, and commercial real estate equity because their pension liabilities are so long term. On the other hand, both consumer and commercial finance companies have much of their assets in short-term nontraded loans, so they raise funds by issuing short-term debt, particularly commercial paper. With mutual funds, interest rate risk is effectively eliminated because the right-hand side of the balance sheet is all equity. Thus there are no liabilities requiring fixed-dollar payments, so there is no risk to the fund itself when interest rates move up or down. Of course the investors in the mutual fund (the equity shareholders) make more or less as rates fluctuate.

Now that we have completed this overview of financial intermediaries, we can turn to a more detailed analysis of the structure and performance of the most important institutions. Chapter 12 focuses on depository institutions, while Chapter 13 deals with the nondeposit variety.

Assets shown on left-hand side of T-account, and liabilities and equity on right-hand side of T-account

Depository Financial Intermediaries

Commercial Banks

Gov't Securities	Deposits
Consumer Loans	Equity
Commercial Loans	
Mortgages	

Savings & Loans Associations

Gov't Securities	Deposits
Mortgages	Equity*

Mutual Savings Banks

Gov't Securities	Deposits*
Consumer Loans	
Mortgages	

Credit Unions

Gov't Securities	Deposits*
Consumer Loans	

Nondepository Financial Intermediaries

Life Insurance Companies

Securities	Insurance Policies
Private Placements	Annuities
Real Estate Equity	Equity*
Mortgages	

Property and Casualty Insurance Companies

Securities	Insurance Policies
	Equity*

Pension Funds

Securities	Pension Liability
Real Estate Equity	
Mortgages	

Commercial Finance Companies

Commercial Loans	Debt
& Leases	Equity

Consumer Finance Companies

Consumer Loans	Debt
	Equity

Mutual Funds

Securities	Equity

Money Market Mutual Funds

Money Market	Equity
Instruments	

Investment Banks

Securities	Debt
	Equity

Venture Capital Funds

Nontraded Equity in	Equity
Start-Up Firms	

*Mutuals do not issue equity but are technically owned by their depositors or their policyholders.

FIGURE 11.5 Selected intermediary balance sheets.

SUMMARY

1. Asymmetric information presents a major challenge to lenders in credit markets, particularly to those making loans to individuals and small businesses. Asymmetric information comes in two forms, adverse selection and moral hazard. Adverse selection arises before a loan is extended because lenders cannot easily distinguish between high- and low-quality borrowers. Moral hazard arises after the loan has been made because borrowers have an incentive to become riskier.

2. Financial intermediaries exist in part because they are specialists in the production of information. Intermediaries also reduce transactions costs and facilitate diversification.

3. The mix of financial intermediaries since World War II has changed significantly. In particular pension funds, stock and bond mutual funds, and money market mutual funds have grown significantly while depository institutions and life insurance companies have declined in relative importance.

4. The increased level and volatility of interest rates, which began in the mid-1960s and subsided in the mid-1980s, led to the creation of the money market mutual fund, which altered the structure of the financial system. Following skyrocketing interest rates beginning in 1979, Regulation Q was dismantled, the S&L industry nearly collapsed, and banks significantly changed the menu of liabilities they offered to their depositors.

5. The rising importance of pension funds, life insurance companies, and mutual funds led to the institutionalization of financial markets as funds flowing through these institutions increasingly displaced direct investment in stocks and bonds by individual investors.

6. The decline of banking's share of intermediated assets over the past fifty years suggests that if the trend continues banks may become a less significant player on the financial landscape. However, the importance of banks as lenders to small businesses and individuals (in conjunction with offering checking account services) suggests that they will be around for a long time.

7. Unlike other types of companies, financial intermediaries typically have financial instruments on both sides of the balance sheets. This creates special challenges for these institutions including the necessity to manage credit risk and interest rate risk.

QUESTIONS

11.1 One of the principal reasons for imposing Regulation Q deposit ceilings was to prevent destructive competition among depository institutions. Do you agree with this logic?

11.2 By some estimates the S&L crisis would have cost us $150 billion (in 1981 dollars) if we had shut down all of the economically insolvent S&Ls in 1981. It now turns out that it is likely to cost us on a present value basis somewhere around $150 billion (in 1995 dollars). Did we win or lose by procrastinating?

11.3 We noted in Chapter 6 that the quicker the market absorbs new information, the more efficient it is. Do you think institutionalization has had any impact on the informational efficiency of the stock and bond markets?

11.4 Asymmetric information is much less of a problem for large companies than for small companies. How difficult do you think it would be for you as a private investor to assess the true credit quality of your neighborhood bicycle shop or your local greeting card store?

11.5 *Discussion question:* We have witnessed a phenomenal growth in private pension plans, particularly the newer defined contribution plans, which offer flexibility in asset allocation. These private plans were promoted by government tax policy. Given their extraordinary success, should policymakers consider downsizing social security by increasing the amount of eligible contributions allowed to private plans?

CHAPTER 12

Depository Financial Institutions

Depository institutions are the most important sources of credit to consumers and small businesses. In addition, the deposit liabilities of these institutions form the cornerstone of the money supply. Because commercial banks are by far the largest depository institutions in the United States, we spend most of our time on them—examining how they are managed and exploring key industry trends. We then turn briefly to nonbank depository institutions to complete the picture.

THE FUNDAMENTALS OF BANK MANAGEMENT

Banks are business firms. Like Frisbee manufacturers, fast-food chains, and textbook publishers, bankers buy inputs, massage them a bit, burn a little incense, say the magic words, and out pops some output from the oven. If their luck holds, they can sell the finished product for more than it cost to buy the raw materials in the first place.

For bankers, the principal raw material is money. They buy it at a long counter they set up in the store, then rush around to the other side of the counter, sit down behind a huge desk (a little out of breath), and sell it as soon as they can to someone else. If they're really good at their business, sometimes they can even sell it back to the same person they bought it from (a trick bankers picked up from Los Angeles' used-car dealers). About the only way you can tell whether bankers are buying money or selling it is to observe whether they're standing up or sitting down. For some unknown reason, probably an inherited trait, bankers always stand up when they buy your money (take your deposit at the teller's window) but invariably sit down when they sell it (make loans or buy securities).

We can think of banks as repackagers of money. This makes them a financial intermediary because they have financial claims on both the asset and liability sides of their balance sheet. The liabilities represent a bank's *sources of funds* and the assets represent a bank's *uses of funds*. Banks engage in this process of buying and selling money for one simple reason: They hope to make a profit by buying money from Peter at a lower price than they sell it to Paula. Our first task is to see how bankers manage to pull this off. We then turn to some of the major trends in banking and discover that in addition to standing up and sitting down, bankers have had to start doing serious gymnastics just to stay competitive.

Uses of Bank Funds

Tables 12.1 and 12.2 show the assets that banks invest in and the major trends in asset allocation over the past 25 years. Table 12.1 contains the dollar amounts and Table 12.2 shows the percentage distribution. What trends are apparent over the past two and a half decades? We mentioned in the previous chapter that banking began to change dramatically in the mid-1960s as loan demand increased. This trend continued in the 1970s and 1980s as the proportion of total loans (business plus mortgage plus consumer plus others) increased from 54 percent of total assets in 1970 to 65 percent of total assets in 1990, with most of the increase during this period concentrated in mortgages. The increase in mortgages, particularly commercial real estate mortgages, turned out to be a big problem for banks during the 1990–1991 recession when real estate values plummeted—most dramatically in the Northeast and Southwest. The increase in loans was mirrored by a decline in cash and investments in state and local government securities. Bank holdings of U.S. gov-

TABLE 12.1 Assets of Insured Commercial Banks, 1970–1994 (in billions of dollars)

	1970	1980	1990	1994
Cash assets	93	202	318	304
U.S. govt. and agency securities	75	163	427	644
State and local govt. securities	69	146	84	77
Other securities	3	15	94	102
Business loans	112	283	615	589
Mortgage loans	73	263	829	998
Consumer loans	66	182	403	487
Other loans	63	184	355	381
Miscellaneous assets	22	101	264	429
Total	576	1,539	3,389	4,011

Source: FDIC *Annual Reports.* All figures are as of year end.

TABLE 12.2   Assets, 1970–1994 (percentage distribution)

	1970	1980	1990	1994
Cash assets	16	13	9	8
U.S. govt. and agency securities	13	11	13	16
State and local govt. securities	12	9	2	2
Other securities	1	1	3	3
Business loans	19	18	18	15
Mortgage loans	13	17	24	25
Consumer loans	11	12	12	12
Other loans	11	12	11	9
Miscellaneous assets	4	7	8	10
Total	100	100	100	100

Source: See Table 12.1.

ernment securities, which are highly marketable and can be liquidated on short notice, remained roughly constant.

In addition to the long-term trends, there are also cyclical fluctuations that are not captured by the tables. For example, between 1990 and 1994 total loans declined from 65 percent to 61 percent, with the bulk of the drop accounted for by the decline in *business loans* from 18 percent to 15 percent. This drop and the associated increase in the securities portfolio occurred during and immediately after the 1990–1991 recession, which is perfectly consistent with the historical substitution of securities for loans that occurs when loan demand declines during a recession. In other words, banks have traditionally treated their government securities portfolio as a residual use of funds—buying government securities during recessions when private loan demand is slack, and then selling them off during business recoveries, when private loan demand is vigorous.[1]

Why is it that no *stocks* (equities) are included among bank assets? The reason is that commercial banks traditionally have been barred by law from owning stocks on the ground that stocks are too risky. This prohibition dates from the National Currency Act of 1863 and the National Bank Act of 1864 and has been reaffirmed repeatedly in subsequent legislation. Banks *do* buy billions of dollars worth of stocks, but not for themselves; they buy them for the trusts, estates, and pension funds that they manage for others. Such trust department holdings are not included among a bank's own assets.

---

[1]For a more detailed discussion of this explanation and the empirical evidence regarding the reduction in lending during the 1990–1991 recession, see "Did Risk-based Capital Allocate Bank Credit and Cause a 'Credit Crunch' in the U.S.?" by Allen N. Berger and Gregory F. Udell in the *Journal of Money, Credit and Banking* 26 (1994).

Sources of Bank Funds

Tables 12.3 and 12.4 show the sources of bank funds and their changes over the past 25 years. Table 12.3 contains the dollar amounts and Table 12.4 the percentage distribution. Notice first how **transactions deposits,** which used to be *the* major source of bank funds—43 percent in 1970—have dropped in importance, declining to 21 percent by 1994. Transactions deposits are deposits with unlimited check-writing privileges. The bulk of the decline occurred in the 1970s and is directly attributable to Regulation Q combined with the general increase in interest rates on other types of assets that occurred over this period. Even in today's low interest rate environment, individuals and business firms are reluctant to hold any more transactions deposits than they re-

TABLE 12.3   Liabilities and Capital of Insured Commercial Banks, 1970–1994 (in billions of dollars)

	1970	1980	1990	1994
Transactions deposits	247	432	684	853
Savings deposits*	99	201	577	740
Time deposits	110	321	716	626
Large-size negotiable CDs	26	238	380	224
Miscellaneous liabilities†	54	239	813	1,256
Equity capital	40	108	219	312
Total	576	1,539	3,389	4,011

*Includes money market deposit accounts.

†Includes deposits in foreign offices.

Source: FDIC *Annual Reports.* All figures are as of year end.

TABLE 12.4   Liabilities and Capital of Insured Commercial Banks, 1970–1994 (percentage distribution)

	1970	1980	1990	1994
Transactions deposits	43	28	20	21
Savings deposits	17	13	17	18
Time deposits	19	21	21	16
Large-size negotiable CDs	5	15	11	6
Miscellaneous liabilities	9	16	24	31
Equity capital	7	7	7	8
Total	100	100	100	100

Source: See Table 12.3.

ally need for their day-to-day payments. They have learned that it pays to economize on their checking accounts because to hold more than is absolutely necessary means sacrificing interest income.

Savings and **time deposits,** on the other hand, continue to be a major source of bank funds—about 40 percent in 1994. Savings and time deposits are frequently lumped together, but in the tables we have disaggregated them into three components: savings deposits, small-denomination time deposits, and large-denomination time deposits (that is, **negotiable certificates of deposit,** or **negotiable CDs,** with denominations usually greater than $100,000). With savings accounts, funds can be withdrawn at any time. Included in this category are **money market deposit accounts** (first permitted in December 1982), which pay a money market rate and offer limited checkability. With time deposits, on the other hand, depositors who want to withdraw funds before the scheduled maturity date are subject to substantial penalties, such as the forfeiture of interest.

The negotiable CD was a particularly important source of funding for banks in the late 1970s and early 1980s. As we noted in the previous chapter, the negotiable CD represented the first major loophole in Regulation Q. Usually issued in denominations of $100,000 and higher, the negotiable CD can be sold in a secondary market if one has to raise cash before it matures. Thus it serves as an alternative to Treasury bills for corporate treasurers with excess funds to invest for a short time. Its importance as a funding source has declined more recently. *"Miscellaneous"* liabilities, however, have become increasingly important over the past 25 years. These include a wide variety sources of funds other than domestic deposits, such as:

1. Borrowings from the Federal Reserve.
2. Borrowings in the **federal (Fed) funds market.** Federal funds are unsecured loans between banks (often on an overnight basis) that are settled by transfers of funds the same day a loan is made.
3. Borrowings by banks from their foreign branches, their parent holding companies, and their subsidiaries and affiliates.
4. **Repurchase agreements.** Banks often sell securities and agree to buy them back at a later date (often the next day). As we described in Chapter 8, when a bank sells securities to a corporation or to another bank under an agreement to repurchase—called RPs or repos—the bank commits itself to buying the securities back on a specified future date at a predetermined price. In effect, since the bank has the use of the funds until the securities are repurchased, the bank is borrowing funds with the securities as collateral; the interest rate is determined by the difference between today's selling price and tomorrow's higher repurchase price. With overnight RPs, the bank gains access to short-term funds, which it hopes to use profitably, and the corporation earns interest while sacrificing virtually no liquidity. When such a transaction is made between a bank and one of

"If you had an account here, it would be a different story."
Drawing by Weber; © 1988 The New Yorker Magazine, Inc.

its own corporate depositors, the bank's balance sheet shows a rise in borrowings and a corresponding drop in transactions deposit liabilities.

Another source of bank funds, and one that has become increasingly important although it does not show up on the tables, arises from the sale of assets through **securitization.** Securitization involves the transformation of a nontraded financial instrument into a traded security. Banks raise new funds by packaging some of their loans into securities and then selling these securities, which are collateralized by the underlying assets, to investors. In addition to securitizing residential mortgages, banks also securitize commercial mortgages, automobile loans, student loans, and credit card loans. However, some loans, such as those to small and midsize companies, remain difficult to securitize, perhaps because of the nagging unresolved asymmetric information problems discussed in Chapter 11.

The final source of funding comes from equity capital. This represents the amount of ownership interest in the bank.[2] Recall that equity gives the owners

---

[2]More precisely, the equity listed in Table 12.3 is calculated based on accounting rules. These rules, however, suffer from several deficiencies. First, they are so complicated that they can put even the most dedicated accountants to sleep, often for days at a time. Second, they are based primarily on the *historical cost accounting* methods that we discussed in the preceding chapter, which fail to reflect changes in the market value of many bank assets and liabilities. Nor do historical cost accounting rules generally reflect a bank's *franchise value* that may have been built up over the years. Third, the stock market usually ignores the accountants' numbers anyway. The stock market's valuation (which equals the stock price times the number of outstanding shares) is often considerably less (or considerably more) than the accountant's valuation (often called *book value* which equals the equity capital on the balance sheet). This explains why banks often acquire other banks for huge multiples of their book value.

all the fruits of prosperity, including a claim on all future dividends, but limits their liability to the amount invested.

Bank Profitability

As we mentioned at the outset of this chapter, bank management is all about buying money for less than you sell it. Success or failure is recorded in the income statement. Table 12.5 shows the income statement for all commercial banks insured by the Federal Deposit Insurance Corporation (FDIC), which includes virtually all banks in the United States. Table 12.6 shows the income statement expressed as a percentage of total assets.

How much did banks pay for their money? The answer is listed under *interest expense*—$111 billion in 1994. For how much did they sell their money? The answer is listed under *total interest income*—$258 billion in 1994. Note that total interest income is divided into two categories, *interest on loans* and *interest on securities*. The difference between total interest income and interest expense, **net interest income,** is one of the most revealing numbers on a bank's financial statement. It is loosely analogous to a manufacturing company's gross profit. Net interest income expressed as a percent of total bank assets is referred to as a bank's **net interest margin** (**NIM** in Table 12.6). This is the bank's *interest rate spread*. In 1994 the net interest margin for the entire

TABLE 12.5   Income Statement of Insured Commercial Banks, 1970–1994 (in billions of dollars)

	1970	1980	1990	1994
Interest on loans	24	152	235	187
Interest on securities	7	23	69	71
Total interest income	31	175	304	258
Interest expense	13	120	205	111
Net interest income	18	55	99	147
Service charges and fees	2	8	16	15
Other operating income	2	8	56	61
Net operating income before expenses	22	71	171	223
Salaries and wages	8	25	52	61
Other operating expenses	7	26	96	94
Net operating income	7	20	23	68
Securities gains (losses)	0	−1	1	−1
Taxes	2	5	8	22
Net income after taxes	5	14	16	45

Source: FDIC *Annual Reports.*

**TABLE 12.6   Income Statement of Insured Commercial Banks, 1970–1994
(percentage of assets)**

	1970	1980	1990	1994
Interest on loans	4.17	9.88	6.93	4.66
Interest on securities	1.13	1.50	2.04	1.77
Total interest income	5.30	11.38	8.97	6.43
Interest expense	2.17	7.80	6.05	2.77
Net interest income (NIM*)	3.13	3.57	2.92	3.66
Service charges and fees	0.35	0.49	0.47	0.37
Other operating income	0.38	0.53	1.65	1.52
Net operating income before expenses	3.85	4.59	5.05	5.56
Salaries and wages	1.34	1.60	1.53	1.52
Other operating expenses	1.28	1.72	2.83	2.34
Net operating income	1.23	1.27	0.68	1.70
Securities gains (losses)	−0.02	−0.03	0.03	−0.02
Taxes	0.33	0.32	0.24	0.55
Net income after taxes (ROA*)	0.89	0.91	0.47	1.12

*When expressed as a percent of total assets.

Source: FDIC *Annual Reports.*

banking industry was 3.66 percent (= $147 billion ÷ $4,011 billion) compared with 2.92 percent four years earlier.

Many factors affect a bank's net interest margin. If a bank provides better service than its competitors, it may be able to get away with charging a higher rate on its loans and paying a lower rate on its deposits. If it has some *monopoly power,* possibly because its only competitor in town went belly-up, it may be able to take advantage of this—again, by charging a higher rate on its loans and paying a lower rate on its deposits. Banks today, however, are less likely to have monopoly power because of the enormous competition they face from other banks and from *nonbank competitors.*

The net interest margin is also affected by a bank's risk. As discussed in the previous chapter, the interest rate spread will change if the average maturity of assets is different from the average maturity of liabilities *and* the level of interest rates change. This is the consequence of *interest rate risk.* For the S&Ls, the increasing cost of short-term deposits in the early 1980s combined with little improvement in the yield on their mortgages quickly turned their net interest margin negative. *Credit risk* can also affect the net interest margin. If a bank invests more in lower yielding government securities and less in loans, its net interest margin will fall. Likewise the net interest margin will fall if a bank shifts within its loan portfolio from riskier to safer loans.

Moving down the income statement in Table 12.5 we see that *service charges and fees* plus *other operating income* have both become more important in recent decades as banks have shifted from traditional interest income to more nontraditional sources of revenue. (More on this later in the chapter.) If we add these other sources of revenue to net interest income we get *net operating income before expenses*.

The next items are operating expenses. *Salary and wages* are particularly important because banks are very labor-intensive enterprises. In great part banks become successful when their employees are productive and their staffs are lean. Thus the ratio of salary and wages divided by total assets shown in Table 12.6 is a key *efficiency* ratio in banking. Other operating expenses include the amount that banks contribute to their *reserve for loan losses* (called the *provision for loan losses*), the amount of depreciation on equipment, and the amount of building expenses.

Before arriving at the "bottom line," we must add *securities gains* (or subtract losses) and taxes. Because banking statements are partially constructed on the basis of **historical cost accounting,** securities held for investment are shown on the balance sheet at the price at which they were purchased—regardless of whether their market value has increased or decreased. The only time a profit or loss is reflected in the financial statements is when an investment security is sold.[3] If it is sold at a gain over book value (the amount the bank purchased it for), then a "gain" is added on the income statement. If it is sold at a loss over book value, then a "loss" is subtracted on the income statement.

The "bottom line" is *net income after taxes*. When net income after taxes is expressed as a percent of total assets, we have a profitability measure called the **return on assets** or **ROA** (see Table 12.6). An ROA above 1 percent is generally regarded favorably by bank analysts. The ROA for all banks in 1994 was 1.12 percent. Note that the banking industry's ROA in 1990 was only 0.47 percent. This was a reflection of the difficulties banks encountered in the late 1980s as described in the last chapter. ROA can be interpreted as measuring the success of a bank in deploying its assets. If we want to focus more narrowly on a bank's success in earning profits for its shareholders, we would look at the **return on equity** or **ROE.** ROE is net income divided by equity capital and was 14.4 percent (= $45 billion ÷ $312 billion) in 1994 compared to only 7.3 percent in 1990.

Bank Risk

Profitability is only part of the bank performance story. As we discussed in Chapter 7, there is a trade-off between risk and return—higher returns come at the expense of more risk. Thus just because a bank's ROA and ROE go up

---

[3]Some securities are **marked-to-market,** that is, changes in their market value are recorded as they occur. Any securities that are traded actively, or any securities that the bank does not intend to hold until maturity, fall into this category.

does not mean that stockholders will be happy. Any increase in profitability must compensate for the associated increase in risk before handing the bank president a big bonus.

Banks face many kinds of risk. Like any company with debt on its balance sheet, banks are riskier because of their *leverage.* As do other financial intermediaries, banks face *credit risk* and *interest rate risk.* But unlike other financial intermediaries, banks and other depository institutions face a unique form of *liquidity risk.* And large money center banks add still another layer of risk associated with acting as dealers in foreign currencies and securities. We refer to this as *trading risk.* Each of these risks is sufficiently important to warrant separate treatment.

learn this

Leverage Risk.   **Leverage** means that debt is combined with equity to purchase assets. Leverage adds to a firm's risk because debt requires fixed payments from the issuer in the future. Thus more capital on a balance sheet means a firm is less risky because more capital means the firm can absorb a larger loss in asset value without defaulting on its liabilities. The most straightforward measure of leverage risk, therefore, is the ratio of equity capital to total assets, known as the *leverage ratio.* In Table 12.4 the line just above the total shows the leverage ratio for the banking industry—8 percent in 1994.

The leverage ratio in Table 12.4 for the banking industry as a whole masks considerable differences in leverage across banks. In the 1980s, in particular, the leverage ratio for large banks was considerably lower than it was for small banks. This concerned bank regulators, particularly because the assets of large banks also tended to be riskier. As a result, regulators in the United States, as well as in many other countries, imposed **risk-based capital (RBC) requirements** in the early 1990s. The RBC ratios themselves are somewhat complicated and not particularly precise, but the idea is simple: The riskier the assets, the higher the capital requirement. We will discuss RBC in more depth in Chapter 15.

Credit Risk.   **Credit risk** arises because some bank borrowers may not be able to pay back their loans. Moreover, many of these loans are made to borrowers whose risk is difficult to assess and whose performance is difficult to monitor. That is, they are loans characterized by the asymmetric information problems of adverse selection and moral hazard, discussed in the previous chapter. Success in making these loans depends on a bank's ability to produce information about these borrowers and structure their loans appropriately. In particular, the riskier loans should be charged a higher interest rate and/or face higher **collateral** requirements.

How do we know how risky a bank's portfolio is? It's not easy—particularly for outsiders. One measure is **loan charge-offs** as a percent of total loans (see Table 12.7). Loan charge-offs are the amount of the loan portfolio that was "written off" during the year because some borrowers could not repay their loans. The virtue of this ratio is its precision—these are the loans that actually went bad over the past year. However, it is a *backward-looking* measure. It shows how loans made in the past have performed; it does not

TABLE 12.7   **Credit Risk Ratios, 1970–1994 (percentage of loans)**

	1980	1990	1994
Charge-offs	0.65	1.43	0.48
Nonperforming loans	not available	5.97	2.51

necessarily indicate how the bank's current loan portfolio will perform in the future. A *forward-looking* measure of credit risk is the ratio of **nonperforming loans** to total loans. Nonperforming loans are those with interest payments delinquent 30 days or more. Loans that are slow in paying interest today are more likely to default in the future. However, because neither the charge-off ratio nor the nonperforming loan ratio are perfect indicators of risk, both are typically used to assess credit risk.

Interest Rate Risk.   As we discussed in the last chapter, **interest rate risk** stems from a mismatch in the maturity of a bank's assets and liabilities. For example, if interest rates increase, a bank whose assets have a longer maturity than its liabilities will suffer a decline in net interest margin because the bank has to pay higher rates to renew its deposits before it gets a chance to replace its low-yielding assets. In addition, the *present value* of its assets will decline by more than the present value of its liabilities because long-term securities are more sensitive to changes in interest rates than short-term securities (see Chapter 4). Thus interest rate risk affects both the income statement and the market value of assets and liabilities on the balance sheet of a bank.

We can be more precise and identify interest rate risk with differences in the **repricing maturity** of assets and liabilities. *Repricing maturity* is a more accurate term than *maturity* because many bank loans carry a **floating interest rate.** To see why this is important, note that in a floating interest rate loan, the interest rate is linked to an index or benchmark rate that changes from time to time, such as **the prime rate, LIBOR,** or the **federal funds rate.**[4] Thus if the interest rate on a two-year loan is specified as "prime plus 2 percent floating," then the loan rate would be $10\frac{3}{4}$ percent if the bank's prime rate was $8\frac{3}{4}$ percent today. But if the prime rate increases tomorrow to 9 percent, then the interest rate on this loan will increase tomorrow to 11 percent. So, despite a maturity of two years, this loan's *repricing* maturity is really only one day for interest rate risk purposes. Many floating rate loans are adjusted at specified intervals, such as every 90 days or every six months. The repricing maturity for these loans would be 90 days and six months respectively.

There are many measures of interest rate risk. The simplest and most commonly used measure is the **one-year repricing GAP.** It is calculated by taking the bank's assets that will be repriced in less than one year (either because

---

[4]LIBOR and the federal funds rate, as described in Chapter 8, are freely determined in the marketplace, while the prime rate is more of an administered rate that is posted by banks to indicate the cost of borrowing for their most creditworthy borrowers.

they mature in less than one year or because they have a floating rate) and subtracting the bank's liabilities that will be repriced in less than one year. That difference is often expressed as a percent of total assets and is called the **GAP ratio.** For example, if a bank has a negative GAP ratio it means that it will reprice more liabilities than assets over the next year. Only relatively recently have banks been required to furnish the financial information necessary to calculate the GAP ratio. The GAP ratio for the banking industry as a whole was about zero percent in 1994.[5]

Banks can reduce their interest rate risk by changing the maturities of their assets or liabilities. However, if the bank's borrowers and depositors prefer the current maturity structure of loans and deposits, then the bank will not be able to entice them to change without decreasing loan rates and increasing deposit rates, thus narrowing its net interest margin. Banks can avoid this by hedging interest rate risk through the use of derivatives such as interest rate swaps, financial futures, and financial options. Since derivatives can be risky, all bankers should read Chapter 9 before doing anything and then scrupulously adhere to the 55-miles-per-hour speed limit.

Trading Risk.   Banks are exposed to **trading risk** because they act as dealers in financial instruments such as bonds, foreign currency, and derivatives. As was described in Chapter 6, dealers buy at their bid and sell at their offer to accommodate public orders. Somewhat less formally, trading by dealers means buying a financial instrument with the intent of selling it in the immediate future at a higher price. Every so often, of course, prices drop before the dealer sells, and that means losses rather than profits. For larger banks, trading risk can be significant because they are among the biggest dealers in the foreign currency, government bond, and swap markets. Banks and bank regulators are trying to develop improved *forward-looking* measures of trading risk. In particular, the focus is on generating an estimate of a bank's **daily earnings at risk (DEaR).** DEaR represents the amount of money a bank could lose in one day on its trading portfolio if markets move in the wrong direction. The challenge in developing a good measure of DEaR is in estimating statistically the likelihood of adverse price changes in these markets.

Liquidity Risk.   Banks and other depository institutions share **liquidity risk** because transactions deposits and savings accounts can be withdrawn at any time. Thus when withdrawals significantly exceed new deposits over a short period, banks must scramble to replace the shortfall in funds. For years bankers solved this liquidity problem by having lots of government bonds on hand that they could easily sell for cash. It is not surprising, therefore, that the ratio of

---

[5]The GAP ratio tells us nothing about the impact of interest rates on the net interest margin two years or more from now. As a result, the managers of larger and more sophisticated banks often focus on the *duration GAP*, which is a more complicated measure of interest rate risk based on the concept of *duration,* or *average* cash flow maturity. (See the appendix to Chapter 5 for a discussion of duration.) The duration GAP is a measure of the sensitivity of the market value of a bank's equity to changes in interest rates. This implicitly takes into account not only the impact on next year's *net interest margin* but also all succeeding years.

cash plus securities to total assets is a traditional measure of bank liquidity. We see in Table 12.2 that this ratio fell from 42 percent in 1970 to 29 percent in 1994, primarily because banks sold government securities to finance the growth in loan demand during this period. Banks also financed this loan growth with nontraditional sources of funds such as negotiable CDs, repurchase agreements, foreign deposits, and borrowings in the federal funds market. And these new sources of funds became useful tools for liquidity management in their own right. Thus the capacity to borrow in these "nontraditional" markets has become a more important source of bank liquidity than selling government securities, making the traditional (cash + securities) ÷ assets ratio a poor indicator of bank liquidity.

MAJOR TRENDS IN BANK MANAGEMENT

The U.S. banking industry is in a period of transition. For most of this century banking was a comfortable business that consisted of just taking in deposits and making loans. Government regulations insulated banks from competition among themselves and from competition from other financial institutions. Recent changes in these regulations in combination with the dynamic forces at work in the financial marketplace generated three major trends in the industry: consolidation, nontraditional banking, and globalization.

The Consolidation of the Banking Industry

The McFadden Act.   One of the principal inhibitions to competition in banking during most of the twentieth century was the McFadden Act of 1927, which prohibits banks from branching across state lines. Ironically, the McFadden Act was passed to prevent the formation of a few large, nationwide banking conglomerates that might monopolize the financial markets. The McFadden Act prevents a bank in Texas from establishing a branch in Oklahoma, or in any other state for that matter. For years, many states also had restrictions that limited or prohibited branching within their state boundaries. The result of all this? Lots and lots of tiny banks. By the beginning of the 1980s there were about 14,400 banks in the United States, about 40 percent of which had assets less than $25 *million*. In contrast, the average size of the ten largest banks in the United States at the time was about $60 *billion*.

To see the implications of all this, imagine that you owned a small bank in the middle of Illinois in 1970. At the time, Illinois prohibited any branching within the state. Therefore, you did not have to worry about the big Chicago banks such as First National, Continental Illinois, Harris Bank, or Northern Trust stealing your customers. Moreover, the McFadden Act conveniently prohibited Iowa- and Indiana-based banks from setting up shop across the street. There were no automated teller machines yet, and money market mutual funds were still a few years away. Town residents had virtually no choice. Pretty nice time to own a small bank, huh?

The Erosion of McFadden. This tidy world was not destined to last. The McFadden Act had a number of loopholes that were being increasingly exploited over time. Large banks were able to operate *loan production offices* across state borders. All of the major New York banks, for example, had loan production offices in most of the larger metropolitan areas by the 1970s. These offices were used to sell loan services to large and midsize local companies (although they could not accept deposits). Also, the S&L bailout legislation in the 1980s permitted bank acquisitions of failed thrifts across state lines. Most importantly, however, was an exception under the McFadden Act and subsequent legislation, permitting a **bank holding company** to acquire a bank in another state if that acquisition *was expressly permitted by state law.*[6] A bank holding company, by the way, is a parent company that can own one or more subsidiary banks. In 1975, Maine became the first state to permit holding companies effectively to branch across state lines by buying Maine banks, if Maine bank holding companies received reciprocal rights.

Nothing much happened in response to the Maine legislation until 1982 when New York passed a similar reciprocity law and Massachusetts passed legislation inviting a regional reciprocity pact in New England. The New York overture terrorized many state legislators across the country who feared that the big New York banks would take over the banking industry. As it played out, regional pacts were formed all across the country, though not surprisingly, all of the regional pacts formed in the 1980s excluded New York. However, there were some states, in addition to Maine, that passed national reciprocity laws (for example, Kentucky and Louisiana), and some that went even further and permitted acquisitions without reciprocity (for example, Idaho and New Jersey).

As the country became a patchwork quilt of different interstate banking laws, the number of cross-border acquisitions accelerated rapidly. As a result, some banks that were only regional players in the 1970s became *super-regional,* quasi-nationwide players by the 1990s. In the process they also became some of the biggest banks in the country, in part because the New York banks were partially constrained from playing in the acquisition game because they were excluded from many of the regional pacts. The impact on the structure of the banking industry appears in Table 12.8, which shows the top ten banks at the end of 1981 versus the top ten banks as of June 1995. The ten largest banks in 1981 are all located in major financial centers, while in 1995 four of the largest banks were from nonfinancial centers. By the end of 1994, 28 percent of domestic banking assets were owned by out-of-state bank holding companies, and seven bank holding companies (Norwest Corporation, Na-

---

[6]Actually, federal branching laws are contained not only in the McFadden Act of 1927 but also in the National Bank Act of 1864, the Banking Act of 1933, and the Douglas Amendment to the Bank Holding Company Act of 1956. It was the Douglas Amendment that prohibited bank holding companies from acquiring banks across state lines, unless expressly permitted by state law. However, the McFadden Act is commonly understood to mean the whole network of restrictive federal branching laws.

TABLE 12.8   The Ten Largest Banks: 1981 and 1995 (in billions of dollars)

1981 Top Ten		1995 Top Ten	
Bank	**Assets***	**Bank**	**Assets†**
Bank of America (San Francisco)	$119	Chemical-Chase (New York)	$297
Citibank (New York)	105	Citicorp (New York)	257
Chase Manhattan (New York)	77	BankAmerica (San Francisco)	226
Manufacturers Hanover (New York)	54	NationsBank (Charlotte, NC)	184
Morgan Guarantee (New York)	53	J. P. Morgan (New York)	166
Continental Illinois (Chicago)	45	First Union-First Fidelity (Charlotte, NC)	124
Chemical (New York)	44	First Chicago-NBD (Chicago)	120
First National (Chicago)	33	Bankers Trust (New York)	103
Bankers Trust (New York)	32	Banc One (Columbus)	87
Security Pacific (Los Angeles)	30	Key Corp (Albany)	67

*Year end 1981.

Source: The American Banker.

†June 30, 1995.

Sources: SNL Securities; Keefe, Bruyette & Woods, Inc. (as taken from the *New York Times*).

tionsbank Corporation, Banc One Corporation, First Interstate Bancorp, BankAmerica Corporation, Keycorp, and First Union) had banks in ten or more states.[7] Even the large financial center banks got into the act during the 1990s with the mergers of BankAmerica and Security Pacific, Chemical and Manufacturers Hanover, First Chicago and NBD (although NBD was a Detroit-based bank), and Chase and Chemical.

In 1994 Congress passed the Riegle-Neal Interstate Banking and Branching Efficiency Act, which essentially overturned the McFadden Act. Under Riegle-Neal, bank holding companies are permitted to acquire banks in any other state, and on June 1, 1997, banks will be permitted to establish cross-state *branches* of the same banking corporation (unless that state passes legislation prohibiting such interstate banking), without resorting to the holding company charade.

Measuring Consolidation.   How far has consolidation gone? One measure is the number of banks. While there were 14,404 individual banks in the United States in 1980, there were only 10,357 by 1994, a 28 percent decline. However, this measure understates the magnitude of decline because many individually

---

[7]See Allen N. Berger, Anil K. Kashyap, and Joseph M. Scalise, "The Transformation of the U.S. Banking Industry: What A Long Strange Trip It's Been" in the *Brookings Papers on Economic Activities* 2 (1995).

In The News

Bigger Is Better

Biggest Banks Get Bigger by Narrowing Focus to Financial, Geographical Niches

Banking's latest megamerger underscores an urgent message sounding throughout the industry: Pursue a niche or prepare to fall behind.

Size alone is not enough. Rather, the banks that prevail will increasingly be those that shun the all-things-to-all-people approach and specialize in one or two areas. The banking industry's current successes—Citicorp, J.P. Morgan & Co. and Wells Fargo & Co., among them—have all profited by pursuing narrowly focused product lines.

"Smart banks have been reducing their breadth of products," says Bob Mushkin, a bank consultant with Roberts Associates in Providence, R.I. "When you have too many products, too many services and too many variations, you introduce complexity into operating systems and confuse employees and customers."

The proposed merger between Chemical Banking Corp. and Chase Manhattan Corp. was driven by cost savings, but it positions the new institution to dominate at least one area—lending to corporate borrowers. Chemical has a 26 percent market share and Chase an 8 percent market share of syndicated loans, which are generally made to the biggest borrowers. Other specialty areas, such as mortgage lending and consumer finance, have also been enhanced.

Of course, factors such as cost control, effective use of technology and overall management will go a long way in determining who wins in the industry's continued shakeout.

Citicorp, which will be the nation's No. 2 bank in assets, has continued to invest heavily in its retail and consumer-banking franchise here and abroad. Its New York neighbors J. P. Morgan and Bankers Trust have gained prowess as trading houses.

Others are pursuing geographical niches. First Chicago Corp.'s merger with NBD Corp. gives them the largest market share in Illinois and two neighboring states. It followed Fleet Financial Group Inc.'s agreement to acquire Shawmut National Corp., concentrating market share in New England.

Analysts are often skeptical about ballyhooed strategies for revenue growth. "Banking is 98 percent execution," says Chris Kotowski, a bank analyst at Oppenheimer & Co. "What makes the difference is that some companies are disciplined and methodical, and others aren't."

Nonetheless, a growing number of banks are either shedding ancillary businesses or trying to expand areas of strength. Earlier this year, Wells Fargo sold its 50 percent stake in a money-management venture because the business didn't fit the bank's focus on small-business lending and consumers. Bank of Boston Corp. wants to expand its profitable Latin American business so it accounts for as much as 30 percent of earnings over the next two or three years, compared with under 20 percent now.

In most industries, specialization—or doing what a company does best—is common. But banking is different. Many bank executives take pride in running local institutions with a responsibility to the community. And federal regulations, such as those restricting interstate banking, protected banks from competitors.

(Continued)

But the inefficiency of the system has caught up with the industry. Nonbank rivals (such as brokerage firms), deregulation and rapid consolidation have forced banks to change to survive.

By segmenting customers and products, technology has given banks the kind of data they need to pursue niche strategies. "We're in the process of taking the covers off, and it's driving the decision on the part of banks to decide where they have the most value," Mr. McDermott said.

Source: James S. Hirsch, *Wall Street Journal,* Reprinted by permission of *The Wall Street Journal.* Copyright © 1995 Dow Jones & Company Inc. All Rights Reserved Worldwide.

chartered banks are held under the same holding company umbrella. A better measure of consolidation, then, is the number of independent banking organizations, where an independent banking organization is either an independent bank (a bank not owned by a holding company) or a holding company that owns subsidiary banks. Under this measure, a holding company which owns 20 banks would only be counted as one independent organization. The number of independent banking organizations declined from 12,380 in 1980 to 7,926 in 1994, a reduction of 36 percent. During this same period the percentage of total assets in banking organizations of $100 million or less dropped from 17 percent to 7 percent.

The Economics of Consolidation.   What's behind this consolidation? Nearly everyone agrees that the artificial walls built by the McFadden Act created too many banks. But most bankers provide more fundamental justifications for consolidation. Some argue that banks must be large enough to offer a wide menu of different products. Others argue just the opposite—that while banks have to get big, financial supermarkets do not work. Instead banks must focus on a niche at which they are particularly good. Interestingly, there is one thing that most bankers believe as an article of faith: **economies of scale** in banking. Economies of scale means that the average cost of production falls as more is produced, implying banks will get more efficient as they get larger. Conventional wisdom in the industry also argues that there are significant **economies of scope** in banking. Economies of scope means that offering two or more products is more efficient than offering just one. Banks have always been providers of a variety of products related to banking (commercial loans, consumer loans, checking accounts, CDs, and so on) and recently the menu has expanded to include a variety of nontraditional activities (which we describe in the next section). Therefore, it seems quite plausible that banks may enjoy economies of scope, with mergers offering a quick means to expand product menus.

There is only one problem with the scale and scope argument—a lack of empirical evidence. Academics' studies suggest that significant economies of scale exist *but* only for banks with assets *below $100 million.* For banks with assets above $100 million the evidence is mixed, and if scale economies exist

TABLE 12.9   Size Distribution of Insured Commercial Banks (end of 1994)

Asset size	No. of banks	% of total banks	% of total assets
Less than $25 million	2,020	19	1
$25–50 million	2,597	25	2
$50–100 million	2,641	25	5
$100–500 million	2,543	24	13
$500 million–1 billion	257	3	4
Over $1 billion	392	4	75
Totals	10,450	100	100

Source: FDIC.

for these banks, they do not seem large enough to be the main motivation be-hind the recent spurt in mergers of very large banks. To get a sense of the size of a $100 million bank, note that the 1995 Chemical-Chase Manhattan combi-nation was a $300 *billion* merger. There is also relatively little empirical evi-dence to suggest that there exist any economies of *scope* in banking.

So how can we reconcile the academic view with the bankers' view? First, the $100 million level still includes an enormous number of banks. Table 12.9 shows the size distribution of individual banks at the end of 1994. Of the 10,450 banks in the United States, 69 percent are under $100 million in asset size. For these banks, the economies of scale argument may hold and many, if not most, of them are likely to disappear. Second, mergers and ac-quisitions involving banks with assets greater than $100 million, such as the Chemical-Chase Manhattan merger of 1995 and the Chemical-Manufactures Hanover merger that preceded it in 1991, produce leaner and meaner bank-ing organizations by eliminating jobs and streamlining back office opera-tions. However, bankers may be incorrect to attribute these savings to *economies of scale and scope.* If one or both parties to a megabank merger are inefficient before they merge, then the merger may prove an opportunity to do *precisely what they should have done* prior to the merger: Cut costs and streamline operations.

Recent evidence suggests that while economies of scope and scale do not seem to characterize banks with assets greater than $100 million, inefficiencies do.[8] This explains why an efficient bank may want to acquire an inefficient bank (at a cheap price), throw out the old management, and impose its own operating system to make the acquired assets more efficient. Why were there so many inefficient banks? Quite probably because bank regulations such as Regulation Q and the McFadden Act protected inefficient bankers for years.

---

[8]See Allen N. Berger and David Humphrey, "The Dominance of Inefficiencies over Scale and Product Mix in Banking," *Journal of Monetary Economics* 28, 1991, and the *Journal of Banking and Finance* (Special Issue on Efficiency), 1993.

Nontraditional Banking

For most of this century banks have been severely limited in terms of permissible activities. The bank holding company form of organization mentioned earlier, however, has provided banks with more regulatory freedom. The Federal Reserve has the power to determine what activities are permissible in a bank holding company beyond the narrowly restricted banking activities conducted in the bank subsidiary. A permissible activity, however, must be "closely related to banking." For example, bank holding companies can offer data processing services, credit insurance, credit card services, and investment advice. However, the **Glass-Steagall Act** of 1933 prevented large commercial banks from engaging in the activity they seemed to covet most, investment banking—although there are some important exemptions. Banks could underwrite municipal general obligation bonds and banks could also act as agents for private placements (unregistered securities that cannot be sold to the public at large). For years, however, the Glass-Steagall Act prohibited one of the most lucrative parts of the investment banking business—the underwriting of domestic corporate debt and equity.

The forces of competition, however, are hard to suppress. Beginning in 1963 banks embarked on a strategy of testing the gray areas of Glass-Steagall and letting the court serve as arbiter. Banks challenged restrictions on a wide variety of activities including municipal revenue bond underwriting, commercial paper underwriting, discount brokerage, managing and advising open- and closed-end mutual funds, and underwriting mortgage-backed securities. In some cases they were successful; in other cases they were not.

Finally in 1987, the Federal Reserve succumbed to the pressure (or recognized the inevitable, depending on your view) and allowed bank holding companies to form investment banking subsidiaries, or **Section 20 affiliates,** to engage in so-called *ineligible activities* (should these now be called "eligible" activities?). The Federal Reserve granted corporate bond underwriting privileges to a handful of commercial banks in 1989 and soon thereafter, J. P. Morgan was granted the right to underwrite corporate equity. Essentially the Federal Reserve reinterpreted the meaning of "closely related to banking," but kept Glass-Steagall alive by limiting Section 20 activity in corporate underwriting and other ineligible activities to 5, and then 10 percent (or less), of total investment banking revenues. Despite this constraint, J. P. Morgan ranked ninth and Citibank ranked thirteenth in 1994 among underwriters of domestic debt and equity. Commercial banks never have been prohibited from underwriting in foreign securities markets. J. P. Morgan, for example, has long been a force in the Eurobond market (which we discuss below), ranking seventh among underwriters of Eurobond and foreign bonds in 1994, ahead of such prominent U.S. investment banks as Morgan Stanley, Lehman Brothers, and Salomon Brothers.

Another major push into nontraditional banking has been in the area of **off-balance sheet** activities. Broadly defined, off-balance sheet activities create a potential (or contingent) exposure to the bank but are not classified for accounting purposes as an asset or a liability. Thus, during the 1970s and 1980s, banks became major players in selling and trading new instruments such as interest rate swaps, financial futures, and financial options. Banks also dramatically increased their guarantee and commitment business. A good example is a stand-by **letter of credit** to back a municipal bond issue. A municipality issues bonds backed by a guarantee in the form of a bank letter of credit. If the municipality defaults, the owners of the bond can seek payment from the bank.

Why did banks, particularly larger ones, pursue nontraditional activities so earnestly? One reason is the loss of the large corporate loan business to the financial markets, as we noted in Chapter 11. Another factor was the new capital adequacy (leverage) requirements imposed during the early and mid-1980s, as bank regulators increased the minimum required ratio of equity capital to total assets. This constrained "on-balance sheet activities" of larger banks that were less well capitalized than smaller banks and promoted nontraditional banking activities that did not affect "on-balance sheet" bank asset size.

Globalization

Only 30 years ago, U.S. banks, with few exceptions, stayed within their own national borders. The field of international banking was dominated by British banks. But things have changed dramatically since then. Now many large U.S. banks do a significant part of their business overseas, lending to foreigners and underwriting securities in foreign markets. Similarly, foreign banks do a lot of business in this country, lending to Americans and underwriting in domestic U.S. markets.

American Banks Abroad. In 1960 only eight U.S. banks had branches abroad, and the assets of those branches totaled less than $4 billion. Now more than 200 American banks have foreign branches, and the assets of those branches total over $500 billion. What accounts for this remarkable expansion of U.S. banks into foreign countries? One reason is the rapid growth of foreign trade and expansion of U.S. multinational corporations that has taken place since 1960. American firms engaged in importing or exporting as well as American multinationals with subsidiaries and affiliates abroad often need banking services overseas. Foreign banks can do the job if necessary, but a branch of an American bank abroad can be even more convenient: There are no language problems; the firm and the branch share common business customs and practices; and, in the case of multinationals, the parent firm and parent bank may already have longstanding ties with each other.

In addition to branches abroad, U.S. banks also participate in international financing through Edge Act corporations, which are domestic subsidiaries engaged strictly in international banking operations. In 1919 Congress passed the Edge Act (named after Senator Walter Edge of New Jersey) to allow U.S. banks to establish special subsidiaries to facilitate their involvement in international finance. **Edge Act** corporations are located in the United States, but they have been exempt from the McFadden Act's prohibition against interstate branching, so that a bank can have Edge Act subsidiaries in several different states—one in Florida, for example, specializing in financing trade with Latin America, one in New York, one on the West Coast, and so on.

Foreign Banks in the United States. Just as U.S. banks have a major presence abroad, so foreign banks play a significant role in this country. For example, in a typical year about a third of the dollar volume of all commercial bank business loans in the United States is made by branches or subsidiaries of foreign-owned banks. Many large and well-known banks are foreign-owned: Marine Midland of Buffalo is owned by the Hong Kong and Shanghai Banking Corporation; Union Bank of Los Angeles is British-owned; California First Bank of San Francisco is Japanese-owned; Harris Trust of Chicago is owned by the Bank of Montreal; and the European-American Bank in New York is owned by a consortium of six foreign banks whose home bases are in Austria, Belgium, England, France, Germany, and the Netherlands. All in all, close to a thousand offices of foreign banks are currently operating in the United States.

Foreign banks do business here through four main organizational forms: They may open a *branch* of the parent bank, open or buy a *subsidiary* bank, establish an *agency,* or open a *representative office.* A branch is an integral part of the foreign bank and usually carries that bank's name. A subsidiary is legally separate from the foreign bank that owns its stock; the subsidiary usually has its own charter and may or may not carry the name of its foreign owner. Both branches and subsidiaries are full-service banking institutions. Agencies have more limited powers than either branches or subsidiaries; they can make loans but cannot accept deposits. Representative offices cannot accept deposits or make loans; they mostly make contacts with potential customers of the parent organization (by holding dinner parties) and perform public relations functions (by sponsoring rock or philharmonic concerts). Foreign banks can also complicate matters further by having Edge Act corporations in the United States.

Until 1978 foreign banks operating in the United States were largely unregulated. They did not have to hold reserves with the Federal Reserve, they were able to branch across state lines, and they had numerous other rights and privileges denied to domestic banks. This was changed by the International Banking Act of 1978, which brought foreign banks under essentially the same federal regulations that apply to domestic banks. However, there was a very important grandfather provision included in the act. This provision allowed foreign banks to keep their "illegal" interstate branches and continue their securities-activity operations. That is, interstate banking and securities-activities restrictions only applied to *new* foreign banks operating in the United States that started operations after 1978.

The Euromarkets. The spread of international trade and the growth of American multinationals encouraged branching by American banks overseas, but these were not the only factors stimulating foreign branches. The maximum deposit rates prescribed by Regulation Q played a part as well.

In the 1960s when Regulation Q still imposed interest-rate ceilings in the United States, European banks were able to offer more attractive yields to potential depositors than U.S. banks were allowed to pay. Not only were there no interest-rate ceilings in most countries abroad, but other regulations, such as reserve requirements against deposits, were typically less onerous than in the United States. As a result, foreign banks could outbid American banks for time deposits.

These deposits in foreign banks, mainly in London, not only paid higher yields than American banks, but, as an added inducement for the convenience and safety of Americans, were recorded as payable *in dollars* rather than in pounds or francs or whatever the money of the host country. Naturally enough, such deposits came to be known as **Eurodollars.** The term has since been broadened to mean deposits in banks abroad—still mostly in London, but now in other places in Europe and in Asia and the Caribbean as well—that are on the banks' books as payable in U.S. dollars rather than in the money of the country where the bank is located.

As we noted back in Chapter 8, Eurodollars are created when an American transfers a dollar deposit from an American bank to a foreign bank and keeps it there in dollars (rather than switching to pounds, say, if the bank to which the money is transferred is in London). Eurodollars are also created when a foreign holder of a deposit in a U.S. bank does the same thing, as when a French exporter gets paid with a check drawn on an American bank and deposits the check in a Parisian bank with instructions to retain it as a dollar deposit instead of exchanging it into an equivalent amount of francs. Why would anyone want to do this? Because dollars are still considered safer than most other kinds of money and are still more generally acceptable in international transactions than any other kind of money.

In response, many American banks decided to open their *own* branches abroad to escape domestic regulations and to bid for funds on a more equal basis with their foreign competition. During periods of tight money, when their ordinary domestic sources of funds dried up because of Federal Reserve restraint, Regulation Q, and financial disintermediation, American banks turned around and borrowed these Eurodollars back from their foreign branches. As we noted earlier in this chapter, these loans from foreign affiliates became an important new source of bank funding and are included under "miscellaneous liabilities" in Tables 12.3 and 12.4.

Of the $527 billion held in foreign branches of U.S. banks at the end of 1994, $265 billion was in London branches and $190 billion in branches in the Bahamas plus the Cayman Islands in the Caribbean. Branches in London are easy to understand: London has been an international financial center for centuries and remains the heart of the Eurodollar market. But how did the Bahamas and the Caymans ever get into the act? The Bahamas and the Caymans are tax havens, with almost zero taxation and practically no regulation. Virtually all the assets in branches there are held not by full-service branches but by "shell" branches, which are primarily bookkeeping operations with fund-raising and lending decisions emanating from the banks' head offices in the United States. A rise in British taxes in the early 1970s led to a substantial shift in loan operations from London to the Bahamas. The Cayman Islands subsequently came into the picture when the Bahamas achieved their independence, giving rise to anxiety (since proven to be unfounded) that this might lead to increased Bahamian regulation and taxation.

Just as the Eurodollar market is the *money market* of the **Euromarket,** the **Eurobond** is the *long-term* part of the Euromarket. Eurobonds are bonds that are sold (a) outside a borrowing corporation's home country, and (b) usually outside the country in whose money the bond's principal and interest are expressed. A typical issue today might involve, for example, a bond that is sold to investors in Great Britain by General Mills, a Minneapolis-based corporation, with the principal and interest payable in dollars. The Eurobond market has been increasingly used by American companies because it has a number of tax advantages and relatively little government regulation. The market is not confined to business borrowers; it is also a major source of funds for foreign governments. In fact, the first Eurobond appeared in 1963 when a British investment bank underwrote a U.S. dollar–denominated bond issue for the Italian highway agency.

Eurobonds are frequently brought to market by consortiums that cooperate across several national boundaries. For instance, dollar-denominated bonds (meaning that the principal and interest are expressed in dollars) could be issued by a Swedish corporation or by a Latin American government. They might be sold through an underwriting group that consists of the overseas affiliate of a New York investment banking firm, several banks in France and Italy, and a consortium of German banks. Parts of the issue thus wind up in the hands of individual and institutional investors in a number of different European nations. The overseas affiliates of several large U.S. commercial banks are quite active as underwriters in the Eurobond market.

In 1981 in an effort to bring some of the offshore Euromarket business back home, the Federal Reserve approved the establishment of **International Banking Facilities (IBFs)** on American soil. Caribbean branches flourished because they operate in an environment almost entirely free from regulation and taxation. The purpose of IBFs is to offer banks comparable conditions here and thus lure offshore banking back to the United States. Both American and foreign banks can now have IBFs that are within the geographic confines of the United States but are regulated *as though* they were located abroad. In effect, an IBF is a domestic branch that is treated by the Federal Reserve as if it were a foreign branch. Their transactions are considered offshore transactions, free from such domestic regulations as reserve requirements and deposit insurance assessments.

It is not necessary for a parent bank to open up a separate office to establish an IBF. Essentially, IBFs are bookkeeping operations, just like shell branches. A bank wanting to start an IBF simply notifies the Federal Reserve and then segregates its IBF assets, liabilities, and related transactions from all others. This creates a new set of books that are exempt from the usual rules and regulations that apply to domestic transactions. Moreover, many states have enacted legislation exempting the income of IBFs from state and local taxes, thereby providing an environment that closely resembles tax havens abroad.

So much for the good news; the bad news is that the services of IBFs are not available to domestic residents. IBFs can transact only business that is international in nature with respect to both sources and uses of funds. They are permitted to accept deposits from and lend funds to foreign-based customers only. Foreign subsidiaries of American multinationals are included among the eligible depositors and borrowers, provided the funds do not come from domestic sources and are not used for domestic purposes.

NONBANK DEPOSITORY INSTITUTIONS—THE THRIFTS

In addition to commercial banks there are three other types of depository institutions: savings and loan associations, mutual savings banks, and credit unions. Together these three institutions comprise the *thrift* industry. They are called thrifts because their principal source of funds is consumer deposits. On the asset side, savings and loans principally invest in residential mortgages and are constrained today to having at least 70 percent of their assets in housing-related loans. Mutual savings banks, which exist mostly in the East, are similar to savings and loans although they have historically had more power to make consumer loans. Credit unions principally invest in consumer loans.

As we discussed in Chapter 11, the savings and loan industry all but collapsed during the 1980s. In the early part of that decade it faced the consequences of an extreme balance sheet maturity mismatch (long-term, fixed-rate mortgages financed by short-term deposits) combined with a huge spike in interest rates. In the second half of the decade it suffered big losses in newly permitted activities, particularly commercial mortgages and real estate. While the industry started the decade with assets that were 43 percent as large as the commercial banking industry, it finished the decade with assets only 32 percent as large. The mutual savings bank industry suffered a similar fate, with assets declining relative to commercial banks from 11.8 percent to 9.3 percent. During the 1990s the trend has accelerated to the point where by 1994 the *combined* assets of the savings and loan associations and mutual savings banks were less than 25 percent of bank assets. In fact, many of the best savings and loans have converted their charters to commercial banks.

Credit unions were unaffected by the problems suffered by the saving and loan associations and mutual savings banks because they didn't have mortgages on their balance sheets when interest rates soared in the early 1980s. Credit unions are cooperatives organized around a common group (most often employees of the same company). Most credit unions are quite small although some exceed $1 billion in assets.

The management issues for the thrifts are similar to commercial banks. Like commercial banks their success depends on their ability to lend money for more than it costs, which is reflected in their *net interest margin*. Also, like banks the thrifts face leverage risk, credit risk, interest rate risk, and liquidity risk. Because of their extensive investment in mortgages, interest rate risk is a particularly important problem for mutual savings banks and the savings and loans. Thus our earlier discussion regarding the GAP ratio also applies to these thrift institutions. In view of their declining importance in the financial landscape, however, little more needs to be said about them.

SUMMARY

1. Over the past few decades, commercial banks have reduced their holdings of cash and state and local securities and increased their holdings of loans, especially real estate loans.

2. On the liabilities side, transactions deposits, which were 43 percent of bank liabilities in 1970, declined to 21 percent in 1994. Their place was taken by large-size negotiable CDs and miscellaneous liabilities, such as federal funds purchases and the sale of securities under repurchase agreements.

3. Key determinants of bank profitability include: (a) the net interest margin, which measures the spread between the yield on assets and the cost of liabilities; (b) the provision for loan losses; and (c) salary and wages.

4. Successful bank management requires good risk management. There are five major sources of risk in banking: leverage risk, credit risk, interest rate risk, trading risk, and liquidity risk.

5. Since the early 1980s, banking has experienced a period of consolidation, stemming in part from the erosion of regulatory barriers to interstate banking. This consolidation will produce industrywide gains in efficiency from economies of scale at small banks and from the elimination of inefficient management at both small and large banks.

6. Over the past two decades, as regulatory barriers have come down, banks increasingly pursued nontraditional off-balance sheet activities, such as underwriting and investment advisory services.

7. Since the 1960s U.S. banks have become much more active in foreign markets and foreign banks have become much more active in U.S. markets.

QUESTIONS

12.1 How have the major sources of bank funds changed in the past 30 years?

12.2 Why do bank regulators generally want banks to have more equity capital, while bankers usually want to have less?

12.3 Why have banks replaced many fixed-rate loans with floating-rate loans?

12.4 Bankers hold more liquid assets than most business firms. Why?

12.5 Bankers insist there are economies of scale in banking. Academics insist there are none except below the very small bank-size levels. Who is correct? Why?

12.6 Why should a consumer patronize a credit union rather than a real bank?

12.7 *Discussion question:* Has the reduction of regulatory barriers, including deposit rate ceilings, restrictions on interstate banking, and restrictions against nontraditional activities, produced a safer or riskier financial system?

CHAPTER 13

Nondepository Financial Institutions

Once upon a time, so the story goes, there were deposit financial institutions and nondeposit financial institutions and never the twain did meet. Those days began to disappear several decades ago. The sharp differences between deposit and nondeposit institutions have faded, as various financial institutions have aggressively invaded each other's territories. In this chapter we will look at each of the major nondeposit financial institutions as well as the overlaps and conflicts that have erupted.

LIFE INSURANCE COMPANIES

The first **life insurance company** in the United States (the Presbyterian Ministers' Fund) was established shortly before the Revolutionary War and is still in existence. There are now more than 2,000 life insurance companies in the country, with combined assets of about $2.1 trillion at the end of 1995. Some, like Prudential Insurance Company and Metropolitan Life, are among the largest and best-known corporations in the world.

Life insurance companies are structured as either stock companies or mutual associations. In stock companies the business is owned and controlled by regular stockholders; in mutuals, ownership and control technically rest with the policyholders. More than 90 percent of the life insurance companies now in existence are stock companies, but the mutuals are much larger and control almost half the assets.

Life insurance companies are supervised and regulated almost entirely by the states in which they operate. A company must be licensed and file reports in all states in which it sells life insurance. Regulation covers virtually every aspect of the business, including sales practices, premium rates, and allowable investments, and is usually overseen by a state insurance commissioner, who is sometimes also the state banking commissioner.

Firms marketing life insurance used to specialize almost exclusively in selling **whole life** policies to individuals. Such policies have a constant premium, which the policyholder pays through the entire life of the policy. In the early years of the policy, this constant premium is higher than actuarial probabilities warrant, but later on it becomes lower than required by actuarial probabilities. (Actuaries are statisticians who specialize in mortality probabilities.) Since the earlier premiums are higher than necessary in terms of actuarial statistics, whole life policies build up reserves. These reserves provide savings that yield a cash value the policyholder can borrow against or take outright at any time by canceling the policy.

Whole life policies contrast with **term life insurance,** in which premiums are relatively low at first but then rise as policyholders grow older and have a higher statistical probability of dying. Term life insurance policies are pure insurance and involve no reserves or savings element.

In the 1980s the life insurance industry increasingly emphasized group insurance (offered through employers, for example) as much as policies for individuals. In addition, life insurance companies began offering new types of life insurance policies, called **universal life** and **variable life** insurance policies. Up until then, whole life had been a very profitable product for life insurance companies, in great part because these policies paid so little interest on the savings component.[1] Most consumers, however, were quite unaware of this because the effective interest rate was not disclosed. But in a low and stable interest rate environment no one really seemed to care. However, in the rapidly rising interest rate environment of the late 1970s (see Chapter 11) the small saver took notice. Many small savers canceled their whole life policies (or borrowed against their cash values), and bought a combination of a term life insurance and money market mutual funds.

The life insurance industry responded by creating the universal life policy and the variable life policy. The universal life and variable life policies essentially "unbundle" the term insurance and the tax-deferred savings component found in the whole life insurance policy. The savings component in a universal life policy pays a money market rate of interest that changes with market conditions. The savings component in a variable life policy is allocated among a menu of investment options, including a money market mutual fund, a bond fund, and at least one stock fund.

---

[1] To be fair, it should be noted that the U.S. tax laws gave (and still give) the purchasers of many life insurance products (including whole life insurance) a tax break. Income taxes on the earnings of the accumulated cash value is deferred until the cash value is paid out at the end of the policy or when the policy is canceled. Even with this tax break, however, the after-tax yield on the savings component of a whole life insurance policy in the mid-1970s was considerably below market rates.

In line with these developments, life insurance companies have also altered their investment policies. Traditionally they used the policy premiums they received (in excess of what they paid in benefits) mainly to buy long-term corporate bonds and commercial mortgages. Lately, however, they have branched out into riskier ventures, such as common stocks and real estate. Metropolitan Life, for instance, paid $400 million in 1981 to buy the Pan Am Building in New York City.[2]

PENSION FUNDS

A lot of people are financially better off dead than alive, because when they die their life insurance policies pay out a hefty amount. Problems arise when they stay alive too long after they've finished their working careers and find out that social security doesn't come anywhere close to meeting their day-to-day retirement needs, not to mention buying an occasional luxury item. *Pension plans* are intended to fill this gap, enabling retirees to maintain a decent standard of living.

Most **pension fund** assets are in employer-sponsored plans. These plans come in two varieties, as discussed in Chapter 11: **defined benefit plans** and **defined contribution plans.** In a defined benefit plan, retirement benefits are defined (specified by the plan) and employer contributions are adjusted to meet those benefits. In a defined contribution plan the contributions are defined (specified by the plan) and the benefits depend on the performance of the assets in the plan. Until the 1980s the vast majority of private pension assets were in defined benefit plans. Since then, however, defined benefit plans have been eclipsed in terms of new pension contributions by defined contribution plans. (Some employers, however, offer both.) Now the amount of funds in defined contribution plans is about equal to the amount of funds in defined benefit plans.

Defined benefit pension plans involve the twin problems of **vesting** and **funding** of future benefits. An employee's pension benefits are said to be vested when the employee can leave the job and still retain pension benefits already earned. Many firms require that a person be on the payroll for a given number of years before benefits are vested; if he or she quits or is fired before then, all pension rights are forfeited. Other plans provide for something like 25 percent vesting after so many years, with a gradual increase to 100 percent after a number of additional years. The specific provisions about vesting are obviously among the most important clauses in any pension plan contract. Employers generally prefer to delay vesting as long as possible so that an employee will think twice (or three times) before quitting to go elsewhere.

---

[2]In 1992 the company changed the name to the Met Life Building.

Equally important are stipulations about funding. A defined benefit pension liability is fully funded when enough money has been set aside so that, after earning an assumed rate of return, there will be sufficient funds to pay the promised pension when it comes due. Because of the power of compound interest over time, the entire final amount does not have to be set aside today. If the money is expected to earn 7 percent interest, then only $1,000 has to be set aside today to fully fund a pension of $1,070 due a year from now . . . or a pension of $7,612 due 30 years from now (because $1,000 $(1 + .07)^{30}$ = $7,612).

Given those figures—$1,070 a year from now or $7,612 thirty years from now, and an assumed 7 percent yield—if *less* than $1,000 is set aside today, then the pension is said to be only partly funded. Many companies have a low level of funding in their defined benefit plans, planning to meet their pension commitments mainly out of current earnings when the pensions come due. This works, of course, only if earnings remain sufficient to meet such liabilities. Clearly, the higher the level of funding the safer the pension. Defined benefit pension plans invest in a variety of financial assets including stocks, bonds, and other instruments.

Because of abuses and mismanagement in many private pension plans, in 1974 Congress enacted the **Employee Retirement Income Security Act (ERISA),** which established minimum reporting, disclosure, vesting, funding, and investment standards to safeguard employee pension rights. The same legislation also created the **Pension Benefit Guaranty Corporation**—known, believe it or not, as Penny Benny. It guarantees some benefits in defined benefit plans in case a company goes bankrupt or is otherwise unable to meet its accrued pension liabilities.

One aspect of pensions worthy of special mention is the matter of gender. Women, on average, live seven years longer than men. Because of this, many defined benefit pension plans used to pay a smaller monthly retirement income to women than to men (because on average women live to collect more monthly checks). In 1983, however, the U.S. Supreme Court, by a 5 to 4 vote, ruled that unequal monthly benefits for men and women are illegal on the grounds that it is a form of discrimination based on sex. The Court held that an *individual* woman may not be paid lower monthly benefits than a man simply because women *as a group* live longer than men. It ruled that monthly benefits have to be equal, even though this means that on average women will collect more than men over their lifetimes.

Similar gender issues also exist in the field of insurance, by the way, where premiums based on relative risk are standard practice. Life insurance policies typically cost women less than men in monthly premiums because, since women live longer than men on average, their premiums will earn interest for the insurance company longer before they have to be used to pay death benefits. In other words, because they live longer, women are better life insurance risks than men. In auto insurance women also generally pay smaller premiums than men of the same age because accident records show that women are better risks—that is, they are involved in fewer accidents. On the other hand, health insurance policies are often *more* expensive for women than for men. There is considerable controversy about these sex differentials in insurance; unlike the controversy over pensions, however, thus far they have not been resolved by either legislation or court decision.

Legislation in the early 1980s made *defined contribution plans* a very attractive alternative to defined benefit plans. Defined contribution plans avoid the problems of vesting and funding because the benefits depend solely on the performance of the assets in the individual's account within the plan. In addition, each individual employee covered under a defined contribution plan has the ability to choose (within limits) the assets in which he or she wishes to invest. The menu of choices can be quite extensive depending on the plan set up by the employer. One employee's asset choices may (and probably will) be quite different than another's, even though they are covered under the same employer plan. Moreover, most plans permit employees to shift asset allocation. Ultimately the benefits for each individual retiree, therefore, will depend on the performance over time of the specific assets chosen by the individual.

Under defined contribution plans, *employees*, as well as employers, can contribute funds to the plan. This is a particularly appealing feature of these plans. Employer contributions are tax deductible to the employer, and employee contributions are exempt from personal income tax when they are made. As with defined benefit plans, employees do not pay income taxes on pension benefits until they receive them after retirement. That is, dollars contributed to pension plans are *tax-deferred* until retirement. The two major defined contribution plans are the 403(b) plan for employees of nonprofit organizations and the 401(k) plan for employees of for-profit organizations. As we noted in Chapter 11, an increasing amount of defined contribution plan funds go into mutual funds.

In addition to employer-sponsored pension plans, some individuals are also given tax incentives to set up their own pension plans—**Keogh plans** for self-employed people and **Individual Retirement Accounts (IRAs)** for working people who are not covered by company-sponsored pension plans.[3] These are usually established in the form of a deposit account in a bank or thrift institution or in the form of shares in a mutual fund of some sort, with the interest or dividends tax-deferred until retirement.

PROPERTY AND CASUALTY INSURANCE COMPANIES

Property and casualty insurance companies cannot plan ahead as easily as life insurance companies because they have no simple equivalent of actuarial mortality tables to tell them how much they will probably have to pay out

---

[3]Keogh plans are named after Representative Eugene F. Keogh of New York, who sponsored the legislation that created pension plans for self-employed individuals.

In The News

It's All in the Family

Trying to Avoid Being Caught in the Middle: Mutual Funds Seek Mergers to Grow and Capitalize on 401(k) Retirement Plans

The Contractors Supply Company of Kansas City, Mo., knows about building for the long term. It sells everything from hammers to backhoes in Kansas, Missouri, and Arkansas.

But until recently, Contractors Supply lacked a basic building block in the retirement plan it offered its 160 employees: bond mutual funds. With Twentieth Century Investors handling their 401(k) and profit-sharing plans, employees had few investment choices beyond the high-growth stock funds for which that fund company is best known. Last month they got that choice, though, a few months after Twentieth Century took over the Benham Group of mutual funds, a bond specialist.

Twentieth Century is not alone in its push to expand. Mutual fund companies that have grown steadily by carving out their own niches are now, increasingly, turning to mergers and acquisitions for growth, particularly to capitalize on the rise of 401(k) programs.

"A 401(k) program is often an investor's first brush with mutual funds," said W. Gordon Snyder, executive vice president of Twentieth Century. By offering a full array of funds in a retirement program, he said, a fund company stands a better chance of being selected for an individual's other investments.

And as investors continue to pour money into funds at a record pace, the gap is growing between full-service behemoths, like the FMR Corporation's Fidelity Investments and the Vanguard Group, and small, niche providers. Fund companies, increasingly aware that the broad middle of that range might be the worst place to be, are being forced to decide whether to be huge or tiny.

But those fund companies choosing to grow by acquisitions or mergers are encountering a paradox. Fidelity and Vanguard did not grow by buying rival funds; their businesses are home-grown. And some fund families, like the Crabbe Huson Group of Portland, Ore., have started down the road to merger only to find that the frustrations of trying to become part of a large, ponderous brokerage firm outweighed the advantages of having a bigger sales force.

Fund companies have been taking a growing share of the expanding business, at the expense of insurance companies, banks and other financial institutions. According to Access Research Inc. of Windsor, Conn., fund companies last year controlled 28 percent of the assets of 401(k) plans, double the level in 1988. Over the same stretch, insurance companies' share fell to 32 percent from 40 percent, and banks' share slipped to 27 percent from 32 percent.

At the same time, companies are offering more investment options to 401(k) participants. A recent survey of 50 large American companies by Watson Wyatt Worldwide, a benefits consulting firm, showed that the number of companies offering 401(k) participants five or more investment options rose to 60 percent this year from 32 percent two years ago.

(Continued)

More Funds, More Choices

The largest mutual fund companies, ranked by assets, are expanding their lines to better compete in the market for 401(k) retirement plans.

			Number of funds	
Largest Companies in 1995			**1990**	**1995**
Fidelity Investments	$324.0	billion	161	**224**
Vanguard Group	160.0		52	**85**
Merrill Lynch Asset Management	135.8		63	**119**
Capital Research & Management	129.5		32	**37**
Franklin/Templeton Group	95.7		71	**112**
Putnam Funds	72.8		51	**67**
Dreyfus Corporation	71.8		91	**162**
Dean Witter Intercapital Inc.	61.5		38	**102**
Smith Barney Inc.	59.9		68	**87**
Federated Investors	59.7		81	**214**

Source: Investment Company Institute

The fastest-growing part of that business is the market for small-company 401(k) programs, for companies with fewer than 500 employees. While 96 percent of companies with more than 5,000 employees already have 401(k) plans, according to Access Research, only one-third of the companies with fewer than 500 workers now have plans. And only 11 percent of companies with fewer than 50 employees have a 401(k) plan.

Source: Edward Wyatt, *New York Times,* September 19, 1995. Copyright © 1995 by The New York Times Co. Reprinted by permission.

every year into the indefinite future. About 4,000 companies nationwide offer insurance against casualties such as automobile accidents, fire, theft, personal negligence, malpractice, and almost anything else you can dream up. Lloyd's of London, it is said, will insure against *any* contingency—at a price.

In dollar terms, automobile liability insurance is the most important of all forms of property and casualty insurance. The most unusual insurance policy of all time is probably the retroactive fire insurance the MGM Grand Hotel in Las Vegas purchased *after* its disastrous 1980 fire, in which 84 people died and 700 were injured. Since there was uncertainty about how much the fire might cost the hotel as the result of negligence lawsuits, the hotel insured itself against payments above a certain amount.

Property and casualty insurance companies, like life insurance companies, are regulated and supervised almost exclusively by the states in which they operate. There is little federal involvement. State insurance commissions set ranges for rates, enforce operating standards, and exercise overall supervision over company policies. Their investment policies reflect the fact that they are fully taxed and that casualty losses can be unexpected and highly variable. Thus they are heavy buyers of tax-free municipal bonds and liquid short-term securities.

MUTUAL FUNDS

Money market mutual funds have been prominent on the American financial scene since the 1970s, as we saw in Chapter 11, but way back in the 1950s stock market mutual funds—generally called just **mutual funds** or *investment companies*—were all the rage. A mutual fund pools the funds of many people; the managers of the fund invest the money in a diversified portfolio of securities and try to achieve some stated objective, like long-term growth of capital or high current income or perhaps only modest current income but minimum risk.

Open-end mutual funds, which are the typical kind, sell redeemable shares in the fund to the general public. Such shares represent a proportionate ownership in a portfolio of securities held by the mutual fund. With an open-end fund, a shareholder can at any time go directly to the fund and buy additional shares or cash in (redeem) shares at their **net asset value (NAV).** The NAV per share is what each share is worth; it is calculated daily on the basis of the market value of securities owned by the fund and is published each day in the financial section of major newspapers.

Suppose a mutual fund owns securities with an aggregate market value of a million dollars at the close of today's stock market, that it has no liabilities, and has 10,000 shares outstanding. The NAV of one share in this particular fund would be a million dollars divided by 10,000 shares, or $100 a share. If the stocks that make up the fund's portfolio fall in value, its NAV per share will drop correspondingly.

Many funds sell their shares directly to the public at the current NAV. These are called **no-load funds.** Others, however, known as **load funds,** charge a sales commission, often as much as 8.5 percent of NAV.

Closed-end investment companies, which are in the minority, are completely unlike those just described. Closed-end funds issue only a limited number of shares and do not redeem their own shares on demand, like open-end funds. Instead, the shares of closed-end funds are traded in the stock market, and if you want to buy or sell them you have to deal with a third party, just as you would in buying or selling shares in IBM or Xerox.

Mutual funds are regulated by the Securities and Exchange Commission under the provisions of the Securities and Exchange Acts of 1933 and 1934 and the Investment Company Act of 1940. The primary objective of regulation is the enforcement of reporting and disclosure requirements and protection of investors against fraudulent practices by fund managers.

Mutual funds grew very rapidly in the 1950s and most of the 1960s, but they came on hard times in the 1970s and early 1980s (aside from money market mutual funds, which grew for very special reasons, as we saw in Chapter 11). However, the resurgence of the stock market in the 1980s and 1990s carried mutual funds to new heights of popularity. Many investors have been especially attracted in recent years to *families* of mutual funds, where a number of mutual funds operate under one management umbrella and where investors can easily transfer money among funds within the family. Typically a family of mutual funds will include bond and money market funds along with a variety of stock mutual funds. The two largest fund families, Fidelity Investments and the Vanguard Group, had 224 and 85 different funds, respectively, in 1995. Having a large menu of funds in the family is particularly valuable to mutual funds trying to capture assets invested in defined contribution pension plans.

FINANCE COMPANIES

There are two broad categories of **finance companies, commercial finance companies** and **consumer finance companies,** although both are often contained under the same corporate umbrella. Consumer finance companies make consumer loans; commercial finance companies make commercial loans usually on a secured (collateralized) basis. The loans made by finance companies have traditionally been riskier than those made by commercial banks. Because much of their lending is short term, finance companies borrow substantial amounts in the commercial paper market. In fact, they are the largest category of commercial paper issuer. Some of the most successful financial institutions in the United States are finance companies, the most notable being General Electric Capital Corporation.

Historically, commercial finance companies have played an important role in financing growing undercapitalized companies. Many people believe that the **leveraged buyout (LBO)** started with Michael Milken and the investment bank that he worked for, Drexel Burnham Lambert, in the late 1970s. In an LBO the acquisition of a company is financed substantially with debt. In the process, the company is transformed from having low leverage (low debt-equity ratio) to having very high leverage. If the acquirers in the LBO are the firm's former managers, then it is referred to as a *management LBO.* In fact,

LBOs existed for many years prior to Milken's arrival on the scene. However, they went by a different name: *bootstrap financings.* Instead of the debt being provided by junk bonds (see Chapter 8), the debt was typically provided by a commercial finance company. There was one other important difference: Commercial finance company bootstrap financing was (and is) offered to small and midsize companies in deals typically involving $50 million or less. The junk bond–financed LBO market, which roared through the mid-1980s and has enjoyed a resurgence in the 1990s, is designed for larger companies. In fact, the true insight of Milken was recognizing that LBO financing for large companies could be conducted in the *traded* securities markets through junk bonds, while it formerly had been limited to *nontraded loans* to smaller companies extended by commercial finance companies.

Some finance companies are referred to as **captive finance companies.** General Motors Acceptance Corporation (GMAC) is a good example. GMAC is the finance company subsidiary of General Motors. Its principal activities are financing car loans and leases to purchasers of GM cars and financing the inventory of GM dealers. Many different types of commercial- and retail-oriented businesses have captive finance companies, for example, J.C. Penney and Caterpiller companies.

SECURITIES BROKERS AND DEALERS AND INVESTMENT BANKS

Securities brokers, dealers, and **investment banks** are crucially important in the distribution and trading of huge amounts of securities, including corporate stocks, bonds, state and local government securities, and U.S. government securities. The difference between investment banks on the one hand and brokers and dealers on the other involves the distinction between *primary* and *secondary* securities markets. As discussed in Chapter 6, primary markets refer to the sale and distribution of securities when they are *originally issued* by the money-raising corporation or governmental unit. Secondary markets involve the *subsequent trading* of those securities once they are already outstanding. The New York Stock Exchange is an example of a secondary market.

Investment banks operate in primary markets, selling and distributing new stocks and bonds directly from the issuing corporations to their original purchasers. Their success is most often measured by the volume of securities they underwrite in various categories as reflected in the **league tables** shown in Figure 13.1. Underwriting is typically conducted through a **syndicate,** which includes many investment banks and brokerage firms. The syndicate is organized by a *managing group* of investment banks with one manager designated as the *lead manager.* The lead manager has special responsibilities that involve determining the final allocation of securities in the syndicate. League tables come in two forms: full credit to each manager and full credit to the lead manager. Figure 13.1 displays rankings by lead manager volume.

Common Stock*

Manager	01/01/94-12/31/94			01/01/93-12/31/93	
	$ Amount	%	Issues	$ Amount	Rank
Merrill Lynch	9,800.4	15.9	86	18,943.3	1
Goldman, Sachs	7,722.1	12.5	44	12,903.6	2
Morgan Stanley	6,331.1	10.3	47	5,504.7	6
CS First Boston	3,561.4	5.8	36	6,087.9	5
Smith Barney	3,487.9	5.6	42	4,868.2	7
PaineWebber	3,224.2	5.2	34	6,123.8	4
Lehman Brothers	3,190.4	5.2	40	7,826.0	3
Salomon Brothers	2,488.8	4.0	23	4,865.2	8
Donaldson, Lufkin & Jenrette	2,050.5	3.3	23	4,156.1	9
Montgomery Securities	2,004.3	3.3	39	2,547.1	12
Alex. Brown & Sons	1,639.1	2.7	36	2,560.9	11
Bear, Stearns	1,224.5	2.0	26	2,513.7	13
Oppenheimer	1,049.0	1.7	14	2,218.1	14
Morgan Keegan	950.7	1.5	14	82.2	53
Robertson Stephens	887.7	1.4	19	899.7	18
Top 15 Totals	49,592.2	80.6	523	82,100.5	—
Industry Totals	61,564.7	100.0	1,049	102,412.6	—

Investment-Grade Debt*

Manager	01/01/94-12/31/94			01/01/93-12/31/93	
	$ Amount	%	Issues	$ Amount	Rank
Merrill Lynch	61,912.6	18.5	410	81,154.7	1
Lehman Brothers	45,095.7	13.5	391	54,699.5	3
CS First Boston	40,357.3	12.0	324	28,494.8	6
Morgan Stanley	38,028.5	11.4	315	36,133.8	5
Goldman, Sachs	34,379.4	10.3	246	65,511.9	2
Salomon Brothers	30,855.3	9.2	350	39,864.8	4
J.P. Morgan	17,941.2	5.4	138	13,435.8	7
Bear, Stearns	8,195.3	2.4	103	8,265.2	9
First Tennessee Bank, N.A.	8,119.3	2.4	109	5,105.6	11
PaineWebber	6,406.2	1.9	108	12,535.0	8
Smith Barney	5,498.5	1.6	81	2,269.6	13
UBS	5,235.4	1.6	82	1,144.4	19
Citicorp	4,547.7	1.4	98	3,531.3	12
Donaldson, Lufkin & Jenrette	3,572.6	1.1	92	1,964.6	15
Dean Witter Reynolds	2,925.1	0.9	60	5,630.3	10
Top 15 Totals	313,070.1	93.5	2,907	359,741.2	—
Industry Totals	334,970.2	100.0	3,245	377,931.0	—

Non-Investment-Grade Debt*

Manager	01/01/94-12/31/94			01/01/93-12/31/93	
	$ Amount	%	Issues	$ Amount	Rank
Merrill Lynch	4,638.0	16.8	21	8,040.3	2
Donaldson, Lufkin & Jenrette	4,213.8	15.3	26	8,176.6	1
Solomon Brothers	3,788.5	13.7	16	3,009.0	5
Goldman, Sachs	2,918.4	10.6	18	3,755.6	4
Morgan Stanley	2,605.1	9.5	17	6,231.6	3
CS First Boston	1,802.3	6.5	11	2,068.6	7
Bankers Trust	1,561.4	5.7	11	1,884.6	8
Lehman Brothers	1,288.6	4.7	8	1,349.9	11
Bear, Stearns	1,178.5	4.3	6	2,498.6	6
Smith Barney	885.0	3.2	7	360.0	15
Citicorp	400.0	1.5	3	1,827.5	9
Dillon, Read	361.5	1.3	3	1,265.0	12
Chemical Banking	360.0	1.3	3	—	—
PaineWebber	337.5	1.2	2	1,731.1	10
Alex. Brown & Sons	300.1	1.1	3	350.0	16
Top 15 Totals	26,836.6	96.8	155	42,598.4	—
Industry Totals	27,565.1	100.0	166	44,877.6	—

*Full credit to lead manager.

FIGURE 13.1 League tables, 1994.

Source: Corporate Financing Week, published by *Institutional Investor*, January 9, 1995.

Brokers and dealers are involved in secondary markets, trading "used" or already outstanding securities. The difference between brokers and dealers is that brokers do not buy or sell for their own account. They match buyers and sellers of a particular security and earn a commission or fee for bringing the two together. Dealers, on the other hand, "take positions" in securities, as described in great detail in Chapter 6. In particular, dealers post bid prices at which they will buy from the public and offer (or ask) prices at which they will sell to the public. Somewhat less formally, they buy securities for their own account and hope to resell them quickly at a higher price. If they are wrong and the price falls before they can unload, their hoped-for profit becomes a loss instead.

Many of the nationwide stock exchange firms, like Merrill Lynch, Smith Barney, and PaineWebber, act in all of these capacities. They are called broker-dealers because sometimes they act as agents (brokers) in executing orders to buy or sell securities on the various stock exchanges and sometimes they act as dealers, quoting prices for various stocks and bonds. They also act as investment bankers for some of the securities they deal in.

A number of large stock exchange firms have branched out to provide new kinds of financial services that were once considered beyond their province. Merrill Lynch was the innovator, starting the ball rolling in 1977 with its Cash Management Account (CMA). The CMA consists of a financial package that includes a credit card, instant loans, check-writing privileges, investment in a money market mutual fund, and complete record keeping—including monthly statements. Today many brokerage firms market families of their own mutual funds. Merrill Lynch, Dean Witter, and Smith Barney were all ranked in the top ten providers of mutual fund families in 1995.

VENTURE CAPITAL FUNDS AND MEZZANINE DEBT FUNDS

The amount of assets in **venture capital funds** and **mezzanine debt funds** are too small to be recorded separately in our tables on intermediary assets in Chapter 3. Nevertheless, these funds provide an important source of funding to small and midsize companies. These funds are usually not available to the public investor and, therefore, are not registered with SEC. Their funding typically comes from wealthy individuals or other financial institutions. Many are sponsored by brokerage firms and banks.

The assets in these companies are quite risky. Specifically, venture capital funds invest in the equity of *start-up* companies. Start-up companies are firms in the very early stages of growth, typically after product development but before implementation of a market plan. Bank financing for firms at this stage will be limited. *Venture capitalists* (the managers of these funds) provide funds to these firms in return for a substantial equity stake in the firm. Most of the companies that a venture capital fund invests in will eventually fail. However, the fund makes its money on the considerable profits it receives on the relatively few firms that succeed. It receives those profits when it takes the successful companies public in an **initial public offering (IPO).** An IPO occurs when a company's stock is sold to the public for the first time (underwritten by an investment bank). The proceeds from the IPO pay off the venture capital fund and the entrepreneur who started the company.

Mezzanine debt funds get their name because they provide debt funds to small and midsize companies with claims on assets that lie somewhere between the "upper level" of financing (straight debt) and the "lower level" of financing (equity). The two best examples are **convertible debt** and **subordinated debt.**[4] Sometimes the managers of mezzanine funds simply invest a combination of high-yielding debt and equity issued by the same company. Though separately these would not be mezzanine instruments, buying them in combination makes them a form of mezzanine financing. Mezzanine fund financing is used to provide long-term funds for small and midsize companies, sometimes as part of a management-buyout financing package. Like venture capital equity, mezzanine financing is *nontraded* and held until maturity by the fund. Fund managers of both venture capital funds and mezzanine debt funds are typically active participants in the management of the firms in which they are invested.

BANKS VERSUS NONDEPOSITORY INSTITUTIONS

Many of these nondepository institutions offer services that compete directly with banks. For example, banks today compete with finance companies for loan business. Traditionally, however, these markets were segmented. Finance companies made the risky class of loans, while banks made the safe loans. Today they often compete for the same business. In fact, some of the largest finance companies are now owned by banks. On the liability side, banks have been forced to compete with many institutions for consumer savings. For example, money market deposit accounts at banks compete directly with money market mutual funds. Since 1986 banks have been allowed to offer their own mutual funds. In the investment banking arena some banks have been allowed to underwrite corporate securities since 1989. They can also offer merger and acquisition advisory services.

Real barriers, however, still exist. Despite legislative attempts in recent years, banks are not allowed to underwrite life insurance. Banks cannot own equities nor can they provide full-service brokerage. The regulatory constraints on underwriting place a binding limit on how much underwriting banks can do. Interestingly, other countries do not always impose these types

---

[4]Subordinated debt is a class of debt whose repayment priority in bankruptcy is behind, or junior to, other classes of debt. Convertible debt is a debt instrument that can be converted into equity (at a predetermined price) if the investor chooses to do so.

of restrictions on their financial institutions. For example, the European Union has adopted the **universal banking** regulatory model. Under universal banking, commercial banks can engage in corporate securities underwriting. Are there risks associated with permitting commercial banks to compete directly with other financial intermediaries? What are the benefits? These questions will be discussed more fully in Chapter 16.

SUMMARY

1. Defined contribution pension plans have become more popular than defined benefit plans. With defined contribution plans, employees can choose the assets they invest in. They also have some flexibility in making their own tax-deferred contributions.

2. Mutual fund families have become increasingly important as a marketing tool. The fact that some funds offer dozens of different choices, from bond funds to stock funds, has been particularly important in capturing the defined contribution pension plan business.

3. Finance companies play an important role in providing funds to consumers and businesses. Some finance companies, known as captives, provide financing for the customers of their parent companies.

4. Venture capital funds and mezzanine debt funds are important long-term financing sources for small and midsize companies. The managers of these funds typically take an active role in the firms to which they supply funds.

5. Over the past several decades, banks have faced increasing competition from other financial institutions to the point where the line between banking and these other institutions has become blurred. Nevertheless, real barriers still exist, especially in the areas of securities underwriting and life insurance.

QUESTIONS

13.1 Under most defined contribution plans, employees have a number of different investment options. How many options should employees be given?

13.2 Explain the meaning of net asset value (NAV) per share for mutual funds.

13.3 Life insurance companies and pension plans offer individuals the ability to save money for retirement with tax-deferred dollars. Are tax incentives really necessary to induce people to save for retirement?

13.4 The business loans that commercial finance companies make have been traditionally riskier than the business loans that commercial banks make. Is the commercial finance company business, therefore, a good business to be in?

13.5 *Discussion question:* Some financial institutions focus on a very few lines of business. Others have become financial supermarkets, combining many different kinds of activities under one corporate umbrella (usually a parent holding company). Which approach is better?

Financial System Architecture

CHAPTER 14

Understanding Financial Contracts

If you're thinking of pursuing the American dream to run a family business, this chapter is a must. Even if your professor doesn't assign it—read it. You'll learn a lot about financial contracts, which is a crucial subject if you ever want to negotiate a bank loan. From a somewhat broader perspective, financial contracts are the glue that holds the financial system together.

In Part II of this book we examined how the financial markets work. In Part III we examined how the intermediated markets work. Now, in Part IV, we put it all together under the umbrella called *financial system architecture* to see how the financial system as a whole operates. Although we address a number of issues in this part of the book, one of the most important focuses on the relative advantages and disadvantages of a financial **markets-oriented system,** as exists in the United States, versus an intermediary or **banking-oriented system,** as exists in Germany. We can then draw implications for the emerging economies of Eastern Europe and Asia. Should they model themselves after the United States or Germany?

But first we must discuss the subject of financial contracts. As we noted in Chapter 11, some borrowers obtain funds directly from the financial markets using traded securities, while other borrowers must obtain funding from financial intermediaries using nontraded financial contracts. These nontraded financial contracts are tailor-made to fit the characteristics of the borrower. It is now time to examine precisely what this means. In this chapter we will focus principally on business financing where the differences in contracting can be striking, both in terms of how the financial instruments are originated and in terms of contract characteristics. Much of the story stems from our old friend from Chapter 11, *asymmetric information*, or, more specifically, the problems associated with the availability of information about the borrowers who seek funding. We will also briefly apply this analysis to consumer financing to highlight key differences from business financing and to explore the limits to securitization of both markets imposed by financial contracting considerations.

In the next three chapters we complete our analysis of financial system architecture. In Chapter 15 we examine the regulation of both the intermediated markets and the financial markets in the United States. We are then prepared to analyze overall financial system design in Chapter 16, which focuses on a comparison of the U.S. financial system with several other major economies. We use that comparison as a basis for examining alternative ways of achieving the fundamental goal of getting funds from saver-lenders to borrower-spenders in the most efficient way possible. It turns out, however, that financial system architecture is not static; we have already seen that the U.S. financial system today is not the same as the U.S. system in the 1950s. In Chapter 17 we examine why financial system architecture changes and the role of innovation in that process.

HOW BUSINESS OBTAINS FINANCING

Businesses need funds for a variety of reasons. They may have to finance permanent assets such as plant and equipment. Sometimes they require funding to finance the acquisition of another business. Many need funding to finance their inventory and their accounts receivable.[1] While financing needs are common to all size companies, the way each individual business does its financing and the markets each accesess vary directly with firm size. For that reason we will consider separately how small-, medium-, and large-size businesses get their funds.

Financing Small Businesses

Before examining small, medium, and large companies, let's first define these categories. Unfortunately, there is no universal definition. The Federal Reserve Board in its survey of small business uses the number of employees as a measure of smallness. In the Fed's view, a firm with fewer than 500 employees is considered small. The problem with this definition is that there are some relatively large firms with fewer than 500 employees. We prefer a definition based on asset size because asset size is probably the most important factor in determining where businesses seek external financing. Our cutoff point for small firms is $10 million in assets.[2]

---

[1]Accounts receivable are funds that are owed to a firm by its customers (to whom the firm has extended "trade credit")

[2]Much of our description of small-firm financing is based on data in the National Survey of Small Business Finance conducted in 1988–1989 by the Federal Reserve Board and the Small Business Administration. This survey is unique among business data sets in that it contains extensive information about both the characteristics of surveyed firms *and* the characteristics of the financial contracts that they used to finance themselves.

What do firms with assets less than $10 million look like? Statistically, the vast majority are privately owned (they do not issue publicly traded stock), with ownership concentrated in a single family. In addition, the overwhelming majority are managed by their owners. They include everything from yogurt stores to bowling alleys to small textile manufacturers.[3]

Many small firms do not need external financing beyond trade credit, namely the delayed payment offered by a company's suppliers. Some small firms that have been consistently profitable over a long period of time often have sufficient capital to be self-financing. However, many small firms do not have that luxury and require external financing. For the tiniest firms that financing is often provided by the owner's credit cards. For those other than the tiniest, banks are the most likely source of external financing, although commercial finance companies also lend to riskier small businesses.

Banks provide working capital financing either via a separately negotiated short-term loan or via a **line of credit (L/C).** *Working capital financing* refers to financing accounts receivable and inventory. With a separately negotiated short-term loan, the bank makes a one-time loan with a short maturity, most often 90 days or less. Under an L/C, the bank extends a credit *capacity* for a specified period of time. For instance, a $1 million, one-year L/C gives the borrowing firm the preapproved ability to borrow up to $1 million at any time during the year. It borrows and pays interest, however, only when it needs the money. It may borrow $200,000 for two weeks and then pay it off, in which case it pays only two weeks' interest. Once the L/C is approved, the borrowing firm can *draw down* funds with a simple telephone request. Firms with a continuing need for working capital financing usually prefer a line of credit. This reduces the headaches associated with getting an approval from the bank each time the firm wants to borrow. It also provides a form of insurance

---

[3]A numerically small exception to this profile are those young companies with new products or technologies that are rapidly moving through the early stages of firm growth. The entrepreneurs who start these companies may turn to a high net worth individual investor for very early-stage equity financing. These investors are called "angels" and this type of equity investment (sometimes up to a $1 million) is called **angel financing.** Perhaps a year or two later the entrepreneur, if successful, will turn to a venture capital fund for more external equity. Venture capital funds provide equity financing, usually in the $1 million to $4 million funding range, typically under the condition that fund managers actively participate in the management of the firm. Because of their high risk, most of these companies eventually fail. For those that succeed, however, the venture capitalist is rewarded handsomely when the company is "taken public" in an *initial public offering (IPO).* As we noted in Chapter 13, an IPO occurs when a company's stock is sold to the public for the first time with the proceeds often being in the $5 to $20 million range. The proceeds from the IPO pay off the venture capital fund and the entrepreneur who started the company. While venture capital-financed start-up firms are a tiny fraction of the small business population, their new product/new technology orientation makes them disproportionately important economically because they represent the Microsofts of the future. For a further discussion of private equity and venture capital see Silvia B. Sagari and Gabriela Guidotti, "Venture Capital: The Lessons from the Developed World for the Developing Markets" in *Financial Markets, Institutions & Instruments,* 1, 1992, and George W. Fenn, Nellie Liang, and Stephen Prowse, "The Economics of the Private Equity Market," Federal Reserve Board *Staff Study* 168 (1995).

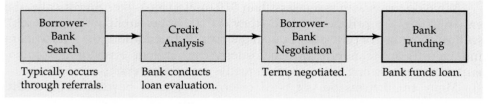

FIGURE 14.1   **Bank loan origination.**

against *credit rationing*, that is, the bank must honor its loan commitment even if the bank would prefer to curtail new lending in general.[4]

In addition to working capital loans, banks also extend funding to small companies to purchase or lease plant and equipment. The maturity of loans to finance plant and equipment is typically less than the life span of the assets themselves.

The process of commercial bank lending is depicted in Figure 14.1. The first step involves finding a bank to fit the borrower. When the owner of a small business becomes dissatisfied with her current bank, she will turn to her most trusted financial advisor. This usually means, for better or worse, her accountant. A good accountant has cultivated relationships with loan officers at different banks and will recommend two or three to choose from. Thus the first step in arranging a bank loan, "borrower-bank search" in Figure 14.1, is usually accomplished through referrals—most often through the firm's accountant, and if not the accountant, the firm's lawyer.

Once the connection is made, the bank's *loan officer* conducts a complete credit analysis of the borrower. This typically starts with a review of the borrower's financial statements followed closely thereafter with a visit to the borrower's place of business. During that visit the loan officer tries to assess the managerial strengths and weaknesses of the owner/manager. This visit also gives the owner/manager a chance to meet her prospective loan officer and evaluate his ability (what's good for the goose is good for the gander).

The loan officer will usually want additional information about the firm in order to assess its future prospects. This includes information about the firm's product or service, as well as its customers, suppliers, production capabilities, and track record. It may also include supplementary financial information, such as a cash flow projections, and computer printouts of accounts receivable, accounts payable, and inventory. In addition, the loan officer may purchase a *credit report* from a commercial credit agency, such as Dunn & Bradstreet, which contains a variety of information including how promptly the firm pays its bills and whether or not it has any lawsuits pending. During this process of credit evaluation the loan officer will probably question the owner/manager several times to clarify the accumulated information—so don't get nervous when the telephone rings and the loan officer is on the line.

---

[4]For a further discussion of credit rationing see Allen N. Berger and Gregory F. Udell, "Some Evidence on the Empirical Significance of Credit Rationing" in *Journal of Political Economy* 100 (October 1992), pp. 1047–1077.

The loan must then be approved internally by the bank. If the loan is small enough, the loan officer may have the authority to approve it on his own. Larger loans may require the approval of more senior loan officers. And, in most banks, loans above a certain amount must be approved by a *loan committee,* which will typically be composed of bank managers and loan officers. If the loan requires committee approval, the loan officer will present the loan to the committee and try to convince committee members that the loan should be approved.[5] The loan officer is likely to negotiate the terms with the owner/manager prior to the loan committee meeting under the assumption that the final contract will be approved. The loan committee can then accept, reject, or modify the loan proposal. Once all the details are approved, the loan is funded, which means you get the money and have the honor of starting to pay interest.

Several features of small business loans distinguish them from loans to larger companies. Perhaps the most important is the relationship that develops between the loan officer and the owner/manager during the process of originating the loan. Over time that relationship will grow as the loan officer monitors borrower performance and assesses future loan requests. Bankers have an advantage in developing a relationship with their business borrowers because the banks provide a whole menu of services, such as checking accounts, retirement products, trust activities, and payroll processing. This makes it easier for banks to learn about a company and its owner/managers. It is not surprising to find, therefore, that small businesses with longer-term bank relationships will on average pay a lower interest rate on their bank loans and will be less dependent on expensive trade credit for external financing.[6]

A second distinguishing feature of the small business loan is the nature of the loan contract itself, specifically, the terms of the contract. Small business loans are very often *collateralized,* are frequently *guaranteed* by the owner/manager, and often contain restrictive *covenants.* Let's take a look at each of these items.

Over one-third of all bank L/Cs to small businesses are collateralized, that is, secured, by accounts receivable and inventory. Typically, riskier firms that want an L/C will be required to *pledge* these assets as collateral. Most loans to purchase plant and equipment, regardless of firm risk, are secured by the plant and equipment purchased with the proceeds. When a company pledges any or all of these assets as collateral to a lender, that lender then has a more

---

[5]A minority of banks do not have loan committees. These banks give individual loan officers credit approval authority, usually depending on their seniority. Sometimes for large loans, approval from two loan officers may be required. See Gregory F. Udell, "Designing the Optimal Loan Review Policy: An Analysis of Loan Review in Midwestern Banks," *Prochnow Reports* monograph 1987.

[6]See Mitchell N. Petersen and Raghuram G. Rajan, "The Effect of Credit Market Competition on Firm-Creditor Relationships," University of Chicago working paper (February 1993); Mitchell N. Petersen and Raghuram G. Rajan, "The Benefits of Firm-Creditor Relationships," *Journal of Finance* 47 (March 1994), pp. 3–37; and Allen N. Berger and Gregory F. Udell, "Relationship Lending and Lines of Credit in Small Firm Finance," *Journal of Business* (July 1995), pp. 351–381.

advantageous position than other creditors should the company enter bankruptcy. The **secured lender** has the right to petition the bankruptcy court to sell the collateral and use the proceeds to pay off its loan (or to obtain value equivalent to this). If the proceeds from selling the collateral are not sufficient, then the remaining balance reverts to the status of an **unsecured loan** with a claim equal to all other unsecured loans. If the proceeds from the sale of the collateral exceed the outstanding balance of the secured loan, then the excess becomes available to pay off the unsecured lenders.[7]

It is not uncommon in small business lending for the bank to require that the owner/manager pledge some of her *personal* assets as collateral. This type of collateral is referred to as *outside* collateral because it represents pledged assets outside of the firm. This is quite different from pledging company assets, or *inside* collateral, such as accounts receivable or inventory, because with inside collateral, the bank gains security at the expense of other firm creditors, while with outside collateral the bank gains security at the expense of the owner/manager. Stocks, bonds, and real estate are typical forms of outside collateral.

Another contract feature often found in small business loans is the requirement that the owner of the borrowing firm *guarantee* the company's loan. When a bank requires an owner/manager to guarantee the loan personally, then the owner will become *personally liable* for any unpaid balance. To assess the value of the owner's guarantee, the bank often requires a personal financial statement showing the owner/manager's personal assets, liabilities, and income. About 40 percent of all L/Cs to small businesses are **personally guaranteed** by the owner.[8]

Bank loans to small businesses frequently contain **restrictive covenants.** Covenants are essentially promises that the company makes to the bank. Many covenants restrict certain types of actions or strategies. For example, the company may be prohibited from selling certain fixed assets or from spending too much money on new fixed assets. The company may not be allowed to acquire other companies. It may be prohibited from paying the owner/managers too much in dividends and/or salaries or from pledging company assets as collateral to some other company. To help the bank monitor the covenants, the firm must submit *audited* financial statements to the bank. These are financial statements prepared by a certified public accountant who *verifies* that the numbers reflect accurately the condition of the company. Au-

---

[7]Commercial finance companies also lend to riskier small and midsize businesses under collateralized loans and L/Cs.

[8]It should be noted that there is a subtle, but important, difference between when an owner/manager personally guarantees and when she pledges outside collateral. In both cases the owner/manager puts her own wealth at risk. However, with a personal guarantee, the owner/manager still has control over all of her assets. However, if she pledges any of these assets as outside collateral, then she cannot sell them without the bank's permission. For example, when personal stocks and bonds are used as collateral, they are held in the bank's vault. Sometimes a bank will require that the owner/manager *both* guarantee the loan and pledge some of her assets as outside collateral.

dited financial statements are quite expensive to prepare. They would be prohibitively expensive, in general, for most companies much below $1 million in assets, which is why covenants are not feasible for companies below this size.

In general, covenants are linked to actions indicating that the company has become riskier. When a covenant is violated the bank typically has the right to demand immediate payment of the loan. The violation, or the potential violation, of a covenant can occur for one of two reasons—either the company is in financial distress, or the company wants to pursue a new activity that is currently restricted. If the reason is financial distress, the covenant violation gives the bank the power to cut its losses rather than waiting until the loan or L/C matures.

In the vast majority of cases, however, the violation of a covenant is by design: The company wants to do something new. The owner/manager will try and convince the bank that the new strategy will improve the firm's value. The bank's loan officer, on the other hand, needs assurance that the new strategy will not make the loan riskier. In order to make this assessment, he will probably conduct a thorough examination similar to the initial credit analysis. If the new strategy does not make the loan riskier, he will waive or relax the covenant. If the new strategy increases the riskiness of the loan, then the loan officer can either deny the request to waive the covenant or renegotiate the terms of the loan (or L/C) to reflect this risk.

One other characteristic of small business loans is that the maturity of the loan rarely extends beyond five years. The reason for this relatively short maturity compared with the longer-term debt of larger companies will be discussed below.

Before leaving the subject of small business financing, we should say a word about *very* small firms, like your local bakery shop or laundromat. For firms with assets below about $100,000, outside financing becomes a very different ball game. In this size range it is difficult to distinguish between the activities of the business and the activities of the owner/manager. For example, many firms in this size range are effectively financed through the owner's personal credit cards and lines of credit. The owner/managers often operate without a clear distinction between the accounts of the business and personal accounts. As a result, banks will often base loans to companies of this size on the creditworthiness of the individual and not on a separate evaluation of the company.

Financing Midsize Businesses

We choose an asset range of $10 million to $150 million to identify midsize businesses because companies that fall into this asset category are usually big enough that they are no longer bank-dependent for external debt financing but are not big enough to issue *traded* debt in the public bond market. Although these companies usually can't issue bonds, some are likely to be publicly owned—that is, they can and do issue equity in the primary market which is traded over-the-counter. Therefore, some midsize companies are managed by someone other than the owner while some are owner managed.

For short-term debt financing, midsize companies, like small businesses, principally turn to commercial banks. The origination of bank loans to midsize businesses is similar to the process we described for small businesses. Also, like small businesses, midsize companies at the small end of the range tend to borrow from local banks *if* local banks are large enough to provide the needed funding, while larger midsize companies are more likely to seek financing from nonlocal banks.

Bank L/Cs to midsize companies typically have covenants of the same type we discussed above. The restrictiveness of these covenants vary with the riskiness and size of the borrower—smaller and riskier businesses will have more restrictive covenants, all other things being equal. Riskier midsize business may also be required to pledge collateral to secure their L/Cs.

Midsize businesses differ from small businesses in one very important way. They have access to longer-term debt financing (beyond equipment loans and mortgages), such as through a financing package from their commercial banks that combines an L/C with an intermediate-term loan. These packages are often referred to as **revolving lines of credit.** A typical "revolver," for example, might give a company a $20 million credit line for three years with the ability to convert any portion of it into a five-year term loan.

Long-term debt financing to midsize companies is often provided by non-bank institutions. *Mezzanine debt funds*, discussed in Chapter 13, provide long-term debt to midsize companies at the smaller end of the midsize range. A much more important source of long-term debt financing to midsize companies comes from the **private placement** market.[9] A private placement is a bond (in our case) that does not have to be registered with the Securities and Exchange Commission. Private placements, therefore, avoid SEC registration costs (which we will discuss later in this chapter) and they avoid the *public* disclosure of financial information that is required of registered bonds. However, private placements can be sold only to financial institutions and high net worth, "sophisticated" investors, and they cannot, in general, be resold by the original investor for at least two years. In short, there is no public secondary market for private placements. Over 80 percent of all private placements are purchased by life insurance companies and the vast majority of these are held until maturity.

If you want to raise money via a private placement, you've got to think big. Almost all issues exceed $10 million, so this source of funds is generally unavailable to small businesses. Firms with access to this market typically get their short-term financing from a commercial bank as described above, and get their long-term financing (usually above seven years to maturity) by issuing a private placement. Like commercial bank loans, private placements have covenants although they are generally somewhat "looser" (less restrictive)

---

[9]Much of our discussion of the private placement market is taken from "The Economics of the Private Placement Market," Federal Reserve Board *Staff Study* 165, by Mark Carey, Stephen Prowse, John Rea, and Gregory Udell (1993).

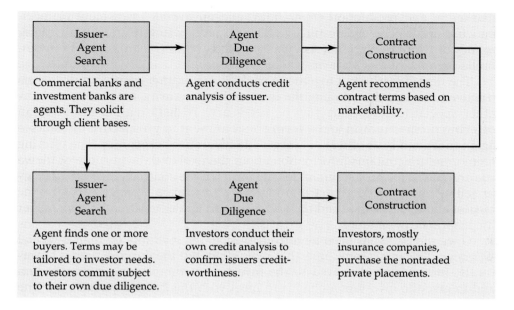

Issuer-Agent Search	Agent Due Diligence	Contract Construction
Commercial banks and investment banks are agents. They solicit through client bases.	Agent conducts credit analysis of issuer.	Agent recommends contract terms based on marketability.

Issuer-Agent Search	Agent Due Diligence	Contract Construction
Agent finds one or more buyers. Terms may be tailored to investor needs. Investors commit subject to their own due diligence.	Investors conduct their own credit analysis to confirm issuers credit-worthiness.	Investors, mostly insurance companies, purchase the nontraded private placements.

FIGURE 14.2   Private placement origination.

than bank loan covenants.[10] The terms of the typical private placement will be *renegotiated* one or more times during its life span, usually because the company wishes to embark on a new strategy that would violate one or more covenants. Many private placements are collateralized. In general, the riskier the borrower, the more restrictive the covenants and the more likely that collateral will be pledged.

As described in Figure 14.2, private placements are originated in a markedly different way than commercial bank loans. In particular, private placements are issued through agents, commercial banks or investment banks, who structure the contract and market it to investors, such as wealthy individuals and life insurance companies. It pays to hire an agent and pay their (often outrageous) fee because agents are far better informed about current pricing and current investor tastes than the issuing company. Commercial banks and investment banks actively solicit client business by regularly calling on midsize and large companies trying to sell them their private placement expertise.

Once an issuer chooses an agent, Figure 14.2 shows that the agent conducts its **due diligence.** Due diligence is just a fancier term for an overall credit analysis of the borrower, but because it's fancy it costs more. Due diligence includes an evaluation of the firm's management, its financial condition, its

---

[10]Typically there will be *cross-default covenants* in the bank loan and private placement contracts that give the private placement holder the right to declare default if the bank loan is in default (because of a covenant violation), and vice versa.

marketing and production capabilities, and an overall assessment of its financing needs. The end result is a formal credit rating from a credit rating agency or from the National Association of Insurance Commissioners (an umbrella organization of state insurance regulators).

The next step is to put together a package of contract terms that will be attractive to investors, including the interest rate, maturity, covenants, and any other special features that may be necessary. To help market the issue an **offering memorandum** and a **term sheet** are sent to prospective investors—again mostly to loan officers of larger life insurance companies. The offering memorandum contains information about the firm and the purpose of the issue and the term sheet summarizes the terms of the contract. A clever strategy in selling the issue is to get one large life insurance company to take the biggest chunk of the deal and then offer the remainder to several other smaller life insurance companies.

Once the issue has been tentatively placed, the investors do their own due diligence. This may seem somewhat redundant, but the purpose here is to verify the information conveyed to the investors in the offering memorandum and to give the investors a chance to meet with the firm's management. The whole process takes about six to eight weeks and results in a "tailored contract," like the commercial bank loan, which meets both the needs of the investors and the needs of the borrower.

Financing Large Businesses

A company with assets exceeding $150 million qualifies for the label "large business" principally because at about this size it becomes cost effective to enter the *public* bond market. For large businesses, debt financing in the public bond market is attractive because *liquid instruments* can be issued at a lower yield than illiquid, nontraded instruments (such as private placements and commercial bank loans). This yield difference due to liquidity was discussed in Chapter 6 and occurs because investors demand compensation for buying a security that they can not easily sell in a secondary market.

So why don't smaller companies issue in the public bond market? One reason is that the distribution costs associated with *underwriting* a public issue are much higher than the distribution costs in the private markets. This is because selling a new private placement to a handful of life insurance companies is a lot easier than selling a bond to hundreds (and sometimes thousands) of different investors, and because of the rather substantial costs associated with registering the bond with the Securities and Exchange Commission (SEC). We will get to the details of SEC registration in a moment, but because some of these registration costs are fixed, the *per dollar* cost of underwriting a publicly traded bond declines with issue size. For issue sizes much below $100 million, the lower distribution costs in the private placement market (principally the agent's fee) more than offsets the higher liquidity premium.

Figure 14.3 shows the process of issuing a corporate bond. First, the issuer chooses an **underwriter,** usually an investment bank, but recently a handful of commercial banks have also entered the picture. Underwriters actively market

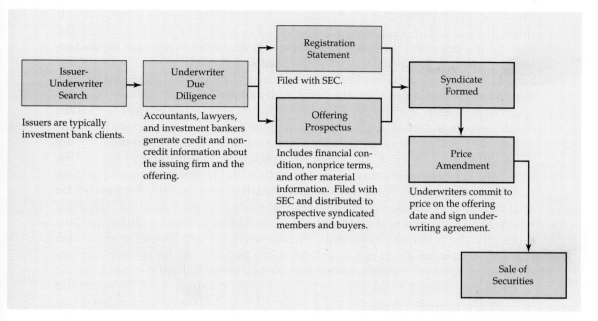

FIGURE 14.3   Securities underwriting.

their services to companies large enough to issue in the public bond market, so big firms will be inundated by underwriters trying to solicit their business.

Once the firm chooses its favorite, the underwriter then does its *due diligence* in much the same way that agents do their due diligence in the private placement market. There are some differences, however. In the public bond market the process of due diligence culminates in a formal document, called a **registration statement,** rather than the offering memorandum of a private placement market. The registration statement must conform to specific disclosure requirements. Included in the registration statement is an **offering** (or **preliminary**) **prospectus** containing all relevant factual information about the firm and its financing. The registration statement is blessed by the underwriter, the accountants, and the issuing firm's attorneys, all of whom become liable for any misrepresentation of facts once they have signed the document. Another difference between the *prospectus* in a public bond issue and the *offering memorandum* in a private placement is that a prospectus may not contain any projections about the company's future while there is no such restriction in an offering memorandum.

Once the registration statement has been approved by the SEC, the bond can be distributed. An underwriting syndicate is formed by the *managing underwriter* to share the responsibility for distributing the security and to share the underwriting risk. Underwriting risk occurs when the underwriters provide the issuer with a *firm commitment* to sell the bonds at an agreed-upon *commitment price,* which is implicitly an interest rate on the bond. If the underwriters sell the bonds for a lower price, they have to make up the loss.

Thus the underwriters buy the bonds for the *commitment price* and try to sell them (they hope) at a somewhat higher *offering price.* The difference between the offering price and the commitment price is the underwriter's fee, or **underwriting spread.** Underwriters try to minimize their risk by waiting to set the commitment price until just before the underwriting (typically the morning of the offering). If all goes well, the issue is distributed in a day or two, and the underwriters earn the spread. Occasionally, however, a big change in market conditions or a company-specific event may prevent the underwriter from selling the issue at the offering price and losses drown out the spread.

Another reason small and midsize companies do not issue in the public bond market is the difficulty of incorporating highly restrictive covenants in publicly traded bonds. There is a straightforward reason for this. Because bonds are often held by thousands of different investors, renegotiation of a covenant, which as we saw above is often necessary, would be extremely difficult. Consequently, the restrictive covenants that are needed when financing small and midsize companies could not be provided in a public bond issue—even if issuing a small amount of public bonds was cost effective (which it is not).

A major change in the underwriting process occurred in 1982 when the SEC, in response to competition for issuers from the largely unregulated Eurobond market, introduced Rule 415, also known as **shelf registration.** Shelf registration permits the issuer to register a dollar capacity with the SEC, then draw down on this capacity (take bonds "off the shelf") at any time without any additional registration requirements. For example, if a company does a $2 billion shelf registration, it may issue $1 billion tomorrow, then draw down another $500 million six months from now, and the final $500 million a year from now. Thus issuers who have done a shelf registration can respond instantaneously to changing market conditions. All the issuer has to do is call several investment bankers to get competitive bids and complete the entire transaction in a matter of hours. The investment banks evaluate market interest in the issue by calling a number of large institutional investors (mutual funds, pension funds, and life insurance companies) before entering a bid. The winning underwriter puts together a very small syndicate and commits to the deal. In many cases the syndicate is formed *after* the winning investment bank has won the bidding. This is referred to as a *bought deal.* A bought deal occurs because of the competitive pressure to commit quickly.

Unlike small- and medium-size companies, large companies with good credit ratings tend to rely on the commercial paper market for short-term financing. Many large commercial paper issuers use a commercial bank or an investment bank as an agent to operate a *commercial paper program.* These agents will then distribute their paper to investors (mostly money market mutual funds). Commercial paper ranges in maturity from one day to 270 days with a significant concentration at the short end of this range. Issuers set their maturities based on their financing needs and the daily (hourly) fluctuations in investor appetite—hungry investors will get lower yields for lunch. A handful of the largest commercial paper issuers (mostly the biggest finance companies) distribute their own commercial paper without the assistance of an agent.

Some very large businesses also issue **medium-term notes,** which are very much like commercial paper except they have maturities ranging from one year to five years. Companies set up *medium-term note programs* with agents in a fashion similar to commercial paper programs.

Most large businesses are publicly held, so that issuing equity is another form of external finance. The process described in Figure 14.3 also applies to equities, but because companies issue new equity much less frequently than new debt, shelf registration, for the most part, is irrelevant. Equity underwriting involves relatively large syndicates of underwriters who conduct *road shows* in big hotels across the country where they trumpet equity issues that they are bringing to market. The underwriting spreads on equity issues are much larger than debt issues because they have to pay for the hotels and trumpets and because equity underwriting is riskier than bond underwriting because stock prices are so volatile.

THE ECONOMICS OF FINANCIAL CONTRACTING

Our discussion thus far is summarized in Figure 14.4, showing how the method and nature of financial contracting differs according to firm size. Now it is time to formulate a framework explaining why these differences exist. Why don't small firms issue public equity? Why do bank loans and private

Characteristic	Small-size Businesses (Bank Loans)	Medium-size Businesses (Privates)	Large-size Businesses (Publics)
Maturity	short	long	long
Rate	floating	fixed	fixed
Covenants	many, tight	fewer, looser	fewest
Collateral	very often	often*	infrequent*
Monitoring by Investors	intensive	significant	minimal
Renegotiation Frequency	high	medium	low
Origination	direct	agents	underwriters

* excluding asset-backed securities

FIGURE 14.4   Credit market comparison.

placements have covenants, and why are they sometimes collateralized? Why not just raise the loan rate instead of imposing restrictive covenants or taking collateral? Why do very large firms sometimes issue in the private placement market and not public bond market?

The answer to some of these questions is related to transactions costs, such as the nontrivial expenses associated with registering with the SEC and distributing securities to hundreds of investors. But transactions costs are not an entirely satisfying explanation. For example, it is hard to see why transactions costs makes it more likely that collateral will be pledged by small companies (for their bank loans) than large companies (for their bonds). Nor can transactions costs easily explain the presence of restrictive covenants in bank loans and private placements. Nor can they explain why small businesses do not have access to long-term debt. To really understand what's going on we have to resuscitate the subject of asymmetric information from Chapter 11. Recall that asymmetric information occurs when buyers and sellers are *not* equally informed about the true quality of what they are buying and selling, or in our case when the issuer has more information than the investor about the issuer's quality and likely future performance.

Asymmetric Information and Financial Contracting

There are two forms of asymmetric information: **adverse selection** and **moral hazard.** Adverse selection is caused by asymmetric information *before* a transaction is consummated, such as when bank loan officers cannot easily tell the difference between high-quality (that is, low-risk) borrowers and low-quality (high-risk) borrowers. Part of the loan officer's job during the credit analysis stage is to uncover information so that safer borrowers are charged an appropriately low interest rate and risky borrowers are forced to pay a high interest rate.

Asymmetric information is particularly acute for small firms because there is very little publicly available information that can be used to assess credit quality. Moreover, no matter how many questions the loan officer asks, and no matter how much financial information the loan officer digests, only the borrower knows the whole truth (and nothing but the truth)—particularly if the bank has not had a long relationship with the company. As a result, credit analysis by itself cannot solve the adverse selection problem. Thus loans are often structured in such a way that borrowers can *signal* their true quality by the types of terms they are willing to accept. For example, an owner who is willing to pledge her own personal assets as collateral (like marketable securities or real estate), and/or is willing to be personally liable for her own company's bank loan, sends a powerful and positive signal about the true (but unobservable) quality of her firm. On the other hand, an owner who is unwilling to put up such *outside collateral* and/or is unwilling to offer a *personal guarantee* indicates clearly that the firm's future prospects are uncertain at best.

The moral hazard problem occurs *after* the loan is made. It arises because the loan contract may give the firm (the owner/manager in the case of a small business) the incentive to pursue actions that take advantage of the lender, and which are not easily observable or controllable by the lender. This is best illustrated by way of a specific numerical example.

Consider the case of the Opaque Manufacturing Corporation, a small company owned and managed by Ian Slick, who has put $200,000 into the company. Before opening for business the company's balance sheet looks like this:

Opaque Manufacturing Corporation
December 31, 1996

Assets		Liabilities and Equity	
Cash	$200,000	Debt	$ 0
		Equity	200,000
Total	$200,000	Total	$200,000

To keep things simple, let's assume that Slick meets with his trusting loan officer, Dave Checkette, at Safe and Sound National Bank and convinces him that with an $800,000 loan, Opaque can deploy its total of $1 million in a riskless venture called SS1 (Secret Strategy 1), which will yield a net return on assets of 10 percent in one year. Checkette agrees to give Opaque Manufacturing Corporation an $800,000 one-year commercial loan at the bank's best rate of 5 percent because he believes Slick's 10 percent return calculation for SS1. In effect, Checkette believes the firm's balance sheet would look like this at the end of the year, just before paying off the bank (Opaque owes $840,000 at that time—the $800,000 principal plus 5 percent of $800,000, or $40,000, in interest):

Opaque Manufacturing Corporation
December 31, 1997

Assets		Liabilities and Equity	
Assets (Strategy SS1)	$1,100,000	Debt	$ 840,000
		Equity	260,000
Total	$1,100,000	Total	$1,100,000

If Slick sticks to his word, our story ends with the bank loan being paid off just as promised. However, suppose that after obtaining the loan, Slick can switch *without the bank's knowledge or control* to another strategy, say, 3S1 (Super Secret Strategy 1), which is considerably riskier and has an expected return on assets of only 7.5 percent.[11] In particular, 3S1 has a 50 percent chance of *increasing* the firm's assets to $1,650,000, and a 50 percent chance of *reducing* the firm's assets to $500,000. Thus the expected value of assets at the end of the year will be $1,075,000 = ([0.5 × $1,650,000] + [0.5 × $500,000])—an expected increase of 7.5 percent. It would appear that SS1 clearly *dominates* 3S1

---

[11]The example that begins here and continues for the next few paragraphs uses the principals of expected return and risk aversion from the section entitled *Consequences of Uncertainty and Risk Aversion* in Chapter 7.

because the expected year-end asset value is higher under SS1 *and* it is riskless. Would it ever make sense for Slick to switch secretly to 3S1 and expose his firm to a 50 percent chance of bankruptcy? Let's see.

If the firm pursues 3S1 and is successful, it will look like this at year's end:

Opaque Manufacturing Corporation
December 31, 1997

Assets		Liabilities and Equity	
Assets (Strategy 3S1,	$1,650,000	Debt	$ 840,000
Success)		Equity	810,000
Total	$1,650,000	Total	$1,650,000

If the firm pursues 3S1 and is unsuccessful, it will look like this:

Opaque Manufacturing Corporation
December 31, 1997

Assets		Liabilities and Equity	
Assets (Strategy 3S1,	$500,000	Debt	$840,000
Failure)		Equity	−340,000
Total	$500,000	Total	$500,000

Several things should be noted about the firm if it pursues 3S1 and is unsuccessful. As can be seen in the above balance sheet, the firm is insolvent because its stockholders' equity is negative. Slick, as the sole shareholder, gets what he deserves—nothing, and the bank gets what's left, which is only $500,000. Because of limited liability, Slick can lose no more than his original investment ($200,000), but the bank takes a loss of $300,000 on its principal plus a $40,000 loss on accumulated interest, for a total loss of $340,000.[12]

Now we can answer whether it pays Slick to be true to his name and to switch to 3S1. Let's focus on the equity account. Our first balance sheet shows that SS1 generates equity of $260,000. Our next two balance sheets show that 3S1 is a gamble. The gamble pays $810,000 with a 50 percent probability and nothing with a 50 percent probability. Is the gamble worth it? The answer depends on how risk-averse Slick is. In this case, however, he'd have to be *very, very* risk-averse not to take the gamble. His expected return on SS1 is only 30 percent ($= 100 \times [[\$260,000 - \$200,000] \div \$200,000]$) on his original $200,000 investment. However, his expected return on 3S1 is 102.5 percent ($= 100 \times [.5 \times [(\$810,000 - \$200,000) \div \$200,000] + 0.5 \times [(\$0 - \$200,000) \div \$200,000]])$!

This example illustrates how the debt contract itself provides an incentive for Ian Slick to alter his investment strategy. Note that the bank did not jack

---

[12]Although −$340,000 appears in the equity account, this is not Slick's personal obligation because of limited liability. Therefore, it must be absorbed by the bank.

up the loan rate to reflect the switch to 3S1 because our hard-working loan officer, Dave Checkette, just couldn't detect the deception no matter how much he checked it out (sorry about that). Thus it made sense for Slick to switch from SS1 to 3S1— *even though* the firm can now be expected to fail 50 percent of the time! All of this because owners disproportionately share in the upside of increased risk, while lenders disproportionately share in the downside.

Carried to its logical extreme, this risk-shifting problem forces all of the Dave Checkettes of the world to assume the worst. Namely that all small business borrowers like Opaque Manufacturing will secretly switch to the riskiest investment strategy they can hide. Thus banks must charge all small firms a commensurately high interest rate. What does Opaque (even without Slick) do in response? The answer: It still chooses the riskiest strategy—after all, it's being charged for it, so why not?

Contracting and the Firm Continuum

Fortunately, there are some things firms can do to convince potential lenders that they won't resort to bait-and-switch investment tactics. In fact, because the activities of large firms are relatively easy to observe, *any* risk shifting by them is easily detected. Their labor contracts are often public knowledge; their supplier relationships are often well known; and their marketing success or failure is regularly documented in the financial press. Most large firms therefore cannot *covertly* switch from low-risk to high-risk strategies and maintain their reputations in the process. Thus the public market for stocks and bonds for the most part reflects the true riskiness of the underlying investment strategies, with prices and yields determined accordingly.

For small firms, however, external reputations are much more difficult to establish. Much of what they do lies beyond the public's scrutiny. These firms need mechanisms to demonstrate that they are low risk and to credibly commit to not shifting their risk profile. It is in this context that the contract features we observed earlier in this chapter make sense. In particular, *outside collateral* and *personal guarantees* reduce the incentive to understate risk during loan negotiations and diminish the incentive to risk shift after the loan is made. The more of the owner's wealth at risk, either directly in the form of more equity in the company, or indirectly in the form of outside collateral or a personal guarantee, the lower the incentive to deceive the lender.

Inside collateral can also be useful in preventing unwanted risk shifting. When a company pledges some of its assets to the bank as collateral, the bank notifies public authorities by filing a *lien* on the collateral. This publicly filed lien effectively restricts the company from selling the asset in order to change the firm's risk profile. To sell the asset the company must get the lien released by the bank, which the bank could refuse to do.

Finally, loan covenants prevent risk shifting by explicitly constraining borrower behavior. For example, by restricting the plant and equipment that a firm can buy or sell over the duration of the loan, the bank can prevent its favorite dry cleaning establishment from entering the motorcycle leasing business. However, even with restrictive covenants and collateral the information asymmetry is typically too difficult to justify long-term debt for small businesses. There is simply too much flexibility in a long-term debt contract given the incentives to shift risk. Therefore, bank loans to small business are typically made on a short-term basis. And if the borrower wants to renew the loan, the bank will conduct a complete credit analysis to assure, as much as possible, that the company's risk profile has not changed. Over time and after many renewals, the company should build up a relationship with the bank, establishing a sort of private reputation to behave responsibly. This explains the empirical observation of lower interest rates and less collateral as the bank-borrower relationship grows over time.

Midsize companies tend to lie somewhere between small companies and large companies in terms of their information problems. They are more visible publicly than small companies but are still more *informationally* impaired than large companies. Therefore, they still need a financial intermediary to scrutinize them at the origination stage to address the adverse selection problem and to design a tailor-made contract with covenants (and possibly inside collateral) to address the moral hazard (risk-shifting) problem. However, there is less of an informational gap associated with lending to midsize companies so they have access to long-term debt in the private placement market.

The relationship between information and market access is described in Figure 14.5 in terms of a *firm continuum*. On the left-hand side we have the tiniest of businesses. These are start-up firms with no track record—Bill Gates with nothing but an idea. It is often impossible for an outsider to assess the prospects for a new genetically engineered vaccine or a new software program when these are mere ideas in some inventor's mind. Financing at this stage must be internal—the owner's own capital or personal credit cards or friends and relatives. Small companies beyond infancy, however, begin to have access to the short-term bank loan market. Start-up companies with a prototype product and a marketing plan can go to a venture capitalist for outside equity. Somewhat larger firms may be able to get an intermediate term loan from a commercial bank or a combination of subordinated debt and equity from a mezzanine debt fund.

As firms mature into midsize companies they gain access to a long-term debt contract from a life insurance company in the private placement market. Midsize companies are likely to "go public," that is, issue public equity for the first time. Large companies, of course, have access to the traded securities markets because there is a wealth of information about them. They get their short-term credit from the money markets by issuing commercial paper, their intermediate term credit from the medium-term note market, their long-term debt from the bond market, and their equity from the stock market. These are all liquid instruments that can be traded in a secondary market. Large companies do not need the specialized information production services of a financial intermediary like a commercial bank or a life insurance company.

Occasionally, there are exceptions. For example, sometimes large firms prefer to issue debt in the private placement market when the transactions are

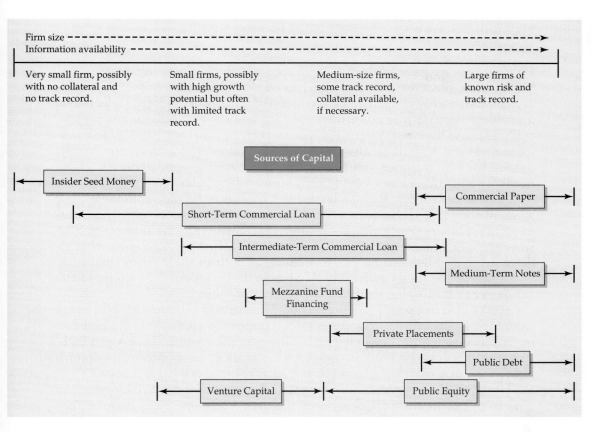

FIGURE 14.5   Firm continuum.

Source: Mark Carey, Steven Prowse, John Rea, and Gregory Udell "The Economics of Private Placements," *Financial Markets, Institutions & Instruments* 2 (1993).

complex. However, this is perfectly consistent with the spirit behind the firm continuum. A "complex transaction" is just the market's phraseology for lack of information, that is, when a transaction is so complicated that it is difficult to assess its true risk. That is precisely the type of transaction that requires a tailored contract and the specialized services of a financial intermediary—a private placement purchased by a life insurance company.[13]

---

[13]For an empirical analysis of large firms who access the private placement market, as well as an overall empirical analysis of the firm continuum, see Mark Carey, Stephen Prowse, John Rea, and Gregory Udell, "The Economics of the Private Placements: A New Look," *Financial Markets, Institutions & Instruments* 2, (1993). Also for an empirical analysis of the firm continuum, see "Securitization, Risk, and the Liquidity Problem in Banking" by Gregory Udell and Allen N. Berger in *Structural Change in Banking*, edited by Michael Klausner and Lawrence J. White (New York: Business One Irwin, 1993).

Consumer Lending, Financial Contracting, and Securitization

Up until now we have focused exclusively on business financing. Asymmetric information, however, also characterizes consumer lending. Some consumers are low-risk borrowers and some are high-risk borrowers. Adverse selection is a problem because it is not always easy for lenders to tell them apart, especially because high-risk borrowers will try their best to look like low-risk customers. Moral hazard is also a problem because consumers may borrow money for one purpose—an SAT preparatory course—and then use those funds for something else—buying high-speed rollerblades.

Consumer lenders, such as banks and consumer finance companies, use some of the same techniques as business lenders to solve asymmetric information problems. For example, in mortgage financing, the homeowner always pledges a house as collateral for the loan. Invariably, auto financing always involves a lien on the car. Moreover, in both of these cases the lender will disburse the funds with a check payable to the seller of the house or the car dealer to insure that the funds are used as promised.

Banks also use subtle pricing mechanisms to *sort* out low-risk borrowers from high-risk borrowers. *Sorting* is a good thing because if a loan package can be designed so that low-risk customers, for example, choose Bank A and high-risk customers choose Bank B, then each bank can price its customers according to their true risk characteristics, and each group gets what it deserves.

How can such contracts be designed? Suppose that high-risk customers tend to overdraw their checking accounts frequently—possibly because they are somewhat irresponsible. When someone writes checks in an amount that exceeds the balance in their checking account, the bank will "bounce" these checks, that is return them unpaid, stamp them "not sufficient funds" (NSF), and charge an NSF fee for each check. Low-risk borrowers, we assume, never overdraw their checking account.

Now suppose Bank A offers customers a low-interest, three-year loan provided that the borrower also opens a checking account with a very high NSF fee. Bank B, on the other hand, offers a high-interest loan combined with a checking account having a low NSF fee. If these rates are set just right, they will encourage high-risk borrowers to choose Bank B to avoid the NSF fee, while low-risk customers are attracted to Bank A because of the low interest rate. Thus the loan rates are set to reflect the respective risks of the two types of customers *even though the customer's true risk is not observable by the two banks.*[14]

Somewhat more generally, asymmetric information is arguably less of a problem in consumer lending than in business lending. First, it is probably

---

[14]For a further analysis of the nature of asymmetric information in consumer lending see Gregory F. Udell, "Pricing Returned Check Charges Under Asymmetric Information," *Journal of Money, Credit and Banking* (November 1986); and Linda Allen, Anthony Saunders, and Gregory F. Udell, "The Pricing of Retail Deposits: Concentration and Information," *Journal of Financial Intermediation* (December 1991).

easier to assess consumer risk than business risk because personal financial information is much less complex than business financial information. Second, there are relatively few types of consumer loans while there are many types (and subtypes) of business loans, so that evaluating consumer risk lends itself to statistical analysis much more easily than business risk. In short, consumer loans tend to be generic while business loans, particularly to small and midsize businesses, are more idiosyncratic. Third, collateral often virtually eliminates the asymmetric information problem in consumer lending while it is less likely to do so in business lending. For example, a residential mortgage may require that the loan not exceed 80 percent of the purchase price of the house thereby eliminating much of the risk. Business collateral, such as inventory and accounts receivable, is much harder to evaluate and is arguably much more volatile in value than a single family home. Thus there is a much higher probability that the value of the collateral may fall below the value of the loan in business lending compared with consumer lending.

Given these differences, it is not terribly surprising that consumer loans have been securitized while small and midsize business loans have not. As we first discussed in Chapter 3, **securitization** involves pooling a group of loans into a trust and then selling securities issued against the trust. A prerequisite for securitization is the ability to standardize the asset. Because of their generic characteristics it has been possible to securitize mortgages, auto loans, credit card receivables, and student loans. But because loans to small and midsize businesses are tailored contracts that require frequent renegotiation, they do not lend themselves to securitization. Our analysis suggests there is little chance this will change in the future.

SUMMARY

1. Small businesses are typically owner managed. They are generally bank-dependent although some borrow from commercial finance companies. Their loans are often collateralized, personally guaranteed, covenant restrictive, and usually have a short maturity. The covenants are frequently renegotiated.

2. Midsize businesses have access to the private placement market where they borrow (with some restrictive covenants) on a long-term basis from life insurance companies under terms that are typically renegotiated several times during the life of the loan. Midsize businesses obtain their short-term financing from banks and often issue publicly traded equity.

3. Large businesses are usually publicly owned and have access to the public bond market. Public bonds contain few covenants, and those they do contain are not very restrictive. Therefore, there is little need to renegotiate publicly issued bonds.

4. Information asymmetry plays a major role in determining which markets businesses have access to. Firm size, in great part, determines the degree of information asymmetry. Much of what large firms do is visible to the public and is often reported in the financial section of the newspaper. Small firms, on the other hand, operate mostly beyond the public view.

5. Information asymmetry explains much of the observed difference in the financial contracts. Collateral, personal guarantees, restrictive covenants, and short maturities are all used in small business loans to undermine adverse selection and moral hazard. These contract terms are not necessary in public bonds because large companies are more easily evaluated and monitored.

6. Consumer lending is also characterized by information asymmetry, but the problems are less acute and the loans tend to be more generic than business lending. As a result, many types of consumer loans have been securitized while business loans have not, and most likely will not, be securitized.

QUESTIONS

14.1 Since the agent's fee in a private placement offering is less than the underwriter's fee in a public bond issue, why don't large companies prefer to issue in the private placement market rather than in the public bond market?

14.2 Bank loans and private placements will often have a covenant restricting the amount that the company can pay in dividends in any given quarter. Why?

14.3 Many small business owners do not want to raise money by issuing more stock. They would rather borrow from a bank even though it will make their company more leveraged. Why do you think this is so?

14.4 What is the incentive for a small business owner to understate the risk of his or her company?

14.5 *Discussion question:* Does the owner of a small business have an obligation to tell the bank that the company is changing its risk strategy if this change will not violate a covenant?

14.6 *Discussion question:* There have been some recent proposals to securitize small business loans that involve a government guarantee. Specifically, the U.S. government would guarantee investors in a securitized pool of small business loans against default. The philosophy behind these proposals is to ensure that small businesses always have access to credit. Is this a good idea?

CHAPTER 15

The Regulation of Markets and Institutions

Governments have followed a simple rule when it comes to regulating the financial sector: If something moves, regulate it; and if it doesn't move, keep your eye on it until it does, and *then* regulate it. There is little doubt that the financial system is one of most intensely regulated sectors of the U.S. economy. As in other areas, there are regulations designed to promote competition and regulations aimed at protecting individual consumers, in this case, investors. However, there are two additional reasons for regulating the financial sector: to assure financial system stability and to facilitate monetary policy. To accomplish all of these goals, the government has established a number of different agencies with specific regulatory authority, as summarized in Table 15.1.

Table 15.1 shows that regulation of the U.S. financial system can be divided into two parts: the regulation of *financial markets* and the regulation of *financial intermediaries*. This chapter will begin by looking at the regulation of financial markets and then turn to the regulation of financial intermediaries, especially commercial banks. Our chapter ends with a discussion of a distinguishing feature of the U.S. regulatory structure: the separation of commercial banking and investment banking as mandated by the *Glass-Steagall Act* of 1933. In contrast with our structure, many other countries, such as those in the **European Union,** have not segregated their banking system from the rest of the financial services industry. Thus our discussion provides a prelude to Chapter 16, where we compare the U.S. financial system with that of other countries and consider the broader issue of designing the optimal regulatory framework.

TABLE 15.1   Principal Financial Regulators in the United States

Regulator	Regulatory scope	Type of regulations
Financial Markets		
Securities and Exchange Commission (SEC)	Primary and secondary securities markets	Disclosure requirements and restrictions on insider trading
Commodities Futures Trading Commission (CFTC)	Futures markets	Regulates futures trading
Self-regulatory organizations (such as New York Stock Exchange and National Association of Securities Dealers)	Secondary Markets	Monitors trading activity
Intermediated Markets		
Office of the Comptroller of the Currency	Federally chartered banks	Charters, examines and regulates federally chartered banks
Federal Reserve System	All commercial banks	Examines and regulates state chartered member banks; regulates all bank holding companies and determines permissible activities*
Federal Deposit Insurance Corporation (FDIC)	All commercial banks, mutual savings banks, and savings and loan associations	Provides explicit deposit insurance up to $100,000 per depositor; examines and regulates state-chartered, nonmember banks
State banking commissions	State-chartered commercial banks	Examines and regulates state-chartered commercial banks
Office of Thrift Supervision	Savings and loan associations	Examines and regulates savings and loan associations
National Credit Union Administration (NCUA)	Credit unions	Examines and regulates credit unions
State insurance commissions	Insurance companies	Examines and regulates insurance companies

*Also sets reserve requirements and discount rate (see Chapter 20).

THE REGULATION OF FINANCIAL MARKETS IN THE UNITED STATES

Much of the regulation of U.S. financial markets is driven by the desire to protect individual investors *and* the philosophy that the best protection is through information about the securities in the marketplace. Regulation in the United States is also guided by a corollary philosophy that financial markets will benefit from full disclosure because that broadens investors' participation in the financial markets. Let's first look at regulation in the *primary markets* and then turn to the *secondary markets*.

The Regulation of the Primary Market

The disclosure of information for newly issued securities is required under the provisions of the Securities Act of 1933. A second piece of legislation, the Securities Exchange Act of 1934, created the **Securities and Exchange Commission (SEC)** to administer the provisions of the 1933 Act. In particular, a publicly traded security must file a **registration statement** and a **preliminary prospectus** with the SEC disclosing all material information about the issue. The only thing missing in the preliminary prospectus is the final interest rate for a bond issue and price for equity issues. The preliminary prospectus is made available to potential investors so they can decide whether to buy the security. If the SEC determines that there has been adequate disclosure, it approves the registration statement and the issue can be sold to the public (see Chapter 14 for more detail). By way of contrast, a privately held firm that borrows only in the bank loan and private placement markets is not required to reveal financial information to the public at large, although it will certainly be required by its lenders (banks and life insurance companies, respectively) to provide financial information to them.

What sort of information must be revealed in a public offering of corporate securities? In short, any factual information that investors may need to make an informed decision about purchasing the security. This includes, but is not limited to:

1. Audited financial statements for up to as many as five years.
2. Information on and terms of any outstanding financial obligations.
3. All employment contracts including pension obligations, stock options, and stock purchase plans.
4. The names of highly compensated employees and officers and the amount of their compensation (check to see if there's anyone you know).
5. Shareholder rights beyond those of ordinary stockholders.
6. Justification for any contracts with firm insiders (for example, leases on buildings owned by firm officers or major shareholders).

It is important to note that SEC approval of the prospectus does not imply that the SEC views the new issue as an attractive investment. It merely means that the disclosure of information in the prospectus is satisfactory to the SEC.

The Regulation of the Secondary Markets

Full disclosure does not end with the filing of the prospectus. The Securities Exchange Act of 1934 extended the provisions in the 1933 Act to include periodic disclosure of relevant financial information for firms trading in the secondary market. Issuers of publicly traded securities must file an annual public report with the SEC known as a *10K report,* which discloses its most recent financial statements and other relevant information about the firm's performance and activities.

To further ensure that individual investors are not taken advantage of, **insider trading laws** prohibit so-called insiders from trading on private information they may have about the firm and its future prospects. Unfortunately, there is some ambiguity as to the precise definition of insider trading. It is clear, however, that certain parties are unambiguously considered insiders—for example, officers, directors, and major stockholders—and they are prohibited from trading on private information that has not yet been released to the public. To further minimize any advantage that insiders might have, the SEC requires all officers, directors, and major stockholders to report all of their transactions in their own firm's stock. A summary of these reports is published monthly by the SEC in its *Official Summary of Securities Transactions and Holdings.* The idea is to expose favorable or unfavorable "votes" that might be indicated by these transactions. Insider trading laws, therefore, do not prohibit all trading in firm shares by insiders, rather they only prohibit trading based on private information that has not been divulged to the public.

OFF THE RECORD

Insider Trading: Efficiency Versus Equity

A number of insider trading scandals wracked the securities industry during the 1980s. Indictments and jail sentences were handed out to lawyers, traders, and even newspaper columnists who fell victim to the temptation to misappropriate privileged information for personal profit. The violations in each case are less important than the legal principle: It is a criminal offense to trade on information that is considered confidential. Although the precise definition of confidential information is subject to legal interpretation, it clearly includes information received by officers, directors, lawyers, and investment advisers working directly or indirectly for a company that might affect the price of the company's stock.

The curious thing about the prohibition against insider trading is that it has nothing to do with promoting the efficiency of stock prices. As we have seen in Chapter 6, stock prices are efficient if they fully reflect all available information. Prices will be efficient if either public investors bid up the price of a stock or if insiders bid up the price when favorable information is uncovered. In fact, some have argued that if insiders were allowed to trade on confidential information, prices would be more efficient because insiders with access to such information would force up stock prices instantaneously.

Why then the laws against insider trading? Fairness, not efficiency, is the key. As a matter of public policy, we would like investors to feel that in the stock market they have a fair chance to earn a decent return for their risks. More particularly, public investors should not feel that they are always at a disadvantage relative to insiders who can dump stocks of companies about to disclose unfavorable information or who will snap up bargains prior to the disclosure of favorable information. Without an impression of fairness, investors might be reluctant to participate in securities markets—making it difficult for companies to raise capital.

The problem is, of course, that there are considerable monetary incentives to circumvent the law. Are public investors better off with an impression of fairness when deception is rampant? Or are investors better off following the ancient dictum "let the buyer and seller beware"? Unfortunately, there is no simple answer.

The 1934 Act also empowered the SEC with the authority to regulate securities exchanges, over-the-counter (OTC) trading, dealers, and brokers. The SEC shares this power, to some extent, with other regulatory agencies. For example, the **Commodities Futures Trading Commission (CFTC)** regulates trading in futures markets and the **Federal Reserve** has responsibility for setting margin requirements on stocks (where margin specifies how much of the purchase price of the security an investor can borrow). For the most part, the SEC relies on self-regulation. It delegates daily oversight to the exchanges themselves, so that the New York Stock Exchange monitors itself, for example, while daily oversight for equities traded over-the-counter is delegated to the **National Association of Securities Dealers.**

THE REGULATION OF COMMERCIAL BANKS IN THE UNITED STATES

The protection of individual depositors, fostering a competitive banking system and above all ensuring bank safety and soundness, are the main goals that have shaped U.S. bank regulatory policies. It will be helpful first to summarize the relatively complex nature of the bank regulatory apparatus and then follow with a discussion of how each goal has been translated into specific policy. Our primary focus will be on the regulation of commercial banks, but for the most part, the regulation of thrifts parallels that of commercial banks.

The U.S. Banking Regulatory Structure

The American commercial banking system is known as a **dual banking system** because one of its main features is side-by-side federal and state chartering (and supervision) of commercial banks. It has no counterpart in any other country. Indeed, it arose quite by accident in the United States, the unexpected result of legislation in the 1860s that was intended to shift the authority to charter banks from the various state governments to the federal government.

The National Currency Act of 1863, the National Bank Act of 1864, and related post-Civil War legislation established a brand-new federally chartered banking system under the supervision of the **Comptroller of the Currency** (within the U.S. Treasury). The idea was to drive the existing state-chartered banks out of business by imposing a prohibitive tax on their issuance of state banknotes (currency issued by state-chartered banks), which in those days was the principal form of circulating money. However, state-chartered banks survived and eventually flourished, because public acceptance of demand deposits instead of currency enabled state banks to remain in business despite their inability to issue banknotes.

Thus today we have a dual banking system: federally chartered banks, under the umbrella of the Comptroller of the Currency, and state-chartered

TABLE 15.2   Status of Insured Commercial Banks, 1994 (dollars in billions)

All commercial banks	Number of banks 10,450		Total assets $4,011	
	No.	Percent	Amount	Percent
National banks	3,075	29	$2,256	56
State banks	7,375	71	1,755	44
F.R. member banks	4,050	39	3,101	77
Nonmember banks	6,400	61	910	23

Source: Federal Deposit Insurance Corporation, data for December 31, 1994.

banks, under the supervision of each of the various states. Federally chartered banks are, for the most part, the larger institutions, but state-chartered banks are more numerous. At the end of 1994, as Table 15.2 shows, 71 percent of the commercial banks had state charters, but the 3,075 with national charters held 56 percent of the assets in the banking system.

In 1913 with the passage of the Federal Reserve Act, another supervisory layer was added as national banks were required to become member banks of the Federal Reserve system, while state banks were permitted the option of joining or not. At present, as can be inferred from Table 15.2, most state banks are not members of the Federal Reserve system. Nevertheless, member banks, both state and national, hold 77 percent of the total assets in the banking system.

An additional supervisory structure was laid atop the entire edifice with the establishment of federal deposit insurance in the 1930s. All Federal Reserve member banks, and thus all national banks, are required to be insured by the **Federal Deposit Insurance Corporation (FDIC).** State nonmembers retain the option of having federal deposit insurance or not, but virtually all commercial banks have chosen to have federal deposit insurance coverage, because it would be difficult to attract deposits without it.

You don't have to be a genius to recognize that the current regulatory apparatus is cumbersome at best. All banks, regardless of charter, have a primary federal regulator who imposes federal regulation and is principally responsible for ensuring compliance. For federally chartered banks, the primary federal regulator is the Comptroller of the Currency. For state-chartered banks who are members of the Federal Reserve system, the primary federal regulator is the Federal Reserve. And, for state-chartered banks who are not members of the Federal Reserve system, the primary federal regulator is the FDIC. In addition, state-chartered banks are regulated by their state banking authorities.[1]

---

[1]If we include other depository institutions in our description, the regulatory landscape becomes even more cluttered. Mutual savings banks are regulated by their state banking authorities as well as the FDIC. Savings and loan associations are regulated by state banking authorities as well as the Office of Thrift Supervision, and they are insured by the Savings Association Insurance Fund, which is managed by the FDIC. Credit unions are regulated by the National Credit Union Administration and state banking authorities.

Moreover, the Federal Reserve is responsible for determining what sort of activities are permissible for banks to engage in. It's hard to believe anyone can figure out what to report to whom.

Even though regulators try to coordinate their activities, differences are bound to arise (and have arisen) in terms of regulatory policies and the quality of supervision. As a result there have been periodic attempts to unify the regulatory structure. Three of the most notable were the Bush Commission proposal in 1984, the U.S. Treasury Proposal in 1991, and the D'Amato proposal (by Senator Alfonse D'Amato of New York) in 1995. To date, all of these have failed—in great part over the issue of which supervisory agency would emerge as the surviving *numero uno*. So far, the legislative will to dismantle the regulatory apparatus and replace it with a more straightforward unified structure has been lacking.

Regulations to Protect Individual Depositors and Financial System Stability

In contrast with the regulation of financial markets, the thrust of bank regulation has not been focused on disclosure.[2] In fact, the most important information about a bank's financial condition—the results of a regulator's **bank examination**—are not divulged to the public by explicit regulatory policy. Banks are "examined" periodically by regulators to determine whether the bank is solvent and whether its business practices are prudent and safe.

Instead, much of the regulatory emphasis in banking focuses on limiting depositor risk with two goals in mind: to protect unsophisticated individual depositors and to protect the safety and soundness of the overall financial system. These two goals are closely linked because the bank's chief liability—the checking account—is paid on a *first-come/first-serve basis*. This characteristic creates the potential for a *run on the bank* and, in the extreme, a systemwide *bank panic*.

To be more specific, banks are obligated to pay their checking account customers on demand. If depositors fear that a bank may be insolvent, they may all literally line up at the tellers' windows and demand their deposits, which is their right. Because most bank assets are in illiquid form (nontraded loans), they cannot be sold quickly for what they are worth. Thus banks will find it extremely difficult to pay out depositors if all depositors show up at once. All of this means that it is quite rational for depositors to lead a so-called run on a bank that may be insolvent because those at the head of the line will be paid out in full, while those at the end of the line will suffer losses.

Bank panics arise when runs spread from bad banks to good banks, because no one can tell the difference between the two types of institutions. Bank runs are potentially *contagious* because the quality of bank loans are so hard to assess.

---

[2]There are, however, regulations designed to promote full disclosure of the *terms* of financial contracts offered to consumers. These regulations require that banks and other financial institutions accurately, uniformly, and completely disclose the yields on products that they offer their consumer customers, such as the interest rates and fees on loans and mortgages.

"There's a run on the bank!"
Drawing by Robt. Day; © 1969 The New Yorker Magazine, Inc.

Deposit Insurance.   In the United States deposit insurance provided by the FDIC is the principal mechanism designed to protect individual depositors and prevent bank panics. The FDIC was created by the Banking Act of 1933 in response to the painful experience of the 1920s, when bank failures averaged 600 a year, and the catastrophic experience of 1930 to 1933, when bank failures exceeded 2,000 a year! Read that sentence over again, so you really appreciate how huge those numbers are and get some idea of how many people lost their life savings as bank after bank disappeared. At the end of 1933 there were fewer than 15,000 commercial banks remaining out of 30,000 that had been in existence in 1920. It is not surprising, therefore, that Congress established the FDIC in response to this historic debacle. Companion legislation created the Federal Savings and Loan Insurance Corporation (FSLIC) to do the same for savings and loan associations. Following the savings and loan crisis in the 1980s, the FSLIC was eliminated and deposit insurance for savings and loan associations is now provided through the FDIC. In 1970 the National Credit Union Administration initiated deposit insurance through the National Credit Union Share Insurance Fund (NCUSIF) for federally chartered credit unions.

   Deposit insurance accomplishes two things. First, by insuring deposits up to a maximum amount per account—currently $100,000—deposit insurance protects unsophisticated small savers (presumably if you have more than $100,000 you are smart enough to look after yourself). Second, it reduces the incentive for insured depositors to join a bank run. However, a substantial number of U.S. bank deposits exceed $100,000 and are thus not explicitly covered by deposit insurance. The FDIC estimates that while 99 percent of all *depositors* are fully insured (because their deposits are less than $100,000), the 1 percent of depositors not fully covered hold *uninsured* balances that constitute one-fourth of the dollar value of total deposits. A depositor who is not fully insured, for example, is someone holding a $150,000 negotiable certificate of deposit (which is insured for $100,000 and uninsured for the remaining $50,000 balance).

Uninsured deposits made bank regulators concerned about runs and panics, so regulators have administered bank failures in ways that expanded de facto insurance. In particular, most bank failures have been handled under the *purchase and assumption* method rather than the *payoff* method. Under the payoff method the FDIC sends its agents to the bank, verifies the deposit records, and then pays out funds directly to each depositor up to a limit of $100,000. Deposits above $100,000 must share in the losses of the bank. However, under the purchase and assumption method, the FDIC provides compensation to a healthy bank to merge with a failed bank and in the process to take over all of the deposit obligations of the failed bank. The net effect under the purchase and assumption method has been 100 percent deposit coverage.[3]

When Continental Illinois Bank failed in 1984 bank regulators went beyond just insuring the bank's depositors. They insured (after the fact) just about everyone Continental owed money to. Regulators felt that because Continental was one of the ten largest banks in the United States, there would be serious economic repercussions not only for the U.S. financial system but the entire global financial system if depositors and other creditors were exposed to losses. Soon thereafter the FDIC articulated a "too big to fail" doctrine providing insurance for all deposits at the largest banks in the country. While the FDIC has not explicitly clarified which banks fall into this category, the too big to fail doctrine was applied to the Bank of New England in 1991 when it was only the thirty-third largest bank in the country.

Moral Hazard and Deposit Insurance.   A compelling argument can be made that deposit insurance has been extremely successful in achieving its dual goals of protecting small depositors and preventing bank panics. After all, we have not seen anything comparable to the banking crisis of 1930 to 1933. Nevertheless, deposit insurance may be a double-edged sword. When depositors are fully insured by a government guarantee, they have little incentive to monitor the riskiness of their banks, creating a *moral hazard* problem very much like the problem in lending that we discussed in the previous chapter. As long as deposit insurance premiums do not depend on risk, that is they are fixed (which had been the case until quite recently), bank stockholders have every

---

[3]This failure policy was changed by the FDIC Improvement Act of 1991, which required federal regulators to use a least cost resolution (LCR) strategy for all but the biggest banks. Under LCR a *modified payoff* might be used in which the uninsured depositors are exposed to losses but the insured deposits are assumed by another bank.

incentive to make their banks riskier at the expense of the FDIC. And that is because stockholders share disproportionately in the upside (success) while the FDIC shares disproportionately in the downside (failure).[4]

There may, of course, be offsetting forces that would discourage banks from irresponsible risk taking. For small banks that tend to be privately owned, the owners' aversion to risk may act as a brake. For larger banks that are professionally managed, keeping a well-paid job may prevent promiscuous behavior. Owner and manager risk aversion, therefore, plus bank examinations and other regulatory efforts, may be enough to offset the moral hazard problem.

Ultimately, the issue of whether moral hazard has been a serious problem in bank regulation is empirical. However, empirical investigation is extremely difficult because it is not easy to tell, even *after the fact*, whether a bank failed because of *deliberate risk taking* or whether it failed because of *bad luck*. Investment strategies that are deemed safe at the time of their implementation (like lending to Mexico in the 1970s) can later backfire (when Mexico defaulted in 1982).

Until the 1980s, concern with the potentially perverse incentives associated with deposit insurance was understandably minimal because the bank failure rate was so low. However, as we saw in Chapter 11, during the 1980s the situation changed dramatically. First, it became apparent that losses from the S&L crisis would far exceed the accumulated funds in FSLIC. In addition, consistent with the predictions of the moral hazard argument, S&Ls seemed to have taken advantage of the new freedoms to invest in risky assets granted in the Garn–St. Germain Act of 1982. Second in addition to the S&L crisis, the banking industry itself suffered more than it had since the Great Depression. As we discussed in Chapter 11, commercial banking had become a much riskier business, and, not surprisingly, by the end of the 1980s 200 banks were failing per year versus fewer than ten per year in earlier decades.

These events stimulated the sentiment for a new approach to bank regulation. Moreover, the moral hazard argument, which seemed unconvincing until the mid-1980s, suddenly became part of the language of bank regulators and policymakers in Washington. Thus a coalition was born, not to be confused with the Moral Majority, aimed at regulatory reform. But unlike the regulatory reform of the 1930s that invented deposit insurance to protect the safety of the banking system from runs and panics, the motivating force in the 1980s was to protect the integrity of the deposit insurance fund (and ulti-

---

[4]The development of the formal economic model of moral hazard is relatively recent, but the basic idea and its specific application to deposit insurance can be traced all the way back to the original debate over the initiating legislation. Consider the typical point of view of the banking community in 1933, with respect to the feasibility of federal deposit insurance, as summarized in this gloomy conclusion: "The plan is inherently fallacious . . . one of those plausible, but deceptive, human plans that in actual application only serve to render worse the very evils they seek to cure" (*The Guaranty of Bank Deposits*, Economic Policy Commission, American Bankers Association, 1933, p. 43). On this basis, organized banking groups generally opposed legislation establishing the FDIC.

mately U.S. taxpayers) from the moral hazard problem caused by fixed-rate deposit insurance. Let's look at the regulatory policies that resulted.

Risk-Based Capital Requirements.   Bank capital essentially provides a cushion against failure. Up until the 1990s, U.S. bank regulators based their **capital adequacy** policy principally on the simple leverage ratio defined as:

$$Leverage\ Ratio = \frac{Capital}{Total\ Assets}$$

The larger this ratio, the larger the cushion against failure. The definition of capital varied somewhat over time and across regulators. However, in general capital meant stockholders equity plus loan loss reserves plus (sometimes) a limited number of liabilities that were considered permanent capital, such as subordinated debt. Regulators required banks to have sufficient capital to meet a minimum leverage ratio (which sometimes varied by bank size category) plus additional capital based on a *qualitative* assessment of the bank's asset and management quality. This qualitative assessment stemmed from the bank's risk profile drawn from recent bank examinations.

This approach to capital adequacy fundamentally changed in 1990 with the implementation of **risk-based capital requirements.**[5] Risk-based capital requirements were agreed to by the United States and other members of the **Bank for International Settlements** so that capital requirements would be linked to objective measures of bank risk in a consistent way across national boundaries. In particular, bank assets were classified into different risk classes (an example appears in Table 15.3), and riskier assets would require more capital. Thus a ratio is formed with capital in the numerator and risk *adjusted* assets in the denominator, producing

$$Risk\text{-}Based\ Capital\ Ratio = \frac{Capital}{Risk\text{-}Adjusted\ Assets}$$

What is important here, rather than exactly how to calculate risk-based capital ratios,[6] is that this change in regulatory policy directly addresses the moral hazard problem. In particular, as a bank's assets get riskier (as measured by the risk categories), the risk-based capital ratio declines because the denominator, risk-adjusted assets, has increased. Regulators will then force banks to offset this increased asset risk with more capital to restore the ratio to the proper level. Theoretically, if the asset risk categories and the capital definitions are set precisely enough, these two forces would offset each other, thereby eliminating the moral hazard problem altogether. In particular, whenever a bank elects to get *riskier* by investing in riskier assets, it would be required to get *safer* by having more capital. In practice, the risk categories

---

[5]Just for good measure, bank regulators still impose a traditional leverage ratio along with the newer risk-based capital ratio.

[6]For the gory details, see Anthony Saunders, *Financial Institutions and Management* (Burr Ridge, Illinois: Irwin, 1994).

TABLE 15.3 Capital Ratios—An Example

Safety First National Bank, December 31, 1997 (dollars in millions)			
Assets		**Liabilities and Equity**	
Cash	$ 100,000	Deposits & Other Liabilities	$ 950,000
U.S. Treasury Securities	300,000		
General Obligation Municipal Bonds	100,000		
Residential Mortgages	200,000		
Consumer and Commercial Loans	300,000	Capital	50,000
Total	$1,000,000	Total	$1,000,000

Leverage Ratio. The leverage ratio is simply:

$$\text{capital}/(\text{total assets}) = \$50{,}000/\$1{,}000{,}000 = 0.05$$

Risk-Based Capital Ratio. The risk-based capital ratio is capital divided by "risk-adjusted assets." Risk-adjusted assets is calculated by weighting the dollar amount in each asset category by the risk weight assigned to that category. There are four risk categories for assets:

Risk category	Description	Weight
Category 1	Cash & Treasuries	0%
Category 2	Municipal Securities	20%
Category 3	Mortgages	50%
Category 4	Loans	100%

In our example, Safety First National Bank's assets fall neatly into these categories. Risk-adjusted assets are calculated by multiplying the dollar amount in each category by risk weight, and summing up, as follows:

Asset	Risk category	Dollar amount		Risk weight		Adjusted Assets
Cash	1	100,000	×	0	=	0
U.S. Treasury Securities	1	300,000	×	0	=	0
General Obligation Municipal Bonds	2	100,000	×	0.20	=	20,000
Residential Mortgages	3	200,000	×	0.50	=	100,000
Consumer and Commercial Loans	4	300,000	×	1.00	=	300,000
				Risk Adjusted Assets	=	420,000

The risk-adjusted capital ratio is:

$$\text{capital}/(\text{risk-adjusted assets}) = \$50{,}000/\$420{,}000 = 0.119$$

Note: The minimum acceptable ratio for what is called the Tier I risk-based ratio is 4 percent so Safety First, with an 11.9 percent ratio, passes muster. There is also a total risk-based ratio (not shown), which is currently set at 8 percent, that includes other items in the numerator.

are too broad to capture differences in asset risk entirely (for example, all commercial loans are grouped together regardless of any differences in risk among them), but at least the regulators are moving the banks in the right direction by forging a link between bank risk and capital adequacy.

Prompt Corrective Action.   The FDIC Improvement Act of 1991 established a new set of procedures to handle troubled banks called **prompt corrective action (PCA).** This is obviously a great name for a program designed to close banks and thrifts before they expose the FDIC to excessive losses. PCA addressed two problems associated with closing failed banks. The first problem is *identifying* insolvent banks. In the past banks have been closed when an examination revealed that a bank's assets were worth less than its liabilities; otherwise it was permitted to operate. Bank examinations, however, are expensive—so they are conducted only about once per year, suggesting that a bank could deteriorate significantly before regulators know about it. Because banks were not closed until bank capital had entirely disappeared, the FDIC lost money when banks failed. A second problem arose over a fear that bank regulators would adopt a *forbearance* policy as the S&L regulators did in the 1980s. Regulatory forbearance occurs when regulators keep an insolvent institution operating in the hope that it can return to solvency. In reality, this is the "hope springs eternal" approach to bank management—which, you may recall from Chapter 12, was not one of the preferred methods of dealing with asset-liability mismatches.

Congress introduced PCA to solve these problems by *forcing* regulators to make timely adjustments to problem banks as they become riskier. It accomplishes this by establishing five categories, or zones, of capital adequacy, extending from the safest banks in the first zone (classified as *well capitalized*) to the riskiest banks in the fifth zone (classified as *critically undercapitalized*). As illustrated in Table 15.4, when banks fall below the *well-capitalized* zone, regulators are *required* to take specific remedial actions. The further a bank's capitalization deteriorates, the more severe the actions become, that is, the more the bank's activities will be restricted. Finally, if the bank drops into the worst zone (where its leverage ratio is below 2 percent), regulators are forced to begin closure proceedings, except under specific conditions.[7] PCA thus addresses regulatory forbearance by substantially limiting regulator discretion, and it addresses the consequences of the identification problem by changing the closure rule. Under the old closure rule, banks were only closed when their capital fell below zero. Under PCA banks are forced to take remedial actions gradually and are closed when the leverage ratio falls below 2 percent even though equity is still positive.

---

[7]Of course, there are the normal loopholes and legal tactics that managers and stockholders may use to delay the closure of their bank, which is why Congress is also considering a bill to execute all lawyers (except those that are members of Congress).

TABLE 15.4   Summary of Prompt Corrective Action[*]
(any restrictions in one category apply to all lower categories as well)

Zone	Mandatory provisions	Discretionary provisions
1. Well capitalized	—	—
2. Adequately capitalized	No brokered deposits except with FDIC approval[†]	—
3. Undercapitalized	Subject to increased monitoring Suspend dividends and management fees Must submit capital restoration plan within 45 days Restrict asset growth Prior supervisory approval needed for acquisitions, new branches, and new lines of business No brokered deposits	Order recapitalization Restrict interaffiliate transactions Restrict deposit interest rates Replacement of senior officers and directors Require divestiture or sale of the institution Restrict certain other activities Other actions that would better carry out prompt corrective action
4. Significantly undercapitalized	Bonuses and raises for senior officers restricted Order recapitalization[‡] Restrict interaffiliate transactions[‡] Restrict deposit rates[‡]	Require reduction in total assets Restrict any activity that poses excessive risk Prohibit deposits from correspondent depository institutions[§] Prohibit holding company from paying dividends without prior Federal Reserve approval Require divestiture or liquidation of any subsidiary
5. Critically undercapitalized	Must be placed in conservatorship or receivership within 90 days unless appropriate agencies concur that other action would better achieve the purpose of prompt corrective action Continual review by heads of banking agencies must occur to avoid receivership after 90 days Prohibited from paying principal or interest on subordinated debt without FDIC approval Certain other activities restricted	Additional restrictions may be placed on activities

[*]This table includes all provisions of the FDIC Improvement Act of 1991 that are commonly referred to as part of prompt corrective action.

[†]In a brokered deposit an investor gives money to a stockbroker who purchases a certificate of deposit on behalf of her client.

[‡]May not be required if certain conditions are met or if implementation would be inconsistent with purpose of prompt corrective action.

[§]A correspondent depository institution is a depository institution that regularly buys (or sells) services from the bank. Many banks sell services to other banks.

Source: Federal Reserve press releases.

Risk–Based Deposit Insurance Premiums.   The FDIC Improvement Act of 1991 also required that the FDIC establish **risk-based deposit insurance premiums.** In the past, all banks paid the same premium per dollar of deposits—regardless of their risk. As we noted above, this *fixed premium* feature of deposit insurance helped create a moral hazard problem because banks could get riskier without paying for it. In theory, however, if deposit insurance premiums were precisely set so that any increase in bank risk were fully priced into an increase in the deposit insurance premium, then the benefits to stockholders from risk shifting would be exactly taxed away by the insurance premium. Thus precisely set risk-based deposit insurance premiums would not only protect the deposit insurance fund by charging *actuarially sound* premiums but would simultaneously attack the moral hazard problem.

Practically speaking, it would be very difficult to link premiums precisely with risk. Risk in banking, particularly the credit risk associated with non-traded loans, is quite difficult to quantify. Nevertheless, some linkage between premium levels and risk would be an improvement over the status quo. The FDIC now relates deposit insurance premiums to risk through the PCA capitalization zones and qualitative regulator judgment.

Theoretically, imposing *both* risk-based capital requirements and risk-based deposit insurance premiums is not necessary. After all, either one could theoretically eliminate the moral hazard problem; imposing both smacks of overkill. However, as we noted earlier, the risk-based capital requirements fall far short of fully incorporating all of the differences in risks across banks. The same is true for risk-based deposit insurance premiums. The existence of these measurement problems suggests that simultaneously implementing both risk-based capital and risk-based deposit insurance premiums, each linked to risk in a somewhat different way, may be a more effective way of dealing with the moral hazard problem.

REGULATION OF NONDEPOSITORY FINANCIAL INTERMEDIARIES

How nondepository financial intermediaries are regulated depends very much on the types of liabilities they issue. Pension funds and life insurance companies, for example, are heavily regulated because their liabilities are purchased by small investors. Thus, a key goal driving the regulation of these two institutions is the protection of small investors—just as with bank regulation. Finance companies, on the other hand, get their funds by issuing debt and equity, pretty much like any manufacturing company, so we find virtually no regulation beyond the securities laws governing publicly traded securities.

Because of the importance of protecting the small investor, there are close parallels between the way pension funds and life insurance companies are regulated and the way commercial banks are regulated. The most striking similarity is the existence of a government-sponsored guarantee of the liabilities. In the case of pension funds, the **Employee Retirement Income Security Act (ERISA)** of 1974 established the Pension Benefit Guaranty Corporation (called Penny Benny by her friends), which guarantees defined benefits pension plans currently up to just over $30,000 per person. The guarantee is a bit more complicated in the case of life insurance companies which, for the most part, are regulated at the state level.

In order to manage the risk of failure and protect the guarantors, the activities of pension funds and life insurance companies are highly regulated. ERISA established minimum reporting, disclosure, and investment standards. State insurance commissions impose risk-based capital requirements and perform periodic audits much as bank regulators do in their regulation of commercial banks. Insurance regulation typically extends beyond financial restrictions to include implicit and explicit restrictions on pricing of particular products.

Mutual funds are regulated by the SEC under the provisions of the Securities Act of 1940, and they are also subject to state regulations. The motivation behind mutual fund regulation is similar to securities regulation—the protection of individual investors *through full disclosure*. This, of course, is different from banks, pension funds, and life insurance companies where regulation is designed to protect small individual investors and policyholders by circumscribing risk taking by the intermediary. The similarity between mutual fund regulation and individual securities regulation stems from the fact that mutual funds invest almost exclusively in traded securities.[8]

WHERE SECURITIES MARKET AND BANKING REGULATION MEET: THE GLASS-STEAGALL ACT

Legislation passed in 1933 and 1934 provided the regulatory framework for much of the financial services industry for a half century. A big part of that framework, the Glass-Steagall Act of 1933, segregated the banking industry from the rest of the financial services industry, especially the securities and insurance businesses. Banks are also barred from owning corporate stock and other activities deemed too risky, with the Federal Reserve acting as referee. In this section we continue the discussion of Chapter 12 and examine the restrictions that split the financial services industry, why they were imposed, and why there is increasing pressure to dismantle them.

---

[8]Money market mutual fund regulation is somewhat different. Specifically, money funds are prohibited from investing any of their assets in noninvestment grade instruments. The logic behind this restriction stems from the nature of money market fund liabilities. Because investors can redeem their shares at a fixed value (often by check), these shares are very much like bank deposits. So like demand deposits, regulation is focused on eliminating investor risk.

The Genesis of Glass-Steagall

Prior to 1933, investment banking and commercial banking were conducted under the same roof. J. P. Morgan & Company, for example, was both an investment bank and a commercial bank. Congress passed the Glass-Steagall Act in 1933 after congressional hearings laid the blame for the financial collapse of the 1930s at the feet of commercial banks and their securities activities. The prevailing sentiment at the time was that investment banking, particularly corporate securities underwriting, was just too risky for banks, and thus represented a substantial threat to financial system stability. Although hard empirical evidence supporting this contention was in short supply, passionate rhetoric was not—and Congress needed a fall guy. The result: Glass-Steagall specifically prohibited commercial banks and securities firms from playing in each other's backyard, including prohibiting banks from underwriting corporate debt and corporate equity. As a direct consequence of that legislation, the mighty house of Morgan was split in two—J. P. Morgan (the bank), which retained the right to issue checking accounts, and Morgan Stanley (the investment bank), which took over all corporate underwriting.

The Erosion of Glass-Steagall

To counter the competitive inroads from less-regulated institutions, commercial banks have exerted pressure on the Federal Reserve and the courts to push back the barriers imposed by Glass-Steagall and related legislation. More specifically, in the 1960s banking organizations began using *one-bank holding companies* as a means of entering *nonbank* activities, such as mortgage banking, leasing, and data processing. Specifically, the holding company would conduct these activities through nonbank subsidiaries. This raised the concern of regulators and bank competitors (not necessarily in that order) that expansion of nonbank activities would break down the barriers established by Glass-Steagall. These concerns led to the passage of the 1970 amendments to the Bank Holding Company Act, which gives the Federal Reserve the power to determine what activities are permissible in all bank holding companies.

For an activity to be permissible, the Federal Reserve had to determine whether the activity was "closely related to banking." This effectively created a game between banks, regulators, and the courts. Banks would test the waters by engaging in a new activity, and then wait to see (after the fact) whether the Federal Reserve would oppose them. Sometimes the securities industry or other affected groups would protest the Federal Reserve's decision, leaving the final resolution to the courts. Through this process, which is described in detail in Chapter 12, banks acquired more and more freedom in the 1970s and 1980s to engage in nontraditional banking activities.

The biggest breakthrough came in 1989 when the Federal Reserve granted five banks the power to underwrite corporate debt. The underwriting had to be done in a subsidiary of the holding company, called a **Section 20 affiliate,** and there were limitations on the volume of underwriting and on interaffiliate transactions. Nevertheless this was a watershed event. The Federal Reserve subsequently granted permission to still more banks to underwrite corporate debt, relaxed the volume restrictions somewhat, and even granted permission to a few banks to underwrite corporate equity.

To date, the Glass-Steagall Act still exists although Congress seems to come closer every year to fully repealing it. Only a small handful of banks, as of now, have been able to crack into the big leagues of securities underwriting. While several dozen of the largest banks have Section 20 subsidiary underwriting privileges, the vast majority do not. Nevertheless, these affiliates are the focal point of attention.

To minimize the risk to commercial banks (and to the FDIC), the Federal Reserve requires that Section 20 affiliates be insulated from the activities of the commercial bank. For example, Figure 15.1 shows a bank holding company that owns a bank subsidiary and an investment banking (Section 20) subsidiary, with barriers, called *firewalls,* separating the operations of the investment banking subsidiary. Firewalls are designed to insulate the commercial bank from the effects of a failure of the investment bank. They include a prohibition on the bank lending any money to the securities affiliate or the bank buying any assets from the securities affiliate. As shown in Figure 15.1, there are also restrictions that prevent the bank from channeling funds to the securities affiliate through the bank holding company. Altogether there are some 20 different firewalls, which all bank employees must repeat whenever there is a fire drill (just kidding).

The Risk of Universal Banking

The issue of risk has become a key issue in the debate over Glass-Steagall. Some argue that the risk of securities activities, especially the underwriting business described in Chapter 14, would jeopardize the stability of the bank-

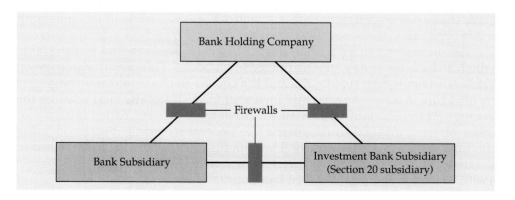

FIGURE 15.1   Bank holding company organization.

ing system. With deposit insurance and the "too big to fail doctrine," however, system risk is not the real issue. The more relevant issue is the exposure of the deposit insurance fund, that is, would bank losses in securities activities lead to more bank failures and significant losses to the FDIC?

Our discussion of modern portfolio theory in Chapter 7 showed that the risk of a portfolio of securities depends not only on the riskiness of the returns of the individual securities, but also on the correlation of returns among those securities. Substitute the word *activities* for *securities* in the last sentence and apply it to a banking organization viewed as a portfolio of activities. The implication is clear: Just because investment banking is riskier than commercial banking does not mean that the *combination* of the two will necessarily be riskier than banking by itself. If the correlation of returns in these two activities is low enough, then the benefits of diversification may produce a safer organization when commercial banking and investment banking are combined under the same umbrella. Moreover, permitting other nonbank activities beyond investment banking may produce further diversification benefits. Many countries in the European Union, for instance, permit **universal banking** organizations in which commercial banking can be combined with investment banking and life insurance activities.

Ultimately, then, the issue of risk and universal banking is an empirical one. There is no doubt that the securities business is one of the riskiest financial service activities—riskier, in particular, than banking, life insurance, and fire and casualty insurance. However, there is evidence suggesting that there are benefits to diversification. Specifically, there are combinations (that is, portfolios) of banking and other nonbanking activities that would reduce the risk of the combination below the risk of banking by itself and might still increase expected return.[9] Whether these risk-reducing combinations would, in fact, be the ones chosen if banks were allowed to participate fully in these activities is not as clear. But it seems like the time has come to let banks decide for themselves.

SUMMARY

1. The driving motivation behind securities market regulation is the protection of the individual investor. For the most part this is accomplished by promoting full disclosure of information both in the primary market when securities are issued and after origination when the securities are traded in the secondary markets.

---

[9] See Anthony Saunders and Ingo Walter, *Universal Banking in the United States* (New York: Oxford University Press, 1994).

2. Banks can be nationally or state chartered. The primary regulator for nationally chartered banks is the Office of the Comptroller of the Currency. State-chartered banks are regulated by their respective state banking authority and by a federal regulator, either the Federal Reserve (if they are a member of the Federal Reserve system) or the FDIC (if they are not a member of the Federal Reserve system).

3. Protection of individual depositors and safeguarding the stability of the banking system are two of the most important goals of bank regulation. Federal deposit insurance is the cornerstone of regulation designed to address these goals. Deposit insurance has been very successful in preventing bank panics. However, it causes moral hazard because it removes the incentive of depositors to discipline the bank against excessive risk taking. Significant changes in bank regulation were implemented in the early 1990s, in great part to address the moral hazard problem. The three most important changes were *risk-based capital requirements, prompt corrective action,* and *risk-based deposit insurance premiums.*

4. The Glass-Steagall Act of 1933 split the commercial banking industry and the investment banking industry. In the past several decades this split has been eroded by loopholes and changes in Federal Reserve policy. Debate continues over whether to entirely dismantle Glass-Steagall. There is evidence of gains from diversification to giving banks full authority to engage in investment banking activities.

QUESTIONS

15.1 What type of information are companies that issue traded securities required to disclose?

15.2 What events in the early 1930s prompted the regulatory legislation that has shaped a half century of regulation in the United States?

15.3 How does deposit insurance prevent a bank run?

15.4 How do risk-based capital requirements, prompt corrective action, and risk-based deposit insurance address the moral hazard problem associated with deposit insurance?

15.5 What is a universal bank and why might it be safer than a commercial bank by itself?

15.6 *Discussion question:* Disclosure requirements in the United States impose a number of costs on issuers, including registration filing costs and accounting and reporting costs. Are the benefits worth these costs? If so, why have the Eurobond markets been so successful without imposing disclosure requirements?

CHAPTER 16

Financial System Design

Can you imagine someone asking you to design a financial system from scratch? Believe it or not, that's just the kind of question that has been asked a lot recently, especially by Eastern Europeans whose countries have abandoned communism and central economic planning in favor of capitalism. Quite literally, these countries are faced with the challenge of building a financial system from square one.

On second thought, this might not be such a big deal. After all, you've just finished reading 15 chapters in your favorite textbook that covered all the key components. Build a new financial system—no problem. Just model it after the U.S. financial system. Start with a stock market like the New York Stock Exchange. Then add some laws patterned after the Securities Act of 1933 to protect investors through full disclosure and create a regulator like the SEC to enforce those laws. For the banking business, establish a deposit insurance system to protect small depositors and to ensure financial stability. To make sure that banks don't take advantage of deposit insurance by becoming too risky, follow U.S. banking laws that restrict banking activities, such as preventing banks from owning equity in other (nonfinancial) companies and restricting bank involvement in the securities or insurance businesses.

End of story? Not quite—things are rarely that simple. As it turns out, the U.S. model is not the only one in town. In fact, some of the most advanced economies have chosen a system very different from ours. For example, the German and Japanese economies follow a *banking-oriented* financial system. The United States and the United Kingdom, on the other hand, have a decidedly *markets-oriented* system. Why? Which is best? And which is a better fit for the new Eastern European economies and other emerging capitalistic countries? These are the questions we address in this chapter.

Because banking-oriented systems and markets-oriented systems are the two major choices, we begin our discussion by analyzing the pluses and minuses of each. Then we take a look at the four most advanced financial systems in the world, Germany, Japan, the United Kingdom, and the United States, to see why Germany and Japan are banking-oriented systems and why the United Kingdom and the United States are markets-oriented systems. Finally, we return to the emerging capitalistic countries with some observations about how to design a financial system of their very own.

INFORMATION AND FINANCIAL SYSTEM DESIGN

Financial systems have many things in common. For example, all financial systems have a *payments system*—that is, a system that facilitates the processing of checks and electronic transfers of funds among consumers and businesses. Most have specialized financial intermediaries, such as savings institutions and credit cooperatives. Virtually all have some form of deposit insurance. Also, they all have *central banks*. Despite these similarities, however, there are also very significant differences, especially related to how businesses obtain financing. In particular, private ownership of business leads to two fundamental problems that must be handled by the financial sector: stockholder-lender conflict and manager-stockholder conflict. Not surprisingly, our old nemesis, asymmetric information, is at the root of both. First, we review how the information asymmetries create stockholder-lender and manager-stockholder conflicts and then turn to how a financial system can be organized to address these problems.

Stockholder-Lender Conflict

We first introduced the problem of asymmetric information in lending in Chapter 11 and discussed it at greater length in Chapter 14. In this chapter we will refer to it by a new name, **stockholder-lender conflict,** because this highlights precisely which parties are involved, namely, stockholders and lenders. By way of review, recall that asymmetric information in business lending comes in two varieties. *Adverse selection* occurs because firm owners (stockholders) have an incentive to understate their true riskiness in order to borrow on a more favorable basis. *Moral hazard* means that firms have an incentive to become riskier after their loans are funded because limited liability makes stockholders more interested in the chances of success than they are worried about failure. Recall also that the magnitude of these problems is much greater for small companies than for large ones because there is much more publicly available information about large companies. This means that it is easier for lenders (before they lend any money) to assess firm risk when the firm is large than when it is small, and it is much easier for lenders (after the loan has been made) to observe any change in firm behavior when the firm is large than when it is small.

Manager-Stockholder Conflict

The stockholder-lender conflict is not the only challenge rooted in information asymmetries. A similar problem emerges because in most large businesses, stockholders delegate the management of the company to a professional manager. The owners would like the manager to operate the firm in the owners' best interests. That is, they would like the manager to maximize the value of the firm, sometimes referred to as maximizing shareholder wealth by maximizing the value of the stock.

Unfortunately, the manager may have other objectives in mind, for example, firm managers may want to *minimize* their own effort and *maximize* their salary and the time they spend on the golf course or running charity tennis tournaments. Managers may want to maximize firm size—not because it will increase shareholder wealth but because it will maximize the manager's personal power and possibly the manager's visibility on national TV commercials. They may want to maximize the so-called "perks" that come with the job, such as driving the most expensive company car, or flying in the most expensive corporate jet, or sitting in the fanciest office. Most importantly, managers want to preserve their jobs. This may result, for example, in the manager choosing excessively safe strategies for the firm as opposed to value-maximizing strategies that may involve more risk—but also substantially more expected return.

It might seem that differences between stockholder and manager objectives would be easy to resolve. If a manager refuses to run the company in the best interest of the stockholders: *Fire the manager!* However, several considerations make this harder than it sounds. First, *asymmetric information* makes it very difficult to monitor the activities of a firm's CEO (chief executive officer) to determine whether the manager's actions are value enhancing or self serving. For example, golf games can bring in a lot of new business and charity tennis tournaments can generate a lot of goodwill. Corporate jets may save precious executive time. Rapid firm growth *is* sometimes the best strategy for maximizing shareholder wealth. And sometimes the safest project is the best project.

Stockholders must actively monitor their manager's performance to pierce this veil of asymmetric information—but this is hard work. And here's where the second problem arises. In large publicly traded companies with thousands of stockholders, there may be no incentive for any individual to monitor the manager. Each shareholder thinks, "I own only a little piece of the company, why should I spend half my life psychoanalyzing management motives when the benefit to me is too small to justify the cost. Let somebody else do it." This is a perfectly rational decision. Unfortunately, every stockholder reaches the same conclusion, and the CEO and other managers are then free to do as they please.

In closely held firms where a significant amount of stock is held by one investor, however, there is usually sufficient incentive to monitor because the owner has enough stock so that the stock price increase stemming from improved managerial efficiency more than offsets the cost of monitoring. Moreover, the owner in a closely held firm often has the power to control the firm's board of directors and fire management when they are behaving in a self-serving way. In privately held firms, where the owner and the manager are

Conflict/Firm	Smaller Firms	Larger Firms
Stockholder-Lender Conflict (risk shifting)	major problem	minor problem
Manager-Stockholder Conflict (corporate governance)	none	major problem

FIGURE 16.1   Financial system design: the problems.

often the same person, the problem (of course) entirely disappears—the manager should always act in the best interest of the owner, because *the manager is the owner!* Thus, the manager-stockholder problem is really a large-firm problem that is most acute in diffusely held publicly traded firms run by professional managers.

Conflict Resolution and Financial System Design

Figure 16.1 summarizes the relationship between firm size and the two problems just identified. Stockholder-lender conflict, sometimes referred to as the *risk-shifting problem*, is significant for small firms (upper left-hand cell) because there is so little information available about them, but not for large firms (upper right-hand cell) because information is easily accessible. Manager-stockholder conflict, sometimes labeled the corporate governance (who's in charge here?) problem, typically does not arise for small firms (lower left-hand cell) because they are managed by their owners but is pervasive for large firms (lower right-hand cell) because they are professionally managed and their ownership is so diffuse.

It is interesting to note that these two conflicts are associated with external finance—the fact that almost all firms raise funds from outsiders in the form of debt and/or equity. From our perspective, what is most interesting is that the two conflicts are dealt with very differently in banking-oriented financial systems compared with markets-oriented financial systems. For example, in Germany and Japan which are banking-oriented systems, banks actually own companies they monitor, and the stock and bond markets are relatively underdeveloped. In the United States and United Kingdom, which have markets-oriented systems, banks do not own companies and the public bond and stock markets are very prominent institutions.

How do these two systems resolve stockholder-lender and manager-stockholder conflict? Let's look at small firms first, then large firms.

Small Firms: Stockholder–Lender Conflict.   Basically, both systems treat small firms similarly. The only relevant problem for small firms is stockholder-lender conflict, and this is addressed by having small firms borrow from banks and other monitoring-intensive financial intermediaries, such as life in-surance companies and commercial finance companies. Because banks are specialists in information production, they are ideally suited to assess bor-rower risk before making the loan, and they also design the loan contracts to minimize the incentive to get riskier after the loan is made. As we saw in Chapter 14, these tailor-made contracts often require that the firm, or the owner of the firm, pledge collateral to secure the loan and that the owner per-sonally guarantee the firm's loan. These tailored contracts also frequently in-clude restrictive covenants that are often renegotiated as banks continuously monitor their customers.

Figure 16.2 summarizes how banking-oriented systems (a) and markets-oriented systems (b) solve the stockholder-lender and manager-stockholder conflicts. Our discussion thus far is reflected in identical entries under the col-umn for small firms in both (a) and (b). More specifically, stockholder-lender conflict for small firms is solved in both systems by having them borrow from financial intermediaries who intensively *monitor* and lend under tailored con-tracts. Manager-stockholder conflict, of course, is "not applicable" for small firms.

Large Firms: Stockholder–Lender Conflict.   While the two types of financial systems treat small firms similarly, they differ significantly in the way they

(a)
Banking-Oriented Systems

Conflict/Firm	Smaller Firms	Larger Firms
Stockholder-Lender Conflict (risk shifting)	financial intermediation (monitoring)	financial intermediation (ownership consolidation)
Manager-Stockholder Conflict (corporate governance)	not applicable	financial intermediation (ownership consolidation)

(b)
Markets-Oriented Systems

Conflict/Firm	Smaller Firms	Larger Firms
Stockholder-Lender Conflict (risk shifting)	financial intermediation (monitoring)	Reputation and rating agencies
Manager-Stockholder Conflict (corporate governance)	not applicable	Takeover market and managerial compensation

FIGURE 16.2   Financial system design: conflict resolution.

treat large firms. Turning first to the stockholder-lender conflict, in Chapter 14 we showed that under a markets-oriented system, large firms tend to borrow short term in the commercial paper market and borrow long term in the corporate bond market, with the production of information about business risk delegated to a third party—the bond rating agency (see the upper right-hand cell in Figure 16.2(b)). Bond rating agencies, you may recall from Chapter 5, measure risk when corporate bonds are first issued and they monitor changes in risk afterwards. The widespread availability of public information, plus the information produced by credit rating agencies, enables large firms to develop reputations for not becoming too risky.

For large firms in banking-dominated systems, the solution to stockholder-lender conflict is different. When the lender and the stockholder are one and the same (the bank), as is often the case in banking-oriented systems, the problem entirely disappears, that is, there is no incentive for stockholders to exploit *themselves*. Practically speaking, this is an oversimplification because in most banking-oriented systems the bank doesn't own *all* of the firm's equity. Usually some of the equity is owned by individual investors, and the stock is traded publicly. Nevertheless, consolidation of ownership is often large enough so that the bank owns a controlling interest. Thus the upper right-hand cell of (a) records financial intermediation as the solution to the stockholder-lender conflict in banking-oriented systems.

Large Firms: Manager–Stockholder Conflict. The solution to manager-stockholder conflict for large firms is also quite different in banking-oriented versus markets-oriented systems. In banking-oriented systems the solution to the manager-stockholder conflict is driven principally by the bank's ownership of the business. By owning a significant amount of a firm's equity, the bank has an incentive to monitor the behavior of the firm's management. The bank also has *control* so it can fire an incompetent or misbehaving manager. Thus, the two right-hand cells of (a) in Figure 16.2 reflect the fact that stockholder-lender conflict and manager-stockholder conflict are both resolved in banking-oriented systems via consolidation of firm ownership in a financial intermediary.

The solution to the manager-stockholder conflict in markets-oriented systems is strikingly different. Because ownership is diffuse, that is, not consolidated, there is little incentive for individual stockholders to monitor a manager. To make matters worse, in a markets-oriented system, managers often influence who is picked to serve on a company's board of directors and if the board is mostly composed of a CEO's golfing buddies, they may turn a blind eye to poor performance.[1] This creates the distinct possibility that inefficient managers may become *entrenched* and the firm becomes *manager-controlled* as opposed to *stockholder-controlled*.

---

[1]While a company's board of directors technically must be approved by a vote of stockholders, the ability of senior management to nominate a slate of board members, and the inability of thousands of stockholders to monitor management and nominate their own slate, often effectively conveys to senior management control over the board.

How are entrenched underperforming managers eliminated? Principally through the **corporate takeover** market, that is, when a company is purchased by another company or by a group of private investors.[2] These new owners, then, can replace the old entrenched management and unlock the efficiency gains that were denied under the old management. Not surprisingly, entrenched managers typically will resist corporate takeovers with various legal and financial maneuvers so that a company is often taken over against the current management's wishes. Quite naturally this is called a **hostile takeover.**

To minimize manager-stockholder conflict, markets-oriented systems also place more emphasis on management compensation packages that link compensation to firm performance than do banking-oriented systems. This is accomplished principally by giving managers stock and stock options in the companies they manage. All of this is recorded in the lower right-hand cell of Figure 16.1(b).

FINANCIAL SYSTEM DESIGN: A DESCRIPTIVE SUMMARY OF GERMANY, JAPAN, THE UNITED KINGDOM, AND THE UNITED STATES

In the previous section we analyzed the two biggest challenges in financial system design, stockholder-lender conflict and manager-stockholder conflict. We have seen that there are two models to choose from to solve these problems jointly, a banking-oriented system and a markets-oriented system. It is now time to see how real countries fit these alternatives by examining the countries with the four largest and most well-developed economies in the world—Germany, Japan, the United Kingdom, and the United States. First we provide an overview of each system and then turn in the next section to a specific analysis of how they compare with each other in terms of conflict resolution.[3]

Germany

Germany is very much a banking-oriented financial system. At the core of the system is the **Hausbank.** Under the *Hausbank* concept a business relies on a single bank (its *Hausbank*) as its primary source of all forms of external finance, including both debt and equity finance. Thus the relationship between a business firm and its *Hausbank* is a very powerful one. Unlike countries

---

[2]When a group of investors buys the outstanding stock of a company (takes over the company) and finances the acquisition mostly with debt, the takeover is called a *leveraged buyout.*

[3]Much of the information contained in this section and in the following section is based on three sources. They are: Anthony Saunders and Ingo Walter, *Universal Banking in the United States* (Oxford: Oxford University Press, 1994); Itzhak Swary and Barry Topf, *Global Financial Deregulation* (Cambridge: Blackwell Publishers, 1992); and Stephen Prowse, "Corporate Governance in an International Perspective: A Survey of Corporate Control Mechanisms Among Large Firms in the U.S., U.K., Japan, and Germany," in *Financial Markets, Institutions and Instruments* 4 (1995).

where banking relationships are strictly limited to debt financing, the *Hausbank* system fosters bank participation in the strategic activities of German firms through stock ownership and control; bankers can also sit on company supervisory boards (the German equivalent of a board of directors).

Bank ownership participation is both direct and indirect. It is direct because banks can, and do, own a significant share of many German companies; in particular, banks own about 10 percent of public companies in Germany. However, indirect ownership is even more important. Many individuals and institutions in Germany deposit their stock holdings in a trust account with a bank. As part of this *custody* arrangement, the voting rights associated with these shares are conveyed to the bank. Thus banks exercise control over German companies by combining the direct voting rights from share ownership with the proxy votes they acquire through their custody accounts. These proxy votes add about another 14 percent to the amount of equity controlled by German banks, for a total of 24 percent.[4]

The German banking system is so important, it makes sense to go into it in some detail. Banks are organized into four major categories: commercial banks, savings banks, cooperative banks, and specialized banks. They represent 24, 38, 15, and 22 percent of the system's total assets, respectively. Commercial banks consist of the three biggest German banks (the *Grossbanken*) and a number of regional banks and private banks. You may have heard of one or more of the *Grossbanken:* Deutsche Bank, Dresdner Bank, and Commerzbank. These three banks are also significant players internationally. Some of the regional banks are also quite large and are active participants in international markets. The savings banks are typically owned by regional or town governments and operate locally. Originally established as thrift institutions (collecting deposits and making mortgage loans), they now offer full commercial banking services although their orientation still emphasizes thrift activities. The cooperative banks were first established in the nineteenth century to collect savings and extend credit to individuals. The most important type of specialized banks are the mortgage banks that make residential mortgage loans and other real estate loans. The mortgage banks are financed principally by bonds. They also include banks that emphasize consumer lending, small business loan guarantees, export finance, and industry-specific finance.

The dominance of banks in Germany comes at the expense of the securities markets. The stock, bond, and commercial paper markets in Germany can best be described as suppressed. There are eight regional stock exchanges, dominated by the Frankfurt exchange. Less than a quarter of the largest German companies are listed on an exchange. Even among those listed, a large proportion are not actively traded. The corporate bond market is minuscule, as is the commercial paper market, perhaps because until 1992 regulations and taxes made it ridiculously expensive to issue these securities. As a result, most German companies are highly dependent on their banks for credit (which is just fine with the banks).

---

[4]See Prowse (1995).

The dominance of the banking system in Germany is enhanced by a regulatory framework that permits *universal banking*. As we discussed in the last chapter, a universal bank engages in a variety of financial service activities. In Germany banks are not only permitted to own nonfinancial companies, but they are also permitted to underwrite corporate securities and to underwrite insurance through a subsidiary. The ability to underwrite securities enables a German bank (the *Hausbank*) to handle all of a company's financial needs effectively throughout its business life cycle.

Many who advocate giving U.S. banks full underwriting privileges cite German universal banking as the model of success. Some caution, however, should be exercised in drawing strong conclusions based on the German system. While it is true that German banks have long had the ability to underwrite corporate securities, they have done so in a decidedly *banking-oriented* system in which the stock and bond markets are poorly developed. It is not obvious that this success would translate to a system with well-developed stock and bond markets.

Japan

The two most important features of the Japanese financial system are the **keiretsu** form of industrial organization and the emphasis on a firm's relationship with its *main bank*. A *keiretsu* is a group of companies that are controlled through interlocking ownership, that is, the companies own stock in each other. This form of industrial organization encourages strong loyalty among the companies in the group, including favoritism in customer-supplier relationships.

Like the German financial system, the Japanese system emphasizes firm loyalty to a single bank, the main bank. In fact, each *keiretsu* has a main bank that typically owns stock in other members of the keiretsu. The current structure of the banking system emerged immediately prior to World War II when the government consolidated power in both the industrial and the financial sectors and reinforced the existing ties between the main banks and their company groups, then called *zaibatsu* (now, in its weakened form, called *keiretsu*).

As in Germany, Japanese banks may own equity in nonfinancial companies, although in 1987 the maximum investment permitted in any *single* firm was reduced to 5 percent. This, however, understates the control exerted by a main bank through the *keiretsu*. Every month the top managers of the firms in the *keiretsu* get together with large shareholders and chief creditors at the *Presidents Club* meeting. While these meetings are not part of the formal governance structure, they act very much like the supervisory board in German companies where planned projects and general firm policy are discussed.

The banking system is divided into three basic categories, the very largest *city banks*, the *regional banks*, and the *special-purpose financial institutions*. The three groups comprise 30, 18, and 52 percent of the banking sector, respectively. A disproportionately large fraction of the world's biggest banks are

Japanese city banks. Possibly you've heard of some of these, such as Sanwa Bank, Dai-Ichi Kangyo Bank, Fuji Bank, and Sumitomo Bank? The special-purpose institutions include the three long-term credit banks, specialized small business institutions, and specialized agriculture, forestry, and fishery institutions.

Historically, the corporate debt markets have been suppressed in Japan much as they have been in Germany, further enhancing the power of commercial banks. Only relatively recently (1987) have Japanese regulations permitted companies to issue commercial paper and corporate bonds. As a result the vast majority of debt financing comes from the banking system.

Unlike Germany, the stock market in Japan is quite large. The Tokyo Stock exchange is comparable in size to the New York Stock Exchange (and is sometimes larger depending on stock price levels and the exchange rate). However, some caution should be exercised in comparing the U.S. and Japanese equity markets because the extensive cross-ownership of shares through *keiretsu* masks the high degree of concentration of ownership of large Japanese firms.

Japan has also adopted laws similar to the U.S. Glass-Steagall Act separating commercial banking from investment banking. As in the U.S. system, however, the separation between securities underwriting and commercial banking is eroding. As of 1993, commercial banks in Japan were permitted to underwrite corporate securities in an affiliate, subject to specific permission from the Ministry of Finance (the regulator of banks in Japan along with the Bank of Japan).

United Kingdom

Unlike the economies in Germany and Japan, the financial system of the United Kingdom is very much markets-oriented, although banks still play a very important role. London is somewhat unique because it serves as *both* a domestic financial market for U.K. business as well as the center of the Eurobond market. Because of a regulatory environment that encourages foreign participation and competition in financial services, the domestic markets are not really distinct from the foreign markets. U.K. companies issue in the Eurobond market and foreign companies, as well as domestic, list stock on the London Stock Exchange.

The banking system consists of five categories: *clearing banks, merchant banks*, other British banks, foreign banks, and other deposit-taking institutions. They comprise 28, 4, 4, 46, and 18 percent of banking system assets, respectively. The clearing banks, dominated by Barclays Bank, National Westminister, Midland Bank, and Lloyds Bank, are universal banks and conduct securities activities through investment banking subsidiaries, in addition to having extensive branch networks throughout the United Kingdom. The merchant banks provide *wholesale* banking services to large corporations, including offering loan commitments and guarantees, derivatives products, and international trade finance. In many ways they are more like U.S. investment banks than traditional commercial banks. The "other" British banks, as their name implies, are an eclectic group consisting of some institutions similar to the merchant banks and others, which are specialized institutions that emphasize such activities as consumer lending. The other deposit-taking institutions are mostly building societies, which are mutual organizations similar (for better or worse) to savings and loan associations in the United States.

Banks in the United Kingdom do not, for the most part, own nonfinancial corporations. While there are no explicit restrictions prohibiting bank equity ownership, the Bank of England (the regulator of banks in the United Kingdom) has generally discouraged the practice in order to promote a safer banking system. The lack of formal restrictions explicitly prohibiting bank stock ownership must be viewed in the overall context of British bank regulation. Historically, the Bank of England has supervised banks on an informal basis by influencing banks through that great English tradition—"the old boy network." Thus through meetings and consultation with management, the Bank of England exercises "moral suasion" over its flock. While the supervision process has become more formalized in recent years, it would still be misleading to consider only explicit restrictions in analyzing constraints on bank ownership of business, as well as other bank activities.

United States

We have extensively examined the U.S. financial system in Chapters 11 through 15. Suffice it to say that the very large stock, bond, and commercial paper markets make the United States the prototype of a markets-oriented system. Moreover, the securitization of residential mortgages and other types of financial assets, such as credit card receivables and auto loans, have further strengthened the importance of the traded securities markets. On the other hand, although U.S. banks are not the primary providers of external finance to large corporations, they do play a key role in external finance for small and midsize companies. And, of course, the Glass-Steagall Act prohibits commercial banks from owning equity in nonfinancial companies, although bank holding companies are permitted very limited ownership privileges.

FINANCIAL SYSTEM DESIGN AND CONFLICT RESOLUTION: GERMANY, JAPAN, THE UNITED KINGDOM, AND THE UNITED STATES

As we have just seen, Germany and Japan have banking-oriented economies and the United Kingdom and the United States have markets-oriented economies. One way to measure the extent of these differences is to look at the relative sizes of the banking sector and the stock markets in each of these countries. The columns in the foreground of Figure 16.3 show the size of the stock markets measured in dollars in each of these four countries at the end of 1994. The columns in the background show the size in dollars of the banking

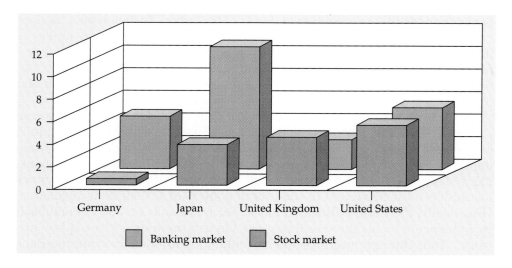

FIGURE 16.3   Size of banking and stock markets (in trillions of dollars), 1994.

sectors (total bank assets) at the end of 1994. As you can see, banking clearly dominates the stock market in Germany and Japan while the two markets are much more comparable in size in the United Kingdom and the United States.

A second measure distinguishing banking-oriented versus markets-oriented systems is *bank ownership of nonfinancial firms*. In banking-oriented systems we should expect to see a substantial amount of firm ownership by banks while in markets-oriented systems bank ownership should be negligible. Estimated ownership patterns for the four countries are shown in Table 16.1, which requires some explanation. The first category (Individuals) is an estimate of the direct ownership by individuals who make their own investment decisions. The second category (Financial institutions—agents) includes both ownership by financial intermediaries who act as agents and ownership by individuals whose investment decisions are based on advice from their brokers. The financial intermediaries and brokers in this category are not actively involved in monitoring or supervising firm management, that is, they are not involved in *corporate governance*. This category, for instance, includes mutual funds acting as passive owners. The third category (Financial institutions—ownership/control) includes financial intermediaries such as banks or insurance companies, which either own shares outright or exercise voting control through proxy rights. This category includes the shares that German banks control through their custody accounts. The fourth category (Nonfinancial corporations) is stock ownership by nonfinancial companies. The final two categories are self-explanatory.

The key conclusion from Table 16.1 is the substantial ownership control by financial institutions (Financial institutions—ownership/control) in Germany and Japan and the insignificant amount in the United Kingdom and the United States. In Germany and Japan, financial intermediaries either own or

TABLE 16.1   Estimated Ownership Patterns

	Germany	Japan	United Kingdom	United States
Individuals	3.0	22.4	22.4	30–55
Financial institutions—agents	3.0	9.5	57.8	55–62
Financial institutions—ownership/control	33.0	38.5	0.7	2.0
Nonfinancial corporations	42.0	24.9	10.1	7.0
Foreign	14.0	4.0	6.5	5.4
Government	5.0	0.7	2.5	0

Note: Financial institutions—agents are institutions such as pension funds, mutual funds, or other money managers that hold equity as agents for other investors. Financial institutions—ownership/control are institutions that hold equity for their own accounts. For the United Kingdom and the United States, individual and corporate ownership of shares has been reduced (and added to the financial institutions as agents category) by the estimated proportion of shares that are traded on brokers's recommendations. For Germany, the total for institutional owners includes stock which is owned by individuals but held and voting rights exercised by banks (approximately 14 percent of outstanding equity).

Source: Reprinted from Prowse (1995).

control 33.0 and 38.5 percent of the outstanding shares, respectively, while in the United Kingdom and the United States financial intermediaries control only 0.7 and 2.0 percent, respectively. Thus the evidence strongly supports labeling financial systems in Germany and Japan as banking-oriented and in the United States and the United Kingdom as markets-oriented.

Conflict Resolution in the Big Four

Let's go back to Figure 16.1 and summarize how our four favorite financial systems resolve the stockholder-lender conflict and the manager-stockholder conflict identified there. This is a recap for those of you who have fallen asleep trying to design the most exciting financial system. The four financial systems are remarkably similar in providing financing to small businesses. Each country has a tier of banks and other financial intermediaries that emphasize lending to this sector of the economy. These institutions design tailored contracts to address the asymmetric information problems that lead to stockholder-lender conflict, and they continuously assess the riskiness of the borrowing firms.

For large companies, however, substantial differences emerge. In bank-controlled Germany and Japan, the stockholder-lender conflict disappears because banks are owners and creditors at the same time. For companies in these countries that are not bank controlled, and there are some of these, the stockholder-lender conflict is relevant—although Figure 16.1 indicates that the problem is not as acute as it is in small firms. Nevertheless, the solution to

TABLE 16.2   Merger and Acquisition Activity: 1985–1989

	United States	United Kingdom	Japan	Germany
Volume (in billions of US$)	$1,070.0	$107.6	$61.3	$4.2
Percentage of total market capitalization	41.1%	18.7%	3.1%	2.3%

Note: Dollar values calculated at current exchange rates for each of the five years covered. Market capitalization figures are for 1987, converted to dollars at prevailing exchange rates.

Source: Reprinted from Prowse (1995).

stockholder-lender conflict for nonbank-controlled large firms in the banking-oriented systems is the same as for small firms: tailored contracts offered by banks that monitor borrower performance.

For the markets-oriented economies of the United Kingdom and the United States, on the other hand, stockholder-lender conflict is still something of a problem even for large firms. Large companies in these countries are, for the most part, publicly owned, and company performance is monitored by independent credit rating agencies, such as the U.S.'s Moody's and Standard & Poor's.

An interesting dimension to the stockholder-lender conflict is how *financial distress* is managed. A company is in distress (deep trouble) when poor performance jeopardizes the firm's ability to meet its financial obligations. During these periods, stockholder-bondholder (lender) conflict is extreme because the owners have very little stake left in their firm. However, in the banking-oriented systems of Germany and Japan, it might be much easier for a company to navigate through troubled times under the protective wing of its *Hausbank* or main bank. On the other hand, when companies rely on widely held debt, as in the United Kingdom and the United States, it is often very difficult to get large numbers of bondholders to agree on a strategy that will enable a company to work its way out of trouble—short of bankruptcy, that is.

Turning now to manager-stockholder conflict, once again there are substantial differences between the two competing systems when it comes to large firms. The concentration of ownership under the German and Japanese financial systems gives banks a major incentive to monitor corporate managers actively. In the United Kingdom and the United States, however, diffuse ownership of company stock eliminates much of the incentive for any individual shareholder to monitor a firm's management, leaving the corporate takeover as the most powerful mechanism for solving manager-stockholder conflict.[5] It is not surprising, therefore, that Table 16.2 shows a substantially larger volume of mergers and acquisitions in the markets-oriented economies

---

[5]Another mechanism used in markets-oriented systems, particularly the United States', is linking managerial compensation to firm performance through stock-based compensation packages.

of the United Kingdom and the United States than in the banking-oriented economies of Germany and Japan.

And the Winner Is . . .

Now that we've been through the theory and practice of banking-oriented and markets-oriented financial systems, how do they measure up against each other? Unfortunately, the game is still underway, so it's too early to declare a winner. However, there are a few qualitative conclusions we can draw. First, financial intermediaries (like banks) with substantial ownership stakes in firms are better at solving stockholder-lender or manager-stockholder conflicts than are rating agencies or individual stockholders. However, this type of intensive monitoring is expensive. Continuous scrutiny of financial information, periodic compliance checks, and active participation in firm management all require a substantial investment in time and resources by the intermediaries.

Second, stocks and bonds issued by firms in banking-oriented systems are much less liquid than securities issued in markets-oriented systems—either because they are not traded at all or because they are traded less frequently. And illiquidity is costly because issuers must compensate investors for the inability to resell their securities easily. Some estimates put this liquidity cost at more than 30 percent, implying that a $100 stock would sell for only $70 if it could not be sold in a secondary market.[6]

Thus there is a trade-off: The cost of raising capital is higher in Germany and Japan because of poor liquidity, while in the United States and the United Kingdom the cost of raising capital is higher because investors must be compensated for unresolved stockholder-bondholder-manager conflicts. Although there is no definitive answer to which of these forces dominates, some of the trends in the marketplace provide a clue.

First, as described in previous chapters, *securitization* is on the rise in U.S. financial markets and is starting to catch on elsewhere. Securitization is a distinct movement away from banking-oriented finance toward markets-oriented finance. However, securitization may never catch on for small business lending because these companies are too information problematic. Second, the Eurobond markets have increasingly provided a markets-based alternative to domestic bank financing in Germany, Japan, and other developed banking-oriented economies. As more and more German and Japanese companies seek such financing, the tight grip of the *Hausbanks* and main banks could very well diminish. Finally the very recent increase in the level of merger and acquisition activity, particularly in Europe—though still at a relatively low level compared to the United States—indicates that the takeover market may provide an alternative to bank monitoring even in banking-

---

[6]See William L. Silber, "Discounts on Restricted Stock: The Impact of Illiquidity on Stock Prices," *Financial Analysts Journal*, July–August 1991, and Francis A. Longstaff, "How Much Can Marketability Affect Security Values?" *Journal of Finance*, December 1995.

oriented economies. Of course, it would be unwise to celebrate victory for markets-oriented systems because we're still in the first half of the game, so just about anything can happen.

FINANCIAL SYSTEM DESIGN FOR EASTERN EUROPE AND OTHER EMERGING ECONOMIES

With the breakup of communism and the Soviet Union, the Eastern European countries were faced with the daunting challenge of building a financial system from square one. One of the first initiatives was to develop *privatization* programs designed to transform government-owned companies into privately owned firms. These privatization programs typically involved the distribution of shares (or vouchers for shares) to the major stakeholders (employees, managers, and creditors) in the industrial firms that were privatized. Most of the early privatization efforts focused on small and midsize companies rather than the large industrial companies.

Some Western economic advisors emphasize that privatization must go hand in hand with the development of new securities markets—particularly equity markets in which the stock of companies could be traded. After all, what could be more symbolic of capitalism than an active stock market? However, there is a growing sentiment that banking-oriented financial systems may make much more sense for these formerly planned economies. Not surprisingly, the argument boils down to asymmetric information.

At best, Eastern Europe can be viewed as an *information-poor* environment where even the activities of large firms are cloaked in a dense fog. Most Eastern European countries, for example, have just recently adopted accounting rules. Rating agencies, for the most part, don't exist. Reputation building is extremely difficult because most Eastern European companies haven't existed long enough to develop reputations—except for producing shoddy goods under communism. Moreover, the lack of managerial talent and experience in Eastern Europe suggests that investor monitoring will be especially critical in these countries. All of these factors indicate that a banking-oriented system like Germany and Japan may be much more suitable for Eastern Europe and other formerly planned economies. Although it might be nice to play the Russian stock market, the odds of success in that arena are much lower than the odds you get in Atlantic City or Las Vegas (which, as we know from elementary statistics, virtually guarantees that you will be a loser if you play long enough). So sit back and relax before taking a flyer in some Eastern European stock market.

SUMMARY

1. There are two types of financial systems to choose from. In banking-oriented systems banks are the principal lenders to both small and

large businesses, and banks own and control large corporations. In markets-oriented systems large companies are diffusely held, and they borrow most of their funds in the securities markets rather than from banks.

2. Financial systems must solve two fundamental problems related to asymmetric information. The first, stockholder-lender conflict, occurs because business owners have an incentive to understate firm risk to their lenders and to get riskier after their loans have been funded. The second, manager-stockholder conflict, occurs because professional managers have an incentive to manage firms in their own best interest, rather than in the interest of the firms' owners.

3. The stockholder-lender conflict is a more severe problem for small firms than large firms. The manager-stockholder conflict does not typically arise in small firms because they are usually either owner managed or because they are tightly controlled by their owners.

4. Stockholder-lender conflict for small firms is resolved under both banking-oriented and markets-oriented systems by financial intermediaries that specialize in producing information about borrower quality and tailoring loan contracts to minimize the conflict. The solution to the stockholder-lender problem for large firms depends on the financial system. In a markets-oriented system credit rating agencies and reputation building are used to resolve the conflict. In banking-oriented systems the problem largely disappears because the bank becomes both the owner *and* the lender.

5. Manager-stockholder conflict is resolved differently under the two systems. In banking-oriented systems, business ownership is consolidated in the bank (that is, the bank owns a controlling interest in companies). This allows the bank to participate on boards of directors and provides an incentive to monitor manager performance. In markets-oriented systems, there is little incentive for any individual shareholder to monitor firm managers because they typically own such a small fraction of the firm. The principal mechanism for resolving manager-stockholder conflict in markets-oriented systems is the hostile takeover.

6. With their huge banking systems and extensive bank ownership of business enterprise, Germany and Japan are decidedly banking-oriented systems. The relative importance of securities markets in the United Kingdom and the United States make these systems markets-oriented.

7. Although much of the publicity about Eastern Europe has focused on privatization and the birth of their stock markets as a symbol of capitalism, a strong argument can be made that a banking-oriented system may make more sense than a markets-oriented one. The information-poor environment that characterizes these formerly communist countries suggest that the more powerful monitoring capacity of a banking-oriented system may be worth the costs it imposes.

QUESTIONS

16.1 Why is stockholder-lender conflict less acute for large firms than for small firms?

16.2 Does stockholder-lender conflict arise in those large German firms that are either privately owned or controlled by a small group of nonbank investors? How is it solved?

16.3 Why isn't it in every stockholder's best interest to monitor the managers of the firms they invest in? How hard is it in the United States for individual stockholders to observe the behavior of corporate CEOs and to evaluate the motivation behind their actions?

16.4 Why are mergers and acquisitions so prevalent in the United Kingdom and the United States and much less so in Germany and Japan?

16.5 What sorts of characteristics make Eastern Europe an "information-poor" environment?

16.6 *Discussion question:* In recent years there has been a considerable amount of publicity surrounding the perception that senior management compensation in Japan is much less than it is in the United States. To what factors might such a difference be attributable? From an investor's point of view, is this a good thing or a bad thing?

CHAPTER 17

Financial Innovation

Not too many years ago, financial transactions were relatively simple matters. To earn interest, you went to a bank with cash and opened a savings account. To capture capital gains in the stock market, you bought some shares of IBM or General Motors. And to pay for everyday expenses, you either dug into your wallet or wrote a check on your commercial bank checking account (hoping your last deposit would cover it).

Now things are different. A savings account is no longer the only choice open to savers: Money market deposit accounts and money market mutual funds offer higher earning alternatives. In the stock market, you no longer have to like IBM or General Motors in order to make a killing; financial futures and options and some mutual funds allow you to buy or sell the *entire* market, all at once, without playing favorites. You can open an account with a mutual fund family and switch your money from a bond fund to an international fund or a stock growth fund by phone—anytime you want (but not at any price). And if you are afraid you don't have enough in the bank to cover that last check, you can always rush down to the automatic teller machine— even at 2 A.M.—and add a few dollars so the check doesn't bounce.

As we've seen in the last few chapters, the financial system has changed a great deal in recent years. Financial innovation has spawned new *institutions* (such as money market mutual funds), new *products* (such as defined contribution pension plans), and new *markets* (such as exchange-traded options and financial futures), thereby transforming conservative, old-fashioned industries like banking and insurance into the new and highly sophisticated *financial services industry*. In this chapter let's step back for a moment and see how it all came about. In other words, what have been the causes of financial innovation? Why did all these changes take place when they did? Although we have discussed these innovations in previous chapters, we now let the innovative *process* take center stage.

CIRCUMVENTING REGULATION

One explanation for financial innovation is that it is a response to excessively constricting government regulation. In particular, innovation is a means of *avoiding* regulation! Take money market mutual funds as an example: They are institutions that probably never would have come into existence if it hadn't been for Regulation Q. Bank depositors were frustrated in the 1970s because the interest rate ceilings imposed by Regulation Q meant that they could not get competitive market interest rates on their money. Even banks that *wanted* to pay market interest rates in order to keep their old depositors or to attract new ones weren't allowed to do so. Within that environment, money market mutual funds were established by entrepreneurs who saw an unfilled need in the financial system and figured out a way to satisfy it. Since money market mutual funds were brand new and politicians had not yet decided to shackle them with regulations, they were free to offer competitive market interest rates. Their usefulness was demonstrated by their rapid growth.

Other innovations are also traceable to the ramifications of Regulation Q. For instance, as interest rates on securities rose during the 1960s and 1970s, Regulation Q ceiling's severely limited the ability of banks to obtain additional funds. After all, who would want to deposit money in a bank when they could earn twice as much by purchasing Treasury bills or by putting their funds into a money market mutual fund? As banks found themselves with profitable loan opportunities but not enough funds to satisfy them, they had no alternative but to devise new ways to raise money. In fact, just about all the instruments of liability management discussed in Chapter 12 came into being in response to this need for additional funds. In particular, negotiable CDs were "invented" in 1961, and Eurodollars became a source of bank funds shortly thereafter. American banks established branches abroad partly because foreign countries did not have deposit rate ceilings like Regulation Q. Banks lured funds into their foreign branches by offering attractive interest rates to depositors abroad and then transferred these funds to the United States to make domestic loans.

The development of the Eurobond market also stems from regulation avoidance, both here in the United States and abroad. In particular, because domestic European and Japanese bond markets were suppressed by taxes and various regulatory constraints, the unregulated Eurobond market offered a competitive alternative to domestic bank financing in these countries. U.S. corporate issuers also found the Eurobond market an attractive alternative to the SEC-regulated domestic corporate bond market. As we discussed in Chapter 14, cumbersome SEC registration requirements imposed a three- to four-week waiting period before a security could be underwritten in the United States, making it very difficult for U.S. companies to time their offerings to coincide with favorable market conditions. Because Eurobond offerings had no comparable registration requirements or waiting period, issuers could float a bond precisely when they wanted to. Thus in 1982, the SEC created shelf registration in order to restore the competitiveness of the U.S. domestic bond market by effectively eliminating the waiting period.

Circumventing regulatory constraints has been an important element in stimulating recent financial innovation, but it has not been the sole motivating factor. Other forces, such as the double-digit inflation that characterized the late 1970s, progressive legislation, the philosophy of deregulation, and the burst in technological advances, were important as well. Each of these will be discussed in turn.

DOUBLE-DIGIT INFLATION

The double-digit inflation of the late 1970s and early 1980s had profound social and economic consequences, including stimulating innovations that have shaped the financial environment ever since. It's hard to imagine that inflation averaged 11 percent per annum between 1978 and 1981, given that inflation has averaged less than 3 percent in recent years. The immediate consequence of double-digit inflation was double-digit interest rates to compensate investors for the erosion in purchasing power. As a result, a number of financial institutions, especially mutual savings banks and savings and loan associations, found themselves in deep trouble because they were paying more to retain deposits than they were earning on most of their assets. The problem was that most assets of these institutions consisted of *long-term* mortgages they had acquired in the 1950s and 1960s, when inflation was in single digits and interest rates were relatively low. In the late 1970s and early 1980s, however, the double-digit interest rates that accompanied double-digit inflation turned these previously profitable thrift institutions into losers. They were still earning the *old* interest rates on their long-term assets, mostly 25- and 30-year mortgages, but they had to pay the newer and higher interest rates on a substantial portion of their liabilities.

The innovative response was a shift from *fixed-rate mortgages* in favor of *floating-rate* (also called *adjustable-rate*) *mortgages*. With floating-rate loans, the interest rate is tied to some competitive market rate, such as the Treasury bill rate. The mortgage loan rate therefore rises and falls with the general level of market interest rates. Even today with lower interest rate levels, many mortgages are still of the adjustable rate variety. Banks reacted in a similar fashion. While in 1977 only about one-third of all business loans carried a floating rate, by the late 1980s about 75 percent were floating-rate loans. As a result of these changes, financial institutions are no longer caught in a "rate squeeze," in which they take in less interest than they pay out. The interest they take in on their assets is closely linked to the interest they pay out on their liabilities, so whenever the interest rate on their liabilities goes up, the interest rate on their assets rises, too.

Financial innovation was stimulated not only by high interest rates but also by the wide *fluctuations* in interest rates during the early 1980s. Widely

Financial Innovation in Action

The United States Is Altering Rules to Accommodate Growing Market in 'Zero-Coupon' Bonds

WASHINGTON—The Treasury Department, as expected, is moving to accommodate the growing market in "zero-coupon" bonds.

The Treasury said yesterday that it will allow banks and securities dealers to sell separately the interest payments and principal of the 10-year notes and 30-year bonds it will auction next month.

The plan for separate interest-payment sales was first disclosed last August. Zero-coupon securities pay no interest but are sold at deep discount from their face value.

Institutions buying Treasury securities will be able to request that each semiannual interest payment and the principal be registered separately by Federal Reserve banks. Each payment may then be sold as a zero-coupon bond.

The program will be known as Separate Trading of Registered Interest and Principal of Securities, or "Strips"—an acronym that reflects the market jargon for the practice of selling separate bond interest payments, known as stripping.

Currently, some dealers buy Treasury securities, put them in special trusts and then sell claims on individual interest payments or on the principal, using trade names like "CATS" and "Tigrs" for the claims. The Treasury plan will eliminate the need for such elaborate trust arrangements.

Cutting Financing Costs

By facilitating trade in Treasury zero coupons, department officials hope to cut the interest costs of financing the federal debt and make zero-coupon securities less expensive and more readily available.

"Over time, we plan to make all the securities for which there is an interest payment eligible" for Strips, Mr. Healey said.

Purchase Minimum

The minimum amount of a security that a bank or broker must buy to qualify for Strips will vary with the interest rate. The minimum, which will be announced by the Treasury along with the results of each auction, will be set to produce a semiannual interest payment of $1,000 or a multiple of $1,000. The securities themselves are generally sold in multiples of $1,000.

Thus, if a security carries a coupon rate of 10%, an institution wishing to sell separate interest payments must buy at least $20,000 of the security, resulting in semiannual interest payments of $1,000. If a security carries an interest payment of, say, 11.25%, the Treasury will set a minimum of $160,000, producing semiannual interest payments of $9,000. Banks and brokers will then be allowed to sell zero-coupon bonds in $1,000 denominations.

Zero-coupon bonds have become increasingly popular in recent years, especially with such investment institutions as pension funds, which project their capital needs far into the future. A zero-coupon bond is appealing to such investors because it lets them assure future payment by investing a fraction of that amount now.

Since mid-1982, about $45 billion of Treasury securities have been turned into zero-coupon bonds.

Source: Alan Murray, *Wall Street Journal*, January 16, 1985. Reprinted by permission of *The Wall Street Journal.* Copyright © 1995 Dow Jones & Company, Inc. All Rights Reserved.

fluctuating interest rates imply greater risk because they mean widely fluctuating securities prices, as we saw in Chapter 4. Among many innovative responses in the market designed to reduce this additional risk are (1) zero-coupon bonds, (2) the development of widespread trading in financial futures, and (3) interest rate swaps. Zero-coupon bonds enable investors to lock in a specific yield for a stated period of time, often as long as 20 or 30 years, regardless of what happens to market interest rates during that interval. With ordinary coupon bonds, the purchaser has the problem of reinvesting the interest payments (coupons) to achieve a target yield. This problem does not arise with zero-coupon bonds, because there are no coupons to begin with. Similarly, futures markets enable market participants to agree today on a future transaction price, thereby removing uncertainty as to what that price will be. Interest rate swaps can also eliminate uncertainty, as we saw in Chapter 9, when two parties swap floating-rate payments for fixed-rate payments to avoid maturity mismatches on their balance sheets.

LEGISLATIVE ENCOURAGEMENT

The first section of this chapter focused on regulatory factors that for *negative* reasons provided a stimulus to financial innovation. We saw that attempts to *circumvent* governmental regulations have led to the introduction of new financial institutions, products, and markets. Government is not always such a negative force, however; indeed, in recent years it has also made *positive* contributions to financial innovation.

Example One: Ginnie Mae pass-through securities emerged primarily through government initiative. The Government National Mortgage Association (hence *Ginnie Mae*) pass-through program was inaugurated by the Department of Housing and Urban Development and, as we noted in Chapter 8, increased the liquidity of mortgages, thereby expanding the flow of credit to the mortgage market.

Example Two: In 1976 Congress passed legislation that for the first time allowed mutual funds to pass on to their shareholders the tax-exemption feature of state and local government securities. As a result, many mutual funds have been established that specialize in acquiring state and local bonds, thereby expanding the market for municipal securities because mutual funds offer a more diversified basket of municipal securities to individual investors. This broadening of the marketplace increased the liquidity of the municipal bond market so that state and local governments could now issue municipal securities at lower yields.

Example Three: Retirement fund legislation in the 1970s and 1980s created an alternative to the employer-sponsored defined *benefit* plan called an employer-sponsored defined *contribution* pension plan. Under defined contribution plans, employees choose where to invest their retirement funds and have the flexibility to vary the amount of their own contribution (within prescribed limits). The benefits, of course, depend on how well their asset choices perform. Today these plans (the 401(k) plan for most companies and the 403(b) plan for nonprofit organizations) are the driving force behind the growth in mutual fund contributions.

THE PHILOSOPHY OF DEREGULATION

At least part of the credit (or blame) for the burst of financial innovation at this point in history must go to the widespread acceptance of what has come to be known as the philosophy of deregulation. Over the past 20 years a wave of deregulation swept through the U.S. economy, extending from telecommunications to the airline industry. As far as financial deregulation goes, there has always been a conflict between *safety* and *flexibility*. Thus a considerable amount of government regulation seemed necessary to make sure that banks and other financial institutions handling other people's money were run prudently and safely. In particular, banks are not allowed to invest in the stock market (which is too risky), and they are examined periodically by the supervisory authorities to make sure they follow the rules with respect to the loans they make and the securities they buy. On the other hand, too much regulation can excessively limit bank management discretion and flexibility. Management decision making needs some leeway to be imaginative and forward-looking in coping with short- and long-run problems. Thus too much legislated built-in safety can have negative as well as positive effects.

Historically, the United States has erred on the side of safety in banking and finance, often sacrificing managerial flexibility to gain more safety. In recent years, however, the balance has shifted somewhat. We still want a lot of built-in safety, but we are not willing to give up quite as much flexibility to get it. The basic philosophy underlying deregulation is that free markets and private initiative are better able to cope with changes in the economic environment than a network of rigid and inflexible rules and regulations. Private management is also more motivated to figure out less costly and more productive ways of doing things, because it stands to gain (with higher profits) if new methods of production or new products successfully reduce costs or expand sales.

As the philosophy of deregulation has become more widespread, many financial institutions have been encouraged to experiment and test the limits of governmental rules and regulations. Thus many banks have edged their way into insurance, stock brokerage, and underwriting. The result of all this regulatory erosion has been increased motivation for change and the encouragement of innovation throughout the financial services industry. Were there no spirit of deregulation in the air, such innovations would probably be introduced much more hesitantly, if at all. Of course, there have been costs associated with financial deregulation, as we saw in the discussion of the savings and loan crisis in Chapter 11. Whether the benefits exceed the costs, or vice versa, is still a matter of some controversy.

GOING OUT ON A LIMB

Innovation, Competition, and the Future of Glass-Steagall

Until quite recently the Glass-Steagall Act of 1933 substantially separated the banking industry from the rest of the financial services industry. This legislation could be viewed as the *quid pro quo* for deposit insurance—also implemented in 1933. Banks were given the ability to issue government insured deposits in return for a limitation on the services they could provide.

In the years since 1933 financial innovations have made these limitations more and more onerous. In 1933 small savers had few alternatives to bank deposits. Today, this is anything but the case. Mutual funds—money market, stock, and bond—all represent attractive alternatives to a bank deposit. Moreover, brokerage firms and mutual fund families have the ability to package these products together along with a checking account so that investors can easily move funds from one instrument to another. In addition, life insurance companies offer a variety of products which compete directly with bank deposits *and* many of these have tax benefits that bank deposits don't have.

On the business side, financial and technological innovation has given even smaller companies access to the traded securities markets. Twenty years ago businesses issued relatively little commercial paper. Fueled by the explosive growth of money market mutual funds, however, commercial paper issuance displaced commercial bank loans as the primary source of short-term credit for large businesses.

As a result of these changes, the pressure on regulators and on congress to ease the restrictions on commercial banks has grown. Banks in many other advanced countries are not shackled by these restrictions. As innovations increasingly infringed on the banking franchise, banks have sought innovative loopholes and regulatory relief inching us closer to *de facto* repeal of Glass Steagall. And each year we seem to get closer to its wholesale repeal.

For the first time since 1933 regulations have been put in place that penalize excessive risk taking by banks. Capital requirements and deposit insurance premiums are now linked to bank risk. Distressed banks must be closed before their capital is entirely dissipated. These regulatory innovations give legislators the opportunity to repeal Glass-Steagall without being subject to criticism that risk-related incentives in banking have been neglected. The principal obstacles to Glass-Steagall repeal today are the political constituencies most affected by a more competitive banking industry. As these fall by the wayside, the days of Glass-Steagall may be numbered.

TECHNOLOGICAL CHANGE

Technology is the traditional stimulus to change, and it is as powerful in financial markets as anywhere else. The technological revolution inspired by computers has had an obvious impact in the field of finance. For example, it would be impossible to have automated teller machines without computerization of the deposit/withdrawal functions. Computerization and information technology has also been crucial in the development of credit cards to the advanced level they have reached. Modern computer-generated methods of information storage, retrieval, and transmission underlie many of the changes that have taken place in the financial services industry.

Another type of technology, analytical technology, has also had a big impact on financial innovation. For example, sophisticated mathematical models have been developed to assist portfolio managers in limiting portfolio risk by using swaps, options, and financial futures. Analytical technology has also been instrumental in developing tools to analyze credit risk. Most consumer loan decisions are made today with the assistance of statistical techniques that can more accurately predict default risk. These techniques are more difficult to apply to business lending because it is inherently more complex. Nevertheless, some banks have used them as an adjunct to conventional credit analysis. With the now widespread use of spreadsheet software, all types of credit analysis are substantially easier than in the old days of adding machines, pencils, and erasers.

Advances in information technology and analytical technology have made it easier for investors to acquire information about companies they may want to invest in. Software programs to access on-line credit information and historical performance data have simplified investment decisions and made it easier to track portfolios. It is not surprising, therefore, that more and more companies have been able to raise funds in the traded securities markets. This isn't to say that smaller companies won't depend in the future on the intensive monitoring services provided by financial intermediaries. It does indicate, however, that the line separating companies that are too small, and too informationally opaque, to borrow in the securities markets may be shifting—not only in the United States but in other advanced economies where the trend is toward growth in direct finance through traded securities markets.

Technological change, of course, is generally considered a major source of improvement in economic welfare. Technological innovations expand the proverbial economic pie, allowing everyone to have more without forcing anyone to have less, thereby making it possible for everyone's standard of living to rise. Financial innovations have similar effects. In the case of financial innovation, however, the main areas of welfare gain are improvements in the ability to bear risk (futures markets), lowered transactions costs (automated teller machines), increased liquidity (the growth of the commercial paper market fueled by money market mutual funds), and avoidance of the consequences of outmoded governmental regulation (money market mutual funds as an end run around Regulation Q).

NECESSITY IS THE MOTHER OF INVENTION

We should not leave our discussion of financial innovation without tying it in with the broad principles regarding invention and innovation more generally. The best-known principle is summarized in the popular aphorism "necessity is the mother of invention." It should be clear that new financial institutions, products, and markets come into use and remain there because of a demand for them, a need that keeps them in existence more than temporarily. This point can be illustrated by examples of successful innovations that extend beyond the experience of the past several decades.

Credit cards, introduced during the 1950s and 1960s, could not have become so widespread without the technological computer base that enables them to function so effectively. Nevertheless, no matter how advanced the technology, credit cards would not have become so popular if they hadn't fulfilled an underlying consumer need. People simply enjoy the ability to spend without paying up immediately. And credit cards facilitate that process.

Similarly, banks introduced consumer loans and term loans (business loans with more than one year to maturity) in the 1930s, because they perceived a demand waiting to be satisfied. Banks had tried to confine their business lending to short-term loans, but business borrowers turned elsewhere in search of longer-term funds. In order to keep their customers, banks changed their policies and extended some of their loans to four or five years in place of the one-year loans they had limited themselves to previously.

Returning to a more recent example, money market mutual funds would have faded rapidly from the scene if they had not satisfied a need. In this case, more clearly perhaps than any other, necessity was the mother of invention. Depositors, prevented from getting market interest rates by Regulation Q, turned enthusiastically to money market mutual funds as soon as the alternative became open to them.

On the basis of such evidence, we can conclude that if someone perceives a need that is currently not being fulfilled and can invent a way to satisfy that need, chances are such an innovation will prove successful. Other innovations will probably fall by the wayside. In other words, if you build a better mousetrap, the world will beat a path to your door—provided people need to catch mice![1]

SUMMARY

1. One explanation for financial innovation is that it is a response to outmoded and excessively restrictive governmental regulation. That partially explains the reasons for financial innovation, but it is not a complete explanation. Double-digit inflation, high interest rates, wide fluctuations in interest rates, progressive government legislation, the philosophy of deregulation, and advances in analytical and computer technologies are also important factors that have helped to stimulate financial innovation.

2. Above all, however, necessity is the mother of invention. Unfilled needs stimulate ways to satisfy them; conversely, unless an innovation fills a need it will not become a permanent part of the financial services industry.

---

[1]For a more detailed overview and model of financial innovation see William L. Silber, "The Process of Financial Innovation," *American Economic Review* (May 1983).

QUESTIONS

17.1   Give an example of governmental regulation causing financial innovation.

17.2   What positive results might flow from financial deregulation?

17.3   Might deregulation yield any negative results?

17.4   Why do some innovations become permanent fixtures while others disappear soon after they are introduced?

17.5   *Discussion question:* One frequently hears that "necessity is the mother of invention." Might it also be true that "invention is the mother of necessity"?

PART V

The Art of Central Banking

CHAPTER 18

Who's in Charge Here?

Monetary policy is the responsibility of the Federal Reserve, but to whom is the Federal Reserve responsible? We saw in Chapter 2 of our book that the money supply should be set to give us high employment without inflation. The Federal Reserve checks the money supply, but who checks the Fed?

The answer to that question is so complex that if we unravel it successfully (not very likely), we will either have unveiled one of the great socioeconomic creations in the annals of civilization, comparable to the invention of indoor plumbing, or unmasked one of the most devious schemes ever contrived by the human mind to camouflage the true locus of clandestine power.

According to some, the Federal Reserve is responsible to the Congress. But it is the president, not Congress, who appoints the seven members of the Board of Governors of the Federal Reserve System, who occupy the stately building at Twentieth Street and Constitution Avenue, Washington, D.C. The president also selects from among those seven the chairman of the board of governors, the principal policymaker of the central bank.

On that basis, one might surmise that the Federal Reserve is responsible to the executive branch of government, in the person of the president. However, since each member of the board has a 14-year term, the current president can appoint only two of the seven members of the Board of Governors, unless there are deaths or resignations. Even the chairman may be the appointee of the previous administration. Furthermore, it is Congress that created the Federal Reserve in 1913, and it is Congress, not the president, that has the authority to alter its working mandate at any time. In 1935, for example, Congress chose to throw two administration representatives off the board of governors—the secretary of the Treasury and the comptroller of the currency, both of whom had been ex officio members—simply because they were representatives of the executive branch.

Others, more cynical, have suggested that the Federal Reserve is mostly responsible to the private banking community, primarily the 4,000 or so commercial banks that are member banks of the Federal Reserve system. The member banks do in fact choose six of the nine directors of each regional Federal Reserve bank, who in turn appoint the presidents of the regional Federal Reserve banks, including the president of the most aristocratic of all, the Federal Reserve Bank of New York. It may or may not be significant that the annual salary of the president of the Federal Reserve Bank of New York is about double the salary of the chairman of the Board of Governors in Washington.

Who's in charge here, anyway?

FORMAL STRUCTURE OF THE FEDERAL RESERVE SYSTEM

The statutory organization of the Federal Reserve system is a case study in those currently popular concepts, decentralization and the blending of public and private authority. A deliberate attempt was made in the enabling congressional legislation, the 1913 Federal Reserve Act, to diffuse power over a broad base—geographically, between the private and public sectors, and even within the government—so that no one person, group, or sector, either inside or outside the government, could exert enough leverage to dominate the direction of monetary policy.

As Figure 18.1 shows, the board of governors of the Federal Reserve system consists of seven members, appointed by the president with the advice and consent of the Senate. To prevent presidential board-packing, each member is appointed for a term of 14 years, with one board member's term expiring at the end of January in each even-numbered year. Furthermore, no two board members may come from the same Federal Reserve district. The chairman of the board of governors, chosen from among the seven by the president, serves a four-year term. However, the chairman's term does not coincide with the presidential term, so an incoming president is usually saddled with an already appointed chairman at the beginning of the new administration. The board is independent of the congressional appropriations process and partly exempt from audit by the government's watchdog, the General Accounting Office, because its operating funds come from the earnings of the 12 regional Federal Reserve banks.

The regional Federal Reserve banks, one in each Federal Reserve district, are geographically dispersed throughout the nation—the Federal Reserve Bank of New York, the Federal Reserve Bank of Kansas City, the Federal Reserve Bank of San Francisco, and so on (see Figure 18.2). Technically, each Federal Reserve bank is privately owned by the member banks in its district, the very banks it is charged with supervising and regulating. Each member bank is required to buy stock in its district Federal Reserve bank equal to 6 percent of its own capital and surplus. Of this 6 percent, 3 percent must be paid in and 3 percent is subject to call by the board of governors. However, the profits accruing to ownership are limited by law to a 6 percent annual dividend on paid-in capital stock. The member bank stockholders elect six of the

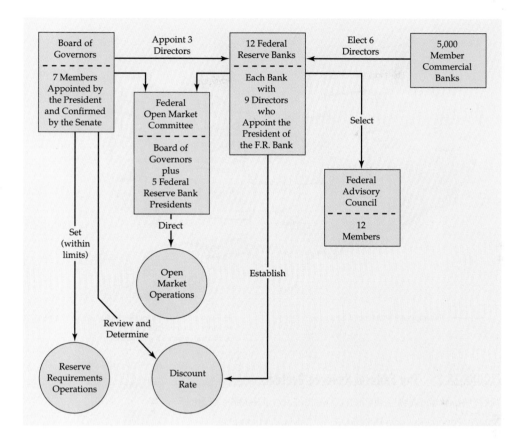

FIGURE 18.1   **The formal structure and policy organization of the Federal Reserve system.**

nine directors of their district Federal Reserve bank, and the remaining three are appointed from Washington by the board of governors. These nine directors, in turn, choose the president of their Federal Reserve bank, subject to the approval of the board of governors.

The directors of each Federal Reserve bank also select a person, always a commercial banker, to serve on the Federal Advisory Council, a statutory body consisting of a member from each of the 12 Federal Reserve districts. The Federal Advisory Council consults quarterly with the board of governors in Washington and makes recommendations regarding the conduct of monetary policy.

Legal authority is similarly diffused with respect to the *execution* of monetary policy, as Figure 18.1 indicates. The board of governors has the power to set **reserve requirements** on bank deposits, for example, but it cannot set them outside the bounds of the specific limits imposed by Congress.

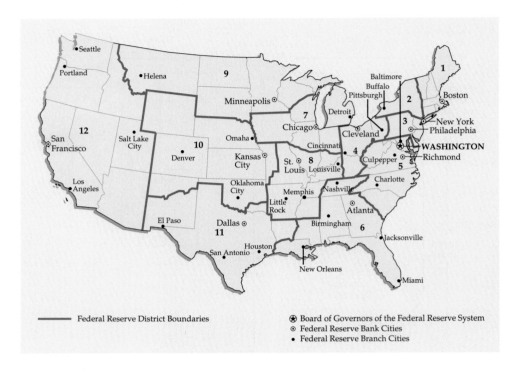

FIGURE 18.2   The Federal Reserve System.

Note: Hawaii and Alaska are in the Twelfth Federal Reserve District.

Source: Federal Reserve Bulletin, R. W. Calvin, Cartographer.

Open market operations (which we will consider in Chapter 20) are directed by a body known as the **Federal Open Market Committee (FOMC),** composed of the seven-member board of governors plus five of the Reserve bank presidents. Although open market operations are directed by the FOMC, they are executed at the trading desk of the Federal Reserve Bank of New York by a person who appears to be simultaneously an employee of the FOMC and the Federal Reserve Bank of New York.

Legal authority over **discount rates** (to be discussed in Chapter 20) is even more confusing. Discount rates are "established" every two weeks by the directors of each regional Federal Reserve bank, but they are subject to "review and determination" by the board of governors. The distinction between "establishing" discount rates and "determining" them is a fine line indeed, and it is not surprising that confusion arises as to precisely where the final authority and responsibility lie.

THE REALITIES OF POWER

So much for the Land of Oz. Actually, the facts of life are rather different, as the more realistic Figure 18.3 illustrates.

By all odds, the dominant figure in the formation and execution of monetary policy is the chairman of the board of governors of the Federal Reserve system. The chairman is the most prominent member of the board itself and the most influential member of the FOMC and is generally recognized by both Congress and the public at large as *the* voice of the Federal Reserve system. Although the Federal Reserve Act appears to put all seven members of the board of governors on more or less equal footing, over the past fifty years strong personalities, outstanding abilities, and determined devotion to purpose have made the chairmen rather more equal than the others. As adviser to the president, negotiator with Congress, and final authority on appointments throughout the system, with influence over all aspects of monetary policy as chairman of both the board of governors and the FOMC, the chairman for all practical purposes is the embodiment of the central bank in this country.

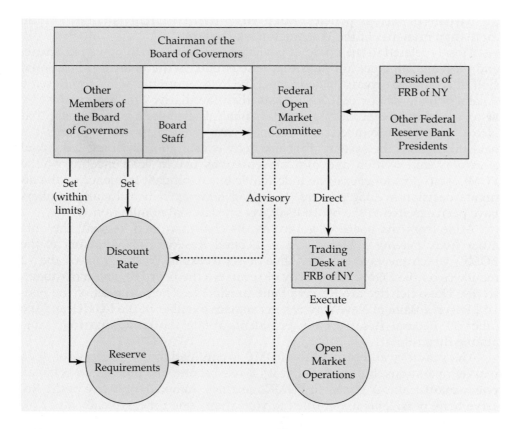

FIGURE 18.3   The realities of power within the Federal Reserve System.

The other six members of the board of governors also exercise a substantial amount of authority, more so than is indicated in the formal paper structure of the system, because with the passage of time primary responsibility for monetary policy has become more centralized and concentrated in Washington. When the Federal Reserve Act was passed in 1913, it was thought that the Federal Reserve system would be mainly a passive service agency, supplying currency when needed, clearing checks, and providing a discount facility for the convenience of the private commercial member banks. At that time there was no conception of monetary policy as an active countercyclical force. Since then the central bank has shifted from passive accommodation to active regulation, from the performance of regional service functions to the implementation of national economic policy. This shift has been accompanied, naturally enough, by a rise in the power of the centralized board of governors in Washington and a corresponding decline in the role of the regional Federal Reserve banks and their "owners," the commercial banks.

It would not be unrealistic to describe the central bank today as headquartered in Washington, with 12 field offices throughout the nation. These field offices may be known by the rather imposing name of *Federal Reserve banks,* and they do indeed retain considerable autonomy in expressing their views on the wisdom of various policies. But even so they essentially amount to little more than branches of the Washington headquarters.

Closely related to the board of governors in the informal power structure, and deriving influence through that association, is the board's professional staff of economic experts and advisers. The long tenure in the Federal Reserve system of many senior staff economists, their familiarity with Federal Reserve history, and their expertise in monetary analysis give them a power base that is to a large extent founded on the respect with which they, as individuals, are held throughout the system. Through daily consultation with the individual governors and written and oral presentations before each meeting of the FOMC, staff personnel exert an indefinable but significant influence on the ultimate decision-making process. In fact, a number of board staff members have been elevated to the board itself, via presidential nomination.

Aside from the board of governors, its chairman, and its staff, the only other body playing a major role in Federal Reserve policy-making is the FOMC, which meets about every five or six weeks in Washington. Of the 12 members on the FOMC, a majority of seven are the board of governors themselves. The other five are Reserve bank presidents. The president of the Federal Reserve Bank of New York is a permanent member of the FOMC, and the other 11 Federal Reserve bank presidents rotate the remaining four seats among themselves.

The statutory authority of the FOMC is confined to the direction of open market operations, but in recent years it has become the practice to bring all policy matters under review at FOMC meetings. Although only five of the Reserve bank presidents are entitled to vote at any one time, typically all 12 attend every meeting and participate in the discussion. Thus potential reserve-requirement and discount-rate changes are, in effect, decided on within the

FOMC, with the 12 Reserve bank presidents participating in an advisory capacity. The board of governors, however, always has the final say on reserve requirements and discount rates if matters should come to a showdown, particularly since legal opinion appears to be that, in case of disagreement, the board's power to "review and determine" discount rates overrides the authority of the individual Reserve banks to "establish" them.

The status of the president of the Federal Reserve Bank of New York in the nation's financial center lends the role a unique position in the hierarchy. A president of the New York Reserve bank who is inclined to use this leverage can mount a substantial challenge even to the chairman of the board of governors. Since such a challenge would have little legal foundation, it would have to be based on the prestige of the presidency of the Federal Reserve Bank of New York and the forcefulness of the person who holds the position.

But where, in the corridors of power, does this leave the member banks, the directors of each Federal Reserve bank, and the Federal Advisory Council? Pretty much shut out, if the truth be known.

The member banks do indeed "own" their district Federal Reserve bank, but such stockholding is mostly symbolic and carries none of the usual attributes of ownership. The member banks also have a major voice in electing the directors of their Reserve bank, but the directors in turn have responsibilities that are largely ceremonial. True, they appoint the members of the Federal Advisory Council, but the Federal Advisory Council serves mostly a public relations purpose and has little to do with actual policy-making. The directors of each Federal Reserve bank also choose the president of their Reserve bank, subject to the approval of the board of governors. But the "subject to approval" clause has meant, in practice, that the most the directors can really do is submit a list of nominees for the position of president. On several occasions the choice of the directors of a Federal Reserve bank has not met with approval from Washington; such cases have made very clear exactly where ultimate authority is lodged.

THE PROBLEM OF FEDERAL RESERVE INDEPENDENCE

The fact that ultimate authority over monetary policy resides in Washington brings to the fore the relationship between the central bank and the other branches of government also responsible for overall national economic policy—the Congress and the administration, the latter personified by the president.

The Federal Reserve is a creature of the Congress. The Constitution gives Congress the power "to coin money and regulate the value thereof." On this basis, in 1913 Congress created the Federal Reserve as the institution delegated to administer that responsibility on its behalf. Congress requires periodic accountability by the Federal Reserve and has the authority to amend the Federal Reserve Act any time it sees fit.

Essentially, Congress has given the Federal Reserve a broad mandate to regulate the monetary system in the public interest and then has more or less

GOING OUT ON A LIMB

Central Bank Independence Abroad

The Federal Reserve is one of the few central banks in the world that is "autonomous" or "independent." In most countries, the central bank is subordinate to the government, frequently being organized as a bureau within the department of the Treasury.

Aside from the United States, the only cases of true central bank independence are Germany and Switzerland. In fact, their central banks are even *more* autonomous than the Federal Reserve. Government authorities can attend policy meetings of the German central bank, the Deutsche Bundesbank, but they are not permitted to vote. The only power the government has is the right to delay the implementation of a Bundesbank decision for up to two weeks.

The Swiss National Bank, Switzerland's central bank, is also constitutionally independent of the Swiss parliament. The Swiss central bank is required to consult with the government on policy matters, but it can proceed on a course of action despite government disapproval.

It is not accidental that of the major industrial nations Germany and Switzerland have experienced the lowest inflation. Their independent central banks are devoted primarily to the goal of price stability. Although German and Swiss central bankers worry about unemployment, this worry is generally overwhelmed by concern about an easy monetary policy rekindling the embers of inflation.

The connection between inflation and central bank independence is emphasized by the accompanying chart, adapted from a study by Alberto Allesina and Lawrence Summers,* which plots the average rate of inflation of various countries during the 1955–1988 period on the vertical axis and an index of central banking independence on the horizontal axis. Not surprisingly, Germany and Switzerland, the countries with

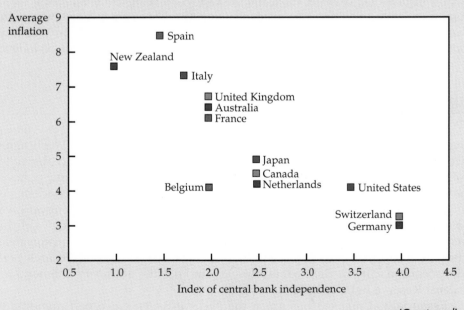

(Continued)

the most independent central banks, had the lowest rate of inflation, while the countries with the least independent central banks during this period (New Zealand, Spain, and Italy) had the highest rates of inflation. Some of these countries (most notably, New Zealand) have made their central banks more independent, perhaps in response to such evidence.

In most democracies, the electorate is usually more upset by unemployment than by inflation. So it probably makes considerable sense to let the central bank have a healthy dose of independence so that shortsighted politicians don't hinder the fight against inflation in order to get elected.

*Alberto Allesina and Lawrence H. Summers, "Central Bank Independence and Macroeconomic Performance: Some Comparative Evidence," *Journal of Money, Credit and Banking,* May 1993.

stood aside and let the monetary authorities pursue this objective on their own and to the best of their abilities. Congress has also attempted to minimize interference from the administration by giving each member of the board of governors a 14-year term, thereby sharply limiting any single president's influence over the board.

This semi-independent status of the central bank is a source of continuous friction. Some members of Congress believe that the Federal Reserve has carried its "independence" too far. There has been concern over its freedom from congressional appropriations and its partial exemption from standard government audit. Also, on occasion the Federal Reserve's responsibility for tight money and high interest rates has stimulated some intensive questioning at congressional hearings, including frequent scoldings of Federal Reserve officials by populist-minded members of Congress who get uptight about tight money.

Others, in Congress and out, have complained that the Federal Reserve simply has not done a very good job, that we would all be better off if Congress laid down some guidelines or rules to limit the discretion available to the monetary authorities in conducting their business. We will discuss such proposals in Chapter 27.

The relationship between the central bank and the president has also aroused controversy. Many feel that the Federal Reserve should be a part of the executive branch of government, responsible to the president, on the grounds that monetary policy is an integral part of national economic policy and should therefore be coordinated at the highest level (that is, by the president), along with fiscal policy, as a component of the administration's total program for economic growth and stability.

The case for central bank independence from the president, on the other hand, rests on the pragmatic basis that subordination of the central bank to the executive branch of government invites excessive money creation and consequent inflation. The charge that an independent Federal Reserve is undemocratic is countered by the reminder that the central bank is still very much responsible to Congress, which can amend the Federal Reserve Act any time it wishes. In addition, the president holds frequent meetings with the chairman of the board of governors, the secretary of the Treasury, and the chairman of the Council of Economic Advisors.

It is feared by many, and not without historical justification, that if the monetary authority is made the junior partner to the president or the Treasury (the fiscal authority), monetary stability will be sacrificed to the government's revenue needs—the government will be tempted to seek the easy way out in raising funds, by printing money or borrowing excessively at artificially low interest rates, in preference to the politically more difficult route of raising taxes or cutting back on government spending. The sole purpose of an independent monetary authority, in brief, is to forestall the natural propensity of governments to resort to inflation.

The rest of Part V takes an intensive look at Federal Reserve methods of control. We will explore how the Fed regulates the money supply and the difficulties the Fed has in trying to hit its monetary targets. To work our way around these important policy issues requires a fair amount of attention to the nitty-gritty, but that's what it's all about.

SUMMARY

1. The dominant figure in the formation and execution of monetary policy is the chairman of the board of governors of the Federal Reserve system. The Federal Open Market Committee is the major policy-making body within the system. It is composed of the seven members of the board of governors and five Reserve bank presidents.

2. The Federal Reserve is accountable to the Congress but is legally independent of the executive branch of government. This semi-independent status of the Federal Reserve has been a source of frequent conflict. It is defended on the ground that the central bank must have considerable independence to counteract the natural propensity of governments to resort to inflationary methods of financing themselves.

QUESTIONS

18.1 Open market operations are the most important policy tool of the Federal Reserve. Who decides what they will be?

18.2 Who is the present chairman of the board of governors of the Federal Reserve system? What president appointed him to that position?

18.3 Is the Federal Reserve more accountable to the legislative branch of government or to the executive branch?

18.4 On what grounds is the semi-independent status of the Federal Reserve justified by those who defend it? On what grounds is that status attacked by those who oppose it?

18.5 What is the status of the president of the Federal Reserve Bank of New York in the central bank's hierarchy?

18.6 *Discussion question:* Country-by-country comparisons show that the more independent a country's central bank, the lower the rate of inflation. But the more independent a central bank, the less responsive it is to the will of the electorate. In a democracy, how independent should a central bank really be?

CHAPTER 19

Bank Reserves and the Money Supply

Now that we know who is responsible for our nation's monetary policy, let's see how the Federal Reserve goes about doing its job. It will take all of four chapters to understand exactly what is going on. We know from our overview in Chapter 2 that the money supply helps to determine overall economic activity. We also outlined the connection between the Federal Reserve, bank reserves, and the money supply. Although it is possible to explore the details in any number of ways, we take the following approach. In this chapter we examine the relationship between bank reserves and the money supply. In Chapter 20 we survey the tools available to the Federal Reserve to carry out its objectives. In Chapter 21 we focus on the connection between the Fed's tools and bank reserves. And finally, in Chapter 22 we tie things together by examining how the Federal Reserve establishes its targets and carries out its game plan.

As we saw in Chapter 2, most of our money supply does not consist of coins and dollar bills. Rather, the money supply (M1) is composed mainly of demand deposits (checking accounts) in commercial banks and in other kinds of financial institutions.[1] We also briefly showed how bank reserves play a crucial role in creating those demand deposits. Now it's time to examine the process in greater detail; it is by regulating the reserves of banks and other financial institutions that the Federal Reserve gets leverage to control the amount of demand deposits in the country and thereby the nation's money supply.

---

[1]Demand deposits as used in this chapter includes two types of transaction accounts: demand deposits and NOW accounts.

CHECK CLEARING AND COLLECTION

We already know a lot about how financial institutions work from Chapter 3 in Part I and from all the chapters in Part III, but a quick review won't hurt. This time we're going to change our perspective and focus on demand deposits in particular and especially on the relationship between reserves and demand deposits. To really understand what's going on, let's go into the banking business.

Assume that we sell stock and raise $5 million to start a bank, that we buy a building for $1 million and open our doors for business. Our bank's balance sheet on opening day would look like this:

Our Bank's Initial Balance Sheet

Assets		Liabilities and Net Worth	
Cash	$4,000,000	Net worth	$5,000,000
Building, etc.	1,000,000		

The balance sheet could stand some improvement. Too much cash. Doesn't earn any interest. So we immediately take three-quarters of the cash and buy government bonds with it. The T-account, showing the *changes* that occur in our balance sheet, looks like this:

Our Bank's Purchase of Government Bonds

A		L & NW	
Cash	−$3,000,000		
Government bonds	+ 3,000,000		

Next, for purposes that will become clear shortly, we take another $900,000 and ship it to our regional Federal Reserve bank, to open up a deposit in our bank's name:

Our Bank's Transfer of Cash to Fed

A		L & NW	
Cash	−$900,000		
Deposit in Fed	+ 900,000		

During the course of the first few days, we gleefully welcome long lines of new depositors who open up accounts with us by depositing $2 million worth of checks drawn on *other* banks—where they are closing out their accounts, because they like our ambience better. Our T-account for these deposits is as follows:

Our Bank's New Cash Deposits

A		L & NW	
Cash items in process of collection	+ $2,000,000	Demand deposits	+ $2,000,000

A demand deposit in a bank is an asset for the depositor. It is part of the depositor's wealth. For the bank, however, it is a *liability*, a debt, because the bank is obligated to pay it—indeed, to pay it *on demand*. A demand deposit must be paid any time the depositor wishes, either by handing out currency across the counter or by transferring the funds to someone else upon the depositor's order. That is precisely what a check is: a depositor's order to a bank to transfer funds to whoever is named on the check, or to whoever has endorsed it on the back.

We now have $2 million of checks drawn on other banks that our new customers have deposited with us. We have to "collect" these checks; so far they are just "cash items in process of collection." If we had the time, we could take each check to the bank on which it is drawn, ask for currency over the counter, and then haul it back to our own bank. Since this would get tedious if we had to do it every day, what we do instead is what other banks do: Rely on the Federal Reserve to help us in the check collection process. Federal Reserve banks play a pivotal role in collecting checks, so pivotal that we must digress a moment to see how they do it.

As we saw in the last chapter, there are 12 Federal Reserve banks around the country—in New York, Atlanta, Dallas, Minneapolis, San Francisco, and so on. Every deposit-type financial institution is affiliated with one of them. The Federal Reserve banks themselves have little direct contact with the public; mostly they deal with the government and with financial institutions. Through facilities they provide, however, checks are efficiently collected and funds transferred around the country. The primary collection vehicle is the deposit that each financial institution maintains with its regional Federal Reserve bank, which is one reason we deposited $900,000 in our Federal Reserve bank two T-accounts back.

Let's see how the collection process works. We take the $2 million worth of checks our new customers have deposited, checks drawn on other banks, and ship the whole batch of them to the Federal Reserve bank. The Fed credits us with these checks by increasing our "deposit in the Fed" by that amount. At the same time, it *deducts* $2 million from the "deposits in the Fed" of the banks on which the checks were drawn. It sends these checks to the appropriate banks, with a slip notifying them of the deduction, and the banks in turn deduct the proper amounts from their depositors' accounts. The T-accounts of the whole check collection process look like this, with the arrows showing the direction in which the checks move:

Check Collection Process, Federal Reserve Bank

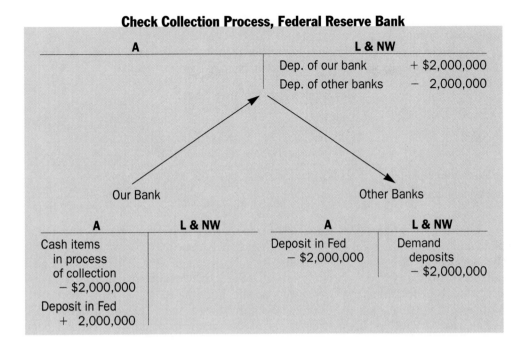

We can summarize this collection process in a few words. When a bank receives a check drawn on another bank, it gains deposits in the Fed equal to the amount of the check. Conversely, the bank on which the check was drawn loses deposits in the Fed of the same amount.[2] We will see soon that deposits in the Fed are part of a bank's reserves. We can rephrase the above into an important banking principle:

When a bank receives a check drawn on another bank, it gains reserves equal to the amount of the check. Conversely, the bank on which the check was drawn loses reserves of the same amount.

Two minor complications. One: What if some of the institutions involved are not members of the Federal Reserve system? No problem. All financial institutions that accept checkable deposits, whether they are member banks or not, must hold reserves in the form of either vault cash or deposits with the Fed (or with another bank that in turn holds them with the Fed). So they will either clear checks directly through the Fed or clear them indirectly through arrangements with a so-called correspondent bank that holds such reserves.

Two: What if the two financial institutions involved are in different Federal Reserve districts, so they have deposits in two *different* Federal Reserve banks? Again no problem. The Federal Reserve has its own Inter-District Settlement Fund, where the 12 Federal Reserve banks all hold accounts, and they

---

[2]Notice that the deposits of banks in the Federal Reserve bank are *liabilities* of the Federal Reserve bank (although assets of the commercial banks), just as deposits of the public in a commercial bank are liabilities of the bank (although assets of the depositors).

settle up in such cases by transferring balances among themselves on the books of the Inter-District Settlement Fund.

So where do we stand now? Let's take a look at our bank's balance sheet, after all the above transactions have been incorporated into it:

Our Bank's New Balance Sheet

A		L & NW	
Cash	$ 100,000	Demand deposits	$2,000,000
Deposit in Fed	2,900,000	Net worth	5,000,000
Government bonds	3,000,000		
Building, etc.	1,000,000		

Looking at this balance sheet reminds us that according to law commercial banks and other deposit-type financial institutions have to hold part of their assets in the form of reserves. As mentioned above, all banks are required to hold reserves—*in the form of either cash or deposits in the Fed*—as specified by the Board of Governors of the Federal Reserve. How does our bank stand with respect to reserves? To simplify matters, let's assume that all banks, ours included, have to hold **required reserves** equal to a flat 10 percent of demand deposits.

We *have* reserves—cash and/or deposits in the Fed—of $3 million. With demand deposits of $2 million, we *need* reserves equal to 10 percent of that figure, or $200,000, to satisfy our legal obligation. Thus we have **excess reserves** of $2.8 million. That simple calculation, computing the amount of a bank's excess reserves, is crucially important in the banking business.

What should we do now? Unfortunately, with this balance sheet we are not too profitable. We have a lot of excess reserves that are earning no interest, and not enough income-producing assets. Let's assume we can find some creditworthy borrowers who want to take out loans. Then a big question faces us: How much can we safely lend without endangering our legal reserve position?

DEPOSIT EXPANSION: THE SINGLE BANK

To answer the question of how much we can safely lend, we need to know two things: (1) how much excess reserves we have, and (2) what happens when we make a loan. We already know how much excess reserves we have—$2.8 million. So let's take a moment to examine what happens when we make a loan.

When a bank lends, the borrower does not ordinarily take the proceeds in $100 bills; more likely, the borrower takes a brand-new checking account instead. On the bank's balance sheet, loans (an asset) and demand deposits (a liability) both rise. A bank *creates* a demand deposit when it lends. In effect, since demand deposits are money, banks create money.

How much, then, can we lend? Since the only limit on our creation of demand deposits appears to be the requirement that we hold a 10 percent reserve, a superficial answer would be that we can lend—and create demand deposits—up to a limit of ten times our excess reserves. We have excess reserves of $2.8 million, so why not lend ten times that, or $28 million? If we did, here is what would happen:

Our Bank's Loan Extension

A		L & NW	
Loans	+ $28,000,000	Demand deposits	+ $28,000,000

And our new balance sheet would look like this:

Our Bank's New Balance Sheet

A			L & NW	
Reserves {	Cash	$ 100,000	Demand deposits	$30,000,000
	Deposit in Fed	2,900,000	Net worth	5,000,000
	Government bonds	3,000,000		
	Loans	28,000,000		
	Building, etc.	1,000,000		

We now have some good news and some bad news. First the good news: We have a fairly large amount of demand deposit liabilities—$30 million—and our reserves, at $3 million, are legally sufficient to support them. It appears we have found a veritable gold mine. In business hardly a month, only a $5 million investment, and here we are collecting the interest on $3 million of government bonds *and* $28 million of loans.

But wait a minute, because here comes the bad news: We haven't really looked into what happens after a borrower takes out a loan. Most borrowers don't take out loans and pay interest on them just to leave the funds sitting there. They want to spend the money. And when they do, they'll write checks on those brand-new demand deposits. The checks will probably be deposited in other banks by their recipients, and when they clear through the Federal Reserve we'll *lose reserves.* (Remember that a bank on which a check is drawn loses reserves equal to the amount of the check.) Thus, for our bank:

Our Bank's Checks Collected

A		L & NW	
Deposit in Fed	− $28,000,000	Demand deposits	− $28,000,000

If our deposits in the Fed are only $2.9 million to begin with, we can hardly stand by calmly while they fall by $28 *million*. We'll wind up in jail instead of on the Riviera. Something has clearly gone very wrong. What has gone wrong, obviously, is that we miscalculated our lending limit, the amount we could safely lend—"safely" meaning without endangering our legal reserve position.

What, then, is our safe lending limit? It is the amount of reserves we can afford to lose, and we already know what that is: our *excess* reserves. A bank can lend up to the amount of its excess reserves, and no more. If it tries to lend more, it will find itself with inadequate reserves as soon as the borrowers spend the proceeds of the loans and the checks are collected through the Federal Reserve's check collection facilities.

So let's start over again. Our excess reserves are $2.8 million. If we lend that amount, our balance sheet entry is:

Our Bank's Loan Extension

A		L & NW	
Loans	+ $2,800,000	Demand deposits	+ $2,800,000

When the borrowers spend the funds, assuming the checks are deposited in other banks, we have:

Our Bank's Checks Collected

A		L & NW	
Deposit in Fed	– $2,800,000	Demand deposits	– $2,800,000

Which leaves our balance sheet as follows:

Our Bank's New Balance Sheet

A			L & NW	
Reserves	Cash	$ 100,000	Demand deposits	$2,000,000
	Deposit in Fed	100,000	Net worth	5,000,000
	Government bonds	3,000,000		
	Loans	2,800,000		
	Building, etc.	1,000,000		

Now, after all checks have cleared, we end up with deposits of $2 million and reserves of $200,000, which is right on the dot; our reserves equal one-tenth of our deposits. But notice that we got there by shrinking our reserves, not by expanding our deposits (as in the previous disastrous example). We shrank our reserves by lending an amount equal to the excess, which resulted in an equivalent reduction in our reserves in the ordinary course of events.[3]

Notice also that the purchase of securities would have the same effect on reserves as lending, except that the drop in reserves would probably occur even more rapidly. If we bought securities for the bank, we would generally not open a deposit account for the seller but simply pay with a check drawn on the bank (payable via our account at the Fed). As soon as the check cleared, our reserves would fall by that amount.

The conclusion of this section is worth emphasizing: A single bank cannot safely lend (or buy securities) in an amount greater than its excess reserves, as calculated *before* it makes the loan. But it can lend or buy securities up to the amount of its excess reserves without endangering its legal reserve position.

An individual bank can therefore create money (demand deposits), but only if it has excess reserves to begin with. As soon as it has created this money—in our case, $2.8 million—it *loses* it to another bank when the money is spent. This is the key to the difference between the ability of a single bank to create money as compared with the banking system as a whole.

DEPOSIT EXPANSION: THE BANKING SYSTEM

When we lent our $2.8 million and created demand deposits of that amount for the borrowers, they soon spent the funds, and we lost both the newly created deposits and reserves of a like amount. That ended our ability to lend. But in the check-clearing process, some other banks *gained* $2.8 million of deposits and reserves, and those other banks can expand *their* lending, for now *they* have excess reserves.

Let's simplify our calculations at this point and assume that instead of having excess reserves of $2.8 million and lending that amount, we had excess reserves of only $1,000 and had lent that. This will make the numbers easier to work with. When the checks cleared, some other banks would have gained $1,000 of deposits and reserves, and those other banks could now continue

---

[3]*An important note:* Calculation of excess reserves to estimate lending ability should always be made *prior* to extending new loans, without including the reserves needed to support the new loan-created deposits. For example, after we made the $2.8 million of loans noted above, demand deposits went up by the same amount, so that required reserves rose by $280,000. But that $280,000 increase in required reserves does not affect our lending ability, because so long as those $2.8 million of deposits are there, our reserves are more than ample. It is not until those loan-created deposits disappear—when the borrowers write checks on their new deposits—that our reserves will drop, as the checks are collected in favor of other banks through the Federal Reserve. By that time, however, we won't need reserves against those deposits, since they will no longer be on our books.

the process, for they now have excess reserves. If the entire $1,000 were deposited in one bank (Bank B), that bank's T-account would look like this:

Deposit in Bank B

A		L & NW	
Deposit in Fed	+$1,000	Demand deposits	+ $1,000

Bank B can now make loans and create additional demand deposits. Assuming it was all loaned up (that it had zero excess reserves) before it received this deposit, how much could Bank B lend? Less than we did, because its excess reserves are not $1,000 but only $900—it has new reserves of $1,000, but it needs $100 of that as reserves against the $1,000 deposit.

If Bank B does indeed make a $900 loan, we should start to sense what is going to happen. Its loans and deposits will both rise by $900, and when the borrowers spend the funds its *reserves* and deposits will both fall by the same amount. Net result: Its demand deposits will drop back to $1,000, its reserves to $100, and its lending (and money-creating) ability will be exhausted.

However, when Bank B's borrowers spend their $900, giving checks to people who deposit them in other banks (such as Bank C), the very check-clearing process that takes reserves and deposits away from Bank B transfers them *to* Bank C:

Deposit in Bank C

A		L & NW	
Deposit in Fed	+ $900	Demand deposits	+$900

Now Bank C can carry the torch. It can lend and create new demand deposits up to the amount of *its* excess reserves, which are $810. As the process is repeated, Bank D can lend $729 (creating that much additional demand deposits), Bank E can lend $656.10, Bank F $590.49, and so on. Because the reserve requirement is 10 percent, each bank in the sequence gets excess reserves, lends, and creates new demand deposits equal to 90 percent of the preceding one. If we add $1,000 + $900 + $810 + $729 + $656.10 + . . . the summation of the series approaches $10,000.

When expansion has approached its $10,000 limit, the banking *system* will have demand deposits that are a multiple of its reserves—demand deposits will be $10,000 on the liabilities side and reserves $1,000 on the asset side for all banks taken together. (At the same time, of course, banks will also have $9,000 in other assets—loans, in our example.) For the banking system, this final stage is reached not by shrinking reserves, as in the case of a single bank, but by expanding deposits. The key: While each bank loses reserves after it lends—in the check-clearing process—some bank always gains the reserves another bank loses, so reserves for the entire banking system do not change. They just get transferred from bank to bank. However, as banks lend more and more, demand deposit liabilities grow, thereby reducing *excess* reserves. This continuous decline in excess reserves eventually sets a limit on further expansion.

In more general terms, how much can the banking system expand demand deposits? While a single bank can lend (and create demand deposits) only up to the amount of its excess reserves, the banking *system* can create demand deposits up to a multiple of an original injection of excess reserves.

The particular expansion multiple for the banking system depends on the **required reserve ratio.** In our example, with a reserve requirement of one-tenth, the multiple is ten (an original increase of $1,000 in excess reserves can lead to an eventual $10,000 increase in demand deposits). If the reserve requirement were one-fifth, the multiple would be five (an original increase of $1,000 in excess reserves could lead to a potential $5,000 increase in demand deposits).

In general, *the* **demand deposit expansion multiplier** *is always the reciprocal of the reserve requirement ratio.* In brief, for the entire banking system:

$$Original\ Excess\ Reserves \times \frac{1}{Reserve\ Ratio} = \frac{Potential\ Change\ in}{Demand\ Deposits}$$

We can derive this formula more formally. We have been assuming that each bank lends out all of its excess reserves. The process of deposit expansion can continue until all excess reserves become required reserves because of deposit growth; then no more deposit expansion can take place. At that point, total reserves (R) will equal the required reserve ratio on demand deposits (r_{dd}) times total demand deposits (DD). That is:

$$R = r_{dd} \times DD$$

Dividing both sides of the equation by r_{dd} (which is a legal operation even in the banking business) produces:

$$\frac{R}{r_{dd}} = \frac{r_{dd} \times DD}{r_{dd}}$$

$$R \times \frac{1}{r_{dd}} = DD$$

Using the familiar delta (Δ) sign to denote "change in," we have:

$$\Delta R \times \frac{1}{r_{dd}} = \Delta DD$$

where the change in reserves initially produces excess reserves in that amount until demand deposits are created in sufficient magnitude by the banks to put all the reserves in the required category.[4]

DEPOSIT CONTRACTION

A change in demand deposits can, of course, be down as well as up, negative as well as positive. If we start with a *deficiency* in reserves in the formula, a negative excess, the potential change in demand deposits is negative rather than positive. Instead of money being created by banks when they lend or buy securities, money is *destroyed* as bank loans are repaid or securities sold.

When someone repays a bank loan, the bank has fewer loans outstanding and at the same time deducts the amount repaid from the borrower's demand deposit balance. There are fewer demand deposits in existence; money has disappeared. Similarly, if a bank sells a bond to one of its own depositors, it takes payment by reducing the depositor's checking account balance. If it sells a bond to a depositor in another bank, the other bank winds up with fewer demand deposit liabilities.

The potential multiple *contraction* in demand deposits follows the same principles discussed above for the potential expansion of demand deposits, with one exception: The entire downward multiple change in demand deposits could conceivably take place in one single bank.

Say that a bank has a $1,000 reserve deficiency. It is then faced with two stark alternatives: It must either (a) increase its reserves by $1,000, or (b) decrease its demand deposits by ten times $1,000, or $10,000 (assuming a reserve requirement of 10 percent).

Let's take the second alternative first. The bank could decrease its demand deposits by the entire $10,000 by demanding repayment of that many loans or by selling that many securities *to its own depositors*. Loans (or bonds) would drop by $10,000 on the asset side, demand deposits would drop by the same

---

[4] An even more formal derivation of the relationship between changes in reserves and changes in deposits uses the formula for the sum of the (geometric) series discussed above in the text. In particular, the change in demand deposits due to an increase in reserves can be expressed as follows:

$$\Delta DD = \Delta R[1 + (1 - r_{dd}) + (1 - r_{dd})^2 + \cdots + (1 - r_{dd})^n]$$

There is a formula which gives the sum of the geometric progression within the brackets. As n gets infinitely large, the formula becomes:

$$\frac{1}{1 - (1 - r_{dd})} = \frac{1}{r_{dd}}$$

or, believe it or not:

$$\Delta R \times \frac{1}{r_{dd}} = \Delta DD$$

amount on the liabilities side, and the reserve deficiency would be eliminated. In this case the single bank alone bears the entire multiple decrease in the money supply.

It is more likely that the bank will choose the first option, increasing its reserves by $1,000. One way it could go about this is by borrowing $1,000 in reserves from the Federal Reserve, an alternative we will discuss more fully in the following chapter. Another way is by selling $1,000 of bonds on the open market, making the reasonable assumption that they will be bought by depositors in other banks (our bank being just a little fish in a veritable sea of banks). After the checks are cleared, the bank's deposits in the Fed will be $1,000 higher, and its reserves will be adequate once again.

But the reserves gained by Bank A will be another bank's loss. Some other bank—the bank where the purchaser of the bond kept the account—has lost $1,000 of deposits and $1,000 of reserves. Assuming that this second bank, Bank B, had precisely adequate reserves before this transaction, it now has a $900 reserve deficiency. It has lost $1,000 of reserves, but its requirements are $100 lower because it has also lost $1,000 of demand deposits, so its deficiency is only $900.

Bank B will now have no choice but to (a) get $900 in additional reserves, or (b) reduce its demand deposits by ten times $900, or $9,000. If it sells $900 of bonds to depositors in other banks, it gets its reserves, but in doing so it puts the other banks $810 in the hole. Thus the multiple contraction process continues very much like the multiple expansion process ($1,000 + $900 + $810 + $729 + $656.10 + . . .), and the summation of the series again approaches $10,000. At each stage, the bank that sells securities gains reserves, but at the expense of other banks, since the buyers of the bonds pay by checks that are cleared via the transfer of reserves on the books of the Federal Reserve bank. Reserve deficiencies are passed from bank to bank, just as in the expansion process reserve excesses are passed from one bank to another.

There is a difference, however. When banks get *excess* reserves, they *may* lend more and increase the money supply; when they have *deficient* reserves, they *must* reduce their demand deposits. We usually assume that banks will want to lend out all their excess reserves and expand demand deposits to the maximum, because they earn interest on the loans generated in the process. But there can be exceptions, as we will see in the appendix to this chapter, which add a few complicating elements to deposit creation that we have so far ignored in the interest of simplicity.

SUMMARY

1. All deposit-type financial institutions are legally required to hold reserves, in the form of either vault cash or deposits in their local Federal Reserve bank.

2. When a bank receives a check drawn on another bank, it gains reserves (through the check collection process) equal to the amount of the check. Conversely, the bank on which the check is drawn loses reserves of the same amount.

3. A single bank can safely lend and create demand deposits up to the amount of its excess reserves. If it tries to lend more, it will find itself short of reserves as soon as the borrowers spend the proceeds of the loans and the checks clear through the Fed's check collection facilities.

4. However, the banking system as a whole can lend and create demand deposits up to a multiple of an original injection of excess reserves. The demand deposit expansion multiplier is the reciprocal of the reserve requirement ratio.

5. A bank with deficient reserves must either (a) increase its reserves by the amount of the deficiency, or (b) reduce its demand deposits by a multiple of the deficiency. Again, the multiple is the reciprocal of the reserve requirement.

6. Banks with excess reserves *may* lend more and increase the money supply. Banks with deficient reserves *must* either increase their reserves or reduce their demand deposits.

QUESTIONS

19.1 Why is the check collection process the key to how much a single bank can *safely* lend?

19.2 Why is the check collection process also the key to how much potential deposit expansion can take place in the whole system?

19.3 Should the amount of a bank's excess reserves (as the basis for an estimate of a bank's lending ability) be calculated before or after making a new loan? Why?

19.4 When a bank has deficient reserves, its behavior is more predictable than when it has excess reserves. Why?

19.5 Are there any differences between the multiple contraction of deposits and their expansion?

19.6 *Discussion question:* Check collection obviously plays a crucial role in the payments system. Would it be a good idea to "privatize" the entire check collection process?

The Complete Money Supply Process

This chapter has suggested that it would be fairly easy for the Fed to generate just about any money supply it wanted. In this appendix we show that such a view is rather naïve. It turns out that the money supply is also influenced by people's preferences for checking accounts, currency, and time deposits as well as by how bank lending responds to movements in interest rates. Each of these complications makes the Fed's job more difficult.

In terms of our formula from the chapter, a change in bank reserves (ΔR) times the reciprocal of the demand deposit reserve ratio (r_{dd}) gives us the maximum potential change in demand deposits (ΔDD). Say the reserve requirement against all checking accounts is 15 percent and the Fed increases bank reserves by $1,000:

$$\Delta R \times \frac{1}{r_{dd}} = \Delta DD$$

$$\Delta R \times \frac{1}{0.15} = \Delta DD$$

$$\Delta R \times 6\frac{2}{3} = \Delta DD$$

$$\$1,000 \times 6\frac{2}{3} = \$6,667$$

The actual change in demand deposits will reach the maximum of $6,667 as long as banks lend out all their excess reserves. If we were to draw up a consolidated T-account for the entire banking system following this $1,000 injection of reserves, showing the changes that take place in the balance sheets of all banks taken together, our formula tells us it would look like this:

Final Position, All Banks Taken Together
($1,000 change in reserves; r_{dd} = 15 percent)

A		L & NW	
Reserves		Demand deposits	+ $6,667
(cash + deposit in Fed)	+ $1,000		
Loans and securities	+ 5,667		

But this is just the first approximation. Looking a bit deeper, we find that fundamental difficulties face the Fed in its efforts to control the money supply, even with such precisionlike formulas. These problems can be categorized into three main complications.

SHIFTS BETWEEN CURRENCY AND CHECKING DEPOSITS

The simple case abstracts from the fact that, as demand deposits expand, the public is likely to want to hold part of its increased money supply in the form of currency. When people need more currency, they simply go to their bank and cash a check. On the bank's balance sheet, both cash (an asset) and demand deposits (a liability) fall. The bank's excess reserves also fall by 85 percent of the withdrawal, assuming a 15 percent reserve ratio.

Notice that a $100 currency withdrawal does not directly change the public's money holdings; it simply switches $100 from demand deposits to dollar bills, leaving the total money supply unaltered. But it *does* deplete bank excess reserves by $85, because a $100 demand deposit uses up only $15 in reserves, whereas a $100 cash withdrawal subtracts a full $100 of reserves (remember that cash in bank vaults counts as reserves). Draining of currency into the hands of the public thus depletes bank reserves dollar for dollar and thereby cuts back the expansion potential of the banking system.

Let's assume that for every $1 in demand deposits, the public wants currency holdings of about 30 cents. That is, the ratio of currency to demand deposits (c/dd) is about 30 percent. This, of course, alters our demand deposit expansion formula. It is fairly easy to see the changes that are necessary: What we have to do is incorporate the currency/demand deposit ratio into the formula.

We continue to assume that banks lend out all their excess reserves. We saw in the chapter that demand deposits could expand until all excess reserves become required reserves (because of deposit growth)—that is, until the demand deposit reserve requirement (r_{dd}) times the growth in demand deposits (ΔDD) equals the change in reserves (ΔR).

But now, when reserves rise initially by ΔR, not only will they be absorbed by demand deposit growth but in addition some of these reserves will *leave* the banking system as the public holds more currency (equal to c/dd times the growth in demand deposits). Although banks will still expand their demand deposits until all reserves are in the required category, they will be unable to retain all the initial change in reserves. Since the initial injection of reserves eventually winds up as either required reserves or as currency held by the public, we have:

$$\Delta R = (r_{dd} \times \Delta DD) + (c/dd \times \Delta DD)$$

Factoring out the ΔDDs gives us:

$$\Delta R = (r_{dd} + c/dd) \times \Delta DD$$

and finally:

$$\Delta R \times \frac{1}{r_{dd} + c/dd} = \Delta DD$$

where the *initial change* in reserves (ΔR) is no longer fully retained within the banking system, because part leaks out into currency holdings outside the system. This total—reserves plus currency outside the banks—is called the **monetary base (B).** When the Federal Reserve injects reserves, it is really adding to the monetary base, since some of these reserves will shift over into the form of currency holdings outside the banking system.

Let us now return, with our new formula, to our illustrative example. Assume a currency/demand deposit ratio of 30 percent, along with our 15 percent demand deposit reserve requirement, and our familiar injection of $1,000 of reserves by the Fed. Because of the currency drain, the $1,000 of additional reserves are not all kept by the banks, so that in our new formula we should properly refer to a $1,000 increase in the monetary base (B) rather than in reserves. What we get, after all is said and done, is a multiple expansion potential for demand deposits that is considerably smaller than before—now it is not 6.67, but only 2.22:[1]

$$\Delta B \times \frac{1}{r_{dd} + c/dd} = \Delta DD$$

$$\Delta B \times \frac{1}{0.15 + 0.30} = \Delta DD$$

$$\Delta B \times \frac{1}{0.45} = \Delta DD$$

$$\Delta B \times 2.22 = \Delta DD$$

$$\$1,000 \times 2.22 = \$2,222$$

Now an initial $1,000 injection of reserves produces an eventual maximum increase in demand deposits of only $2,222. If we again draw up a consolidated T-account for all banks, following a $1,000 initial boost to reserves, the final results will look like this:

---

[1]This multiplier is strictly correct only if ΔB is initially all reserves.

Final Position, All Banks Taken Together
($1,000 initial change in reserves; r_{dd} = 15 percent;
and now adding cash drain: c/dd = 30 percent)

A		L & NW	
Reserves		Demand deposits	+ $2,222
(cash + deposit in Fed)	+ $ 333		
Loans and securities	+1,889		

Memorandum: Currency drain (i.e., currency outside the banks, held by the public): + $667

Notice that, because of the currency drain, the banking system *retains* as reserves only $333 of the original $1,000. With a 15 percent reserve requirement, this amount can support demand deposits of only $2,222. The other $667 has moved *out* of the banking system into the hands of the general public, on the premise that the public wants to hold 30 cents more currency when it gets $1 more demand deposits ($667 = 30% of $2,222).

The total change in the M1 measure of the *money supply* due to the *initial* change in reserves (= change in the monetary base) is the sum of the change in demand deposits and the change in currency. We have just seen that currency goes up by 30 percent of $2,222, or more generally:

$$\Delta Currency = c/dd \times \Delta DD = c/dd \times \frac{1}{r_{dd} + c/dd} \times \Delta B$$

Hence, the total change in the money supply (ΔM) due to the initial change in reserves is:

$$\Delta M = \Delta DD + \Delta Currency$$

$$= \frac{1}{r_{dd} + c/dd} \times \Delta B + \frac{c/dd}{r_{dd} + c/dd} \times \Delta B$$

which simplifies to:

$$\Delta M = \frac{1 + c/dd}{r_{dd} + c/dd} \times \Delta B$$

Using our numbers, the M1 money supply multiplier is 2.889:

$$\Delta M = 2.889 \times \$1,000 = \$2,889$$

which is $2,222 in demand deposits and $667 in currency.

This formula relating the change in money supply to an initial change in reserves is a lot more complicated than the simple inverse of the required reserve ratio that we derived in the chapter. Moreover, as Figure 19A.1 shows, the ratio of currency to demand deposits has fluctuated considerably over time, making the money supply multiplier not only more complicated but somewhat unstable as well.

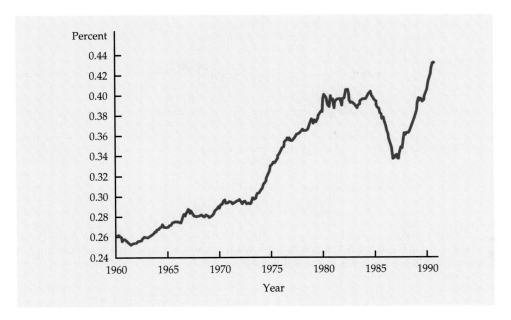

Percent

Year

FIGURE 19A.1   The currency ratio (*c/dd*) has varied considerably over time.

SHIFTS BETWEEN TIME DEPOSITS AND CHECKING ACCOUNTS

We also have to recognize that banks have business-owned time deposits that often require reserves. Assume a reserve requirement on time deposits of 3 percent. While this is smaller than the reserve requirement against demand deposits, it does absorb bank reserves and further reduces the demand deposit expansion potential of the system. Assume that the public wants to hold a ratio of time deposits to demand deposits (*td/dd*) of two to one. Since the reserve requirement against such deposits (r_{td}) is 3 percent, this has to affect our demand deposit expansion formula. The new demand deposit multiplier turns out to be 1.961:[2]

---

[2]The derivation is as follows: The initial injection of reserves (ΔB) now gets absorbed by required reserves against demand deposits ($r_{dd} \times \Delta DD$); by currency ($c/dd \times \Delta DD$); and by required reserves against time deposits. The increase in time deposits (ΔTD) equals $td/dd \times \Delta DD$, and reserves against time deposits equal $r_{td} \times td/dd \times \Delta DD$. Therefore, we have:

$$\Delta B = (r_{dd} \times \Delta DD) + (c/dd \times \Delta DD) + (td/dd \times r_{td} \times \Delta DD)$$

Factoring out the ΔDDs gives us:

$$\Delta B = [r_{dd} + c/dd + (td/dd \times r_{td})] \times \Delta DD$$

and finally:

$$\Delta B \times \frac{1}{r_{dd} + c/dd + (td/dd)(r_{td})} = \Delta DD$$

$$\Delta B \times \frac{1}{r_{dd} + c/dd + (td/dd)(r_{td})} = \Delta DD$$

$$\Delta B \times \frac{1}{0.15 + 0.30 + 2(0.03)} = \Delta DD$$

$$\Delta B \times \frac{1}{0.15 + 0.30 + 0.06} = \Delta DD$$

$$\Delta B \times \frac{1}{0.51} = \Delta DD$$

$$\Delta B \times 1.961 = \Delta DD$$

$$\$1{,}000 \times 1.961 = \$1{,}961$$

We can extend this expression to the M1 measure of the money supply as a whole (not just demand deposits) by adding the increase in currency in circulation to the increase in demand deposits:

$$\Delta M = \Delta DD + \Delta Currency = \frac{1}{r_{dd} + c/dd + (td/dd)(r_{td})} \times \Delta B$$

$$+ \frac{c/dd}{r_{dd} + c/dd + (td/dd)\,(r_{td})} \times \Delta B$$

which simplifies to:

$$\Delta M = \frac{1 + c/dd}{r_{dd} + c/dd + (td/dd)\,(r_{td})} \times \Delta B$$

If you work it out, you'll find that this yields an M1 money supply multiplier of 2.549.

The consolidated bank T-account for an initial $1,000 reserve increase under these circumstances is interesting:

Final Position, All Banks Taken Together
($1,000 initial change in reserves; $r_{dd} = 15$ percent; currency drain $c/dd = 30$ percent; and now adding time deposit growth: $td/dd = 2$ and $r_{td} = 3$ percent)

A		L & NW	
Reserves (cash + deposit in Fed)	$412	Demand deposits	+ $1,961
For demand deposits:	+ $294		
For time deposits:	+ 118		
Loan and securities	+5,471	Time deposits	+ 3,922

Memorandum: Currency drain (i.e., currency outside the banks, held by the public): + $588 (= 30% of $1,961)

These results—fewer demand deposits but more total deposits and more bank lending compared with the previous T-account—reflect two things. The currency drain is now less, so the banking system retains more reserves.

(The currency drain is less even though the *c/dd* ratio is the same, because currency outflows depend, by assumption, on the growth of demand deposits only.) And time deposits, while they use up reserves and thereby inhibit potential demand deposit expansion, do not remove reserves from the banking system the way currency drains do; with time deposits, banks can continue lending, and indeed they can lend even *more* than with an equivalent amount of demand deposits, because the reserve requirement against time deposits is lower.

This suggests that the reserve multiplier consequences for broader money supply definitions are still more complicated than for M1. In our last example, associated with a demand deposit multiplier of 1.961 and an M1 multiplier of 2.549, we have an M2 multiplier that is quite a bit larger: namely, 6.471. How do we know? Because we can see that an original reserve injection of $1,000 results in a $588 expansion of currency in circulation, a $1,961 increase in demand deposits, *and* a $3,922 increase in time deposits. These add up to a $6,471 increase in M2.

THE ROLE OF INTEREST RATES

Finally, a last complication: Banks may not always be willing to expand their loans (or securities purchases) up to the full amount of their excess reserves. If some banks don't lend all their excess reserves (perhaps because they cannot find enough creditworthy borrowers) and don't buy additional securities (perhaps because they expect bond prices to fall), the whole sequence of lending and demand deposit creation cannot reach its theoretical maximum.

Banks that do not fully expand their loans won't lose all their excess reserves to other banks, so the other banks will be unable to lend as much. In addition, banks that do lend are likely to lose some reserves to the nonlenders, thereby rendering such reserves immobile. Thus the potential multiple can be realized only if *all* banks are willing to lend and/or buy securities up to the *full* amount of their excess reserves.

In the 1930s idle excess reserves were plentiful. In the past few decades most banks have stayed rather fully loaned up, but it is quite possible that bank holdings of excess reserves could be a function of interest rates, high rates inducing banks to make more loans and hold less excess reserves, and low rates making it less costly for banks to hold excess reserves (they are not giving up much interest income by not lending). This raises the possibility that the money supply is a function of interest rate levels. This is confirmed by Figure 19A.2, which plots historical movements in the ratio of excess reserves to checking deposits as well as showing the level of the Treasury bill rate. Broadly speaking, higher interest rates are associated with smaller excess reserve ratios. Thus money supply will react positively to interest rates as banks lend out more of their excess reserves. Moreover, as we will see in the next chapter, banks borrow more reserves from the

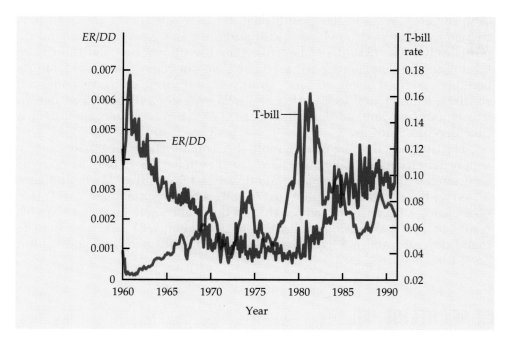

FIGURE 19A.2   Excess reserves as a percent of checking deposits tend to be high when the level of the three-month Treasury bill is low, and vice versa.

Federal Reserve through the discount window when interest rates go up, providing still another mechanism for higher interest rates to expand the money supply.

What do all these complications mean for the Federal Reserve, these successive modifications of our original simple demand deposit expansion multiplier? (Remember when it was just the reciprocal of the demand deposit reserve requirement?) They mean, most important, that the Fed's ability to control the money supply, even in its narrow definition, is not nearly as precise as we had originally thought. As it attempts to control the money supply, the central bank has to deal with currency drains, time deposit growth, and even movements in interest rates. We can get away with using hypothetical numbers for the multipliers, but for the Fed that is simply not good enough. It has to predict with accuracy the various ratios for the coming weeks and months if it is to succeed in making the money supply what it wants it to be.

CHAPTER 20

The Instruments of Central Banking

In the last chapter we saw that bank lending and the money supply were related by some multiple to the level of bank reserves. The Federal Reserve exercises control over bank lending and the money supply by altering the reserves of commercial banks and of other deposit-type institutions and by influencing the deposit creation multiplier. The Fed accomplishes these objectives by changing reserve *requirements* relative to deposits and by changing the actual *amount* of reserves that financial institutions hold. First we'll look at reserve requirements and then we'll see how the Fed varies the actual amount of reserves through the discount rate and open market operations.

RESERVE REQUIREMENTS

Within limits established by Congress, the Federal Reserve can specify the reserve requirements that banks and other deposit-type institutions must hold against deposits. Congressional limits for bank reserves were first established in the Federal Reserve Act of 1913 and have been reset a number of times since, most recently in the Banking Act of 1980 and the Garn–St. Germain Depository Institutions Act of 1982. This most recent legislation provides that *all* depository institutions—savings banks, savings and loans, and credit unions, as well as *all* commercial banks, whether members of the Federal Reserve system or not—are subject to the Fed's reserve requirements. As of 1995 each depository institution had to hold reserves (in the form of vault cash or deposits in a regional Federal Reserve bank) as follows:

1. Against *demand deposits* and other transactions accounts, reserves equal to:

    a.   3 percent of its *first $52.0 million* of demand deposits.[1]

    b.   10 percent of its demand deposits *in excess of that amount*. The Fed can vary this latter percentage within a range of 8 to 14 percent, and under emergency circumstances it can go as high as 18 percent.

2. Against *business-owned time and savings deposits,* reserves are zero. The Fed can vary reserves against such deposits within a range of zero to 9 percent.

3. Finally, regardless of the above requirements, the first $4.3 million of reservable liabilities is *exempt* from reserve requirements. The Fed adjusts this $4.3 million figure upward annually by 80 percent of the annual percentage increase in total reservable liabilities in the country (similar to the annual adjustment mentioned in footnote 1).

Lowering the required reserve ratio for demand deposits—for example, from 12 to 10 percent—does two things. First, it instantly and automatically increases banks' excess reserves, since fewer reserves are now required against any given volume of demand deposits. A bank with demand deposits of $1,000 and reserves of $120 is all loaned up when the reserve requirement is 12 percent; lowering it to 10 percent suddenly provides $20 of excess reserves. More excess reserves, of course, enable banks to make more loans, buy more securities, and expand demand deposits.

In addition, lowering the required reserve ratio also increases the demand deposit expansion *multiplier* for the entire banking system. As we saw in the previous chapter, the multiplier—at least in its simple form—is the reciprocal of the required reserve ratio. The smaller the ratio, the larger its reciprocal. Thus a decrease in the required reserve ratio from 12 percent (or about one-eighth) to 10 percent (one-tenth) would raise the deposit expansion multiplier from about eight to ten.

Raising the required reserve ratio—for example, from 10 to 12 percent—would have the opposite effects. It would create reserve deficiencies, or at least reduce excesses, *and* lower the potential for multiple expansion. Putting banks into a deficit reserve position would *force* them to call in loans and sell securities, bringing about a reduction in demand deposits, while smaller excesses would at least restrain lending and deposit creation.

Since the same reserve requirements apply to nonmember as well as to member commercial banks, membership in the Federal Reserve system has become essentially irrelevant. The problem of dropouts from the Federal Reserve system that occurred during the 1960s and 1970s has been resolved. Banks can no longer escape the requirement to hold zero-interest-bearing re-

---

[1] The $52.0 million figure is adjusted annually by 80 percent of the annual percentage change in total transactions accounts in the country. Example: If total transactions accounts in the country rise by 5 percent, the $52.0 million figure will be increased by 80 percent of 5 percent, which equals 4 percent. Four percent of $52.0 million equals $2.1 million. Accordingly, at the beginning of 1996 the amount would be increased from $52.0 million to $54.1 million.

serves by leaving the system. Also, since the same requirements apply to thrift institutions as to commercial banks, the distinction between them—as far as reserves go—has become less important.[2]

How crucial are reserve requirements for monetary policy? What would happen if the Federal Reserve eliminated reserve requirements entirely in order to increase bank profits?

Actually, even without formal reserve requirements the Fed would still be in business. Financial institutions would still need both cash to meet customer withdrawals and balances in the Fed to clear checks. As long as they have a demand for claims against the central bank, and as long as the central bank controls the supply of such claims, monetary policy can still work. While the Fed would lose one tool of monetary policy if it could no longer change reserve requirements, it could still influence the behavior of financial institutions.

There is one qualification: The size of the multiplier relationship between reserves and money supply might fluctuate considerably. This would make the job of controlling the money supply more difficult. Not impossible, but more difficult. And as we saw in the appendix to the previous chapter, things are tough enough already.

DISCOUNTING AND THE DISCOUNT RATE

The Federal Reserve can also alter the excess reserves of banks and other depository institutions by changing the actual amount of reserves that financial institutions hold. One way this is accomplished is through the discount mechanism, by which the Fed lends reserves, temporarily, to the banks. The Fed charges an interest rate, called the **discount rate,** on such loans. In other words, banks faced with reserve deficits can temporarily borrow reserves from their regional Federal Reserve bank at a price (the discount rate).

---

[2] Recall that reserve requirements are satisfied by holding vault cash or deposits in a bank's regional Federal Reserve bank, neither of which earn any interest. Higher reserve requirements thus lower bank profitability by increasing the proportion of assets that yield no income.

The differential impact of reserve requirements on bank profitability was one of the main reasons behind passage of the Banking Act of 1980. Until it was enacted, the Fed's reserve requirements applied only to commercial banks and, further, only to those commercial banks that were members of the Federal Reserve system.

The adverse effect of the Fed's reserve requirements on their earnings led many member banks to reconsider their membership in the Federal Reserve system. About one-third of the commercial banks in the United States are chartered by the federal government (national banks) and two-thirds are chartered by the state in which they operate (state banks). National banks are *required* to be members of the Federal Reserve system, but state banks are free to join the system or not, as they wish. During the 1960s and 1970s many state banks withdrew from the Federal Reserve system, giving up their membership to escape the Fed's reserve requirements.

Say that a bank in Cucamonga, California, has a reserve deficiency of $1,000 (it needs $1,000 more reserves than it has). Rather than take the drastic step of calling in loans, and preferring not to sell securities, it can borrow the reserves it needs from the Federal Reserve Bank of San Francisco at the prevailing discount rate. If it did so, the T-accounts would look like this:

Commercial Bank Discounting from the Fed

Federal Reserve Bank

A		L & NW	
Loan to Cucamonga bank	+ $1,000	Deposit of Cucamonga bank	+ $1,000

Cucamonga Commercial Bank

A		L & NW	
Deposit in Fed	+ $1,000	Due to Fed	+ $1,000

When a manufacturer borrows from a bank, the manufacturer receives a brand-new deposit at the bank. A bank is in the same position relative to the Federal Reserve: When it borrows from its friendly neighborhood Federal Reserve bank, it receives a brand-new deposit at the Fed which increases its legal reserves.[3] The ability to borrow these reserves—to discount from the Fed—means that when it is faced with a reserve deficiency the Cucamonga bank does not have to call in loans or sell securities, and thus the money supply can remain unchanged.

The Federal Reserve tries to influence the willingness of banks to borrow reserves by changing the interest rate it charges on such loans (the discount rate). A lower discount rate will make the borrowing of reserves more attractive to banks, and a higher discount rate will make it less attractive.

The effectiveness of the discount mechanism as a means of injecting or withdrawing reserves is limited by the fact that the initiative for borrowing from the Fed rests not with the Fed but with the banks. Banks will want to borrow reserves only when they need them. If they already have ample reserves, there is no reason for them to borrow more, no matter how low the discount rate.

The Banking Act of 1980 expanded access to borrowing from the Federal Reserve to *all* depository institutions that have to hold reserves—which means nonmember as well as member commercial banks and also thrift institutions. Previously, only member banks had access to discounting—the **discount window**—although in emergencies others could sometimes use it, too. Now, however, nonmember banks and thrift institutions have the same access to bor-

---

[3] Notice that the Cucamonga bank's deposit in the Fed is an asset of the Cucamonga bank, but a liability of the Fed (just as your deposit in a local bank is your asset but the bank's liability).

GOING OUT ON A LIMB

The Discount Window Prevented a Financial Meltdown in 1987

On Monday, October 19, 1987, prices on the New York Stock Exchange fell by more than 20 percent, the single largest daily decline in history. Although most investors viewed Blue Monday as a nightmare, the real financial catastrophe threatened to erupt the following day.

It is now well documented that because of customer losses, a number of firms associated with the nation's futures and options exchanges were threatened with bankruptcy on October 20, 1987. Moreover, many stock exchange firms were concerned that securities purchased on the 19th would not be paid for. If these defaults had occurred, financial obligations that most market participants take for granted would have gone unfulfilled, and the implicit trust that underlies all financial transactions would have disappeared.

With the financial system on the brink of a standstill on the morning of October 20, 1987, officers of the Federal Reserve system announced both publicly and privately that the central bank would provide whatever liquidity was necessary to keep financial markets afloat. In particular, the Fed's discount window would be made available to brokerage firms to help them meet their obligations.

The Federal Reserve executed its role as "lender of last resort" to avert a breakdown of the payments system. Had the Fed hesitated, the financial system as we know it would have disappeared. Such decisive action should be applauded.

rowing from the Federal Reserve that member banks have, and on exactly the same terms.

It has been recognized for a long time that discount policy has two dimensions: The first is *price*, the discount rate, the rate of interest the Federal Reserve charges financial institutions when they borrow from the Fed. The second dimension has to do with the *quantity* of Federal Reserve lending, including Federal Reserve surveillance over the amount that each institution borrows and the reasons why it borrows. Let us examine quantity first and price second.

Historically, the primary function of a central bank has been to stand ready to supply funds—promptly and in abundance—whenever the economy is in danger of coming apart at the seams because of a shortage of cash. While that is no longer its sole function, it is still one of its most important. The central bank is the ultimate source of liquidity in the economy, because with its power over bank reserves it can increase (or decrease) the ability of the banking system to create money. Since no one else can do the job, it is the central bank that must be responsible for supplying funds promptly on those rare but crucial occasions when liquidity shortages threaten economic stability: "financial panics," the history books call them. Because of this responsibility, the central bank has traditionally been called the **lender of last resort.**[4]

---

[4] The principle of the central bank as "lender of last resort" was eloquently articulated as long ago as 1873 by Walter Bagehot in *Lombard Street,* the first full-blown exposition of what central banking is all about. Many of his ideas stemmed from Henry Thornton's *An Enquiry into the Nature and Effects of the Paper Credit of Great Britain,* which was published in 1802.

The discount facilities instituted by the passage of the Federal Reserve Act in 1913 were supposed to provide a vehicle through which the Federal Reserve could quickly inject funds precisely where needed in order to stop a panic from spreading. Banks threatened with cash drains could borrow what they needed from the Fed—the lender of last resort. Thus they could get more reserves without any other bank losing them and thereby prevent an infection from becoming a plague.

In the ordinary course of events, however, bank use of the discount facility is rather routine, not at all panic-oriented, with banks borrowing here and there to make short-run adjustments in their reserves with no fuss or bother. A bank may find itself with an unexpected reserve deficit, for example, and need to borrow a few million to tide itself over the weekend.

The Fed has always stressed that ordinary run-of-the-mill borrowing of this sort (as contrasted with crisis situations) should not be used *too* often to get banks out of reserve difficulties. Banks should run their affairs so they do not have to rely on the Fed to bail them out every few weeks. Or, as the Federal Reserve usually puts it, discounting is considered a privilege, not a right, and privileges should not be abused. Federal Reserve surveillance enforces the "privilege, not a right" concept by checking up on banks that borrow too much or too frequently.[5] A bank is supposed to borrow only because of *need*, and not go out and make a *profit* on the deal.

In particular, the Fed is sensitive to the possibility that banks may borrow from it and then turn around and use the money to purchase higher-yielding securities. The Fed does not want a bank borrowing from it at a 6 percent discount rate and then using the funds to buy a short-term security yielding 8 percent. Nor does the Fed like it when a bank borrows from it too often, in effect using the discount facility as a more or less permanent source of funds.

One Fed method of preventing "abuse" of the discount facility is to tighten surveillance procedures: It checks up on why banks are borrowing and what they are doing with the money. Another way is simply to raise the price of borrowing—which brings us to the discount rate itself.

The Discount Rate and Market Interest Rates

The objective of changing the discount rate is just what the Federal Reserve says it is: A higher discount rate discourages borrowing from the Fed, and a lower discount rate encourages it. These results flow from the least-cost alternatives facing banks with reserve deficiencies. A higher discount rate makes it relatively more advantageous to sell securities to get additional reserves, and a

---

[5] In 1973, however, the Fed introduced a special "seasonal borrowing privilege" that encourages small banks to borrow to cover most of their recurring reserve needs arising from seasonal swings in loans or deposits (as happens to banks in agricultural and resort areas).

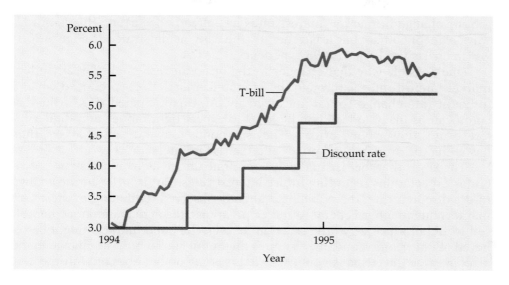

FIGURE 20.1   Movements in the discount rate tend to come after Treasury bill rates.

lower discount rate makes it relatively more advantageous to borrow from the Fed. Actually, "higher" and "lower" in absolute terms are not as important as the relationship between the discount rate and market interest rates.

In some countries the discount rate is often kept above short-term market interest rates, so that it is a *penalty rate,* a means of restraining excessive commercial bank use of the central bank's borrowing facilities. In the United States, on the other hand, the discount rate is usually, although not always, held below the Treasury bill rate, so that the Fed has to rely more on surveillance than cost to prevent "abuse of the discount privilege."

How does a change in the discount rate affect market interest rates? The two are not *directly* connected. A higher or lower discount rate alters bank borrowing from the Fed, thereby changing bank reserves, bank lending, the money supply, and finally market interest rates. This is a rather weak linkage, however, since a change in the discount rate affects reserves and the money supply far less than other tools available to the Federal Reserve.

Careful examination, however, reveals that *changes* in Treasury bill yields typically *precede* changes in the discount rate. Treasury bill yields rise, probably because of Federal Reserve open market operations (which we discuss in the next section), and then—after they have risen quite a while and often quite a bit—the discount rate moves up. Or bill rates fall and then the discount rate is lowered. In other words, a change in the discount rate is likely to come *after* a basic change in market interest rates has already occurred. This is not always true, of course, but it is generally the case, as illustrated in Figure 20.1, which charts the 1994 to 1995 experience.

One possible way that changes in the discount rate might directly affect market interest rates is through the "announcement effect" produced when a discount rate change comes unexpectedly. An unanticipated rise in the discount rate is likely to lead bondholders to expect tight money and higher interest rates (lower bond prices). They sell bonds to avoid capital losses, thus hastening the drop in bond prices and the rise in interest rates.

The key is that the rise in the discount rate under such circumstances generates expectations regarding future interest rates. But if, prior to the change in the discount rate, the public had already observed tightening in the credit markets due to other Federal Reserve operations, the actual announcement itself would produce very little reaction. In fact, the bond markets might be relieved of uncertainty, and interest rates might fall back a bit. The change in the discount rate thus usually confirms what is going on but does not initiate it.

OPEN MARKET OPERATIONS

The most important way the Federal Reserve alters the actual amount of reserves the banks hold is not by discounting, but by buying and selling government securities—technically known as **open market operations.** Undertaken at the Fed's own initiative, open market operations are the mainstay of Federal Reserve policy.

About $4,000 billion worth of marketable government securities are outstanding. They are held as investments by the public—by individuals, corporations, financial institutions, and so on. Over $300 billion are held by the Federal Reserve system. These government securities came into being when the U.S. Treasury had to borrow to finance budget deficits. This pool of widely held marketable securities, with many potential buyers and sellers, offers an ideal vehicle through which the Federal Reserve can affect bank reserves. Federal Reserve purchases of government securities increase bank reserves, and Federal Reserve sales decrease them. Here's how it works:

When the Federal Reserve *buys* $1,000 of government securities, much as you might buy a stock or a bond on one of the stock exchanges, it pays with a check drawn on itself. If the Fed buys the securities directly from a commercial bank—say, from a bank in Succasunna, New Jersey—the Succasunna bank sends the Fed's check to its regional Federal Reserve bank (the Federal Reserve Bank of Philadelphia) and has its deposit at the Fed—its reserves—increased by $1,000. The Succasunna bank's excess reserves rise by the full amount of the transaction, and with more excess reserves it can make more loans and increase its demand deposits.

The T-accounts for a Federal Reserve purchase of government securities directly from a commercial bank are:

Fed Open Market Purchase of Securities Directly from a Commecial Bank

Federal Reserve

A		L & NW	
Govt. securities	+ $1,000	Deposit of Succasunna bank	+ $1,000

Succasunna Commercial Bank

A		L & NW
Deposits in Fed	+ $1,000	
Govt. securities	− 1,000	

But what the central bank giveth, the central bank can taketh away. When the Federal Reserve *sells* government securities out of its portfolio, it *gets paid* for them, and everything is reversed. Say the Fed sells $1,000 of government securities directly to our friendly Succasunna bank; the Succasunna bank now has gained $1,000 worth of securities, which is good, but it has to pay for them, which is bad. The Fed takes payment by deducting that sum from the Succasunna bank's deposit at the Federal Reserve, thus diminishing its reserves. If you were to draw up the T-accounts for the transaction, everything would be exactly the same as the T-accounts above, except that every plus sign would become a minus and every minus sign a plus. The Succasunna bank's excess reserves fall by the full amount of the transaction; if it had no excess reserves, now it has a $1,000 reserve deficiency.

Note that the Federal Reserve could achieve the same ends—that is, change bank reserves—by buying or selling any asset, such as any type of bond or stock, or even CD recordings. The reason for limiting its open market operations to the purchase and sale of government securities is quite obvious: Who would determine whether the Federal Reserve should buy Michael Jackson or Bruce Springsteen albums? General Motors stock or IBM? The Federal Reserve is smart enough, at least in this respect, not to get involved in the really important decisions.[6]

Of course, when the Federal Reserve buys (or sells) government securities, it has no assurance that a bank will be the other party to the transaction. But it doesn't matter whether the securities the Fed buys are being sold by a bank or by someone else, nor is it important whether the securities the Fed sells are ultimately bought by a bank or by someone else. In either case, when the Fed buys, bank reserves go up, and when the Fed sells, bank reserves go down.

For example, suppose that when the Fed bought $1,000 of government securities, the seller of the securities wasn't the Succasunna bank but an insur-

---

[6] Actually the Federal Reserve occasionally buys and sells securities denominated in foreign currencies in connection with its foreign exchange operations. The effect on reserves is exactly the same as if it had purchased or sold U.S. Treasury securities. The only difference in the T-accounts would be that foreign government securities would replace the government securities entry.

OFF THE RECORD

Three Key Interest Rates

The *prime rate*, the *discount rate*, and the *federal funds rate* are referred to in newspapers so often that they deserve special mention, particularly since they are frequently confused with each other.

The **prime rate** is the interest rate that commercial banks charge on loans to their most creditworthy business customers, most creditworthy meaning financially strongest and therefore most likely to repay on time. Banks charge higher rates than the prime for loans to corporations without such strong credit ratings. The prime rate is an *administered* rate in that banks set it and it stays there until they decide to raise or lower it; thus the prime rate typically stays the same for weeks or even months at a time.

The **discount rate** is the interest rate that the Federal Reserve charges on loans to commercial banks. The Federal Reserve makes short-term loans to banks when the banks need funds for relatively brief periods of time. Thus the prime rate involves a payment commercial banks receive, while the discount rate is a cost, something they pay out. Like the prime rate, the discount rate is also an administered rate, set in this case by the Federal Reserve and often staying unchanged for months.

Finally, the **federal funds rate**—often called just the *funds rate*—is the interest rate that banks charge each other on very short-term loans among themselves. Usually the loans are "overnight"—made on one day and paid back the next. Unlike the prime rate and the discount rate, the federal funds rate is not an administered rate; rather, it is a *market-determined* rate, fluctuating continuously depending on the relationship between the demand for loans (by banks who need to borrow) and the supply (from banks who want to lend).

ance company in Mishawaka, Indiana. It wouldn't matter if the insurance company were in Cut Off, Louisiana; Zap, North Dakota; Searchlight, Nevada; or even Eureka, California. However, *this* insurance company happens to be in Mishawaka, Indiana.[7]

In any case, when the Fed buys, it still pays for the securities with a check drawn on itself. When the insurance company deposits the check in its local commercial bank, the Mishawaka bank now has the Federal Reserve's check (an asset), and it gives the insurance company a demand deposit. In turn, the Mishawaka bank sends the check to its regional Federal Reserve bank (the Federal Reserve Bank of Chicago) and receives in exchange a $1,000 addition to its reserves.

The T-account for the insurance company shows that it now has $1,000 less in government securities and $1,000 more in its demand deposit account at its local commercial bank. For the Federal Reserve and the Mishawaka bank, the T-accounts for such a Federal Reserve purchase look like this:

---

[7] Speaking of place names reminds us of Zzyzx Road (pronounced Zzyzx), which you will encounter on Interstate 15 about fifty miles out of Barstow on the way to Las Vegas.

Fed Open Market Purchase of Securities from a Nonbank

Federal Reserve

A		L & NW	
Govt. securities	+ $1,000	Deposit of Mishawaka bank	+ $1,000

Mishawaka Commercial Bank

A		L & NW	
Deposits in Fed	+ $1,000	Demand deposit of ins. co.	+ $1,000

Notice that in this case the commercial bank's excess reserves go up, but not by the full amount of the transaction. The bank has $1,000 more of reserves, but it needs $100 more (assuming a 10 percent reserve requirement), because its deposits have gone up by $1,000; thus its *excess* reserves have risen by $900. However, the money supply has *already* risen by $1,000, so the ultimate potential effect on the money supply is the same regardless of where the Fed buys its securities. To summarize:

1. If the Fed buys $1,000 of government securities directly from commercial banks, bank excess reserves rise by the full $1,000 and the banking system can then create $10,000 of new money (assuming a 10 percent reserve requirement).

2. If the Fed buys from nonbanks, bank excess reserves rise by only $900 and the banking system can create $9,000 of new money. But the money supply has already gone up by $1,000, and $9,000 + $1,000 also equal $10,000. So, in the end, the ultimate effect on the money supply of either type of open market purchase turns out to be the same.[8]

Commercial banks are unable to do anything to offset these measures. If the Fed wants to reduce bank reserves by open market sales, there is nothing the banks can do about it. By lowering its selling price, the Fed can always unearth a buyer. Since it is not in business to make a profit, the Fed is free to alter its selling price as it wishes. And while any single commercial bank can replenish its own reserves by selling securities to other banks—or to individuals who keep their accounts in other banks—the reserves of the other banks will then decline. Reserves replenished by one bank are lost by others.

---

[8] Similarly, were the Fed to *sell* securities to an insurance company, everything would be exactly the same as the T-accounts immediately above, except the signs would be reversed. Our Mishawaka bank would find its excess reserves diminished by $900 (not by $1,000, because although its reserves would be $1,000 lower, its deposit liabilities would also be that much lower). When the Fed sells securities directly to commercial banks, on the other hand, bank excess reserves fall by the full amount of the sale. However, in the two cases the potential effect on the money supply is the same.

Total bank reserves must fall by the value of the securities sold by the Federal Reserve.

As suggested in Chapter 2, it should now be clear why a contraction or expansion in the money supply via pure monetary policy does not change the total size of the public's portfolio (its wealth) directly. The public gives up an asset, or incurs a liability, as part of the very process through which currency or demand deposits rise; the reverse occurs when demand deposits decline. For example, if the money supply is increased by the Federal Reserve's open market purchases of securities, the increased demand deposit acquired by the public is offset by the reduction in its holdings of government securities (they were purchased by the Federal Reserve). In any subsequent expansion of demand deposits by bank lending or security purchases, the public acquires an asset (demand deposits) but either creates a liability against itself in the form of a bank loan or sells to the bank an asset of equal value, such as a government bond.

A Day at the Trading Desk

Now that we understand the mechanics of open market operations, let's see how the Federal Reserve implements its policies. Although monetary policy is made in Washington, open market operations are actually conducted in New York—in a well-guarded trading room on the eighth floor of the Federal Reserve Bank of New York, which is only a few blocks from Wall Street. The Federal Open Market Committee (FOMC) in Washington decides on the general aims and objectives of monetary policy, but then it is up to the manager of the System Open Market Account, who is located at the Federal Reserve Bank of New York, to do the actual buying and selling to carry out the FOMC's intentions.

The location in the heart of the New York financial district puts the manager of the System Open Market Account in close contact with the government securities dealers the Fed does business with. Every morning of the work week, the account manager meets with some of the securities dealers to get the "feel of the market," and even the opening handshakes (firm or limp? dry or sweaty palms?) probably reveal a hint of whether the market is likely to be strong or weak, bullish or bearish.

Feedback from the securities dealers is only one component of the vast array of data and information marshaled by the account manager in mapping plans for open market operations on any given day. The starting point, of course, is the stance of monetary policy as expressed by the FOMC with respect to bank reserves, the money supply, and interest rates. Given these targets, the account manager has to figure out how to achieve them by open market operations—whether to buy or sell, how much, from or to whom, and when.

Each morning, a little after 9:30, the account manager receives a report on the reserve position of the banking system as of the night before. A key indicator of whether the quantity of reserves is high or low relative to demand is provided by the federal funds rate, the rate charged on funds lent by one bank to another. If many banks have excess reserves and only a few have deficiencies, the federal funds rate is likely to fall, because there will be many eager lenders and few borrowers. On the other hand, if many banks have reserve deficiencies and only a few are in surplus, the rate will rise, because there will be many eager borrowers and few lenders. The federal funds rate thus provides the Fed with a sensitive barometer of reserve supply relative to demand.

A little later in the morning, the account manager is provided with a detailed projection covering expected movements in various items that can affect the reserve position of the banking system—including currency holdings of the public (which show considerable seasonal variation), deposits in foreign accounts at the Federal Reserve banks, and other technical factors. As we will see in the next chapter, a change in any of these can cause reserves to go up or down and thereby affect bank lending capabilities, interest rates, and growth in the money supply. For example, as the public cashes checks in order to get more currency, commercial banks must pay out vault cash and thereby suffer a loss in reserves.

A call is also made to the U.S. Treasury to determine what is likely to happen to Treasury balances in **tax and loan accounts** at commercial banks—deposits of the U.S. government generated by tax payments of the public and receipts from bond sales—and to find out what is likely to happen to Treasury balances at the Federal Reserve banks, from which most government expenditures are made. As funds are shifted from Treasury tax and loan accounts in commercial banks to Treasury balances at the Federal Reserve, the commercial banking system loses reserves.[9]

By 11:00 A.M., the account manager has a good idea of money market conditions, including what is happening to interest rates, and of anticipated changes in the reserve position of the banking system. The manager also knows what the FOMC wants. If the FOMC had asked for moderate growth in reserves to sustain moderate growth in the money supply, and if all the other technical factors just discussed are expected to pour a large volume of reserves into the banking system, the account manager may decide that open market *sales* are necessary to prevent an excessive expansion in reserves. If, on the other hand, reserves are expected to go up too little or even to decline as a result of these other forces, the Fed may engage in large-scale open market purchases. It is clear, therefore, why knowledge of the amount of government securities that the Federal Reserve bought or sold on a given day, or during a given week, in itself tells us almost nothing about the overall posture or intent of monetary policy. Many purchases and sales are used to offset technical influences on reserves.

At 11:15 it is time for a daily long-distance conference call with a member of the board of governors in Washington and one of the Federal Reserve bank presidents. The account manager outlines the plan of action for the day and explains the reasons for this particular strategy. Once the decision is approved, the purchase or sale of securities (usually Treasury bills) takes place.

---

[9] The discussion of the last two paragraphs on the impact of various items on bank reserves will be explained in detail in the next chapter.

The account manager instructs the traders in the trading room of the Federal Reserve Bank of New York to call the primary government securities dealers and ask them for firm bids for stated amounts of specific maturities of government securities (in the case of an open market sale) or for their selling price quotations for stated amounts of specific maturities (in the case of an open market purchase).

The account manager may instruct the Fed's traders to buy or sell securities outright—that is, involving no additional commitments. Or they might decide to inject or withdraw reserves only *temporarily,* say for several days. One type of open market operation is particularly well suited to the temporary injection of reserves, namely, buying government securities under **repurchase agreements.** With a "repo" the Fed buys the security with an agreement that the seller will repurchase it on a specific date in the future, usually within a week or so. When the Fed buys, reserves go up, but when the security is sold back to the dealer a week or so later, reserves drop back down again.[10]

A **reverse repo** is designed to do the opposite. It *withdraws* reserves from the banking system temporarily. With a reverse repo, also called a **matched sale-purchase agreement,** the Fed sells securities but simultaneously agrees to buy them back at a specific date in the future. When the Fed sells, reserves fall; but later when the Fed buys the securities back, reserves are restored.

In recent years, the Fed has relied to an increasing extent on repos and reverse repos. In terms of the dollar volume of open market operations, they now greatly exceed outright purchases and sales.

It takes only about half an hour for the traders to complete their "go-around" of the market and execute the open market operation. By 12:30 the account manager is back to monitoring bank reserve positions via the federal funds rate and to keeping track of trends in financial markets in general. If necessary to implement the original objective, the manager is prepared to engage in further open market operations during the afternoon.

SUMMARY

1. The Federal Reserve regulates bank lending and the money supply through its control over bank reserves and the deposit creation multiplier. All depository institutions are equally subject to the Fed's reserve requirements, regardless of whether they are commercial banks, savings and loans, savings banks, or credit unions, and regardless of Federal Reserve membership.

---

[10] The term *repo* takes its name from the dealer's point of view. That is, the dealer sells to the Fed under an agreement to repurchase the securities. As we saw in Chapter 8, dealers do repos with many market participants as a way of financing their securities holdings.

2. By changing the required reserve ratio, the Fed alters bank excess reserves and simultaneously changes the deposit expansion multiplier for the banking system. Lower required reserve ratios mean easier money, while higher ratios imply tighter money.

3. Discounting and the discount rate have a long and distinguished history, dating back to the nineteenth-century concept of the central bank as a "lender of last resort." By changing the discount rate, the Fed affects the willingness of banks to borrow reserves from the Federal Reserve. Reducing the discount rate usually confirms an easier monetary policy, while increasing the discount rate usually confirms tighter money.

4. Most important, by buying or selling government securities (called open market operations), the Fed supplies banks with additional reserves or takes away some of their reserves. Fed buying increases bank reserves (easier money), while Fed selling decreases reserves (tighter money).

5. Open market operations are not conducted in Washington but at the Federal Reserve Bank of New York. Repos and reverse repos have become much more important than outright purchases and sales in recent years.

6. By changing bank reserves and thereby the money supply, the Fed alters people's liquidity and, it is hoped, their spending on goods and services, which in turn helps determine GDP, the level of unemployment, and the rate of inflation.

QUESTIONS

20.1 If banks did not legally have to hold any required reserves at all, would monetary policy still be able to function?

20.2 What is meant by a penalty discount rate? Is that what we have in the United States?

20.3 Does the discount rate usually provide a good early warning signal of Federal Reserve policy intentions?

20.4 How does the account manager decide whether to buy or sell securities in open market operations?

20.5 What is meant by a Federal Reserve repurchase agreement?

20.6 *Discussion question:* Does the Federal Reserve have enough policy tools at its command to do a good job of controlling the money supply? Should Congress give it additional policy instruments—such as direct control over consumer credit or over interest rates on credit cards?

CHAPTER 21

Understanding Movements in Bank Reserves

Adding and subtracting bank reserves are simple matters when all that's needed are pluses and minuses on textbook T-accounts. But in the real world simple T-accounts are replaced by complicated balance sheets that frequently seem to hide the truth. To understand the specific factors influencing bank reserves, we must look at the balance sheet of the Federal Reserve.

In the previous chapter we noted that both open market operations and lending at the discount window can change the volume of bank reserves and, therefore, the potential level of the money supply. Not surprisingly, we will see that both open market operations and discounting show up in specific items on the Fed's balance sheet. But there are other entries on the Fed's balance sheet that can offset or exacerbate these movements in reserves. Some are not even under the discretionary control of the Federal Reserve. Thus we have to examine the Fed's balance sheet to help explain why the central bank sometimes has difficulty controlling total bank reserves.

As if this weren't sufficiently complicated, it is also true that activities of the U.S. Treasury can add or absorb bank reserves. It is therefore necessary to expand the determinants of bank reserves beyond the Fed's balance sheet to get the entire picture. This expanded view goes by the rather imposing name of the **bank (or depository institutions) reserve equation.** In fact, it is nothing more than a tally sheet of the sources and uses of reserves. Nevertheless, it is so useful for monitoring trends in reserves that it is often billed as the fundamental framework of monetary control.

In the first two sections of this chapter we present the Fed's balance sheet and the monetary accounts of the U.S. Treasury. We use T-accounts to show how the specific items influence reserves. In the next two sections we combine these balance sheets into the reserve equation and show how it can be used to monitor Federal Reserve policies.

TABLE 21.1   The Federal Reserve's Balance Sheet (mid-1995; in billions of dollars)

Assets		Liabilities & capital accounts	
Gold certificates (including special drawing rights)	$19.0	Federal Reserve notes outstanding	$382.8
Coin	0.4	Bank deposits (reserves)	26.3
Loans	0.2	U.S. Treasury deposits	8.2
U.S. govt. and agency securities			
Owned outright	372.4	Foreign and other deposits	0.5
Held under repurchase agreements	2.8		
Items in process of collection	4.3	Deferred credit items	4.0
		Miscellaneous liabilities and	
Other assets	35.7	capital accounts	13.0
	$434.8		$434.8

Source: Federal Reserve Bulletin.

THE FED'S BALANCE SHEET

Table 21.1 is the somewhat simplified balance sheet of the Federal Reserve system in mid-1995.[1] Each of the items on both the assets and the liabilities sides deserves some explanation, since each of them reflects something that has an effect on reserves.

The general proof of that last statement—that every item on the Fed's balance sheet has an effect on reserves—is so obvious it's easy to overlook. So here it is:

1. By definition, on *any* balance sheet, total assets = total liabilities (including net worth or "capital accounts").

2. With respect to the Fed, its total liabilities include reserves—they are "bank deposits" in the Fed plus that part of "Federal Reserve notes outstanding" which is in bank vaults.

3. Therefore, bank reserves must equal total Federal Reserve assets minus all other Federal Reserve liabilities (and capital accounts) besides bank reserves.

From this accounting gem, it is clear that anything affecting a Fed asset or a Fed liability has to alter reserves *unless it is offset somewhere else in the balance sheet.* If total Fed assets rise, for example, and there are no changes in

[1] If you look in the back of the *Federal Reserve Bulletin*, you will find the Fed's balance sheet in a table labeled "Federal Reserve Banks: Condition and Federal Reserve Note Statements."

"other liabilities," then reserves have to rise. Or if Fed liabilities other than reserves rise, and no asset changes, then reserves have to fall. It all follows from the fundamental accounting identity: total assets = total liabilities plus capital accounts.

To understand the mechanics underlying the process, it will be useful to examine more closely each of the major items on the Fed's balance sheet. We will see exactly how increases in each of the Fed's assets expand bank reserves and how increases in "other liabilities" decrease bank reserves. We can then isolate the uncontrollable items that complicate the Fed's influence over reserves.

1. *Gold certificates (including special drawing rights),* equal to $19.0 billion in Table 21.1, are Federal Reserve assets that arise in connection with U.S. Treasury gold purchases, regardless of whether the gold is purchased from abroad or from domestic mines. Say the U.S. Treasury buys $100 million of newly mined gold from the Get Rich Quick Mining Company in Dodge City, Kansas. The Treasury pays for the gold with a check drawn on its deposit in the Federal Reserve; the Get Rich Quick Mining Company deposits the check in its local commercial bank, which sends it to the Fed for collection, and as a result bank reserves rise by $100 million, as we see in the following T-accounts:

T-Accounts for a Treasury Purchase of Gold

U.S. Treasury		Federal Reserve		Commercial Bank	
A	**L**	**A**	**L**	**A**	**L**
Gold + $100			Dep. of commercial bank + $100	Dep. in FRB + $100	Dep. of mining co.
Dep. in FRB − 100			Dep. of Treas. − 100		+ $100

So far, this illustrates that if a Fed liability other than bank reserves falls, and there are no offsetting entries, then bank reserves must rise. But when gold is involved, that is not the end of the story. The Treasury has used up part of its checking account balance at the Fed. To replenish it, the Treasury issues to the Fed a "gold certificate" (a claim on the gold) equal in value to the dollar amount of gold purchased, and the Fed in exchange credits the Treasury's deposit account by a similar amount, as follows:

T-Accounts for Treasury Issuance of Gold Certificates

U.S. Treasury		Federal Reserve	
A	**L**	**A**	**L**
Dep. in FRB + $100	Gold certif. outstanding + $100	Gold certif. + $100	Dep. of Treas. + $100

In this latter transaction, Federal Reserve assets (namely, gold certificates) have risen but reserves are not affected, because a liability other than reserves (namely, Treasury deposits) has risen simultaneously.[2] However, the net result of both of these transactions is still an increase in bank reserves. (A gold *sale* by the Treasury would *reduce* bank reserves, with all the above entries being the same except opposite in sign.)[3]

2. *Coin* on the asset side of the Federal Reserve balance sheet consists of coins and bills issued by the U.S. Treasury (a liability of the Treasury) that the Fed happens to have in its vaults (equal to $0.4 billion in Table 21.1). Mostly it consists of coins. If some bank sends a truckload of pennies to the Fed, cash goes up on the asset side of the Federal Reserve's balance sheet and that bank's reserves go up on the liability side.

3. *Loans* (or bank borrowings), totaling $0.2 billion in Table 21.1, have been examined in detail via T-accounts in the last chapter. When banks borrow from the Fed the banks' reserves rise, and when they repay such debts their reserves decline.

4. *U.S. government and agency[4] securities* are acquired by the Fed when it engages in open market operations, as we saw in the T-accounts of the last chapter. When the Fed buys securities, bank reserves expand; when the Fed sells securities, bank reserves contract. Table 21.1 shows that in mid-1995, $372.4 billion of securities were held outright and none were held as part of repurchase agreements (more on this toward the end of the chapter).

5. *Items in process of collection* on the asset side of the Fed's balance sheet is an entry that arises in the course of clearing checks. The entry "deferred credit items" on the liabilities side is generated by the same process. Although each of these entries is rather obscure, the difference between them—"float"— is well known and has often caused serious short-term disruptions in bank reserves. A somewhat detailed treatment, therefore, is worthwhile.

Let's take a specific example. Say you have an account in the Safe & Sound National Bank and you see in the local newspaper that for only $100 you can get an antique spittoon and bedpan (matching set, last one left, accept no substitutes!). So you rush downtown and are lucky enough to get them, paying the $100 by check. The store has its checking account at the Last Laugh National Bank, in a neighboring town. It deposits your check in Last Laugh, which sends it in to the Fed for collection.

---

[2] As you can see, this step is nothing more than a sterile bookkeeping operation since this "monetization of gold" comes *after* the gold stock has already affected bank reserves. In fact, some gold purchases are not "monetized" by the Treasury (no gold certificates are issued for them), and yet they affect bank reserves just the same.

[3] Special drawing rights (SDRs) constitute $8 billion of the $19 billion in Table 21.1. SDRs result from international monetary arrangements made in recent years. They are a supplement to gold in international finance, and an increase in U.S. holdings of SDRs affects bank reserves exactly the same as an inflow of gold.

[4] Agency issues are securities of government-sponsored institutions, such as the Federal Home Loan Banks and the Federal National Mortgage Association. Agency obligations account for only about $4 billion of the $372 billion in Table 21.1.

So far so good, and indeed we saw all this before in Chapter 19. But in reality things are just a bit more complicated. Back in Chapter 19 we said that the Fed would simply add $100 to the Last Laugh Bank's deposit in the Fed, deduct that amount from your Safe & Sound Bank's reserve account, and that would be that. Although the end results are accurate enough, the mechanics are not quite that simple, as the T-account below indicates:

T-Accounts for Federal Reserve Float

Federal Reserve Bank

	A		L	
(a)	Items in process of collection: Safe & Sound Bank	+ $100	Deferred credit items: Last Laugh Bank	+ $100
(b)			Deferred credit items: Last Laugh Bank	− 100
			Bank deposits: Last Laugh Bank	+ 100
(c)	Items in process of collection: Safe & Sound Bank	− 100	Bank deposits: Safe & Sound Bank	− 100

When the Fed receives your check from Last Laugh, it doesn't *immediately* credit Last Laugh's reserve account and reduce Safe & Sound's reserve account. What it does is give Last Laugh "deferred credit," meaning that Last Laugh's reserve account will be credited in due course, according to a prearranged time schedule. At the same time it considers the check "in process of collection" from Safe & Sound. Thus the first pair of entries, labeled (a), in the Fed's T-account.

Next step: After a day or two, depending on the time schedule, Last Laugh will formally receive an addition to its reserve account—the pair of entries labeled (b) above. Notice that, for the moment, *after* step (b) but *before* step (c), "items in process of collection" on the Federal Reserve's balance sheet exceeds "deferred credit items" by $100. This $100 difference is known as Federal Reserve **float,** and it adds to total bank reserves because it means that one bank's reserves have been increased, but so far no other bank's reserves have been reduced.

Finally, when the check is actually collected from Safe & Sound, then Safe & Sound's reserve account will be reduced, which is step (c). At that time, "items in process of collection" will also decline, and both float and total reserves will fall by $100, returning to their original amounts.

Float—the difference on the Fed's balance sheet between the asset "items in process of collection" and the liability "deferred credit items"—arises because many checks are not collected within the time period established for crediting the reserves of banks depositing checks with the Fed. According to the time schedule now in use, all checks must be credited to a depositing bank's reserve account no later than two days after they are received by the Fed.

With respect to its effect on bank reserves, adding $0.3 billion in mid-1995 according to Table 21.1, the importance of float is not so much that it exists but that it fluctuates considerably. Float usually rises when bad weather grounds planes and causes delays in the mails, since this interferes with the delivery of checks en route for collection. A rise in Federal Reserve float increases total bank reserves, but such gains are temporary since subsequent declines in float reduce reserves.

6. *Other Federal Reserve assets*, totaling $35.7 billion in mid-1995, consists primarily of securities denominated in foreign currencies. As shown in the T-accounts of the last chapter (also see footnote 6), whenever the Federal Reserve buys any security there is an increase in reserves and whenever the Federal Reserve sells there is a decrease in reserves. Purchases and sales of foreign securities usually occur in connection with foreign exchange operations of the Fed.[5]

7. *Federal Reserve notes outstanding* are most of our $1, $2, $5, $10, and $20 bills (and so on up the ladder), an asset to those of us who are fortunate enough to have any. But to the Fed they are just another liability, totaling $382.8 billion in Table 21.1. When your local bank finds itself running short of currency, it cashes a check at its regional Federal Reserve bank, and the Fed sends an armored car to deliver some more tens and twenties. This is recorded as shown in the following:[6]

T-Accounts for Shipment of Currency from Fed to Banks

Federal Reserve Bank		Commercial Bank	
A	**L**	**A**	**L**
	F.R. notes outstanding + $100	Cash in vault + $100	
	Dep. of bank − 100	Dep. in FRB − 100	

When commercial banks or thrift institutions ship currency back to the Fed, of course, the entries are the same but opposite in sign. Which means

---

[5] On the Fed's balance sheet, the sum of bank borrowing, U.S. government and agency securities, float and other assets is often referred to as *Federal Reserve credit.*

[6] What if the Fed includes in its shipment some Treasury-issued coin or some Treasury-issued $5 or $10 bills? To the extent that this occurs, then instead of the Fed liability "Federal Reserve notes outstanding" rising, what happens is that the Fed asset "coin" falls. In *either* case, bank deposits at the Fed fall.

that when the Fed receives an inflow of Federal Reserve notes, its assets do not rise; instead, its Federal Reserve note liabilities decline, because there are fewer Federal Reserve notes *outstanding*. (Federal Reserve notes in the possession of the Federal Reserve are just so much paper. If they are frayed or worn, they are burned; if they are still serviceable, they are stored awaiting the day when banks will want them again.)

So when the item "Federal Reserve notes outstanding" rises, bank deposits at the Fed fall, and vice versa. But these transactions—shipments of currency back and forth between depository institutions and the Federal Reserve banks—do not in themselves alter bank reserves. They just exchange one kind of reserve (a deposit at the Fed) for another (cash in vault). However, if the *public* decides to hold more currency—perhaps because Christmas is approaching and people need more coins and bills to spend—then bank reserves fall dollar for dollar with the currency drain:

T-Accounts for Public Holding More Currency

Commercial Bank		Public	
A	**L**	**A**	**L**
Cash in vault − $100	Demand deposits − $100	Demand deposits − $100	
		Currency + 100	

When currency is returned to the banking system, as in the weeks after the Christmas season ends, then bank reserves rise dollar for dollar with the currency reflow. The T-accounts are the same as above, but opposite in sign. If the currency is then shipped back to the Fed, banks are merely exchanging reserves in the form of currency for reserves in the form of deposits at the Fed.

8. *U.S. Treasury deposits*, amounting to $8.2 billion in Table 21.1, are just what the name implies: deposits of the Treasury held in the Federal Reserve banks. The Treasury keeps most of its working balances in "tax and loan accounts" at many commercial banks throughout the country. This is where tax payments and the receipts from bond sales are initially deposited. But when the Treasury wants to spend the money, it first shifts its funds to a Federal Reserve bank and then writes a check on its balance at the Fed. The Treasury can shift its balances from commercial banks to the Fed prior to making payments by writing a check on its balance at commercial banks and giving the check to the Fed.[7] As a result, Treasury deposits at the Fed rise and bank reserves fall:

---

[7] The Treasury's balances are actually shifted by electronic instructions wired to banks, not by writing paper checks.

T-Accounts for Shift in Treasury Balances from Banks to Fed

U.S. Treasury		Federal Reserve Bank		Commercial Banks	
A	L	A	L	A	L
Dep. in comm. bank − $100			Comm. bank dep. − $100	Dep. in FRB − $100	Dep. of Treasury − $100
Dep. in FRB + 100			Treasury dep. + 100		

However, when the Treasury actually spends the funds, then its deposits at the Fed fall and reserves rise again. Say the Treasury spends $100 on paper clips. It pays a supplier of paper clips with a check drawn on its balance at the Fed, the supplier deposits the check in his or her local commercial bank, the bank sends it in to the Fed, and—*voilà!*—as Treasury deposits at the Fed decline, bank reserves are increased:

T-Accounts for Treasury Spending

U.S. Treasury		Federal Reserve Bank		Commercial Banks	
A	L	A	L	A	L
Dep. in FRB − $100			Comm. bank dep. + $100	Dep. in FRB + $100	Demand dep. + $100
Paper clips + 100			Treasury dep. − 100		

This completes our analysis of bank reserves and the balance sheet of the Federal Reserve. In addition, however, many transactions of the U.S. Treasury also affect bank reserves. Some of these transactions we have already discussed, but they bear repeating from the independent viewpoint of the Treasury; others—like the issuance of Treasury currency—have not yet been taken into account. Let's turn to the Treasury's influence on bank reserves. In the appendix to this chapter we describe the somewhat broader issue of how the Treasury finances government spending and how that affects reserves and money supply.

THE U.S. TREASURY'S MONETARY ACCOUNTS

First of all, strictly speaking, it is the Treasury, not the Fed, that officially buys and sells gold on behalf of the government. As we have seen, after it buys some gold, the Treasury usually issues an equal amount of gold certificates (a Treasury liability) and hands them to the Fed (for whom they are an asset), so that the Treasury can replenish its deposit account at the Fed. However, as the T-accounts at the beginning of this chapter show, it is really the gold purchase that increases bank reserves, not the subsequent issue of gold certificates. Since gold, per se, does not appear on the balance sheet of the Fed, we had to talk about the gold certificates while we were confining ourselves to the Fed's balance sheet. But now that we are bringing the Treasury explicitly into the picture, we can go right to the heart of the matter: When the Treasury buys gold, bank reserves rise, and when the Treasury sells gold, bank reserves fall.[8]

A second aspect of Treasury operations that affects bank reserves is changes in the Treasury's deposits at the Federal Reserve banks. Since we have just seen the T-accounts illustrating this process, there is no need to repeat them.

Finally, we have to take account of the fact that the Treasury also issues a small amount of our currency, including all of our coins. Actually, the Bureau of Engraving and Printing operates the printing presses for bills (this is not the same thing as the Government Printing Office, although for all practical purposes maybe there isn't much difference), and the Bureau of the Mint manufactures the coins in three coin factories that are located in Denver, Philadelphia, and San Francisco. Both of these bureaus are departments of the U.S. Treasury.

The impacts on bank reserves of changes in Treasury currency outstanding are the same as the effects of Federal Reserve notes. Thus the T-accounts presented above apply here as well. The reason is straightforward: There is no difference between currency that is in the form of Federal Reserve notes and currency (such as U.S. notes or silver certificates) that is issued by the U.S. Treasury. Regardless of who issued it, all coin and bills in bank vaults count as reserves. Thus when the public decides it wants to hold more currency—because a trip to the supermarket calls for a fifty-dollar bill rather than a twenty—then bank reserves fall dollar for dollar with the drain of currency out of bank vaults into the purses of the public. It doesn't matter whether the currency leaving the banks is in the form of Federal Reserve notes or Treasury-issued money. And conversely, when the public redeposits its change—nickels, quarters, and a few dollar bills—back in the banking system, bank reserves rise dollar for dollar with the currency reflow regardless of the type of currency being redeposited.

THE BANK RESERVE EQUATION

We have now become acquainted with all the factors that affect depository institutions' reserves, and we can put them together in a full and complete "bank (or depository institutions) reserve equation." The reserve equation is

---

[8] You can confirm the ultimate significance of gold rather than gold certificates by noting that if you were to consolidate the balance sheets of the Treasury and the Fed, gold certificates would cancel each other—since they are a liability of the Treasury and an asset of the Fed—leaving only the gold itself.

TABLE 21.2   The Bank Reserve Equation (mid-1995; in billions of dollars)

Factors Supplying Reserves:

Federal reserve credit:	
U.S. govt. and agency securities	$375.2
Loans	0.2
Float	0.3
Miscellaneous Federal Reserve assets	35.7
Gold stock (including SDRs)	19.0
Treasury currency outstanding	23.3
	453.7

Less Factors Absorbing Reserves:

Currency in circulation (i.e., outside the Federal Reserve, the Treasury, and bank vaults)	371.0
Treasury cash holdings	0.3
Treasury, foreign, and other deposits with Federal Reserve banks	8.7
Miscellaneous Federal Reserve liabilities and capital	13.0
	393.0

Equals Bank Reserves:

Bank deposits with Federal Reserve banks	24.1
Currency in bank vaults	36.6
	$60.7

Source: Federal Reserve Bulletin.

nothing more than a record of the sources and uses of bank reserves. It is simple to visualize conceptually, as long as you remember the accounting at the beginning of this chapter plus the fact that Treasury currency in bank vaults also counts as reserves.

Thus, bank reserves = total Fed assets *minus* all Fed liabilities and capital accounts *other than* those Fed liabilities that constitute bank reserves *plus* Treasury currency in bank vaults. This is usually put more formally, as in Table 21.2, but it amounts to the same thing.[9]

Table 21.2, the bank reserve equation, looks a bit different from Table 21.1, the Fed's balance sheet, but the differences are really minor. "Factors supplying reserves" in Table 21.2 correspond roughly to Federal Reserve assets, and "factors absorbing reserves" correspond roughly to Federal Reserve liabilities; in addition Treasury-issued currency is also incorporated into Table 21.2.

In brief, Table 21.2, the bank reserve equation, is the consolidation of the Fed's balance sheet with the Treasury's monetary accounts. Some of the altered items are as follows. Federal Reserve float in Table 21.2 is the excess of

---

[9] You can find the reserve equation in the *Federal Reserve Bulletin* in a table titled "Reserves of Depository Institutions and Reserve Bank Credit."

the Fed asset from Table 21.1 called "items in process of collection" over the Fed liability "deferred credit items." Gold stock in Table 21.2 replaces gold certificates in Table 21.1 because it is the purchase or sale of the gold itself that affects bank reserves, not the issuance of gold certificates. "Treasury currency outstanding" in Table 21.2, the only really new item as compared with Table 21.1, includes all Treasury-issued currency regardless of who holds it; that is, it is counted here whether it is held by the public, commercial banks, the Federal Reserve, or even the Treasury itself. Thus under the "Factors absorbing reserves" in Table 21.2 we include both Federal Reserve notes and Treasury-issued currency as part of "Currency in circulation." This item absorbs reserves because it refers to currency held by the nonbank public—that is, currency that is *outside* the Federal Reserve, the Treasury, and the banks. Currency of any sort that may be held by the Treasury is included in the figure for "Treasury cash holdings."[10]

Thus, the reserve equation presented in Table 21.2 is really just a formal summary of the sources and uses of reserves. As we mentioned in the beginning of the chapter, other factors besides Federal Reserve decisions can influence bank reserves. The Federal Reserve, in fact, uses the reserve equation to keep track of these forces. Let's see how it is done.

PUTTING IT ALL TO USE

In Chapter 19, when we related demand deposits to reserves via the deposit expansion multiplier, we assumed that the Fed could control the volume of reserves by judicious use of open market operations. But from the reserve equation, we see that this is no simple matter. Movements in float, gold, Treasury deposits, currency in circulation, and the other items listed in Table 21.2 have to be forecast and monitored. Only then can Fed open market operations hope to come close to the mark in terms of bank reserves.

---

[10] For more detail on the consolidation of the Fed's balance sheet with the Treasury's monetary accounts, see Arthur W. Samansky, *Statfacts: Understanding Federal Reserve Statistical Reports* (Federal Reserve Bank of New York, 1981). To *really* understand the accounting nitty-gritty you'll have to dig into the *Supplement to Banking and Monetary Statistics*, Section 10 (Board of Governors of the Federal Reserve System, 1962), pp. 1–13.

We should mention that in the bank reserve equation as published by the Federal Reserve, the term *currency in circulation* is defined as Federal Reserve notes and Treasury-issued currency held outside the Fed and the Treasury. In other words, currency in circulation as published by the Fed includes currency held by the banks as well as by the nonbank public. From the point of view of bank reserves this is illogical, as the Fed itself admits, because currency in circulation is treated as an entry that reduces reserves in the reserve equation, but in fact currency held by banks is part of their reserves. The Fed's published version winds up with reserves held in the form of deposits at the Fed, to which vault cash is added back in to get total reserves. Our version amends the reserve equation, redefining *currency in circulation* as only currency held by the nonbank public. The Fed's reasons for its form of presentation are mainly historical, as explained on page 7 of the *Supplement to Banking and Monetary Statistics* mentioned above.

OFF THE RECORD

Why Did Germany Let the Pound Sink in September 1992?

According to its 1979 charter, all members of the European Monetary System (EMS) were committed to supporting agreed-upon ranges for exchange rates between member countries. For example, in 1992 both Germany and the United Kingdom were required to intervene in the foreign exchange market if the exchange rate between the British pound and the German mark threatened to move outside of the following boundaries: 2.778 marks per pound and 3.132 marks per pound. More specifically, if the mark strengthened and the pound weakened to the point that fewer than 2.778 marks were needed to buy one British pound, then both the Bundesbank and the Bank of England were obligated to buy British pounds with marks to prop up the value of the pound. As we explained in Chapter 10's discussion of fixed-exchange rates, buying pounds with marks could be a problem for the Bank of England since the Bank of England has a limited quantity of marks; only the Bundesbank can print marks.

Thus in September 1992, as the pound weakened to 2.778 marks, the main burden of supporting the British pound fell to the Bundesbank. But when the Bundesbank buys pounds in the foreign exchange market it also means that it is buying British securities. As we just saw in the text, the purchase of anything by a central bank increases its assets and hence increases reserves to the domestic banking system. Thus, the Bundesbank's purchase of pounds meant that Germany's banking system winds up with more reserves. This is exactly what the Bundesbank could not tolerate in September 1992 because it was still fighting the inflationary effects of the 1990 unification of East and West Germany. More bank reserves would mean faster German money supply growth and more potential inflation.

This was the explanation offered by most commentators on September 15, 1992, for why the Bundesbank (and the Bank of England) stopped supporting the British pound, forcing the United Kingdom to withdraw from the EMS. Of course, the Bundesbank could have neutralized (sterilized) the effect on bank reserves of its purchases of pounds by conducting defensive open market operations—by selling bonds in the open market.* So why, after all is said and done, did the Bundesbank abandon its support of the British pound? Perhaps the Bundesbank just didn't believe the pound was worth 2.778 marks. And they were right, because the pound promptly declined to under 2.40 pounds soon after the United Kingdom withdrew from the EMS.

*When intervention in the foreign exchange market is offset by defensive open market operations it is called sterilizing the foreign exchange intervention.

For example, if reserves are rising because of a temporary decline in the Treasury's balance at the Fed, open market sales may be used to offset such influences. Open market operations of this type are called *defensive* because they are aimed at defending a target level of reserves from "outside" influences. Another example would be increased Fed purchases of government securities in December to offset seasonal increases in currency holdings by the public. December may mean mirth and cheer to most of us, but to practitioners of the dismal science in the Fed's trading room it means "pump up reserves to offset currency drains."

In The News

The Holiday Shopping Season Causes Defensive Open Market Operations

Prices Rise on Fed Purchases Treasury Issues Benefit

Prices of Treasury securities rose slightly yesterday, with all of the gains coming in the second half of the day after the Federal Reserve bought an undisclosed amount of notes and bonds for its own account.

The Fed's purchases were welcomed by securities dealers, as it was an opportunity to them to reduce their holdings from the auction last week of $16 billion of 3-, 10- and 30-year Treasury issues. After declining by about one-third point prior to the Fed's 1:30 P.M. purchases, all three of the new issues closed with price gains of one-third to one-fourth point.

Economists and Fed watchers said the purchases were not a sign of any change in monetary policy, although the effect of the Fed's purchases will be to increase the supply of reserves in the banking system during the week beginning tomorrow, and put downward pressure on short-term interest rates.

"The Fed's purchases are viewed as a purely technical operation, and did not signal any change in monetary policy," said Albert Gross, senior vice president and economist at Refco Inc., a securities firm.

The Fed typically buys Treasury securities at this time of year, analysts explained, because it needs to provide the banking system with enough reserves to offset the funds drained from the banking system as the public increases its holdings of cash during the holiday shopping season. "They did the same thing this time last year," Mr. Gross said.

Source: Michael Quint, *New York Times*

As we saw in the previous chapter, there is a special type of open market operation that particularly lends itself to defensive uses, namely, buying government securities under repurchase agreements. Under a repo the Fed buys the security with an agreement that the seller will repurchase it on a specific date in the future (usually within seven days). As Table 21.1 indicates, $2.8 billion of government securities were held under repurchase agreements in mid-1995. A reverse repo is designed to sop up reserves over a short interval; that is, the Fed sells government securities and agrees to repurchase them at some date in the near future (this is also called a *matched sale-purchase agreement*).

By their very nature, repos and reverse repos are *temporary* injections or deletions of reserves and might be interpreted as always being in the defensive category. But that would be falling into the well-known pitfall of identifying a specific Federal Reserve action with a particular objective. Never, never, never do that. Once you do, the Fed denies it and then makes sure you're wrong by going out and doing just the opposite—using repos and reverse repos continuously to change reserves over a long period of time. In fact, in terms of volume of transactions, repos and reverses far outweigh outright purchases and sales.[11]

Which brings us to the *dynamic* variety of open market operations. Dynamic open market operations are aimed at either increasing or decreasing the overall level of bank lending capacity by changing the level of bank reserves. Even here, the volume of purchases or sales must be undertaken in light of movements in all the other factors in Table 21.2 that affect bank reserves. For example, if an increase in reserves is desired and the reserve equation shows that all other sources of reserves will be expanding, open market purchases may be completely unnecessary.

FOCUSING ON THE MONETARY BASE

There has been considerable controversy over what specific variable the Fed should try to control in order to regulate the money supply. The control variable is often called an *operating target* because it is the *immediate* objective of open market operations. We can show how to change Table 21.2 to focus on one popular alternative to bank reserves—the **monetary base.**

The definition of the monetary base is total reserves plus currency held by the nonbank public. The reserve equation can be altered quite easily to focus on the monetary base; just shift "Currency in circulation" down to the bottom of Table 21.2, to join bank reserves. Then, in terms of Table 21.2, what we would have is (Federal Reserve credit + gold stock + Treasury currency outstanding) *less* (Treasury cash holdings + Treasury, foreign, and other deposits with the Federal Reserve banks + miscellaneous Federal Reserve liabilities and capital) = the monetary base (i.e., bank reserves + currency in circulation).

The pros and cons of alternative targets in helping the Fed achieve its goals will be explored in the next chapter.

SUMMARY

1. The main message of this chapter is that hitting a particular target for bank reserves takes a fair amount of work, planning, and coordination. The Fed cannot simply assume that changes in its holdings of government securities will translate into reserve movements. The Fed must look at all the sources and uses of bank reserves.

---

[11] Table 21.1 shows that the volume of securities *held* under repurchase agreements at any given time can be very small, even though the number and volume of repo transactions are enormous. The reason all transactions don't appear on the Fed's balance sheet is that repos expire and the securities are returned to their original owner.

2. We showed via T-accounts that all the items on the Federal Reserve's balance sheet, as well as some U.S. Treasury operations, have a potential effect on bank reserves. A convenient summary of the influences on bank reserves is provided by the bank reserve equation.

3. The most important item supplying reserves is U.S. government and agency securities held by the Federal Reserve. The largest alternative use of reserves is currency in circulation. Thus open market operations and the public's use of currency are key factors in the reserve equation. This does not mean, however, that the other entries can be ignored. Whenever these other factors fluctuate without warning, as float often does, there can be significant complications for the Federal Reserve.

4. The Fed maintains a particular target level of reserves by conducting *defensive* open market operations to offset movement in other items in the bank reserve equation. *Dynamic* open market operations are used to alter the overall level of reserves.

QUESTIONS

21.1 When the U.S. Treasury buys some gold, it doesn't cost the Treasury anything. How is this possible?

21.2 When the public withdraws currency from banks, bank reserves fall. Is the money supply directly and immediately affected by this transaction?

21.3 What is Federal Reserve float and how does it come into existence?

21.4 What is the difference between the monetary base and bank reserves?

21.5 What must the Fed usually do during December to keep monetary policy unchanged?

21.6 *Discussion question:* Explain why someone who knows what the bank reserve equation is will not necessarily pay very much for information about whether the Fed is buying or selling government securities, even if it were legal to puchase such information.

Monetary Effects of Treasury Financing

When the government spends more than it receives in tax receipts, it runs a deficit. The easiest way to finance the deficit is to print up the money and pay the bills. But that option is not open to the U.S. Treasury. Congress in its infinite wisdom conferred on the Federal Reserve system, not the U.S. Treasury, the responsibility of printing money and regulating its supply. What the Treasury *can* do is to sell bonds and use the proceeds to meet its obligations. In the process of carrying out its debt finance and spending functions the Treasury complicates the Fed's job of controlling the money supply. In this appendix we examine alternative procedures for financing government spending in general, and a deficit in particular, and explore their effects on bank reserves and the money supply.

It is useful to identify five ways available to the U.S. Treasury to finance government spending: (1) collecting taxes; (2) borrowing from the nonbank public; (3) borrowing from the banking system; (4) borrowing from the Federal Reserve; and (5) printing money. Each method has somewhat different implications for bank reserves and the money supply.

1. *Taxation.* Assume the government decides to spend an additional $100 million on water pollution control equipment and chooses to raise the money by levying taxes on everyone who takes more than one shower a week. As the taxes are collected, they are initially deposited in the Treasury's accounts at commercial banks throughout the country, called the Treasury's "tax and loan accounts." Thus demand deposits (DD) at commercial banks are transferred from private ownership to Treasury ownership. The relevant T-accounts look as follows:

T-Accounts for Taxation

U.S. Treasury		Fed. Res. Banks		Commercial Banks		Nonbank Public	
A	L	A	L	A	L	A	L
DD in comm. bank +$100					DD of public −$100	DD in comm. bank −$100	Taxes due − 100
Taxes due − 100					DD of Treasury + 100		

As a result of this step alone, the money supply falls by $100 million, since government deposits are not counted in the money supply.[1] Bank reserves, however, are not yet affected.

Before the Treasury spends the money, it usually shifts the funds from the commercial banks to a Federal Reserve bank so that it can make its disbursements from a central account. *This* step depletes total bank reserves by $100 million, as the following T-accounts show:

T-Accounts for Shifting Funds to the Federal Reserve

U.S. Treasury		Fed. Res. Banks		Commercial Banks		Nonbank Public	
A	L	A	L	A	L	A	L
DD in comm. bank −$100		Comm. bank dep. −$100	Dep. in FRB −$100	DD of Treasury −$100			
DD in FRB + 100		Treasury deposit + 100					

Having raised $100 million and shifted it from commercial banks to its account at the Federal Reserve, the government now spends it. When expenditures are made, the Treasury writes checks on its demand deposit account at the Fed to pay its suppliers. The suppliers deposit the checks in commercial banks, and the banks send the checks to the Fed for collection. The result is that the money supply *and* bank reserves go back up by $100 million:

---

[1]The money supply is defined as currency and demand deposits owned by the nonbank public, because it is designed to measure the *private* sector's liquidity.

T-Accounts for Government Spending

U.S. Treasury		Fed. Res. Banks		Commercial Banks		Nonbank Public	
A	**L**	**A**	**L**	**A**	**L**	**A**	**L**
DD in FRB −$100			Comm. bank deposit +$100	Dep. in FRB +$100	DD of public +$100	DD in comm. bank +$100	
Goods & services + 100			Treasury deposit − 100			Goods & services − 100	

By combining all the effects of acquiring funds via taxation and spending the money, we see that after all is said and done neither the money supply nor bank reserves are altered. The money supply falls when taxes are collected, but it rises by the same amount when the government spends the proceeds. Similarly, bank reserves at first decline when the Treasury shifts the funds to its account at the Fed, but then reserves are replenished when the Treasury spends the money.[2]

2. *Borrowing from the nonbank public.* Alternatively, suppose that people who take more than one shower a week amount to a substantial voting bloc (not very likely), and Congress decides it would be the better part of valor not to tax them. Instead, the Treasury finances its spending—now *deficit* spending—by borrowing, specifically by selling bonds to the nonbank public. The T-accounts are the same as for taxation, except that this time people get a government security for their money instead of a receipt saying they paid their taxes:

T-Accounts for Borrowing from Nonbank Public

U.S. Treasury		Fed. Res. Banks		Commercial Banks		Nonbank Public	
A	**L**	**A**	**L**	**A**	**L**	**A**	**L**
DD in comm. bank +$100	Debt outst. +$100				DD of public −$100 DD of Treasury + 100	DD in comm. bank −$100 Govt. bond + 100	

---

[2]While the end result of the government's taxation and spending is to leave the money supply and bank reserves unchanged, the *timing* of the shifting of funds from tax and loan accounts at commercial banks to the Fed, and of subsequent expenditures, creates reserve management problems for the Federal Reserve, as we saw in the chapter.

Again, as with taxation, this action reduces the money supply, transferring it from the pockets of the public to the accounts of the Treasury. When the Treasury shifts the funds to the Fed, bank reserves are also reduced, but as soon as the government spends the funds the money supply and bank reserves bounce back to where they had been originally (we have already seen the T-accounts for both of these transactions). The net result of the government's financing its deficit by borrowing from the nonbank public: Just as in the case of taxation, after all is said and done neither the money supply nor bank reserves are altered (although this time the public does wind up with more government bonds than before).

3. *Borrowing from the banking system.* The Treasury need not sell its securities to the nonbank public. Instead of the public, the commercial banks might buy them. The ultimate net effects would depend on whether the commercial banks (a) are fully loaned up to begin with (zero excess reserves), or (b) have excess reserves. To see why this is so, let's examine each possibility.

a. If the banking system is fully loaned up to begin with, it will not be able to buy the government securities unless it first disposes of other assets. This is because the purchase of the government securities would result in an increase in Treasury demand deposits at commercial banks, against which required reserves must be held. To release sufficient reserves, private deposits have to be reduced by a corresponding amount. By selling $100 million of other investments to the public, the banks can now buy $100 million of government bonds from the Treasury. The relevant T-accounts are as follows, with the banks' liquidation of other investments above the dashed line and their subsequent acquisition of government securities below it:

T-Accounts for Borrowing from the Commercial Banking System
(zero excess reserves)

U.S. Treasury		Fed. Res. Banks		Commercial Banks		Nonbank Public	
A	L	A	L	A	L	A	L
				"Other" securities − $100	DD of public − $100	DD in comm. bank − $100	
						"Other" securities + 100	
DD in comm. banks + $100	Debt outst. + $100			Govt. bonds + $100	DD of Treasury + $100		

In effect, the banks have sold some of their other securities and replaced them with new government bonds. These transactions, by themselves, decrease the money supply, because the public has fewer deposits. (Although the

Treasury has gained deposits, Treasury deposits are not counted as part of the money supply, as we pointed out earlier.) But, as in our previous cases, the Treasury shifts its funds to its account at the Fed and then spends them. When the funds are spent, the public's money holdings are restored to their former level. Once again, there is no change in either total bank reserves or the money supply.

b. On the other hand, if banks have excess reserves to begin with, then they will not have to dispose of other securities or call in loans in order to make room for their new purchases of Treasury securities. Thus that part of the T-accounts above the dashed line will not be necessary. The banks buy the Treasury bonds and open up a new deposit for the Treasury; the Treasury shifts its balance to the Fed and then spends the money. When the Treasury spends, individuals receive brand-new demand deposits (for which they give up goods and services). Under these circumstances, financing a deficit by borrowing from the banks *increases the money supply* by as much as the deficit (although it does not alter total bank reserves).[3]

4. *Borrowing from the Federal Reserve.* The Treasury could borrow the money directly from the Federal Reserve:

T-Accounts for Borrowing from the Federal Reserve

U.S. Treasury		Fed. Res. Banks		Commercial Banks		Nonbank Public	
A	**L**	**A**	**L**	**A**	**L**	**A**	**L**
DD in FRB + $100	Debt outst. + $100	Govt. bonds + $100	Treasury deposit + $100				

In this case the Treasury does not have to shift the funds to the Federal Reserve before spending them; they are already there. Also, this method of borrowing reduces neither the money supply nor bank reserves. The government merely sells some bonds to the Fed, gets a checking account for them, and is in business.[4] Painlessly. Thus, when the Treasury *spends* the funds, the public winds up with more demand deposits and the banks with more reserves, as our T-accounts for government spending (which we saw earlier)

---

[3]Note that since banks had excess reserves to begin with, the money supply could have increased without any Treasury financing. The only role played by the deficit in this case is to induce banks to lend out all excess reserves.

[4]In ordinary circumstances, the Treasury does not sell securities *directly* to the Federal Reserve. Rather, newly issued bonds are brought to market through auctions held by the Federal Reserve banks. The Fed acts as the Treasury's fiscal agent, distributing issues to ultimate buyers, as we saw in Chapter 8. Securities dealers buy newly issued Treasury obligations for their inventory, to distribute to their customers. Our example in the text would be implemented if the Federal Reserve bought back some of these newly issued securities from dealers.

show. Indeed, this way of financing a deficit has the same effects as printing greenbacks. It increases both the money supply *and* bank reserves.

5. *Printing money.* Instead of borrowing from the Federal Reserve, the Treasury could (if Congress permitted it) do the same thing by printing currency, depositing it with the Fed, and then spending from its account at the Fed. The T-accounts for printing money are almost the same as those for borrowing from the Fed; the only difference is that the Treasury would give the Fed noninterest-bearing currency instead of interest-bearing bonds. But that is a meaningless difference, since at the end of the year the Federal Reserve turns over most of its interest earnings to the Treasury anyway:

T-Accounts for Printing Money

U.S. Treasury		Fed. Res. Banks		Commercial Banks		Nonbank Public	
A	L	A	L	A	L	A	L
DD in FRB + $100	Currency outst. + $100	Treasury currency + $100	Treasury deposit + $100				

In the end, therefore, it is the Federal Reserve and not the Treasury that decides whether or not deficit financing will be tantamount to printing money. If the Fed buys the securities, new money is created; if the Fed refuses and the public buys the securities, no additional cash is created.

Obviously the deficit has to be financed in some way. We have just seen, however, that it is the Federal Reserve's prerogative to decide how much will come in the form of new money and how much must come through the ultimate sale of bonds to the public. The Fed can make the Treasury's financing job easier by **monetizing the debt,** that is, by buying some of the newly issued securities. But turning new debt into new money may not be in the public interest. After all, in the long run, just about everyone agrees that excess money creation is inflationary (see Chapter 2). In fact, the reason Congress created the Federal Reserve was to keep the printing press away from the Treasury: to make deficit spending costly by forcing the Treasury to pay interest on its debt. In that way the inflationary consequences of a deficit would be mitigated.

When the Federal Reserve monetizes the debt by buying Treasury securities, it lets the Treasury get to the printing presses through the back door. And that's precisely what Congress doesn't want (or at least says it doesn't). Thus there is frequent tension between the Treasury and the Federal Reserve that sometimes spills over into a public spat. So keep your eyes and ears open for some fancy fisticuffs between the secretary of the Treasury and the chairman of the Federal Reserve.

CHAPTER **22**

Monetary Policy Strategy

In Chapter 20 we spoke of the important daily conference call between the manager of the System Open Market Account, located in the Federal Reserve Bank of New York, a member of the board of governors in Washington, D.C., and a president of one of the other Federal Reserve banks currently serving on the Federal Open Market Committee (FOMC). We have never listened in to what is said during one of these calls, but we can make a pretty good guess at the conversation, much as sports commentators are able to surmise what is said at those all-important conferences between the quarterback and coach in the closing minutes of a game, or the even more important huddle between a pitcher and catcher with runners on second and third and none out. It probably goes something like this:

OPERATOR: Kansas City and Washington are standing by, New York. Will you deposit $3.35, please?

NEW YORK: You mean it's our turn to pay? Hold on a minute, operator, we don't seem to have enough change here.

WASHINGTON: This is Chairman Greenspan on the line.

NEW YORK: Sorry, there's no one here by that name.

WASHINGTON: No, you don't seem to understand, I'm Chairman Alan Greenspan and I want. . . .

NEW YORK: Hello, Alan. Sorry for the mix-up, but we've just hired a few Ph.D.s to answer the phones, and they haven't gotten the hang of it quite yet. Anyway, we have a problem here. Reserves are increasing but so is the federal funds rate.

WASHINGTON: I know the problem but our staff thinks that reserve demand should slacken and the funds rate will decline soon.

KANSAS CITY: Hello? Hello? When do we start?

As we said, we've never listened in, but the implication that the Federal Reserve may not be able to get exactly what it wants contains an element of truth. In the preceding chapters we described who runs the Federal Reserve, the tools at the Fed's disposal, and the way Federal Reserve actions influence bank reserves and the money supply. It is now time to put it all together to see how well the Federal Reserve meets its obligations. First, we take a more detailed look at the formulation of policy through what is known as the Federal Open Market Committee's directive. Second, we review the reasons for the particular game plan that is followed. We then analyze the linkages between Fed operating targets and its ultimate economic objectives. At the end we should have a pretty good idea of why the Fed sometimes has trouble hitting its targets.

THE FOMC DIRECTIVE

The FOMC meets in Washington about once every five or six weeks. At the beginning of each meeting the staff of the FOMC, comprising economists from the Board of Governors and the district Federal Reserve banks, presents a review of recent economic and financial developments—what is happening to prices, unemployment, the balance of payments, interest rates, money supply, bank credit, and so on. Projections are also made for the months ahead. The meeting then proceeds to a discussion among the committee members; each expresses his or her views on the current economic and financial scene and proposes appropriate monetary policies.

The FOMC directive, embodying the committee's decision on the direction of monetary policy until the next meeting, is voted on toward the end of each meeting, with dissents recorded for posterity. If economic conditions are proceeding as expected the month before and the current stance of monetary policy is still appropriate, the previous directive may remain unaltered. If conditions have changed, the directive is modified accordingly.

In recent years, the FOMC directive has usually contained five or six paragraphs. The first few review economic and financial developments, including the behavior of real output, inflation, monetary aggregates, and interest rates. The third or fourth paragraph then turns to a general qualitative statement of current policy goals. For example, at the meeting on February 1, 1995, the goals of the FOMC were set forth as follows:

> The Federal Open Market Committee seeks monetary and financial conditions that will foster price stability and promote sustainable growth in output.

Immediately following this general statement, the directive presents long-run target ranges for the monetary aggregates that are thought to be consistent with the broadly stated goals. At the meeting of February 1, 1995, the annual targets were stated as follows:

In furtherance of these objectives the committee . . . established ranges for growth of M2 and M3 of 1 to 5 percent and 0 to 4 percent respectively, measured from the fourth quarter of 1994 to the fourth quarter of 1995. The monitoring range for growth of total domestic nonfinancial debt was lowered to 3 to 7 percent for the year.

There are four important points to recognize in this statement. First, the goals for the monetary aggregates are stated for M2 and M3, rather than for a single measure of money supply. Second, the target growth ranges for each monetary aggregate are rather broad. Third, just for good measure, the committee throws in a target for total debt growth during the year. Finally, because of uncertainties associated with behavior of transactions balances, the committee does not set a specific target for M1. These sources of flexibility reflect the Fed's uncertainty over the precise linkages between the aggregates and the ultimate goals of policy.

The last order of business in the FOMC directive is to specify the immediate prescription for implementing these longer-run objectives. In that February 1995 meeting, the immediate targets were described:

In the implementation of policy for the immediate future, the Committee seeks to increase somewhat the existing degree of pressure on reserve positions. . . . The contemplated reserve conditions are expected to be consistent with moderate growth in M2 and M3 over the coming months.

Two points are worth emphasizing here. First, while the Fed's immediate objectives are still couched in terms of money supply growth, the directive also mentions reserve targets to implement the desired growth in the aggregates. Thus in outlining its so-called **operating targets,** the committee states that behavior of reserve aggregates should be consistent with targeted money supply growth. The numerical reserve targets are not disclosed publicly with any greater precision.

The second point is that although the FOMC directive clearly emphasizes the monetary and reserve aggregates, in practice, the Fed operates on interest rates. This message is delivered quite clearly in the press release that since 1994 has accompanied every FOMC meeting in which a policy shift has occurred. For example, in our favorite February 1, 1995, meeting, the Fed's press release at the close of the meeting indicated that "interest rates in the reserve market" would be increased by one-half percent. Although this is consistent with the directive's call for increased pressure on reserve positions, the Fed is much more precise about its interest rate targets than its reserve targets.

In the next section we illustrate how the Fed conceptualizes its monetary policy plan. We then turn to a series of subissues concerning the detailed implementation of that plan that demonstrates, among other things, that the Fed cannot have it both ways: It must choose to target either reserves or interest rates. For now, rates seem to rule the roost, despite all the lip service given to the monetary aggregates.

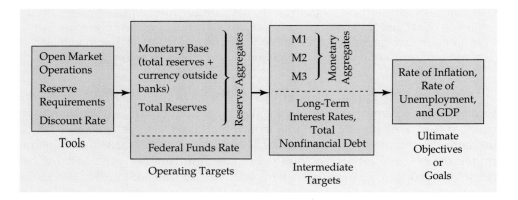

FIGURE 22.1   The Fed's game plan.

THE FED'S STRATEGY

Figure 22.1 summarizes the FOMC game plan as described in the directive. Notice that the ultimate goals are separated from the Fed's tools by two sets of intervening targets. These operating and intermediate targets are more immediately responsive to Federal Reserve actions than the ultimate goals regarding inflation and unemployment. Fed officials believe that by formulating these intermediate steps they can more easily and quickly judge whether they are on the right track than if they waited for a signal from overall economic activity. As long as the linkages work reasonably well, it makes sense to use the intervening objectives.

The Fed's plan is established in the following way (more or less). First, it decides upon the rate of growth in GDP that is most consistent with the rates of inflation and unemployment that are the objectives for the year. Then the Fed sets the range for monetary growth that is expected to generate the target rate of GDP growth. Given that desired range for monetary growth—say 5 to 8 percent for M2—the Fed then sets a target range for the growth in reserves—say 3 to 5 percent—which will produce the desired rate of growth in money.

The key to the usefulness of both operating and intermediate targets rests with the connecting linkages on each side: from the tools to operating targets, from the operating targets to the intermediate targets, and finally to the ultimate goals. Each of these steps has been fraught with controversy in the past. In fact, in each of the target boxes in Figure 22.1 there is a list of alternative objectives that can be pursued. The operating targets include alternative reserve measures, while the intermediate targets list the conventional measures of money supply. In addition, below the dashed line in each of the boxes, the interest rate and credit alternatives to the reserve and monetary aggregates are included as well. The advantages and disadvantages of these alternatives will be discussed in the next three sections.

Reserves Versus the Federal Funds Rate

The Federal Reserve has had trouble deciding which operating target it prefers:

1. Before October 1979, the Fed favored the federal funds rate as its main operating target.

2. However, the 1970s were marked by double-digit inflation. In an effort to gain better control over the money supply and thereby tame inflation, in October of 1979 the Fed switched its operating target from the federal funds rate to the reserve aggregates. Reserve aggregates were the dominant operating target from October 1979 until mid-1982.

3. By mid-1982, double-digit inflation had been replaced by double-digit unemployment as the major economic problem in the country. The Fed reacted by trying to lower interest rates in an effort to stimulate more borrowing and spending. It thus started to pay attention again to the federal funds rate as an operating target. The Fed still pays considerable lip service to the reserve aggregates, as the February 1995 directive indicates, but since mid-1982 the federal funds rate has been the dominant operating target.

This approach gives rise to a problem, however, inasmuch as there is often an irreconcilable conflict between federal funds rate targets and reserve targets. To understand why this is so, let's review how the federal funds market works.

Federal funds are immediately available funds that are lent, usually on an overnight basis, between banks. Thus, in the simplest case, if Banc One (Columbus, Ohio) needs funds and Fifth Third (Cincinnati) has an excess, then Fifth Third can "sell" funds to Banc One for immediate delivery. The exchange of funds is accomplished by a transfer of reserves on the books of the Federal Reserve system today and will be returned tomorrow, unless another transaction is made. The interest rate charged on such overnight transactions is called the federal funds rate. Alternatively, an overnight transfer of reserves can occur with a sale of government securities and an agreement to repurchase them (at a higher price, to reflect the interest rate) on the following day. As explained in Chapter 8, this so-called "repo" market is closely linked with the federal funds market, since they are both sources of overnight funds. In the rest of this discussion, we use the federal funds rate to represent all sources of overnight funds.

Because the federal funds market is an immediate source of reserves to individual banks, the federal funds rate directly reflects Federal Reserve pressure on bank reserves. The best way to see this is through a simple model of the supply of and demand for bank reserves. Figure 22.2 shows reserves on the horizontal axis and the federal funds rate on the vertical axis. The supply of reserves is described by a vertical line at $50 billion in Figure 22.2, reflecting the Fed's control over reserves via the bank reserve equation of Chapter 21. The demand for reserves, labeled *D* in Figure 22.2, is negatively related to the federal funds rate for two reasons. First, banks hold required reserves

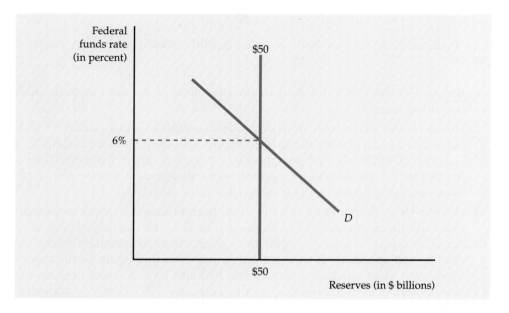

FIGURE 22.2   The supply and demand for reserves produces the equilibrium federal fund rate.

against checking accounts, and the demand for checking accounts, especially by businesses, declines as the overnight interest rate goes up. Because business firms economize on their checking account balances to take advantage of higher overnight rates, banks, in turn, are able to demand fewer reserves as the federal funds rate increases. A second reason that the demand for reserves declines as the overnight rate rises is that banks pare their excess reserves to the bare minimum (see the appendix to Chapter 19) when the opportunity cost, the federal funds rate, increases.

Figure 22.2 shows the equilibrium federal funds rate at 6 percent, the intersection point of the supply and demand curves. If the rate were lower than 6 percent the demand for reserves would be greater than the supply made available by the Fed, banks would try to borrow reserves in the federal funds market (like Banc One above), and that would drive up the federal funds rate. If the rate were higher than 6 percent, the Fed's supply of reserves would be greater than the demand, banks would try to lend reserves in the federal funds market, and that would drive down the federal funds rate. Only at the intersection of the supply and demand curves for reserves will there be a balance between borrowers and lenders in the federal funds market, hence no upward or downward pressure on the funds rate.

At first glance, our simple model suggests that targeting the federal funds rate or a particular level for bank reserves produces exactly the same result. For example, Figure 22.3 shows that if the FOMC decides to increase the supply of reserves from $50 to $55 billion, this implies that the funds rate will decline from 6 percent to 5 percent. Alternatively, the FOMC can specify that the

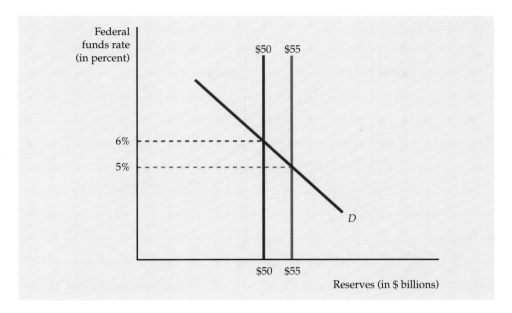

FIGURE 22.3   An increased supply of reserves lowers the federal funds rate; a lower federal funds rate requires an increased supply of reserves.

federal funds rate should decline from 6 percent to 5 percent, which means that the supply of reserves must increase from $50 to $55 billion. Because the level of reserves and the federal funds rate are uniquely related in Figures 22.2 and 22.3, it makes no difference which one the FOMC focuses on.

But the world is more complicated than Figures 22.2 and 22.3 suggest. At the very least, the demand curve for reserves fluctuates with the pace of economic activity. At any given federal funds rate the demand for reserves will be higher if economic activity requires larger checking account balances and the demand for reserves will be lower if economic activity requires smaller checking account balances. Figure 22.4 illustrates this with three demand curves labeled *D*, *D'*, and *D''*, with *D'* representing demand for reserves with the faster pace of economic activity, *D''* with the slower pace of economic activity, and demand curve *D* representing the average pace of economic activity. Now the FOMC has a problem. If it targets reserves of $50 billion (see panel (a) in Figure 22.4), it will have to live with a federal funds rate that fluctuates between 5½ percent and 6½ percent, depending on the pace of the economy. On the other hand, specifying that the federal funds rate must be 6 percent (see panel (b) in Figure 22.4) means that the FOMC must permit reserves to increase to $52 billion if reserves demand is *D'* and must permit reserves to decline to $48 billion if reserves demand is *D''*. In other words, targeting reserves means that the FOMC must tolerate fluctuations in the federal funds rate because it doesn't really know the exact pace of economic activity. Similarly, targeting the federal funds rate means that the FOMC must accept variability in the level of bank reserves.

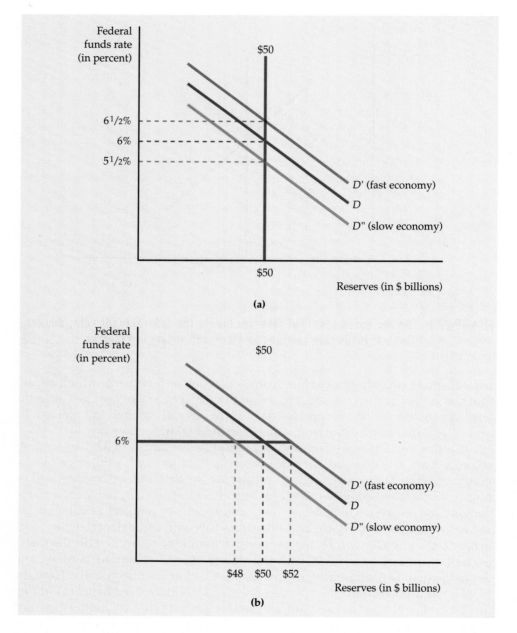

Under the current operating procedures, the FOMC chooses a specific federal funds rate target, say 6 percent, and adjusts bank reserves to hit that objective. The problem with this approach is that the Fed cannot simultaneously guarantee $50 billion in reserves even if that level of reserves is necessary to hit the longer-term money supply targets specified in the FOMC's directive. For example, if the pace of economic activity produces demand curve D' in Figure 22.4, then $52 billion in reserves will be needed to hit the 6 percent funds rate target, and that may generate higher monetary aggregates than the FOMC's directive indicates is consistent with its longer-run objectives. Of course, the FOMC can adjust its federal funds rate target once it recognizes the faster pace of economic activity, but that means monetary policy is delaying its battle to control economic activity.

Why doesn't the Fed specify its objectives in terms of reserves? The answer to that comes in two parts. First, our discussion just suggested that a shortcoming of focusing on the federal funds rate is that it may not produce the level of reserves needed to hit a particular monetary aggregate. But that does not mean that targeting reserves will automatically generate a specific monetary aggregate. Second, there is less certainty nowadays that the monetary aggregates are reliably linked to economic activity. Thus, the Fed may not lose very much by keeping overnight interest rates relatively stable because whatever volatility is introduced to reserves and the monetary aggregates is not worth worrying about. We elaborate on these points in the next two sections.

Linking Reserves and the Monetary Aggregates

Even if the Fed were to choose reserves as its sole operating target, there would still be the task of implementing the next linkage—between reserves and the various measures of money supply as intermediate targets. There are two major problems in this area. First, the Federal Reserve is not able to control total reserves precisely. As we saw in Chapter 20, for example, banks can borrow reserves from their regional Federal Reserve banks. Discounting adds to reserves just as open market operations do, but discounting is at the individual bank's initiative rather than the Fed's. The Fed discourages such borrowing either by raising the discount rate or, after some demonstrated abuse, by refusing to lend to the offending bank. In the meantime, however, the level of reserves goes off track.

The second problem in the linkage between a reserve target and the intermediate money supply objective has to do with instability in the multiplier relationship between reserves and deposits. The discussion in the appendix to Chapter 19 showed that only in the simplest case were demand deposits equal to total reserves multiplied by the inverse of the required reserves ratio. There were numerous complications in the relationship. For example, if banks don't make loans based on all of their reserves, but instead hold some reserves in excess of what is required, the multiple expansion in deposits is cut short. Moreover, to the extent that the public withdraws currency from the banking system, the process of deposit creation with a given level of initial reserves is short-circuited; banks lose reserves dollar for dollar when currency leaks out of the system (see the T-accounts in Chapter 21). Finally, if M1 is the intermediate target, the reserve multiplier may be relatively simple, while if M2 or M3 is the preferred monetary aggregate (for reasons given in the next section), the reserve multiplier linkage will be much more complicated, and will depend, in part, on the mix of deposits with different reserve requirements.

To summarize: A given level of total reserves can support more or less deposits depending on (1) the mix of deposits with different reserve requirements, (2) the propensity of banks to hold excess reserves, and (3) the leakage of reserves into currency. In fact, the currency drain has led some critics to propose that the Fed focus its attention on the sum of reserves plus currency—the monetary base.

How Useful Are the Monetary Aggregates?

Suppose the Fed can have its way with reserves (as it probably can) and suppose the reserve multipliers are sufficiently stable to generate a particular money supply target (which may also be reasonable). The problem confronting the Federal Reserve is that it is no longer so sure that the monetary aggregates are reliably linked to economic activity. In the good old days this linkage used to be a straightforward proposition. M1, consisting of currency and checking accounts, was widely acknowledged as the best measure of immediately spendable funds. Hence the linkage between M1 and GDP was accepted as the most reliable relationship between a financial aggregate and spending, and M1 was considered the best monetary target. But the growth of savings deposits and time deposits as close substitutes for checking accounts forced many economists to reconsider their devotion to the M1 definition. As far back as the mid-1950s, John Gurley and Edward Shaw, Keynesian economists at Stanford, popularized the notion that the deposit liabilities of savings and loan associations, savings banks, and other financial intermediaries must be monitored in order to get an accurate fix on whether monetary policy was expansionary or contractionary. In recent years, with still newer financial instruments on the scene, the Gurley-Shaw argument would favor either the M2 or M3 definition of money. For somewhat different reasons, Milton Friedman has long advocated that both commercial bank demand deposits and savings deposits paint a better monetary picture than M1 alone. It is not surprising, therefore, that M1 has disappeared entirely from the FOMC's directive.

Now let's turn to the credit side of the picture. The intermediate targets listed below the dashed line in Figure 22.1 include both long-term interest rates and a credit aggregate. In fact, this second item under the dashed line in the intermediate target box is something of a hybrid: It is an aggregate—*total nonfinancial debt*—but it is a *credit*, rather than monetary, aggregate. While its precise orientation is, therefore, somewhat in doubt, its lineage is unambiguous: Ben Friedman, a prominent Keynesian from Harvard (and no relationship to Milton except that they are both first-rate economists) has long ad-

---

GOING OUT ON A LIMB

Rip Van Winkle Rips Fed

When Rip Van Winkle emerged from his twenty-year slumber in 1995, he felt right at home with the conduct of monetary policy. Back in 1975 the Fed had been using the federal funds rate as the primary monetary lever, just as it had ever since the early 1950s; in 1995, the Fed also focused on the federal funds rate. Some deference was surely paid to the monetary aggregates under Chairman Alan Greenspan in the 1990s, but similar lip service was accorded to the aggregates during the 1970s as well. Monetary policy was delicately inched up and down via changes in the federal funds rate in the 1990s, just as in the good old days. Rip felt right at home.

What had happened to the lessons of the Volcker years, when focusing on the money supply and permitting wide gyrations in the federal funds rate to the tune of supply and demand was the only way to keep inflationary pressures under control? Rip Van Winkle could hardly tell that Chairman Paul Volcker had tamed the inflation tiger with the money supply. Indeed, he wasn't even sure who Paul Volcker was.

Once he had heard the full story, however, Rip could hardly believe the current state of affairs. Although inflation hadn't been a problem for a number of years, that situation could easily change—and inflation could accelerate once it got started. Moreover, focusing on the money supply was just as important in averting deep recession as in fighting inflation. After all, the 1930s had illustrated how a collapse in the money supply could contribute to a collapse in the overall economy.

Convinced that the Fed had forgotten the painful lessons, Rip sent letters to just about everyone in Congress to force the Fed to follow the wisdom of the money supply targets. But no one would take him seriously. After all, it was he who had been asleep for twenty years, not the Fed. Or was it the other way around?

---

vocated the use of credit aggregates to supplement the purely monetary side of the picture.

Since interest rates seem to be the focal point of the Fed's procedures let's review the advantages and disadvantages of the alternate intermediate targets. The main virtue of using a monetary aggregate target is that it helps to insulate automatically the overall level of economic activity from unanticipated shifts in business or consumer spending. Thus if the Fed's ultimate goal is some level of economic activity that reflects its desired inflation/unemployment combination, pursuit of a monetary aggregate target will help to sustain that level of economic activity from uncontrolled shifts in spending. Let's look at an example of how the monetary aggregate target automatically provides stability compared with the interest rate target.

Suppose there is a burst of unanticipated investment spending because business firms expect higher sales next year. As long as reserves and the money supply are kept on target, the jump in business demand for credit to carry out the spending plans will cause interest rates to rise. This will force others to rethink their spending plans, thereby mitigating the inflationary burst in the economy. But if the Fed had targeted on interest rates, then the unanticipated jump in interest rates would require the Fed to push them back

OFF THE RECORD

Should the Fed Target Exchange Rates?

During the first half of the 1990s, newspaper headlines frequently lamented the declining value of the dollar in foreign exchange markets. On the other hand, during the first half of the 1980s newspaper headlines complained about the rising value of the dollar. In 1985 a meeting of the United States, Great Britain, Japan, Germany, and France (known as the G-5), took place at the Plaza Hotel in New York. The resulting Plaza Accord announced that these nations would intervene in the foreign exchange markets to lower the international value of the dollar in order to spur U.S. exports and reduce U.S. imports. Thus 1985 marks the formal beginning of the "managed floating" exchange rate regime mentioned in Chapter 10. Many commentators, in fact, view the decline in the international value of the dollar after the Plaza Accord as an indication that central banks can manipulate exchange rates.

During 1995 the value of the dollar declined from about 100 Japanese yen to the dollar at the beginning of the year to a low of 80 Japanese yen to the dollar by mid-April. This sharp depreciation of the dollar occurred despite frequent purchases of the dollar and sales of yen on the foreign exchange market by both the Bank of Japan and the Federal Reserve. What happened to the power of the central banks?

The main lesson is that central banks can manipulate foreign exchange rates only if they follow underlying monetary policies designed to reinforce the stated objectives. Thus in 1985 short-term interest rates in the United States declined, convincing investors to sell dollars and buy other currencies to earn higher returns. Thus the value of the dollar declined because it was supposed to. The problem during the first half of 1995 was that many participants in the foreign exchange markets viewed U.S. monetary policy as too easy and Japanese monetary policy as too tight. Both central banks were focusing their interest rate policies primarily on domestic considerations. Thus global investors shunned the United States in favor of Japan, producing an excess demand for Japanese yen and an excess supply of dollars, generating a depreciating dollar despite central bank intervention.

Only time will tell whether these conditions are reversed. But the lesson is clear: A central bank's interest rate policies can satisfy either domestic targets or international targets. It is fortuitous when both objectives can be implemented simultaneously. When there is a conflict, most central banks focus on domestic targets.

down again. Thus the Fed would be led to supply more bank reserves to support a higher level of money supply, thereby sanctioning an inflationary jump in economic activity. Interest rate targets, then, are poor protection against unanticipated changes in real spending decisions.

An interest rate target would, however, insulate the economy from unanticipated shifts in the demand for money. For example, if people reduced their cash balances and started to spend more, the declining demand for money would push down interest rates. The Fed would cut back on reserves and money supply if it were following an interest rate target, which is precisely what it should do to keep spending from accelerating. In this case, the interest rate target insulates the economy from unanticipated shifts in money demand.

Whether the Federal Reserve should focus on money supply or on interest rates depends, therefore, on whether money demand is more or less predictable

<u>TABLE 22.1</u>   **Growth Ranges for Monetary and Debt Aggregates (in percent)**

	1993	1994	1995
Aggregate			
M2	1–5	1–5	1–5
M3	0–4	0–4	0–4
Debt	4–8	4–8	3–7

than business investment plans. Congress is sufficiently impressed by the need to focus on the monetary aggregates to require the Federal Reserve to testify regarding its target growth rates for various measures of the money supply. Let's see how the Fed has performed in recent years.

THE FED'S TRACK RECORD

Table 22.1 records the Federal Reserve's target ranges for the monetary aggregates as reported to Congress from 1993 to 1995. The numbers seem to suggest that virtually no change in monetary policy occurred during those years. Figure 22.5, on the other hand, shows that the Fed's discount rate and the federal funds rate moved sharply higher, especially during 1994, as the Fed tried

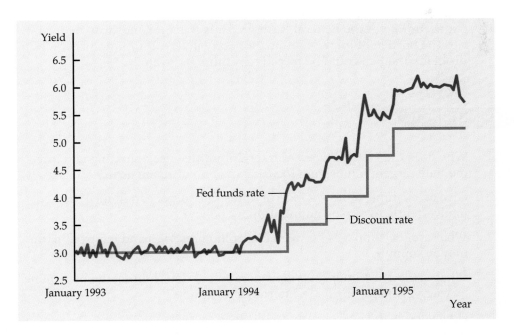

FIGURE 22.5   **The Federal Reserve tightened monetary policy considerably during 1994 according to movements in the federal funds and discount rates.**

to rein in emerging inflationary pressure associated with the rapid expansion in economic activity.

Quite obviously, the monetary aggregate targets do not describe what the Fed wanted to do during 1994. Every time the Fed raised short-term interest rates during that year, the stated objective was to restrain inflationary pressures. And thus far the Fed has succeeded in keeping inflation under control. Under such conditions, Congress will permit the Fed to pay mere lip service to the monetary aggregates. But if inflation surfaces as a problem, Congress might very well force the Fed to mend its schizophrenic ways.

SUMMARY

1. The Federal Reserve's strategy for implementing monetary policy is summarized in a directive issued about once every five weeks by the Federal Open Market Committee. Operating targets for reserves are set so that the Fed can best hit its intermediate money supply targets. Despite this apparent emphasis on the aggregates, the federal funds rate is the focal point of Fed policy.

2. Focusing on reserves as an operating target requires that the Fed tolerate some variability in the federal funds rate, while targeting the funds rate means that it must accept volatility in reserves.

3. The monetary aggregates are no longer reliably linked to economic activity, according to the Federal Reserve. Thus it is the funds rate that carries the burden of implementing monetary policy. If inflation becomes a problem, the Fed could be forced to rethink its strategy.

QUESTIONS

22.1 Why does the Federal Open Market Committee use operating and intermediate targets rather than focusing only on ultimate goals?

22.2 Give an example of how a federal funds rate target can induce the Fed inadvertently to pursue an inflationary policy?

22.3 What are the slippages between controlling reserves and controlling the money supply?

22.4 What is the most important consideration in determining the best monetary aggregate for the Fed's intermediate targets?

22.5 How good is the Fed's record in hitting its targets?

22.6 *Discussion question:* Is the conduct of monetary policy more art than science, or vice versa?

PART VI

Monetary Theory

CHAPTER 23

The Classical Foundations

One of the first questions we asked in this book was: What is the "right" amount of money? The answer depends on how money influences the economy, which monetary theorists have wondered about ever since economic science emerged from moral philosophy. The origins of monetary theory lie in the **classical economics** of Adam Smith (1723–1790) and his friends. The two cornerstones of the classical system are **Say's law,** which deals with interest rates, employment, and production, and the quantity theory, which explains the role of money. Both concepts are essential to the proper functioning of the classical world; both were attacked by John Maynard Keynes when the classical wisdom was supposedly laid to rest in 1936; and both were resurrected and refined by modern monetarists and new classical macoreconomists during the 1970s, 1980s, and 1990s. Obviously, this is the place to start.

To understand the role of money according to classical thinking, we must first see what determines **gross domestic product, GDP** (the total value of goods and services domestically produced). We start, therefore, with Say's law of markets and work our way toward the somewhat more famous **quantity theory of money.** Along the way we'll stop to consider some specifics: classical interest theory as well as the demand for money.

SAY'S LAW

Jean Baptiste Say (1767–1832) summarized the classical school's income and employment theory with the now familiar maxim, "Supply creates its own demand." Dubbed Say's law, it meant quite simply that the economy could never suffer from underemployment or succumb to Thomas Malthus' fear of underconsumption. Total spending (demand) would always be sufficient to justify production at full employment (supply). Let's spend some time making clear why this is the case.

Given current technology, potential output of the economy is determined by the size of the labor force available to work with the existing stock of capital goods (plant and equipment). This production function, in technical terms, defines the total supply of goods and services that can be produced. Say argued that production would be at the full employment level, since spending would always be great enough to buy all the goods and services that could be produced. Why? Because of the interplay of market forces, guided by what Adam Smith referred to as an *invisible hand*.

If people who wanted to work couldn't find a job, they would offer their services for less money and would be snapped up by eager entrepreneurs. Entrepreneurs who found it difficult to sell slow-moving items would promptly lower their prices and watch their inventories disappear. Flexible wages and prices would assure that all markets would be cleared, all goods sold, all people employed—except economists, who would have nothing to do, since everything worked just fine without them. The interplay of market forces under the guiding principle of **laissez-faire** (noninterference) would bring about the best of all possible worlds.

To represent classical economics as having an entirely uniform outlook, however, would be unjust to some prominent precursors of modern Keynesian ideas. The Reverend Thomas Malthus (1766–1834) could hardly believe that *he*, a man of the cloth, was unable to see the invisible hand, so he proceeded to launch a sustained and vigorous attack on it. Spurning the microeconomic details, Malthus argued as follows: While the production of goods and services generates *income* in the same amount as total output, there does not seem to be anything to force *spending* to equal total production. Supply might create its own purchasing power (income), but not its own demand (spending). In particular, if people try to save too large a fraction of their income—more than firms want to invest—part of the goods produced will be left unsold, entrepreneurs will cut back their production, and unemployed labor and capital will result. This argument was later refined and formalized by Keynes, as we shall see in the next chapter.[1]

However, the classical economists cannot be disposed of so simply. People save part of their income, but such funds do not disappear. They are borrowed by entrepreneurs to use for capital investment projects. Savers receive interest on their funds, and borrowers are willing to pay, as long as they expect to earn a return on their investment in excess of the rate of interest.

But what made the classical economists so sure that all saving would actually be invested by entrepreneurs? If saving went up, would investment go up by the same amount? In classical economics, the overall level of the *rate of interest* is the key; according to classical theory, interest rates would fluctuate

---

[1] There is a distinction between the accounting identity that income or output equals actual expenditure and the possibility that income may not equal *desired* expenditure. The appendix to this chapter discusses these relationships, which are relevant both for classical and Keynesian economics. Because of the accounting identity between income and output, we use these terms interchangeably throughout the text.

to make entrepreneurs *want to invest* what households *wanted to save*. As is emphasized in the appendix to this chapter, this equality between desired saving and desired investment is sufficient to maintain production at the assumed level—in this case, full employment. The next section explains in greater detail this classical theory of interest rate determination. It is really an elaboration of one of the market mechanisms underlying Say's law.

CLASSICAL INTEREST THEORY

Back in Chapter 4 we described how the overall level of interest rates was determined by the supply of and demand for loanable funds. Classical economists obviously recognize the importance of supply and demand but focus their attention on saving and investment—the two main factors that, in the long run, underlie the supply of and demand for loanable funds. With saving creating a supply of funds and investment generating the demand for funds, classical economists had a firm handle on the forces underlying the level of interest rates. Let's see how classical economists presented this more fundamental approach to interest rate determination in the long run. Note that throughout this discussion as well as in almost all of Part VI, we refer to the interest rate as a proxy for the overall level of rates. Return to Chapter 5 to explore the details on the structure of interest rates.

   Saving, according to classical economics, is a function of the rate of interest. The higher the rate of interest, the more will be saved (see Figure 23.1),

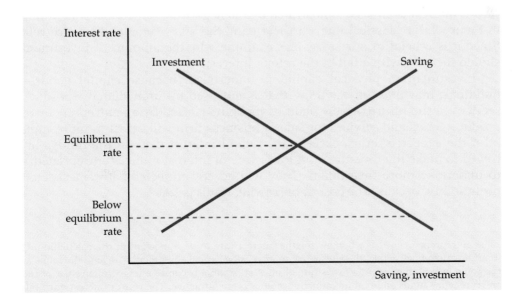

FIGURE 23.1   Classical interest theory.

OFF THE RECORD

Investment Versus Investment

It is obvious from the text that monetary theorists use the word *investment* to mean purchasing resources for production rather than consumption. Throughout Parts I–V of this book, investment referred to purchasing financial assets, such as stocks and bonds, just as the word is used in conversation. From now on, unless indicated otherwise, investment will take on its formal meaning in monetary theory: spending on real resources that generate services in the future.

It is not unusual, by the way, for the same word to have different meanings, even in the same sentence. For example, the well-known warning to children: "Don't go out in the cold without a coat or you will catch a cold." We all recognize (except perhaps for parents) that the two meanings for the word *cold* in that sentence may not have anything to do with each other. Similarly, investment in the sense of people purchasing stocks and bonds may not necessarily mean greater spending by business on plant and equipment. In fact, this distinction is what underlies much of the debate between John Maynard Keynes (see the next chapter) and the classical economists.

since at higher interest rates people will be more willing to forgo present consumption. The rate of interest is an inducement to save, a reward for not giving in to baser instincts for instant gratification by consuming all your income. It does not pay, by the way, to make too much of this classical assumption, because classical interest theory worked just as well if saving did not depend on the interest rate—that is, if saving were a vertical line in Figure 23.1.

As long as investment is a function of the rate of interest, increasing as the rate of interest declines (as illustrated by the negatively sloped investment line in Figure 23.1), classical interest theory and Say's law remain alive and well. Since it is crucial to our story, let's examine why the amount of investment should increase with a fall in the rate of interest.

Investment in physical capital is undertaken because capital goods—buildings, machines, or anything that is not used up immediately—produce services in the future. A new plant or machine is used by an entrepreneur to produce goods and services for sale. A business firm will invest in more capital if the expected return exceeds the rate of interest paid on the funds borrowed to make the investment. A lower rate of interest induces entrepreneurs to undertake more investment. They will accept projects of lower expected profitability, because the cost of borrowing funds is less.[2]

---

[2] The entrepreneur need not borrow for the interest rate to be important in the calculation. If funds are already available, the alternative to increasing capital equipment is to lend the funds at the going rate of interest. At a lower rate of interest, lending becomes a less attractive use of the entrepreneur's funds and real investment becomes more attractive. The rate of interest *must* fall to elicit more investment spending because of our old friend from microeconomics, the law of diminishing returns. More investment means a larger capital stock, and, given the labor force and current technology, there is reduced marginal productivity (profitability).

Figure 23.1 includes a supply of funds curve (people's saving) and a demand for funds curve (entrepreneurs' demand for investment). The rate of interest is in equilibrium (no tendency to change) at the point of intersection between saving and investment, where total saving is equal to total investment: Everyone who wants to borrow funds is able to, and everyone who wants to lend can do so. If the rate of interest were below equilibrium, as shown in Figure 23.1, entrepreneurs would want more funds than savers were ready to provide, and competition would force the interest rate upward. If the rate of interest were above equilibrium, savers would want to lend more funds than entrepreneurs wanted to invest, and competition would force the cost of funds downward.

But things don't usually stay in equilibrium for very long. If people really listened to some of Thomas Malthus' dire predictions of the consequences of unrestrained population growth, they might decide to save more at every rate of interest. The entire saving function would then shift to the right (Figure 23.2). At the old equilibrium interest rate, desired saving now exceeds the amount of investment that entrepreneurs are ready to make. That is precisely what Thomas Malthus said was wrong with the classical system—people would spend too little in the form of consumption, they would save too much (more than entrepreneurs cared to invest), and unemployment would follow.

But not really. The excess of saving over investment puts downward pressure on the rate of interest, as savers try to lend out their funds. As the rate of interest declines, some people will give in to their baser instincts and spend a greater part of their income (saving less and enjoying it more). At the same

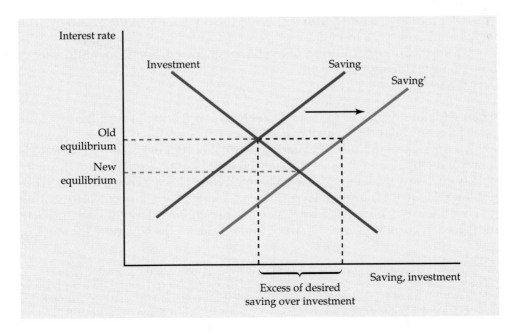

FIGURE 23.2   Increased saving calls forth increased investment.

time, the decline in the rate of interest will encourage business firms to expand their investments. As Figure 23.2 shows, the rate of interest will settle at a lower equilibrium, at which point all that is saved out of current income is still invested by entrepreneurs.

Where in all this does money fit in? The interest rate is influenced in the long run only by the saving of the public (determined by their habits of thriftiness) and by capital investment of entrepreneurs (determined by the productivity of capital). Money plays no role in this area of the classical system. It influences neither employment, the rate of interest, nor production. Real things are determined by real forces. Total goods and services produced and total employment are determined by the supply of capital, the labor force, and existing technology; the interest rate is determined by the thriftiness of the public and the productivity of capital. Money plays no role in the real sector of the economy. Instead it is treated separately—via the second pillar of the classical edifice, the quantity theory—where it determines the price level.

THE QUANTITY THEORY OF MONEY

Money, according to the classicists, is a veil that must be pierced to examine the determinants of real economic activity. Money affects the price level, but nothing else. An increase in the supply of money leads to an increase in the prices of all goods and services, but everything else—most notably the level of real economic activity, the rate of interest, and people's real income—remains unchanged. This conclusion expresses the quantity theory of money. It implies that money is *neutral* with respect to the real sector of the economy. The logic behind this is as follows.

We start with the **equation of exchange,** which is not the quantity theory but simply an identity, a truism:

$$MV = PY \tag{1}$$

where M is the supply of money, V is **velocity** or its rate of turnover, P is the price level, and Y is the level of *real* income.

On the right-hand side of equation (1) total output of goods and services is represented by Y; that is what is produced by labor and capital given the technology currently available. Y is usually referred to as *real* gross domestic product, or real GDP. The price level, P, is an index of the current prices of all goods. When Y is multiplied by P we have the *nominal* level of GDP, or GDP measured in current prices.[3] On the left-hand side of the equation, the stock of

---

[3] Throughout this book when we use the term *GDP* by itself we mean the real value of goods and services produced. The phrase *nominal GDP* is used to distinguish real output from the nominal value. As long as prices remain unchanged, movements in nominal GDP and real GDP are one and the same. When the price level changes, movements in real GDP and nominal GDP differ, as we will see with concrete examples in the rest of this chapter. For a discussion of how price indices are constructed, see any basic text on economics.

money (in dollars) is represented by *M*. When multiplied by its velocity, the number of times such dollars are used in the purchase of goods and services, the product *MV* also equals total spending. The equation of exchange says that total spending (*MV*) equals the value of what is bought (*PY*).

The equation of exchange was originally put forth in a slightly different form. The level of real income on the right-hand side was replaced by *T*, the total level of transactions. The total level of transactions exceeds the level of GDP, because there are many transactions that are excluded from GDP. Purchases and sales of *financial* assets and of *existing* assets—such as stocks and bonds, old homes, and works by the Great Masters, are not part of current production and hence are not included in GDP. When the equation of exchange is written as:

$$MV = PT \qquad (2)$$

the velocity figure on the left-hand side is called *transactions velocity*.

Equation (1) is the most frequently used version of the equation of exchange. It is really the most meaningful approach, since our main concern is with GDP and not with total transactions. Thus all our subsequent discussion will be in terms of equation (1) and the "income" velocity of money. Irving Fisher, the brilliant Yale economist who is unfortunately known for his advice to buy just before the stock market crashed in 1929, was the most eloquent expositor of the equation of exchange as we have just presented it.

The Cambridge Approach

There is still another version of the equation of exchange, however, associated with economists at Cambridge University in England. So before discussing how we progress from the simple identity expressed by equation (1) or (2) to the quantity theory as used by Fisher and other classical economists, let us give equal time to our friends across the Atlantic.

The Cambridge economists viewed the equation of exchange in a slightly different light. Instead of concentrating on the rate of turnover of a given stock of money during the year (its velocity), they concentrated on the fraction of total expenditure that people hold in the form of money. Simple algebraic manipulation of equation (1) produces the Cambridge **cash-balance approach** to the equation of exchange:

$$M = kPY \qquad (3)$$

where *k* is the fraction of spending that people have command over in the form of money balances. Obviously $k = 1/V$, so equations (1) and (3) are equivalent from an algebraic standpoint (for some unknown reason, when the Cambridge economists divided both sides of equation (1) by *V* they changed $1/V$ to the letter *k*). And (3), like its predecessors, is still a truism—an identity that must be true by definition. This latest version does represent a different orientation, however. In fact, equation (3) readily lends itself to interpretation as a **demand for money equation.**

But we are running a bit ahead of ourselves. It is time to convert the equation of exchange, whatever its form, from an algebraic identity—which it has been so far—into an analytical tool. Let's move, in other words, from the *equation of exchange* (an identity) to the *quantity theory of money* (a cause-and-effect hypothesis).

We started this section by saying that the quantity theory implied that increases in the supply of money cause increases in the price level. We can now be even more precise: According to the quantity theory of money, a change in the money supply produces a *proportionate* change in the price level—for example, if the money supply doubles, so does the price level. This cause-and-effect conclusion follows from two basic propositions (a nice word for *assumptions*) of the classical school. First, on the right-hand side of equation (1), $MV = PY$, Y is assumed fixed at full employment (now you know why we started out with Jean Baptiste Say). Second, velocity is assumed to be fixed by the payment habits of the community. If $MV = PY$, and V and Y are assumed to be fixed, then if M doubles it follows that P *must* double. For example, if V and Y are fixed at 4 and 100 respectively, then a supply of money equal to 25 is consistent with a P equal to 1. If M doubles to 50, P must double to 2.

To understand the process involved, we need only recall the discussion in Chapter 2 of how people react to changes in the money supply brought about by central bank operations. Start out in equilibrium, with all people satisfied with the liquidity of their portfolio. Assume the Federal Reserve doubles the money supply. Liquidity rises. If people were formerly satisfied with their liquidity position, now they will try to get rid of their excess money balances by spending more. This increase in the demand for goods and services drives up prices, because total real output cannot expand—it is fixed at the full employment level by virtue of Say's law. If people were in equilibrium before a doubling of M, they will stop trying to spend the increased money balances only after their total expenditures have also doubled. Since real output is fixed, a doubling of total spending must cause prices to double. End result: Money stock held by the public has doubled, nominal GDP has doubled, the price level has doubled, V is the same as before, and so is **real GDP.**

Note carefully that classical economists insist on clearly distinguishing the real versus nominal consequences of anything in general, and money in particular. A change in the money supply leaves the real amount of goods and services produced (real GDP) unchanged, but increases the dollar value of GDP (nominal GDP).

MONEY DEMAND AND THE QUANTITY THEORY

The two versions of the quantity theory, $MV = PY$ and $M = kPY$, are algebraically equivalent and also produce the same cause-and-effect implications for the relationship between money and prices. For explaining the transmission mechanism as we just have, and for what is to come later, the cash-balance version ($M = kPY$) is superior (in keeping with the best British tradition). The cash-balance equation can be interpreted as a demand for money function, as we mentioned above. Assume that $k = \frac{1}{4}$. Then if PY or **nominal GDP** equals $400, this means that people want to hold one-fourth of nominal GDP, or $100, in cash balances; if GDP climbs to $600, the amount of money demanded rises to $150; and if GDP doubles to $800, money demand doubles to $200.

The fraction of nominal GDP that people want to hold in the form of money, k, is determined by many forces. It is essentially a **transactions demand** for money. Thus, since money is used as a medium of exchange, the value of k is influenced by the frequency of receipts and expenditures; if you are paid weekly, you can manage with a smaller daily average cash balance than if you are paid monthly. Second, the ease with which you can buy on credit (the use of credit cards) also influences k by permitting people to reduce the average balance in their checking accounts. Money is also used as a temporary abode of purchasing power—waiting in the wings until you summon it and exercise control over real goods and services. Thus an individual may hold more or less, depending on whether he or she expects to be out of a job for four months or two months of the year. For the community as a whole, so the argument goes, all these factors average out and are fairly stable, hence the public winds up wanting to hold a stable and/or predictable level of money balances.

Looking at the cash-balance version of the quantity theory ($M = kPY$) as a demand for money equation, it is easy to see that the doubling of prices (and hence nominal GDP) produced by a doubling of the money supply follows directly from the equilibrium condition that the amount of money demanded must equal the supply. When M doubles, people have twice as much money as they want to hold (money supply exceeds the amount demanded), given that nothing else has changed. So they start to spend it. They stop spending when they want to hold the increased money supply (when the amount of money demanded grows into equality with the supply). That occurs when nominal GDP has doubled.

It is also possible to look at this new equilibrium position in a slightly different way. Namely, the *real* amount of money that people hold is the same in both the initial and final positions. The real amount of money is given by the actual money supply deflated by the price level, or M/P, where that tells you the amount of real goods and services that is "controlled" by the cash balances people hold. For example, if you hold a $1,000 checking account you control $1,000 worth of goods and services; if you have a $2,000 checking account but the price level has doubled, you still control the same real volume of goods and services.

The cash-balance version of the quantity theory, in fact, emphasizes that people try to fix their real money balances, not the dollar value of their cash holdings. Thus when the supply of money doubles, the public has twice as many *real* balances as it wants, given the old price level and real GDP. People try to get rid of those excess real balances by spending. But since the real output of goods and services is fixed at full employment, only prices respond to the increased demand for goods. Prices will continue to rise until people stop trying to spend those extra real balances. And that happens when they have none left, that is, after prices have doubled so that real balances are back to their original level ($M/P = 2M/2P$ is a famous theorem in Boolean algebra).

AGGREGATE DEMAND AND SUPPLY: A SUMMARY

In keeping with the best traditions of economics, it is useful to summarize the discussion thus far within an aggregate supply/demand framework. This will serve us well later in explaining policy debates in Chapter 27 and will also form the foundation for analyzing inflation.

Figure 23.3 may not look exactly like the supply/demand graph you learned to love in basic economics, but it really is. Price is measured on the vertical axis and quantity is on the horizontal axis. In the macroeconomic framework, price refers to the price level of all goods, P, and quantity refers to the aggregate real output of all goods and services, Y. Since output (or production) and income are one and the same (two ways of measuring GDP—as shown in the appendix to this chapter), we label the horizontal axis income. However, in our discussion we will use the terms *income* and *output* interchangeably.

The supply schedule in Figure 23.3 is a vertical line to represent the classical assumption that the volume of goods and services that can be produced is fixed at full employment (Y_{FE}). In particular, changes in the price level do not influence the supply of goods and services. (We encounter similar vertical

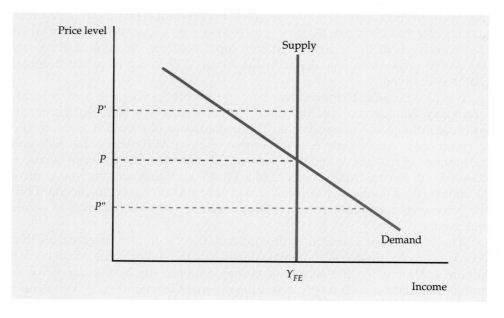

FIGURE 23.3   The equilibrium price level.

supply schedules at the microeconomic level for many commodities in the very short run as well as for things like land in the long run.)

The demand schedule in Figure 23.3 is negatively sloped. While this is the normal shape, the reason is somewhat different in the macroeconomic context. The aggregate demand schedule is drawn for a given level of the money supply (M). And as we have just seen, a given stock of money buys more goods and services with a lower price level. Hence a lower price level means that the amount of goods and services demanded is greater.[4]

The intersection of supply and demand in Figure 23.3 indicates the equilibrium price level. Since the supply of goods is fixed by Say's law, the demand schedule tells us only what price level will clear the market. If the price level were higher than P (as at P' in Figure 23.3), the aggregate demand for goods and services would be too low, and businesses would have to lower prices to sell all their output. If the price level were lower than P (as at P''), the aggregate demand for goods and services would exceed what is available, and businesses would raise prices to ration the existing supply (and to make a handsome profit). Thus P is the equilibrium price level.

Note that price flexibility is the key to the classical school's argument that the level of real output would be at full employment. If the price level in Figure 23.3 were for some reason stuck at P', then aggregate demand for real goods would be below full employment output (Y_{FE}). That's why we said earlier, in our discussion of Say's law, that flexible wages and prices would ensure that all goods would be sold and all labor employed. Now we see clearly that if this weren't the case, aggregate demand for real goods would be too low. Downward rigidity in prices is one of the elements Keynes focused on in analyzing the behavior of economic activity at less than full employment, as we'll see in the next chapter.

Figure 23.4 allows us to identify the demand schedule more precisely. In particular, when there is a shift in the entire demand curve, we see that the price level rises from P to P'. Our discussion in the previous sections showed that increases in the money supply raise the price level. From Figure 23.4 we see that this occurs because higher levels of M increase the aggregate demand for goods and services. In particular, in Figure 23.4 at the old price level, P,

---

[4] Note that the normal microeconomic reasons for demand rising when prices fall are not relevant in the macroeconomic context. First, lower prices usually generate a larger amount demanded because a particular commodity is cheaper and consumers substitute it for other goods. But in the macro framework we are dealing with all goods together, and all prices are falling, hence the "substitution effect" is not relevant. Second, lower prices usually increase the amount demanded because people's incomes can now buy more. But in the macro framework all prices, including the price of labor (wages), are falling. Thus the "income effect" of price decreases is irrelevant. That's why we appealed to our real money supply discussion. In particular, even though prices are falling, the stock of money is fixed by the central bank. Thus, as the value of real balances increases, because prices are falling, the amount demanded for all goods taken together rises.

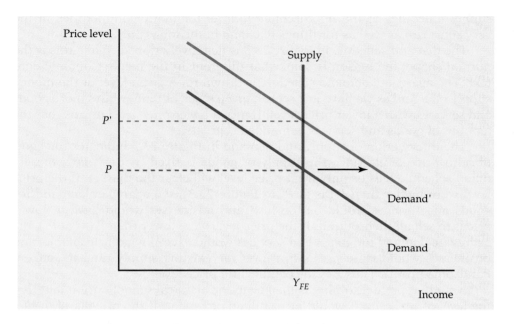

FIGURE 23.4   An increase in aggregate demand raises prices.

the public had just the right amount of real cash balances (given the old money supply). When the supply of money is increased, the demand for goods and services at every price level goes up, because real cash balances are higher. This is represented in the figure by a rightward shift of the demand curve. The net result of this increased demand, however, is simply to raise the price level to P' because the aggregate supply of goods and services is fixed at full employment.

Our algebraic discussion in the previous sections was more specific than the graphics, because we could show that changes in the money supply lead to proportional changes in prices under the quantity theory. But the pictures emphasize an important dimension as well: The quantity theory is really a specific statement of the aggregate demand for goods and services. In particular, this theory emphasizes that changes in the money supply raise prices by changing aggregate demand.

We have also just identified the source of the popular notion that inflation stems from "too much money chasing too few goods." In the context of classical thinking, continued expansion in the money supply raises the aggregate demand for goods; with a fixed supply of goods, the result is rising prices, which is exactly what we mean by inflation. The classical message, therefore, is that inflation is a monetary phenomenon: Unless the money supply increases, the price level is stable. As we will see in Chapter 27, this is not the same conclusion reached by the Keynesian story on inflation.

REAL VERSUS NOMINAL RATES OF INTEREST

Once inflation enters the picture, we must return to amend our discussion of interest rate determination. Until now there was no need to consider the distinction between the real rate of interest and the nominal rate. The reason is that real and nominal yields are the same when the inflation rate is zero. Thus our discussion above, showing how saving and investment determine the rate of interest, is unambiguous: A given nominal rate of interest (in terms of dollars earned) is the same as the real yield (in terms of real goods and services earned) when the price level remains unchanged.

We pointed out in Chapter 4, however, that if inflation occurs, the real yield on a bond is not equal to the nominal rate. In particular, a $1,000 one-year bond that promises $50 in interest and costs $1,000 has a 5 percent nominal yield. But if the rate of increase in the price level is 2 percent, then it takes $1,020 next year just to buy what $1,000 would have purchased a year earlier. Thus only $30 of the $50 interest payment represents additional real goods and services that can be bought. A convenient rule of thumb is as follows: The real yield is approximated by the nominal rate minus the rate of inflation; in our case, the real yield is 3 percent.

All of this is more arithmetic than economics. But Irving Fisher, of quantity theory fame, was the first to put the commonsense arithmetic together with some economic analysis. In particular, Fisher argued that if savers and investors expected inflation, they would force up the equilibrium nominal rate of interest to include an inflation premium. The equilibrium real rate would remain unchanged at the level determined by saving and investment, just as the nineteenth-century classical economists said. But the nominal rate would increase by the expected rate of inflation.

The argument is as follows. Savers who were previously satisfied with, say, a 5 percent yield on bonds when inflation was zero will save less and lend less when the expected rate of inflation jumps to 2 percent—after all, their savings will buy fewer real goods next year. Investors, meanwhile, will want to borrow even more funds when they expect 2 percent inflation—after all, they'll be investing in goods and services that can be sold at even higher prices next year. Thus at the old interest rate of 5 percent there is a greater demand for funds and a smaller supply. The level of interest rates is forced up to bring saving and investment back into equality. When the nominal yield rises to 7 percent, and the real rate of interest is back at 5 percent, lenders and borrowers will once again have consistent saving and investment plans.

More specifically, unless the nominal rate of interest rises by the expected rate of inflation, the real rate of interest (the nominal rate minus the expected rate of inflation) will be too low. As we saw in Figure 23.1, when the real rate is below equilibrium, desired investment exceeds saving and the real rate of interest is pushed up. So Fisher's addendum to the purely classical interest theory was that, in equilibrium, the nominal rate of interest would increase by the expected rate of inflation and the real rate would remain unchanged (determined by saving and investment at full employment).

MODERN MODIFICATIONS: MONETARISTS AND NEW CLASSICISTS

From the late 1940s through the 1990s, a group of economists, associated in varying degrees with the University of Chicago, built upon the traditions of classical economics with the benefit of modern theoretical and statistical techniques. Originally labeled the Chicago school, but currently referred to either as monetarists or new classical macroeconomists, this informal group has produced a set of ideas with important implications for the role of money in the economy. For simplicity we sometimes refer to this group as **monetarists.**

Monetarists adhere to virtually all the tenets of classical economics. However, they have made some modifications. For example, some have used the quantity theory as a framework for describing the relationship between M and PY rather than just M and P. This approach recognizes the fact that real output may deviate temporarily from full employment and represents an attempt at describing what influences overall economic activity rather than just the price level.

It must be emphasized, however, that this broader view of the quantity theory can never wander very far from the first pillar of classical economics: Say's law. Modern monetarists still view the invisible hand as pushing the economy toward the full employment level of production (Y_{FE}). Any increases or decreases in Y stemming from expansions or contractions in M are viewed as temporary. As we will see in Chapter 27, much of this discussion hinges on a more precise specification of the aggregate supply and demand schedules that were just introduced.

A second modification of classical thought occurred with Milton Friedman's revival of the quantity theory during the 1950s. Friedman replaced the idea of the stability of velocity with the less militant notion that it is predictable. Or, looked at another way, money demand may not be a fixed fraction of total spending, but it is related to PY in a close and predictable way. Obviously this provides a looser linkage between changes in money and prices, one that must be described in statistical terms rather than with a simple arithmetical example. Nevertheless, if people respond in a predictable way to changes in the money supply, much of the classical heritage is sustained.

Perhaps the most important classical tradition that is upheld by modern monetarists is the inherent stability of the economy at full employment. This explains the monetarist rejection of governmental attempts to fine-tune economic activity. A higher level of economic activity requires more capital and labor or technological improvements; more money only leads to inflation. The

GOING OUT ON A LIMB

The Money Supply and the Great Depression

Most people believe that the Great Depression of the 1930s was started by the stock market crash of 1929. In fact, although the stock market crash might have initiated the depression, according to many economists the depth and duration of the depression must be largely attributed to the major contraction in the money supply that followed in the wake of the stock market's collapse.

First the dimensions of the depression. Gross domestic product in the United States was $104 billion in 1929. In 1930 it declined 13 percent to $90 billion, and in the three subsequently years GDP continued to shrink to a low point of only $56 billion in 1933. Unemployment soared from 3 percent of the civilian labor force in 1929 to an intolerable 25 percent in 1933!

In 1939, a decade after the stock market crash GDP was still below its 1929 level and unemployment was still 17 percent of the civilian labor force.

To a large extent, the depth and duration of the depression were due to what happened to the money and the associated impact on spending. M1 (currency plus checking accounts) was $26 billion in 1929. By 1933, though, M1 had declined by 23 percent, to only $19 billion. In other words, almost a fourth of the money supply simply disappeared.

This money supply contraction resulted from the collapse of the banking system. In the four years 1930 through 1933, more than 9,000 commercial banks failed, wiping out billions of dollars of deposits (there was no federal deposit insurance yet, since the FDIC didn't begin operations until 1934).

It was 1936 before the money supply recovered to its 1929 level. No wonder the depression was so deep and lasted so long.

---

answer to cyclical downturns is to wait for the natural upturn. Government intervention is unnecessary and potentially damaging.

The new classical macroeconomists have added still another wrinkle to the futility of government efforts at fine-tuning—**rational expectations.** This perspective, as we will see in greater detail in Chapter 28, emphasizes that people formulate expectations based on all available information, including their knowledge of how the economy behaves. Recognizing that the economy tends toward full employment implies that any attempt at increasing the money supply to reduce unemployment will not be successful. People will immediately equate increases in money supply with an offsetting rise in prices. Thus there will not be any expansionary impact on real economic activity, because increases in money supply simultaneously generate expectations of higher prices.

To some extent, these are the implications of classical economics that sparked the Keynesian revolution. In the next chapter we outline the Keynesian viewpoint and then turn to the current policy debate in Chapters 27 and 28.

"Mr. Semple, who wants to stimulate the economy, help the cities, and clean up the environment, I'd like you to meet Mr. Hobart, who wants to let the economy, the cities, and the environment take care of themselves. I'm sure you two will have a lot to talk about."

Drawing by Stan Hunt; © 1976 The New Yorker Magazine, Inc.

SUMMARY

1. The two main concepts of classical thinking on money and aggregate economic activity are Say's law and the quantity theory. Say's law emphasizes that the economy is inherently stable at full employment. Any deviations from that level of economic activity are only temporary. A key mechanism promoting stability is the flexibility of interest rates. Saving and investment are brought into equality through variations in the interest rate.

2. The quantity theory of money states that the impact of money in classical economics is limited to the price level. Increases in the money supply raise prices, and decreases in money reduce the price level. Money is neutral with respect to the real sector of the economy. There is a clear distinction between real and nominal magnitudes.

3. At the heart of the quantity theory is a stable demand for money. More particularly, the demand for real cash balances is a predictable fraction of real GDP. The quantity theory can also be viewed as a statement about what determines the aggregate demand for goods and services. In particular, it says that increases in the money supply raise aggregate demand. With aggregate supply fixed at full employment, the impact of an increase in the money supply is to raise prices.

4. The real rate of interest is determined by saving and investment. When expectations of inflation emerge, the nominal rate of interest is forced up to include an inflation premium, leaving the real rate unchanged.

5. Modern monetarists treat the quantity theory more flexibly than their classical ancestors did. Money influences spending in a predictable way rather than in a rigid numerical fashion. Moreover, if the economy is at less than full employment, even real output might respond to changes in the money supply. But the natural tendency toward full employment eliminates any systematic impact on real output of changes in money supply.

QUESTIONS

23.1 Explain why an increased desire to save (implying less desired consumption spending) would not generate unemployment according to classical economists.

23.2 Why do classical economists maintain that prices would double if the money supply doubles?

23.3 What factors determine the demand for money according to the original quantity theory?

23.4 Use aggregate supply and demand curves to show why classical economists contend that inflation is a monetary phenomenon.

23.5 Explain why the equilibrium nominal rate of interest will rise by the expected rate of inflation.

23.6 *Discussion question:* Are wages, prices, and interest rates sufficiently flexible to maintain full employment most of the time?

GDP Definitions and Relationships

This is a review of aggregate economic relationships from basic economics. We discuss the circular flow of income and output, the separation between saving and investment, and other macroeconomic relationships needed for the next few chapters.

THE CIRCULAR FLOW OF SPENDING, INCOME, AND OUTPUT

Let's start by taking a simplified view of the economy, dividing its participants into two groups: business firms and households. Firms produce goods and services for sale; households buy these goods and services and consume them. Households are able to buy the goods and services produced by firms because they also supply firms with all the land, labor, capital, and entrepreneurship required for production; hence they receive as income the total proceeds of production. The total value of the goods and services produced within the United States is called gross domestic product (GDP), or more simply national income (Y), and it can be measured by either the total output sold by firms *or* the total income received by households (in the form of wages, rent, interest, and profits).

These relationships are summarized in Figure 23A.1, the inner circle recording flows of *real* things (factors of production to firms and goods and services to households), the outer circle recording the associated *money* flows (income payments to households and money expenditures to firms). The money flow relationship can be written symbolically as $C = Y$, where C stands for household spending on consumer goods and Y stands for national income or GDP.

As long as firms sell all their output, they will continue to produce at that level. As long as we assume that all the income received by households is spent

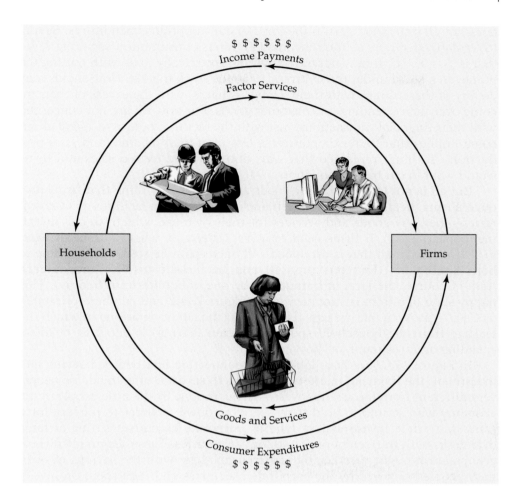

FIGURE 23A.1   The circular flow of spending, income, and output.

on the goods and services produced, production equals sales, output equals demand, and we are in equilibrium (there is no tendency for anything to change). But if we keep this up much longer, you will have fallen asleep in the very position you are now in, maybe still holding this book (also equilibrium). So we modify things a bit to make our hypothetical economy more like the real one.

SAVING AND INVESTMENT

Households don't spend all their income; they usually save some fraction. Saving represents a leakage in the circular flow. Total income of households (which is equal to the total value of goods and services produced by firms) does not all return to firms in the form of consumption expenditures. Saving (S) is defined simply as total income (Y) minus consumption spending (C)—that is, $S = Y - C$. It may not have anything specifically to do with putting the money in a bank, under the mattress, or in the stock market. Households may do any of these things with their savings—that is, with the excess of their income over their spending on consumer goods. For now we are not concerned with their financial transactions, just with the fact that failure to spend all income implies that total expenditure is less than total income (and total production). If things remained that way, output would exceed sales and firms would want to cut back production.

But all is not lost. Consumer goods are not the only thing that firms produce. Firms themselves add to their stock of production facilities or to inventories—they buy goods and services for their own use, which we call investment spending (I). If firms *want to invest* (I) exactly what households *want to save* (S), then all that is produced will once again be sold, but this time to both households (for consumption) and business firms (for investment). And, of course, the level of output will be one of equilibrium (hooray). This happy state of affairs is summarized in Figure 23A.2 and can be represented as $C + I = Y$. Note that we can also describe the situation as one in which the leakage from the household spending stream (saving) is equal to business spending on investment, or, in symbols, $S = I$.

In Figure 23A.2 we have labeled the connecting link between saving and investment the financial markets. Decisions to save are often made by people very different from those who invest—saving is done by the little people in the economy who scrimp to hold their spending down in order to prepare for a rainy day, while investment is done by corporate executives sitting at huge oval desks with thirteen phones and four secretaries. These seemingly diverse groups are brought together by financial markets, with the savings of ordinary people borrowed by the corporate executives and then spent on investment goods, so that both groups may continue along their merry way.

The word *investment* is frequently confusing, because it is used to mean different things. Here it means the purchase of "real" productive facilities, like factories and machine tools, whereas in common usage investment often refers to purely financial transactions, like buying stocks and bonds. Buying stocks and bonds can have implications for real investment (the purchase of factories and machine tools), but they are clearly different things. Throughout Part VI investment refers to the purchase of productive facilities.

It is important to emphasize that for equilibrium output to occur when saving equals investment it is necessary that households *want to save* the same amount as business firms *want to invest*. As we noted earlier in this chapter, classical economics assumed that the interest rate would bring desired saving and investment together.

We have to distinguish this condition (where desired $S = $ desired I) from one in which S and I are equal simply by definition. That is, saving is defined as $Y - C$. But $C + I = Y$, so that I also equals $Y - C$. Thus, by definition, S

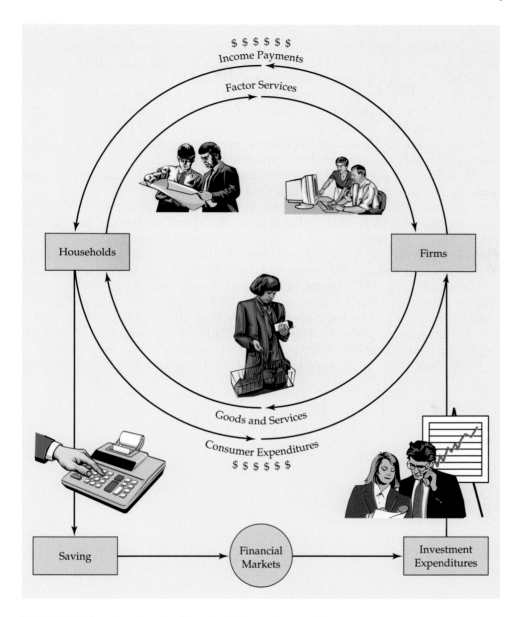

FIGURE 23A.2   The circular flow including saving and investment

must always equal *I*, since both equal *Y* − *C*. But *this* equality is an ex post accounting identity, always true by definition. It is not an ex ante behavioral equality arising from what people *want* to do. Only when people *want* to save what firms *want* to invest will income be in equilibrium (remain unchanged). A concrete example is given in the next chapter.

So far we have ignored the government (wishful thinking?). It, too, introduces a leakage between income payments and household consumption expenditures—namely, taxes (T). When the government collects taxes, households have less to spend on consumer goods (and less to save). If some other form of spending did not increase when taxes were levied, production once again would exceed the sum of all types of expenditures, and economic activity would decline. But the government could lend these funds to business firms so they could increase investment spending, or the government itself could buy goods and services from business firms.

If *desired* spending in the form of consumption (C), investment (I), and government expenditure (G) equals total output, or $C + I + G = Y$, then that level of production will be maintained. Note that we can also describe the situation as one in which total leakages from the spending stream, saving plus taxes, equal total spending injections in the form of investment and government expenditure, or $S + T = I + G$. For simplicity, we may sometimes refer to the left-hand side as total saving and the right-hand side as total investment.

One final note: Our exports to foreign countries minus our imports from foreign countries, referred to as net exports (NX), also adds to aggregate demand (imports must be subtracted because they are included in C, I, and G but do not generate domestic production). Thus our new equilibrium including the foreign sector is as follows: If desired spending in the form of $C + I + G + NX$ equals what is produced, then that level of output will be maintained.

CHAPTER 24

The Keynesian Framework

John Maynard Keynes, first baron of Tilton (1883–1946), did many things differently. We are not concerned here with his ability to make a fortune speculating in the market while simultaneously teaching at King's College, Cambridge; nor with his infatuation with the finer things in life—ballet, drama—and his editorial supervision for many years of the technical *Economic Journal;* nor with his unique abilities in the fields of mathematics, philosophy, and literature. Rather, we are concerned with his contribution to economics in his book *The General Theory of Employment, Interest and Money,* published in 1936: how it revolutionized the thinking of all economists since, how it replaced classical economics as the conventional wisdom, and how it led to a different outlook on employment, interest, and money.

Before going into the details of Keynes's contributions to monetary theory and the refinement of his ideas at the hands of other economists (collectively labeled **Keynesians**), it will be helpful to set the stage by noting an essential difference in Keynes's outlook compared with that of his classical teachers. Keynes was concerned with the short run, while classical economists were preoccupied with the long run. Keynes's attitude toward the concern of his classical mentors is best illustrated by his now-famous dictum: "In the long run, we are all dead."

Classical economics explained why fluctuating prices and interest rates would continuously push economic activity toward full employment. But Keynes argued that these free market forces could take considerable time to work themselves out. And in the short run there could be lengthy periods of underemployment. While it is difficult to delineate the borderline between the short run and long run, the six years of worldwide depression preceding the publication of Keynes's magnum opus seemed too long to wait for classical market forces to restore full employment.

Keynes was preoccupied with what determined the level of real economic activity during those lengthy recession or depression intervals between the full employment points of the classical school. Real output could increase

without any increase in the price level if we started out in a sufficiently depressed state. *All of Keynes's basic analysis assumes that the price level is fixed.*[1]
Therefore, throughout this chapter, all changes in GDP represent real
changes. Moreover, throughout this book, whenever GDP appears without a
modifier, it refers to *real GDP*. As in the last chapter, real GDP is represented
by the letter Y.

Keynes obviously had to focus on the aggregate demand for goods and
services, since full employment supply was irrelevant for his particular problem. Theoretically, he could have chosen the quantity theory to describe aggregate demand, just as he had done in his classical life before 1936. But in
his new incarnation he had other plans for money, quite different from the
quantity theory. Moreover, he believed he had to introduce a new set of analytical tools to deal with unemployment, since classical economics had almost
nothing to say about such matters. Keynes wanted to design a model of GDP
determination that would explain how economic activity could be in equilibrium at *less* than full employment. Who or what was to blame for a depressed
level of economic activity? To what extent is money the culprit?

WHEN SAVING DOESN'T EQUAL INVESTMENT

The appendix to the previous chapter showed that for GDP to be at an equilibrium level—that is, no tendency for change—all that is produced must be sold
to consumers or willingly added to the capital stock as investment by business
firms. We also said that this equilibrium condition could be stated in another
way: Total saving *desired* by households must equal total investment *desired*
by firms. In that way the leakage out of the spending stream in the form of
saving would be made up by desired investment spending by firms, and everyone would be happy.

We also mentioned in the appendix that ex post (after all is said and done)
saving is always equal to investment. Only in the ex ante (desired) sense is
equality of saving and investment an equilibrium condition. Let's take a very
specific example of these relationships to set the stage for our discussion in
the rest of the chapter.

Assume entrepreneurs produce $1,000 billion of output (Y) at full employ-
ment and expect to sell $800 billion to consumers (C) and want to use the re-
maining $200 billion for investment (including inventory accumulation). They
will continue producing at that rate only if their sales are realized. If consumers plan to buy $800 billion in consumer goods and services and therefore
desire to save $200 billion, all is well. But what if consumers decide they want
to spend only $700 billion on consumer goods, which means they want to save
$300 billion? What will give?

---

[1] Toward the end of this chapter we will describe how this looks in terms of the aggregate supply
and demand framework introduced in Figure 23.3.

Assuming that consumers succeed in implementing their spending plans, entrepreneurs will wind up selling only $700 billion, although they have produced $800 billion in consumer goods and services. Clearly their selling plans have been disappointed, and they wind up with an *extra* $100 billion in (unwanted) inventories. In fact, they *wind up* investing $300 billion (the same as saving): their planned capital accumulation of $200 billion plus $100 billion of *unintended* inventory accumulation. Saving (S) equals investment (I) ex post, but *desired* saving exceeds *desired* investment by $100 billion.

The key classical-Keynesian confrontation involves precisely such circumstances: What happens when *desired* saving exceeds desired investment? The classics had a series of simple answers based on a single principle—*prices adjust* when there is an excess supply of or demand for any good (or all goods together). Therefore, when there is an excess supply that isn't being sold, entrepreneurs reduce their prices to get rid of unsold inventories, workers lower their wage demands to stave off unemployment, and the rate of interest (the *price* of borrowing) decreases when saving exceeds investment. The fall in the interest rate lowers desired saving (increasing desired consumer spending directly) and raises desired investment, until desired saving and investment are again equal and entrepreneurs are content with their previous (full employment equilibrium) level of production. All of this was stated more formally in the preceding chapter.

But Keynes was not sympathetic. Prices are sticky and probably wouldn't decline as inventories piled up. Wages are notoriously resistant to decreases and, even more important, fluctuations in the rate of interest do not equilibrate desired saving and desired investment. The rate of interest is determined in the money market; it equilibrates the supply and demand for money, not saving and investment. (And that is why Keynes dropped the quantity theory, as we will see in greater detail later.)

Assuming that the rate of interest doesn't bring saving into equality with investment, what happens as a result of the undesired inventory accumulation? Keynes thought that the level of real output, rather than prices, would respond most quickly. Entrepreneurs with unwanted accumulating inventories would probably cut back production. Output would fall as long as desired saving exceeded desired investment. Since the price level was unchanged, both real output and income would decline. How far? Until desired S equaled desired I, when a new equilibrium GDP, lower than before, would be reached. To help us see how far GDP would fall when desired saving exceeds desired investment, Keynes invented the consumption function (or, looked at another way, the saving function).

CONSUMPTION AND SIMPLE GDP DETERMINATION

We start by determining equilibrium production, or GDP, where GDP is measured by both income received and output sold (as described in the appendix to the previous chapter). Figure 24.1 is the familiar Keynesian cross diagram.

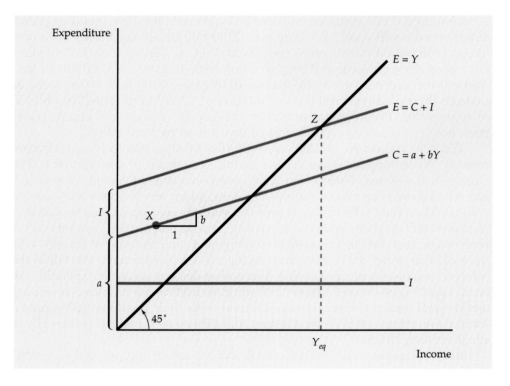

<u>**FIGURE 24.1**</u>   <u>**Spending determines income.**</u>

On the horizontal axis we measure real income and real output (both represented by Y) and on the vertical axis we measure different types of expenditure. For simplicity we label the horizontal axis income and the vertical axis
expenditure. The line drawn from the origin at an angle of 45 degrees marks
off equal magnitudes on each axis (remember isosceles triangles from basic
geometry?), hence it traces the equilibrium condition $E = Y$, or expenditure
equals income.

Expenditure takes two forms: **consumption** and **investment** (we'll ignore
the government and foreign sectors for a while). Keynes argued that consumption spending (C) depends mainly on the level of income (Y)—more income, more consumption. In Figure 24.1, therefore, desired consumption is a
simple linear function of Y:

$$C = a + bY$$

The letter b is the slope of the line, or $\Delta C/\Delta Y$), the change in consumption per
unit change in income (see point X in Figure 24.1). It is called the **marginal
propensity to consume** and is assumed to be less than 1. For example, if b is
0.8, that means an increase in Y of \$100 raises C by \$80. (It also means that
saving goes up by \$20.)

The *a* in the **consumption function** is the constant term. It records the level of *C* if *Y* were zero (presumably people eat even if they have no income—many of us have relatives like that), and it also sums up all other influences on consumption besides income. For example, if you had bought Xerox when it was $1 a share (only as far back as 1958), you would now be consuming a lot more than if you bought silver when it was $50 an ounce (January 1980). Thus the consumption function might shift up or down, recorded by larger or smaller values for *a*, if people are wealthier or poorer, although our equation still says they would consume $8 out of every $10 *increment* in earned income.

As far as investment (*I*) is concerned, Keynes agreed with the classics that it is a function of the rate of interest on bonds. Entrepreneurs compare the expected rate of return on a prospective investment with the rate of interest.[2] They invest as long as the rate of return exceeds the rate of interest and continue up to the point at which the expected return on the last investment just equals the rate of interest. If the rate of interest declines, then investment projects with lower expected returns become profitable and investment will increase. For now we take the rate of interest as given. We also take expectations as given, which is an even more questionable proposition. Under such conditions, investment is some constant amount (say $200 billion), as indicated by the horizontal line labeled *I* in Figure 24.1.

---

[2] The rate of return on an investment is determined by the expected future dollar revenues on the project and the current cost of the investment. In particular, if an investment is expected to generate $105 next year and requires a cash outlay of $100, we can calculate the rate of return quite simply. It is that rate of discount which equates the expected future revenues with the current cost, or $100 = \dfrac{105}{1 + q}$, where *q* is the rate of discount or, in our terminology, the rate of return. In our case it is clearly equal to 0.05, or 5 percent. We call *q* the rate of discount because it reduces (discounts) the $105 that is due next year to its current value (time is money).

Looked at another way, $100 put out at 5 percent for 1 year (100×1.05) produces $105 one year hence. This perspective also gives a clue as to how one ought to treat revenues two years hence. Namely, $100 left at 5 percent for two years produces 100×1.05 after one year, or $105, which is then reinvested and generates $110.25 after the next year ($105 \times 1.05 = 110.25). In general, therefore, if R_2 is the expected revenue two years from now, it must be discounted twice or

$$C = \frac{R_2}{(1 + q)(1 + q)} = \frac{R_2}{(1 + q)^2}$$

The general formula for the rate of return is as follows. If revenues of $R_1, R_2, \ldots, R_n$ are expected over the next *n* years, then the rate of discount *q* which equates *C*, the current cost, to the expected stream of revenues, as in

$$C = \frac{R_1}{(1 + q)} + \frac{R_2}{(1 + q)^2} + \cdots + \frac{R_n}{(1 + q)^n}$$

is called the rate of return on the investment project. Relax—you have at least 13 seconds to perform the necessary computations.

Those of you who still remember Chapter 4 may recall that this equation is very similar to the one used to calculate the yield (rate of return) on a bond. Just substitute *P* (the price of the bond) for *C*, put the coupons (C_1 through C_n) where the *R*s are, and replace *q* with the rate of interest (*r*). In fact, once you do that, the formulas are the same, which is just fine since in both cases we're measuring rates of return. Of course, that doesn't make it any easier to calculate these things.

Equilibrium output is represented by the line $E = Y$, where total desired expenditure (E) equals total income, Y. Total desired expenditure is the sum of desired C and desired I, or, in Figure 24.1, line $E = C + I$, which is the vertical addition of $C \ (= a + bY)$ and I. The point at which the total desired expenditure line $(E = C + I)$ crosses the expenditure-equals-production line $(E = Y)$ is equilibrium income (Y_{eq}). Point Z in Figure 24.1 is an example. At the level of production Y_{eq}, desired expenditure equals income.

It is also true that *desired* saving equals desired investment at that same income level. Desired saving is given by the difference between income and desired consumption (that is, $S = Y - C$). It can be measured by the vertical difference between the 45-degree line and the consumption function. In Figure 24.1 the only point at which saving (the vertical difference between the 45-degree line and the consumption function) equals investment (the difference between the $E = C + I$ line and the consumption function) is at income Y_{eq}.

In Figure 24.2 we have plotted the saving function explicitly, where Y is measured along the horizontal axis and dollars saved or invested are on the vertical axis. Saving is defined as $Y - C$, so that desired saving, S, equals $Y - (a + bY)$. Rearranging terms (and factoring the Y term) gives:

$$S = -a + (1 - b)Y$$

which is called the **saving function.** The **marginal propensity to save** equals 1 minus the marginal propensity to consume (out of each dollar increment in Y, a person spends b cents and saves $1 - b$ cents). From Figure 24.2 it is also

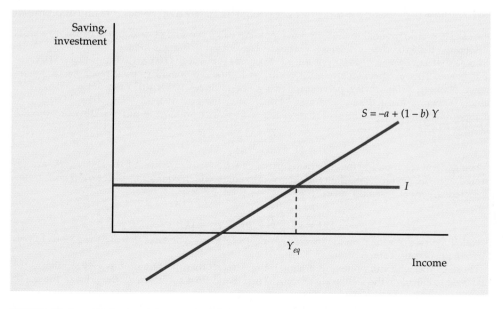

FIGURE 24.2   Saving and investment determine income.

clear that only at income Y_{eq} is desired saving equal to investment. At higher levels of income, desired saving exceeds desired investment; at lower levels of income, desired saving is less than desired investment.

CHANGES IN GDP

Will production and income stay at level Y_{eq} in Figure 24.1 forever? It will if the consumption function (and hence the saving function) remains where it is, and if desired investment is also unchanged. Is that good? Yes, *if Y_{eq} is the full employment level of economic activity.* But not only wouldn't Keynes guarantee that it would be full employment, he was convinced that it would be only a fortuitous accident if it were. He reasoned that the level of economic activity is subject to wide swings because the level of investment is highly unstable. The consumption function is quite stable—you can always count on dumb households to consume a predictable percentage of income. But if entrepreneurs became uncertain about future sales prospects, for example, then desired investment spending would decline and GDP would fall.

There are two ways to see *how far* GDP declines when desired investment spending falls. Let us first look at what happens in terms of total spending (investment and consumption) when desired investment falls—the wide-angle approach of Figure 24.1. We can then look at it from the standpoint of the investment-saving relationship—the isolated camera on S and I of Figure 24.2.

In Figure 24.3 we have replotted Figure 24.1's equilibrium point Z and the equilibrium income associated with the old total spending function $E = C + I_{old}$. If desired investment now falls to I_{new}, then the total desired spending function declines to $E = C + I_{new}$, the new equilibrium point is at N, and income declines to $Y_{new\ eq}$. The decline in income is written as ΔY (the change in Y) and is measured by the change in income along the horizontal axis or by the distance MN (constructed parallel to the horizontal axis). As can be seen in Figure 24.3, the decline in income *exceeds* the decline in investment: The decline in income is ZM, which is equal to MN by construction, while the drop in investment is only part of ZM.

Why does income change by some *multiple* of the change in investment spending? Quite simply, because when investment changes and income begins to decrease (or increase), there is a further *induced* change in consumer spending. Consumption is a function of income, and whenever there is a change in Y, consumption spending is affected by the amount $b\Delta Y$, where b is the marginal propensity to consume.

How large is the ΔY associated with a particular ΔI? GDP will change by the sum of the changes in both components of expenditure, namely $\Delta I + \Delta C$. Algebraically:

$$\Delta Y = \Delta I + \Delta C$$

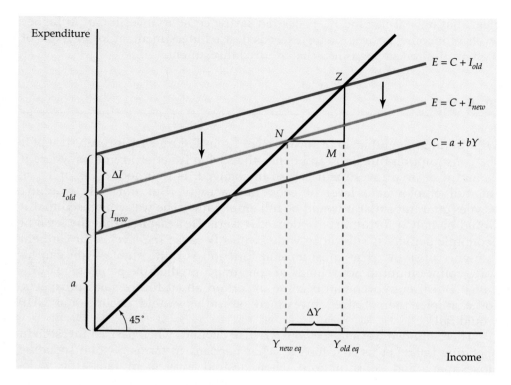

FIGURE 24.3 **A decline in investment spending reduces *Y* by a multiple of the change in investment.**

But we know that, after all is said and done, $\Delta C = b\Delta Y$ (from our consumption function). Substituting $b\Delta Y$ for ΔC we have:

$$\Delta Y = \Delta I + b\Delta Y$$

We can now solve for the unknown value of ΔY by isolating the ΔY terms on the left side. We do this by subtracting $b\Delta Y$ from each side, which yields:

$$\Delta Y - b\Delta Y = \Delta I$$

Factoring the ΔY terms on the left side gives us:

$$\Delta Y(1 - b) = \Delta I$$

Dividing both sides by $(1 - b)$ produces:

$$\Delta Y = \Delta I\frac{1}{1 - b}$$

where $1/(1 - b)$ is known as the **multiplier.** If b, the marginal propensity to consume, equals 0.8, then the change in income will be five times the initial

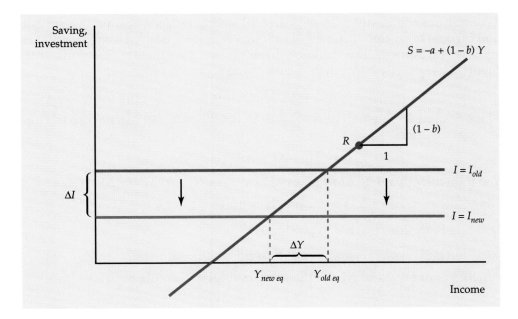

$$S = -a + (1 - b)\, Y$$

FIGURE 24.4   A decline in investment spending reduces *Y* by a multiple of the change in investment.

change in investment. If $b = 0.5$, the change in income will be two times the initial ΔI.[3]

The second way of looking at this process is to impose our desired S equals desired I condition for equilibrium. In Figure 24.4 we see that at income $Y_{old\ eq}$ investment I_{old} equals desired saving. When investment falls to

---

[3] The multiplier is sometimes derived by more explicit use of the successive rounds of consumption flowing from the initial ΔI. For example, initially ΔI produces a direct change in income, ΔY, equal to the ΔI. But then consumption changes by $b\Delta Y$ (which is equal to $b\Delta I$). This leads to a further change in consumption, $b\,(b\Delta I)$. This goes on, with the successive additions to GDP getting smaller and smaller because b is less than unity, hence b^2 is smaller than b, b^3 is smaller than b^2, and so on. The total ΔY is equal to the initial change in investment plus all of the subsequent changes in consumption (which stem from the initial $\Delta I = \Delta Y$). Or $\Delta Y = \Delta I + b\Delta I + b^2\Delta I + b^3\Delta I + \ldots + b^n\,\Delta I$. The right-hand side is a geometric progression whose sum is given by

$$\Delta I \times \frac{(1 - b^n)}{(1 - b)}$$

Since b is less than unity, b^n approaches zero as n gets large; hence we have

$$\Delta Y = \Delta I \times \frac{1}{(1 - b)}$$

which (surprisingly enough) is the same expression we derived in the text! These successive rounds of consumption were lumped together in the text into one $b\Delta Y$, by saying "after all is said and done," while here we build it up from each round of ΔY.

I_{new} and income is still at $Y_{old\ eq}$, desired saving exceeds desired investment and income must fall. Income falls enough to reduce desired saving until it is equal to investment. But we know from our saving function (see point R in Figure 24.4) exactly how much saving changes per unit ΔY:

$$\Delta S = (1 - b)\Delta Y$$

Since desired ΔS must equal desired ΔI in equilibrium, we can impose the following condition:

$$\Delta I = \Delta S$$

and then directly relate ΔI to ΔY by substituting $(1 - b)\ \Delta Y$ for ΔS. Hence:

$$\Delta I = (1 - b)\Delta Y$$

Dividing both sides by $(1 - b)$ produces:

$$\Delta Y = \Delta I \frac{1}{1 - b}$$

which, to our great chagrin, is the same multiplier formula as before.

AUTONOMOUS VERSUS INDUCED CHANGES IN GDP

Figures 24.3 and 24.4 suggest that anything that shifts the *position* of the total desired spending function will alter GDP. Such shifts in the position of the spending function are produced by **autonomous spending changes** (autonomous = independent; in our case, independent of GDP). The larger the size of the autonomous change in spending, the greater will be the change in economic activity.

But the multiplier story was based on the fact that autonomous spending changes also *induce* further changes in spending—in our case, via the consumption function. The larger the propensity to spend out of increments in income, or the larger the *slope* of the spending function (the larger b is), the greater will be the induced change in spending, and thus the greater will be ΔY.

Now you can see why Keynes divided spending into the two categories of consumption and investment. What he was really interested in was induced versus autonomous spending decisions. He argued that consumption spending is largely induced, while investment spending is largely autonomous (independent of income, but a function of the expected rate of return on capital and the rate of interest). Of course, investment prospects might be influenced by sales (current and future), which are certainly related to GDP. Similarly, desired consumption may change independently of current income; the constant term in the consumption function, a, shifts when Xerox goes from $10 per share to $100 per share. Nevertheless, Keynes still felt consumer spending was largely induced (by Y), while investment spending was largely independent (of Y).

Exports and Imports

It is worth noting that the multiplier expression derived above can be modified quite simply to take account of other sources of ΔY. In particular, ΔY is related to *any* autonomous change in spending (ΔA) by the same $1/(1 - b)$ factor. Or:

$$\Delta Y = \Delta A \frac{1}{1 - b}$$

For example, exports add to aggregate demand as exporters buy goods domestically and ship them abroad, while imports reduce domestic aggregate demand because spending by importers on consumption or investment is directed overseas. Thus in the appendix to the last chapter we noted that net exports (NX), exports minus imports, adds to domestic aggregate demand. Thus an autonomous increase in net exports will generate a multiple increase in GDP while an autonomous decrease in net exports will produce a multiple decrease in GDP.

What might cause shifts in net exports? Our discussion on foreign exchange in Chapter 10 emphasized that when foreigners want more of our products, either because of changing tastes or prices, our exports increase, while when we want more foreign products because of changing tastes and prices, our imports go up.

Although changes in net exports can clearly influence aggregate demand, most of our discussion (with the exception of monetary policy effectiveness) proceeds with net exports in the background. Somewhat more formally, unless we say otherwise we assume $NX = 0$, or net exports equals zero, or our exports just about equal our imports.

GOVERNMENT TO THE RESCUE

The great problem of macroeconomics, according to Keynes, was that changes in autonomous spending would spark fluctuations in economic activity—rather wide fluctuations, via the multiplier, if the induced component of expenditure were large. These wide fluctuations in GDP would be associated with unemployment when GDP fell below its full employment level as a result of a decline in autonomous spending. What to do? The classical response to such a situation was to do nothing—laissez faire. Keep hands off and let the long run work things out. But that was not the Keynesian response.

Keynes was the original Big Spender. If the private sector doesn't spend enough to keep everyone employed, let George do it (King George, of course). Government spending and taxation could be manipulated to offset the autonomous forces buffeting GDP and thereby restore full employment.

It is not very difficult to add government expenditure and taxes to our simple model. GDP is equal to the total of all expenditures in the economy—consumption, investment, and government:

$$C + I + G = Y$$

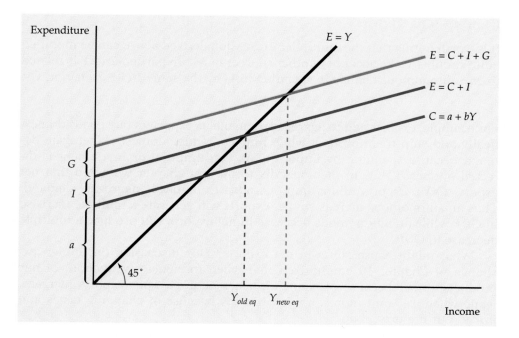

FIGURE 24.5   Adding government spending raises income.

Assuming that government spending is some fixed level *G*, we can simply add another line to Figure 24.1 for autonomous government spending. This is done in Figure 24.5, where $Y_{new\ eq}$ is the new equilibrium level of income when government spending is added.

The government usually finances its expenditures by taxation. Taxes do not lower spending directly, in the same sense that government expenditure directly changes spending. Rather, taxes reduce the amount of income that households have available for consumption expenditure. Consumption is not so much a function of GDP but of **disposable income,** where that is defined as equal to income minus taxes ($Y - T$). We therefore have a new consumption function, written as:

$$C = a + b\,(Y - T)$$

Or, after carrying out the multiplication we can write the consumption function as:

$$C = a + bY - bT$$

It is easy to see that when taxes go up by \$10, consumption declines by *b* times that amount (or if *b* = 0.8, by \$8). The reason is quite simple: People treat a dollar of income taken away by the government the same way they treat any other decline of a dollar's worth of income—they reduce consumption expenditure by the marginal propensity to consume times the change.

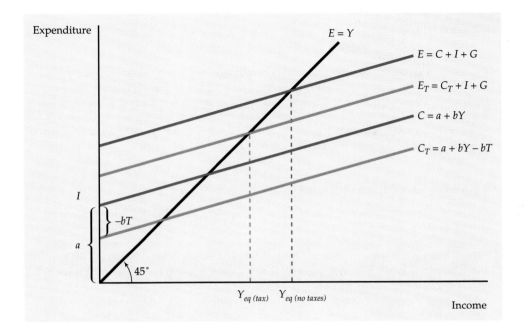

FIGURE 24.6   Introducing taxes lowers income.

Taxes, in fact, introduce the same type of leakage between income and spending that saving does. From the standpoint of our model it makes no difference whether people reduce their consumption because they just happen to feel like it or because the government says it would be nice if they did (curiously, if you don't feel like it in the second case, you wind up getting a striped uniform and free room and board for between one and five years). In either case, the consumption function shifts downward. Figure 24.6 shows the equilibrium levels of GDP with and without taxes. Figures 24.5 and 24.6 also suggest that changes in both government spending and taxes produce multiplier effects on GDP. In this respect they are just like any other kind of autonomous expenditure. But there is one big difference: Both taxes and government spending can be changed by government policy.[4]

The moral of the model of GDP including government expenditure and taxation is that the economy need not be buffeted about by autonomous changes in investment spending. Entrepreneurs may cut their desired investment spending if they get nervous, but nothing need happen to GDP as long as the government keeps its collective head and either increases *its* spending or lowers taxes so that consumers can increase theirs. In either case, the autonomous decline in investment spending could be offset by government

---

[4] We will ignore the fact that taxes vary with the level of income. It does change the nature of the model slightly, but for our purposes we are better off without that complication.

OFF THE RECORD

Taking the Pulse of the Economy

Reading the financial news is somewhat complicated when the subject is overall economic activity. In fact, when measuring the performance of the aggregate economy there is no single number that does the job. Instead, a variety of statistics released by the government on a monthly or quarterly basis, and published in major newspapers, serve as important indicators. It is useful to divide these statistics into measures of aggregate output and unemployment on the one hand, and the price level and inflation on the other.

Aggregate Output and Unemployment

The most comprehensive measure of economic activity is real GDP. Estimates are released in April for the first quarter (January–March), in July for the second quarter (April–June), and so on. Although real GDP is released as a dollar figure, the most important feature is its rate of growth. Thus, if real GDP grows at an annual rate of 4 percent during a quarter, that is considered a fast pace of economic activity; if it grows by only 1 percent that would be slow.

The most important number released on a monthly basis is the unemployment rate. An unemployment rate between $5\frac{1}{2}$ and 6 percent is considered both politically acceptable as well as indicative of no inflationary pressures. An increase in the unemployment rate of one-half of one percent during a one- or two-month period implies that economic activity is slowing down sufficiently to take its toll on the work force.

The Price Level

The GDP deflator is the most comprehensive measure of the price level. It is a weighted average of prices of all goods and services produced in the economy. It is released quarterly along with data on GDP. A rate of increase in the deflator of about 3 percent on an annual basis has been considered acceptable in recent years.

Two somewhat narrower measures of inflation are released monthly: the consumer price index and the producer price index. As suggested by their names, the former measures the rate of change in prices of goods purchased by the typical consumer (as defined by the Department of Commerce), while the latter measures price changes at the wholesale level. For obvious reasons, although the consumer price index is a less comprehensive measure of the price level than the GDP deflator, it receives the lion's share of attention because it measures how inflation influences each of us directly in our role as a consumer. Once again, a 3 percent increase on an annual basis is considered acceptable; 5 or 6 percent is not.

fiscal policy (*fiscal* means pertaining to the public treasury or revenue, from the Latin *fiscus*). Whether or not the timing and magnitude of changes in *G* and *T* would be appropriate, given the institutional setup, is another matter (and will be discussed in later chapters). But the possibility of improving on the workings of the free market is certainly evident.

This returns us to an important issue mentioned earlier: Is fiscal policy even necessary? Why doesn't income remain at full employment, with desired

"There are plenty of jobs around. People just don't want to work."
Drawing by Drucker; © 1972 The New Yorker Magazine, Inc.

saving and investment brought into equality via fluctuations in the rate of interest, as the classical economists said would happen? Why did Keynes, a truly classical economist before he became a Keynesian, reject the classical theory of interest rate determination? And what did he put in its place?

MONEY AND THE RATE OF INTEREST

Our exposition of the Keynesian model so far is very much like its classical counterpart in at least one respect: Money doesn't matter. While the classics said economic activity was set at the full employment level, and Keynes said it would settle at the point where total desired expenditure equaled production—which might be less than full employment—up to this point *neither* model has the money supply affecting real economic activity. The classics, as we saw in the previous chapter, deflected its impact to the price level. Keynes, the financial wizard of Cambridge, took a bolder position: The rate of interest is a monetary phenomenon. It is not determined by saving and investment, the way the classics said, but by the supply of and demand for money.[5] Keynes also said that money might affect the level of real economic activity, but only to the extent that it first influenced the rate of interest. Changes in the rate of interest would then alter desired investment spending and thereby change the level of GDP.

---

[5] Obviously, since prices are fixed and inflation is not part of the picture, Keynes is referring to the real rate of interest when claiming it is a monetary phenomenon. The classical picture of the real rate is Figure 23.1, which shows saving and investment as determining the real rate of interest.

The first order of business in investigating the rate of interest is to establish the framework by noting how Keynes divided the decision making in his model of macroeconomic activity. So far, the analysis of income and expenditure revolves around two decisions: (1) household choice between spending income and saving it, with the latter defined simply as nonconsumption; and (2) business firm decisions regarding the level of investment spending. These parts of the Keynesian system deal only with *flows:* consumption, saving, investment, and income over a given time period. It is, in the accountant's terminology, the "income statement" of the economy, with an implicit time dimension. We have also noted that none of these decisions involve any financial transactions; they deal only in *real* goods and services.

Money introduces an entirely new dimension to the macro model. Money is a **financial asset,** which is held in an individual's portfolio just as one holds a savings account at a bank, corporate equity, or Treasury bond. In other words, money is part of an individual's wealth—part of a person's balance sheet, in accountant's terms. The interest rate is determined by the third decision in the Keynesian scheme of things: (3) decisions of the public regarding the composition of its financial asset holdings.

Let's divide the public's portfolio into two types of assets: money and everything else. As we've seen before, money can be defined in many specific ways. For our purposes, the main distinction is that money has a fixed rate of interest, without any risk. Sometimes the rate is fixed at zero, as with currency, but that's not necessarily so, as with some checking accounts. The key is that no capital losses or gains are incurred on the asset called money. Money is also used as the medium of exchange (to conduct transactions). Thus money is the most liquid of all assets, where liquidity is defined as the ability to turn an asset into the medium of exchange quickly with little or no loss in value. For lack of a better name, we'll call all other assets "bonds." The price of a bond can vary in terms of the medium of exchange, so the owner can suffer capital losses or reap capital gains. The return on a bond can be above or below what was expected at the time it was purchased, depending on whether interest rates rise or fall subsequently (as we saw in Chapter 4).

Money is a riskless asset, and bonds are risky assets. If people are risk averters—that is, if they dislike risk—then they will demand a higher expected return on risky assets compared with riskless assets.[6] Thus a choice is necessary: How much of one's portfolio should go into money and how much into bonds?

It is important to note that the more bonds and less money held in a portfolio, the greater the uncertainty over total portfolio return. For example, if I have $100, all in cash, my return is certain. If I put it all into bonds yielding 10 percent, I expect my return to be just that: 10 percent. But if interest rates rise

---

[6] Those of you who have read Chapter 7 recognize that risk aversion and higher expected returns on risky securities are sophisticated components of modern portfolio analysis, in addition to their commonsense interpretations.

substantially after my purchase, my $100 bond might be worth (could be sold for) only $75. In this case my expected 10 percent return would be reduced by the capital loss of $25. If I had held $50 in cash and invested only $50 in bonds, I would have lost only half as much. More bonds in a portfolio mean more risk.

Our composite bond in this analysis includes all risky assets—equities, corporate bonds, municipals, even long-term government bonds. We'll assume that an efficient combination of risky assets has been derived. Back in Chapter 6 we discussed the structure of yields on different types of bonds. For now we are concerned only with the choice between money and the composite bond of Keynes. It is this decision that determines the overall expected return, the "average" interest rate, on bonds.

The demand for money, called **liquidity preference** by Keynes, is a function of the rate of interest. In Figure 24.7 the horizontal axis measures the quantity of money, while the rate of interest is on the vertical axis. The demand-for-money function is negatively sloped—the lower the rate of interest, the larger the amount of money demanded.

There are a number of reasons for this negative relationship between quantity of money demanded and rate of interest. Keynes argued that people had an idea of some "normal" rate of interest, as though the rate of interest were attached to its "normal" level by a rubber band. When the rate of interest *declines,* more and more people become convinced that it will snap back to its "normal" level, that is, that interest rates *will rise in the future.* If they hold bonds when rates are rising, they will suffer capital losses. In other words, the

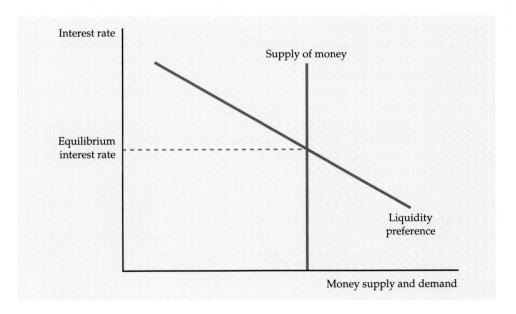

FIGURE 24.7   Keynesian interest theory.

public, trying to avoid capital losses, would want to hold fewer bonds (but more money) as interest rates decline. This relationship has been called the **speculative demand for money** because people are speculating on future bond prices.

A more general approach to the negative relationship between demand for speculative money balances and the interest rate stresses interest rates as compensation for risk bearing.[7] A high rate of interest means that the cost of being liquid and safe (holding money) is great, in terms of the interest forgone. A high interest rate is an inducement to hold a large portion of one's assets in bonds (bond demand is high) and only a little in cash. At lower interest rates, the opportunity cost of (what one gives up by) holding money is much less. Since it feels good to be liquid, the amount of money demanded is greater at lower rates of interest. In more formal terms, people are risk averse—they don't like risk. There must be an inducement to hold a riskier portfolio, one with a larger amount of bonds. The inducement is a higher rate of interest.

Either approach to the demand for money explains its negative relationship to interest rates (as interest rates fall the amount of money demanded rises). Coupled with a fixed supply of money, determined by the central bank (a rather bold assumption), the rate of interest is in equilibrium when the amount of money demanded equals the supply. We know that the interest rate is in equilibrium then (as in Figure 24.7), because below the equilibrium rate the demand for money exceeds the fixed supply. If the rate of interest momentarily fell *below* the equilibrium rate, people would want more money than they have and would try to sell bonds to get it. The attempt to sell bonds drives bond prices down and interest rates up, until—at the equilibrium rate—people are satisfied with their portfolios of money and bonds.

At a rate of interest *above* the equilibrium rate, people would have more money than they want. They would try to get rid of their excess money balances by purchasing bonds. Bond prices would be driven up and interest rates down, until people were again happy with their holdings of money and bonds. This is at the equilibrium interest rate, of course.

Our introductory discussion in Chapter 4 described the interest rate as determined by the supply of and demand for loanable funds, or looked at another way (see footnote 5 of Chapter 4) by the supply of and demand for bonds. It should not be too difficult to see why Keynesian analysis can look at the supply of and demand for money, rather than looking at the bond market directly, and say that the rate of interest is determined by equilibrium in the money market. As long as the total size of the public's portfolio, its wealth, is fixed—and in the short run this is a reasonable assumption—then a change in the demand for money relative to supply would be reflected in a one-to-one

---

[7] This approach was first formally presented in James Tobin's article "Liquidity Preference as a Behaviour Toward Risk," *Review of Economic Studies* (1958). The modern discussion of the pricing of risky financial assets was presented in Chapter 7 of our text.

relationship by an opposite change in the demand for bonds relative to supply. In other words, if the demand for money goes up, it necessarily implies that people want to hold fewer bonds, and vice versa. Looking only at the supply of and demand for money is perfectly consistent with our earlier discussion, because a change in one market is automatically reflected in the other.

MONETARY POLICY

What causes the rate of interest to change? Clearly, if either the demand for money or the supply of money shifts position, the equilibrium interest rate would change. For now, assume that the money-demand function is given, and let us examine the impact of changes in the money supply on interest rates and economic activity.

In Figure 24.8, let's start out with the money supply at $60 billion and the equilibrium interest rate as indicated. Assume the central bank increases the money supply from $60 to $70 billion. At the old rate of interest, the amount of money that people are now holding is greater than what they want. People try to dispose of their excess money balances (reduce their liquidity) by buying bonds, driving the price of bonds up and the interest rate down until the interest rate has fallen sufficiently to make people content to hold the new level of cash (and stop trying to buy bonds). This happy state of affairs occurs

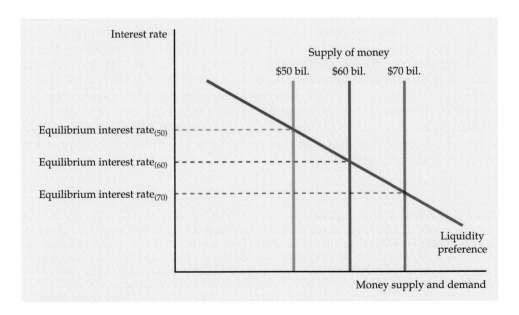

FIGURE 24.8   Effect of changing the money supply on the interest rate.

at the lower equilibrium interest rate$_{(70)}$, when the amount of money demanded now equals the new supply.[8]

The implications of the increased money supply for economic activity are clear—a lower interest rate on bonds means higher investment spending, *ceteris paribus* (a key phrase meaning everything else held constant, often used by economists to produce unexpected results). In terms of our GDP-determining diagrams earlier in the chapter, the investment line shifts up and GDP goes up by the increase I (induced by the decline in the interest rate) times the multiplier.

A decrease in the money supply produces just the opposite results. We start once again with a money supply of $60 billion in Figure 24.8, and this time let the central bank *decrease* the money supply to $50 billion. At the old equilibrium rate of interest, the amount of money that people are now holding is less than the amount they want to hold. People try to sell bonds to get more cash, bond prices decline, and interest rates rise until people are satisfied with their new money balances. They stop trying to sell bonds when a new equilibrium is established at the higher interest rate$_{(50)}$.

The implications for aggregate economic activity are the reverse of the case in which the money supply was increased. This time we have a higher interest rate on bonds, and investment will decline; GDP goes down by the drop in I (induced by the rise in the interest rate) times the conventional multiplier.

The negative relationship between the demand for money and the rate of interest is an important component of the Keynesian model of GDP determination. It provides a link between changes in the supply of money and the level of economic activity.

But what Keynes giveth, Keynes can take away. If an increase in the money supply does *not* lower the interest rate, investment spending will not be affected. Keynes proceeded to question the efficacy of monetary policy under certain conditions. He argued, for example, that at very low interest rates the money-demand function becomes completely flat. In Figure 24.9 it is easy to see that a very flat demand-for-money function means that increases in the money supply could no longer reduce the rate of interest. In particular, an increase in the money supply from $50 billion to $60 billion lowers the interest rate, but a further increase to $70 billion fails to produce any additional decline.

---

[8] Since some forms of money balances pay interest—such as some checking accounts—it is at least conceivable that the larger supply of money could be absorbed by a higher interest payment on money balances rather than a lower interest rate on bonds. The excess supply of money requires only a decrease in the differential between the rate on bonds and the rate on money (so that people are induced to hold relatively more of the latter). One reason all bond rates fall, rather than the rate on money rising, has to do with the zero interest rate on currency and the fact that currency and demand deposits exchange on a one-to-one basis. Thus the rate of interest paid by banks on demand deposit balances cannot wander very far from the zero rate paid on currency. As a result, the major burden of adjustment to changes in the supply of money falls on all other rates of interest, rather than the own-rate on money.

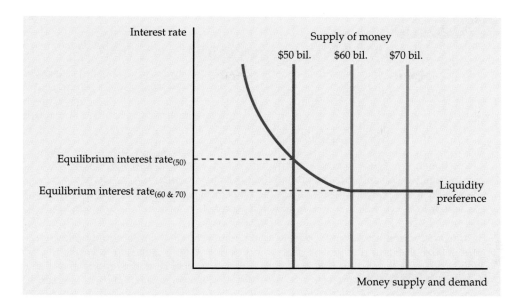

FIGURE 24.9   Keynesian liquidity trap.

What causes the money-demand function to enjoy the horizontal position? Keynes argued that at very low interest rates everyone would expect interest rates to rise to more "normal" levels in the future. In other words, everyone would expect bond prices to fall, therefore no one would want to hold bonds and the demand for liquidity (money) would be infinite. Any increase in money supply would simply be held by the public (hoarded), and none of the increased liquidity would spill over to the bond market. No one, in fact, would willingly hold bonds. In this **liquidity trap,** as Keynes called the flat portion of the money-demand function, monetary policy does not alter interest rates and therefore is completely ineffective. More generally, the flatter the liquidity-preference function, the less effective monetary policy is in changing interest rates, hence in influencing GDP.

It should be obvious that monetary policy will also be less effective in changing GDP if investment spending is not very responsive to changes in the rate of interest. An interest-insensitive investment function means that even a large change in the rate of interest will not alter investment spending very much. Thus a given change in the money supply will raise GDP by less if investment spending does not respond to interest rates.

Modern Keynesians have pointed out, however, that investment spending is not the only linkage between money supply and GDP. Consumers may also change their spending in response to variations in the interest rate. In particular, we noted above that consumer wealth—the value of stocks and bonds—influences consumption expenditure. A lower rate of interest means that the prices of bonds rise. Thus consumers will spend more when interest

OFF THE RECORD

Was 1995 the Japanese Year of the Liquidity Trap?

The investment banking firm Goldman, Sachs issued a 1995 research report entitled "The Japanese Liquidity Trap." It describes Japan's inability "to change the direction of the real economy and the yen ever since 1993." It goes on to say that "there are fears that the economy is now stuck in a Keynesian liquidity trap."

John Maynard Keynes invented the liquidity trap to illustrate why expansionary monetary policy, such as a level of short-term interest rates below 1 percent in the United States during the Great Depression, could not jump start the economy. Keynes never did say that the liquidity trap actually existed back then nor did his followers present evidence that it ever existed. Nevertheless, the power of suggestion obviously still lives as the liquidity trap is resuscitated as a possible explanation for Japanese stagnation during the 1990s.

Despite short-term rates at $3/4$ percent during the first half of 1995 and despite negative inflation and no real growth, there is no evidence that Japan suffered from a liquidity trap in 1995. And despite its title, the Goldman, Sachs research report draws the same conclusion. In fact, short-term interest rates were driven down from over 2 percent to below 1 percent by a rapidly expanding Japanese money supply during the first half of 1995. This is precisely what should not happen during the Keynesian liquidity trap.

Why then did Goldman, Sachs' well-respected research staff raise the specter of the liquidity trap? One answer is that the stagnation of investment spending in the face of declining interest rates prompts analogies with the Great Depression, even though the problem is not a liquidity trap but an interest-insensitive investment function. Of greater importance, however, is concern with the next step in Japan's effort to stimulate its economy: If another $3/4$ percent drop in rates is implemented and fails to jump start the economy, what next?

rates fall because they feel wealthier. In terms of our earlier diagrams, this wealth effect of a decrease in the interest rate causes the consumption function to shift upward.

Monetary Policy and International Trade

We mentioned earlier in the chapter that an increase in exports, or more precisely net exports (exports minus imports), adds to aggregate demand just like any category of autonomous spending. Although exports and imports comprise smaller segments of the U.S. economy than in most other countries of the world, modern Keynesians invoke the potentially significant impact of monetary policy on GDP through net exports. This so-called exchange rate effect works as follows.

Recall our discussion back in Chapter 10 about how the exchange rates between the dollar and, say, the German mark or the French franc are influenced by the expected returns investors earn on domestic and foreign bonds. More specifically, when U.S. interest rates go up because of a decrease in our money supply, foreigners will now want to buy U.S. bonds because they can earn a higher return on them, assuming nothing else changes. This means that German and French investors, for example, must go into the foreign exchange market to buy U.S. dollars with marks and francs, so they can pay for the now attractive U.S. securities. When exchange rates are flexible, the increased demand for dollars and increased supply of marks and francs in the foreign exchange market will drive up the cost of dollars in terms of foreign currencies; that is, the dollar will appreciate. This appreciation of the dollar reduces our exports of goods and services to Germany and France because our products become more expensive to them (because dollars cost more) and it increases our imports of goods and services from Germany and France because their products are less expensive for us (because francs and marks are cheaper). Thus net exports decline when domestic interest rates rise, driving down GDP.

When interest rates go down because of an expansion in the money supply, the reverse happens. U.S. investors buy foreign bonds because they earn more abroad. This drives down the value of the dollar in the foreign exchange market, making our exports more attractive and discouraging imports. Thus when domestic interest rates fall, net exports increase, driving up GDP.

We can conclude by summing up all of the channels through which monetary policy influences GDP. A change in money supply will have a larger effect on GDP when interest rates change by a lot and when *investment, consumption,* and *net exports* are very sensitive to interest rates. These three components of monetary policy are sometimes referred to as the **transmission mechanisms of monetary policy** and are often referred to by special names. The effect on investment spending is often called the **cost of capital effect** because monetary policy influences investment through the cost of raising capital to business. The effect on consumption is referred to as the **wealth effect** because monetary policy operates through interest rates on consumer wealth and how that affects their spending. And of course, the effect on net exports is called the **exchange rate effect.**

Transactions Demand and Monetary Policy

The concept of a speculative demand for money, related to the rate of interest, was a Keynesian innovation. Before Keynes came along, classical economists had emphasized that the only reason people would want to hold money was for transactions purposes—to buy goods and services—as we saw in the previous chapter. An increase in GDP leads to an increase in the amount of money demanded (at every rate of interest), because people need more cash to carry out the higher level of transactions. Keynes also acknowledged this *transactions demand,* although he did not himself appear to realize all its implications.[9]

---

[9] Keynes also discussed a precautionary demand for money: People hold cash to provide for unforeseen contingencies. This demand was considered constant or was lumped together with transactions balances. In the next chapter we expand on the implications of transactions demand. In particular, since changes in income alter transactions demand and interest rates, we determine the level of income and interest rates simultaneously.

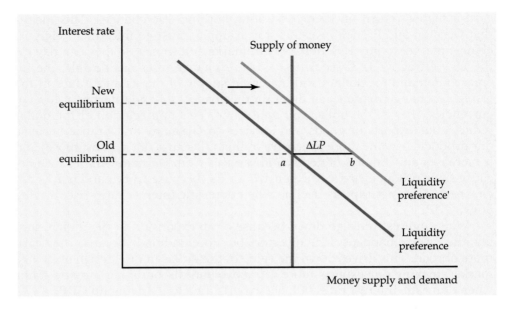

FIGURE 24.10   A shift in the demand for money changes the interest rate.

Figure 24.10 shows how a change in the demand for money (at every rate of interest) affects the interest rate. We start out with a given money supply and a given money-demand (liquidity-preference) function. Together they determine the equilibrium interest rate. Now suppose that people become more nervous than normal, perhaps because they expect a decrease in money supply. They seek ultimate relief by building up the proportion of cash in their portfolios. In other words, at every rate of interest people want more money (and fewer bonds) than before. Say the demand for money increases (ΔLP) by the amount *ab*. This happens at each rate of interest, so that we now have a new money-demand function to the right of the old. At the old equilibrium rate of interest, the amount of money demanded is larger than the fixed supply. To get more cash, people try to sell bonds, driving bond prices lower and interest rates higher until a higher equilibrium interest rate is established. The case of a decrease in the demand for money can be treated symmetrically. The money-demand function shifts to the left and the interest rate declines.

Something similar happens when the level of income changes. Let's say that income rises. People now demand more money balances at every rate of interest to carry out the higher level of transactions, the demand-for-money function shifts to the right, and the rate of interest rises. In an economy that is growing, perhaps because investment spending is rising, the rate of interest would rise because of the increase in transactions demand for money—unless, of course, the central bank expands the supply of money to provide for those transactions balances.

Now you know why we said back in Chapter 2 that "easy" or "tight" money is not really a matter of increases or decreases in the money supply in an absolute sense, but rather of increases or decreases relative to demand. In a growing economy, the money supply must increase because the demand for money will rise along with the growth in GDP. Unless the central bank increases the money supply, interest rates will rise.

The transactions demand for money is probably affected by the interest rate as well as by income. It is very likely that higher interest rates reduce the demand for transactions balances. For example, assume you are paid $4,000 monthly. You deposit the entire amount in the bank, spend it evenly over the month, and wind up at zero. Your *average* daily cash balance is $2,000. This is your transactions demand. But if interest rates on bonds were sufficiently high, you'd be willing to go to the cost and trouble to take half your salary at the beginning of the month ($2,000) and buy a bond, put the other $2,000 in your bank to be spent during the first 15 days, and then when that runs out sell the bond and spend the second $2,000 over the last half of the month. What this means is that your average daily cash balance is only $1,000 (you go from $2,000 to zero evenly over 15 days). What you gain from this is the higher interest on the funds invested in the bond market. And as long as the gain exceeds the costs, it's worth doing.

Your initial reaction might be: It would take an awfully high rate of interest to make me go through such shenanigans. That could be. But if you were a large corporation with a few million dollars in idle cash, the investment of that money could be very profitable. Most economists agree that the transactions demand for money, like the speculative demand, is a function of the rate of interest. For some purposes it can be ignored or played down—but not if you are a corporate treasurer.

An interesting sidelight on the transactions demand discussion is the role played by credit cards. The easiest way to look at this is that credit cards permit a transaction to take place without a cash balance. In other words, people could theoretically invest all their cash at the beginning of the month in bonds, pay for everything via those little plastic cards, and then at the end of the month sell the bonds, put the proceeds into the bank, and write one check to the credit card company (which could be the bank itself). Although this is an extreme example, it indicates how credit cards get into the model and how their growth affects the economy. Greater use of credit cards reduces the demand for money (at every interest rate), thereby lowering interest rates, permitting investment and GDP to increase.

Expectations and Monetary Policy

Most simple economic models assume that expectations are exogenous, that is, they are determined outside the system.[10] This one is no exception. An important implicit assumption is that changes in the money supply are imposed

---

[10] More sophisticated economic models require that expectations for variables in the model (such as interest rates) conform with the predictions of the model. This is called *rational expectations* and will be discussed in Chapter 28.

by our central bank, the Federal Reserve, and that such policy changes are *unanticipated*. Under such circumstances, monetary policy alters the interest rate by more or less, depending on the conditions described above.

But whether an increase or decrease in the stock of money causes a *simultaneous* movement in interest rates in the predicted direction depends crucially on whether or not the change in policy was anticipated. In particular, if everyone expects the Federal Reserve to cut back on the money supply next week or next month, a change in interest rates is likely to occur beforehand, with little or no effect at the time the money supply is actually altered. The reasoning is straightforward: If everyone expects the Fed to reduce the money supply in the future—and therefore expects interest rates to rise—then profit-maximizing bondholders will try to sell bonds *now* to avoid expected capital losses. Bond sales will drive down bond prices, driving up interest rates until they just about equal the expected rate next period. Thus when the money supply is, in fact, cut back next week or next month, rates don't move at all.

Incorporating expectations about policy movements into our model is possible but cumbersome. It is simulated by a shift in the demand-for-money function at every interest rate. In our particular example, when we say that bondholders want to sell to avoid capital losses, we are saying, in effect, that the demand for bonds decreases—or, in terms of our picture, that the demand for money increases at every rate of interest. That means the money-demand function shifts to the right, as in Figure 24.10, increasing the rate of interest with the same supply of money.[11]

Thus an anticipated monetary policy will change interest rates before it is implemented. This is not especially surprising once it is put into the framework of our model, but it can be troublesome for policymakers when portfolio managers get into the habit of forecasting stabilization behavior. More on this in Chapter 28.

AGGREGATE DEMAND AND SUPPLY

So far we have described all the factors that can influence the aggregate demand for goods and services according to Keynes. As we mentioned at the very beginning of this chapter, since Keynesian analysis assumes prices are fixed because of a depressed state of the economy, all the impacts on aggregate demand discussed up to now correspond to changes in real income and output as well. It will be useful, nevertheless, to put the Keynesian model into a formal supply/demand framework, just as we did for classical economics in

---

[11] In the example of the previous paragraph, when the *anticipated* decrease in the money supply actually takes place, there is no increase in the level of rates at that time precisely because the demand for money simultaneously decreases by the same amount at that time. The reason is that people no longer expect the Fed to reduce the money supply. Thus the demand for money returns to its original position.

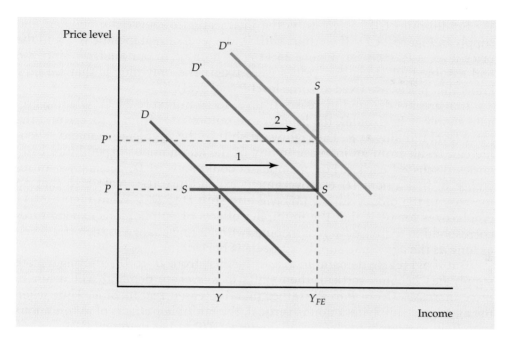

FIGURE 24.11   **Increases in aggregate demand raise real income or prices, depending on the shape of aggregate supply.**

Chapter 23. This will highlight the similarities and differences between Keynes and the classics, permit a brief insight into Keynesian causes of inflation, and also let us see what is meant by supply-side economics.

In Figure 24.11 we put the price level on the vertical axis and GDP on the horizontal axis, just as we did in Figure 23.3. Don't get nervous simply because until now aggregate spending $(C + I + G)$ has been plotted in the figures against income (Y). Now we are interested in how aggregate demand varies when the price level changes, so Figure 24.11 plots income (output) as a function of price. We have different pictures tailored to answer different questions.

The aggregate supply schedule in Figure 24.11 is in two parts: a horizontal segment, which reflects the fact that prices do not increase at less than full employment, and a vertical part, which is the classical school's supply schedule, showing that only prices (not real income) increase after full employment (assumed equal to Y_{FE}) is reached.

The aggregate demand schedule (D) is negatively sloped for the same reason as in the classical world: A lower price level raises the real supply of money balances, which in turn increases the aggregate demand for goods and services. But in the Keynesian world, this rise in the real supply of money has a very specific channel of influence on GDP. It occurs through the impact of rising real balances on the interest rate (as in Figure 24.8) and the impact of a lower interest rate on investment spending and hence GDP.

Equilibrium GDP is given by the intersection of aggregate demand and supply in Figure 24.11. If we start with *D*, the level of real income is *Y* and the price level is *P*. Thus far, Figure 24.11 adds nothing to our analysis, since we had assumed all along that prices were fixed. The only plus is that we now know that prices are fixed at some level *P* (big deal).

If aggregate demand increases from *D* to *D'* in Figure 24.11, when aggregate supply is horizontal, the level of real output rises from *Y* to Y_{FE} and the price level remains at *P*. The rightward shift in the aggregate demand schedule can result from an increase in any of the autonomous expenditure categories discussed earlier. For example, *D* could shift to *D'* because of an increase in investment (*I*) or government expenditure (*G*). Note also that an increase in the money supply (*M*) will also shift *D* to *D'*.[12] What Figure 24.11 emphasizes for us is that the multiplier effects of autonomous expenditures correspond to increases in real income (without any change in the price level) as long as the aggregate supply schedule is horizontal.

But if aggregate demand increases further, from *D'* to *D''*, after aggregate supply has become vertical, then shifts in aggregate demand will result in price increases (from *P* to *P'*) rather than increased real income. Thus when the aggregate supply function is vertical, the multiplier effects of autonomous spending translate into changes in *nominal* GDP rather than real GDP.

What emerges from this is that when the economy is at or near full employment, Keynesian aggregate demand analysis can be used together with the aggregate supply curve to explain upward pressure on prices, or inflation. Anything that shifts the aggregate demand schedule to the right—whether it is increased government spending, increased consumer spending, or increased money supply that increases investment spending—will force up the price level. Notice that this explanation of what influences the price level is somewhat different from that of classical economics. In Chapter 23 we showed that, according to classical thinking, shifts in the aggregate demand schedule reflect changes in the money supply; in fact, the aggregate demand schedule embodies the quantity theory. This is a fundamental distinction between the classical/monetarist view of inflation and the Keynesian theory and will be discussed again in Chapter 27.

At this point it is appropriate to mention the role of so-called *supply-side policies* in macroeconomics. Keynes himself had little reason to focus on aggregate supply, since in the depressed economy of the simple Keynesian model there are more than enough goods and services to go around. But in a full employment setting, the only way to increase real output is to expand productive capacity. That would be represented in Figure 24.11 by a rightward shift in the vertical segment of aggregate supply (Y_{FE} would shift to the right). **Supply-side economics** focuses primarily on the impact of government poli-

---

[12] Recall that an increase in *M* shifts *D* because at *every* price level there are more real cash balances, which lowers interest rates and raises investment spending.

cies on the aggregate supply schedule. Although this is very different from the Keynesian focus, the two are by no means contradictory.[13]

As we mentioned early in Chapter 23, the productive capacity of the economy is determined by the supply of labor, capital, and available technology. Policies that increase any of these production factors will increase potential real output. The government does not directly control any of these, but its tax policies influence the willingness of households and business firms to supply labor and invest in capital. In particular, higher tax rates may very well discourage work and investment, because labor and entrepreneurs are denied some fraction of the income they earn.

According to supply-siders, the main consequence of reducing tax rates is increased production incentives. This view contrasts with the Keynesian emphasis that a reduction in taxes raises aggregate demand. Up to now we have considered the effect of a tax reduction only on the aggregate demand schedule in Figure 24.11; supply-siders contend that the tax impact on the aggregate supply schedule can be even more important. Thus they *could* argue that reducing taxes when the economy is at full employment need not cause prices to rise. In particular, if the vertical portion of the aggregate supply schedule shifted to the right by more than the movement in aggregate demand, prices could even fall. Whether this is in fact the case can be clarified only by empirical evidence.

The role of Keynesian, monetarist, and supply-side mechanisms in the inflationary process will be discussed in greater detail in Chapter 27. Meanwhile, in the next chapter we treat you to the pleasure of a more complicated Keynesian aggregate demand model.

SUMMARY

1. Keynesian analysis maintains that the level of production is determined by the aggregate demand for goods and services. This differs from classical economics, which argued that production occurs at full employment. The main difference between Keynes and the classics is that Keynes did not think that fluctuating prices and interest rates would push the level of economic activity toward full employment, especially in the short run.

2. The Keynesian model focuses on the determinants of aggregate demand in order to pinpoint the level of production. Demand is divided into consumption, investment, and government expenditure. To Keynesians the consumption function is a key behavioral relationship, because it allows them to explain how consumer spending varies with income. Thus when

---

[13] Note that the quantity theory is in the same boat as Keynesian analysis, because it focuses almost exclusively on aggregate demand.

there is a change in autonomous spending (such as an increase in investment), income changes by some multiple (because of induced consumption spending).

3. Government expenditure and taxation play an important role in influencing the level of aggregate demand. Changes in taxes and government expenditures have multiplier effects on income and can be used to offset the effects on GDP of autonomous changes in investment.

4. According to Keynesians, the demand for and supply of money determine the level of interest rates. This view differs from the classical quantity theory, in which the supply of and demand for money determine the price level. The Keynesian result stems from the behavioral assumption that the demand for money is interest-sensitive plus the fact that the price level does not vary.

5. Changes in the money supply alter the level of interest rates in the Keynesian world. The impact on economic activity is then determined by the response of investment spending and the subsequent multiplier effects on GDP. The greater the impact of money supply changes on interest rates, and the larger the sensitivity of spending to interest rate changes, the larger the effect of monetary policy on GDP.

6. There are actually three transmission mechanisms linking monetary policy to GDP. The cost of capital channel through investment spending, the wealth channel through consumption, and the exchange rate channel through net exports.

7. All Keynesian analysis focuses on the aggregate demand for goods and services. It assumes that aggregate supply is sufficient to accommodate increased demand without raising prices. Any increases in aggregate demand at full employment will raise prices and cause inflation. Supply-side policies emphasize the need to generate increased real output at or near full employment.

QUESTIONS

24.1 What happens, according to Keynes, when desired saving exceeds desired investment? Is this view different from classical economics?

24.2 Why does a change in investment spending produce a change in GDP by some multiple, according to Keynes?

24.3 Explain how the equilibrium rate of interest is determined by the supply of and demand for money, according to Keynesian analysis.

24.4 Show geometrically that if there is a so-called liquidity trap, monetary policy cannot lower interest rates.

24.5 Explain why the transactions demand for money falls as the rate of interest rises.

24.6 Is it correct to say that if a change in the money supply is fully anticipated, then there will be no impact on the interest rate at the time of the change?

24.7 What does Keynesian analysis assume about the shape of the aggregate supply schedule? How does this assumption produce different results from those of classical economics?

24.8 *Discussion question:* Put yourself into Keynes's shoes and try to explain what it was about classical economics that forced you to change your outlook. Was it the quantity theory, Say's law, or the shape of the aggregate supply curve?

CHAPTER 25

The *ISLM* World

Why confuse things with a more complicated model of GDP determination? Is it worth the effort? Haven't we said that a good model is like a good map—it tells you how to get from one place to another without detailing every curve in the road, every bump in the terrain? True enough. But sometimes a few complications make life more interesting. Versatility is the password. Being adaptable to more than one use is a desirable characteristic for a model.

The more complex model of GDP determination is known as ***ISLM* analysis.** Among its many attractions, it shows how monetary and fiscal policy interact with each other; it shows what determines the relative multiplier effects of each; it provides a partial integration of the classical and Keynesian systems into one conceptual framework; and it demonstrates some of the fundamental features distinguishing the classical and Keynesian outlooks. As in the previous chapter, most of the analysis assumes a fixed price level, so that we still are concerned with the level of real GDP. In the next-to-last section we will analyze the implications of flexible wages and prices, and at the end we will show how the *ISLM* model collapses into an aggregate demand schedule.

MONEY, INTEREST, AND INCOME

In Chapter 23 we noted that the classical economists stressed the transactions demand for money. Keynes, as we saw in Chapter 24, also discussed this transactions demand, although he did not himself seem to perceive all its ramifications. In particular, because transactions demand increases with income, the rate of interest rises as income rises. Thus not only does the interest rate help determine income; in addition, income helps determine the interest rate.[1] Causation runs both ways—from the interest rate to income and from

---

[1] The one exception is the liquidity trap, introduced in the last chapter, where the rate of interest is given and is independent of everything except public psychology.

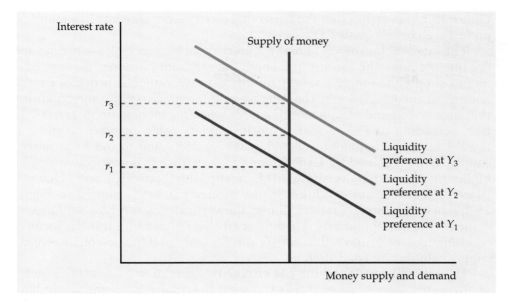

FIGURE 25.1   How to derive the *LM* curve: At higher levels of income, the demand for money rises and so do interest rates.

income to the interest rate. Fortunately, this is not an insurmountable problem. The economy winds up with a determinate level of each, but our model must be reformulated to take this into account.

We begin, in Figure 25.1, with three alternative money-demand functions, each associated with a different level of economic activity.[2] The liquidity-preference function associated with Y_1 is for a level of GDP that is less than Y_2, which in turn is less than Y_3. Each level of GDP has its own liquidity-preference function, because at higher income levels more money is demanded for transactions purposes (at every rate of interest). The horizontal distance between any two demand-for-money functions is equal to the difference in the demand for money at the two levels of GDP. If we use the classical formulation coming out of Cambridge (as discussed in Chapter 23), we can write:

$$Demand\ for\ Money = kY$$

or

$$\Delta Demand\ for\ Money = k\Delta Y$$

The latter implies that the demand for money will change by k times the change in the level of GDP (where k equals, for example, 0.25). In terms of

---

[2] The discussion in the remainder of this chapter will be based on geometric analysis. For those who prefer algebra, the appendix to the chapter presents the entire model, and its implications, in equation form.

Figure 25.1, this means that the horizontal distance between any two liquidity-preference curves equals $k\Delta Y$.

The demand for money is really a function of two variables—income and the interest rate. The equilibrium condition (amount of money demanded = money supply) no longer provides an interest rate; rather, it provides combinations of income (Y) and the interest rate (r) which satisfy the condition that money demand equals money supply *when the money supply is fixed*. In fact, according to Figure 25.1, a positive relationship between Y and r is needed to keep the amount of money demanded equal to the fixed money supply. A higher level of GDP (compare Y_2 with Y_1) is associated with a higher interest rate (r_2 versus r_1). This relationship between Y and r that satisfies the equilibrium condition in the money market is plotted in Figure 25.2, where the interest rate is still on the vertical axis but now we have income on the horizontal axis. The line is labeled *LM* because it is the locus of combinations of Y and r that satisfy the *l*iquidity-preference-equals-*m*oney-supply equilibrium condition.

How should you "read" the **LM curve?** In either of two ways. For a series of alternative interest rates, it tells you what the resulting income would have to be to make the demand for money equal to the (fixed) supply of money. *At higher interest rates,* there is less money demanded, *so income must be higher* to increase the demand for transactions balances if the total demand for money is to remain equal to the (fixed) supply. *Or,* for a series of alternative income levels, Figure 25.2 tells you what the resulting interest rate would have

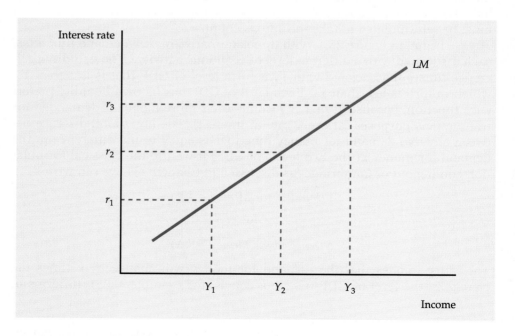

FIGURE 25.2   The *LM* curve.

to be to make the demand for money equal to the fixed supply. *At higher income levels,* more transactions money is desired, *so the interest rate must be higher* to shrink the demand for money balances if total demand is to remain equal to the fixed supply.

Before you write to the folks back home and tell them that an increase in the interest rate raises GDP, or that an increase in GDP raises the interest rate, rest assured that nothing of the sort has been said—so far. In fact, we can't even determine Y and r as yet, much less say anything about how each of these variables changes. All we have is one relationship (equation or equilibrium condition) and two variables, Y and r, and you remember enough high school algebra to know that you need at least two equations to determine the equilibrium values of two variables.

We *will* produce another relationship between Y and r, based on the equilibrium condition in the market for goods and services (the $C + I + G = Y$ or the $I = S$ equilibrium condition). This great unification and solution, which will knock your socks off, is scheduled to take place in about ten pages. But before that cataclysmic experience, it will be helpful for subsequent policy discussions to elaborate on the factors determining the slope of the *LM* curve and shifts in its position. Both of these help determine the relative size of monetary and fiscal policy multipliers.

ALL ABOUT *LM*

The determinants of the slope of the *LM* curve are best illustrated by going over the reasons for its positive slope. Take point *A* in Figure 25.3. Assume that the amount of money demanded equals the fixed money supply at that point, hence combination Y_1 and r_1 lies on the *LM* curve. To see whether a second (Y, r) combination that also satisfies the equilibrium condition (money demand = money supply) lies above and to the right of *A* (like point *B*), or below and to the right (like point *D*), let us first pick a point *C* which differs from *A* only in the level of income.

At point *C*, the rate of interest is still r_1 but income is Y_2 (above Y_1). Since income is higher at point *C* than at point *A*, the transactions demand for money is greater at *C*. Nothing else is changed, so point *C* must have a larger demand for money than the (fixed) supply. To set matters right, the interest rate must *rise* to reduce the demand for money and thereby restore the equality between demand and supply.

The slope of line *AB* (the *LM* curve) in Figure 25.3 is determined by two factors. *The first is the size of the gap between money demand and supply at point C.* If the increment in the amount of money demanded per unit ΔY is large, then the amount demanded will be a lot higher at *C* than at *A*, and the increase in r needed to restore equilibrium (to lower the amount demanded) will be large. In other words, if transactions demand is great, then the level of

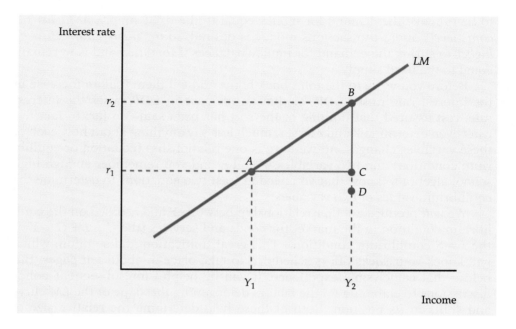

FIGURE 25.3   The slope of the *LM* curve.

r needed to maintain demand-supply equality at Y_2 will be great, point B will be higher than otherwise, and the slope of the *LM* curve will be steeper.

The second factor influencing the slope of the LM curve is the interest-sensitivity of money demand. For a given excess of money demand over supply at point C in Figure 25.3, the greater the interest-sensitivity of liquidity preference, the *smaller* the necessary increase in the rate of interest to restore equilibrium. This is so because when liquidity preference is highly interest-sensitive, then even a small increase in r reduces the amount of money demanded by a lot. In other words, at Y_2 the rise in r needed to ensure demand-supply equality will be smaller the greater is the sensitivity of demand to r; point B will be lower than otherwise, and the slope of the *LM* curve will be flatter.

To summarize: The slope of the *LM* curve will be steeper the greater is the income-sensitivity of demand for money, and the less is the interest-sensitivity of demand for money; the *LM* curve will be flatter the less is the income-sensitivity of the demand for money, and the greater is the interest-sensitivity.

Monetary Policy and the *LM* Curve

What causes the *LM* curve to shift *position* (in contrast to a change in its slope)? It does get boring in the same position, so the monetary authorities rush to the rescue. An increase in the supply of money moves the *LM* curve to the right, and a decrease in the money supply moves the *LM* curve to the left. *By shifting the position of the LM curve, the Federal Reserve can increase or de-*

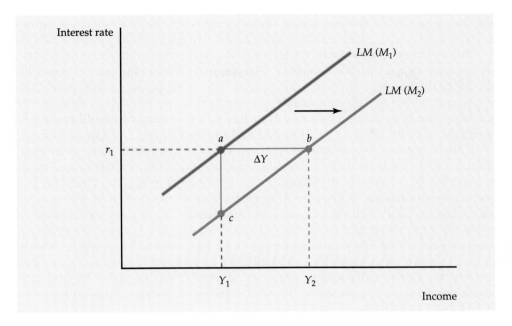

FIGURE 25.4 **An increase in the money supply shifts the *LM* curve to the right.**

crease the potential equilibrium level of GDP associated with a given interest rate. Let's see why a change in the money supply shifts the *LM* curve.

In Figure 25.4 we start with the *LM* curve associated with money supply M_1. All points on that curve satisfy the condition that the amount of money demanded $= M_1$. Take point *a*, with interest rate r_1 and income Y_1. Now increase the money supply to M_2. At point *a* the new larger money supply now exceeds the demand for money. What can restore equilibrium between the demand for money and money supply? Clearly, if *income* rises, the transactions demand for money will go up, hence some point to the right of *a*, say point *b*, will now represent equilibrium between demand and supply. Therefore, the new *LM* curve, *LM*(M_2), the one with combinations of *Y* and *r* that satisfy demand equal to the new larger money supply, must be to the right of the old *LM* curve. (A similar argument shows that the *LM* curve must shift to the left if there is a decline in money supply.)

We can say exactly how far to the right (or to the left) the new *LM* curve must be. If the supply of money increases by ΔM, the amount of money demanded must change by the same amount in order to restore equilibrium. But we know that the transactions demand for money changes by *k* times the change in income ($k\Delta Y$). So income must change until $k\Delta Y$ equals ΔM (assuming nothing else changes, which is what we are doing by looking at the horizontal differences between two *LM* curves, with the interest rate held constant). The demand for money will increase to match the enlarged supply when $k\Delta Y = \Delta M$, or when $\Delta Y = \Delta M/k$, which we can also write as $\Delta Y = 1/k \times$

ΔM. In other words, the horizontal distance between two *LM* curves is equal to $1/k \times \Delta M$ (or the difference in Figure 25.4 between Y_1 and Y_2 is $1/k \times \Delta M$).[3]

But a change in income is not the only way for a change in the money supply to be absorbed into the economy. The interest rate can fall, and this would also raise the amount of money demanded. This is represented in Figure 25.4 by point *c*, which lies directly below point *a;* that is, we are still at income Y_1, but this time it is the interest rate that has fallen to restore equilibrium between the amount of money demanded and the new (larger) supply of money.

Unfortunately, we cannot as yet say exactly where the new increased money supply leads us. *Will it all be absorbed by increases in GDP, or will it all be absorbed by declines in the interest rate?* That question is a Big One. Our introductory discussion in Chapter 2 suggested that expansion in *M* will lead to *both* a higher GDP and a lower interest rate. Hence, if we start out at point *a* in Figure 25.4, the new equilibrium of the economy lies somewhere *between* points *b* and *c*. The classical economists, however, said an increase in *M* will all be absorbed by transactions demand. We cannot yet answer the question because we don't really know where we started from. In order to find out where the devil we are, we must introduce the goods sector of the economy— saving and investment.

THE GOODS MARKET

Economic activity and interest rates are affected by behavior in the market for goods and services as well as in the money market. The counterpart to the money-demand-equals-money-supply equilibrium condition is the equilibrium between desired saving and investment (or total desired expenditure equals production). The equilibrium levels of GDP and interest rate must satisfy two equilibrium conditions: the condition that $I = S$ as well as money demand = money supply—which is a good thing, because with two variables, *Y* and *r*, we need two equations if both variables are to be determined simultaneously.

To describe the combinations of *Y* and *r* needed for equilibrium in the goods market, we must recall the investment function from Chapters 23 and 24. Desired investment spending is negatively related to the rate of interest; a fall in the rate of interest raises the level of investment spending. A higher level of investment spending, in turn, implies a higher level of GDP. These relationships are best depicted graphically. We will then discuss them in more general terms.

In Figure 25.5(a) the saving function is drawn together with three alternative levels of investment, each one associated with a different rate of interest.

---

[3] Recall from Chapter 23 that when there is no interest-sensitivity of the demand for money, then $1/k$ equals velocity. Under those conditions, the horizontal distance (which holds the rate of interest constant) between the two *LM* curves equals ΔM times velocity. This will be important in the next chapter, unless you decide not to read it because things are complicated enough as is.

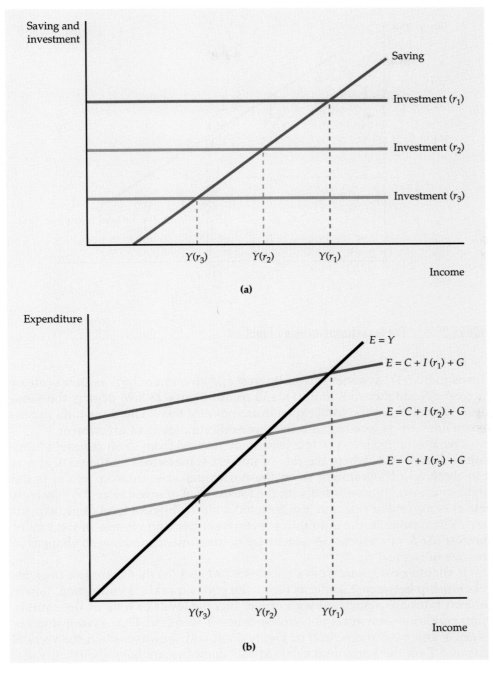

FIGURE 25.5 **How to derive the *IS* curve: At lower rates of interest the level of investment is higher, and so is the level of income.**

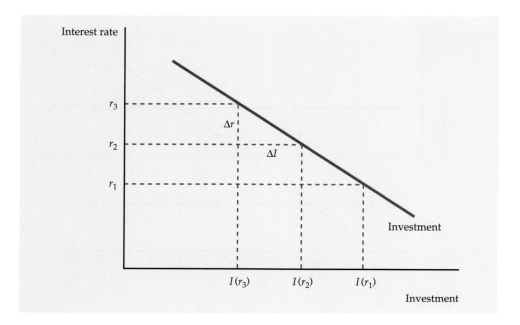

FIGURE 25.6   The investment-demand function.

"Investment (r_1)" assumes rate of interest r_1, "investment (r_2)" assumes rate of interest r_2 (a higher rate than r_1), and so on. Figure 25.5(b) depicts the same situation, but from the total expenditure point of view. The three total expenditure lines are associated with the three different levels of investment.

   The alternative levels of investment are derived from the investment function in Figure 25.6, where the rate of interest is measured on the vertical axis and the level of investment is on the horizontal axis. Interest rate r_3 is the highest rate and is associated with the lowest level of investment $I(r_3)$; interest rate r_1 is the lowest rate and is associated with the highest level of investment $I(r_1)$. The change in the amount of investment per unit change in the rate of interest $(\Delta I/\Delta r)$ measures the sensitivity of investment spending to changes in the rate of interest.

   It should be obvious from Figures 25.5(a) and (b) that there is a negative relationship between Y and r as far as the goods market is concerned. Lower interest rates are associated with higher income levels as long as the equilibrium condition—saving equals investment—is satisfied. This relationship between Y and r is summarized in Figure 25.7, with r measured on the vertical axis and Y on the horizontal axis. (At this point, *we* are having difficulty distinguishing the horizontal from the vertical and who's on what—so keep your eyes open.) The locus of points satisfying the investment-equals-saving equilibrium condition is called the **IS curve.**

   How should you "read" the IS curve? As with the *LM* curve, in either of two ways. For a series of alternative interest rates, it tells you what income must be to make saving equal to investment. *At higher interest rates,* there is

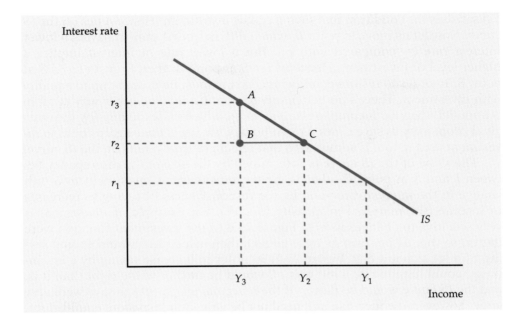

FIGURE 25.7   The *IS* curve and its slope.

less investment, *so income must be lower* to shrink saving (which is a function of income) to the point where it equals the smaller volume of investment. *Or, for a series of alternative income levels, it tells you what the interest rate must be to make saving equal to investment. At higher income levels,* saving is larger, *so the interest rate must be lower* to expand investment to the point where it equals the larger volume of saving.

Perhaps now you can appreciate our advice earlier in the chapter, with respect to the *LM* curve, suggesting that you not pass on that particular information about the relationship between Y and r. Now there are two relationships between Y and r. While more of a good thing is usually better, it can lead to embarrassing situations. In our case, however, it will rescue our model from indeterminacy. But before presenting the Missouri Compromise (named after those who refused to believe it was possible), let's take a quick look at the factors that determine the slope and position of the *IS* curve; these are the things, along with the factors that determine the slope and position of the *LM* curve, that influence the relative magnitudes of the monetary and fiscal policy multipliers on GDP.

ALL ABOUT *IS*

To see why the *IS* curve looks the way it does, what makes it flatter or steeper, what moves it to the right or to the left, let us examine its negative slope in greater detail. Take point A in Figure 25.7 and assume that combination (r_3,

Y_3) satisfies the condition that saving equals investment: Hence A lies on the *IS* curve. Now let us move to point B, which differs from A only in having a lower interest rate (r_2 compared with r_3). But a lower rate of interest implies a higher level of investment. Hence, if $I = S$ at point A, then I must *exceed* S at point B. In order to restore equilibrium, saving must be brought up to equality with investment. There's no better way to do it (in fact, no other way at all in our model) than for income to rise, say to Y_2, which raises saving (by the marginal propensity to save times ΔY). At point C saving is once again equal to investment, and it, too, is admitted to that select group of points on the *IS* curve.

The slope of the *IS* curve is determined by the size of the discrepancy between I and S at point B—that is, by the sensitivity of investment to a unit change in the interest rate—and by the responsiveness of saving to increases in income (the marginal propensity to save). For example, if investment is very sensitive to changes in r (in Figure 25.6, if the investment function were flatter, so that ΔI per unit Δr were larger), then investment would exceed saving by a lot at point B in Figure 25.7. In order to increase saving by a lot, income would have to rise a lot; point C would be further to the right than it is, and the *IS* curve would be flatter. If the marginal propensity to save were very large, however, the increase in Y need not be very large to restore equilibrium, point C would be more to the left, and the *IS* curve would be steeper.

All of this could be said in somewhat less formal terms. The fall in the rate of interest at point B compared with point A raises investment spending. This ΔI, in turn, raises the level of GDP by ΔI times the "simple" multiplier, $1/(1 - b)$, of the previous chapter. This increase in GDP is measured from point B to point C. (Note that this assumes quite explicitly that the rate of interest remains the same both before and after the increase in Y, and that is accomplished by drawing a *horizontal* line from B to C.) Hence, the more sensitive investment spending is to changes in the rate of interest, the flatter the slope of the *IS* curve will be and the larger the multiplier effect. This is perfectly consistent with the story just told in terms of the marginal propensity to save, because the larger the marginal propensity to save ($= 1 - b$), the smaller the multiplier of the simple Keynesian model.

To summarize: A *highly* interest-sensitive investment function and a *low* marginal propensity to save imply a flat *IS* curve; a low interest-sensitivity of investment and a high marginal propensity to save imply a steep *IS* curve.

The *position* of the *IS* curve (in contrast to its slope) is altered by any change in autonomous spending, such as government spending, private investment that is independent of the rate of interest, or private consumption spending that is independent of income (or, looked at from another standpoint, private saving that is independent of income, such as changes induced by government taxation). Such shifts in autonomous spending disturb the $I = S$ (or $E = Y$) equilibrium condition. The equilibrium combinations of Y and r will, therefore, be altered. This can be seen by looking either at saving-equals-investment equilibrium or income-equals-expenditure equilibrium. We will spare you the agony of doing it both ways (just this once) and concentrate on the expenditure-equals-income approach.

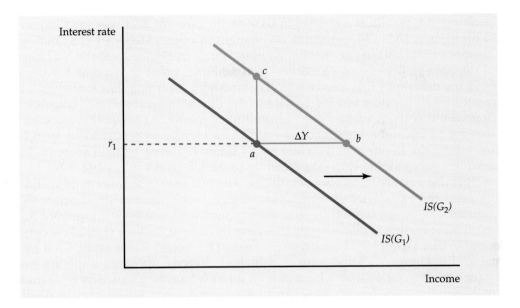

FIGURE 25.8   An increase in government spending shifts the *IS* curve to the right.

In Figure 25.8 let's start out with *IS* curve $IS(G_1)$. At every point, saving equals investment and desired total expenditure equals income. Now assume government spending goes up, from G_1 to G_2. From Figure 25.5(b) it is clear that under such conditions each of the total-expenditure functions would shift upward, producing a higher level of Y for each interest rate. In Figure 25.8, therefore, an increase in G implies a shift to the right of the *IS* curve, say to $IS(G_2)$—that is, a higher level of Y for each rate of interest.[4]

Similar shifts in the *IS* curve would be brought on by increases or decreases in investment spending that are independent of the rate of interest. How might that come about? If entrepreneurs suddenly expect higher future dollar returns on investment projects, the rate of return discussed in Chapter 24 will increase and some investment spending will be undertaken that otherwise would not have been. Keynes thought such shifts would, in fact, occur quite often and in substantial magnitude. Entrepreneurs are a fickle group, very sensitive to anything (war and peace) and anyone (presidents and reporters) that might influence the future profitability of their investments. Their actions tend to shift the investment demand function (Figure 25.6) to the right or left, thereby shifting the *IS* curve to the right or left as well.

We can also say exactly how much the *IS* curve shifts to the right or left because of a change in autonomous spending. A change in autonomous

---

[4] An increase in taxes, on the other hand, implies a lower level of consumption in Figure 25.5(b), hence each of the total expenditure lines is lower than before and the level of Y associated with each rate of interest is less. Result: The *IS* curve shifts to the left.

spending, ΔA, produces a change in GDP by the amount ΔA times the Chapter 24 multiplier, $1/(1 - b)$, assuming no changes in other categories of spending (besides consumption via the change in income). In Figure 25.8, the horizontal distance between two *IS* curves—for example, point *a* to point *b*—measures the difference between two levels of income, assuming that some type of autonomous spending has increased but the rate of interest remains constant. That would equal ΔA times our old multiplier friend $1/(1 - b)$. Therefore, an increase in autonomous spending—such as a change in government spending—shifts the *IS* curve to the right by ΔA times $1/(1 - b)$, while a decrease in autonomous spending shifts the *IS* curve to the left by ΔA times $1/(1 - b)$.

But there really is *another* possibility. The increase in autonomous spending need not raise GDP if some other category of spending simultaneously contracts. If, at the same time that government spending goes up, private investment spending is discouraged (because the rate of interest rises), it is conceivable that GDP could remain unchanged. This possibility is recognized explicitly in Figure 25.8 by point *c*, which is directly above *a*, implying no change at all in GDP. Instead, the rate of interest has risen sufficiently so that total spending remains the same: Income equals desired expenditure at point *c* as well as point *b*, saving equals investment at both points, and so both are on the new *IS* curve.

Keynesians seem to agree that a change in government spending will raise GDP a lot, hence we will wind up near point *b* when *G* goes up. The classical economists, on the other hand, felt that the level of output would be unaffected by changes in any particular category of expenditure. An increase in *G* would be accompanied by a decrease in some other kind of spending, leaving income unchanged (we would move to point *c*). We can't really tell what will happen until we bring the *IS* curve together with the *LM* curve, derive equilibrium *Y* and *r* simultaneously, and then examine the way these variables respond to monetary and fiscal policy within that *general* equilibrium framework.

THE SIMULTANEOUS DETERMINATION OF INCOME AND INTEREST: *IS* AND *LM* TOGETHER

The equilibrium levels of GDP and the interest rate must satisfy equilibrium in the money market (money demand = money supply or $LP = M$), *and* in the product market ($I = S$). In Figure 25.9 we have drawn an *LM* curve for a given money supply and an *IS* curve for a given level of government expenditure and taxation and a given investment function (relating I to r). The equilibrium Y and r must be at the intersection point of the *IS* and *LM* curves, point *E*, since only at that point does saving equal investment *and* liquidity preference (LP) equal the money supply. At any other point, one or both of these equilibrium conditions are violated, and dynamic forces will move income and the interest rate toward point *E*.

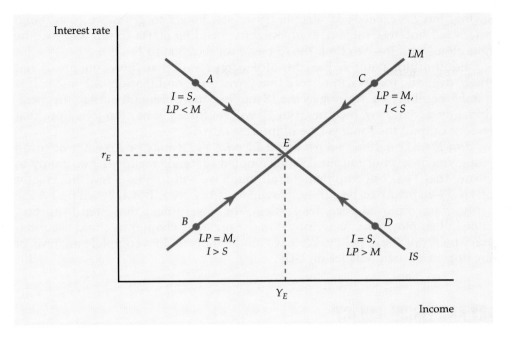

FIGURE 25.9   **The simultaneous determination of income and interest (fantastic!).**

Let's see what happens if the economy is not at point *E* in Figure 25.9. Take point *A* on the *IS* curve. Saving equals investment, but money demand is less than money supply. (The latter is so because point *A* is directly above point *B*, which is on the *LM* curve. At point *B* we know *LP = M*. Since point *A* has a higher rate of interest, the amount of money demanded is less, so with a given money supply we have *LP* less than *M*.) People want to hold less money than they have at point *A*. To get rid of the money they start to buy bonds, driving bond prices higher and the interest rate lower. As the interest rate falls, investment rises and so does income—and, believe it or not, we are sliding down the *IS* curve toward *E*.

At point *B*, money supply equals money demand because we are on the *LM* curve, but investment exceeds saving (point *B* is directly below *A*; at *A* we know *S = I*; at *B* the interest rate is lower, hence *I* exceeds *S*). The excess of *I* over *S* leads to an increase in production as entrepreneurs try to replenish falling inventories. As income rises, the rate of interest is driven up because the money supply is fixed and people start to sell bonds in order to get additional transactions balances. We are now climbing up the *LM* curve toward *E*.

At points to the right of *E*, dynamic forces would lead to a fall in the level of income. At *C* we have *LP = M*, but desired investment is less than desired saving (see if you know why—*hint:* compare with *D*). Entrepreneurs cut back their production in order to reduce inventory accumulation. As GDP falls there is a reduction in the need for transactions balances, people start buying bonds with the extra cash, bond prices rise, and interest rates decline—we return to *E* by sliding down the *LM* curve. Finally, at point *D* investment equals saving, but *LP* exceeds *M*. People try to sell bonds to get more cash, bond prices fall, interest rates rise; investment spending starts to fall and income falls along with it—we climb the *IS* curve until we get to *E*.

Equilibrium point *E* has the nice property that if the economy is not there, dynamic forces will restore that particular combination of *Y* and *r*. It is a *stable* equilibrium. As long as the *IS* and *LM* curves remain in the same position, any deviation of income from Y_E will set forces in motion to restore that level of output; the same is true of interest rate r_E.

But there is nothing sacred about income Y_E. It may or may not be a full employment level of output. We have noted no tendency for the economy to ensure that Y_E is full employment, although we will suggest a few things later on. If Y_E happens to be full employment, all is well. But if it isn't, and the army of unemployed becomes restless, the government may step in to produce full employment. As we noted in the previous chapter, it could use monetary policy or fiscal policy. We have all the tools to do a complete analysis of the impact of such policies on GDP.

MONETARY AND FISCAL POLICY

Monetary Policy

We have now reached the point where we can put all of our slopes and shifts to good use. Figures 25.10, 25.11, and 25.12 summarize the way monetary

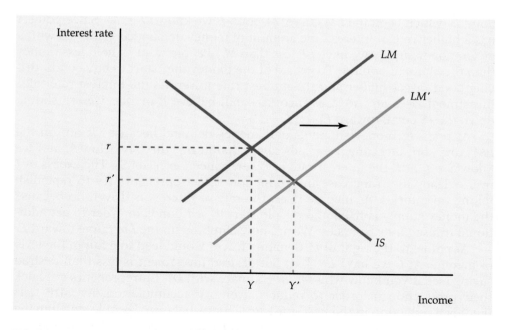

FIGURE 25.10   An expansionary monetary policy.

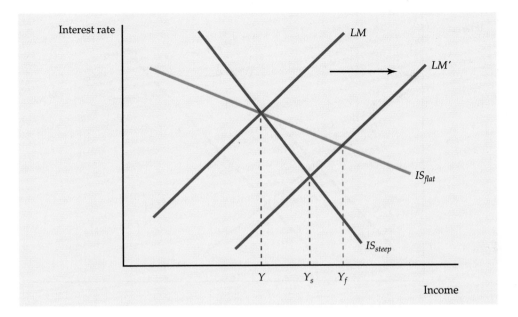

<u>**FIGURE 25.11**</u>   **Monetary policy is more effective the flatter the *IS* curve.**

policy influences economic activity, and the factors affecting the size of the multiplier effects on GDP within the *ISLM* framework.

In Figure 25.10, if we start with *LM* and *IS*, the equilibrium level of income is *Y* and the interest rate is *r*. An increase in the money supply, for example, shifts the *LM* function to *LM'*, reducing the interest rate to *r'* and increasing GDP to *Y'*.[5]

Figure 25.11 shows that an increase in money supply (*LM* shifts to *LM'*) raises GDP by more, the *flatter is the IS curve*. With the relatively steep *IS* curve, the increase in income is only to *Y_s*, while with the flatter *IS* curve the increase is to *Y_f*. The flatter *IS* curve can be due to a highly interest-sensitive investment function.[6] Hence, the fall in *r* due to an increase in *M* raises the level of investment by a lot. The impact of monetary policy on GDP is more powerful under such conditions.

---

[5] All the examples are in terms of increases in the money supply. A decrease would simply shift the *LM* curve to the left and all the changes would be just the reverse.

[6] The **wealth effect** of interest rates on consumption also makes the *IS* curve flatter, thereby increasing the impact of a change in the money supply on GDP. The reasoning is as follows: A decline in the rate of interest not only increases investment spending directly but also increases wealth (by raising bond prices) and thereby induces consumers to spend more. For a given decline in the rate of interest, therefore, both investment and consumption go up, causing income to rise by a larger amount. Similarly, the **exchange rate effect** also makes the *IS* curve flatter. In particular, a decline in the rate of interest lowers the value of the dollar on the foreign exchange market, thereby encouraging net exports, causing GDP to increase more.

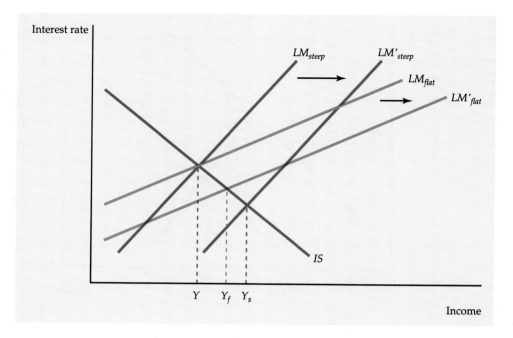

FIGURE 25.12   Monetary policy is more effective the steeper the *LM* curve.

Figure 25.12 is somewhat more complicated. It illustrates that an increase in the money supply is more powerful *the less the sensitivity of money demand* to changes in the interest rate. If the demand for money is rather insensitive to changes in the rate of interest, the *LM* curve is steeper. An increase in money supply would shift LM_{steep} to LM'_{steep} or LM_{flat} to LM'_{flat}.[7] The former implies an increase in GDP from Y to Y_s, while the latter implies a shift from Y to Y_f. The explanation is as follows: The *less* the interest-sensitivity of the demand for money, the *larger* the decline in the rate of interest when money supply is increased (because the amount of money demanded increases only slightly when there is only a small fall in r); therefore, with a big drop in r (needed to increase money demand), the induced increases in investment spending and GDP are large.

Fiscal Policy

The nature of the impact of fiscal policy on GDP is summarized in Figures 25.13, 25.14, and 25.15. An increase in government spending (or a decrease in taxes) shifts the *IS* curve to the right.[8] In Figure 25.13 there is a shift from *IS*

---

[7] Notice that the *horizontal* distances between the curves in the two sets are identical because the income sensitivity of the demand for money is the same in both cases; hence the *potential* increase in GDP due to the increased money supply is the same (at the old equilibrium interest rate).

[8] A decrease in government spending or an increase in taxes shifts the *IS* curve to the left, and all the impacts are the reverse of those in the text.

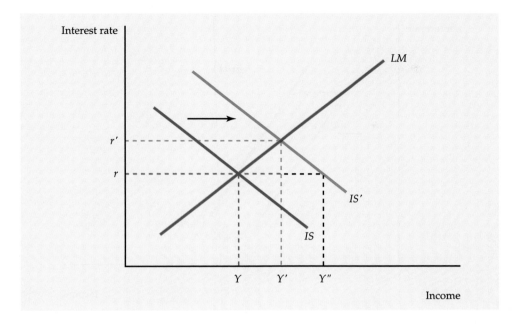

FIGURE 25.13   An expansionary fiscal policy.

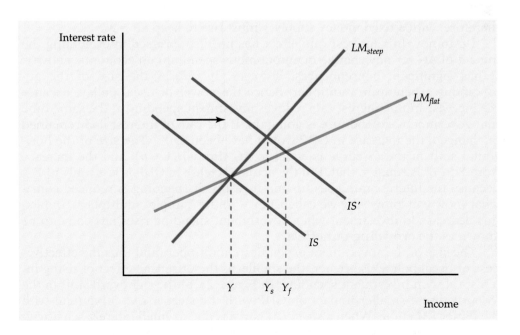

FIGURE 25.14   Fiscal policy is more effective the flatter the _LM_ curve.

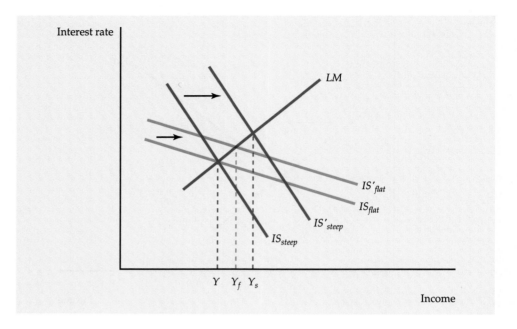

FIGURE 25.15   Fiscal policy is more effective the steeper the *IS* curve.

to *IS'*. Equilibrium GDP goes from *Y* to *Y'* at the same time that the interest rate is driven *up* from *r* to *r'*. The interest rate goes up because there is increased transactions demand for money associated with the rise in GDP; therefore, with a fixed money supply, *r* must rise to keep *LP = M*.

Up to now this interest rate effect has been suppressed in evaluating the impact of ΔG (or any change in autonomous spending) on economic activity. It has significant consequences, however. It *reduces* the size of the autonomous expenditure multiplier, hence the power of fiscal policy, because the increase in the interest rate reduces investment spending at the same time that government expenditure is going up. If the rate of interest had remained unchanged, the increase in GDP would have been to *Y''*. The size of the horizontal shift in the *IS* curve is equal to ΔG times $1/(1 - b)$, and the increase from *Y* to *Y''* is equal to that. But the actual increase in GDP is less (only to *Y'*), because the interest rate goes up and investment spending is reduced somewhat (now you know why we called $1/(1 - b)$ the "simple" multiplier). In fact, this decrease in investment when government spending rises has come to be known as the **crowding-out effect.**

The size of the government expenditure multiplier (and thus the effectiveness of fiscal policy) is greater, the smaller is the offsetting effect of rising interest rates on investment spending. In Figure 25.14 the rightward shift in the *IS* curve has a smaller impact on GDP with the steeper *LM* curve than with the flatter *LM* curve. When a steep *LM* curve is due to small interest-sensitivity of liquidity preference, for example, the increased transactions demand for

TABLE 25.1   A Summary of Monetary and Fiscal Policy Effectiveness

Then	(1) If *LP* is very sensitive to *r*	(2) If *I* is very sensitive to *r*
(A) The *LM* curve is	flatter	—
(B) The *IS* curve is	—	flatter
(C) Monetary policy is	less effective	more effective
(D) Fiscal policy is	more effective	less effective

money as GDP rises requires a large increase in the rate of interest to bring total money demand back into equality with money supply. The large rise in the
rate of interest cuts off a large amount of private investment—there is a large
"crowding-out" effect—hence the net impact on GDP is relatively small.[9]

Figure 25.15 is another rather complicated diagram. It indicates that the
less the interest-sensitivity of investment, the larger is the government expenditure multiplier, and thus the more effective is fiscal policy. If investment
spending is insensitive to changes in the rate of interest, the *IS* curve is
steeper. An increase in government spending either shifts IS_{steep} to IS'_{steep},
raising GDP to Y_s, or shifts IS_{flat} to IS'_{flat}, raising GDP to Y_f. The increase in
the rate of interest cuts off more investment the greater the sensitivity of investment to the rate of interest; hence the rise in income is smaller under such
circumstances.[10]

As a reward for reading this far and still remaining conscious (check your
pulse), Table 25.1 summarizes the factors influencing the relative effectiveness of monetary policy and fiscal policy. Start at the top of columns (1) and
(2), with the statement, for example, "If *LP* is very sensitive to *r*," and then
proceed to the extreme left-hand column for "*Then* (A), (B), (C), and (D)." The
implications of each statement for *ISLM* analysis and monetary and fiscal policy are recorded in the table.

KEYNES AND THE CLASSICS

Velocity, one of the cornerstones of the classical system, seems to have disappeared from our Keynesian framework. Where has velocity gone? It has disappeared behind the *LM* curve. Since a particular *LM* function is drawn for a

---

[9] The steep *LM* curve can also be due to a large transactions demand for money. In this case, the
increase in *Y* produces a large rise in the demand for money, forcing the rate of interest to rise by
a lot in order to bring money demand back into equality with the fixed money supply.

[10] Notice that the horizontal distances between the *IS* curves in the two sets are identical. This is
so because, if the rate of interest is held constant, the *potential* increase in GDP due to an increase
in government spending is the same (because the marginal propensity to consume is assumed to
be the same).

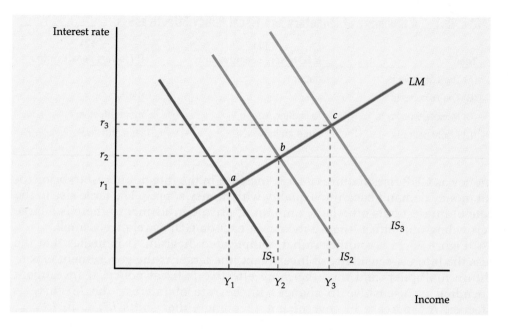

FIGURE 25.16 **When the *IS* curve shifts, both income and velocity rise.**

given money supply, as one moves up along an *LM* function, the income velocity of money is necessarily going up. Income is rising but the money supply is constant, so Y/M ($= V$) has to rise. In Figure 25.16, three different *IS* curves produce three different levels of GDP, as well as three different levels of velocity: V_1 ($= Y_1/M$) at *a*; V_2 ($= Y_2/M$) at *b*; and V_3 ($= Y_3/M$) at *c*.[11] V_3 is greater than V_2, which is greater than V_1.

The rightward shifts in the *IS* curve in Figure 25.16, associated with (for example) increased levels of government spending, succeed in raising GDP by raising velocity. In fact, velocity goes up because the demand for money is sensitive to the rate of interest. The rise in the rate of interest induces the public to hold less speculative balances (or, more generally, to make more economical use of all money balances), permitting more cash to be used for carrying out transactions.

If the demand for money were totally *insensitive* to the interest rate, then velocity would be constant and GDP would not be affected by shifts in autonomous spending. An interest-insensitive demand for money means that money demand depends *only* on income. For a given supply of money, there is only one level of income at which the equilibrium condition, $LP = M$, is satisfied. The *LM* curve is vertical at that level of GDP, as shown in Figure 25.17—

[11] Velocity is properly defined as *PY/M*, but in our discussion prices are fixed so that movements in velocity are identified with *Y*.

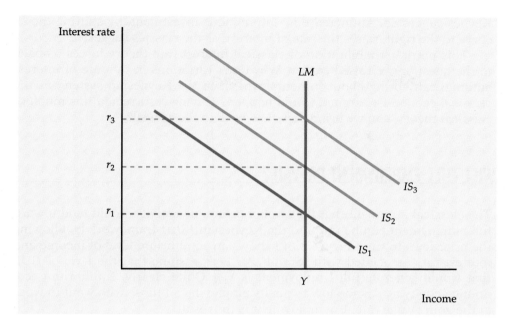

FIGURE 25.17   When the *LM* curve is vertical, shifts in the *IS* curve raise neither income nor velocity.

implying that no matter how high government spending rises, the level of GDP cannot go up because then *LP* would exceed *M*.

It is the fixed money supply that prevents GDP from rising under such circumstances. If autonomous spending goes up, illustrated by the rightward shifts in the *IS* curve in Figure 25.17, the result is an increase in the rate of interest, cutting off investment spending. The rate of interest rises until the drop in interest-sensitive investment spending is equal to the autonomous increase in spending, resulting in no increase in GDP. The "crowding-out" effect is complete. (We will return to the implications of a vertical *LM* curve in the next chapter.)

Another feature of *ISLM* analysis is that it integrates the classical and Keynesian theories of interest rate determination. In Chapter 24 the simplified Keynesian view was that the interest rate was a purely monetary phenomenon, determined by the supply of and demand for money. The classical school, on the other hand, argued that the interest rate was a "real" phenomenon, determined exclusively by saving and investment.[12] In our current treatment both monetary factors, embodied in the *LM* curve, and real factors, embodied in the *IS* curve, affect the interest rate. An increase in the money supply, by shifting the *LM* curve to the right, lowers the rate of interest, as

---

[12] Recall once again that this controversy refers to the real rate of interest. As long as inflationary expectations are zero, real rates equal nominal rates. Moreover, as long as inflationary expectations are unchanged, changes in nominal interest rates correspond to changes in real rates.

Keynes suggested. An increase in autonomous investment, by shifting the *IS* curve to the right, raises the rate of interest, as the classics suggested.

This partial rehabilitation of classical interest rate theory forces us back to the question we raised earlier: Why don't variations in the rate of interest automatically bring about full employment in the Keynesian system, as the classical economists argued would happen? Having resurrected this much of classical theory, can we bring Say's law back to life as well?

WHEN WILL FULL EMPLOYMENT PREVAIL?

The classical argument that the level of economic activity would tend toward full employment can be put into the Keynesian *ISLM* framework by allowing the price level to vary. Figure 25.18 shows an equilibrium level of income and interest rate associated with *IS* and *LM*. Let's assume that the level of GDP that would generate full employment is Y_{FE}. Quite clearly, equilibrium economic activity at Y is too low to justify employing all those who want to work at the going wage rate. Unemployment is the result.

The Keynesian apparatus makes it perfectly clear that the only way employment will increase is for aggregate economic activity to increase; only if desired spending increases will GDP increase beyond Y toward Y_{FE}. So far we have no reason to suspect that either the *IS* curve or the *LM* curve will shift to

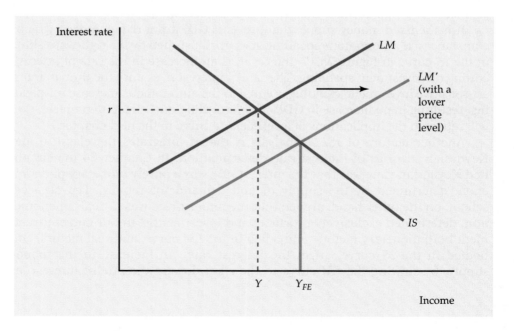

FIGURE 25.18   The classical position: Lower prices shift the *LM* curve to the right and automatically produce full employment.

GOING OUT ON A LIMB

ISLM Analysis Lives

To paraphrase Mark Twain, reports of the death of *ISLM* are greatly exaggerated. The *ISLM* model was invented by Sir John Hicks in a famous 1937 article, "Mr. Keynes and the Classics." It quickly became the standard exposition of the Keynesian viewpoint, although there have always been reservations about how faithfully *ISLM* analysis represented the views of Lord Keynes himself.

Prominent objections to the *ISLM* approach include the following: (1) The analysis of income and expenditure (the *IS* curve) is a flow concept, while money and portfolio balance (the *LM* curve) is a stock concept, and there is no linkage between the flows and stocks; (2) monetary effects are collapsed into a single parameter, the interest rate, with no role for such potentially important factors as bank portfolio composition and the structure of financial markets; (3) money is viewed as a direct substitute for other financial assets, but not for physical assets; (4) prices of goods are either fixed or flexible, rather than flexible in varying degrees.

There is little doubt that each of these objections contains a strong element of truth, and each has spawned more sophisticated approaches to macromonetary analysis. Nevertheless, *ISLM* has stood the test of time. Despite its shortcomings it has been with us for more than fifty years. Odds are that it will last at least another few, so that it will help usher in the new millennium.

the right, hence no reason to suspect that output *Y* will not remain at that level unless there are increases in government spending or the money supply.

But the classical economists said we needn't wait for government intervention. With less than full employment, workers would lower their wage demands and prices would be lowered as entrepreneurs tried to sell the output they produced with the increased labor that they hired (more workers would presumably be hired at lower wage rates). However, if both prices *and wages* are falling, there is no reason to expect consumers to spend more—goods cost less but individuals receive less money for their work, so their *real* income hasn't increased. Investment spending is also not likely to be affected directly. Entrepreneurs pay less for their inputs because of the decline in prices, but they must also expect to receive a smaller dollar return on outputs; the two are likely to cancel each other and expected profitability should be more or less unchanged. Indeed, all our behavioral relationships are in *real* terms; people see through falling prices accompanied by falling incomes, so consumption, investment, and money-holding decisions are unaffected by equal movements in dollar incomes and prices. Thus it seems that both the *IS* and *LM* curves in Figure 25.18 will remain unchanged, aggregate demand will remain at its old level (*Y*), workers just hired will be fired, and the level of employment will be back where it started.

Nevertheless, the classical economists had an ace in the hole: *One thing clearly affected by a fall in the price level is the real value of the supply of money.* As we saw in previous chapters, if the money supply is fixed at $1,000 and the price level is one, its real value (in purchasing power) is the same as if the money supply were $2,000 and the price level were doubled. But if we start out with a $2,000 money supply and the price level is cut in half—presto, the real money supply doubles (for example, from $2,000/2 to $2,000/1)! This increase in the real value of the money supply due to falling prices is the mechanism through which the economy would move itself from a position of less than full employment to full employment. Here's how.

In terms of Figure 25.18, falling prices shift the *LM* curve to the right for the same reason that an increase in money supply does: Falling prices increase the real value of the money supply and thereby create an excess of (real) money supply over the (real) demand for money. Falling prices continue as long as people are unemployed, so that the increased real value of the money supply continues to shift the *LM* curve to the right, lowering the interest rate and increasing desired investment. This process would continue until the *LM* curve in Figure 25.18 is shifted from *LM* to *LM'* (the latter associated with a lower price level than at the original position), at which point economic activity is at full employment.

The Keynesian attack on this classical mechanism was not confined to the argument that prices and wages are sticky and inflexible and not likely to fall very promptly. The classical school, in fact, stressed that unemployment was the result of such downward inflexibility in wages and prices. Keynes said, however, that there were at least two other circumstances that would stall the move toward full employment. The first is the case of a *liquidity trap,* in which an increase in the money supply would not lower the interest rate, as we noted at the end of the last chapter. As long as the liquidity-preference function is perfectly horizontal, an increase in the money supply, real or nominal, is associated with the same rate of interest. The *LM* curve is horizontal under such conditions,[13] and no matter how far the price level declines, the interest rate won't fall, investment spending will remain unaltered, and so will aggregate output and employment. This situation is depicted in Figure 25.19.

The second case in which falling prices fail to work is when investment is highly *insensitive* to the rate of interest. The *IS* curve is very steep. Under such conditions, declining prices and the induced reduction in the rate of interest will be unable to raise investment to a sufficiently high level to generate full employment spending, as in Figure 25.20.

But classical economics wasn't built on such a fragile link between the monetary sector and spending on goods and services. The classical argument that we have just presented based the automatic tendency toward full employment on the rightward shift in the *LM* curve due to increases in the real value of the money supply. This is a thoroughly "Keynesian" mechanism, in the sense that money affects the economy only through the interest rate. But falling prices not only lower the interest rate, they also make people's real money balances worth more, and this might have a more direct impact on economic activity. People would be wealthier in addition to being more liquid. And if more liquidity wouldn't help (because of, say, the liquidity trap), more wealth (in the

---

[13] Recall that the *LM* curve is flatter the greater the interest-sensitivity of money demand. In the liquidity trap, money demand is infinitely interest-elastic, hence the *LM* curve becomes totally flat.

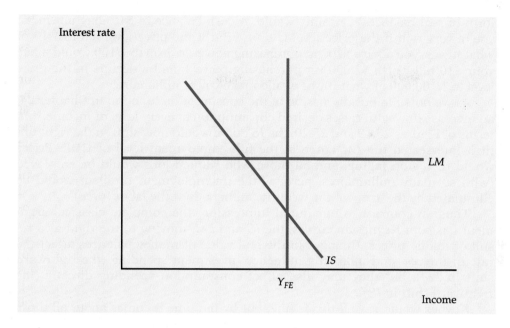

FIGURE 25.19   An extreme keynesian position: A liquidity trap.

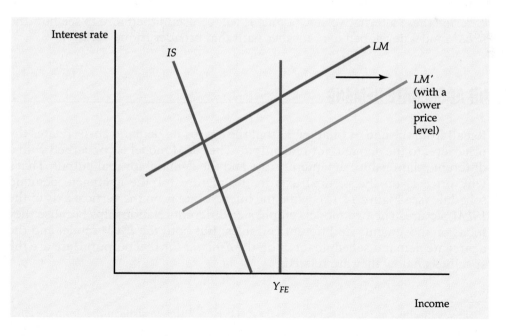

FIGURE 25.20   Another extreme keynesian position: Investment unresponsive to the interest rate.

form of real balances) certainly would. A cash balance of $10 may not mean you're very rich if the price level is unity. But if the price level fell to 1/10 of what it was, you'd have $100 in purchasing power; a drop to 1/100 would make your $10 bill worth $1,000 (in purchasing power); and a decline in the price level to 1/100,000 of what it was would make you a millionaire!

As we noted in our discussion of the consumption function in Chapter 24, an increase in wealth raises desired consumption at every level of income.[14] In terms of Figures 25.19 and 25.20, the *IS* curve would now shift to the right until it intersected the *LM* curve at the full employment level of GDP. Prices would then stop falling, and all those who wanted jobs would be employed (with so many millionaires, perhaps the unemployment problem would be eliminated by the army of the wealthy pulling out of the labor force).

Thus, in contrast to our initial impression, the complete classical argument has *both* Keynesian curves, the *IS* and *LM*, moving to the right as a result of falling prices. Changes in the real value of money balances affect the rate of interest and indirectly influence investment spending (the rightward shift in *LM*), but they may also affect consumption spending directly (the rightward shift in *IS*).

Keynes would say all this is fine, but by the time it comes about all those who wanted jobs will have passed through the Great Unemployment Window in the Sky. The classical "do it yourself" path to full employment is lengthy and arduous. Unemployment can last a very long time if the economy is left to its own devices, with no help from its friends. So the Keynesian prescription is fiscal policy. In Chapter 27 we use aggregate supply and demand analysis to describe these alternative viewpoints. It will be useful therefore to see how the *ISLM* model developed here meshes with that broader framework.

ISLM AND AGGREGATE DEMAND

Recall from the end of Chapter 23 that the aggregate demand curve relates the price level to the demand for real output. The *ISLM* model is concerned with a different relationship: the interest rate and the demand for real output. That's why price is on the vertical axis in the picture for the aggregate demand schedule (see Figure 24.11), while the interest rate is on the vertical axis in the *ISLM* picture. The two models emphasize different relationships because they focus on movements in different variables. But both the *ISLM* model and the aggregate demand schedule focus on the *demand* for real output. Here are the specifics on how they are related.

---

[14] The wealth effect just discussed is called the real balance effect, to distinguish it from the influence of interest rates on wealth. As we mentioned in footnote 6, the interest-rate-induced wealth effect merely changes the slope of the *IS* curve (it depends on the interest rate, and the interest rate is on the vertical axis). The real balance effect *shifts* the *IS* curve because it alters spending at every rate of interest.

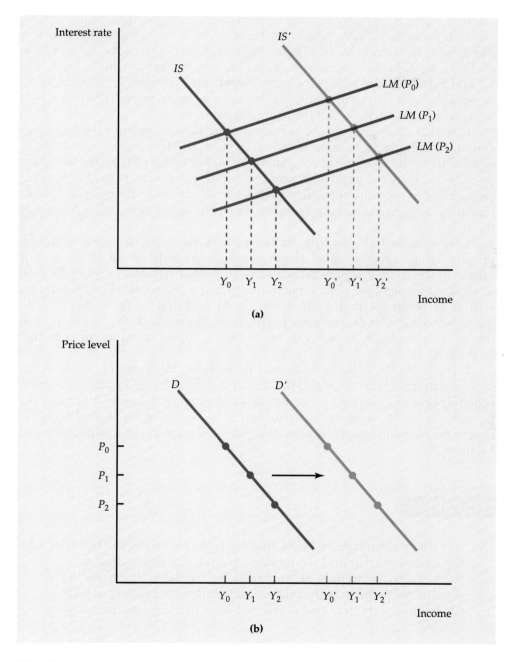

FIGURE 25.21   Deriving aggregate demand from *ISLM*.

It is relatively straightforward to generate a complete aggregate demand schedule from the *ISLM* model. Different price levels are associated with a family of *LM* curves, as in Figure 25.21(a). Given the curve *IS* in Figure 25.21(a), we have a number of equilibrium real income or output levels (Y_0, Y_1, and Y_2) associated with price levels P_0, P_1, and P_2. Figure 25.21(b) plots the demand for real output as an explicit function of those prices. The result is D, which is exactly what we call the aggregate demand curve.

It is also fairly easy to see the underlying factors causing the aggregate demand schedule to change position. Figure 25.21(a) shows that a rightward shift in the *IS* curve to *IS'* generates higher levels of GDP for any given price level. Thus the aggregate demand curve shifts from D to D' when any category of exogenous spending pushes the *IS* curve to the right. It follows that decreases in exogenous spending push the aggregate demand curve to the left.

Less obvious but also true, an increase in the stock of money shifts aggregate demand to the right. The reasoning is as follows: An exogenous increase in the money supply causes *each* of the *LM* curves in Figure 25.21(a) to shift rightward (use your imagination); thus a higher level of demand for GDP is associated with any given price level, and that's represented by a demand schedule like D' compared with D in Figure 25.21(b). Similarly, decreases in the money supply will cause the aggregate demand curve to shift to the left.

It is possible to describe in greater detail how the *IS* and *LM* curves combine to determine the slope and the size of the shifts in the aggregate demand schedule. For our purposes, you are no doubt happy to know, it is more important simply to recognize the connection between the *ISLM* world and the aggregate demand/supply framework. We will explore the implications in Chapter 27.

SUMMARY

1. The main advantage of *ISLM* analysis is that it shows the behavior of the money market and the product market in a single diagram. Keynes's earlier treatment ignored some crucial interactions. An important mechanism is that the interest rate both influences GDP (through investment) and is affected by it (through the demand for money).

2. The simple Keynesian fiscal policy multiplier ignores the fact that an expansion in aggregate demand raises interest rates. Thus in the *ISLM* model the impact of fiscal policy on GDP is tempered by rising interest rates that crowd out private investment.

3. Monetary policy raises GDP by lowering the interest rate and encouraging investment. The impact on GDP will be reduced, therefore, when ei-

ther the interest rate can't be lowered much (because money demand is very interest-sensitive) or when investment spending is relatively insensitive to the interest rate.

4. Velocity, the cornerstone of classical economics, is hidden behind the *LM* curve of the Keynesian model. Fiscal policy raises GDP by increasing the velocity of the existing money supply.

5. Flexible wages and prices will push aggregate demand toward full employment equilibrium even in the Keynesian world. That process is tempered by a very interest-sensitive money demand and by very interest-insensitive investment. Nevertheless, given enough time, wage-price flexibility will generate full employment even according to *ISLM* analysis.

QUESTIONS

25.1 Explain in words what the *LM* curve represents. Do the same for the *IS* curve.

25.2 Explain why the equilibrium level of GDP is at the intersection point of the *IS* and *LM* curves. Take a point on the *IS* curve above and to the left of the intersection point and explain why GDP will increase from that level.

25.3 Show geometrically that a flatter *IS* curve makes monetary policy more powerful, while a flatter *LM* curve makes fiscal policy more powerful.

25.4 What is meant by "crowding out" in the *ISLM* world? What makes it more or less of a problem?

25.5 Is it correct to say that the interest rate is determined by the supply of and demand for money, according to *ISLM* analysis?

25.6 How did Keynes argue that the slopes of the *IS* and/or *LM* curves could prevent falling wages and prices from producing full employment GDP? What did classical economists argue in response?

25.7 Explain the relationship between the *IS* and *LM* curves and the aggregate demand curve.

25.8 *Discussion question:* Do you think that the *ISLM* model is an elegant presentation of overall equilibrium, or is it an unnecessarily complicated statement of obvious relationships?

The Simple Algebra of Income Determination

For the algebraically inclined, much of the discussion can be summarized succinctly in equation form. The economy is divided into two sectors: the goods or product market, comprising the demand for goods and services; and the monetary sector, comprising the demand for and supply of money.

THE MODEL

The product market can be described by four functional relationships (behavior equations) and one equilibrium condition (an identity). All the functional relationships are assumed to be linear, an assumption that simplifies exposition without doing excessive damage to real-world applications. The functional relationships:

(1) $\qquad C = a + b(Y - T) \qquad$ Consumption (C) function

(2) $\qquad I = d - n(R) \qquad$ Investment (I) function

(3) $\qquad T = e + t(Y) \qquad$ Tax (T) function

(4) $\qquad G = \overline{G} \qquad$ Government spending (G)

and the equilibrium condition:

(5) $\qquad C + I + G = Y \qquad$ or $\qquad S + T = I + G$

where Y stands for GDP (income) and R for the interest rate. In each equation, the first lowercase letter represents the constant term of the function, and the second lowercase letter the coefficient of the independent variable (or the slope of the function); that is, b is the marginal propensity to consume ($\Delta C/\Delta(Y - T)$), and n is the interest-sensitivity of the investment function ($\Delta I/\Delta R$). Government spending is indicated by $\overline{G}$ and is exogenously fixed (imposed on the system from outside).

The *monetary sector* of the economy consists of two functional relationships and one equilibrium condition:

(6) $L = f - h(R) + k(Y)$ Liquidity preference (L) or demand-for-money function

(7) $M = \overline{M}$ Money supply (M)

(8) $L = M$ Equilibrium condition

THE *IS* AND *LM* FUNCTIONS

By solving equations (1) through (5), we find the *IS* function:

(9) $$Y = \frac{a - be + \overline{G} + d}{1 - b + bt} - \frac{n}{1 - b + bt}R$$

By solving equations (6) through (8), we find the *LM* function:

(10) $$Y = \frac{\overline{M} - f}{k} + \frac{h}{k}R \quad \text{or} \quad R = \frac{kY + f - \overline{M}}{h}$$

EQUILIBRIUM INCOME AND INTEREST

By solving (9) and (10) simultaneously, we obtain equilibrium income (Y) and interest rate (R):

(11) $$Y = \frac{1}{1 - b + bt + \frac{nk}{h}}\left(a - be + d + \overline{G} - \frac{nf}{h} + \frac{n\overline{M}}{h}\right)$$

(12) $$R = \frac{1}{h(1 - b + bt) + nk}[ka - kbe + kd + k\overline{G}$$
$$+ f(1 - b + bt) - \overline{M}(1 - b + bt)]$$

MULTIPLIER EFFECTS ON INCOME AND THE INTEREST RATE

From (11) one can derive the multiplier effects on income, and from (12) one can derive the multiplier effects on the interest rate, that follow from a change in government spending (ΔG), an autonomous shift in the consumption or investment function (Δa or Δd), a shift in the tax function (Δe), a change in the money supply (ΔM), or an autonomous shift in the demand for money (Δf).

The multiplier effects on income, from (11), are:

(13) $$\frac{\Delta Y}{\Delta G \text{ or } \Delta a \text{ or } \Delta d} = \frac{1}{1 - b + bt + \frac{nk}{h}}$$

$$(14) \qquad \frac{\Delta Y}{\Delta e} = - \frac{b}{1 - b + bt + \frac{nk}{h}}$$

$$(15) \qquad \frac{\Delta Y}{\Delta M \ (\text{or} - \Delta f)} = \frac{n}{h \ (1 - b + bt) + nk}$$

The multiplier effects on the interest rate, from (12), are:

$$(16) \qquad \frac{\Delta R}{\Delta G \ \text{or} \ \Delta a \ \text{or} \ \Delta d} = \frac{k}{h(1 - b + bt) + nk}$$

$$(17) \qquad \frac{\Delta R}{\Delta e} = - \frac{kb}{h(1 - b + bt) + nk}$$

$$(18) \qquad \frac{\Delta R}{\Delta M \ (\text{or} - \Delta f)} = - \frac{(1 - b + bt)}{h(1 - b + bt) + nk}$$

POLICY IMPLICATIONS

A number of policy implications are contained in the above multiplier formulas. Among the more important are the following:

1.   As (13) indicates, in the complete Keynesian system the multiplier effect on income of a change in government spending is *smaller* than the simple $1/1 - b$ that is typically taught in beginning economics courses. It is smaller by the addition of $bt + nk/h$ to the denominator. Here's what it means: t represents tax rates (they cut back consumer spending); k is the transactions demand for money (as income rises, the amount of transactions money desired increases, raising interest rates); n is the interest-sensitivity of investment spending (as interest rates rise, they cut back investment spending); h is the interest-sensitivity of the demand for money (if liquidity preference is very responsive to interest rates, it will take only a small rise in rates to induce people to reduce their cash holdings enough to provide the additional money needed for transactions purposes).

2.   Compare (13) and (14): As long as b is less than unity, an increase in government spending will increase income by more than an equal increase in taxes will lower income. The multiplier for a change in government spending is larger than the multiplier for a tax change.

2a. It follows from the above that a simultaneous and equal increase in both government spending and taxes—that is, a balanced budget change in government spending (financed entirely by higher taxes)—will not leave income unchanged but will increase it. Balanced budgets are not neutral with respect to income.

3.   Equation (15) indicates that monetary policy will be *less* powerful in affecting income the larger is h (the responsiveness of liquidity preference to

interest rates) and the smaller is n (the responsiveness of investment spending to interest rates).[1]

3a. As a special case of the above, if h is *infinite* (Keynesian liquidity trap) or n is *zero* (investment completely insensitive to interest rates), then the multiplier for $\Delta M = 0$ and monetary policy is useless.

3b. Under such circumstances ($h = \infty$ or $n = 0$), it follows that fiscal policy is the only alternative.

4. Conversely, (15) also indicates that monetary policy will be *more* powerful in affecting income the smaller is h and the larger is n.

4a. As a special case of the above, if h is *zero* (liquidity preference completely insensitive to interest rates), then—from (13)—the multiplier for $\Delta G = 0$ and fiscal policy is useless.

4b. On the other hand, under such circumstances ($h = 0$), monetary policy is both necessary *and sufficient* to control income. If $h = 0$, equation (15) indicates that the multiplier for $\Delta M = 1/k$; so long as k is constant in the liquidity-preference function, a change in the money supply will always change income by the constant $1/k$. That is, $\Delta M \times 1/k = \Delta Y$, which is—surprise!—the same as the quantity theory of money ($M \times$ velocity $= Y$, with velocity constant and equal to $1/k$).

---

[1] The effect of changes in h, n, or any of the other coefficients on the size of the multipliers can be verified by numerical examples (putting in actual numbers for each coefficient, calculating the multiplier, and then changing one of the coefficients and recalculating the multiplier), or by using calculus (take the derivative, for example, of $\Delta Y/\Delta M$ with respect to n, h, or k). Note also that the points made under 3a, 3b, 4a, and 4b are not discussed in this chapter. They correspond to points that will be made in the next chapter.

CHAPTER 26

Money and Economic Stability in the *ISLM* World*

Last chapter's *ISLM* model integrated the classical and Keynesian outlooks on the determination of GDP and interest rates. We can now utilize this *ISLM* framework to articulate some of the controversies that have surrounded the debate between the Keynesians and the intellectual heirs of the classical wisdom, known at various times as monetarists or new classical macroeconomists. The first section of this chapter reviews the old debate concerning the relative effectiveness of monetary and fiscal policy. The next section turns to the *ISLM* framework to explain why monetarists and new classicists contend that economic activity is inherently stable while Keynesians emphasize the need for an active attempt at economic stabilization. In the last section we turn to an explicit consideration of price flexibility in the *ISLM* world.

MONETARY POLICY, FISCAL POLICY, AND CROWDING OUT

The oldest controversy articulated within the *ISLM* framework is over the relative effectiveness of monetary and fiscal policy. In fact, near the end of the last chapter (see Figure 25.17) the monetarist "special case" in the Keynesian model was set forth: a demand for money that is unresponsive to interest rates—depending on income only—and that produces a vertical *LM* function.

---

*This chapter uses analytical techniques developed in Chapter 25. If you skipped Chapter 25, skip this one too. All this material is presented in Chapter 27 in a somewhat different framework.

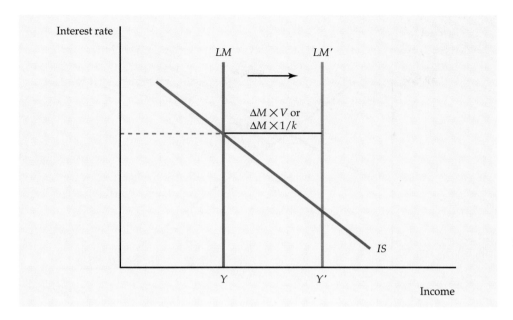

FIGURE 26.1 **When the *LM* curve is vertical, an increase in the money supply increases income by Δ*M* times velocity.**

In that world, things are very simple. Velocity is constant. With a fixed money supply, GDP can't change and neither does velocity. The impact of a change in money supply on the level of income equals Δ*M* multiplied by velocity (*V*). This can be seen in Figure 26.1. Start with *LM* and *IS* and equilibrium income *Y*. An increase in the money supply shifts the *LM* curve to the right by Δ*M* × *V* (see footnote 3 of Chapter 24). The new equilibrium level of income is *Y'*, and it is obvious that the change in income from *Y* to *Y'* equals Δ*M* × *V in this case.* Income continues to rise until all the increased money supply is absorbed into increased transactions demand.

On the other hand, as Figure 26.2 shows, when the *LM* curve is not vertical but is positively sloped (as is the case when the demand for money that underlies it is somewhat responsive to the rate of interest), then the increase in income due to a change in the money supply will be less than in Figure 26.1. In Figure 26.2 we have superimposed a set of positively sloped *LM* curves (*LM* and *LM'*) on the monetarist case of Figure 26.1. While the horizontal distance between the two *LM* curves is the same as before, the increase in income is clearly less than before.[1] Why? Because the increase in the supply of money lowers the interest rate, and at lower interest rates people will hold some of

---

[1] The horizontal distance between the two *LM* curves is the same as before, but now it is simply called Δ*M* × 1/*k*, because 1/*k* = *V* only when the interest-sensitivity of liquidity preference equals zero.

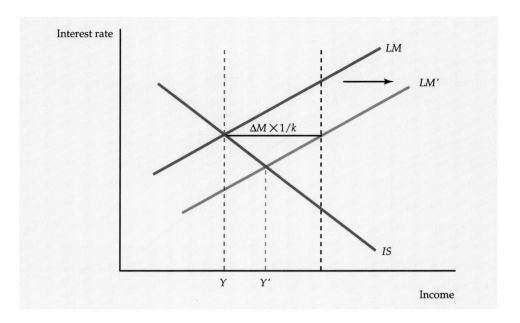

FIGURE 26.2 When the *LM* curve is not vertical, an increase in the money supply is less powerful in increasing income.

the increased money supply in the form of "idle" balances rather than for transactions purposes. Thus the velocity or rate of turnover of the *total* money supply falls (some of it is now being held "idle"). But we are running a bit ahead of ourselves; let's wait until we come to the Keynesian analysis of money to complete this part of our story.

Let us reemphasize that the monetarists are playing the game under protest—they don't like the rules of the Keynesian *ISLM* apparatus. It forces them into a situation where the change in money supply first lowers the interest rate, which increases investment, and thereby GDP. For monetarists, the channels through which money influences spending are not restricted to interest rates, as will be emphasized in the next chapter. Thus while the vertical *LM* curve does convey some of the monetarist flavor—that is, the stability of velocity—it still leaves a Keynesian taste. Moreover, as we stressed in Chapter 23, the assumption of stability in velocity is replaced by predictability in modern versions of monetarism.

The Keynesian reservations about the potency of monetary policy can be summarized in a number of "special cases" in the *ISLM* model. First, an increase in money supply would not affect anything if the *LM* curve were horizontal at the relevant level of GDP, that is, if the liquidity trap were a reality.

Figure 26.3's money-supply-and-demand functions form the basis for constructing Figure 26.4's *LM* functions. If we increase the money supply from *M* to *M'* in Figure 26.3's liquidity trap, then we get no shift in the *LM* function in Figure 26.4. The *LM* curve with *M* (namely, *LM*) is the same as with *M'*

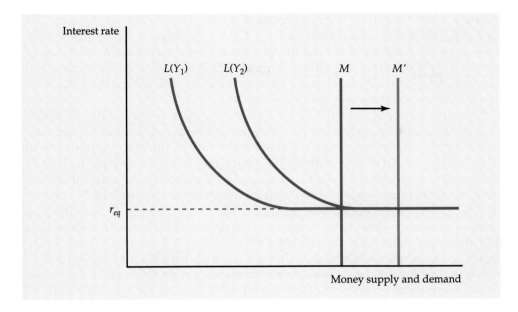

FIGURE 26.3   **With a liquidity trap, an increase in the money supply from *M* to *M'* does not shift the *LM* curve (see Figure 26.4).**

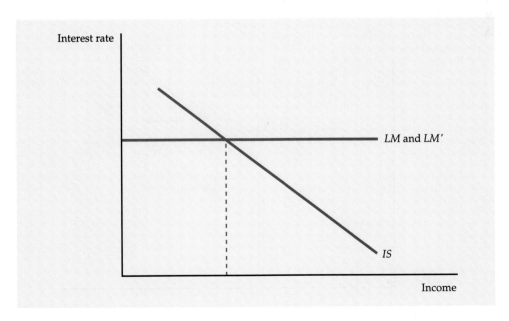

FIGURE 26.4   **With a liquidity trap, an increase in the money supply, because it does not shift the *LM* curve, does not change income.**

(namely, *LM'*). As can be seen in Figure 26.4, when the *IS* curve intersects *LM* (or *LM'*), producing equilibrium income Y_{eq}, an increase in the money supply from *M* to *M'* does not lower the interest rate. All the increased money supply is held as idle balances. Equilibrium income is unchanged. More money and the same level of GDP imply a decrease in velocity—the hallmark of the Keynesian critique of monetary policy.

A second category of pitfalls for monetary policy concerns the *IS* curve. Even if the liquidity-preference function is well behaved, so that an increase in the money supply succeeds in lowering the rate of interest, there may still be no impact on GDP if investment is completely unresponsive to the rate of interest. From Chapter 25 we know that the *IS* curve is very steep if investment has little interest-sensitivity; with zero interest-sensitivity, the *IS* curve is vertical. Under such conditions, changes in the money supply do not affect income even though they may change the rate of interest. Figure 26.5 illustrates that situation. Start with *IS* and *LM* and equilibrium income *Y*. Then, an increase in the money supply causes a rightward shift in the *LM* curve to *LM'*, which merely lowers the interest rate with no impact on GDP. Once again, the money supply has gone up but GDP hasn't, with velocity falling as a result.

To summarize the monetary policy discussion: Monetary stimulus works in the Keynesian world when both the *IS* curve and the *LM* curve are "normal." Pathological cases of horizontal *LM*s and vertical *IS*s render monetary policy impotent. More generally, even when we are untroubled by horizontal *LM* curves and vertical *IS* curves, the impact of money on GDP is not the simple Δ*M* times a fixed velocity. For example, an increase in *M* may very well produce falling interest rates, more investment, and higher GDP. But GDP is

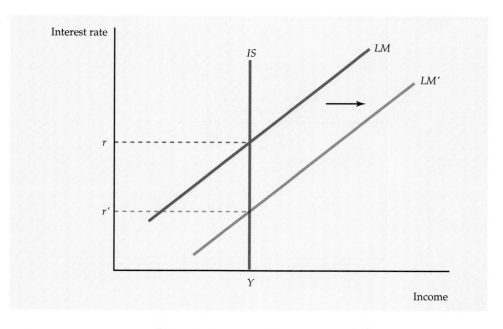

FIGURE 26.5 **When the *IS* curve is vertical, monetary policy is ineffective.**

not likely to rise in direct proportion to the change in *M,* because as interest rates decline, the speculative demand for money increases along with the transactions demand. In other words, velocity is likely to decline.

Turning to fiscal policy, the monetarist and Keynesian polar cases in *ISLM* analysis produce symmetrical results. In particular, fiscal policy has a zero impact with a vertical *LM* curve, while it is completely effective (with no offsetting crowding out due to interest rate effects on private investment) with a horizontal *LM* curve.

Figure 26.6 illustrates these points. Let's start at point *a* with income *Y* and interest rate *r.* An increase in government spending (or a reduction in taxes) shifts the *IS* curve from *IS* to *IS'.* If the *LM* curve were *LM,* the new equilibrium would be at *b,* and the entire impact would be absorbed by a higher interest rate with no increase at all in GDP. In this case there is complete crowding out. But if the *LM* curve were *LM',* the new equilibrium would be at *c* and the impact would be entirely on GDP, with no rise at all in the interest rate; in fact, since the rightward shift in the *IS* curve equals Δ*G* times $1/(1 - b)$, which also equals the change in GDP, the simple multiplier of Chapter 24 has returned in full bloom.

The general case of the positively sloped *LM* curve produces results that lie between the extremes, as we saw in the last chapter. An increase in government expenditure raises GDP, but by less than the "full multiplier" of the simple Keynesian system. This is because the interest rate goes up, cutting off some private investment (there is partial but not total crowding out). The rise in the rate of interest does not lower investment by as much as government

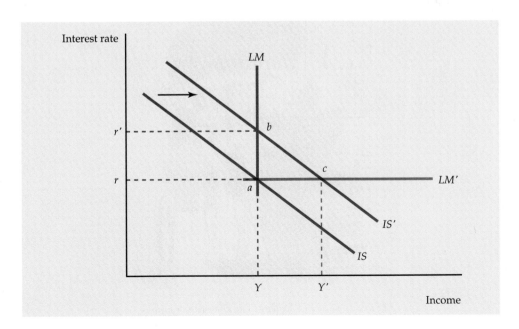

FIGURE 26.6   **When the *LM* curve is vertical, fiscal policy is completely ineffective; when it is horizontal, it is totally effective.**

spending increases, because the higher rate of interest also reduces the demand for money, permitting once-idle speculative balances to be used for carrying out the increased transactions associated with higher levels of GDP. It would seem, therefore, that unless the economy is characterized by the extreme case of zero interest-sensitivity of the demand for money (producing a vertical *LM* curve), even monetarists would agree that fiscal policy could have some impact on GDP.

IS THE PRIVATE SECTOR INHERENTLY STABLE?

Most economists now believe that the *LM* curve is positively sloped, although they may disagree over whether it is very steep or somewhat flat. Such differences of opinion over the steepness of the *LM* curve are sufficient to demonstrate the stability or instability of economic activity in the face of exogenous shifts in private investment.

Figure 26.7 shows two alternative *LM* curves: LM_{steep} and LM_{flat}. There are two *IS* curves representing shifts in autonomous investment. As can be seen in the picture, with LM_{steep} the induced fluctuation in GDP due to the shifting *IS* curve is *S* to *S'*. When the *LM* curve is LM_{flat}, however, the fluctuation in GDP is much wider, between *F* and *F'*. The key to the smaller fluctuation in

"In theory, yes, Mrs. Wilkins. But also in theory, no."

Drawing by Stan Hunt; © 1976 The New Yorker Magazine, Inc.

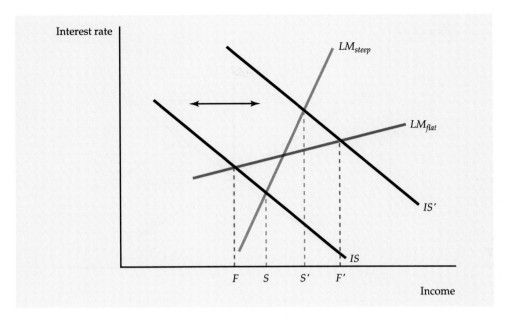

FIGURE 26.7   A flatter *LM* curve means wider fluctuations in GDP associated with exogenous shifts in investment.

GDP with LM_{steep} is that the level of interest rates fluctuates more than with LM_{flat}. Thus when the *IS* curve shifts from *IS'* to *IS*, the interest rate falls a lot, inducing a large amount of endogenous investment to offset a large part of the decline in autonomous investment. With a flatter *LM* curve, the fall in the rate of interest is smaller and induced investment is less. Thus a steeper *LM* curve stabilizes the level of economic activity associated with a particular stock of money, because the interest rate fluctuates more.

When the economy operates near its full employment capacity, fluctuations in the price level help provide self-correcting stabilization. Figure 26.8 shows the intersection of *IS* and $LM(P_0)$ at Y_{FE}. We introduced Y_{FE} at the end of Chapter 25 to represent full employment GDP. The *LM* curve is labeled with a particular price index, P_0, since changes in the price level will affect the position of *LM*. Moreover, at full employment, we assume that prices rise in response to increases in aggregate demand. A shift in autonomous spending pushes *IS* to *IS'* and raises demand to *Y*. As a result, prices rise. With a fixed stock of money, this reduces the *real* supply of money, and the *LM* curve is pushed back toward the full employment line. This process stops once aggregate demand is back at full employment; in our picture this occurs at the intersection between *IS'* and $LM(P_1)$.

At the new equilibrium *E'* we have both a higher price level and a higher rate of interest. The higher price level (caused by an exogenous increase in spending) has reduced the real supply of money, raised interest rates, and

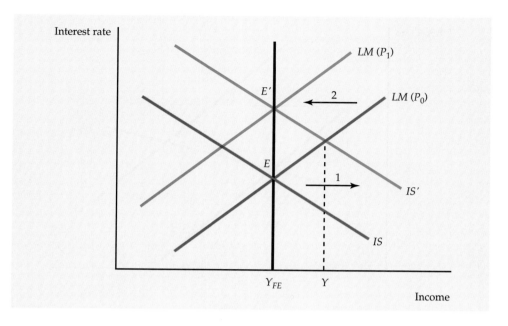

FIGURE 26.8   At full employment, fluctuations in the price level help stabilize economic activity.

pushed back aggregate demand to the full employment level. Thus the fixed supply of money, together with flexible prices and interest rates, insulates full employment economic activity from exogenous changes in investment. The process would be reversed (lower prices and lower interest rates) if there were a decrease in exogenous investment (shifting *IS* to the left). Notice that Figure 26.8 has the elements of an inflation story, as we will see shortly.

FLEXIBLE PRICES, THE NATURAL RATE OF INTEREST, AND REAL CROWDING OUT

Price flexibility has even more startling effects on the impacts of monetary and fiscal policy. In the first instance, when the economy is operating at or near full employment, and prices are flexible, the Keynesian interest rate mechanism gives way completely to purely classical arguments. In particular, at full employment the rate of interest is independent of movements in the money stock. This can be seen in Figure 26.9, starting with *IS* and *LM* intersecting at Y_{FE} and r_{FE}. The latter is the real rate of interest because, as usual, we are assuming the absence of any inflationary expectations. As always, an increase in money supply shifts *LM* to *LM'*, apparently pushing down the in-

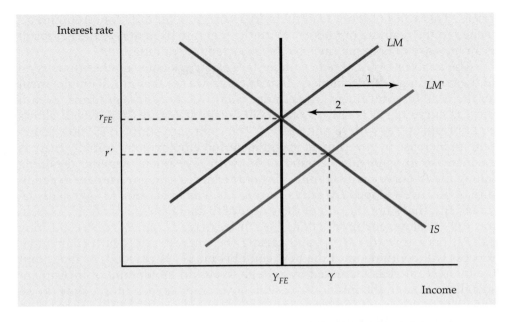

FIGURE 26.9   An increase in money supply at full employment doesn't lower the interest rate.

terest rate from r_{FE} to r' and raising aggregate demand to Y'. But the excess of aggregate demand over Y_{FE} causes prices to rise. This reduces the real supply of money, pushing LM' back toward LM. After all is said and done, prices have risen until the LM curve is back where it started, since otherwise prices would keep on rising. And when LM' is back at LM, the real rate of interest is restored to its original level. Thus, at full employment, increases in money supply cannot reduce the interest rate below r_{FE}. Similar reasoning shows that *decreases* in the money stock will not raise interest rates above r_{FE} if prices fall when aggregate demand is below full employment.

The interest rate r_{FE} has a special name. It is called the **natural rate of interest** and is defined as that rate which equates saving and investment at full employment. It is determined by the intersection point between the IS curve and the Y_{FE} line. Shifts in the money stock can't change r_{FE}. Only shifts in the IS curve can, as we saw earlier in Figure 26.8. Thus at full employment only saving and investment (including government spending) determine the interest rate; money has nothing to do with it. At full employment, classical interest theory pops out of the Keynesian picture!

The implications for the effect of expansionary monetary policy on interest rates at full employment are twofold: (1) the real rate of interest is unchanged by increases in money supply; (2) nominal rates (not shown in the figures) will rise if inflationary expectations are generated by the increased money stock. The latter is quite likely, especially in the long run. Borrowers and lenders recognize that excessive expansion in money stock means rising prices. This will no doubt lead them to agree upon an inflation premium attached to the real rate of interest. With the real rate fixed at r_{FE}, the net result is an increase in nominal rates by the expected rate of inflation.[3]

The analysis of fiscal policy under flexible prices adds another dimension to the crowding-out mechanism. In particular, we see that at full employment an increase in government expenditure is crowded out in *real* terms, even if the *LM* curve has a positive slope. Look again at Figure 26.8, which shows equilibrium at Y_{FE} with *IS* and $LM(P_0)$. The rightward shifts to *IS'* now represent an increase in government spending at full employment. Initially there is an increase in aggregate demand to Y', with investment demand declining (along the *IS* curve) to offset only part of the increase in government expenditure. A positively sloped *LM* curve permits such an expansion in aggregate demand. But that's not the end of the story. With aggregate demand, Y', exceeding full employment production, Y_{FE}, prices rise (from P_0 to P_1), pushing $LM(P_0)$ back toward $LM(P_1)$ and raising the interest rate still further. That process will continue until the new equilibrium, E', is reached. At that point the interest rate has increased by enough to cut off an amount of investment spending equal to the initial increase in government expenditure. How do we know? If that weren't the case, aggregate demand would still be above Y_{FE}, prices would still be rising, and so would the interest rate.

Two points are worth noting in this example. First, the interest rate at full employment is obviously affected by shifts in the real sector of the economy, represented by the *IS* curve (even though it is unaffected by shifts in the monetary sector). Second, notice that nominal GDP is higher at E' compared with E. How do we know? Because real income is still at Y_{FE}, but prices are higher (P_1 versus P_0). Thus while there is real crowding out at full employment even with a positively sloped *LM* curve, there isn't nominal crowding out as with the vertical *LM* curve.

The story at full employment is decidedly classical, even when cloaked in a Keynesian framework. But that's not really as devastating to Keynesian protagonists as it initially seems. After all, at full employment Keynes was as classical an economist as Milton Friedman and John Stuart Mill put together.

SUMMARY

1. The "special" (or extreme) monetarist and Keynesian slopes of the *ISLM* diagram help to highlight the polar positions on monetary and fiscal policy. In particular, a vertical *IS* curve and a horizontal *LM* curve make monetary policy impotent and fiscal policy supreme. A vertical *LM* curve, on the other hand, causes fiscal policy to lose its potency (complete crowding out) and raises monetary policy to its ultimate power (fixed velocity).

---

[3] In the next chapter there is a more detailed discussion of real and nominal interest rate movements. Also, return to Chapter 4 for a simple discussion.

2. The demonstration that a steep *LM* curve insulates GDP from exogenous investment shocks highlights the stabilizing role of fluctuating interest rates on economic activity. Flexible prices add to that stabilizing mechanism.

3. Price flexibility at full employment restores the results of classical interest rate theory: The level of the real rate of interest is determined only by saving and investment. A change in the money supply cannot alter this "natural rate of interest"; it can only influence nominal interest rates by changing inflationary expectations. Price flexibility at full employment also causes fiscal policy's impact on *real* GDP to be completely crowded out even with a positively sloped *LM* curve.

QUESTIONS

26.1   Explain why monetarists would argue that the slope of the *LM* curve determines only part of the real crowding-out effect associated with fiscal policy.

26.2   Explain verbally or geometrically how the slope of the *LM* curve helps determine whether shifts in autonomous investment cause small or large fluctuations in GDP.

26.3   Define the natural rate of interest and show how price flexibility prevents changes in the money supply from influencing the natural rate.

26.4   *Discussion question:* Which do you think is the more powerful force in stabilizing the economy at or near full employment: flexible wages and prices or flexible interest rates?

Interest Rates Versus the Money Supply Under Uncertainty

In Chapter 22 we discussed the advantages and disadvantages of using the money supply versus the interest rate as a target of monetary policy. Monetarists generally prefer a money supply target, while Keynesians prefer an interest rate objective. At this point we can formalize the underlying analysis to demonstrate the pluses and minuses of each.

The issue boils down to this: Is it always better for the Fed to specify a target for the money supply rather than the interest rate, or vice versa? The answer is—it depends. Consider the situation where the major source of instability in GDP comes from unanticipated movements in the *IS* curve. In Figure 26A.1 we have the *IS* curve shifting back and forth between *IS* and *IS'*. With a money supply target set by the Fed and a stable demand function for money, we have the upward-sloping money market equilibrium curve pictured in Figure 26A.1. The level of GDP varies between *A* and *B*.

Compare this variability in GDP with what occurs when the Fed sets the interest rate as its policy target. Under such conditions we have the horizontal money market equilibrium curve in Figure 26A.1.[1] GDP varies between *X* and *Z*. Clearly the money supply target is superior—it ensures a smaller variability

---

[1] The *LM* curve is flat under such circumstances, because the Fed accompanies any increased demand for money with an increased supply. Hence higher levels of *Y* (which increase the demand for money) are associated with the same level of interest, r^*. Notice that the definition of the *LM* curve is slightly different; it is the combination of *Y* and *r* with a *given* Federal Reserve policy and not a *given* money supply. That's why we've called the *LM* curve by its generic name: the money market equilibrium curve.

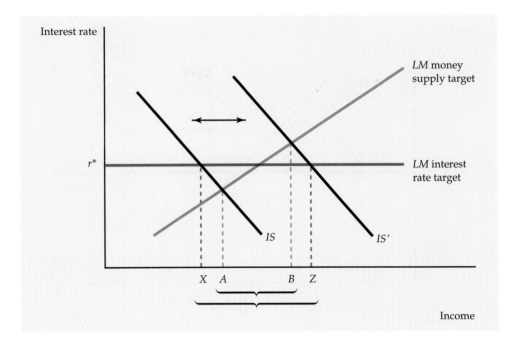

FIGURE 26A.1   With an interest rate target, an unstable *IS* curve leads to wider variation in GDP than if the Fed had a money supply target.

in GDP when the major source of instability is in the *IS* curve (a victory for the monetarists).

When the game is played in the Keynesian ballpark, things turn out just the reverse. Here the demand for money is highly unstable. If the money supply is fixed by the Fed and the demand for money shifts, then the *LM* curve moves between *LM* and *LM'* in Figure 26A.2. With a fixed *IS* curve, GDP varies between *A* and *B*. But if the Fed uses an interest rate target, the relevant "*LM* curve" is again horizontal and there is no instability in GDP whatsoever. It stays put at *X*.

Monetarists insist that the most stable relationship in the economy (if not the world) is the demand for money. The Keynesian consumption function is much less stable. The *IS* curve is therefore the major source of GDP instability. Figure 26A.1 tells the truth—a money supply target is best. Keynesians argue that if anything is unstable it is monetarists themselves. Not being psychiatrists, they'll settle for an unstable demand function for money. The *LM* curve is therefore the major source of GDP variability. Figure 26A.2 tells the truth—an interest rate target is best.

As in most monetarist-Keynesian disputes, the ultimate resolution lies in empirical evidence. Chapter 29 comes as close as we can in letting the numbers speak for themselves.

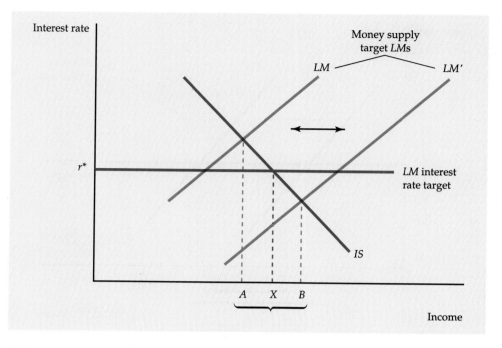

FIGURE 26A.2   **With a money supply target, an unstable *LM* curve leads to wider variation in GDP than if the Fed had an interest rate target.**

CHAPTER 27

An Aggregate Supply and Demand Perspective on Money and Economic Stability

At a conference of professional economists, Robert Solow, a prominent Keynesian from MIT, commented as follows on a paper presented by Milton Friedman: "Another difference between Milton and myself is that everything reminds Milton of the money supply; well, everything reminds me of sex, but I try to keep it out of my papers."

The intellectual traditions represented by these two Nobel prize–winning economists surely extends well beyond the money supply. Robert Solow is a staunch supporter of Keynesian policy activism, while Milton Friedman has long trumpeted the virtues of classical laissez-faire macroeconomics. Nevertheless, there was a time when the importance of the money supply in explaining aggregate economic performance was the defining distinction among these two, as well as all other, macroeconomists. Thus the name *monetarists* came to represent the upholders of the broad classical traditions of nonintervention as well as the narrower notion that the money supply cannot be relegated to a sideshow, as the followers of Keynes had once suggested. Although the so-called new classical macroeconomists have refined monetarist thinking by focusing on rational expectations (as we will see in the next chapter) and the role of prices in clearing imbalances between supply and demand, we nevertheless use the term *monetarists* to represent the entire spectrum of modern classical thinking on money and economic stability.

As it turns out, the most important elements of the monetarist-Keynesian dialogue can be best articulated within the aggregate supply and demand framework discussed toward the ends of Chapters 23 and 24. In the rest of this chapter we put the details of the classical and Keynesian models on the back burner and use the aggregate supply and demand pictures to explain the opposing positions on the stability of the economy, the relative effectiveness of monetary and fiscal policy, the causes of inflation, and the consequences for interest rates. Although these issues have been discussed in previous chapters, the unifying theme of aggregate supply and demand provides a powerful perspective. In the next chapter we will return to these issues from still another vantage point: rational expectations. By that time we should have a clear understanding of the monetarist and Keynesian outlooks on just about everything.

IS THE PRIVATE SECTOR INHERENTLY STABLE?

Monetarists tend to believe that aggregate demand will be relatively unaffected by autonomous shifts in investment spending. Keynesians argue that unless there is an active attempt at stabilization, the level of economic activity and unemployment will fluctuate considerably when buffeted by entrepreneurial animal spirits.

Monetarists, reflecting their classical ancestry, argue that any exogenous decrease in investment spending would be countered automatically by either increased consumption or interest-sensitive investment spending. The mechanism could be attributed, somewhat mysteriously, to the fixed money stock, resulting in a relatively fixed level of aggregate demand based on the quantity theory; or, in keeping with classical interest theory, it could be attributed to a reduction in interest rates that would follow a downward shift in the investment function. The drop in interest rates would, in turn, stimulate investment spending, reduce saving (thereby increasing consumption), and make up for the initial drop in investment.

Keynesians are less impressed with the automatic offsets to gyrations in investment spending. First, the mysterious quantity theory linkage between money and aggregate demand is simply not part of the picture. Moreover, the interest rate does not necessarily respond to a drop in investment. And even if the interest rate did decline, there's no guarantee that it would induce very much additional spending.

Fluctuations in the price level are another source of stability, according to monetarists. If, for example, consumption and investment didn't rise fast enough to offset the initial decline in investment spending, the resulting unemployment would drive down prices. A fixed money stock with lower prices

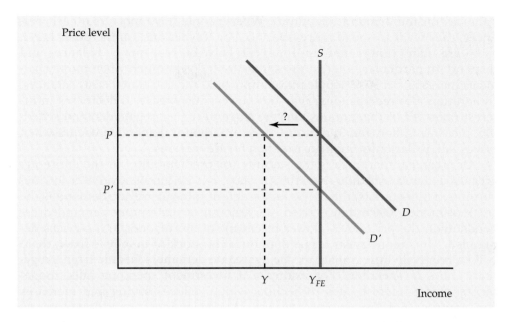

FIGURE 27.1 **Monetarist response to declines in exogenous investment: Income remains at the full employment level.**

means a larger real supply of money. This could stimulate spending directly via the quantity theory. Alternatively, the larger real supply of money would lower interest rates—in good Keynesian fashion—and investment spending would increase still further. The Keynesian response to such expected price effects is twofold: First, prices rarely decline; and second, the spending effects are too slow to rely on to restore full employment.

These arguments can be put somewhat more elegantly in terms of aggregate demand and supply. Recall from our earlier discussions that the aggregate demand schedule, labeled D in Figure 27.1, shows how the quantity of real income (or output) demanded varies with changes in the price level. In particular, decreases in prices increase the amount of goods and services demanded because real money balances increase when the price level falls.[1] The aggregate supply schedule, labeled S, shows how quantity produced varies with price. In Figure 27.1, the supply curve is vertical, reflecting the classical assumption that quantity supplied is fixed at full employment.

First let's focus on aggregate demand. The quantity theory approach of monetarists assumes a direct and powerful impact of increased real money

---

[1] Recall that a decrease in the price level does not increase people's real income directly, because a falling price level means both goods prices and factor prices (wages) are falling. Thus falling prices do not directly expand aggregate demand via a simple Keynesian consumption function argument.

balances on the demand for output. When people have more real cash balances, they want to spend more—period. For Keynesians, on the other hand, there are many things that can intervene between real money balances and demand. In particular, interest rates may not fall very much when money balances increase, because people may simply hold the additional cash balances. In addition, desired spending may not be very responsive to decreases in interest rates. All of this implies that the slope of the aggregate demand schedule, measuring how much of an increase in amount demanded occurs when prices fall, is flatter for monetarists than for Keynesians.

Of greater importance is the stability (or predictability) of the entire aggregate demand schedule—whether it stays put or jumps around a lot. According to monetarists, the major factor determining aggregate demand is the stock of money. Once that is fixed, the amount of real output demanded depends upon the price level—lower prices mean more goods and services demanded. Thus monetarists argue that, once the stock of money is fixed, there will be relatively little impact on the aggregate demand schedule from exogenous shifts in spending. For example, if investment spending falls, monetarists expect interest rates to decline, which reduces saving and increases consumption. For Keynesians, however, changes in investment do not necessarily generate offsetting movements in consumption expenditures. Thus the aggregate demand schedule will be pushed to the left if exogenous investment falls, because at every price level fewer goods are demanded.

Now let's put the economy through its paces. Our objective is to see whether GDP is stable at full employment. Obviously, this depends on the behavior of the aggregate demand schedule, but it also depends on the shape of aggregate supply. Thus Figure 27.1 has the monetarist vertical aggregate supply curve, while Figure 27.2 has the simple Keynesian horizontal supply curve (S) as well as a somewhat more realistic upward-sloping supply curve (S').

Start with aggregate demand curve D in each figure, so that GDP is at the full employment level. Now ask what happens if businesses suddenly decide to invest less than they have been. From the monetarist view of Figure 27.1, the demand schedule, D, may simply stay put, in which case aggregate economic activity remains at Y_{FE}. Some other form of spending will increase to take the place of the drop in investment. But if the aggregate demand curve does shift to D' in Figure 27.1, and the level of aggregate demand falls to Y at the old price level P, the resulting unemployed labor and unused capacity cause wages and prices to fall toward P'. As prices fall, the real quantity of money expands and aggregate demand increases along the new demand curve D'. Prices fall until demand is brought back into equality with aggregate supply at Y_{FE}.

In the Keynesian presentation of Figure 27.2, the leftward shift from D to D' most certainly takes place as a result of the fall in exogenous investment. If that happens, the story can end right there, when it has hardly begun. If prices are rigid even in the face of unemployment and excess capacity, the supply curve is S and aggregate demand and GDP remain at the depressed level Y. The monetarist incentive to increase spending—falling prices—never appears.

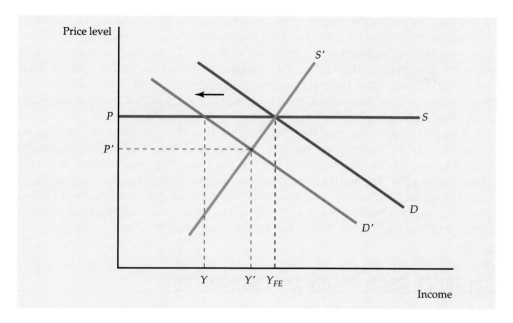

FIGURE 27.2   Keynesian response to declines in exogenous investment: Income falls below the full employment level.

The more realistic Keynesian case occurs when prices fall somewhat when production is below full capacity, and wages also decline *but at a slower pace.* This produces an aggregate supply curve that looks like S' in Figure 27.2.[2] With supply curve S', aggregate real output is above Y (where it would be if prices didn't fall) but is still below full employment income, Y_{FE}. The problem is that wages and prices do not fall far enough to stimulate sufficient new aggregate demand along D' to offset the decrease in exogenous investment.

Note that in both of the figures, if the demand curve were flatter, the fall in prices would not have to be that large to encourage more aggregate demand along the new demand curve D'. This would also reflect the monetarist point of view: Falling prices with a fixed stock of money will generate full employment because aggregate demand is very sensitive to increases in real money balances.

An important point to remember is that the upward-sloping Keynesian aggregate supply curve S' is only a short-run relationship. Even Keynesians recognize that with production below full employment there will be continued

---

[2] Here's one way of looking at why the supply curve is positively sloped. When wages (W) and prices (P) fall at the same rate, business firms' *real* wage expense (W/P) remains unchanged and they will hire the same number of workers as before. On the other hand, if wages fall less than prices, then firms will fire some workers and cut back their output of goods and services. That is precisely the implication of the positive slope in supply curve S': When prices fall, the supply of real output declines below the level that would fully employ all labor (and capital). We will return to this issue in our discussion of inflation later in this chapter.

downward pressure on wages. As wages fall more, there will be an incentive for producers to move back to full employment production. Eventually, therefore, the vertical aggregate supply curve of Figure 27.1 comes into the picture, even for Keynesians. But the essential message is that the entire process takes time, and during that time the aggregate supply curve is not vertical. Thus, Keynesians argue, we should try to push up aggregate demand by monetary and fiscal policies.

To summarize: monetarists tend to think that the aggregate demand curve is stable, given a particular money supply, and that the aggregate supply schedule is vertical. These conditions imply that exogenous shifts in investment leave GDP unchanged. Keynesians argue that the aggregate demand curve is quite sensitive to exogenous changes in investment and that the aggregate supply schedule is not vertical. These circumstances imply that entrepreneurial animal spirits buffet the level of real income.

MONETARY POLICY, FISCAL POLICY, AND CROWDING OUT

Suppose the Keynesians have a point, and aggregate demand shifts to D' when business people are discouraged and cut back on their investment expenditures. Let's also put the economy into Figure 27.2 with the upward-sloping supply schedule S'. Thus the reduction in aggregate demand reduces income to Y'. If we don't want to wait for further price adjustments to set matters right, then something must be done to push up aggregate demand. Monetary and fiscal policies are the two discretionary tools available to government policymakers for precisely such circumstances.

According to the monetarists, if the central bank increases the money supply, the aggregate demand schedule shifts to the right, reflecting increased demand for goods and services.[3] The transmission mechanism of an increase in money to spending is direct. It isn't necessary for extra cash balances to first go into the bond market (as with Keynesians), where prices are forced up and interest rates pushed down. Rather, there can be direct substitution between money and real goods.

For Keynesians, on the other hand, an increase in the money supply may very well shift the aggregate demand schedule rightward, but the impact is less certain than for monetarists. The problem is that the transmission mechanism between money and spending is not quite so direct. According to Keynesians, falling interest rates can generate increased spending in a number of ways. The so-called cost-of-capital effect is the traditional impact of lower

---

[3] Do not be confused on this point. Increases in real balances caused by falling prices are reflected in the *slope* of the aggregate demand curve, because prices are on the vertical axis; increases in real balances caused by an increase in the stock of money *shift* the aggregate demand curve, because at each price level (on the vertical axis) more goods and services will be demanded (measured on the horizontal axis).

borrowing costs on the demand for investment goods. The wealth effect focuses on the impact of interest rates on securities prices: Lower interest rates mean higher bond prices, and people respond to such capital gains by consuming more. The exchange rate effect implies that with flexible exchange rates, lower interest rates drive down the value of the dollar on foreign exchange markets, increasing our net exports. Finally, the credit availability effect asserts that lenders may simply increase the amount of funds offered to borrowers, thereby permitting them to expand their spending plans. When all these channels of money to spending are operative, then the impact of expanding the money supply on aggregate demand is quite potent. But in this very specific outlook, there's many a possible slip 'twixt the cup and the lip.

The Keynesian answer to the somewhat less certain effects of monetary policy is to focus on fiscal policy to stimulate aggregate demand. We started out with a reduction in autonomous investment expenditure that pushed the aggregate demand curve to the left. A simple solution is to offset that decrease by exogenously increasing government spending or raising consumer expenditure by a discretionary reduction in tax rates.

A monetarist questions whether *any* exogenous shift in expenditure, whether generated by business firms or by the government, influences aggregate demand. We saw earlier that, according to monetarists, interest rates would fall to counteract the effects of decreased investment on aggregate demand. A symmetrical argument maintains that interest rates will rise when government spending goes up. Thus the government spends more, but others—business firms and consumers—are induced to spend less because interest rates rise.

This process has often been called by a special name: *crowding out*. Because in the past it has received considerable attention as a central issue dividing monetarists and Keynesians, it is worth some further elaboration.

We begin by noting that, initially, an increase in government spending raises aggregate demand directly, before anything else has happened. But the public's need for day-to-day transactions money is likely to rise along with aggregate demand. If the supply of money does not increase simultaneously, the public will find itself short of cash, will presumably sell off some financial assets to try to get additional money, and will thereby drive up interest rates. This crowding-out effect may inhibit private investment spending, at least partly offsetting the expansionary impact of the government's spending. In brief, both the execution and the net impact of fiscal policy appear to be inextricably bound up with monetary implications. Moreover, it is especially important to consider how the government finances the increased expenditure (or the reduction in taxes).

The Keynesian position on these matters is that any fiscal action, no matter how it is financed, will have a significant effect on aggregate demand. Keynesians do not deny that interest rates are likely to rise unless new money is forthcoming to meet cash needs for day-to-day transactions. Thus they admit that a government deficit financed by money creation is more expansionary than one financed by bond sales to the public, and that both are more expansionary than increased government spending financed by taxation. But higher

GOING OUT ON A LIMB

Are Bank Loans Special?

There has been a long-simmering debate between some monetarists and Keynesians over whether bank loans matter. Most Keynesians feel that bank loans are special because borrowers at banks often have few alternative sources of funds. Therefore, an expansion or contraction of money supply associated with movements in bank loans will have more powerful effects on spending compared with money supply movements based on bank purchases or sales of securities. Most monetarists, on the other hand, argue that money is money, no matter how it comes about. The security seller receiving cash is just as likely to spend as someone who has taken out a bank loan.

Empirical evidence leaves little doubt that bank borrowing is the major source of funds for small and intermediate-size businesses. Our discussion in Chapter 14 on asymmetric information explained why this is not surprising. Thus tight money that restricts bank lending is likely to squeeze these spenders out of the marketplace; they cannot turn to the money or bond markets to raise funds, as the IBMs of the world can. On the other hand, large firms can and do extend credit, called *trade credit,* to smaller firms, thereby providing indirect access to the money and bond markets. In addition, large firms compete with small firms, so that if the latter do less business, the former will make it up. So, the question remains, are bank loans special?

The answer: probably, at least in the short run. Large firms cannot fully replace small firms without substantial time for adjustment. Moreover, small firms prefer bank loans to trade credit because bank loans are cheaper. Thus an expansion or contraction in money supply associated with movements in bank loans has a more powerful effect on spending than a monetary expansion or contraction based on bank purchases or sales of securities.

interest rates have dual effects. They may reduce private investment spending, but they may also lead people to economize on their cash balances, thereby supplying part of the need for new transactions money from formerly idle cash holdings.

As the monetarists see it, a fiscal deficit financed by selling bonds to the public will not affect aggregate demand. True, the government will be spending more. But others will wind up spending less. Net result: No change in total spending. The rise in government spending will *initially* increase aggregate demand. However, this will increase the demand for cash for transactions purposes and drive up interest rates, and bond sales to finance the government's expenditures will drive up rates still further. The public will be buying government bonds and financing the government, instead of buying corporate bonds and financing business firms. Business firms will be crowded out of financial markets by the government. The rise in interest rates will reduce private investment spending by as much as government spending is increased, and that will be the end of the story. Government fiscal policy, unaccompanied by changes in the supply of money, merely changes the proportion of government spending relative to private spending.

It is useful to summarize the monetary and fiscal issues with a chronological flavor. The first leg of the debate focused on Keynesian skepticism over whether changes in the money supply influenced aggregate demand. The next step was the monetarist counterattack on fiscal policy because of crowding out. And just as the respective positions on these items came under control, a third, as yet undiscussed, issue emerged as a focal point of concern: whether *countercyclical* policy has any impact on spending at all. The problem usually focuses on whether countercyclical movements in the money supply are anticipated and whether such anticipations lead to expected inflation and hence neutralize the money supply changes. To deal with this latest development properly, we first turn to issues of inflation and countercyclical policy. In the next chapter we extend the discussion to include rational expectations.

INFLATION, MONEY, AND THE PHILLIPS CURVE

The first issue dividing monetarists and Keynesians is whether or not inflation is purely a monetary phenomenon. This issue turns on what influences the aggregate demand schedule. This is evident in Figure 27.3, which shows that if we start at full employment (where we always tend to be), with aggregate demand *D* and price level *P*, anything pushing demand to *D'* and *D"* raises prices to *P'* and *P"*. The dynamics of *P* rising to *P'* and then *P"* is precisely what we mean by inflation: rising prices. Thus monetarists contend that since the aggregate demand schedule is likely to be stable at *D* unless the money supply changes, the main culprit behind shifts to *D'* and *D"* is the Federal Reserve.

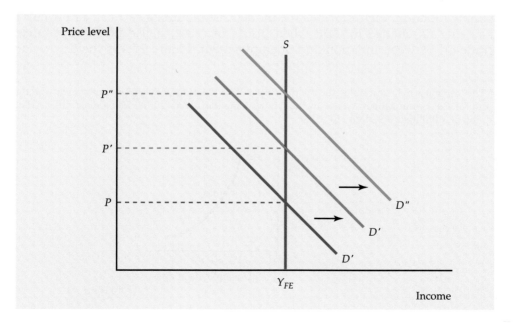

FIGURE 27.3   Anything shifting aggregate demand to the right causes inflation.

Keynesians, on the other hand, are not so quick to blame the Fed when inflation gets out of control. Any group of suddenly overexuberant spenders—government, business, or consumers—can push up aggregate demand and generate increases in prices. Obviously, the Keynesian position permits the blame for inflation to be attributed to expanding government deficits when the economy is at full employment. Monetarists, on the other hand, cannot rail against deficits per se as causing inflation. Only if the deficit induces the Federal Reserve to expand the money supply will inflation follow.

Shifts in the aggregate supply schedule can also be charged with generating inflation. In fact, the so-called cost-push variety of inflation forces up prices precisely because it shifts the supply schedule in Figure 27.3 to the left. Higher costs (such as occurred with energy during the 1970s) restrict production, producing a period of rising prices. But monetarists stress that such a once-and-for-all "supply shock" cannot account for persistent inflation; it is more of a one-shot deal.

A second issue dividing monetarists and Keynesians on inflation concerns the possibility of a trade-off between inflation and unemployment. Keynesians have supported the notion of a trade-off, known as a **Phillips curve** after Professor A. W. Phillips, who popularized the relationship. The Phillips curve suggests that lower rates of unemployment could be obtained if only we were willing to tolerate a faster rate of increase in prices.[4] Monetarists deny that there is a permanent trade-off between inflation and unemployment, arguing instead that once inflation was incorporated into people's expectations, the unemployment rate would return to its "natural" level.

Once again we can explain the underlying conflict in terms of our aggregate supply/demand framework, but this time the issue turns on the shape of supply function. Figure 27.3 is the monetarist picture: a vertical supply curve showing no change in GDP when prices increase, hence no Phillips curve trade-off between inflation and unemployment. Figure 27.4 is the Keynesian

---

[4] The original article describing the relationship is "The Relation Between Unemployment and the Rate of Change in Money Wages in the United Kingdom, 1861–1957," *Economica* (1958). The graph of a Phillips curve looks like this:

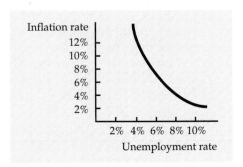

The negatively sloped curve shows that lower rates of unemployment are associated with higher rates of inflation.

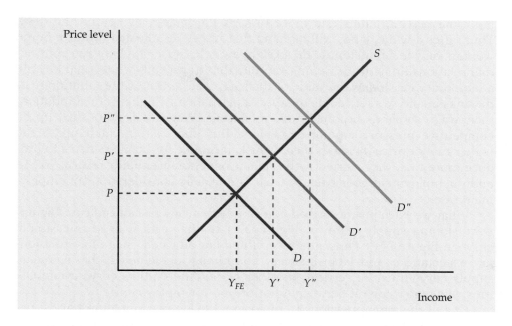

FIGURE 27.4   Inflation causes higher income (and lower unemployment) with a positively sloped supply curve.

picture: a positively sloped supply curve showing that as prices rise because of shifts in aggregate demand, real output expands *beyond* Y_{FE}. This higher level of income is produced by reducing the unemployment rate below what is normally considered full employment. Or, more generally, more inflation means less unemployment, as in the Phillips curve.

This situation, unfortunately, requires some explaining in terms of worker behavior, wage-price lags, and inflationary expectations. Rest assured, however, that we will expose you to only the bare minimum (we really don't know very much more ourselves). The key to the debate focuses, once again, on whether the aggregate supply curve is vertical or positively sloped. A positive slope implies that real output varies positively with the price level. Our discussion back in footnote 2 showed that output varies positively with prices when wages change more slowly than prices. And that's reasonable, according to Keynesians, because many wage rates are set contractually, and contracts are not adjusted continuously. What this means is that when the price level falls, declining wages lag behind falling goods prices, and the real value of labor's compensation increases. That's why fewer workers are employed and less is produced when the price level declines. The other side of the coin is that when the price level rises, wages increase more slowly than prices, labor's real compensation falls, more workers are hired, and GDP goes up. And that's why the Keynesian picture shows a trade-off between inflation and unemployment.

Monetarists have emphasized, and economists of all persuasions now recognize, that a lower real wage cannot permanently induce workers to spend less time playing tennis and more time at the factory or behind the desk. Thus, after a while, labor will demand that wages be adjusted upward. Some workers may feel reluctant to do so right away because of a long-run contractual relationship with their employer, one that transcends what could be only a temporary erosion in the value of their paychecks. But as the inflation reality sinks in and workers come to *expect* a permanently higher rate of inflation, their wage demands become more vociferous. Wages will be pushed up by competitive pressure among employers. But once wages catch up to the higher rate of price increase, there is little incentive for business firms to produce more than they started with. Thus production eventually returns to Y_{FE} and unemployment goes back to what is normally considered a full employment rate.

What we have just described is a slow but steady transition from the upward-sloping supply curve in Figure 27.4 to the vertical aggregate supply curve in Figure 27.3. Thus, after everything has adjusted, including inflationary expectations and labor-business contractual agreements, the aggregate supply curve must be vertical. In other words, the Phillips curve eventually must show no trade-off between inflation and unemployment.

One of the main questions is, of course, how long can a temporary situation last? A more intriguing possibility is that if everyone knows that the trade-off is temporary, it may not even get started! In the next chapter we return to this discussion within the framework of rational expectations. For now let's turn our attention to the consequences of inflation and inflationary expectations for the level of interest rates.

INFLATION AND INTEREST RATES

Inflationary expectations are crucial to explaining how interest rates respond to changes in the money supply. In this area, however, we cannot appeal to the aggregate supply/demand framework for expositional help. English will have to suffice (sorry; we don't like it any more than you do).

Milton Friedman has argued that an *expansionary* monetary policy *raises* interest rates and a *contractionary* monetary policy *lowers* interest rates—just the reverse of standard Keynesian analysis. How does Milton do it? Here's the point: An increase in the money supply *may initially* lower interest rates, if the increased liquidity is spent on financial assets. But that is only the beginning. Once aggregate demand responds to the increased money supply (as it must in the monetarist world), the transactions demand for money will increase, thereby driving interest rates upward. But this is hardly new. Mainstream Keynesians certainly wouldn't disagree. The monetarists argue, however, that the "income effect" of the increased money supply will overwhelm the initial "liquidity effect," so that the interest rate will snap back past its original level.

If pressed on this last point, Keynesians might even acquiesce again. After a while interest rates *could* pass the original equilibrium, but it all depends on the speed and strength of the response in GDP to monetary expansion. Keynesians would focus their attention on the interim period—before GDP expands. And this interim period is sufficiently long to justify the statement: Expansionary monetary policy *means* lower interest rates, and contractionary policy *means* higher rates.

But there's more to the monetarist story, namely, inflationary expectations. In particular, if expectations of inflation are generated by an expansionary monetary policy, then this will cause a *further* increase in the level of *nominal* interest rates. The reason is as follows: Suppose that when the expected rate of inflation is zero, the equilibrium interest rate is 5 percent. As we said in Chapter 23, if lenders expect prices to rise by 2 percent during the next 12 months and want to receive 5 percent in real terms, they will demand 7 percent from borrowers. As long as borrowers expect the same rate of inflation, they will go along with the higher nominal rate of interest. After all, if they were ready to pay 5 percent with no inflation, they should be equally eager to borrow money at 7 percent with 2 percent inflation—they will be paying off the loan in "cheaper" dollars.[5]

What might lead *both* borrowers and lenders to expect inflation and then arrive at a higher nominal rate of interest? You guessed it—an expansionary monetary policy. When such inflationary expectations are tacked onto the income effect, monetarists contend that it is virtually certain that these two will dominate the initial liquidity impact and expansionary monetary policy will lead to higher nominal interest rates. An analogous argument can be made for contractionary monetary policy lowering interest rates.

Notice, by the way, that the distinction between real and nominal rates is crucial in these arguments. Increases in money lead to inflation via the quantity theory. The real interest rate is determined by savers and investors. They "pierce the veil" of money and refuse to let inflation interfere with their agreed-upon *real* rate of interest. Thus when the "inflation premium" described by Irving Fisher (see Chapter 23) is added to the real rate, we see that increases in money supply raise the nominal rate of interest. Therefore, Milton Friedman, with an assist from Irving Fisher, concludes that an expansionary monetary policy raises interest rates.

The story just told, of nominal interest rates rising because of the inflationary expectations generated by expansionary monetary policy, can take on still another dimension. In particular, if policymakers are *expected* to increase the money supply in an effort to lower interest rates, there will, in fact, not even be any temporary liquidity effect on real interest rates, since such anticipated money stock movements will have already been incorporated in portfolio decisions. For example, the liquidity effect of the anticipated increase in

---

[5] Borrowers would like to pay only 5 percent. But as we saw in Chapter 23, competition for funds forces them to pay what lenders demand, unless they are willing to pass up some investment projects. But inflation will increase the expected *dollar* returns on investments, so that if a project was worth undertaking before it would be just as worthwhile with inflation and the higher nominal interest rate.

money stock will have already raised bond demand to take advantage of anticipated capital gains; thus no further bond price increases occur when the money stock actually increases. All that's left is the quantity theory effect, which says that increases in money stock raise prices. Thus the anticipated rate of inflation generated by expansionary monetary policy pushes up nominal interest rates. There simply aren't any intermediate steps.[6]

Although the expectations story sounds convincing, remember that Keynesians argue that the simple quantity theory operates only at or near full employment. At lower levels of economic activity, there is considerable slippage between money and prices. Even near what we designate as full employment there are wage and price rigidities because of contractual arrangements that interfere with any proportional relationship between money and prices.

Most observers contend, therefore, that it takes time for the inflation premium to be fully reflected in nominal interest rates. In the short run, lenders may have to settle for lower real interest rates. Instead of the nominal rate rising by 2 percent in our example above, it may rise by less, and therefore the real rate would fall somewhat when expected inflation jumped by 2 percent. Eventually, as lenders adjust their cash balances and borrowers alter their investment plans, the real rate returns to its long-run equilibrium level and the nominal rate rises above the real rate by the full expected rate of inflation.

How long is the long run? Ah, if we only knew the answer to that question, how simple life would be. We get closer to Irving Fisher's result even in the short run—say, within six months—as the delay in borrower and lender reactions gets shorter. Furthermore, when expectations of inflation respond quickly to economic forces, the Fisher result is likely to occur still more quickly. On the other hand, when delays are long and expectations of inflation respond slowly, then it takes longer for nominal rates to rise by the full amount of the expected inflation. As a general rule, it is a good bet that an increase in nominal rates of interest will closely follow a jump in inflationary expectations, but nominal interest rates are unlikely to respond immediately by the full amount Fisher suggested.

Can we really be this far into a book on money and not be sure which way interest rates respond to monetary ease or stringency? Yes and no—unequivocally.

We can summarize the discussion as follows. An increase in the money supply will immediately reduce both the nominal rate and the real rate of interest because of a liquidity effect. As inflationary expectations respond to the monetary expansion, nominal rates are driven up but by less than the inflationary surge. Thus the nominal rate could very well be above the original level of nominal (and real) rates while the real rate can be below it. After borrowers and lenders have completed all their adjustments, the real rate of interest will be back where we started and the nominal rate will have increased

---

[6] This discussion has applied the rational expectations argument to interest rates. More on this in the next chapter.

by the expected rate of inflation.[7] So now you can answer just about anything you want to the question of what happens to interest rates when the money supply expands, as long as you keep the real and nominal straightened out (don't worry, not many people can do that). To really confuse matters you might try to explain how decreases in the money supply produce an opposite set of results.

SHOULD A ROBOT REPLACE THE FEDERAL RESERVE?

We started this chapter with a discussion of whether the private sector is inherently stable. If the self-correcting mechanisms described above operate properly, there is little need for active monetary and fiscal policies to prevent economic fluctuations. In fact, these stabilizing mechanisms form the foundation for the monetarist argument against government attempts at fine-tuning the economy. It's simply not needed.

Keynesians claim that since the strength of these self-correcting forces is uncertain, we should use **countercyclical monetary and fiscal policies** to help ensure full employment production. They implicitly assume that attempts at leaning against the economic trends—expansionary policy in recessions and contractionary policy during inflations—can only help. The problem is that attempts at countercyclical policy can actually wind up causing greater instability than would have otherwise been the case.

Milton Friedman was the first to point out the potentially destabilizing impacts of government countercyclical policy. To explain the argument we must recognize that the effects of changes in monetary policy or fiscal policy take time to work themselves out. In particular, there are lags in the impacts of monetary and fiscal policy on GDP. The empirical evidence on lags is presented later, in Chapter 29. For now it is sufficient to recognize that it takes time for changes in interest rates to alter business spending decisions and it takes time even for households to adjust their consumer expenditures to increased disposable income. In a moment we will see that putting this little addendum on lags together with our aggregate demand story, we are able to show the potential damage of stabilization efforts. An alternative philosophy—rules rather than discretion—is proposed by monetarists to mitigate the problem.

Assume that the Federal Reserve forecasts a recession six months from now. If the forecast is correct, and if a current expansion in the money supply would have an impact six months hence, well and good. But what if the Federal Reserve's crystal ball is not clear, and it is more than a year before the main impact of today's monetary policy is reflected in the economy? Then the

---

[7] The fact that expansionary monetary policy cannot reduce interest rates permanently explains why it is impossible for the central bank to make Congress happy by forcing down the cost of credit. It also explains why bondholders will not be forever wealthier because of increases in the money supply.

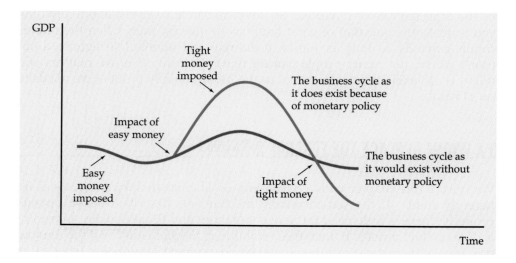

FIGURE 27.5 <u>**Friedman's alleged perverse effects of countercyclical monetary policy.**</u>

effects of today's expansionary monetary policy are likely to be felt *after* the economy has passed the trough and is already on its way up.

As Figure 27.5 illustrates, the impact of today's easy money may exacerbate tomorrow's inflation. Tight money will have similarly delayed effects; it may be imposed with the best of intentions, to curtail a boom, but its real impact, being delayed, might accentuate a recession. Monetary policy is a destabilizer rather than a stabilizer!

On these grounds—the precarious nature of economic forecasting and the alleged length, variability, and unpredictability of the time lags involved—monetarists have given up on orthodox monetary policy. Friedman argues that the economy has been and is now inherently stable and that it would automatically tend to stay on a fairly straight course, as Figure 27.5 indicates, if only it were not being almost continuously knocked off the track by erratic or unwise monetary policies. Conclusion: Quarantine the central bank. The best stabilization policy is no stabilization policy at all. Hasn't it all been said before:

> They also serve who only stand and waite.

John Milton

What monetarists propose instead is that the Federal Reserve be instructed by Congress to follow a fixed long-run rule: Increase the money supply at a steady and inflexible rate, month in and month out, year in and year out, regardless of current economic conditions. Set the money supply on automatic pilot and then leave it alone.

The specific growth rate—3, 4, or 6 percent—is less important than the principle. Once a figure is decided upon, no tinkering is permitted. In point of fact, the actual money supply growth rate is intended to keep prices stable and employment high by allowing aggregate demand to grow at the same rate as the economy's real productive capacity. This is illustrated in Figure 27.6

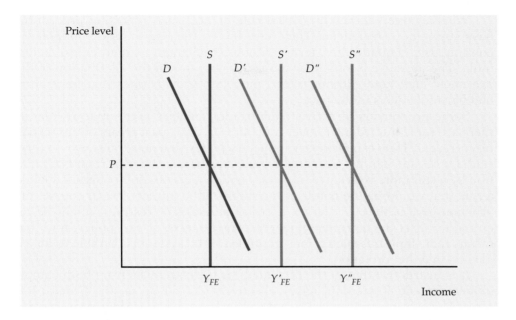

FIGURE 27.6   Aggregate demand and supply shifting together over time according to a fixed monetary rule.

with our by now familiar aggregate supply and demand framework. But in this context, we allow the aggregate supply curve to shift rightward to reflect growth in capital and the labor force. Stable prices and full employment will be achieved when growth in the money supply pushes the aggregate demand schedule to the right along with aggregate supply (as in Figure 27.6).

The main advantage of a rule is that it would eliminate forecasting and lag problems and therefore remove what monetarists see as the major cause of instability in the economy—the capricious and unpredictable impact of discretionary countercyclical monetary policy. As long as the money supply grows at a constant rate each year, be it 3, 4, or 6 percent, any decline into recession will be temporary. The liquidity provided by a constantly growing money supply will cause aggregate demand to expand. Similarly, if the supply of money does not rise at a more than average rate, any inflationary increase in spending will burn itself out for lack of fuel. Discretionary deviations by the central bank would interfere with the natural course of the economy and only make matters worse.

The U.S. Congress has been impressed enough to come part of the way toward a rule, in preference to allowing the Federal Reserve to rely entirely on its own judgment and discretion. In March 1975 both the House of Representatives and the Senate passed House Congressional Resolution 133, which instructed the Federal Reserve to "maintain long-run growth of the monetary and credit aggregates commensurate with the economy's long-run potential to increase production." It also required that the Fed report to Congress on its target monetary and credit growth rates. In November 1977 these provisions were incorporated into the Federal Reserve Act itself.

Whether one believes in a fixed rule or not, such reporting procedures have surely been beneficial. They have forced the Fed to assess its policies continuously in quantitative terms without shackling it with an inflexible formula. The objective is smoother monetary growth and the elimination of the extremely high (and extremely low) monetary growth rates that have often had harmful effects in the past.

Some proponents of activist stabilization policies argue that as long as there are some immediate impacts of policy on GDP, past errors of timing can be corrected. Thus expansionary monetary policy that acts too slowly to forestall a recession can be prevented from exacerbating the next round of inflation by a still more restrictive monetary policy. This possibility argues against a rule that would tie the hands of the stabilization authorities. Of course, the problem here is that ever-larger doses of stimulus or restraint might be required to offset the detrimental lagged consequences of past policy. And that means that slight miscalculations might leave the system vulnerable to an explosion in either direction.

It is instructive that in the final analysis the extremists from both camps, monetarist and Keynesian, have collectively ganged up on the Federal Reserve. The extreme monetarists want to shackle it, because their concern with time lags leads them to believe it is both mischievous and harmful, and the extreme Keynesians want to subordinate it to fiscal policy. In the middle, squabbling but making more common cause than they had thought possible, are the moderates: moderate monetarists, who believe that the forecasting-lag problem is not so great as to negate all the stabilizing effects of countercyclical monetary policy, and moderate Keynesians, who believe that monetary policy has a powerful impact on spending and should be used along with fiscal policy with considerable caution.

It seems clear, after all is said and done, that central banking is still at least as much art as science. We simply do not know enough yet to legislate an eternal rule, or even a rule for the next six months, that the Federal Reserve must follow under any and all circumstances. Meanwhile, for better or worse, we appear to have no alternative but to rely on our best knowledge and judgment in the formulation of monetary policy. We can only try to make sure that the decision makers are able and qualified men and women with open minds and the capacity to learn from experience.

SUMMARY

1. The monetarist argument that the private sector is inherently stable stems from the automatic tendency for falling interest rates and prices to raise aggregate demand whenever exogenous spending falls. Keynesians claim that in the short run wages are less flexible than prices and that therefore exogenous shifts in aggregate demand will produce variations in GDP.

2. Monetarists claim that the transmission mechanism between money and spending is direct. Additional cash balances are spent directly on real

goods and services. According to Keynesians, however, the linkage between money and spending occurs through the interest rate, and in this
case there is room for considerable slippage.

3.   Keynesians contend that fiscal policy has a direct and powerful impact
on spending. Monetarists claim that much of the expansionary impact of
fiscal policy disappears because rising interest rates crowd out private
investment.

4.   Inflation is basically a monetary phenomenon, according to monetarists,
because aggregate demand depends primarily on the money supply.
Keynesians claim that fiscal policy or other exogenous spending can
cause inflation as well.

5.   The existence of a Phillips curve trade-off between inflation and unemployment depends upon the lags of wages and expectations behind
changes in the price level. Even Keynesians would agree that in the
long run there is no trade-off, but in the short run there is considerable
disagreement.

6.   Real interest rates initially fall after an increase in the money supply,
but once inflationary expectations take hold, nominal rates rise. After
a while the real rate will return to its original level, but as long as inflationary expectations remain, the nominal level of rates will be
higher.

7.   The monetarist case for a fixed rule to circumscribe stabilization policy
stems from the possibility that the lagged effects of policy changes might
cause greater instability in GDP. The key problem is accurately anticipating the timing of policy impacts on aggregate demand. Monetarists
propose a fixed rule to prevent destabilizing effects. Keynesians believe
the inflexibility imposed by a rule cannot be justified, given the present
state of knowledge about the impact of policy on demand.

8.   Many of these monetarist-Keynesian arguments can be traced to differing views of the aggregate supply and demand curves. Monetarists tend
to believe aggregate demand is stable once money supply is fixed; Keynesians see no reason to assume such stability. Monetarists say the aggregate supply curve is usually vertical; Keynesians claim it is horizontal
some of the time and upward sloping much of the time.

QUESTIONS

27.1   How does the slope of the aggregate supply curve help determine
whether GDP will be stable at full employment?

27.2   What is the Phillips curve, and how is it related to the aggregate supply
curve?

27.3 Does an increase in money supply increase interest rates or decrease interest rates? (*Hint:* Be careful to identify real versus nominal interest rates.)

27.4 What is meant by crowding out? How many different types of crowding out can you identify?

27.5 Why should the money supply grow in the long run?

27.6 *Discussion question:* Do you believe we would be better off with a monetary policy that follows a fixed rule for money supply growth? Explain why we do not (and are not likely to) have one.

CHAPTER 28

Rational Expectations: Theory and Policy Implications

Rational expectations, ice cream, and apple pie have at least one thing in common: It's hard to be against them. But the similarity ends there, because the implications of rational expectations are far more controversial than either of the other two—even if you're serious about counting calories.

Throughout our discussion of the monetarist and Keynesian viewpoints, expectations have never been far from the surface. We saw in the last chapter that inflationary expectations are crucial determinants of the nominal interest rate. We also showed how inflationary expectations enter into wage agreements and thereby influence the shape of the aggregate supply curve and hence the Phillips curve trade-off between inflation and unemployment. Finally, back in Chapter 24 we indicated that expectations of monetary policy actions could affect the timing of interest rate responses to changes in the money supply.

In all these earlier discussions we never were very particular about how these expectations were formulated. Implicit in most discussions was the assumption that expectations of the future are based on the past: If price increases have been accelerating, for example, then inflation is *expected* to get worse. As it turns out, this seemingly innocuous formulation of expected inflation is not terribly rational, because it ignores other pieces of information that might be important to a proper estimate of future inflation.

The first order of business, therefore, is to describe precisely what is meant by rational expectations. We then turn to the implications for monetary and fiscal policy, the ability to control inflation, and the consequences for interest rates.

WHEN ARE EXPECTATIONS RATIONAL?

If people use all available information to formulate expectations (of prices, interest rates, money supply, or anything else), then their expectations are considered rational. If people ignore information, then expectations are not rational. People are likely to be rational in formulating their expectations, because ignoring something is usually costly. For example, ignoring the news report of a freeze in Florida in formulating your expectation of orange juice prices next month is likely to cost you money. A rational forecast would suggest stocking up on orange juice before prices go up. Ignoring the information and relying on recent price trends to guide your spending plans will lead to inferior results. Thus people have strong incentives to make rational forecasts and can be relied upon to act accordingly. If our models are to describe economic activity accurately, then the behavioral relationships must be based on rational expectations.

Let's examine in somewhat greater detail how inflationary expectations are formulated. Extrapolating recent price trends is often referred to as *adaptive* expectations. Thus if inflation has been on the rise, adaptive expectations suggest that people expect inflation to continue to go up. But if at the same time that inflation is increasing the Federal Reserve restricts the money supply, and people are aware of this policy, then on the basis of their knowledge of how the economy works, people would probably expect the inflation rate to go down rather than up. Such expectations would be considered rational because they include information—what is happening to the money supply—that is relevant for properly forecasting inflation. Moreover, people will utilize that information, because spending, investing, and business decisions depend upon inflation forecasts. If inflation is expected to go down, certain job opportunities become more or less attractive, some investments become more or less attractive, and so on.

Notice that rational inflationary expectations include at least two items that were ignored by the less rigorous adaptive approach to forecasting: the behavior of the monetary authority and the structure of the economy. Since knowledge of what policymakers will do and what economic models suggest are the consequences of such actions is potentially important for the future course of prices, it is crucial that rational expectations incorporate that information. The reason is not that we say so but that people will find it optimal (and profitable) to behave according to rational expectations.

ANTICIPATED VERSUS UNANTICIPATED MONETARY POLICY

Perhaps the most stunning implication of rational expectations is that when it is combined with the classical world's assumption of completely flexible wages and prices, the result is that an *anticipated* monetary policy will have no impact on economic activity. The argument is complicated, so we will have

OFF THE RECORD

Applying Rational Expectations to the Securities Markets

It makes considerable sense to apply the principle of rational expectations to securities prices. Every scrap of information is likely to be exploited in formulating expected bond prices or stock prices, because there are direct, and often immediate, profit opportunities available in acting upon such information. This idea has an interesting implication for current securities prices: They will reflect all currently available information. For example, suppose a secret Federal Reserve document describing a surprise reduction in money supply growth was discovered in a Washington, D.C., trash can and were then published in the *Wall Street Journal.* Since a less expansionary monetary policy would lead to less inflation and lower nominal rates of interest, hence higher bond prices in the future, the demand for bonds would increase right now and bond prices would rise until there was no longer an opportunity to earn a profit. Thus the information about the Federal Reserve's new policy would be incorporated in bond prices immediately upon its release. In other words, securities prices fully reflect all available information. Thus the application of rational expectations to securities markets produces what we called *efficient capital markets* back in Chapter 6.

to pay attention. It goes like this. Recall from the last chapter that the positively sloped aggregate supply curve implies that faster money supply growth leads to higher output and less unemployment as long as wages go up more slowly than prices. The argument is straightforward: If wages go up more slowly than prices it will pay business firms to hire more workers. The problem is that workers will permit their wages to rise more slowly than prices only as long as their inflationary expectations lag behind actual inflation. People will not work more if they expect a decline in their *real* wages (money wages adjusted for inflation to provide a measure of the goods and services the money wages can buy). But according to rational expectations, workers recognize the connection between inflation and money supply growth. Thus if we start with an *anticipated* increase in the money supply, then the subsequent inflation will also be anticipated. And in that case, inflationary expectations keep pace with actual inflation and, because wages and prices are completely flexible, workers make sure that wages move up simultaneously with prices. Under those circumstances there won't be any increase in output or reduction in unemployment as a result of the anticipated increase in the money supply.

Note that if the money growth is not anticipated, the increased aggregate demand leads to higher prices that are not anticipated. Wages do, in fact, lag behind prices, and business firms hire more workers. The result: higher output and lower unemployment when money supply growth is not anticipated.

It is possible to illustrate the entire story within the aggregate supply and demand model as long as we remember to label each aggregate supply curve with the appropriate expected price level. In Figure 28.1 start with aggregate demand curve D_1 and aggregate supply curve $S(P_1^e)$, where P_1^e indicates that

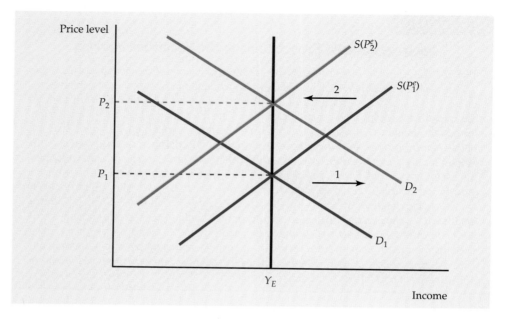

FIGURE 28.1   Anticipated monetary policy shifts aggregate supply along with aggregate demand, leaving GDP unchanged.

the expected price level is P_1. The equilibrium price level given by the intersection point between D_1 and $S(P_1^e)$ is P_1 and equilibrium income is Y_E. An increase in the money supply shifts D_1 to D_2 and would raise output above Y_E if the aggregate supply curve remained $S(P_1^e)$. But if the change in money supply is anticipated, the aggregate supply curve no longer is $S(P_1^e)$ because the increased money supply is expected to increase the price level above P_1. The new aggregate supply curve under rational expectations is $S(P_2^e)$, where the new equilibrium price level is equal to P_2. Thus the end result of an anticipated change in the money supply is an unchanged level of economic activity and a higher price level.[1]

IMPLICATIONS FOR STABILIZATION POLICY

The distinction between anticipated and unanticipated monetary policy takes on still greater significance once we recognize that stabilization policy usually falls under the category of anticipated policy. If unemployment be-

---

[1] The proof that the new aggregate supply curve must be exactly $S(P_2^e)$ is fairly complicated. It is based on the notion that the expected price level P_2^e must be consistent with the actual new equilibrium price level P_2, and that neither has any tendency to change. This will occur where the level of output Y_E has no tendency to change as well, that is, Y_E is the full employment level of output.

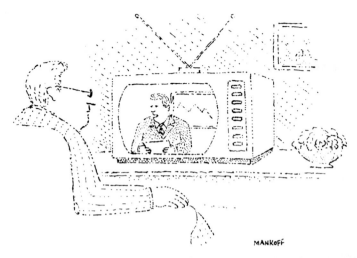

"On Wall Street today, news of lower interest rates sent the stock market up, but then the expection that these rates would be inflationary sent the market down, until the realization that lower rates might stimulate the sluggish economy pushed the market up, before it ultimately went down on fears that an overheated economy would lead to a reimposition of higher interest rates."

Drawing by Mankoff; © 1981 The New Yorker Magazine, Inc.

gins to rise and the Federal Reserve is known to pursue countercyclical monetary policy, then everyone expects the Federal Reserve to expand the money supply. As long as wages and prices are flexible, however, the expansion in money supply will lead to higher prices. Because people are aware of these relationships, expected inflation occurs simultaneously with the expansion in money supply, wages move up in tandem with prices, and the impact of the expansionary monetary policy on real economic activity is neutralized.

The cruel facts of rational expectations are that only random acts by the central bank—"erroneous" increases or decreases in the money supply—influence the level of economic activity. Systematic policies are useless. From this perspective, the discussions in the last chapter on rules versus discretion and whether the Federal Reserve should be a robot are irrelevant. No matter what systematic decision rule the Fed follows, it will not influence real economic activity—for better or worse.

The outcome of the rational expectations world is decidedly classical-monetarist rather than Keynesian. Although rational expectations do not necessarily support Milton Friedman's contention that the attempt at economic stabilization is destabilizing (since any systematic policy is neutralized), the close connection between money supply and inflation and the inherent stability of the economy at full employment are decidedly monetarist-classical propositions. Rational expectations theory is sometimes considered the main component of the new classical macroeconomics.

But all is not lost for proponents of Keynesian thinking. Rational expectations combined with contractual rigidity in wages and prices modify the stark conclusions just described. In particular, even though inflationary expectations follow directly from expansionary monetary policy, and even though countercyclical policy will be anticipated, wages and prices are not determined by an auctioneer. Unlike prices of stocks and bonds, wages are frequently set by contractual agreement. If that's the case, then wages may very well lag behind prices even if expectations of inflation are formed rationally. Somewhat more concretely, even when workers expect inflation to rise, they do not force up their wage demands instantaneously. Similarly, even if business firms expect a decrease in inflation, they do not reduce wages paid instantaneously. These sluggish adjustments are part of the implicit and explicit contractual arrangements in labor markets.

Without instantaneous adjustments in wages to reflect expected inflation, the positively sloped aggregate supply curve does not shift to the left in Figure 28.1. Thus when D_1 shifts to the right, the equilibrium level of output does, in fact, increase. From our new perspective these results occur not because expected inflation lags behind actual inflation—rational expectations do not permit that—but because wages simply do not adjust completely. Corporations hire more workers and output rises until the contractual arrangements run their course.

The battlefield between monetarists and Keynesians over the effectiveness of stabilization policy has shifted once again. Instead of inflationary expectations, the area of contention now is labor contracts and rigid wages. For some reason, that has a familiar ring to it. And for good reason, because wage rigidity is exactly where Keynes and his classical mentors originally parted company.

INFLATION, THE PHILLIPS CURVE, AND CREDIBILITY

In the last chapter we described the controversy over the Phillips curve: Keynesians argued that a trade-off existed between inflation and unemployment, while monetarists claimed that there was no long-run trade-off. The key was the shape of the aggregate supply curve and whether inflationary expectations lag behind actual inflation. According to the Keynesians, the aggregate supply curve is positively sloped because expectations of inflation adjust more slowly than actual inflation to changes in underlying economic activity. Under such circumstances, policymakers could increase the level of economic activity and reduce unemployment as long as they were ready to tolerate an increase in the rate of inflation. Monetarists argued that in the short run this might be so, but after expectations have adjusted, the aggregate supply curve is vertical and no permanent trade-off is possible.

The rational expectations story pushes the monetarists' long-run analysis into the short run by transforming a series of upward-sloping aggregate supply curves into a vertical one. We begin, once again, with a change in the money supply that is fully anticipated. The increased money supply shifts the aggregate demand curve to the right. But as we saw in Figure 28.1, if wages and prices are flexible, whenever the Federal Reserve embarks on a counter-cyclical expansion in the money supply, the rightward shift in aggregate demand is met by a leftward shift in aggregate supply. In Figure 28.2, we illustrate these simultaneously shifting aggregate supply and demand curves that leave income and output at the "natural" full employment level Y_{FE}. The simultaneous shifts in aggregate supply and demand occur because the expansionary monetary policy that shifts D_1 to D_2 to D_3 produces rational inflationary expectations that shift $S(P_1^e)$ to $S(P_2^e)$ to $S(P_3^e)$. The equilibrium points in Figure 28.2 show an unchanged level of output at Y_{FE} combined with ever-increasing price levels. The result is that even though we have individual positively sloped aggregate supply curves, the outcome of a countercyclical monetary policy is a de facto vertical aggregate supply curve produced by simultaneous shifts in S and D. Thus policymakers are not confronted by a Phillips curve trade-off between inflation and unemployment, because the positively sloped aggregate supply curve does not stay put.

Keynesians, of course, would respond that as long as wages and prices are set contractually, shifting aggregate supply curves would not eliminate the

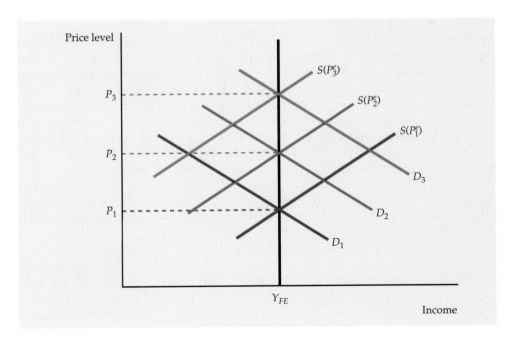

FIGURE 28.2   Anticipated monetary policy can affect only the price level.

Phillips curve trade-off between inflation and unemployment. Even under rational expectations, the contractual rigidities remain and provide policymakers with an avenue for influencing real economic activity.

For those of you with a soft spot for policy-making, do not think that a Phillips curve is necessary to provide a meaningful life. Although the absence of a trade-off between inflation and unemployment under rational expectations (with flexible wages and prices) deals a devastating blow to policymakers trying to reduce unemployment, it creates a pleasant surprise for the inflation fighters. In particular, reducing inflation is accomplished painlessly. Let the central bank embark on a contractionary monetary policy and make certain that *everyone knows about it.* As long as the Federal Reserve's policy is credible, the leftward shift in the aggregate demand schedule produced by a reduction in the money supply is accompanied by a rightward shift in the aggregate supply curve. For example, if we start in Figure 28.2 with $S(P_3^e)$ and D_3 and price level P_3, the reduction in money supply shifts D_3 to D_2. Since everyone now expects the lower price level P_2, the aggregate supply curve also shifts to $S(P_2^e)$. The economy moves from price level P_3 to price level P_2 painlessly—without any decrease in economic activity and without any increase in unemployment.

The key to this happy result is *credibility*. If the public suspects that the Federal Reserve will not stick to its guns, perhaps because the Fed is afraid that unemployment will increase, then the expected price level will not fall to P_2^e, and the aggregate supply curve will stay where it is. The result will be costly: a reduction in output and increased unemployment. Only if the Fed announces its policy and the public is convinced that it will pursue it at all costs will the costs turn out to be negligible.

How is this credibility accomplished? Rhetoric is usually not sufficient, especially in democratic societies where considerable political pressure can be brought to bear on policymakers. Concrete policy changes are necessary to alter ingrained inflationary expectations. This is especially so in the case of hyperinflation, where exorbitant rates of inflation have taken hold of an economy. Under such circumstances, changing the monetary unit, introducing a truly independent central bank, and invoking severe fiscal restraint to balance the budget have had the desired effect. The hyperinflations suffered by Germany, Austria, Poland, and Hungary in the aftermath of World War I were reversed with hardly any reduction in real output as a result of an overhaul in the monetary-fiscal regimes in each of those countries. Under more mundane circumstances, however, the search for a credible policy proceeds with much more caution. And that often dooms the experiment before it gets started.

At this point our discussion of the trade-off between inflation and unemployment sounds more like topics in advanced psychology than anything resembling economic policy. In part, that is the message of rational expectations. Economic policy-making is far more complicated than the Keynesian revolution had anticipated. And while wages and prices might not be sufficiently flexible to drive out countercyclical policy completely, the effectiveness of the conventional Keynesian models must be modified by rational inflationary expectations.

INTEREST RATES AND ANTICIPATED MONETARY POLICY

The rational expectations message for interest rates is not much brighter than for countercyclical policy in general. Recall our discussion in the last chapter on how a change in the money supply affects the level of interest rates. We identified the Keynesian liquidity effect, which links an increase in money supply with a decline in both real and nominal interest rates. The monetarists stress that this liquidity effect is only transitory, soon to be swamped by inflationary expectations that drive nominal rates above real rates. Keynesians have a short-run "liquidity" perspective when claiming that expansionary monetary policy lowers interest rates, while monetarists have a longer-run perspective when emphasizing that interest rates go up because of inflationary expectations.

The rational expectations world is much simpler. An anticipated increase in the money supply leads to higher nominal interest rates immediately, while unanticipated increases in money supply produce lower nominal interest rates. The reasoning is straightforward. Anticipated increases in money supply produce inflationary expectations simultaneously with the expansion in money supply. Under such circumstances, lenders are reluctant to part with funds unless interest rates reflect the expected inflation and borrowers agree to pay higher rates because of the expected inflation. The liquidity effect never reduces interest rates, because inflationary expectations respond instantaneously. When the money supply jumps without warning, however, then the liquidity effect produces a drop in rates. In fact, if the expansion in money supply occurred without rhyme or reason, inflationary expectations might not get started until aggregate demand pushed up economic activity. And that might take sufficient time for the liquidity effect to remain for a while.

The lesson of the rational expectations story is harder to avoid in financial markets than in labor markets. When it comes to stocks and bonds, prices are not set by contractual agreement. Thus the rational expectations distinctions between the impacts of anticipated and unanticipated monetary policy on interest rates are important lessons. Nevertheless, the story cannot end here. Empirical evidence is the only way to resolve the policy disputes between monetarists and Keynesians, with or without rational expectations. And for answers we must turn to the next chapter.

SUMMARY

1. Expectations are rational when people take account of all available information in forecasting economic variables. In forecasting inflation, for example, rational expectations reflect information on what is happening to the money supply and what economic models predict the consequences will be for prices.

2. When expectations are rational and when wages and prices are completely flexible, anticipated monetary policies have no effect on economic activity. The result for stabilization policy, which is usually anticipated, is decidedly monetarist-classical: There is no impact of countercyclical policy on the level of economic activity.

3. The Keynesian viewpoint is that even if expectations are rational, wages and prices are not completely flexible because of contractual arrangements in labor markets. Under such circumstances, even an anticipated countercyclical monetary policy will have an impact on economic activity.

4. The rational expectations perspective eliminates even a temporary trade-off between inflation and unemployment. This means policymakers cannot reduce unemployment below some natural level by increasing the rate of inflation. There is no short-run Phillips curve under rational expectations.

5. A contractionary monetary policy can reduce inflation without an increase in unemployment in the rational expectations world. As long as the anti-inflationary policy has credibility, the reduction in inflation will be painless.

6. Prices and yields in financial markets are sufficiently flexible to make the rational expectations world a reality. Under such circumstances, an anticipated monetary policy cannot influence real interest rates even in the short run. Anticipated monetary policy influences interest rates only through inflationary expectations.

QUESTIONS

28.1 Define rational expectations and explain why it is reasonable to assume people formulate expectations rationally.

28.2 Explain why an anticipated monetary policy will have no effect on the level of economic activity if people formulate price expectations rationally.

28.3 What behavioral assumption do Keynesians propose that revives the case for the effectiveness of countercyclical policy despite rational expectations? Explain.

28.4 How does credibility in fighting inflation reduce the likelihood that unemployment will accompany anti-inflationary monetary policies?

28.5 *Discussion question:* If everyone agrees that rational expectations make sense, why is it that our government still practices countercyclical monetary (and fiscal) policy?

CHAPTER 29

Empirical Evidence on the Effectiveness of Monetary Policy

Theory, like punishment, is said to be good for the soul. But even the most philosophical among us realize that humans—and yes, even students—also require rewards that are somewhat more concrete. Having poked into every nook and cranny of the monetarist-Keynesian dialogue over the effectiveness of monetary and fiscal policy, the time has come to reveal the Truth (with a capital T). Since many people believe that numbers are Truth, here they are aplenty.

What are the facts about the behavior of velocity? How powerful is the impact of monetary policy on economic activity? How are interest rates affected? What particular categories of spending are most influenced by money? After all, if monetary policy is to alter GDP, it cannot do it by mystic incantations; it has to do it by changing the consumer spending of households, the investment spending of business firms, or the expenditures of governments—federal, state, or local. In contrast to the theoretical discussion of previous chapters, we now turn to the *empirical* evidence.[1]

---

[1] Our discussion draws on a number of studies, including: Patricia C. Mosser, "Changes in Monetary Policy Effectiveness: Evidence from Large Macroeconometric Models," Federal Reserve Bank of New York *Quarterly Review*, Spring 1992; Benjamin M. Friedman, "Changing Effects of Monetary Policy on Real Economic Activity," in *Monetary Policy Issues in the 1990s*, Federal Reserve Bank of Kansas City; Eric M. Leeper, "Facing Up to Our Ignorance About Measuring Monetary Policy Effects," Federal Reserve Bank of Atlanta *Economic Review*, May/June 1992.

LIVING WITH VELOCITY

We have seen that part of the monetarist-Keynesian debate hinges on the behavior of velocity—monetarists contending that it is relatively stable and that any changes are highly predictable, and Keynesians arguing that either contention is an exaggeration. The facts are that velocity is neither perfectly stable nor fully predictable. The Federal Reserve, unfortunately, does not operate in a world designed for its own convenience. With a money supply of $500 billion, a miscalculation of only 0.1 in velocity means a $50 billion swing in GDP. And with a money supply of $1,000 billion, the GDP jump is twice as large. But all is not necessarily lost. While velocity is not fixed, neither do its movements appear to be obviously random or perverse. If the Federal Reserve could discover the underlying determinants of fluctuations in velocity, it might still be able to coexist with such a moving target.

With that in mind, examining the past may provide a clue to developments in the future. Figure 29.1 plots the historical course of two measures of velocity, each one associated with a different money supply concept. The velocity figures for V1 are based on M1 and V2 on M2. Two broad generalizations emerge from the picture. First, while none of the velocity measures has been completely stable, the meanderings of V2 have been quite tame. Of course, we just pointed out that even small miscalculations in velocity mean wide swings in GDP, especially for the more inclusive definition of money. Nevertheless, the rather narrow range of movement in V2 is impressive. The

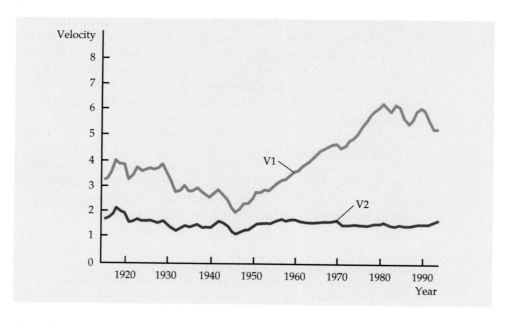

FIGURE 29.1   Historical movements in M1 and M2 velocities.

second glaring message of Figure 29.1 is that V1 looks highly unpredictable. Those who prefer the narrow definition of money have some explaining to do.

First the facts. Velocity of M1 reached a peak of about 4 with the onset of the 1920s. It fell almost continuously during the Great Depression and World War II to an all-time low of about 2 in 1946. Since then, however, V1 has sky-rocketed. It rose to 2.5 in 1950 and to 3.5 in 1960, passed its previous peak of 4 in 1965, pushed past 5 in the early seventies, touched 6 in the 1980s and then declined somewhat in recent years. Why has the velocity of M1 gone on its own trip, apparently giving monetarism a bad name and making life difficult for the Federal Reserve? If we have a reasonable explanation, we may be able to claim that V1's behavior is predictable, and that's enough for most reasonable people.

The main reason for the post–World War II rise in velocity of M1 lies in the relatively narrow historical definition of M1—demand deposits plus currency—and the increasing attractiveness of other categories of financial assets—bonds as well as stocks, money market mutual funds and money market deposit accounts—as prudent and desirable outlets in which to invest excess cash. These assets are highly liquid, almost as liquid as money, and yet they offer much higher interest rates than demand deposits. Attractive yields on financial assets other than money have led more and more people to wonder why they should ever hold any idle cash aside from what they need for day-to-day transactions purposes. Traditional concepts about how much cash on hand is really necessary for doing business have also come under reexamination. If money for day-to-day transactions purposes can be pared down, then some of it can be lent to earn higher interest. The money then moves to borrowers who can use it for current purchases. As a result, a larger volume of current spending flows from the same stock of money.

Corporate treasurers, in particular, have found that it pays dividends to scrutinize their cash holdings intensively. Could they manage to get along with somewhat less in the till than they had previously thought of as "normal" and invest a portion in high-yielding time deposits at commercial banks or in U.S. Treasury bills? Increasingly the answer has been yes, and imaginative new techniques of cash management have been developed to facilitate the process (as well as some not-so-imaginative old techniques, such as becoming "slow payers" when bills come due).

This trend has not escaped the attention of consumers. They have learned to economize on money by substituting lines of credit at retail stores and financial institutions in place of cash reserves; in addition, the growing use of credit cards has drastically reduced household needs for day-to-day transactions money. What was formerly held in the form of demand deposits or currency, for emergency use or for current payments, now shifts to interest-bearing savings deposits or higher-yielding money market mutual funds and money market deposit accounts.

In summary, there has been a pattern in the movements of M1 velocity since the end of World War II—a persistent long-run rise with minor short-run dips during recessions. Even though we may not be able to pinpoint all the specific determinants, we can still see broad cause-and-effect relationships.

Higher interest rates lead to an increase in velocity by inducing business firms and households to economize on money. They hold less, lend out the excess, and others (the borrowers) can then spend it. Once learned, techniques of cash management are not easily forgotten, so that even in recessions, when interest rates fall, velocity does not drop back very far.

The problem is that for no apparent reason, since the mid-1980s M1 velocity has reversed its post–World War II uptrend. This behavior has been sufficiently puzzling to force the Federal Reserve to abandon setting M1 targets, as we saw in Chapter 22. On the other hand, M2 velocity in Figure 29.1 has been rather stable even in recent years. The problem here is that even small movements in this number can be troublesome for the Fed.

When it comes to practical policy, however, the Federal Reserve may be able to live with such moving targets. By gaining further insight into what makes velocity move, the central bank might be able to establish a range of probabilities as to where velocity is likely to be tomorrow and the day after and to act on that basis. In other words, a morning line on velocity (not unlike the one your local bookie puts out on the races at Hialeah)—provided the odds were unemotionally calculated and continuously reassessed in the light of emerging evidence—might still enable the Federal Reserve to come out a winner.

THE DEMAND FOR MONEY

We have just suggested that the historical movement in the velocity of M1 stems from many factors, including movements in interest rates, technology, and innovations in financial markets. To focus more precisely on the relative importance of each of these requires that we disentangle their separate influences. Only a formal application of statistical techniques to historical data on the money stock, interest rates, income, and other variables will permit us to identify the individual relationships. Indeed, economists have spent considerable effort estimating statistical counterparts to the money demand equations discussed in earlier chapters. And the reasons for the effort are not difficult to understand—after all, the monetarist and Keynesian heritages have a large stake in the outcome of such studies.

Just about every statistical study has shown that both the interest rate and the level of GDP influence money demand. In particular, higher interest rates significantly reduce the demand for cash balances. This result, by itself, contradicts extreme forms of monetarism, which assume zero interest-sensitivity of money demand. On the other hand, none of the empirical investigations has ever isolated the Keynesian liquidity trap. Thus the monetarist outlook gains support as well.

The question of the interest-sensitivity of money demand has historically been an important issue dividing monetarists and Keynesians. But once the extreme positions—zero and infinite interest-elasticity—have been ruled out, the more sophisticated problem focuses on the *stability* of the money demand equation. After all, given the statistical results, the specific numbers are less important than their reliability in forecasting future money demand. As long as the historical estimates are reliable predictors of money demand, then the Federal Reserve can gauge the proper amount of money to add to or subtract from the economy in order to hit a particular target of economic activity. On the other hand, if the particular estimates change a lot, or if the demand for money jumps around for no apparent reason, then changes in the money supply will be useless predictors of economic activity. Monetarists would obviously be unhappy at such results, and so would ecumenical Keynesians, who view both monetary and fiscal policies as potentially important stabilization weapons.

Most of the evidence suggests that the demand for money was quite stable until the mid-1970s; the predictive power of statistical money demand equations was quite good. Then, about the middle of 1974, the estimated demand equations for money went adrift. People were holding smaller money balances than the historical relationships suggested. The 1980s were also not

---

GOING OUT ON A LIMB

Where Is All That Cash Hiding?

In 1960, 20 percent of the U.S. money supply (M1) was in the form of currency (including coins). We had $29 billion of currency in circulation and $112 billion of checking accounts. The population of the United States at the time was 180 million people, so that the $29 billion of coin and bills amounted to an average of $160 for each man, woman, and child in the country.

By contrast, in 1995 about 33 percent of the money supply consisted of currency ($370 billion of currency in circulation and $750 billion of checking accounts). The population of the United States was then 260 million people, so that the $370 billion of coin and bills amounted to a startling average of $1,480 for each man, woman, and child in the country.

Perhaps people are holding so much more cash today because prices are higher now than they were in 1960. In any event, the effect of higher prices should be at least partly offset by the increased use of credit cards, enabling people to hold *less* cash than they used to carry. Also, a lot of U.S. currency is hoarded abroad, as a store of value for residents of inflation-prone countries like Russia and Brazil.

But no doubt much of the reason for the increase in cash is activity in the covert "underground" economy—that part of the economic system that never uses checks as a means of payment. *Cash only, please!* Cash leaves no paper trail. The underground economy includes illegal transactions, such as gambling, prostitution, and drug dealing; home-repair types of activities, such as gardening and carpentry, where payment in cash is requested in order to evade taxes; and even the labor of an untold number of industrious and otherwise honest college students (and maybe some of their professors) who work "off the books" for tax evasion purposes.

No one knows for sure how large the underground economy is, but we calculate that it could be as big as 10 to 15 percent of the officially reported gross domestic product.

helpful. In fact, the problem was just the opposite of the 1970s: too much money rather than too little. This is reflected in the decline in M1 velocity since the mid-1980s in Figure 29.1. The inability to explain movements in M1 demand is one of the reasons the Federal Reserve dropped M1 targeting in its execution of monetary policy.

COMPUTER SIMULATIONS AND TIME LAGS

The empirical evidence just presented on velocity and money demand provides only modest comfort to those promoting the relationship between money and economic activity. Moreover, the simple velocity and money demand approaches, even with carefully calculated probabilities, leave much to be desired as a guideline for Federal Reserve policy-making. In particular, they ignore time lags between changes in monetary policy and the impact on economic activity. They also ignore the more sophisticated statistical methodology that can be used together with modern computer technology to simulate the impact of monetary policy on economic activity via a formal econometric model. Both lags and econometric models add flesh to the skeleton of our theoretical models. First we look at lags, and then we introduce the power of econometric modeling.

By their own admission, Federal Reserve officials are not omniscient. If the economy starts to slip into a recession, it takes time before the experts realize what is happening so they can take steps to correct it. Similarly, if inflation begins to accelerate, it takes a while before the evidence verifies the fact.

Prompt recognition of what the economy is doing is not as easy as it sounds. For one thing, the available data are often inadequate and frequently mixed: New car orders will rise while retail department store sales are falling; farm prices may be dropping while employment in urban areas is rising. Furthermore, the economy rarely proceeds on a perfectly smooth course, either up or down. Every upsweep is interrupted from time to time by erratic dips; every decline into recession is punctuated irregularly by false signs of progress, which then evaporate. Is a change only a brief and temporary interruption of an already existing trend, or is it the start of a new trend in the opposite direction? No one is ever perfectly sure. This problem of getting an accurate "fix" on what is happening in the economy, or what is likely to happen in the near future, is called the **recognition lag** in monetary policy.

As soon as the recognition lag ends, the **impact lag** begins, spanning the time from when the central bank starts using one of its tools, such as open market operations, until an effect is evident on the ultimate objective—aggregate spending in the economy. It may take weeks before interest rates change significantly after a monetary action has begun. Changes in credit availability and money supply also take time. And a further delay is probable before actual spending decisions are affected. Once monetary policy does start to influence spending, however, it will most likely continue to have an impact on GDP for quite a while. All of this was swept under the rug in the theoretical models discussed in earlier chapters. But now it's time to add some flesh to that bare-bones description of the real world.

Regarding the *recognition* lag, rough impressionistic evidence suggests that the Federal Reserve generally starts to tighten only a few months after a business cycle has reached its trough, while its move toward easing after a peak in the cycle is somewhat more delayed. This evidence is less than definitive, and it is likely that under some circumstances the monetary authorities will sense what is going on and take action more promptly than under other circumstances. Nevertheless, the inference that the central bank is typically more concerned with preventing inflation than with avoiding recession probably contains a grain of truth.

The *impact* lag is most conveniently discussed, along with the strength of monetary policy, in terms of the results that formal econometric models of the economy have produced. An econometric model is a mathematical-statistical representation that describes how the economy behaves. Such a model gives empirical content to theoretical propositions about how individuals and business firms, lenders and borrowers, savers and spenders react to economic stimuli. After such relationships are formalized in mathematical expressions, data on past experience in the real world are used to estimate the precise behavioral patterns of each sector. A model, therefore, is based on real-world observations jelled into a formal pattern by the grace of statistical techniques. Thrown into a computer, the model simulates the economy in action and grinds out predictions based on the formal interactions the model embodies.

Our knowledge of how best to construct such a model is far from complete. The same data can produce different results, depending on the theoretical propositions used to construct the model. As one cynic put it, "If one tortures the data long enough, it will confess."

A Keynesian model, for instance, would incorporate behavioral assumptions different from those of a monetarist model and hence grind out a different set of predictions. Monetarist models frequently relate total GDP to money supply directly, on the basis of a predictable velocity assumption. Keynesian models, on the other hand, involve considerable efforts to explain the determinants of consumption spending, investment spending, and liquidity preference. With regard to monetary policy in particular, the Keynesians' model tries to show explicitly the linkages between money supply, interest rates, and real spending decisions. And if something is left out, they have only themselves to blame.

Since both monetarists and Keynesians are presumably interested in the truth, it is reasonable to assume that their models have been specified with that objective in mind. Let's review the evidence to see if some consensus emerges.

THE IMPACT OF MONETARY POLICY ON GDP

The Federal Reserve board, working with economists at several universities, has developed an econometric model of the behavior of economic aggregates in the United States. Many other economists have done similar work at universities and financial institutions. But our discussion will be based primarily on the Federal Reserve model, which was prepared specifically to evaluate the impact of stabilization policies on economic activity.

It is important to emphasize at the outset that these econometric models are evolutionary phenomena, constantly revised and altered to reflect new and different perspectives about economic reality. Moreover, the computer-generated numerical estimates of how the economy responds to a change in monetary policy (and fiscal policy as well) vary with the specific conditions of economic activity. Thus the numbers reported later provide a general flavor of how the models simulate economic and financial responses to policy, but they should be viewed as impressionistic. In fact, we should always stamp our computer output with the technician's favorite warning: GIGO.[2]

The Federal Reserve's model articulates rather carefully the impact of monetary policy on various categories of spending. Indeed, the channels of transmission are clearly set out in mathematical splendor. We will give some of the details later, but at this point it is best to concentrate on an overview of the model's findings for monetary policy.

The latest version of the Fed's model shows that a 1 percent increase in the money supply raises real GDP by about $\frac{1}{2}$ percent after one year. During the next two years, GDP continues to rise until it increases by the same 1 percent as the money supply after a total of three years.

Earlier versions of the Fed model took longer for monetary policy to work its way through the economy. Back then monetarists were unhappy with such results and suspected that the architects of the Federal Reserve's model unwittingly left something out of their complicated system of equations. As a result monetarist economists at the Federal Reserve Bank of St. Louis developed a simple model that related GDP directly to the money supply, without any intervening steps. And after all was said and done, this model also showed that a 1 percent change in money supply increased GDP by about 1 percent after a year.

The surprising outcome is an apparent consensus that monetary policy has a significant impact on economic activity even within a year. The problem is that after this initial period the impact of the monetary expansion probably continues and this can cause difficulties for policymakers, as we saw in our discussion of lags in Chapter 27.

FISCAL POLICY AND CROWDING OUT

The theoretical discussions in earlier chapters indicated a clear distinction between monetarist and Keynesian views on the effectiveness of fiscal policy. Monetarists contend that tax and expenditure policies merely displace private

---

[2] GIGO, of course, means *Garbage In, Garbage Out*. In our terms, if the economic assumptions underlying the model are bad, so are the simulations.

spending, leaving little net impact of fiscal policy on GDP. Keynesians, on the other hand, argue that the "crowding-out" effects of government policies are incomplete, implying that fiscal policy generates much of the traditional multiplier effect on GDP. It should be clear by now that this dispute can be resolved only by resort to empirical evidence.

Experiments with the Federal Reserve model show that, holding the money supply constant, an increase in government spending by 1 percent of GDP increases the level of real GDP by about 1 percent for at least two years. It takes more than three years for crowding out to reduce the impact on real GDP to zero. An alternative experiment shows that if the money supply varies so that the level of interest rates is held constant, then the multiplier effects on GDP are enormous: Even after four years GDP is 4 percent higher than without the expansion in government spending. These results suggest that according to the Federal Reserve's model, fiscal policy has a multiplier of about one without any help from monetary policy, but that an accommodating monetary authority can make fiscal policy even more effective.

The original version of the monetarist model developed at the Federal Reserve Bank of St. Louis was much more pessimistic about fiscal policy: It reported complete crowding out of fiscal effects within the first year after government spending was increased. One of the problems with this revolutionary result was that the St. Louis model was silent on the specific categories of private spending that were crowded out by the government's expenditure. This agnosticism of the St. Louis model made its results highly suspect, according to most Keynesians.

It seems that the empirical evidence on fiscal policy confirms the crowding-out effect, but only if the contractionary effects on private spending are given substantial time to work themselves out. This brings us to the question of the role of interest rates within the framework of our models. First let's look at how changes in money supply influence the level of rates, and then we can turn to the specific categories of spending that are most sensitive to interest rate movements.

THE IMPACT OF MONEY ON INTEREST RATES

According to both monetarists and Keynesians, the initial liquidity impact of an expansionary monetary policy reduces the level of interest rates. Similarly, both monetarists and Keynesians recognize that inflationary expectations generated by excessively expansionary monetary policy will raise interest rates. The key difference of opinion, as we explained back in Chapter 27, focuses on how long it takes for inflationary expectations to counteract the initial liquidity effects.

Figure 29.2 illustrates that the levels of short-term interest rates have been rather closely related to actual movements in the rate of inflation. Thus a

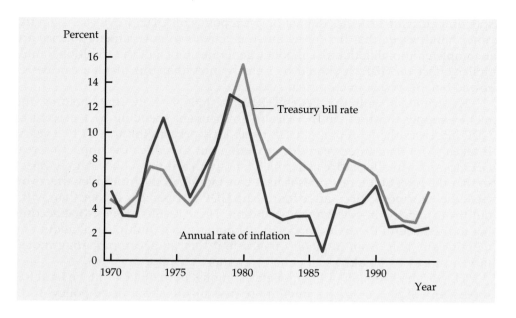

FIGURE 29.2   Interest rates move with the rate of inflation.

broad sweep of the data clearly shows the impact of inflation on the rate of interest. But the chart also shows substantial intervals of independent movements in the level of interest rates. And to identify the separate role of monetary policy in this area, it is once again necessary to consult the statistical evidence.

Most econometric models, including that of the Fed, report that interest rates decline and remain below their original levels for six months to a year after an expansionary monetary policy and that they are above their original levels for a similar period after a contractionary monetary policy. After a year, however, the initial liquidity effect is reversed, and interest rates move in the opposite direction. In contrast, there are some monetarist models that show the Treasury bill rate snapping back to its original level and going above it within three months after an expansionary monetary policy.

It should be emphasized that the response of inflationary expectations depends crucially on the initial state of the economy. At levels of economic activity that are very close to full employment, or when saver and investor concerns about inflation are especially strong, an upward jump in inflationary expectations due to expansionary monetary policy can be even quicker than we just indicated. Thus while the formal models show a relatively slow adjustment, their predictions are based on the average historical experience. Any particular historical event can show more sensitivity than the average if the specific conditions are ripe.

At this point it seems useful to go one step further in examining the behavior of interest rates. Rising rates should cut off some spending and falling rates should be stimulative. Let us see which categories of spending are most sensitive to movements in interest rates. In this way we can isolate the channels through which monetary policy operates, as well as identify the categories of private spending that are likely to be crowded out by fiscal actions.

BUSINESS INVESTMENT

One would expect interest rates and all types of investment spending to move in opposite directions: An increase in interest rates, for example, should lower business spending on plant and equipment. If the cost of borrowing rises, so our theory said, business firms should presumably be less willing to incur new debt to build new factories or buy new machines. The simple historical record shows, however, that interest rates and business investment almost always move in the *same* direction. As in most cases where fact contradicts economic theory, one of them must give ground—and it is usually fact.

In the historical record, many things are happening simultaneously, so separate strands of cause and effect are not sorted out. Investment spending on plant and equipment is influenced by a number of factors besides interest rates—sales expectations, changes in anticipated profitability, pressures from competitors, the degree of capacity currently being utilized, and expectations regarding inflation, to name only some. An increase in interest rates may inhibit investment, and yet investment may, in fact, rise if a number of these other elements shift sufficiently to offset its effect.

Econometric methods, such as those used in constructing the Federal Reserve model, permit us to sort out the effects of individual variables. For our particular concern, we can examine the impact of interest rates on investment, holding all other influences constant. The Fed model shows, for example, that an increase of 1 percentage point (say from 8 to 9 percent) in the corporate bond rate lowers business spending on new plant and equipment by nearly 5 percent after three years, but almost all of that effect occurs in the last year.

In this instance, the time delay of interest rate effects is clearly quite substantial. Most investment decisions are not made today and executed tomorrow. Decisions regarding installation of new machinery and construction of new plants are usually made far in advance. Thus an increase in interest rates does not promptly affect investment in plant and equipment. What it does affect is current decisions that will be implemented months or years in the future.

RESIDENTIAL CONSTRUCTION

The impact of monetary policy is felt more promptly and more powerfully on residential construction expenditures. In particular, an increase of 1 percentage point in the interest rate lowers spending on housing by approximately 9 percent within a year. Part of this effect on residential construction occurs through **credit rationing** activities by financial institutions engaged in mortgage lending. In fact, credit availability is often emphasized by modern Keynesians as a significant channel through which monetary policy influences spending. But this specific case of mortgage credit rationing is less important now that financial institutions are less specialized.

Construction expenditures by state and local governments also appear sensitive to the actions of the monetary authorities. Municipal bond flotations are often reduced, postponed, or canceled during periods of high and rising interest rates. Many municipal governments have self-imposed interest rate ceilings that eliminate them from the market when rates go up. In other instances, when interest costs become too large, local voters are reluctant to approve bond issues for school construction and other projects, since the higher interest burden implies the immediate or eventual imposition of higher property or sales taxes.

CONSUMER SPENDING

The last major item on the monetary policy hit list is consumer spending. In this case the Federal Reserve model includes the wealth effect of modern Keynesians to channel the impact of interest rates to spending. In particular, a lower interest rate raises the value of stocks and bonds, according to the model, and this increases the level of consumer spending.

The importance of the wealth effect in the overall impact of monetary policy is quite substantial, according to the Federal Reserve's formulation. About one-quarter of the impact of monetary policy on GDP after one year stems from the effects of changes in wealth on consumer spending. This is more than four times the response in plant and equipment expenditure and just about equal to the powerful effect of monetary policy on residential construction.

Perhaps the most important message of the entire set of empirical results is that there are significant impacts of monetary policy on spending. While at first glance this seems to bolster the role of the Federal Reserve in the countercyclical efforts of the government, the potentially destabilizing impacts discussed in Chapter 27 become even more threatening. The Federal Reserve model suggests that monetary policy is a force to be reckoned with but might be too powerful to harness for delicate fine-tuning of economic activity.

SUMMARY

1. The historical behavior of GDP relative to M1 rules out the simple notion that velocity is fixed and unchanging. Although M2 velocity is somewhat more stable historically, it is more important to concentrate on the predictability of velocity, rather than its stability.

2. Statistical investigations of money demand suggest that the demand for money is less stable than was once thought, although M2 has fewer problems than M1.

3. The impact of monetary policy on economic activity, as well as the associated time delays, is best illustrated by the results of econometric models. The main implication of the Federal Reserve's model is a rather substantial impact of money on GDP.

4. Fiscal policy has an impact on GDP, according to the models, but there is also evidence of significant crowding out. In particular, if government spending increases when the money supply is held constant, the rising rates of interest will cut off substantial amounts of private spending.

5. Interest rates increase and decrease with the rate of inflation. The relationship is not close enough, however, to negate the fact that increased money supply growth will lower short-term interest rates for a while (perhaps six months) before inflationary expectations take over.

6. Tight monetary policy and rising rates of interest have significant contractionary effects on residential construction. Consumer spending is also discouraged through a wealth effect of higher interest rates on stock and bond values. Business plant and equipment spending responds to higher interest rates with a significant delay.

QUESTIONS

29.1 Why has the velocity associated with M1 increased from about 2 immediately after World War II to about 6 during the 1980s?

29.2 What is the evidence from computer simulations of econometric models regarding the time lags between a change in money supply and a response in GDP?

29.3 Do historical movements in the Treasury bill rate seem to reflect changes in the rate of inflation?

29.4 Which is more responsive to tight money, residential construction or business investment? Why do you think this is so?

29.5 Is the demand for money stable and predictable?

29.6 *Discussion question:* Now that you've seen the numbers from formal econometric models, do you really believe that they tell the truth?

PART VII

Grand Finale

CHAPTER 30

Tying It All Together

The alarm rings and your eyelids open slowly. Last night is a vague memory. You stumble into the kitchen to get that all-important cup of coffee. Just a few peaceful moments alone with the morning paper—that's all you ask. But there it is—front page—staring you right in the face. Another **economic indicator!** This time it's the "**purchasing managers index.**" Bad news, too. The index fell from 46.8 percent to 44.2 percent. So how did the market react? Bonds up! Doesn't seem to make sense. You read on and find that money managers feel that if the employment numbers scheduled for release on Friday are *worse* than expected, the bond market is going *up even more.* Is the world upside down? Bad news is good news? It's too early for this!

Early or not, this is the stuff of the morning's business news. Nearly every day the front page of the *Wall Street Journal* shows an economic indicator, perhaps one of those in Figure 30.1, that was released the previous business day. Often the headlines relate that indicator to movements in the stock and bond markets. But what are the linkages?

We have waited until now to address this question because all bases had to be covered: markets and instruments, banks, central banking, and, of course, monetary theory. Now we can tie it all together. We begin by discussing some of the key economic indicators and then turn to explaining how these indicators influence securities prices.

THE ECONOMIC INDICATORS

An economic indicator measures economic performance. Some indicators are obviously important, such as GDP growth, unemployment, and inflation. In fact, as you may recall from Chapter 22, these economic aggregates embody the ultimate objectives or goals set by the Federal Reserve when it establishes

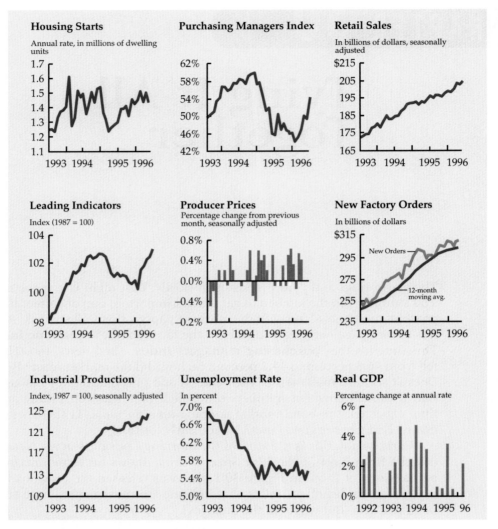

a game plan for monetary policy. Other economic indicators are more focused but still measure how well the economy and its components are doing. Some of these indicators you may have heard of, such as **new car sales** and **new home sales.** Others you may not have heard of before, such as the **purchasing managers index, housing starts/building permits,** and the **index of leading economic indicators.**

Table 30.1 lists the most important economic indicators, with the source of the data shown in column 2 and the frequency of the release dates in column 3. Column 4 records our "expected" response for the stock and bond markets, which we will come back to shortly.

TABLE 30.1   Key Economic Indicators

Name	Source	Availability/ release date	Predicted market response to "good" news*
GDP/GNP	Dept. of Commerce -BEA**	Monthly 21st–30th	Bonds–dn Stocks–up
Employment	Dept. of Labor -BLS	Monthly 1st–7th	Bonds–dn Stocks–up
Personal inc. & consumption	Dept. of Commerce -BEA	Monthly 22nd–31st	Bonds–dn Stocks–up
Car sales	Auto Makers	Every 10 days	Bonds–dn Stocks–up
Purchasing managers index	NAPM	Monthly 1st bus. day	Bonds–dn Stocks–up
Retail sales	Dept. of Commerce -BOC	Monthly 11th–14th	Bonds–dn Stocks–up
Industrial production	Federal Reserve	Monthly 14th–17th	Bonds–dn Stocks–up
Capacity utilization	Federal Reserve	Monthly 14th–17th	Bonds–dn Stocks–up
Durable goods orders	Dept. of Commerce -BOC	Monthly 22nd–28th	Bonds–dn Stocks–up
New home sales	Dept. of Commerce -BOC	Monthly 28th–4th	Bonds–dn Stocks–up
Housg strts/ bldg permits	Dept. of Commerce -BOC	Monthly 16th–20th	Bonds–dn Stocks–up
Construction spending	Dept. of Commerce -BOC	Monthly 1st bus. day (2 mo. lag)	Bonds–none Stocks–none
Business inventories & sales	Dept. of Commerce -BOC	Monthly 13th–17th (2 mo. lag)	Bonds–uncertain Stocks–none
Factory orders & mfg inventories	Dept. of Commerce -BOC	Monthly 30th–6th (2 mo. lag)	Bonds–dn Stocks–up
Index of leading econ. indicators	Dept. of Commerce -BEA	Monthly last bus. day	Bonds–dn Stocks–up
Consumer price index	Dept. of Labor -BLS	Monthly 15th–21st	Bonds–up Stocks–up
Producer price index	Dept. of Labor -BLS	Monthly 9th–16th	Bonds–up Stocks–up

*Market response is in terms of probable securities' price reaction to good news about the indicator. Good news means news that is better than expected. Bond yield reaction is the opposite of bond price reaction. Bond price reaction is shown here. "dn" equals down.

**BEA: Bureau of Economic Analysis of the U.S. Department of Commerce; BLS: Bureau of Labor Statistics of the U.S. Department of Labor; NAPM: National Association of Purchasing Management; BOC: Bureau of the Census of the U.S. Department of Commerce.

Every stock and bond trader knows exactly (to the minute in most cases) when these indicators will be released. They sit behind their computers with bated breath and the instant the data hit the screens they buy or sell, depending on the news. Thus it is not surprising that news gets impounded in stock and bond prices nearly instantaneously.

To understand how the markets react to a particular indicator requires a two-step procedure. First we have to understand what the indicator is and then determine its connection to securities prices. We start with the details of a particular indicator—more specifically, who produces it, how accurate it is, and how often it is revised. And then, of course, we determine how the indicator behaves relative to changes in the economy. A detailed description of each of the indicators listed in Table 30.1 is beyond our scope, so we'll focus on some of the most important of them.[1]

The Employment Report

The monthly employment report is compiled by the Bureau of Labor Statistics (BLS) of the U.S. Department of Labor. It is usually released on the Friday of the first week of the month (showing data for the previous month). The report contains information on employment and average workweek and hourly earnings, with the **unemployment rate** and the level of **payroll employment** getting the most press coverage. In many ways the employment report can be viewed as the most important economic indicator of all.

Unlike the GDP numbers, which are released quarterly, the employment statistics are released every month, so they offer a frequent update on the pulse of economic activity. Because the employment numbers indicate how many people are looking for jobs, they are the most politically sensitive of all the indicators. Washington pays attention when the employment data are released because the whole nation pays attention!

The employment numbers show why it's important to know the details behind each economic indicator before placing your bets on the market. The two key bits of information, the unemployment rate and the level of payroll employment, are actually based on two surveys: a household survey and an establishment survey (both conducted by the BLS).

The household survey is based on a monthly sample of 59,500 households. The BLS uses this survey to estimate the unemployment rate based on the answers to two questions: Are you employed? And, if you are not, are you looking for work? The unemployment rate is then calculated as the ratio of the number of people unemployed to the number of people in the labor force. To be counted in the labor force you must either have a job or be looking for one.

The number reported for payroll employment, however, is not calculated from the household survey but from the establishment survey, which can-

---

[1] For further details, see W. Stansbury Carnes and Stephen D. Slifer, *The Atlas of Economic Indicators* (New York: HarperBusiness, 1991).

vasses business establishments rather than households. One might expect both surveys to produce the same results, and often they do; but just as often, they do not. Some of the difference may be due to statistical "noise." But there are other reasons as well. Self-employed and domestic workers are included in the household survey but not in the payroll survey. Also, if a person has more than one job, she will be counted only once in the household survey but may be counted several times in the establishment survey. There may also be bias in the household survey that is avoided in the establishment survey. For example, individuals responding to the household survey may be reluctant to admit that they are no longer looking for a job—possibly out of fear that they might lose their unemployment benefits or endanger their immigration status. Working in the other direction, some respondents to the household survey may have stopped looking for jobs because they view the effort as fruitless.

The net effect of these relative strengths and weaknesses is that while both surveys are considered important, market participants place a little more weight on the payroll numbers compared with the unemployment rate because the measurement problems are probably less severe. Note also that because these data are released before most of the other key indicators, they tend to set the stage for rest of the month. Of course, when interpreting economic developments it is important to remember that the employment numbers tend to be **lagging indicators.** That is, they follow behind changes in overall economic activity. Employment turns up *after* the economy turns up, and employment turns down *after* the economy has peaked.

Housing Starts and Building Permits

The report on housing starts and building permits is important in part because it reflects activity in a very important sector of the economy. In particular, housing accounts for more than 25 percent of the investment component of GDP and more than 40 percent of household budget expenses. Housing is also important because expansion in housing construction *leads* economic upturns, making housing starts and building permits a **leading indicator.** When investment in housing increases, it has a ripple effect throughout the economy via the multiplier discussed in Chapter 24. So when analysts and forecasters see housing activity turn up—typically prompted by low interest rates that are associated with the trough of a recession—they are likely to predict good times ahead.

As you may have guessed, the housing report has two components, *housing starts* and *building permits.* Data on housing starts are collected by the Bureau of the Census, a division of the Department of Commerce, and are released about mid-month. Housing starts are divided into two categories, single-family and multifamily. A 200-unit apartment building, for example, would be categorized as 200 multifamily "starts." A housing start is recorded when excavation begins for a new house or apartment building. Most localities require building permits before excavation so that building permits precede housing starts (usually by about one month). Housing starts are about 10 percent greater than building permits because some localities do not require permits.

Purchasing Manager's Index

The purchasing manager's index is based on a survey conducted by the National Association of Purchasing Management (NAPM). Purchasing executives from more than 250 industrial companies in 21 different industries are surveyed once a month. The survey consists of six questions about production, orders, prices, inventories, vendor performance, and employment. Respondents are asked to characterize each activity as either *up, down,* or *unchanged.* A composite index is formed from the responses to each question so that an index above 50 represents an expanding manufacturing sector and below 50 implies contraction. The NAPM index is viewed by analysts and investors as useful in tracking the overall economy even though it focuses only on manufacturing. It is a **coincident indicator,** which means that its movements occur simultaneously with economic activity.

Index of Leading Economic Indicators

As we noted above, some economic indicators are called leading indicators because they precede changes in economic activity. Wouldn't it be nice, then, if somebody compiled an index of the best leading indicators to predict recessions and economic upturns? Well somebody did, and it's called, not surprisingly, the *index of leading economic indicators* (LEI), released each month by the Bureau of Economic Analysis (BEA) of the Department of Commerce.

Here are some details. The LEI has 11 components:

1. Average workweek—manufacturing
2. Initial unemployment claims
3. New orders for consumer goods
4. Vendor performance
5. Plant and equipment orders
6. Building permits
7. Change in unfilled orders
8. Sensitive material prices
9. Stock prices—S&P 500
10. Real M2
11. Index of consumer expectations

As a general rule of thumb, the LEI turns down before a decline in GDP and turns up before GDP resumes its uptrend. Market participants view three consecutive monthly changes in one direction (for example, −0.4 percent, −1.0 percent, and −0.9 percent) as anticipating a change in economic activity, in this case, predicting a downturn. On average, the LEI seems better in terms of accuracy and lead time in predicting downturns compared with upturns, although neither set of forecasts are all that good.

VALUATION, THE FED, AND MARKET REACTION

How do the stock and bond markets react to improvements in each of these economic indicators? The final column in Table 30.1 shows the "conventional wisdom" about how prices react to good news about an indicator. For example, a higher reading on the purchasing managers index probably triggers a decline in bond prices,[2] while driving up the stock market. Similarly, good news about GDP growth, employment, housing starts and building permits, and the index of leading indicators will all make the bond market go *down* and the stock market go *up*. In general, as we will see shortly, good news about any of the indicators related to expenditure drives up stock prices and drives down bond prices. But that doesn't necessarily mean that an announcement that GDP increased by 2 percent or that employment rose by 50,000 workers will necessarily be followed by a jump in the stock market and a decline in bond prices. To see why this is so, we must dig a little deeper into market psychology.

Good News Versus Bad News: The Role of Expectations

If good news about GDP growth is good news for the stock market, then at first blush we should expect the stock market to go up if GDP goes up. But, as we've stressed in earlier discussions, investor expectations drive decision making so that what really matters is how the numbers that are released compare with what was expected. For example, a company that announces an increase in earnings per share from $5.00 to $8.00 might easily suffer a decline in its stock price if everyone had expected an increase in earnings to $12.00 per share. Similarly, 2 percent growth in GDP could be *bad* news if investors had expected 2½ percent growth. On the other hand, if they had expected 2 percent growth, then there would be little reaction because 2 percent growth had been anticipated—in the language of Wall Street, it would have been *fully discounted* by the market. Fully discounted simply means fully anticipated and therefore embedded in prices because investors have already bought or sold based on their expectations.

Thus markets react only to unanticipated news, or somewhat redundantly, only to *new* news. The LEI, for example, is mostly *old* news because most of the component indicators that make up the LEI have been released earlier. Thus forecasters and investors have reasonably good estimates of

---

[2] Bond traders think in terms of prices instead of interest rates, even though we know from Chapter 4 that one is just the mirror image of the other. So when reading in the business section of our favorite newspaper that bond markets have "fallen," it probably means that *prices* have fallen and *interest rates* have risen.

what the LEI will show ahead of time, so there is less reaction on the day the LEI is released than seems justified for a leading index. By the same logic, housing starts have less of an impact on the market than building permits because this month's housing starts can be partially predicted by last month's building permits.

One last tidbit. Some indicators are less reliable than others because they are subject to substantial future revision. "All other things being equal" (a phrase used by economists who don't want to wager anything on their forecasts), an indicator that is less vulnerable to revision will be more powerful in moving the market. As it turns out, however, in many cases all other things are not equal. For example, the GDP and payroll employment numbers are powerful *despite* their vulnerability to large revisions.

Stock and Bond Valuation—A Refresher

Now let's turn to the heart of the issue—column 4 in Table 30.1, "Predicted Market Response to 'Good' News." We've already explained that "good" news

In The News

Interest Rates Call the Shots for Stocks

Stocks Rally on Expectations of Interest Rate Cut by the Fed

A crop of conflicting economic data hit the financial markets yesterday, but stocks and especially bonds rallied, as traders interpreted the reports to mean the Federal Reserve would cut interest rates, perhaps as early as next month.

The stock market has now recovered nearly all of last week's losses. The Dow Jones industrial average rose 38.05 points yesterday, to 4,484.51, not far from the 4,485.20 record set on June 6. The broader Standard & Poor's 500-stock index gained 5.17 points, to a record 536.05, and the Nasdaq composite index advanced 6.25 points to 894.23, also a record.

The bond market rallied even more than stocks yesterday, helping to fuel the stock rally as corporate borrowing costs fell lower. Bond prices rose sharply and the yield on the benchmark 30-year Treasury bond tumbled to 6.54 percent from 6.70 percent.

But the reports that prompted the stock and bond rallies were far from unambiguous. As many Wall Street economists expected, the Consumer Price Index rose three-tenths of 1 percent in May, indicating that inflation was tame. Moreover, retail sales increased just two-tenths of 1 percent in May, even weaker than expected. Both reports supported the argument that the Fed may cut interest rates later this year to spur a flagging economy.

The Federal Reserve Bank of Atlanta, though, said its May national production index, a measure of manufacturing activity, rose for the first time since January. By signaling growth, this undermined the argument for an imminent rate cut by the Fed.

Whatever the case, some analysts said that bond traders appeared to be betting on too large a Fed cut.

Source: Adapted from Anthony Ramirez, *New York Times,* June 14, 1995. Copyright © 1995 by The New York Times Co. Reprinted by permission.

means *unanticipated* increases in an indicator of economic activity. We've also noted that "good" news drives up stock prices and drives down bond prices. To see how this works, we need to recall our earlier discussions about bond pricing (Chapter 4) and stock valuation (Chapter 8).

The entire process can be illustrated with some simple examples. To represent bonds we take a ten-year zero-coupon government bond, and to represent stocks we assume a company pays out all of its earnings in dividends and that these cash distributions will be the same forever. Chapter 4 shows that the price of the ten-year zero-coupon bond is given by the following formula, where F is the face value paid at maturity and r is the ten-year interest rate:

$$Bond\ Price = F/(1 + r)^{10}$$

Chapter 8 shows that price of a stock comes from a slightly different formula, where D represents the future stream of dividend payments (they are all the same) and k is a discount factor consisting of the risk-free rate (such as on Treasury bills) plus an adjustment for the riskiness of the stock:

$$Stock\ Price = D/k$$

There are, of course, more complicated examples for each type of security but none of these would alter our general conclusions.

Let's take the bond first. The numerator in the formula, the face value of the bond, is a fixed obligation. Whether the economy is heating up, or whether it is slowing down, the U.S. Treasury still has to pay the same amount at the end. So bond prices will change only if the denominator, the ten-year interest rate, is affected by unanticipated readings on an economic indicator. Well, what affects this rate? In great part, you may recall from Chapter 4, it is expectations about the future rate of inflation. Thus good news about the economy drives down bond prices primarily because as the economy heats up expectations are generated of more future inflation (see Chapter 27 to refresh your memory). In addition, good news about the economy also suggests that the Federal Reserve's open market committee (FOMC) may tighten monetary policy to restrain inflationary pressures, as we saw in Chapter 22. This means that the Fed may very well drive up the federal funds rate which, via the term structure of interest rates discussed in Chapter 5, pushes up the ten-year interest rate. Thus fears of emerging inflationary pressure plus concern that the Fed will respond by driving up the federal funds rate will decrease the value of our ten-year zero-coupon bond because the fixed future cash flow (F) will be discounted at a higher rate.

What about stocks? Stocks are a more complicated matter because good news will likely affect both the numerator and the denominator of our formula. Good news about the economy means that companies will earn more, implying that they will pay higher dividends in the future. This will increase stock values because dividends are in the numerator in our stock valuation formula. However, the interest rate is also in the stock valuation formula. In fact, it is in the denominator as part of the discount factor applied to expected future dividends. Thus the denominator of the stock formula behaves just as it does in the bond formula; that is, unanticipated good news drives up the discount factor because of expectations of inflation and anticipated tightening by the Federal Reserve.

Thus in the stock valuation formula there are two effects which work in opposite directions. Unanticipated good news increases the numerator (through dividends) and good news increases the denominator (through interest rates). Which effect dominates? Theoretically, it could be either depending on circumstances. In practice, conventional wisdom on Wall Street is that the effect on the numerator is usually stronger than the denominator, so that stock prices rise on good news.

The effect of good news on stocks and bonds and the linkages just discussed are summarized in Figure 30.2. One notable departure from the pattern that stock and bond prices move in opposite directions when unanticipated news is released is the reaction to inflation. Unanticipated good news about inflation (that is, news that inflation is lower) has a positive effect on both the stock and bond markets. The reason is that favorable news about inflation drives down the level of interest rates and, as we've just seen, the interest rate is in the denominator of both the stock and bond formulas. Thus lower inflation drives up both stock prices and bond prices.

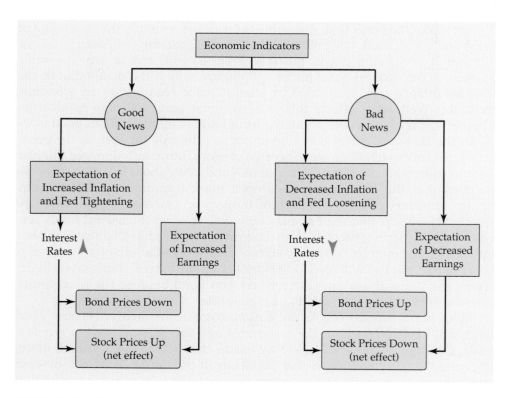

FIGURE 30.2   Economic indicators and market behavior.

PUTTING IT ALL TOGETHER

Economic indicators are at the center of a feedback mechanism operating through economic activity, economic policy, and investor behavior. The indicators measure how the economy is currently performing and suggest how the economy will perform in the future. Investors, forecasters, and analysts all observe these indicators and make assessments about the future—more precisely about future dividends and interest rates. Because the Federal Reserve also monitors the economy through these economic indicators, favorable or unfavorable news triggers new monetary policy settings. Exactly how things work out is the result of a complicated set of interactions.

Here is an example. Consider the case where unanticipated good news about economic activity is released today. This suggests that future inflation will rise, leading to higher interest rates, and also suggests that dividends will increase with faster economic activity. Moreover, investors now expect tighter monetary policy as the Fed moves to offset increased inflationary pressure. Investors and traders, however, are not going to wait until next year's inflation numbers are out, nor even until the next FOMC meeting, to make their investment decisions. They will trade *today* based on updated estimates of Fed monetary policy, dividends, and inflation, including an estimate of how successful the Fed will be in countering emerging inflationary pressures. The net outcome of investor and trader assessments will be recorded in stock and bond markets much like voters casting their ballots in a referendum.

Can we make money based on newly released economic indicators, that is, can we make a killing in the market by buying stocks and selling bonds on good news and vice versa on bad news? Unfortunately, it's not so easy. Remember our discussion of the "newness" of news. By the time we read about an economic indicator in the paper (or hear about it on television), it is now *old* news. The people who are paid to manage the hundreds of millions of dollars of investment funds, such as the pension fund managers, mutual fund managers, insurance company investment managers, and activist Wall Street professional traders, get there first—probably seconds after they saw the news on their computer screens.

Will we always see the stock and bond markets reacting according to Table 30.1 when reading the morning newspaper? Sometimes, but not always. Rarely is a single economic indicator the only event of the day. In our global marketplace, elections in Japan, labor strikes in France, and monetary policy in Germany can all affect the U.S. securities markets—not to mention the budget debates in Washington D.C. The conventional wisdom reflected in Table 30.1, however, rests on the linkages between the institutions and markets that we've discussed in the previous 29 chapters. While you may not be able to outwit the stock and the bond markets, you now have a good sense of the forces at work that influence financial decision making. Our advice is to sit back, relax, and enjoy the next performance. Hopefully, you will now understand what is going on.

SUMMARY

1. Economic indicators are measures of how well the economy, or specific segments of the economy, are doing. There are leading, lagging, and coincident economic indicators. Leading economic indicators precede changes in overall economic activity, while lagging economic indicators follow changes in overall economic activity, and coincident economic indicators move with overall economic activity.

2. The index of leading economic indicators is comprised of 11 separate leading indicators. It performs better as a predictor of economic turning points than any of its component parts.

3. The stock and bond markets react to economic indicators in different ways. Bond market prices fall on good news about the economy because of inflationary expectations and anticipated Federal Reserve tightening while the stock market rises because expected increases in future dividends dominate.

4. The stock and bond markets will react only to unanticipated news. A fully anticipated economic release will not have any effect on the market because the news was already reflected in prices. The news must be "new."

5. It is unlikely that individual investors can profit by trading on newly released economic indicators. Institutional investors respond instantaneously to news releases so that stock and bond prices are driven up or down within minutes of an announcement. By the time you read it in the newspaper it is too late.

QUESTIONS

30.1 Why do markets react to some economic indicators more than others?

30.2 Why do investors care so much about what the Federal Reserve is likely to do in the future?

30.3 Why is "goods news" bad news for bond prices?

30.4 Why isn't "good news" bad news for stock prices?

30.5 *Discussion question:* Many of the economic indicators are produced by government agencies. Should we invest more money in these agencies in order to get more precise estimates, or should we move in the opposite direction and rely more on the private sector for generating measures of economic performance?

Careers in Banking and Financial Markets

There are lots of jobs at banks having nothing at all to do with banking—like repairing computer terminals and running the executive dining room. Although these are important activities, they are not what we usually think of when banking is mentioned as a career. Our most visible contacts with banks—the teller who takes our money and the branch officer in charge of student loans—are somewhat closer to what banking is all about, but these are only two of the many specialized tasks that fall within a banker's purview.

In the few pages that we have left, we cannot offer a comprehensive review of all career opportunities in banking and financial markets. And even if we could, it would turn out to be more tedious than the discussion of the bank reserve equation in Chapter 21 (if that's possible). Instead we will provide a brief overview of the terrain and then offer some details on specific interesting opportunities. In particular, we will *not* describe what lawyers and accountants who work for banks or other financial institutions actually do; rather we'll focus on the derring-do of bond traders and Fed watchers—after all, that's where the money is (or was).

AN OVERVIEW

The first thing to consider with a career in banking and financial markets is whose side you want to be on. Jobs in the private sector with a bank, mutual fund, or insurance company focus on profits; jobs in the public sector with the Federal Reserve system, FDIC, or state insurance departments focus on safety. Although both public and private sector jobs deal with financial institutions and markets, with people on both sides of the fence often looking at similar things, their perspectives are quite different. A bank examiner with the FDIC or Federal Reserve will review a commercial bank's books to determine whether loans with delinquent payments impair the bank's capital; a commercial loan officer at a bank will examine a prospective borrower's books to determine whether timely repayments of interest and principal will add to the bank's profits. Although both the bank examiner and the loan officer use corporate finance and accounting skills, their objectives and motivations are not the same.

Suppose the profit motive is your favorite pastime. You would then have an array of subindustries within financial markets to consider, including commercial banking, investment banking, insurance, and pension funds (see Chapters 11, 12, and 13 for a description of these institutions). Although each of these financial institutions has a different overall objective, there are particular skills that are easily transferable among them. For example, both a bank economist and an insurance company economist would forecast interest rates, talk with the institution's corporate customers about their particular industry's outlook, and evaluate the costs and benefits of some internal investment project. Economic and statistical analyses come into play in each and every case. Similarly, an investment officer or portfolio manager for an insurance company, bank, or pension fund will evaluate the merits of putting money into stocks or fixed income securities and, if the latter, whether the investments should be long term or short term.

Once you focus attention on a particular industry, an equally important decision centers on whether to concentrate on the retail or wholesale end of the business. Most financial institutions operate on both levels. A commercial bank has people dedicated to explaining the advantages of different types of certificates of deposit to depositors with as little as $1,000 to invest. Banks also have CD traders and salespeople who specialize in placing large certificates of deposit ($100,000 and up) with institutional investors, such as money market mutual funds and large corporations. Both activities raise funds for the banks, but they require very different skills. Retail CDs are marketed by people with strong interpersonal skills, while wholesale CDs are sold by people who are equally comfortable with interest rate calculations (see Chapter 4), movements in the term structure of interest rates (see Chapter 5), and whether the Federal Open Market Committee is likely to vote yes or no to a tighter or easier monetary policy (for this you must remember all of Part V). The CD salespeople for commercial banks must be capable of discussing these factors in order to tailor the CDs to the needs of sophisticated corporate treasurers.

A final distinguishing characteristic among institutions, as well as jobs within a particular firm, centers on domestic versus international business. Despite the growing interrelationship between foreign and domestic activities, there are different regulations that apply in each area, as well as foreign exchange rate movements that must be considered when you are dealing with foreign institutions. If you work for an international bank or if you are a foreign exchange trader, you must feel comfortable with the Japanese yen, German mark, Swiss franc, and whatever else comes along (see Chapter 10 for some help).

There are, no doubt, many other ways to categorize the opportunities available within banking and financial markets. But once you've decided upon public versus private, banking versus insurance, wholesale versus retail, and domestic versus international, you've come far enough along to focus on exactly what you might want to do. In the next section we outline one or two glamorous opportunities (at least as far as financial markets are concerned).

SPECIFIC OPPORTUNITIES

As financial markets have moved toward deregulation, business has become more transactions-oriented. The increased emphasis on transactions has generated a bonanza for people with skills in sales and trading, as well as for those with the analytical techniques to support these activities. Sales and trading jobs at the major investment banks and large commercial banks are exciting, well-paid opportunities; so are the jobs as financial economists, statisticians, and mathematicians that form the underlying brain trust. Let's take a somewhat closer look at what these people do and what it takes to get on the road to financial market stardom.

Trading

We've already encountered the role of a trader in Chapter 6, when we described how a dealer makes a market by quoting a bid and offer for a particular security. Many of the large financial institutions are market makers in a wide variety of instruments. For example, commercial banks might be market makers in Treasury securities, mortgage-related instruments, and municipal bonds. Investment banks add corporate bonds to the list, while the major thrift institutions usually restrict their attention to mortgage-backed securities. In addition to buying and selling these investment-type instruments, large banks also make markets in CDs and other short-term money market instruments.

The trader's job at these institutions is to quote bids and offers for securities on a continuous basis and to accommodate incoming purchase and sale orders from other banks, thrifts, pension funds, and insurance companies. Recall from Chapter 6 that the dealer earns a profit by buying securities at the bid price ($97) and turning around and selling at the offer price ($99) before the equilibrium price ($98) has changed. A trader has to be extremely sensitive to shifting market conditions; otherwise a profit can quickly turn into a loss. For example, if a trader for the First National Profit Bank buys some government bonds at a price of $97 from an insurance company, and before the trader has a chance to sell the bonds to an incoming purchase order from a pension fund the government announces a rise in the consumer price index, the equilibrium price of the bonds may drop to $95. With a bid and offer now at $94 and $96, respectively, the dealer winds up selling the securities that were bought at $97 for $96: a one dollar loss instead of a two dollar profit. Although Chapter 30 helps you understand what happened, that doesn't make the loss any easier to accept.

Traders must continuously monitor market conditions and alter their quotes so that they don't get stuck with unwanted inventory. In addition to concentrating on the market, traders must have the discipline to take profits when they are there and cut losses before they turn into disasters. It is sometimes said that the three most important characteristics of a successful trader are discipline, discipline, and discipline.

Traders are frequently viewed as interchangeable parts. A person with discipline, concentration, and sensitivity who can trade government bonds successfully can switch to trading municipals, corporates, or CDs. The details of each instrument can be quickly absorbed (see Chapter 8 first) as long as the trader's intuition is finely tuned.

Traders start their day early—7:30 A.M. on the East Coast, 4:30 A.M. on the West Coast. Much of their time is spent under intense pressure, trying to extract information about likely price movements of the securities they are responsible for from the price movements of related instruments. In trying to gauge market sentiment they work closely with salespeople who deal with their institution's customers. Let's take a closer look at what bond salespeople actually do.

Sales

On the retail level, securities are sold to individuals by people whom we call stockbrokers. They are more formally called account executives by the securities firms that they work for. These investment banks also employ account executives to sell stocks and bonds to institutional investors such as pension funds and insurance companies. Commercial banks and large thrifts similarly employ salespeople to sell government bonds, municipals, and mortgages to institutional investors.

The salesperson's job is twofold: On the one hand, he or she tries to uncover information about the types of securities that institutional investors are most interested in buying and selling; and on the other hand, she or he tries to convince the bank's customers to buy the securities that the bank has already acquired through the activities of its traders. Thus salespeople provide information to traders about the sentiment within the investment community as well as creating an outlet for the securities that traders have acquired. Obviously these two activities go together. If salespeople report little investor interest in long-term government bonds, the commercial bank's traders will be less aggressive buyers of such securities.

People employed in sales have to be gregarious and people-oriented. They spend considerable time talking on the phone to customers throughout the country and must feel comfortable with simple chitchat. In addition, however, salespeople must bring investment ideas to the party. In order to make a sale, the salesperson must convince the insurance company's portfolio manager, for example, that shifting out of a long-term government bond into a GNMA pass-through security will increase yields without unduly increasing risk exposure. To be effective, therefore, salespeople must have some perspective on the likely movements in interest rates over various investment horizons as well as a working knowledge of how specific bond characteristics, such as particular coupons, call provisions, and tax treatment will influence an investment's performance.

Salespeople obviously benefit considerably, therefore, from a solid course in money, banking, and financial markets. In addition, however, they pay close attention to what the bank's brain trust of professional economists, statisticians, and other fixed-income researchers have to say about markets in general and specific instruments in particular. Let's see what kind of information the research staff provides.

Financial Economist

Most fixed-income divisions within large banks and thrift institutions employ an economist who is designated as a Fed watcher. The primary job of this money market specialist is to alert traders and salespeople to the expected activities of the Federal Reserve. Thus the Fed watcher pays close attention to the bank reserve equation (see Chapter 21) as well as to the Federal Open Market Committee's most recent policy directive (see Chapter 22).

Much of the Fed watcher's analysis is communicated to traders and salespeople in brief memos. In addition, when an important news item comes across the news ticker, such as the release of the consumer price index or the employment report, the Fed watcher may use the firm's intercom to provide instant analysis to traders and salespeople. All these items provide salespeople with important discussion points for use with customers. However, salespeople have to translate the Fed watcher's general overview of interest rate movements and economic activity into concrete strategies for institutional investors. For this perspective the salesperson turns to the fixed-income group's rocket scientists.

Fixed-Income Research

Swapping a government bond for a GNMA pass-through security has wide-ranging implications for the composition of a pension fund's portfolio, despite the fact that GNMAs and government bonds are both insured by the federal government. Recall from our discussion in Chapter 8 that the prepayment uncertainty associated with mortgage-related securities makes the maturity of these securities uncertain. The econometricians, statisticians, and mathematicians who work in the fixed-income research area provide, among other things, estimates of prepayments on GNMA pass-through securities so that salespeople can help explain the ramifications of GNMA purchases to their customers.

The fixed-income research group also reports on such obscure items as the probability of a particular corporate bond being called by the issuer prior to maturity, the advantages of swapping low-coupon bonds for high-coupons or vice versa, and the price sensitivity of a bond portfolio to a one-percentage-point change in interest rates. Armed with such precision tools, a bond salesperson can back up simple chitchat with hard facts about how to improve portfolio yields without unduly increasing risk. Thus the rocket scientist econometricians, statisticians, and mathematicians earn their way into the hearts and minds of institutional investors even though their native language is one of differential equations, autocorrelated residuals, and lognormal distributions. Salespeople translate these obscure formulae into higher yields for their customers.

Cooperation between traders and salespeople, Fed watchers, and rocket scientists generates clever investment strategies for institutional investors, consistent profits for large banks and thrifts, and high bonuses for all of the fixed-income employees. It sounds as though life after *Money, Banking, and Financial Markets* can work out pretty well—as long as you know where to look.

Loan Officer

As we discussed in Chapter 14, banks specialize in tailoring commercial loans to businesses. Unlike corporate bonds, commercial bank loans are chock full of special features such as covenants, collateral requirements and guarantees that enable banks to extend credit to companies that are too small, or whose credit characteristics are too challenging, to have access to the public debt markets. The commercial loan officer is responsible for making this happen by working closely with the borrowing company's management—and working within the lending policies of the bank. The loan officer must have a solid understanding of financial accounting, strong interpersonal skills and a knack for negotiating.

At many banks loan officers are also responsible for generating new business. Therefore, this job often has a big sales component. This requires that the loan officer cultivate strong ties with the local business community.

GLOSSARY

accrued interest   Interest accumulated on a bond since the last interest payment.

actuarial probabilities   Calculations of life expectancy based on past experience with respect to age, gender, and similar factors.

adverse selection   A problem of asymmetric information that occurs, in the case of a debt contract, at the origination stage because lenders can not differentiate between high and low quality borrowers.

aggregate demand (supply)   The total amount of goods and services demanded (supplied) in the economy.

allocational efficiency   The tendency of market prices to reflect all information affecting the underlying value of securities.

amortize   To pay off the principal of an indebtedness, along with the interest, during the life of a loan.

angel financing   Financing provided by high net worth individuals (called "angels") who invest in the equity of start-up (new) companies.

annuity   A contract to pay an amount of funds in the future, either in a lump sum or in periodic payments.

appreciate   To increase in value, especially referring to foreign currency.

arbitrageur   One who engages in **arbitrage,** buying something in one market and simultaneously selling it at a profit in another market.

asked price   The price a dealer charges when selling to the public.

asset   (1) An item owned that has value; (2) an item on a balance sheet showing the value of property owned or receivable.

assumption method   A procedure, used in cases of bank failure, in which the failed bank is merged with a healthy one.

asymmetric information   A situation that occurs in any type of contracting when the seller has more information than the buyer.

auction market   A market where buyers and sellers bargain directly with each other.

automated clearinghouse (ACH)   An electronic system for making regular payments or receiving regular credits.

automated teller machine (ATM)   A card-operated facility for making bank deposits and withdrawals.

autonomous spending changes   Changes in spending that are independent of GDP.

balance of payments (national)   A record of payments that one country makes to and receives from all other foreign countries.

balance sheet   A summary statement of an individual's or a business's financial condition on a given date.

bank   *See* **commercial bank.**

bank examination   An audit of the financial condition and overall safety and soundness of a bank by its regulators.

bank failure   Situation in which a bank goes out of business because it cannot meet its obligations. *See also* **assumption method** *and* **payoff method.**

bank holding company   A holding company that owns one or more banks and possibly other (nonbank) subsidiaries.

banking-oriented system A financial system such as Germany or Japan in which the banking market is large relative to the stock and bond markets.

Bank Insurance Fund (BIF) Fund, operated by the FDIC, that insures deposits at commercial banks and most savings banks.

bank (or depository institutions) reserve equation A formal statement of factors affecting bank reserves: Fed assets minus all Fed liabilities and capital accounts, other than those Fed liabilities that constitute bank reserves, plus Treasury currency in bank vaults.

bank reserves *See* **reserves.**

basis point One-hundredth of a percentage point (0.01 percent, or 0.0001). Yields change by one basis point when interest rates go from 9.00 percent to 9.01 percent.

bear market A financial market in which prices are falling.

bid price The price a dealer will pay when buying from the public.

bid-asked spread The difference between the price a dealer is willing to pay for a security (bid price) and the price at which the dealer is willing to sell the security (asked or offer price).

blue-chip stock Stock of a high-quality corporation with a good record of earnings and stability.

Board of Governors of the Federal Reserve System Seven individuals appointed by the President to help run the central bank. *See also* **Federal Reserve System.**

bond A liability issued by a government (government bond) or a business (corporate bond) promising to pay the holder a fixed cash amount at a specified maturity date and (usually) to make regular interest payments in the interim. *See also* **municipal bond** *and* **zero-coupon bond.**

bond-anticipation notes (BANs) Short-term municipal securities issued to raise stopgap funds and paid off when long-term bonds are issued.

bond equivalent yield *See* **coupon equivalent yield.**

Bretton Woods The New Hampshire town where fixed exchange rates and the International Monetary Fund were established by international agreement in 1944. *See* **fixed exchange rates** *and* **International Monetary Fund.**

broker An institution (or individual) who arranges purchases and sales of securities for the account of others and receives a commission on each transaction.

brokerage house A financial institution that acts as a broker, dealer, and underwriter of securities. *See* **broker, dealer,** *and* **underwriting.**

brokered market A market where a person (or institution) called a broker is employed to find the other side of the trade.

bull market A financial market in which prices are rising.

callable *See* **call provision.**

call option An option contract in which the option buyer has the right (but not the obligation) to buy a specified quantity of the underlying asset at a specified price until the expiration date of the option.

call provision A stipulation in a bond that allows the bond issuer to pay off part or all of the bond before the scheduled maturity date.

capital adequacy The sufficiency of a bank's capital to protect the depositors (and the FDIC) against losses.

capital gain The difference between the price paid for an asset and the higher price at which it is sold. If the selling price is lower than the purchase price, there is a **capital loss.**

capital market The market for stocks and long-term debt instruments.

captive finance companies A finance company that is owned by a parent company and whose principal activities are associated with financing the products sold by its parent company.

cash-balance approach A version of the quantity theory of money that focuses on the demand for money. *See also* **demand-for-money equation.**

cash items in the process of collection Checks drawn on one bank and deposited in a second bank but not yet cleared.

caveat emptor et venditor Buyer and seller beware.

central bank A governmental "bank for banks," generally responsible for national monetary policy. *See also* **Federal Reserve System.**

certificates of deposit (CD) Deposits with specific maturities, also referred to as time deposits.

checking (checkable) deposits Accounts at a financial institution (checking accounts) that permit the account holder to transfer funds to a third party via a check (an order to pay).

classical economics A system of economic thought, founded by Adam Smith, that relies on the price system to allocate resources and argues that price flexibility will lead to full employment (Say's law).

clearing corporation Associated with a futures exchange to guarantee rights and obligations of market participants.

clearinghouse A facility for settling transfers of funds between banks.

Clearing House Interbank Payment System (CHIPS) A telecommunications system that transfers funds between banks internationally.

closed-end investment company A mutual fund issuing a limited number of shares that are then traded in the stock market.

collateral Assets such as equipment, accounts receivable, inventory or real estate pledged to a lender to secure a loan.

collateralized mortgage obligation (CMO) A pool of mortgages placed in a trust with a division of claims designed to give investors a more predictable cash flow than individual mortgages.

commercial bank A financial institution that offers a wide variety of services, including checking accounts and business loans.

commercial finance companies Nondeposit financial intermediaries that specialize in making business loans.

commercial paper Short-term debt instruments issued by finance companies and large business firms.

Commodities Futures Trading Commission (CFTC) The government agency that regulates futures trading in the United States.

common stock Ownership interest in a company; such ownership provides a residual claim to the company's earnings, paid in the form of dividends.

compound interest Interest calculated on the sum of the principal and the interest already earned.

consols Perpetual bonds, which have no maturity date but pay a fixed cash flow (interest) forever.

consumer finance companies Nondeposit financial intermediaries that specialize in making consumer loans.

consumption The using up of goods or services by households; more generally, the purchase of goods for immediate use by households.

consumption function The relationship of consumption spending to the level of income, in its simplest form expressed as $C = a + bY$. *See also* **marginal propensity to consume.**

contemporaneous reserves The system of reserve requirements now in effect, which makes required reserves depend on the current level of deposits (but still leaves a small gap between the calculation and the holding of required reserves).

conversion feature (of a bond) The right to convert a corporate bond into shares of the company's stock at a predetermined price.

convertible debt A debt instrument that can be converted into equity (at a predetermined price) if the investor chooses to do so.

convertible preferred stock Preferred stock that can be converted into common stock at a predetermined price.

corporate takeover The acquisition of one company by another company or by a group of investors.

correspondent balances Funds kept by one bank in another (a **correspondent bank**) to facilitate check clearing and other business relationships.

cost of capital effect Impact of a change in interest rates on GDP through investment spending.

countercyclical monetary policy A policy of the central bank designed to stabilize economic activity, usually by increasing the rate of growth of the money supply **(expansionary monetary policy)** during recessions and decreasing the rate of growth of the money supply **(contractionary monetary policy)** in inflationary periods.

counterparties   Two parties to a swap agreement.

coupon equivalent yield (bond equivalent yield)   The difference between the face value and the purchase price of a Treasury bill, divided by the purchase price and annualized using 365 days to the year (366 in leap year).

coupon rate   The interest rate calculated by dividing the annual coupon payment on a bond by the face value of the bond.

coupon securities (coupon-bearing securities)   Bonds that make periodic interest payments prior to maturity. In some cases the bonds have actual coupons attached, which bondholders remove and send in at regular intervals to collect interest.

credit risk   The risk associated with the possibility that borrowers may default on their obligation.

credit unions   Depository institutions specializing in consumer loans that are organized around a common link among depositors—such as a common employer.

crowding-out effect   A decrease in spending (usually investment) resulting from a rise in interest rates caused by an increase in government spending.

currency   Coins and bills used as money.

currency swaps   A contractual agreement between two counterparties to exchange payments in different currencies during a future period.

current coupon   Most recently issued government security of a particular maturity.

current yield   The annual coupon payment on a bond divided by the current price of the bond.

daily earnings at risk   A measure of the amount of potential loss exposure to a financial intermediary over the next day due to trading risk.

dealer   An institution or individual acting as a market-maker by continuously quoting bids and offers on a security, with the objective of earning a profit on the bid-asked spread.

dealer market   A market where a specialized trader called a dealer or market-maker continuously quotes bid and offer prices.

default   To fail to make a payment on schedule.

default risk   The chance that the issuer of a security will default.

defensive open market operations.   *See* **open market operations.**

deferred credit items   An entry on a bank's balance sheet indicating that at a predetermined time it will receive an addition to its reserve account.

deficit nation   A nation that imports more than it exports, resulting in a deficit balance of trade.

defined benefit plans   A pension plan where the benefits paid at retirement are specified.

defined contribution plans   A pension plan where the contributions of the employer and the employee are specified and the benefits depend on the performance of the assets in the plan.

demand deposit   Noninterest bearing checking accounts.

demand deposit expansion multiplier   The number that when multiplied by the level of reserves determines the maximum amount of demand deposits. In its simplest form, it equals the inverse of the required reserve ratio.

demand-for-money equation   An equation explaining how the demand for money varies with other economic variables, especially income and interest rates.

depository institution   An institution that accepts deposits and/or offers services such as checking accounts; includes commercial banks, savings and loan associations, savings banks, and credit unions.

depository institutions reserve equation   *See* **bank reserve equation.**

deposit rate ceilings.   *See* **Regulation Q.**

depreciate   To decrease in value, especially referring to foreign currency.

depression A time span marked by a severe drop in the level of economic activity and very high levels of unemployment.

derivative financial instrument A financial instrument such as a swap or an option or futures contract that derives its value from some other, underlying, financial asset.

devaluation A lowering of the agreed-upon value of a country's money, in a system of fixed exchange rates.

discount bond *See* **zero-coupon bond.**

discount rate The interest rate financial institutions pay to the Federal Reserve to borrow reserves.

discount window The facility that financial institutions are said to use when borrowing reserves from the Federal Reserve.

discretionary funds Bank liabilities and assets that are subject to short-term management control.

dishoarding Decreased money holdings.

disintermediation Removal of funds from financial institutions for direct investment in primary securities.

disposable income Income minus taxes.

dividends Earnings of a corporation that are distributed to stockholders.

dividend yield The current annual dividend of a stock divided by its price.

Dow Jones Industrial Average (DJIA) A measure of the level of stock prices, based on the stock prices of 30 blue-chip industrial companies.

dual banking system The chartering and supervision of commercial banks by both state and federal governments.

due diligence An assessment of a firm's overall quality conducted when its securities are originated.

duration A measure of the futurity of a bond's payment stream that takes into account coupon size as well as time to maturity. It also measures the price sensitivity of the bond to a change in yield.

dynamic open market operations *See* **open market operations.**

Edge Act corporation An international banking subsidiary of a U.S. bank.

efficient capital market A financial market in which securities prices reflect all available information.

efficient portfolio A combination of assets that yields the greatest possible return for a given risk and that carries the lowest possible risk for a given return.

electronic funds transfer system (EFTS) A system in which telecommunications replace checks as the means of transferring funds between banks.

Employee Retirement Income Security Act (ERISA) Legislation enacted in 1974 to safeguard employee pension rights and establish the Pension Benefit Guaranty Corporation.

entrepreneur An individual who as an owner starts, organizes, and manages the risk of a business venture.

equation of exchange $MV = PY$, an expression showing that total spending (the supply of money times velocity) equals the value of what is bought (the price level times the level of real GDP). Sometimes used to relate the price level (P) or nominal GDP (PY) to the money supply.

equilibrium A level or value from which there is no tendency to change.

equilibrium interest rate The interest rate at which the quantity of funds lenders want to lend equals the quantity of funds borrowers want to borrow. At equilibrium, there is no tendency for the interest rate to change.

equilibrium price The price at which the quantity demanded equals the amount supplied, so that there is no tendency for the price to change.

equities *See* **stocks.**

equity capital The difference between total assets and total liabilities on a balance sheet.

Eurobonds Bonds sold outside a borrowing corporation's home country.

Eurodollars Deposits held in dollars in foreign banks.

Euromarket The market for Eurodollars and Eurobonds.

European Monetary System (EMS) A quasi-fixed exchange rate system among several European countries established in 1979.

European Union The formal union of European countries to form a common market for goods and services.

ex ante Planned or expected (contrast with **ex post**).

excess reserves Bank reserves held in excess of what is required. *See* **reserves** *and* **required reserves.**

exchange rate effect Impact of a change in interest rates on GDP through net exports.

exchange rates *See* **foreign exchange rate, fixed exchange rates,** *and* **floating exchange rates.**

exercise price The predetermined price in an option that the underlying asset can be bought at (call) or sold for (put).

expectations hypothesis A theory of the term structure of interest rates stressing that long-term rates will be an average of the current short-term rate and expected future short-term rates.

ex post Actual or realized (contrast with **ex ante**).

face value The final amount of indebtedness (excluding interest) that must be repaid on a bond. *See also* **principal** or **par.**

Fed Federal Reserve System.

Federal Advisory Council A group of commercial bankers that makes recommendations to the Federal Reserve Board of Governors regarding monetary policy.

Federal Deposit Insurance Corporation (FDIC) A federal agency that insures deposits at commercial banks, savings banks and savings and loan associations. It also examines and supervises state-chartered commercial banks that are not members of the Federal Reserve System.

federal funds An unsecured loan between banks where the funds that are lent are transferred the same day the loan is made.

federal funds market The market for unsecured loans between banks, called federal funds.

federal funds rate The interest rate on federal funds.

Federal Home Loan Banks Government sponsored banks from whom savings and loans associations can borrow money.

These banks are members of the Federal Home Loan Bank system.

Federal Home Loan Mortgage Corporation ("Freddie Mac") A subsidiary of the Federal Home Loan Bank that issues debt instruments that provide claims primarily to pools of conventional mortgages.

Federal Housing Finance Board (FHFB) An agency that oversees the Federal Home Loan Banks.

Federal Land Banks Part of the Federal Farm Credit System, these banks make loans to farmers.

Federal National Mortgage Association ("Fannie Mae") A private corporation with certain ties to the government that issues debt instruments that provide claims primarily to pools of government-insured mortgages.

Federal Open Market Committee (FOMC) A policy-making group within the Federal Reserve System that directs the open market operations of the system.

Federal Reserve System ("the Fed") The central banking system and monetary authority of the United States, made up of regional Federal Reserve banks and the Federal Reserve Board of Governors, which supervises and examines state-chartered member banks, regulates bank holding companies, and is responsible for the conduct of monetary policy.

Federal Savings and Loan Insurance Corporation (FSLIC) Government agency that provided deposit insurance for savings and loan associations (replaced by the Federal Deposit Insurance Corporation).

Fed Wire A telecommunications system, operated by the Federal Reserve, that transfers funds between banks.

FHA-VA mortgage A mortgage insured either by the Federal Housing Authority (FHA) or by the Veterans Administration (VA).

finance companies Nondeposit financial intermediaries that specialize in making consumer and business loans.

financial assets *See* **real assets.**

financial disintermediation When funds flowing through the intermediated markets are shifted to flowing through the financial (securities) markets.

financial futures   Futures contracts whose underlying assets are securities or, in index futures, the cash value of a group of securities.

financial institutions   Institutions which engage in activities associated with either the financial markets or the intermediated markets.

financial intermediaries   Institutions with financial claims on both sides of the balance sheet that act as go-betweens in funneling funds from saver-lenders to borrower-spenders.

financial intermediation   The process of funneling funds from saver-lenders to borrower-spenders through a financial intermediary.

financial markets   Markets in which financial assets can be traded.

fiscal policy   Government policy concerning spending and taxation.

fixed exchange rates   An international financial system in which rates of exchange between the values of different countries' currencies are maintained at agreed-upon levels.

fixed-rate loan (mortgage, security)   A loan (mortgage, security) that carries an unchanging interest rate throughout the life of the instrument.

fixed-rate payer   Party in an interest rate swap making fixed payments.

float   The total value of checks that have been credited by the Fed to the banks in which they have been deposited but have not yet been collected from the banks on which they are drawn.

floating exchange rates   An international financial system in which rates of exchange between the values of different countries' currencies fluctuate according to supply and demand in the marketplace.

floating interest rate   A loan whose interest rate is adjusted periodically with changes in market rates.

floating-rate (variable-rate) loan (mortgage, security)   A loan that carries an interest rate that is adjusted periodically to reflect changes in market interest rates in general.

floating-rate payer   Party in an interest rate swap making variable payments.

flower bonds   Government bonds that can be used at par value to settle federal estate taxes.

flow of funds accounting   A record of payments and receipts among the different sectors of the economy.

foreign exchange rate   The value of a unit of one nation's money in terms of another nation's money.

forward contract   A nonstandardized agreement to exchange an asset in the future at a currently agreed upon price.

funding (of pension benefits)   Setting aside funds now to cover future pension liabilities.

futures contract   A standardized agreement, traded on an organized futures exchange, for delivery of a specific commodity or security on a specified future date and at a specified price.

GAP ratio   The one-year repricing GAP divided by total assets. *See* **one-year repricing gap.**

general obligation bonds   Municipal bonds backed by the overall taxing power of the state or local government.

Glass-Steagall Act of 1933   Legislation that separated investment banking from commercial banking.

GNMA ("Ginnie Mae") pass-through securities   Claims to a pool of FHA-VA mortgages insured by the Government National Mortgage Association (GNMA).

gold export point   Under an international gold standard, the limit to which a deficit nation's currency can depreciate before it becomes cheaper to export gold than to purchase foreign currency.

gold import point   Under an international gold standard, the limit to which a surplus nation's currency can appreciate before it becomes cheaper for other nations to pay their trade deficits to it in gold than to purchase its currency.

gold standard   A monetary system in which currency is redeemable in gold at a fixed price.

Government National Mortgage Association (GNMA, "Ginnie Mae")   A division of the U.S. Department of Housing and Urban Development that insures pools of FHA and VA mortgages.

Gresham's law "Bad money drives good money out of circulation."

gross domestic product (GDP) The total value of goods and services produced in the domestic economy in a given year.

group insurance Insurance made available to members of a group, such as employees of a corporation, usually at favorable rates.

Hausbank A German company's principal bank. The company relies on it as the primary source of all forms of external finance, including both debt and equity.

hedger One who tries to reduce the risk of loss resulting from a change in the price of a particular asset. In futures markets, it is someone who sells a futures contract while holding the underlying asset **(short hedger)** or purchases such a contract in anticipation of purchasing the underlying asset **(long hedger).**

high-yield *See* **junk bonds.**

historical cost accounting Accounting rule used for banks and savings and loan associations that values assets and liabilities at their purchase price.

hoarding Increased money holdings.

holding company A corporation set up to hold a controlling interest in one or more other corporations. A **bank holding company** owns one or more banks.

holding period yield The annual return on a bond when it is sold before maturity. *Also see* **return** *and* **yield to maturity.**

hostile takeover The acquisition of one company, against its management's will, by another company or by a group of investors usually associated with the removal of the acquired company's management.

hyperinflation A rapid increase in general price levels, e.g., above 100 percent per year.

impact lag of monetary policy The time between the use of a monetary strategy and its effect on the economy.

income statement A summary statement of an individual's or a business's current receipts and current expenditures during a period of time.

index fund A mutual fund whose goal is to mimic the performance of one of the financial market indices, often the S&P 500.

Individual Retirement Account (IRA) A tax-benefited pension plan for workers.

inflation Generally rising price levels.

initial public offering (IPO) Occurs when a company issues publicly traded stock for the first time.

insider trading Illegal use of knowledge not available to the general public, to gain advantage in buying and selling securities.

institutionalization Shift in flow of funds from investors directly purchasing traded securities to indirectly purchasing traded securities through financial intermediaries such as mutual funds.

insurance company A financial institution providing protection against loss (of life or property) or costs (such as medical or legal costs) by accepting payments (premiums) in return for a guarantee of compensation.

Inter-District Settlement Fund A facility for transferring funds among banks located in different Federal Reserve districts.

interest A charge paid by a borrower to a lender for the use of the lender's money.

interest rate The cost of borrowing expressed as a percent of principal per annum. *See* **yield** *and* **yield to maturity.**

interest rate risk The risk that a change in interest rates may affect the net worth of a financial intermediary because of a mismatch in the maturity of its assets and liabilities.

interest rate swaps A contractual agreement between two counterparties to exchange interest payments during a future period.

intermediated markets Markets in which funds flow from saver-lenders to borrow-spenders through financial intermediaries.

internal rate of return *See* **yield to maturity.**

International Banking Facility (IBF) A domestic branch bank established for international banking and treated for regulatory purposes as a foreign branch.

International Monetary Fund (IMF) An international organization set up in 1944 to supervise exchange rates and to promote orderly international financial conditions.

international reserves Reserves held by one country usually in the form of gold or in the money of another country.

intrinsic value An option's value at expiration (or if it is exercised).

investment banks Financial institutions whose central activity is originating securities in the primary market but often also engage in securities market-making, brokering, trading and advisory services.

investment grade Bonds rated in the top four categories by Moody's or Standard and Poor's.

investment portfolio The collection of securities, such as stocks and bonds, held by an individual or a corporation.

investment spending The purchase of plant, equipment, and inventories by a business.

IOU *See* **promissory note.**

IS **curve** Graph of points showing combinations of level of income and interest rate at which savings equals investment.

ISLM **analysis** A model of the economy that shows the interaction of monetary policy and fiscal policy and partially integrates the classical and Keynesian systems.

junk bonds Risky bonds rated below Baa.

keiretsu A group of Japanese companies that are controlled through interlocking ownership (the companies own stock in each other).

Keogh Plan A tax-benefited pension plan designed for self-employed individuals.

Keynesian Derived from the theories of John Maynard Keynes, advocating government spending and taxation to maintain full employment and a stable economy.

lagged reserves The former system of bank reserve requirements, which left a gap of two weeks between the calculation of required reserves and the time when the reserves had to be held.

laissez-faire "Let (people) do (as they wish)," a policy of government nonintervention in the economy.

league tables The rankings of investment banks by volume of underwriting in specific classes of securities.

legal tender Money that the government requires a creditor to accept in discharge of debts. If it is not accepted, interest need not accrue thereafter.

lender of last resort The Federal Reserve, which acts as the ultimate source of funds to banks and other financial institutions by providing reserves to prevent bank failures.

lesser developed countries (LDCs) Refers to developing countries whose economies and financial systems are still considered immature.

letter of credit A financial guarantee given by a bank to insure payment by one of its customers to a third party.

leverage The degree to which financial intermediaries, or any company, is financed by debt versus equity—often measured in banking by the leverage ratio, which equals stockholders equity divided by total assets.

leveraged buyout (LBO) The acquisition of a company where the acquisition is substantially financed by debt.

liability A financial obligation.

LIBOR London Interbank Offered Rate, the rate charged between banks for Eurodollar time deposits.

life insurance company Companies that sell life insurance, annuities and other savings-oriented products.

line of credit (L/C) A commitment by a bank or other institutional lender that provides a borrower with a *capacity* to borrow up to a specified limit.

liquid asset An asset that can be converted quickly into a medium of exchange without suffering a loss.

liquidity Ability to convert an asset into cash quickly with little loss in value.

liquidity preference Keynes's term for the demand for money, often used in connection with the rate of interest.

liquidity premium   The higher yield on longer-term securities compared with short-term securities, to compensate for the additional risk of long-term issues. Associated with the liquidity premium theory of the term structure of interest rates.

liquidity risk   The risk to a bank that unexpected deposit withdrawals or unexpected loan demand will leave it short of funds.

liquidity trap   In Keynesian theory, the point beyond which an increase in the money supply will no longer cause interest rates to drop.

LM **curve**   Graph of points showing combinations of level of GDP and interest rates at which liquidity preference equals the money supply.

loanable funds   Funds that lenders are willing to make available to borrowers. Can be used as a framework for determining the equilibrium level of interest rates.

loan charge-offs   The amount of the loan portfolio that had to be written down over the past year because some of the bank's borrowers could not pay their loans back.

loan/deposit ratio   The ratio of a bank's total loans to its total deposits, a measure of the bank's liquidity.

loaned up   Said of a bank that has no excess reserves against which it can make loans.

long   The buyer of a financial asset, usually an options or futures contract, who is also said to "take a long position."

M1   *See* **money supply.**

M2   A definition of money supply that adds to M1 such assets as savings accounts, small-denomination time deposits, money market deposit accounts, and money market mutual fund shares.

M3   A definition of money supply that adds to M1 and M2 such assets as large-denomination time deposits.

macroeconomics   The study of whole systems of the economy, such as total income and output, the price level and interest rates, and the interrelationships among them.

Magnetic Ink Character Recognition (MICR)   A system of imprints on checks that allows for machine sorting.

managed floating system   The international financial system currently in use, in which major nations intervene to influence foreign exchange rates by buying and selling currencies.

manager-stockholder conflict   Conflict that arises because of asymmetric information and the difference between a manager's personal objectives and the objective of maximizing stockholder wealth.

margin   (1) A minimum down payment required by law for the purchase of stock; (2) a deposit placed with a clearing corporation by both the buyer and the seller of a futures contract.

marginal propensity to consume   The amount that a person spends out of each dollar of incremental income.

marginal propensity to save   The amount that a person saves out of each dollar of incremental income.

marked-to-market   Accounting rule that changes the value of a security (or any asset or liability) any time its market value changes.

marketability   The ease of buying and selling an asset, associated with narrow bid-asked spreads.

market-maker   *See* **dealer.**

market portfolio   Portfolio consisting of all securities in the marketplace.

market risk (capital uncertainty)   The risk of price fluctuations for a security. For bonds, it is associated with variations in the level of the interest rate.

markets-oriented system   A financial system such as the U.S. or the U.K. in which the stock and bond markets are large relative to the banking system.

mark-to-market settlement   Daily adjustments made in balances at a clearing corporation to reflect price changes in futures contracts.

matched sale-purchase agreement   Open market operation (sale), sometimes called a "reverse repo," in which the Federal Reserve sells securities and agrees to buy them back in the near future.

maturity date   The due date for the final payment on a financial instrument such as a bond or a certificate of deposit.

medium of exchange Something used to finalize payments for goods and services (M1, or currency and checking accounts).

medium-term notes Debt instruments that are similar to commercial paper except their maturities range from 1–5 years instead of 270 days or less.

mezzanine debt funds A fund that invests in subordinated debt, or a combination of debt and equity.

modern portfolio theory Analysis of portfolio decisions under uncertainty and the implications for the returns on risky securities.

monetarism The position, based in classical economics, that an "invisible hand" pushes the economy toward a full employment level of production at which it is inherently stable and that government efforts to affect economic activity through countercyclical policies are unnecessary and potentially damaging. Also associated with the quantity theory of money.

monetary authority An institution responsible for executing national monetary policy, such as the central bank.

monetary base Total bank reserves plus currency held by the nonbank public.

monetary policy Government policy concerning money and credit conditions, especially the rate of growth in the money supply and the level of interest rates. *See also* **countercyclical monetary policy.**

monetizing the debt The government's creation of money with which to buy back interest-bearing government securities.

money Whatever is used as a medium of exchange, unit of account, and store of value. *See also* **legal tender** *and* **money supply.**

money market The financial market for short-term securities.

money market deposit accounts Deposits with limited checking account privileges that typically pay an interest rate comparable to treasury bills or other money market instruments.

money market mutual funds Mutual funds that invest in money market instruments.

money multiplier *See* **demand deposit expansion multiplier.**

money supply (M1) The total of currency outside banks and demand deposits.

monitoring Producing and using information about a borrower or issuer *after* a financial contract's origination.

moral hazard A problem of asymmetric information occurring after a loan is made. In particular, the borrower may become riskier without being detected by the lender.

mortgage A (usually long-term) loan for the purchase of a home or other building, where the home or building serves as collateral in case of default.

mortgage pool A package of mortgages that is sold as a unit.

multiplier The ratio of the change in GDP to a change in exogenous spending; sometimes called expenditure multiplier to distinguish it from the money multiplier.

municipal bond A bond issued by a state or local government, called a tax-exempt because the interest is exempt from federal income tax.

mutual fund A fund that pools the investments of a large number of shareholders and purchases securities such as stocks or, in a money market mutual fund, money market instruments.

mutual fund family A group of mutual funds owned and managed by the same management company.

mutual savings banks Depository institutions that specialize in making consumer and mortgage loans. These thrift institutions are mostly located in the Northeast.

National Association of Securities Dealers An association of securities dealers to whom the Securities and Exchange Commission has delegated oversight of the over the counter equities market.

National Association of Securities Dealers Automated Quotation System (NASDAQ) A computerized system for displaying bid and asked prices for over-the-counter stocks.

natural rate of interest The rate of interest at which savings equals investment at full employment.

negotiable certificates of deposit (CDS) Certificates of deposit that can be traded in a secondary market.

negotiable order of withdrawal (NOW) account An interest-bearing checking account.

net asset value (NAV) The value of a share of a mutual fund, based on the market value of the assets owned by the fund and the number of shares outstanding.

net interest income Interest income minus interest expense on a bank's income statement.

net interest margin (NIM) Net interest income expressed as a percent of total bank assets.

net worth The difference between an individual's or business's assets and liabilities.

New York Stock Exchange Composite Index A measure of the level of stock prices, based on all the stocks listed on the New York Stock Exchange.

no-load funds Mutual funds sold directly to the public with no sales commission.

nominal GDP The gross domestic product measured in current prices.

nominal interest rate Interest rate measured in money terms, as distinct from the real interest rate, which is corrected for changes in purchasing power.

nonbank bank A bank that limits its commercial services (dropping either demand deposits or business loans) in order to bypass various legal restrictions.

nondepository financial intermediaries A financial intermediary that does not issue deposits.

nondiscretionary funds Bank liabilities and assets not subject to short-term management control.

nonperforming loans Loans whose interest payments are delinquent 30 days or more.

nonsystematic risk Risk that is independent of other securities and can be eliminated by portfolio diversification.

nontraded financial contracts A financial claim or contract that cannot be traded in a secondary market but is instead held to maturity by its original investor or lender.

notional principal amount Agreed upon principal in a swap transaction.

off-balance sheet Refers to activities that banks engage in that are not recorded as either assets or liabilities.

offer price *See* **asked price.**

offering memorandum A document used in the origination of private placements that contains information about the issuing firm and the purpose of the issue.

offering (or preliminary) prospectus A public document filed with the registration statement that contains all relevant factual information about the firm and its financing.

Office of Thrift Supervision (OTS) Department within the U.S. Treasury that charters, regulates, examines, and supervises savings and loan associations.

one-year repricing GAP The dollar difference between the amount of a bank's assets that will be repriced in less than one year and the amount of the bank's liabilities that will be repriced in less than one year.

on the run *See* **current coupon.**

open-end mutual fund A mutual fund that offers to the public shares that are redeemable at net asset value.

open interest The number of open long (equal to short) positions for a given option or futures contract.

open market operations The purchase and sale of government securities by the Federal Reserve in order to control levels of bank reserves. Those aimed at defending a target level of reserves from outside influences are **defensive open market operations;** those aimed at changing the level of reserves are **dynamic open market operations.**

operating efficiency (of securities markets) The effectiveness with which markets bring together buyers and sellers.

operating target One of two intermediate objectives of an open market operation, usually either the level of reserves or the federal funds rate.

option contract *See* **call option** *and* **put option.**

option premium The price paid by an option buyer to the option seller for the rights acquired.

over-the-counter market (OTC) Trading in stocks, usually of smaller companies, that are not listed on one of the stock exchanges. Also refers to how government and corporate bonds are traded, that is, through dealers who quote bids and offers to buy and sell "over the counter."

par Face value of a financial asset, especially a bond (often equal to 100)

passbook savings account Name used in the past to refer to bank accounts which carry a specific interest rate and from which funds can be withdrawn at any time.

pass-through securities *See* **GNMA pass-through securities.**

payments system The institutional arrangements for settling transactions in the economy.

payoff method A procedure, used in cases of bank failure, in which the bank goes into receivership and the FDIC pays depositors directly.

peg To hold to a fixed level, as in pegging the foreign exchange rate.

Pension Benefit Guaranty Corporation (Penny Benny) An agency that insures pension benefits against company bankruptcy.

pension (retirement) fund A fund that invests the contributions made by or for workers and makes payments to them when they retire.

personally guaranteed A loan to a business that is also guaranteed by an individual, typically the business' owner.

petrodollars Revenue, in dollars, from OPEC sales of oil.

Phillips curve The relationship between inflation and unemployment, suggesting that lower unemployment is usually accompanied by higher rates of inflation. Originally presented by Professor A. W. Phillips.

point of sale (POS) terminal An electronic device that automatically debits a buyer's checking account and credits the seller's checking account at the time of sale.

portfolio diversification Holding many different types of securities in a portfolio.

preferred habitat theory The theory of the term structure of interest rates that combines supply and demand forces with expectations.

preferred stock Ownership interest in a company that carries a fixed promised dividend payment.

preliminary prospectus *See* **offering prospectus.**

prepayment Payment of an obligation before the payment is due.

present value Value of a future payment discounted by an interest rate to produce its present value (value today).

price-earnings (P/E) ratio The price of a stock divided by its earnings per share.

primary securities Stocks and bonds issued by ultimate borrower-spenders.

primary securities market The financial market for the purchase and sale of stocks or bonds when they are first issued.

prime rate The interest rate that banks charge their "biggest and best" customers, although frequently a bank's very largest customers may pay rates below the prime rate.

principal (of a bond) The amount borrowed, excluding interest. Frequently used interchangeably with the face value of a bond, although they are equal only for a coupon-bearing security that is sold at par.

private placements Nontraded corporate bonds that do not have to be registered with the SEC.

promissory note A written promise to pay a specified sum of money at a specified time or on demand; sometimes called an IOU.

prompt corrective action (PCA) A set of banking regulations that take much of the discretion away from regulators in their handling of failing banks.

property and casualty insurance companies Financial intermediaries that offer insurance against casualties such as automobile accidents, fire, theft, negligence, and malpractice.

put option   An option contract in which the option buyer has the right (but not the obligation) to sell a specified quantity of the underlying asset at a specified price until the expiration date of the option.

quantity theory of money   The theory that a proportional increase in the supply of money leads to a proportional increase in the price level.

rational expectations   Expectations of economic variables that reflect all currently available information. According to some, rational expectations may lead individuals to anticipate monetary policy and neutralize its effects.

real assets   Property such as land or equipment, as distinguished from financial assets, such as stocks and bonds.

real GDP   Gross domestic product, adjusted for the effects of inflation.

real interest rate   The interest rate in terms of goods and services; approximated by subtracting the rate of inflation from the nominal interest rate.

recession   A time span marked by a drop in the level of economic activity and increased unemployment.

recognition lag of monetary policy   The time between a change in economic conditions and the realization by policymakers that the change has occurred.

redlining   Discriminatory practices in mortgage lending.

registration statement   A public document that must be filed with Securities Exchange Commission before a security can be sold to the public.

Regulation Q   The regulation that imposed ceilings on deposit interest rates. Regulation Q was effectively dismantled in the early 1980s.

repricing maturity   The length of time until a loan's interest rate is reset or the loan matures.

repurchase agreement (RP or "repo")   The sale of securities with a commitment to buy them back at a specified date and at a specified price. Repos are used by the Federal Reserve as a type of open market operation and by government securities dealers to finance their inventories of bonds.

required reserve ratio   The ratio of bank reserves to deposits that a bank must hold according to law.

required reserves   Funds that a bank *must* hold in the form of vault cash or deposits at the Federal Reserve to meet its required reserve ratio.

reserve requirements   *See* **required reserve ratio.**

reserves   Funds that a bank holds in the form of vault cash or deposits at the Federal Reserve.

Resolution Trust Corporation (RTC)   An agency that administered the closing or merging of insolvent thrift institutions.

restrictive covenants   Contractual promises agreed to by a corporation when it obtains financing that typically restrict its activities.

retained earnings   Profits of a corporation that are not distributed as dividends to shareholders.

return   Value of an investment at the end of the period minus value at the beginning divided by the value at the beginning. *See* **total return, yield to maturity.**

return on assets (ROA)   Net income after taxes divided by total assets.

return on equity (ROE)   Net income after taxes divided by stockholders' equity.

revenue bond   A bond issued to finance a particular project, such as a toll road, the receipts from which are used to pay the interest and principal on the bond.

reverse repo   *See* **matched-sale purchase agreement.**

revolving lines of credit   A financing package from commercial banks that combines a line of credit with a term loan.

risk aversion   An investor characteristic requiring higher expected returns on risky securities compared with a riskless security.

risk-based capital (RBC) requirements   A regulatory requirement in banking that links minimum capital standards to bank risk.

risk-based deposit insurance premiums   Deposit insurance premiums that vary with the riskiness of the bank, as required under the FDIC Improvement Act of 1991.

risk premium   Extra return above the risk free rate for investing in a risky security.

risk structure of interest rates   The relationship between yields on different types of securities, especially those with different credit ratings.

risky securities   Securities with uncertain returns.

round lot   The unit in which securities are usually traded (100 shares of an equity, $1 million of face value in Treasury bills).

saving function   The relationship between saving and level of income, in its simplest form expressed as $S = -a + (1 - b)Y$. *See also* **marginal propensity to save.**

savings accounts   *See* **savings deposits.**

savings and loan association (S&L)   Depository institutions that are substantially restricted to investing in home-related assets such as mortgages.

Savings Association Insurance Fund (SAIF)   Fund, operated by the FDIC, that insures deposits at savings and loan associations.

savings bank   A financial institution that traditionally was limited to accepting savings deposits and making home mortgage loans.

savings deposit   Nontransactions deposits that can be withdrawn at any time such as a money market deposit account.

Say's law   "Supply creates its own demand," hence total spending (demand) will always be sufficient to justify production at full employment (supply).

secondary securities market   A financial market in which previously issued securities are traded, such as the New York Stock Exchange.

Section 20 affiliates   Investment banking subsidiaries of bank holding companies that can engage in underwriting activities formerly prohibited under the Glass-Steagall Act.

secured lender   A lender whose loans are secured by collateral.

securities   Financial instruments representing ownership or debt, such as stocks and bonds, that provide claims to future expected cash flows.

Securities and Exchange Commission   A federal agency that regulates securities brokers and dealers and securities markets.

securities brokers   Financial institutions (or individuals who work for these institutions) that operate in the secondary market by matching buyers and sellers of a particular security and earn a commission or fee for bringing the two together.

securitization   Pooling a group of loans into a trust and then selling securities issued against the trust, thus transforming non-traded loans into traded securities.

serial maturity   Scheduled retirement of a portion of a bond issue each year until the entire issue has matured.

settlement by offset   The cancellation of rights and obligations in the options and futures market through purchases and sales of identical contracts.

share   A unit of ownership in the capital stock of a corporation.

shelf registration   The process by which a firm registers a dollar *capacity* to issue securities with the Securities and Exchange Commission that it can use in increments, or in total, at any time during the life of the shelf.

shell branch   A banking facility set up abroad to avoid domestic regulation and taxation.

short   The seller of a financial asset who still has an outstanding obligation to buy back the asset, especially an options or futures contract. Also phrased as "take a short position."

simple interest   Interest calculated by multiplying the principal by the interest rate and the time in years. *See also* **compound interest.**

Society for Worldwide Interbank Financial Telecommunications (SWIFT)   A telecommunications system that transfers funds between banks internationally.

sources and uses of funds statement   A financial statement integrating the income statement and balance sheet of a unit or a sector of the economy.

specialist   A dealer who makes a market in stocks traded on an organized exchange (such as the New York Stock Exchange) and who is also responsible for matching public buy and sell orders in an auction format.

speculative demand for money Keynes' notion that people demand cash balances to speculate on future interest rates.

speculators People who take on risk on financial transactions in anticipation of profit.

spot market The market in which an asset is traded for immediate delivery, also called the cash market, as opposed to a market for forward or future delivery.

Standard & Poor's 500 Stock Index A measure of the level of stock prices based on the prices of 500 stocks selected by Standard & Poor's Corporation.

stock flotation The sale of a new stock issue to raise capital for a corporation.

stockholder-lender conflict Conflict between stockholders and lenders that arises because of asymmetric information and the difference in the way risk affects each of them.

stocks (equities) Shares of ownership in corporations. *See also* **common stock.**

store of value The extent to which assets maintain their purchasing power over time. Money must be a good store of value to function well.

strike price *See* **exercise price.**

stripping Removing the interest coupons from bonds and reselling them as separate (zero-coupon) securities.

subordinated debt A class of debt whose repayment priority in bankruptcy is behind, or junior to, other classes of debt.

supply-side economics The theory that reduction in tax rates increases production incentives and encourages expansion of economic activity, resulting ultimately in increased tax revenues.

syndicate A group of investment banks that is put together to share the risk associated with underwriting a security.

systematic risk Risk that is common to all securities that cannot be eliminated by portfolio diversification.

T-account A simple accounting statement that records only changes in balance sheet items from a starting point.

tax and loan accounts Deposits of U.S. government funds, generated by tax receipts and bond sales, in commercial banks.

tax-anticipation notes (TANs) Short-term municipal securities issued to raise stop-gap funds and paid off from tax receipts.

tax-exempts *See* **municipal bond.**

term life insurance Pure life insurance with no savings component included in the policy.

term sheet A short document used in the origination of private placements that summarizes the key terms of the contract.

term structure of interest rates The relationship between yields on different maturities of the same type of security.

thin markets A market with low trading volume.

thrift institutions ("thrifts") Savings and loans associations, mutual savings banks, and credit unions are referred to as the thrift institutions.

time deposits *See* **certificates of deposit.**

total return A security's capital gain plus coupon or dividend income divided by price.

traded securities Financial claims or contracts that are traded in a secondary market such as stocks traded on the NYSE.

trading risk The risk to a financial intermediary associated with trading a financial instrument.

transactions costs Costs, such as commissions and the bid-asked spread, of buying and selling securities. *See also* **marketability.**

transactions demand for money The demand for money associated with the level of economic activity.

transactions deposits Deposits with unlimited checking privileges.

transmission mechanisms of monetary policy The channels through which changes in money affect economic activity.

Treasury bills A zero-coupon obligation of the U.S. government issued with a maturity of one year or less.

Treasury bond   A coupon-bearing obligation of the U.S. government issued with a maturity of over ten years.

Treasury note   A coupon-bearing obligation of the U.S. government issued with a maturity of one to ten years.

underwriter   A financial institution that is hired by a company to sell its securities to the public.

underwriting   The process by which a newly issued security is sold to the public.

underwriting spread   The fee earned by an investment bank or other financial institution for marketing a newly issued security.

unit of account   Something used to measure relative values of goods and services. Money is usually a unit of account.

universal banking   The combination of the traditional activities of a commercial bank and the underwriting activities of an investment bank and possibly other financial services under the same roof.

universal life   A life insurance policy that includes a savings component that pays a money market rate.

unsecured loan   A loan that is not secured by collateral.

variable life   A life insurance policy that includes a savings component that can be allocated among a menu of investment options.

variable-rate loan   *See* **floating-rate loan.**

velocity   The rate of turnover of the money supply; the average number of times per year each dollar is used to purchase goods and services (often measured as GDP divided by the money supply).

venture capital funds   A fund that invests in the equity of new "start-up" companies.

vesting   Rights in a pension fund that are not lost if the employee leaves the job before retirement.

wealth   The total value of the assets owned by an individual or business at a particular point in time.

wealth effect   Impact of a change in interest rates on GDP through the effect of wealth on consumption.

whole life   Life insurance policies with a constant premium and savings component.

World Bank (International Bank for Reconstruction and Development)   An organization funded by developed countries to lend money to developing countries.

yield   The effective rate of return for holding a debt instrument, as distinguished from its coupon rate of interest. *See also* **current yield, yield to maturity,** and **holding period yield.**

yield curve   A graphic representation of the relationship between yield and maturity of securities.

yield on a discount basis   The difference between the face value and the purchase price of a Treasury bill, divided by the face value and annualized using 360 days to the year.

yield to maturity (internal rate of return)   The rate of discount (per annum) that makes the sum of the present values of all future payments of a security equal to its purchase price.

zaibatsu   Large Japanese financial-industrial combines that preceded the keirestu.

zero-coupon bond   A bond issued without interest-bearing coupons, at a discount below face value.

INDEX

(718) 890-1550
Bell Atlantic
Business office